AMERICAN POETRY:
THE NINETEENTH CENTURY

VOLUME ONE

AMERICAN POETRY:
THE NINETEENTH CENTURY

VOLUME ONE
Philip Freneau to Walt Whitman

THE LIBRARY OF AMERICA

The paper used in this publication meets the
minimum requirements of the American National Standard for
Information Sciences—Permanence of Paper for Printed
Library Materials, ANSI Z39.48—1984.

Distributed to the trade in the United States
by Penguin Books USA Inc
and in Canada by Penguin Books Canada Ltd.

Library of Congress Catalog Number: 93-10702
For cataloging information, see end of Index.
ISBN 0–940450–60–7

Second Printing
The Library of America—66

Manufactured in the United States of America

JOHN HOLLANDER
SELECTED THE CONTENTS AND WROTE
THE NOTES FOR THIS VOLUME

This volume has been published with grants from the National Endowment for the Humanities and the Lila Wallace-Reader's Digest Fund.

Contents

PHILIP FRENEAU

(1752–1832)

On the Civilization of
the Western Aboriginal Country

Strange to behold, unmingled with surprize,
Old hights extinguished, and new hights arise,
Nature, herself, assume a different face,—
Yet such has been, and such will be the case.
Thus, in the concave of the heavens around,
Old stars, have vanished, and new stars been found,
Some stars, worn out, have ceased to shine or burn,
And some, relumed, to their old posts return.

Two wheels has Nature constantly in play,
She turns them both, but turns a different way;
What one creates, subsists a year, an hour,
Then, by destruction's wheel is crushed once more.
No art, no strength this wheel of fate restrains,
While matter, deathless matter, still remains,
Again, perhaps, new modelled, to revive,
Again to perish, and again to live!

THOU, who shalt rove the trackless western waste,
Tribes to reform, or have new *breeds* embraced,
Be but sincere!—the native of the wild
If wrong, is only Nature's ruder child;
The arts you teach, perhaps not ALL amiss,
Are arts destructive of domestic bliss,
The *Indian world*, on Natures bounty cast,
Heed not the future, nor regard the past.—
They live—and at the evening hour can say,
We claim no more, for we have had our day.
The *Indian* native, taught the ploughman's art,
Still drives his oxen, with an *Indian* heart,
Stops when they stop, reclines upon the *beam*,
While briny sorrows from his eye-lids stream,

To think the ancient trees, that round him grow,
That shaded *wigwams* centuries ago
Must now descend, each venerated bough,
To blaze on fields where nature reign'd 'till now.

Of different mind, he sees not with your sight,
Perfect, perhaps, as viewed by Nature's light:
By Nature's dictates all his views are bent,
No more *imperfect* than his AUTHOR meant.

All moral virtue, joined in one vast frame,
In 'forms though varying, still endures the same;
Draws to one point, finds but one general end,
As bodies to one common centre tend.

Whether the impulse of the mind commands
To change a *creed*, or speculate in lands,
No matter which—with pain I see YOU go
Where wild *Missouri's* turbid waters flow,
There to behold, where simple Nature reign'd,
A thousand *Vices* for one *Virtue* gained;
Forests destroyed by *Helots*, and by slaves,
And forests cleared, to breed a race of knaves.—
The bare idea clouds the soul with gloom—
Better return, and plough the soil at home.

But, if devoid of subterfuge, or art,
You act from mere sincerety of heart,
If honor's ardor in the bosom glows
Nor *selfish* motives on *yourselves* impose,
Go, and convince the natives of the west
That *christian* morals are the first, the best;
And yet *the same* that beam'd thro' every age,
Adorn the *ancient*, or the modern page;
That, without which, no social compacts bind,
Nor *honor* stamps her image on mankind.

Go, teach what Reason dictates should be taught,
And learn from *Indians* one great Truth you ought,
That, though the world, wherever man exists,
Involved in darkness, or obscured in mists,

The *Negro*, scorching on *Angola's* coasts,
Or *Tartar*, shivering in *Siberian* frosts;
Take all, through all, through nation, tribe, or clan,
The child of Nature is the *better* man.

On the Great Western Canal
of the State of New York

Meliusne sylvas ire per longas
Fuit, an recentes carpere undas?
—HORACE.

i. e. which was best—to travel through tedious,
dreary forests, or to sail on these recent waters?

The nation true to honor's cause,
To *equal rights* and *equal laws*,
Is well secured, and well released
From the proud monarchs of the east.

Thus *Holland* rose from *Spain's* controul,
And thus shall rise from pole to pole
Those systems formed on reason's plan
That vindicate the *Rights of man.*—

Nature, herself, will change her face,
And arts fond arms the world embrace;
In works of peace mankind engage,
And close the despot's iron age.

And *here* behold a work progress,
Advancing through the wilderness,
A work, so recently began,
Where Liberty enlightens man:
Her powerful voice, at length, awakes
Imprisoned seas and bounded lakes.

The great idea to pursue,
To lead the veins the system through;
Such glorious toils to emulate,
Should be the task of every *State*.

From *Erie's* shores to *Hudson's* stream
The unrivalled work would endless seem;
Would *millions* for the work demand,
And half depopulate the land.

To *Fancy's* view, what years must run,
What ages, till the task is done!
Even *truth*, severe would seem to say,
One hundred years must pass away: —

The sons might see what sires began,
Still unperformed the mighty plan,
The impeded barque, in durance held,
By hills confined, by rocks repelled. —

Not *China's* wall, though grand and strong,
Five hundred leagues it towers along,
Not China's wall, though stretching far,
Which this vast object can compare,

With such gigantic works of old
This proud *Canal* may be enrolled,
Which to our use no tyrant gave
Nor owes its grandeur to one Slave. —

If kings their object tribes compell'd
With toil immense, such walls to build,
A *new Republic* in the west
(A great example to the rest)
Can seas unite, and *here* will shew
What Freedom's nervous sons can do.

See Commerce *here* expand her sail,
And distant shores those waters hail,
As wafting to Manhattan's coast
The products that new regions boast.

And hence our fleets transport their freights
To jealous kings and sister states,
And spread her fame from shore to shore,
Where suns ascend, or billows roar,

To make the purpose all complete,
Before they bid *two oceans* meet;
Before the task is finished, all,
What rocks must yield, what forests fall?

Three years elapsed, behold it done!
A work from Nature's *chaos* won;
By hearts of oak and hands of toil
The Spade inverts the rugged soil
A work, that may remain secure
While suns exist and Moon's endure.

With patient step I see them move
O'er many a plain, through many a grove;
Herculean strength disdains the sod
Where tigers ranged or *Mohawks* trod;
The powers that can the soil subdue
Will see the mighty project through.

Ye patrons of this bold design
Who *Erie* to the *Atlantic* join,
To you be every honour paid—
No time shall see your fame decayed:—
Through gloomy groves you traced the plan,
The rude abodes of savage man.

Ye Prompters of a work so vast
That may for years, for centuries last;
Where Nature toiled to bar the way
You mark'd her steps, but changed her sway.

Ye Artists, who, with skillful hand,
Conduct such rivers through the land,
Proceed!—and in your bold carreer
May every Plan as wise appear,
As *this*, which joins to *Hudson's* wave
What Nature to *St. Lawrence* gave.

To Mr. Blanchard,
the Celebrated Aeronaut in America

Nil Mortalibus ard unum lest
Cælum ipsum petimus *stuttistra.*
HORACE.

From Persian looms the silk *he* wove
No *Weaver* meant should trail above
The surface of the earth we tread,
To deck the matron or the maid.

But *you* ambitious, have design'd
With silk to soar above mankind: —
On silk you hang your splendid car
And mount towards the morning star.

How can you be so careless—gay:
Would you amidst red lightnings play;
Meet sulphurous blasts, and fear them not—
Is Phæton's sad fate forgot?

Beyond our view you mean to rise—
And *this Balloon*, of mighty size,
Will to the astonish'd eye appear,
An atom wafted thro' the air.

Where would you rove? amidst the storms,
Departed Ghosts, and shadowy forms,
Vast tracts of æther, and, what's more,
A sea of space without a shore!—

Would you to Herschell find the way—
To Saturn's Moons, undaunted stray;
Or, wafted on a silken wing,
Alight on Saturn's double ring?

Would you the lunar mountains trace,
Or in her flight fair Venus chase;
Would you, like her, perform the tour
Of sixty thousand miles an hour?—

To move at such a dreadful rate
He must propel, who did create—
By him, indeed, are wonders done
Who follows Venus round the sun.

At Mars arriv'd, what would you see!—
Strange forms, I guess—not such as we;
Alarming shapes, yet seen by none;
For every planet has its own.

If onward still, you urge your flight
You may approach some satellite,
Some of the shining train above
That circle round the orb of Jove.

Attracted by so huge a sphere
You might become a stranger here:
There you might be, if there you fly,
A giant sixty fathoms high.

May heaven preserve you from that fate!
Here, men are men of little weight:
There, Polypheme, it might be shown,
Is but a middle sized baboon.—

This ramble through, the æther pass'd,
Pray tell us when you stop at last;
Would you with gods that æther share,
Or dine on atmospheric air?—

You have a longing for the skies,
To leave the fogs that round us rise,
To haste your flight and speed your wings
Beyond this world of little things.

Your silken project is too great;
Stay here, Blanchard, 'till death or fate
To which, yourself, like us, must bow,
Shall send you where you want to go.

Yes—wait, and let the heav'ns decide;—
Your wishes may be gratified,
And you shall go, as swift as thought,
Where nature has more finely wrought,

Her Chrystal spheres, her heavens serene;
A more sublime, enchanting scene
Than thought depicts or poets feign.

On the Conflagrations at Washington

August 24, 1814

——*Jam deiphobi dedit ampla ruinam,*
Vulcano superante, domus; jam proximus ardet
Ucalegon.
VIRGIL.

Now, George the third rules not alone,
For George the vandal shares the throne,
True flesh of flesh and bone of bone.

God save us from the fangs of both;
Or, one a vandal, one a goth,
May roast or boil us into froth.

Like danes, of old, their fleet they man
And rove from *Beersheba* to *Dan*,
To burn, and beard us—where they can.

They say, at George the fourth's command
This vagrant host were sent, to land
And leave in every house—a brand.

An idiot only would require
Such war—the worst they could desire—
The felon's war—the war of fire.

The warfare, now, th' invaders make
Must surely keep us all awake,
Or life is lost for freedom's sake.

They said to Cockburn, "honest Cock!
To make a noise and give a shock
Push off, and burn their navy dock:

"Their capitol shall be emblazed!
How will the *buckskins* stand amazed,
And curse the day its walls were raised!"

Six thousand heroes disembark—
Each left at night his floating ark
And *Washington* was made their mark.

That few would fight them—few or none—
Was by their leaders clearly shown—
And *"down,"* they said, *"with Madison!"*

How close they crept along the shore!
As closely as if *Rodgers* saw her—
A frigate to a seventy-four.

A veteran host, by veterans led,
With *Ross* and *Cockburn* at their head—
They came—they saw—they burnt—and fled.

But not unpunish'd they retired;
They something paid, for all they fired,
In soldiers kill'd, and chiefs expired.

Five hundred veterans bit the dust,
Who came, inflamed with lucre's lust—
And so they waste—and so they must.

They left our congress naked walls—
Farewell to towers and capitols!
To lofty roofs and splendid halls!

To courtly domes and glittering things,
To folly, that too near us clings,
To courtiers who—tis well—had wings.

Farewell to all but glorious war,
Which yet shall guard *Potomac's* shore,
And honor lost, and fame restore.

To conquer armies in the field
Was, once, the surest method held
To make a hostile country yield.

The mode is this, now acted on;
In conflagrating *Washington*,
They held our independence gone!

Supposing *George's* house at Kew
Were burnt, (as we intend to do,)
Would that be burning England too?

Supposing, near the silver *Thames*
We laid in ashes their *saint James*,
Or *Blenheim* palace wrapt in flames;

Made Hampton Court to fire a prey,
And meanly, then, to sneak away,
And never ask them, what's to pay?

Would that be conquering London town?
Would that subvert the english throne,
Or bring the royal system down?

With all their glare of guards or guns,
How would they look like simpletons,
And not at all the *lion's sons*!

Supposing, then, we take our turn
And make it public law, to burn,
Would not old english honor spurn

At such a mean insidious plan
Which only suits some savage clan—
And surely not—the english man!

A doctrine has prevail'd too long;
A king, they hold, *can do no wrong* —
Merely a pitch-fork, without prong:

But de'il may trust such doctrines, more, —
One king, that wrong'd us, long before,
Has wrongs, by hundreds, yet in store.

He wrong'd us forty years ago;
He wrongs us yet, we surely know;
He'll wrong us till he gets a blow

That, with a vengeance, will repay
The mischiefs we lament this day,
This burning, damn'd, infernal play;

Will send *one city* to the sky,
Its buildings low and buildings high,
And buildings — built the lord knows why;

Will give him an eternal check
That breaks his heart or breaks his neck,
And plants our standard on QUEBEC.

JOEL BARLOW

(1754 – 1812)

from *The Columbiad*

From sultry Mobile's gulf-indented shore
To where Ontario hears his Laurence roar,
Stretcht o'er the broadback'd hills, in long array,
The tenfold Alleganies meet the day,
And show, far sloping from the plains and streams,
The forest azure streak'd with orient beams.
High moved the scene, Columbus gazed sublime,
And thus in prospect hail'd the happy clime:
Blest be the race my guardian guide shall lead
Where these wide vales their various bounties spread.
What treasured stores the hills must here combine!
Sleep still ye diamonds, and ye ores refine;
Exalt your heads ye oaks, ye pines ascend,
Till future navies bid your branches bend;
Then spread the canvas o'er the watery way,
Explore new worlds and teach the old your sway.
  He said, and northward cast his curious eyes
On other cliffs of more exalted size.
Where Maine's bleak breakers line the dangerous coast,
And isles and shoals their latent horrors boast,
High lantern'd in his heaven the cloudless White
Heaves the glad sailor an eternal light;
Who far thro troubled ocean greets the guide,
And stems with steadier helm the stormful tide.

Book I, lines 309 – 332

He spoke; and silent tow'rd the northern sky
Wide o'er the hills the Hero cast his eye,
Saw the long floods thro devious channels pour
And wind their currents to the opening shore;
Interior seas and lonely lakes display
Their glittering glories to the beams of day.

Thy capes, Virginia, towering from the tide,
Raise their blue banks and slope thy barriers wide,
To future sails unfold an inland way
And guard secure thy multifluvian bay;
That drains uncounted realms, and here unites
The liquid mass from Alleganian heights.
York leads his wave, imbank'd in flowery pride,
And nobler James falls winding by his side;
Back to the hills, thro many a silent vale,
Wild Rappahanoc seems to lure the sail,
Patapsco's bosom courts the hand of toil,
Dull Susquehanna laves a length of soil;
But mightier far, in sealike azure spread,
Potomac sweeps his earth disparting bed.
  Long dwelt his eye where these commingling pour'd,
Their waves unkeel'd, their havens unexplored;
Where frowning forests stretch the dusky wing,
And deadly damps forbid the flowers to spring;
No seasons clothe the field with cultured grain,
No buoyant ship attempts the chartless main;
Then, with impatient voice, My Seer, he cried,
When shall my children cross the lonely tide?
Here, here my sons, the hand of culture bring,
Here teach the lawn to smile, the grove to sing;
Ye laboring floods, no longer vainly glide,
Ye harvests load them, and ye forests ride;
Bear the deep burden from the joyous swain,
And tell the world where peace and plenty reign.
  Hesper to this return'd him no reply,
But raised new visions to his roving eye.
He saw broad Delaware the shores divide,
He saw majestic Hudson pour his tide;
Thy stream, my Hartford, thro its misty robe,
Play'd in the sunbeams, belting far the globe;
No watery glades thro richer vallies shine,
Nor drinks the sea a lovelier wave than thine.
  Mystick and Charles refresh their seaward isles,
And gay Piscateway pays his passing smiles;
Swift Kenebec, high bursting from his lakes,
Shoots down the hillsides through the clouds he makes;

And hoarse resounding, gulfing wide the shore,
Dread Laurence labors with tremendous roar;
Laurence, great son of Ocean! lorn he lies
And braves the blasts of hyperborean skies.
Where hoary winter holds his howling reign
And April flings her timid showers in vain,
Groans the choked Flood, in frozen fetters bound,
And isles of ice his angry front surround.
    As old Enceladus, in durance vile,
Spreads his huge length beneath Sicilia's isle,
Feels mountains, crusht by mountains, on him prest,
Close not his veins nor still his laboring breast;
His limbs convulse, his heart rebellious rolls,
Earth shakes responsive to her utmost poles,
While rumbling, bursting, boils his ceaseless ire,
Flames to mid heaven and sets the skies on fire.
So the contristed Laurence lays him low,
And hills of sleet and continents of snow
Rise on his crystal breast; his heaving sides
Crash with the weight, and pour their gushing tides.
Asouth, whence all his hundred branches bend,
Relenting airs with boreal blasts contend;
Far in his vast extremes he swells and thaws,
And seas foam wide between his ice-bound jaws.
Indignant Frost, to hold his captive, plies
His hosted fiends that vex the polar skies,
Unlocks his magazines of nitric stores,
Azotic charms and muriatic powers;
Hail, with its glassy globes, and brume congeal'd,
Rime's fleecy flakes, and storm that heaps the field
Strike thro the sullen Stream with numbing force,
Obstruct his sluices and impede his course.
In vain he strives; his might interior fails;
Nor spring's approach, nor earth's whole heat avails;
He calls his hoary sire; old Ocean roars
Responsive echo thro the Shetland shores.
He comes, the Father! from his bleak domains,
To break with liquid arms the sounding chains;
Clothed in white majesty, he leads from far
His tides high foaming to the wintry war.

Billows on billows lift the maddening brine,
And seas and clouds in battling conflict join,
O'erturn the vast gulf glade with rending sweep,
And crash the crust that bridged the boiling deep;
Till forced aloft, bright bounding thro the air,
Moves the blear ice and sheds a dazzling glare;
The torn foundations on the surface ride,
And wrecks of winter load the downward tide.

The loosen'd ice-isles o'er the main advance,
Toss on the surge and thro the concave dance;
Whirl'd high, conjoin'd, in crystal mountains driven,
Alp over Alp, they build a midway heaven;
Whose million mirrors mock the solar ray
And give condensed the tenfold glare of day.
As tow'rd the south the mass enormous glides
And brineless rivers furrow down its sides,
The thirsty sailor steals a glad supply,
And sultry tradewinds quaff the boreal sky.

But oft insidious death, with mist o'erstrown,
Rides the dark ocean on this icy throne;
When ships thro vernal seas with light airs steer
Their midnight march and deem no danger near.
The steerman gaily helms his course along
And laughs and listens to the watchman's song,
Who walks the deck, enjoys the murky fog,
Sure of his chart, his magnet and his log;
Their shipmates dreaming, while their slumbers last,
Of joys to come, of toils and dangers past.
Sudden a chilling blast comes roaring thro
The trembling shrouds and startles all the crew;
They spring to quarters and perceive too late
The mount of death, the giant strides of fate.
The fullsail'd ship, with instantaneous shock
Dasht into fragments by the floating rock,
Plunges beneath its basement thro the wave,
And crew and cargo glut the watery grave.

Say, Palfrey, brave good man, was this thy doom?
Dwells here the secret of thy midsea tomb?
But, Susan, why that tear? my lovely friend,
Regret may last, but grief should have an end.

An infant then, thy memory scarce can trace
The lines, tho sacred, of thy father's face;
A generous spouse has well replaced the sire;
New duties hence new sentiments require.
  Now where the lakes, those midland oceans, lie,
Columbus turn'd his heaven-illumined eye.
Ontario's banks, unable to retain
The five great Caspians from the distant main,
Burst with the ponderous mass, and forceful whirl'd
His Laurence forth, to balance thus the world.
Above, bold Erie's wave sublimely stood,
Look'd o'er the cliff and heaved his headlong flood;
Where dread Niagara bluffs high his brow
And frowns defiance to the world below.
White clouds of mist expanding o'er him play,
That tinge their skirts in all the beams of day;
Pleased Iris wantons in perpetual pride
And bends her rainbows o'er the dashing tide.
Far glimmering in the north, bleak Huron runs,
Clear Michigan reflects a thousand suns,
And bason'd high, on earth's broad bosom gay,
The bright Superior silvers down the day.
  Blue mounds beyond them far in ether fade,
Deep groves between them cast a solemn shade,
Slow moves their settling mist in lurid streams
And dusky radiance streaks the solar beams.
Fixt on the view the great discoverer stood
And thus addrest the messenger of good:
But why these seats, that seem reserved to grace
The social toils of some illustrious race?
Why spread so wide and form'd so fair in vain?
And why so distant rolls the bounteous main?
These happy regions must forever rest
Of man unseen, by native beasts possest;
And the best heritage, my sons could boast,
Illude their search in far dim deserts lost.
For see, no ship can point her pendants here,
No stream conducts nor ocean wanders near;
Frost, crags and cataracts their north invest,
And the tired sun scarce finds their bounds awest.

To whom the Seraph: Here indeed retires
The happiest land that feels my fostering fires;
Here too shall numerous nations found their seat,
And peace and freedom bless the kind retreat.
Led by this arm thy sons shall hither come,
And streams obedient yield the heroes room,
Spread a broad passage to their well known main,
Nor sluice their lakes nor form their soils in vain.
　Here my bold Missisippi bends his way,
Scorns the dim bounds of yon bleak boreal day
And calls from western heavens, to feed his stream,
The rains and floods that Asian seas might claim.
Strong in his march and charged with all the fates
Of regions pregnant with a hundred states,
He holds in balance, ranged on either hand,
Two distant oceans and their sundering land,
Commands and drains the interior tracts that lie
Outmeasuring Europe's total breadth of sky.
　High in the north his parent fountains wed,
And oozing urns adorn his infant head;
In vain proud Frost his nursing lakes would close
And choke his channel with perennial snows;
From all their slopes he curves his countless rills,
Sweeps their long marshes, saps their settling hills;
Then stretching, straitening south, he gaily gleams,
Swells thro the climes and swallows all their streams;
From zone to zone, o'er earth's broad surface curl'd,
He cleaves his course, he furrows half the world,
Now roaring wild thro bursting mountains driven,
Now calm reflecting all the host of heaven;
Where Cynthia pausing, her own face admires,
And suns and stars repeat their dancing fires.
Wide o'er his meadowy lawns he spreads and feeds
His realms of canes, his waving world of reeds;
Where mammoths grazed the renovating groves,
Slakcd their huge thirst and chill'd their fruitless loves;
Where elks, rejoicing o'er the extinguisht race,
By myriads rise to fill the vacant space.
Earth's widest gulf expands to meet his wave,
Vast isles of ocean in his current lave;

Glad Thetis greets him from his finisht course
And bathes her Nereids in his freshening source.
    To his broad bed their tributary stores
Wisconsin here, there lonely Peter pours;
Croix, from the northeast wilds, his channel fills,
Ohio, gather'd from his myriad hills,
Yazoo and Black, surcharged by Georgian springs,
Rich Illinois his copious treasure brings;
Arkansa, measuring back the sun's long course,
Moine, Francis, Rouge augment the father's force.
But chief of all his family of floods
Missouri marches thro his world of woods;
He scorns to mingle with the filial train,
Takes every course to reach alone the main;
Orient awhile his bending sweep he tries,
Now drains the southern, now the northern skies,
Searches and sunders far the globe's vast frame,
Reluctant joins the sire and takes at last his name.
    There lies the path thy future sons shall trace,
Plant here their arts and rear their vigorous race:
A race predestined, in these choice abodes,
To teach mankind to tame their fluvial floods,
Retain from ocean, as their work requires,
These great auxiliars, raised by solar fires,
Force them to form ten thousand roads and girth
With liquid belts each verdant mound of earth,
To aid the colon's as the carrier's toil,
To drive the coulter and to fat the soil,
Learn all mechanic arts and oft regain
Their native hills in vapor and in rain.
    So taught the Saint. The regions nearer drew
And raised resplendent to their Hero's view
Rich nature's triple reign; for here elate
She stored the noblest treasures of her state,
Adorn'd exuberant this her last domain,
As yet unalter'd by her mimic man,
Sow'd liveliest gems and plants of proudest grace
And strung with strongest nerves her animated race.
    Retiring far round Hudson's frozen bay,
Earth's lessening circles shrink beyond the day;

Snows ever rising with the toils of time
Choke the chill shrubs that brave the dismal clime;
The beasts all whitening roam the lifeless plain,
And caves unfrequent scoop the couch for man.
  Where spring's coy steps in cold Canadia stray
And joyless seasons hold unequal sway,
He saw the pine its daring mantle rear,
Break the rude blast and mock the brumal year,
Shag the green zone that bounds the boreal skies
And bid all southern vegetation rise.
Wild o'er the vast impenetrable round
The untrod bowers of shadowy nature frown'd;
Millennial cedars wave their honors wide,
The fir's tall boughs, the oak's umbrageous pride,
The branching beach, the aspin's trembling shade
Veil the dim heaven and brown the dusky glade.
For in dense crowds these sturdy sons of earth,
In frosty regions, claim a stronger birth;
Where heavy beams the sheltering dome requires
And copious trunks to feed its wintry fires.
  But warmer suns, that southern zones emblaze,
A cool thin umbrage o'er their woodland raise;
Floridia's shores their blooms around him spread,
And Georgian hills erect their shady head;
Whose flowery shrubs regale the passing air
With all the untasted fragrance of the year.
Beneath tall trees, dispersed in loose array,
The rice-grown lawns their humble garb display;
The infant maiz, unconscious of its worth,
Points the green spire and bends the foliage forth;
In various forms unbidden harvests rise,
And blooming life repays the genial skies.
  Where Mexic hills the breezy gulf defend,
Spontaneous groves with richer burdens bend.
Anana's stalk its shaggy honors yields,
Acacia's flowers perfume a thousand fields,
Their cluster'd dates the mast-like palms unfold,
The spreading orange waves a load of gold,
Connubial vines o'ertop the larch they climb,
The long-lived olive mocks the moth of time,

Pomona's pride, that old Grenada claims,
Here smiles and reddens in diviner flames;
Pimento, citron scent the sky serene,
White woolly clusters fringe the cotton's green,
The sturdy fig, the frail deciduous cane
And foodful cocoa fan the sultry plain.

Here, in one view, the same glad branches bring
The fruits of autumn and the flowers of spring;
No wintry blasts the unchanging year deform,
Nor beasts unshelter'd fear the pinching storm;
But vernal breezes o'er the blossoms rove
And breathe the ripen'd juices thro the grove.

Beneath the crystal wave's inconstant light,
Pearls burst their shells to greet the Hero's sight;
From opening earth in living lustre shine
The various treasures of the blazing mine;
Hills, cleft before him, all their stores unfold,
The pale platina and the burning gold;
Silver whole mounds, and gems of dazzling ray
Illume the rocks and shed the beams of day.

Book I, lines 501 – 806

Now grateful truce suspends the burning war,
And groans and shouts promiscuous load the air;
When the tired Britons, where the smokes decay,
Quit their strong station and resign the day.
Slow files along the immeasurable train,
Thousands on thousands redden all the plain,
Furl their torn bandrols, all their plunder yield
And pile their muskets on the battle field.
Their wide auxiliar nations swell the crowd,
And the coopt navies from the neighboring flood
Repeat surrendering signals and obey
The landmen's fate on this concluding day.

Cornwallis first, their late all conquering lord,
Bears to the victor chief his conquer'd sword,
Presents the burnisht hilt and yields with pain
The gift of kings, here brandisht long in vain.
Then bow their hundred banners, trailing far

Their wearied wings from all the skirts of war.
Battalion'd infantry and squadron'd horse
Dash the silk tassel and the golden torse;
Flags from the forts and ensigns from the fleet
Roll in the dust and at Columbia's feet
Prostrate the pride of thrones; they firm the base
Of freedom's temple, while her arms they grace.
Here Albion's crimson Cross the soil o'erspreads,
Her Lion crouches and her Thistle fades;
Indignant Erin rues her trampled Lyre,
Brunswick's pale Steed forgets his foamy fire,
Proud Hessia's Castle lies in dust o'erthrown,
And venal Anspach quits her broken Crown.
   Long trains of wheel'd artillery shade the shore,
Quench their blue matches and forget to roar;
Along the incumber'd plain, thick planted rise
High stacks of muskets glittering to the skies,
Numerous and vast. As when the toiling swains
Heap their whole harvest on the stubbly plains,
Gerb after gerb the bearded shock expands,
Shocks, ranged in rows, hill high the burden'd lands;
The joyous master numbers all the piles
And o'er his well earn'd crop complacent smiles:
Such growing heaps this iron harvest yield,
So tread the victors this their final field.
   Triumphant Washington with brow serene,
Regards unmoved the exhilarating scene,
Weighs in his balanced thought the silent grief
That sinks the bosom of the fallen chief,
With all the joy that laurel crowns bestow,
A world reconquer'd and a vanquisht foe.
Thus thro extremes of life, in every state,
Shines the clear soul, beyond all fortune great,
While smaller minds, the dupes of fickle chance,
Slight woes o'erwhelm and sudden joys entrance.
So the full sun, thro all the changing sky,
Nor blasts nor overpowers the naked eye;
Tho transient splendors, borrow'd from his light,
Glance on the mirror and destroy the sight.

Book VII, lines 713–768

Too much of Europe, here transplanted o'er,
Nursed feudal feelings on your tented shore,
Brought sable serfs from Afric, call'd it gain,
And urged your sires to forge the fatal chain.
But now, the tents o'erturn'd, the war dogs fled,
Now fearless Freedom rears at last her head
Matcht with celestial Peace,—my friends, beware
To shade the splendors of so bright a pair;
Complete their triumph, fix their firm abode,
Purge all privations from your liberal code,
Restore their souls to men, give earth repose
And save your sons from slavery, wars and woes.

Based on its rock of right your empire lies,
On walls of wisdom let the fabric rise;
Preserve your principles, their force unfold,
Let nations prove them and let kings behold.
EQUALITY, your first firm-grounded stand;
Then FREE ELECTION; then your FEDERAL BAND;
This holy Triad should for ever shine
The great compendium of all rights divine,
Creed of all schools, whence youths by millions draw
Their themes of right, their decalogues of law;
Till men shall wonder (in these codes inured)
How wars were made, how tyrants were endured.

Then shall your works of art superior rise,
Your fruits perfume a larger length of skies,
Canals careering climb your sunbright hills,
Vein the green slopes and strow their nurturing rills,
Thro tunnel'd heights and sundering ridges glide,
Rob the rich west of half Kenhawa's tide,
Mix your wide climates, all their stores confound
And plant new ports in every midland mound.
Your lawless Missisippi, now who slimes
And drowns and desolates his waste of climes,
Ribb'd with your dikes, his torrent shall restrain
And ask your leave to travel to the main;
Won from his wave while rising cantons smile,
Rear their glad nations and reward their toil.

Book VIII, lines 384–420

But now had Hesper from the Hero's sight
Veil'd the vast world with sudden shades of night.
Earth, sea and heaven, where'er he turns his eye,
Arch out immense, like one surrounding sky
Lampt with reverberant fires. The starry train
Paint their fresh forms beneath the placid main;
Fair Cynthia here her face reflected laves,
Bright Venus gilds again her natal waves,
The Bear redoubling foams with fiery joles,
And two dire Dragons twine two arctic poles.
Lights o'er the land, from cities lost in shade,
New constellations, new galaxies spread,
And each high pharos double flames provides,
One from its fires, one fainter from the tides.

Book IX, lines 1–14

From Mohawk's mouth, far westing with the sun,
Thro all the midlands recent channels run,
Tap the redundant lakes, the broad hills brave,
And Hudson marry with Missouri's wave.
From dim Superior, whose uncounted sails
Shade his full seas and bosom all his gales,
New paths unfolding seek Mackensie's tide,
And towns and empires rise along their side;
Slave's crystal highways all his north adorn,
Like coruscations from the boreal morn.
Proud Missisippi, tamed and taught his road,
Flings forth irriguous from his generous flood
Ten thousand watery glades; that, round him curl'd,
Vein the broad bosom of the western world.

Book X, lines 213–226

Advice to a Raven in Russia

December, 1812

Black fool, why winter here? These frozen skies,
Worn by your wings and deafen'd by your cries,
Should warn you hence, where milder suns invite,
And day alternates with his mother night.
    You fear perhaps your food will fail you there,
Your human carnage, that delicious fare
That lured you hither, following still your friend
The great Napoleon to the world's bleak end.
You fear, because the southern climes pour'd forth
Their clustering nations to infest the north,
Barvarians, Austrians, those who Drink the Po
And those who skirt the Tuscan seas below,
With all Germania, Neustria, Belgia, Gaul,
Doom'd here to wade thro slaughter to their fall,
You fear he left behind no wars, to feed
His feather'd canibals and nurse the breed.
    Fear not, my screamer, call your greedy train,
Sweep over Europe, hurry back to Spain,
You'll find his legions there; the valliant crew
Please best their master when they toil for you.
Abundant there they spread the country o'er
And taint the breeze with every nation's gore,
Iberian, Lussian, British widely strown,
But still more wide and copious flows their own.
    Go where you will; Calabria, Malta, Greece,
Egypt and Syria still his fame increase,
Domingo's fatten'd isle and India's plains
Glow deep with purple drawn from Gallic veins.
No Raven's wing can stretch the flight so far
As the torn bandrols of Napoleon's war.
Choose then your climate, fix your best abode,
He'll make you deserts and he'll bring you blood.
    How could you fear a dearth? have not mankind,
Tho slain by millions, millions left behind?
Has not CONSCRIPTION still the power to weild
Her annual faulchion o'er the human field?

A faithful harvester! or if a man
Escape that gleaner, shall he scape the BAN?
The triple BAN, that like the hound of hell
Gripes with three joles, to hold his victim well.
  Fear nothing then, hatch fast your ravenous brood,
Teach them to cry to Bonaparte for food;
They'll be like you, of all his suppliant train,
The only class that never cries in vain.
For see what mutual benefits you lend!
(The surest way to fix the mutual friend)
While on his slaughter'd troops your tribes are fed,
You cleanse his camp and carry off his dead.
Imperial Scavenger! but now you know
Your work is vain amid these hills of snow.
His tentless troops are marbled thro with frost
And change to crystal when the breath is lost.
Mere trunks of ice, tho limb'd like human frames
And lately warm'd with life's endearing flames,
They cannot taint the air, the world impest,
Nor can you tear one fiber from their breast.
No! from their visual sockets, as they lie,
With beak and claws you cannot pluck an eye.
The frozen orb, preserving still its form,
Defies your talons as it braves the storm,
But stands and stares to God, as if to know
In what curst hands he leaves his world below.
  Fly then, or starve; tho all the dreadful road
From Minsk to Moskow with their bodies strow'd
May count some Myriads, yet they can't suffice
To feed you more beneath these dreary skies.
Go back, and winter in the wilds of Spain;
Feast there awhile, and in the next campaign
Rejoin your master; for you'll find him then,
With his new million of the race of men,
Clothed in his thunders, all his flags unfurl'd,
Raging and storming o'er the prostrate world.
  War after war his hungry soul requires,
State after State shall sink beneath his fires,
Yet other Spains in victim smoke shall rise

And other Moskows suffocate the skies,
Each land lie reeking with its people's slain
And not a stream run bloodless to the main.
Till men resume their souls, and dare to shed
Earth's total vengeance on the monster's head,
Hurl from his blood-built throne this king of woes,
Dash him to dust, and let the world repose.

MANOAH BODMAN

(1765–1850)

from *An Oration on Death*

What rich profusion here,
  Is scatter'd all abroad,
To make us love and fear,
  Obey and worship God.
    And sound his praise,
      Through every clime,
    In constant lays,
      Till end of time.

The huge leviathan,
  The oyster and the eel,
The lion and the lamb,
  Each in their nature feel.
    And go abroad,
      In quest of food,
    Depend on God,
      For every good.

These shining crumbs of clay,
  With yellow, green and gold,
March on their lucid way,
  And day in night unfold.
    And shine so bright,
      And please themselves,
    And fill'd with light,
      They quit their cells.

―――――――

Is dull conformity
   Confin'd to spirits alone,
Who all so clearly see
   The Great, the Three in One?
      Forbid it sense,
         It cannot be:
      In heaven's immense,
         They different see.

JOHN QUINCY ADAMS

(1767–1848)

The Wants of Man

"Man wants but little here below,
Nor wants that little long."
—GOLDSMITH'S HERMIT.

I.

"Man wants but little here below,
    Nor wants that little long."
'Tis not with ME exactly so,
    But 'tis so in the song.
MY wants are many, and if told
    Would muster many a score;
And were each wish a mint of gold,
    I still should long for more.

II.

What first I want is daily bread,
    And canvas backs and wine;
And all the realms of nature spread
    Before me when I dine.
Four courses scarcely can provide
    My appetite to quell,
With four choice cooks from France, beside,
    To dress my dinner well.

III.

What next I want, at heavy cost,
    Is elegant attire;—
Black sable furs, for winter's frost,
    And silks for summer's fire,
And Cashmere shawls, and Brussels lace
    My bosom's front to deck,
And diamond rings my hands to grace,
    And rubies for my neck.

IV.

And then I want a mansion fair,
   A dwelling house, in style,
Four stories high, for wholesome air—
   A massive marble pile;
With halls for banquets and balls,
   All furnished rich and fine;
With stabled studs in fifty stalls,
   And cellars for my wine.

V.

I want a garden and a park,
   My dwelling to surround—
A thousand acres (bless the mark),
   With walls encompassed round—
Where flocks may range and herds may low,
   And kids and lambkins play,
And flowers and fruits commingled grow,
   All Eden to display.

VI.

I want, when summer's foliage falls,
   And autumn strips the trees,
A house within the city's walls,
   For comfort and for ease.
But here, as space is somewhat scant,
   And acres somewhat rare,
My house in town I only want
   To occupy——a square.

VII.

I want a steward, butler, cooks;
   A coachman, footman, grooms,
A library of well-bound books,
   And picture-garnished rooms;

Corregios, Magdalen, and Night,
    The matron of the chair;
Guido's fleet coursers in their flight,
    And Claudes at least a pair.

VIII.

I want a cabinet profuse
    Of medals, coins, and gems;
A printing press, for private use,
    Of fifty thousand EMS;
And plants, and minerals, and shells;
    Worms, insects, fishes, birds;
And every beast on earth that dwells,
    In solitude or herds.

IX.

I want a board of burnished plate,
    Of silver and of gold;
Tureens of twenty pounds in weight,
    With sculpture's richest mould;
Plateaus, with chandeliers and lamps,
    Plates, dishes—all the same;
And porcelain vases, with the stamps
    Of Sevres, Angouleme.

X.

And maples, of fair glossy stain,
    Must form my chamber doors,
And carpets of the Wilton grain
    Must cover all my floors;
My walls, with tapestry bedeck'd,
    Must never be outdone;
And damask curtains must protect
    Their colors from the sun.

XI.

And mirrors of the largest pane
   From Venice must be brought;
And sandal-wood, and bamboo cane,
   For chairs and tables bought;
On all the mantel-pieces, clocks
   Of thrice-gilt bronze must stand,
And screens of ebony and box
   Invite the stranger's hand.

XII.

I want (who does not want?) a wife,
   Affectionate and fair,
To solace all the woes of life,
   And all its joys to share;
Of temper sweet, of yielding will,
   Of firm, yet placid mind,
With all my faults to love me still,
   With sentiment refin'd.

XIII.

And as Time's car incessant runs,
   And Fortune fills my store,
I want of daughters and of sons
   From eight to half a score.
I want (alas! can mortal dare
   Such bliss on earth to crave?)
That all the girls be chaste and fair—
   The boys all wise and brave.

XIV.

And when my bosom's darling sings,
   With melody divine,
A pedal harp of many strings
   Must with her voice combine.
A piano, exquisitely wrought,
   Must open stand, apart,
That all my daughters may be taught
   To win the stranger's heart.

XV.

My wife and daughters will desire
   Refreshment from perfumes,
Cosmetics for the skin require,
   And artificial blooms.
The civit fragrance shall dispense,
   And treasur'd sweets return;
Cologne revive the flagging sense,
   And smoking amber burn.

XVI.

And when at night my weary head
   Begins to droop and dose,
A southern chamber holds my bed,
   For nature's soft repose;
With blankets, counterpanes, and sheet,
   Mattrass, and bed of down,
And comfortables for my feet,
   And pillows for my crown.

XVII.

I want a warm and faithful friend,
   To cheer the adverse hour,
Who ne'er to flatter will descend,
   Nor bend the knee to power;
A friend to chide me when I'm wrong,
   My inmost soul to see;
And that my friendship prove as strong
   For him, as his for me.

XVIII.

I want a kind and tender heart,
   For others wants to feel;
A soul secure from Fortune's dart,
   And bosom arm'd with steel;
To bear divine chastisement's rod.
   And mingling in my plan,
Submission to the will of God,
   With charity to man.

XIX.

I want a keen, observing eye,
    An ever-listening ear,
The truth through all disguise to spy,
    And wisdom's voice to hear;
A tongue, to speak at virtue's need,
    In Heaven's sublimest strain;
And lips, the cause of man to plead,
    And never plead in vain.

XX.

I want uninterrupted health,
    Throughout my long career,
And streams of never-failing wealth,
    To scatter far and near;
The destitute to clothe and feed,
    Free bounty to bestow;
Supply the helpless orphan's need,
    And soothe the widow's woe.

XXI.

I want the genius to conceive,
    The talents to unfold,
Designs, the vicious to retrieve,
    The virtuous to uphold;
Inventive power, combining skill,
    A persevering soul,
Of human hearts to mould the will,
    And reach from pole to pole.

XXII.

I want the seals of power and place,
    The ensigns of command,
Charged by the people's unbought grace,
    To rule my native land.
Nor crown, nor sceptre would I ask
    But from my country's will,
By day, by night, to ply the task
    Her cup of bliss to fill.

XXIII.

I want the voice of honest praise
  To follow me behind,
And to be thought in future days
  The friend of human kind;
That after ages, as they rise,
  Exulting may proclaim,
In choral union to the skies,
  Their blessings on my name.

XXIV.

These are the wants of mortal man;
  I cannot want them long,
For life itself is but a span,
  And earthly bliss a song.
My last great want, absorbing all,
  Is, when beneath the sod,
And summon'd to my final call,
  The mercy of my God.

XXV.

And oh! while circles in my veins
  Of life the purple stream,
And yet a fragment small remains
  Of nature's transient dream,
My soul, in humble hope unscar'd,
  Forget not thou to pray,
That this thy WANT may be prepared
  To meet the Judgment Day.

To the Sun-Dial

*Under the Window of the Hall of the House of
Representatives of the United States*

Thou silent herald of Time's silent flight!
   Say, could'st thou speak, what warning voice were thine?
   Shade, who canst only show how others shine!
Dark, sullen witness of resplendent light
In day's broad glare, and when the noontide bright
   Of laughing fortune sheds the ray divine,
   Thy ready favors cheer us—but decline
The clouds of morning and the gloom of night.
Yet are thy counsels faithful, just, and wise;
   They bid us seize the moments as they pass—
Snatch the retrieveless sunbeam as it flies,
   Nor lose one sand of life's revolving glass—
Aspiring still, with energy sublime,
By virtuous deeds to give eternity to Time.

To Sally

*"Integer vitæ, scelerisque purus
Non eget Mauris jaculis, neque arcu."*

The man in righteousness array'd,
   A pure and blameless liver,
Needs not the keen Toledo blade,
   Nor venom-freighted quiver.
What though he wind his toilsome way
   O'er regions wild and weary—
Through Zara's burning desert stray;
   Or Asia's jungles dreary:

What though he plough the billowy deep
   By lunar light, or solar,
Meet the resistless Simoon's sweep,
   Or iceberg circumpolar.
In bog or quagmire deep and dank,

His foot shall never settle;
He mounts the summit of Mont Blanc,
   Or Popocatapetl.

On Chimborazo's breathless height,
   He treads o'er burning lava;
Or snuffs the Bohan Upas blight,
   The deathful plant of Java.
Through every peril he shall pass,
   By Virtue's shield protected;
And still by Truth's unerring glass
   His path shall be directed.

Else wherefore was it, Thursday last,
   While strolling down the valley
Defenceless, musing as I pass'd
   A canzonet to Sally;
A wolf, with mouth protruding snout,
   Forth from the thicket bounded—
I clapped my hands and raised a shout—
   He heard—and fled—confounded.

Tangier nor Tunis never bred
   An animal more crabbed;
Nor Fez, dry nurse of lions, fed
   A monster half so rabid.
Nor Ararat so fierce a beast
   Has seen, since days of Noah;
Nor strong, more eager for a feast,
   The fell constrictor boa.

Oh! place me where the solar beam
   Has scorch'd all verdure vernal;
Or on the polar verge extreme,
   Block'd up with ice eternal—
Still shall my voice's tender lays
   Of love remain unbroken;
And still my charming SALLY praise,
   Sweet smiling and sweet spoken.

JAMES KIRKE PAULDING

(1778–1860)

from *The Backwoodsman*

Neglected Muse! of this our western clime,
How long in servile, imitative rhyme,
Wilt thou thy stifled energies impart,
And miss the path that leads to every heart?
How long repress the brave decisive flight,
Warm'd by thy native fires, led by thy native light?
Thrice happy he who first shall strike the lyre,
With homebred feeling, and with homebred fire;
He need not envy any favour'd bard,
Who Fame's bright meed, and Fortune's smiles reward;
Secure, that wheresoe'er this empire rolls,
Or east, or west, or tow'rd the firm fixed poles,
While Europe's ancient honours fade away,
And sink the glories of her better day,
When, like degenerate Greece, her former fame
Shall stand contrasted with her present shame,
And all the splendours of her bright career
Shall die away, to be relighted here,
A race of myriads will the tale rehearse,
And love the author of the happy verse.
Come then, neglected Muse! and try with me
The untrack'd path—'tis death or victory;
Let Chance or Fate decide, or critics will,
No fame I lose—I am but nothing still.

Book I, lines 17–40

In truth it was a landscape wildly gay
That 'neath his lofty vision smiling lay;
A sea of mingling hills, with forests crown'd,
E'en to their summits, waving all around,
Save where some rocky steep aloft was seen,
Frowning amid the wild romantic scene,

38

Around whose brow, where human step ne'er trode,
Our native Eagle makes his high abode;
Oft in the warring of the whistling gales,
Amid the scampering clouds, he bravely sails,
Without an effort winds the loftiest sky,
And looks into the Sun with steady eye:
Emblem and patron of this fearless land,
He mocks the might of any mortal hand,
And, proudly seated on his native rock,
Defies the World's accumulated shock.
Here, mid the piling mountains scatter'd round,
His winding way majestic Hudson found,
And as he swept the frowning ridge's base,
In the pure mirror of his morning face,
A lovelier landscape caught the gazer's view,
Softer than nature, yet to nature true.
Now might be seen, reposing in stern pride,
Against the mountain's steep and rugged side,
High PUTNAM's battlements, like tow'r of old,
Haunt of night-robbing baron, stout and bold,
Scourge of his neighbour, Nimrod of the chase,
Slave of his king, and tyrant of his race.
Beneath its frowning brow, and far below,
The weltering waves, unheard, were seen to flow
Round West Point's rude and adamantine base,
That call'd to mind old ARNOLD's deep disgrace,
ANDRE's hard fate, lamented, though deserv'd,
And men, who from their duty never swerv'd—
The HONEST THREE—the pride of yeomen bold,
Who sav'd the country which they might have sold;
Refus'd the proffer'd bribe, and, sternly true,
Did what the man that doubts them ne'er would do.
Yes! if the Scroll of never-dying Fame,
Shall tell the truth, 'twill bear each lowly name;
And while the wretched man, who vainly tried
To wound their honour, and his Country's pride,
Shall moulder in the dirt from whence he came,
Forgot, or only recollected to his shame,
Quoted shall be these gallant, honest men,
By many a warrior's voice, and poet's pen,

To wake the sleeping spirit of the land,
And nerve with energy the patriot band.
Beyond, on either side the river's bound,
Two lofty promontories darkly frown'd,
Through which, in times long past, as learned say,
The pent up waters forc'd their stubborn way;
Grimly they frown'd, as menacing the wave
That storm'd their bulwarks with its current brave,
And seem'd to threaten from their shatter'd brow,
To crush the vessels all becalm'd below,
Whose white sails, hanging idly at the mast,
O'er the still waves a deep reflexion cast.
Still farther off, the Kaatskill, bold and high,
Kiss'd the pure concave of the arched sky,
Mingled with that its waving lines of blue,
And shut the world beyond from mortal view.

Book II, lines 61–122

 'Twas sunset's hallow'd time—and such an eve
Might almost tempt an angel Heaven to leave.
Never did brighter glories greet the eye,
Low in the warm, and ruddy Western sky,
Nor the light clouds at Summer eve unfold
More varied tints of purple, red, and gold.
Some in the pure, translucent, liquid breast
Of crystal lake, fast anchor'd seem'd to rest,
Like golden islets scatter'd far and wide,
By elfin skill in Fancy's fabled tide,
Where, as wild Eastern legends idly feign,
Fairy, or genii, hold despotic reign.
Others, like vessels, gilt with burnish'd gold,
Their flitting airy way are seen to hold,
All gallantly equipt with streamers gay,
While hands unseen, or Chance, directs their way;
Around, athwart, the pure ethereal tide,
With swelling purple sail, they rapid glide,
Gay as the barque, where Egypt's wanton queen

Reclining on the shaded deck was seen,
At which as gaz'd the uxorious Roman fool,
The subject world slipt from his dotard rule.
Anon, the gorgeous scene begins to fade,
And deeper hues the ruddy skies invade;
The haze of gathering twilight Nature shrouds,
And pale, and paler, wax the changeful clouds.
Then sunk the breeze into a breathless calm,
The silent dews of evening dropt like balm;
The hungry nighthawk from his lone haunt hies,
To chase the viewless insect through the skies;
The bat began his lantern loving flight,
The lonely whip-poor-will, our bird of night,
Ever unseen, yet ever seeming near,
His shrill note quaver'd in the startled ear;
The buzzing beetle forth did gayly hie,
With idle hum, and careless blund'ring eye;
The little trusty watchman of pale night,
The firefly, trimm'd anew his lamp so bright,
And took his merry airy circuit round
The sparkling meadow's green and fragrant bound,
Where blossom'd clover, bath'd in balmy dew,
In fair luxuriance, sweetly blushing grew.

Book II, lines 167–208

Here lay dark Pittsburgh, from whose site there broke
The manufacturer's black and sparkling smoke,
Where Industry and useful Science reign'd,
And man, by labour, all his wants sustain'd;
There, mid the howling forest dark and drear,
Rov'd the wild Indian, wilder than the deer,
King of the woods—who other blessings priz'd,
And arts and industry alike despis'd:
Hunting the trade, and war the sport he loved,
Free as the winds, the dauntless chieftain rov'd,
Taunting with bitter ire, the pale-fac'd slave,
Who toils for gold from cradle to the grave.

Extremes of habits, manners, time and space,
Brought close together, here stood face to face,
And gave at once a contrast to the view
That other lands and ages never knew;
Pass but the river, and that world where meet
Of bland society each courteous sweet,
Is left behind, for manners wild and rude,
And scenes of death, or deathlike solitude.

Sweet river of the West! a purer wave,
A fairer region never yet did lave!
Tranquil, and smooth, and clear, its current roves
Through flowery meadows, and long sylvan groves;
Winding in silence on its destin'd way,
Idly it lingers with a sweet delay,
And often turns, as if its course to find,
Back to the smiling scenes it left behind.
Sweet river of the West! though yet unsung
By native bard, thy native vales among—
Though yet no strains of native music pour,
To wake the sleeping echoes of thy shore,
Ere long some minstrel from thy banks shall spring,
And track thy wand'rings with a loftier wing,
In worthier strains thy various charms rehearse,
And in oblivion drown my weaker verse.

Yes! the bright day is dawning, when the West
No more shall crouch before old Europe's crest,
When men who claim thy birthright, Liberty,
Shall burst their leading-strings and dare be free,
Nor while they boast thy blessings, trembling stand,
Like dastard slaves before her, cap in hand,
Cherish her old absurdities as new,
And all her cast-off follies here renew;
Statesmen no more from thence their precepts draw,
And borrow both their reason and their law,
Like advertising quacks, right wond'rous sage,
With the same nostrums cure both youth and age,
And blundering up the lofty steeps of fame,
Break down the vigour of our youthful frame,

With stimulatives, fitted to revive
Some worn out profligate, scarce half alive;
When Mind at last shall break its rusty chain,
And here, our chosen monarch, freely reign.

Book II, lines 553–606

'Tis true—yet 'tis no pity that 'tis true,
Many fine things they neither felt nor knew.
Unlike the sons of Europe's happier clime,
They never died to music's melting chime,
Or groan'd, as if in agonizing pain,
At some enervate, whining, sickly strain;
Nor would they sell their heritage of rights,
For long processions, fetes, and pretty sights,
Or barter for a bauble, or a feast,
All that distinguishes the man from beast.
With them, alas! the fairest masterpiece,
Of beggar'd Italy, or rifled Greece,
A chisell'd wonder, or a thing of paint,
A marble godhead, or a canvass saint,
Were poor amends for cities wrapt in flame,
A ruin'd land and deep dishonour'd name;
Nor would they mourn Apollo sent away,
More than the loss of Freedom's glorious day;
Among them was no driv'ling princely race,
Who'd beggar half a state, to buy a vase,
Or starve a province nobly to reclaim,
From mother Earth, a thing without a name,
Some mutilated trunk decay'd and worn,
Of head bereft, of legs and arms all shorn,
Worthless, except to puzzle learned brains,
And cause a world of most laborious pains,
To find if this same headless, limbless thing,
A worthless godhead was, or worthless king.

Book III, lines 499–526

CLEMENT MOORE

(1779–1863)

A Visit from St. Nicholas

'Twas the night before Christmas, when all through
    the house
Not a creature was stirring, not even a mouse;
The stockings were hung by the chimney with care,
In hopes that ST. NICHOLAS soon would be there;
The children were nestled all snug in their beds,
While visions of sugar-plums danced in their heads;
And Mamma in her 'kerchief, and I in my cap,
Had just settled our brains for a long winter's nap;
When out on the lawn there arose such a clatter,
I sprang from the bed to see what was the matter.
Away to the window I flew like a flash,
Tore open the shutters and threw up the sash.
The moon on the breast of the new-fallen snow,
Gave the lustre of mid-day to objects below,
When, what to my wondering eyes should appear,
But a miniature sleigh, and eight tiny rein-deer,
With a little old driver, so lively and quick,
I knew in a moment it must be St. Nick.
More rapid than eagles his coursers they came,
And he whistled, and shouted, and called them by name;
"Now, *Dasher*! now, *Dancer*! now, *Prancer* and *Vixen*!
On, *Comet*! on, *Cupid*! on, *Donder* and *Blitzen*!
To the top of the porch! to the top of the wall!
Now dash away! dash away! dash away all!"
As dry leaves that before the wild hurricane fly,
When they meet with an obstacle, mount to the sky;
So up to the house-top the coursers they flew,
With the sleigh full of Toys, and St. Nicholas too.
And then, in a twinkling, I heard on the roof,
The prancing and pawing of each little hoof—
As I drew in my head, and was turning around,
Down the chimney St. Nicholas came with a bound.

He was dressed all in fur, from his head to his foot,
And his clothes were all tarnished with ashes and soot;
A bundle of Toys he had flung on his back,
And he look'd like a pedlar just opening his pack.
His eyes—how they twinkled! his dimples how merry!
His cheeks were like roses, his nose like a cherry!
His droll little mouth was drawn up like a bow,
And the beard of his chin was as white as the snow;
The stump of a pipe he held tight in his teeth,
And the smoke it encircled his head like a wreath;
He had a broad face and a little round belly,
That shook when he laughed, like a bowlfull of jelly.
He was chubby and plump, a right jolly old elf,
And I laughed when I saw him, in spite of myself,
A wink of his eye and a twist of his head,
Soon gave me to know I had nothing to dread;
He spoke not a word, but went straight to his work,
And fill'd all the stockings; then turned with a jerk,
And laying his finger aside of his nose,
And giving a nod, up the chimney he rose;
He sprang to his sleigh, to his team gave a whistle,
And away they all flew like the down of a thistle.
But I heard him exclaim, ere he drove out of sight,
"Happy Christmas to all, and to all a good night."

FRANCIS SCOTT KEY

(1779–1843)

Defence of Fort M'Henry

O! say can you see, by the dawn's early light,
   What so proudly we hail'd at the twilight's last gleaming,
Whose broad stripes and bright stars through the perilous
        fight,
    O'er the ramparts we watch'd, were so gallantly
        streaming?
      And the rockets' red glare, the bombs bursting in air,
      Gave proof through the night that our flag was still
        there—
        O! say, does that star-spangled banner yet wave
        O'er the land of the free, and the home of the brave?

On the shore, dimly seen through the mists of the deep,
   Where the foe's haughty host in dread silence reposes,
What is that which the breeze o'er the towering steep,
    As it fitfully blows, half conceals, half discloses?
      Now it catches the gleam of the morning's first beam,
      In full glory reflected now shines on the stream—
        'Tis the star-spangled banner, O! long may it wave
        O'er the land of the free, and the home of the brave.

And where is that band who so vauntingly swore
   That the havock of war and the battle's confusion
A home and a country should leave us no more?
    Their blood has wash'd out their foul foot-steps'
        pollution.
      No refuge could save the hireling and slave,
      From the terror of flight or the gloom of the grave;
        And the star-spangled banner in triumph doth wave
        O'er the land of the free, and the home of the brave.

O! thus be it ever when freemen shall stand
    Between their lov'd home, and the war's desolation,
Blest with vict'ry and peace, may the heav'n-rescued land
    Praise the power that hath made and preserv'd us a
        nation!
      Then conquer we must, when our cause it is just,
      And this be our motto—"In God is our trust!"
        And the star-spangled banner in triumph shall wave
        O'er the land of the free, and the home of the brave.

WASHINGTON ALLSTON

(1779–1843)

from *The Sylphs of the Seasons*

And now, in accents deep and low,
Like voice of fondly-cherish'd woe,
    The Sylph of Autumn sad:
Though I may not of raptures sing,
That grac'd the gentle song of Spring,
Like Summer, playful pleasures bring,
    Thy youthful heart to glad;

Yet still may I in hope aspire
Thy heart to touch with chaster fire,
    And purifying love:
For I with vision high and holy,
And spell of quick'ning melancholy,
Thy soul from sublunary folly
    First rais'd to worlds above.

What though be mine the treasures fair
Of purple grape and yellow pear,
    And fruits of various hue,
And harvests rich of golden grain,
That dance in waves along the plain
To merry song of reaping swain,
    Beneath the welkin blue;

With these I may not urge my suit,
Of Summer's patient toil the fruit,
    For mortal purpose given:
Nor may it fit my sober mood
To sing of sweetly murmuring flood,
Or dies of many-colour'd wood,
    That mock the bow of heaven.

But, know, 'twas mine the secret power
That wak'd thee at the midnight hour,
    In bleak November's reign:
'Twas I the spell around thee cast,
When thou didst hear the hollow blast
In murmurs tell of pleasures past,
    That ne'er would come again:

And led thee, when the storm was o'er,
To hear the sullen ocean roar,
    By dreadful calm opprest;
Which still, though not a breeze was there,
Its mountain-billows heav'd in air,
As if a living thing it were,
    That strove in vain for rest.

'Twas I, when thou, subdued by woe,
Didst watch the leaves descending slow,
    To each a moral gave;
And as they mov'd in mournful train,
With rustling sound, along the plain,
Taught them to sing a seraph's strain
    Of peace within the grave.

And then uprais'd thy streaming eye,
I met thee in the western sky
    In pomp of evening cloud;
That, while with varying form it roll'd,
Some wizard's castle seem'd of gold,
And now a crimson'd knight of old,
    Or king in purple proud.

And last, as sunk the setting sun,
And Evening with her shadows dun,
    The gorgeous pageant past,
'Twas then of life a mimic shew,
Of human grandeur here below,
Which thus beneath the fatal blow
    Of Death must fall at last.

Oh, then with what aspiring gaze
Didst thou thy tranced vision raise
    To yonder orbs on high,
And think how wondrous, how sublime
'Twere upwards to their spheres to climb,
And live, beyond the reach of Time,
    Child of Eternity!

And last the Sylph of Winter spake;
The while her piercing voice did shake
    The castle-vaults below.
Oh, youth, if thou, with soul refin'd,
Hast felt the triumph pure of mind,
And learnt a secret joy to find
    In deepest scenes of woe;

If e'er with fearful ear at eve
Hast heard the wailing tempest grieve
    Through chink of shatter'd wall;
The while it conjur'd o'er thy brain
Of wandering ghosts a mournful train,
That low in fitful sobs complain,
    Of Death's untimely call:

Or feeling, as the storm increas'd,
The love of terror nerve thy breast,
    Didst venture to the coast;
To see the mighty war-ship leap
From wave to wave upon the deep,
Like chamoise goat from steep to steep,
    'Till low in valleys lost;

Then, glancing to the angry sky,
Behold the clouds with fury fly
    The lurid moon athwart;
Like armies huge in battle, throng,
And pour in vollying ranks along,
While piping winds in martial song
    To rushing war exhort:

Oh, then to me thy heart be given,
To me, ordain'd by Him in heaven
    Thy nobler powers to wake.
And oh! if thou with poet's soul,
High brooding o'er the frozen pole,
Hast felt beneath my stern control
    The desert region quake;

Or from old Hecla's cloudy height,
When o'er the dismal, half-year's night
    He pours his sulph'rous breath,
Hast known my petrifying wind
Wild ocean's curling billows bind,
Like bending sheaves by harvest hind,
    Erect in icy death;

Or heard adown the mountain's steep
The northern blast with furious sweep
    Some cliff dissever'd dash;
And seen it spring with dreadful bound
From rock to rock, to gulph profound,
While echoes fierce from caves resound
    The never-ending crash:

If thus, with terror's mighty spell
Thy soul inspir'd, was wont to swell,
    Thy heaving frame expand;
Oh, then to me thy heart incline;
For know, the wondrous charm was mine
That fear and joy did thus combine
    In magick union bland.

Nor think confin'd my native sphere
To horrors gaunt, or ghastly fear,
    Or desolation wild:
For I of pleasures fair could sing,
That steal from life its sharpest sting,
And man have made around it cling,
    Like mother to her child.

When thou, beneath the clear blue sky,
So calm no cloud was seen to fly,
  Hast gaz'd on snowy plain,
Where Nature slept so pure and sweet,
She seem'd a corse in winding-sheet,
Whose happy soul had gone to meet
  The blest Angelic train;

Or mark'd the sun's declining ray
In thousand varying colours play
  O'er ice-incrusted heath,
In gleams of orange now, and green,
And now in red and azure sheen,
Like hues on dying dolphins seen,
  Most lovely when in death;

Or seen at dawn of eastern light
The frosty toil of Fays by night
  On pane of casement clear,
Where bright the mimic glaciers shine,
And Alps, with many a mountain pine,
And armed knights from Palestine
  In winding march appear:

'Twas I on each enchanting scene
The charm bestow'd that banish'd spleen
  Thy bosom pure and light.
But still a *nobler* power I claim;
That power allied to poets' fame,
Which language vain has dar'd to name—
  The soul's creative might.

Though Autumn grave, and Summer fair,
And joyous Spring demand a share
  Of Fancy's hallow'd power,
Yet these I hold of humbler kind,
To grosser means of earth confin'd,
Through mortal *sense* to reach the mind,
  By mountain, stream, or flower.

But mine, of purer nature still,
Is *that* which to thy secret will
    Did minister unseen,
Unfelt, unheard; when every sense
Did sleep in drowsy indolence,
And Silence deep and Night intense
    Enshrowded every scene;

That o'er thy teeming brain did raise
The spirits of departed days
    Through all the varying year;
And images of things remote,
And sounds that long had ceas'd to float,
With every hue, and every note,
    As living now they were:

And taught thee from the motley mass
Each harmonizing part to class,
    (Like Nature's self employ'd;)
And then, as work'd thy wayward will,
From these with rare combining skill,
With new-created worlds to fill
    Of space the mighty void.

Oh then to me thy heart incline;
To me whose plastick powers combine
    The harvest of the mind;
To me, whose magic coffers bear
The spoils of all the toiling year,
That still in mental vision wear
    A lustre more refin'd.

She ceas'd—And now in doubtful mood,
All motionless and mute I stood,
    Like one by charm opprest:
By turns from each to each I rov'd,
And each by turns again I lov'd;
For ages ne'er could one have prov'd
    More lovely than the rest.

"Oh blessed band, of birth divine,
What mortal task is like to mine!"—
    And further had I spoke,
When, lo! there pour'd a flood of light
So fiercely on my aching sight,
I fell beneath the vision bright,
    And with the pain I woke.

On a Falling Group in the Last Judgement of Michael Angelo, in the Cappella Sistina

How vast, how dread, o'erwhelming is the thought
Of Space interminable! to the soul
A circling weight that crushes into nought
Her mighty faculties! a wond'rous whole,
Without or parts, beginning, or an end!
How fearful then on desp'rate wings to send
The fancy e'en amid the waste profound!
Yet, born as if all daring to astound,
Thy giant hand, oh Angelo, hath hurl'd
E'en human forms, with all their mortal weight,
Down the dread void—fall endless as their fate!
Already now they seem from world to world
For ages thrown; yet doom'd, another past,
Another still to reach, nor e'er to reach the last!

On the Group of the Three Angels Before the Tent of Abraham, by Raffaelle, in the Vatican

Oh, now I feel as though another sense
From Heaven descending had inform'd my soul;
I feel the pleasurable, full control
Of Grace, harmonious, boundless, and intense.
In thee, celestial Group, embodied lives
The subtle mystery; that speaking gives
Itself resolv'd: the essences combin'd

Of Motion ceaseless, Unity complete.
Borne like a leaf by some soft eddying wind,
Mine eyes, impell'd as by enchantment sweet,
From part to part with circling motion rove,
Yet seem unconscious of the power to move;
From line to line through endless changes run,
O'er countless shapes, yet seem to gaze on One.

On Seeing the Picture of Æolus by Peligrino Tibaldi, in the Institute at Bologna

Full well, Tibaldi, did thy kindred mind
The mighty spell of Bonarroti own.
Like one who, reading magick words, receives
The gift of intercourse with worlds unknown,
'Twas thine, decyph'ring Nature's mystick leaves,
To hold strange converse with the viewless wind;
To see the Spirits, in embodied forms,
Of gales and whirlwinds, hurricanes and storms.
For, lo! obedient to thy bidding, teems
Fierce into shape their stern relentless Lord:
His form of motion ever-restless seems;
Or, if to rest inclin'd his turbid soul,
On Hecla's top to stretch, and give the word
To subject Winds that sweep the desert pole.

On Rembrant; Occasioned by His Picture of Jacob's Dream

As in that twilight, superstitious age
When all beyond the narrow grasp of mind
Seem'd fraught with meanings of supernal kind,
When e'en the learned philosophic sage,
Wont with the stars thro' boundless space to range,
Listen'd with rev'rence to the changeling's tale;
E'en so, thou strangest of all beings strange!
E'en so thy visionary scenes I hail;

That like the ramblings of an idiot's speech,
No image giving of a thing on earth,
Nor thought significant in Reason's reach,
Yet in their random shadowings give birth
To thoughts and things from other worlds that come,
And fill the soul, and strike the reason dumb.

On the Luxembourg Gallery

There is a Charm no vulgar mind can reach,
No critick thwart, no mighty master teach;
A Charm how mingled of the good and ill!
Yet still so mingled that the mystick whole
Shall captive hold the struggling Gazer's will,
'Till vanquish'd reason own its full control.
And such, oh Rubens, thy mysterious art,
The charm that vexes, yet enslaves the heart!
Thy lawless style, from timid systems free,
Impetuous rolling like a troubled sea,
High o'er the rocks of reason's lofty verge
Impending hangs; yet, ere the foaming surge
Breaks o'er the bound, the refluent ebb of taste
Back from the shore impels the wat'ry waste.

To My Venerable Friend, the President of the Royal Academy

From one unus'd in pomp of words to raise
A courtly monument of empty praise,
Where self, transpiring through the flimsy pile,
Betrays the builder's ostentatious guile,
Accept, oh West, these unaffected lays,
Which genius claims and grateful justice pays.
Still green in age, thy vig'rous powers impart
The youthful freshness of a blameless heart:
For thine, unaided by another's pain,
The wiles of envy, or the sordid train

Of selfishness, has been the manly race
Of one who felt the purifying grace
Of honest fame; nor found the effort vain
E'en for itself to love thy soul-ennobling art.

America to Great Britain

All hail! thou noble Land,
   Our Fathers' native soil!
O stretch thy mighty hand,
   Gigantic grown by toil,
O'er the vast Atlantic wave to our shore:
   For thou with magic might
   Canst reach to where the light
   Of Phœbus travels bright
     The world o'er!

The Genius of our clime,
   From his pine-embattled steep,
Shall hail the guest sublime;
   While the Tritons of the deep
With their conchs the kindred league shall proclaim.
   Then let the world combine—
   O'er the main our Naval Line
   Like the milky way shall shine
     Bright in fame!

Though ages long have past
   Since our Fathers left their home,
Their pilot in the blast,
   O'er untravell'd seas to roam,
Yet lives the blood of England in our veins!
   And shall we not proclaim
   That blood of honest fame
   Which no tyranny can tame
     By its chains?

While the language free and bold
    Which the Bard of Avon sung,
In which our Milton told
    How the vault of Heaven rung
When Satan, blasted, fell with his host;
    While this, with rev'rence meet,
    Ten thousand echoes greet,
    From rock to rock repeat
        Round our coast;

While the manners, while the arts,
    That mould a nation's soul,
Still cling around our hearts—
    Between let ocean roll,
Our joint communion breaking with the Sun:
    Yet still from either beach
    The voice of blood shall reach,
    More audible than speech,
        'We are One.'

Coleridge

And thou art gone most loved, most honor'd friend!
No—never more thy gentle voice shall blend
With air of earth its pure ideal tones—
Binding in one, as with harmonious zones,
The heart and intellect. And I no more
Shall with thee gaze on that unfathom'd deep,
The Human Soul; as when, push'd off the shore,
Thy mystic bark would thro' the darkness sweep—
Itself the while so bright! For oft we seem'd
As on some starless sea—all dark above,
All dark below—yet, onward as we drove,
To plough up light that ever round us stream'd.
But he who mourns is not as one bereft
Of all he loved: thy living Truths are left.

Art

O Art, high gift of Heaven! how oft defamed
When seeming praised! To most a craft that fits,
By dead, prescriptive Rule, the scattered bits
Of gathered knowledge; even so misnamed
By some who would invoke thee; but not so
By him,—the noble Tuscan,—who gave birth
To forms unseen of man, unknown to Earth,
Now living habitants; he felt the glow
Of thy revealing touch, that brought to view
The invisible Idea; and he knew,
E'en by his inward sense, its form was true:
'T was life to life responding,—highest truth!
So, through Elisha's faith, the Hebrew Youth
Beheld the thin blue air to fiery chariots grow.

On the Statue of an Angel, by Bienaimé, in the Possession of J. S. Copley Greene, Esq.

Ah, who can look on that celestial face,
And kindred for it claim with aught on earth?
If ever here more lovely form had birth,—
No, never that supernal purity,—that grace
So eloquent of unimpassioned love!
That, by a simple movement, thus imparts
Its own harmonious peace, the while our hearts
Rise, as by instinct, to the world above.
And yet we look on cold, unconscious stone.
But what is *that* which thus our spirits own
As Truth and Life? 'T is not material Art,—
But e'en the Sculptor's soul to sense unsealed.
O, never may he doubt,—its witness so revealed,—
There lives within him an immortal part!

On Kean's Hamlet

O thou who standest 'mid the bards of old,
  Like Chimborazo, when the setting sun
  Has left his hundred mountains dark and dun,
  Sole object visible, the imperial One,
In purple robe, and diadem of gold,—
Immortal Shakspeare! who can hope to tell,
  With tongue less gifted, of the pleasing sadness
  Wrought in thy deepest scenes of woe and madness?
  Who hope by words to paint the ecstatic gladness
Of spirits leaping 'mid thy merry spell?
When I have gazed upon thy wondrous page,
  And seen, as in some necromantic glass,
  Thy visionary forms before me pass,
  Like breathing things of every living class,
Goblin and Hero, Villain, Fool, and Sage,
It seemed a task not Buonarroti's e'en,
  Nor Raffael's hand could master by their art,—
  To give the semblance of the meanest part
  Of all thy vast creation, or the heart
Touch as thou touchest with a kindred scene.
And vainer still, methought, by mimic tone,
  And feignèd look, and attitude, and air,
  The Actor's toil; for self will have its share
  With nicest mimicry, and, though it spare
To others largely, gives not all its own.
So did I deem, till, living to my view,
  Scorning his country while he sought her good,
  In Kemble forth the unbending Roman stood;
  Till, snuffing at the scent of human blood,
In Cooke strode forth the unrelenting Jew.
But these were beings tangible in vice,
  Their purpose searchable, their every thought
  Indexed in living men; yet only sought,
  Plain as they seem, by genius,—only bought
By genius even with laborious price.
But who, methought, in confidence so brave,
  Doffing himself, shall dare that form assume

So strangely mixed of wisdom, wit, and gloom,—
Playful in misery even at the tomb,—
Of hope, distrust, of faith and doubt, the slave?
That being strange, that only in the brain
   Perchance has lived, yet still so rarely knit
   In all its parts,—its wisdom to its wit,
   And doubt to faith, loathing to love, so fit,—
It seems like one that lived, and lives again!
Who, then, dare wear the princely Denmark's form?
   What starts before me?—Ha! 't is he I 've seen
   Oft in a day-dream, when my youth was green,—
   The Dane himself,—the Dane! Who says 't is Kean?
Yet sure it moves,—as if its blood were warm.
If this be Kean, then Hamlet lived indeed!
   Look! how his purpose hurries him apace,
   Seeking a fitful rest from place to place!
   And yet his trouble fits him with a grace,
As if his heart did love what makes it bleed.
He seems to move as in a world ideal,
   A world of thought, where wishes have their end
   In wishing merely, where resolves but spend
   Themselves resolving,—as his will did lend
Not counsel e'en his body to defend.
Or Kean or Hamlet,—what I see is real!

A Word: Man

How vast a world is figured by a word!
A little word, a very point of sound,
Breathed by a breath, and in an instant heard;
Yet leaving that may well the soul astound,—
To sense a shape, to thought without a bound.
For who shall hope the mystery to scan
Of that dark being symbolized in *man*?
His outward form seems but a speck in space:
But what far star shall check the eternal race
Of one small thought that rays from out his mind?
For evil, or for good, still, still must travel on

His every thought, though worlds are left behind,
Nor backward can the race be ever run.
How fearful, then, that the first evil ray,
Still red with Abel's blood, is on its way!

On Michael Angelo

'T is not to honor thee by verse of mine
    I bear a record of thy wondrous power;
Thou stand'st alone, and needest not to shine
With borrowed lustre: for the light is thine
    Which no man giveth; and, though comets lower
Portentous round thy sphere, thou still art bright;
    Though many a satellite about thee fall,
Leaving their stations merged in trackless night,
Yet take not they from that supernal light
    Which lives within thee, sole, and free of all.

Rubens

Thus o'er his art indignant Rubens reared
His mighty head, nor critic armies feared.
His lawless style, from vain pretension free,
Impetuous rolling like a troubled sea,
High o'er the rocks of Reason's ridgy verge
Impending hangs; but, ere the foaming surge
Breaks o'er the bound, the under-ebb of taste
Back from the shore impels the watery waste.

JOHN PIERPONT

(1785–1866)

from *Airs of Palestine*

Here let us pause:—the opening prospect view:—
How fresh this mountain air!—how soft the blue,
That throws its mantle o'er the length'ning scene!
Those waving groves—those vales of living green—
Those yellow fields—that lake's cerulean face,
That meets, with curling smiles, the cool embrace
Of roaring torrents, lull'd by her to rest;—
That white cloud, melting on the mountain's breast;
How the wide landscape laughs upon the sky!
How rich the light, that gives it to the eye!
    Where lies our path?—though many a vista call,
We may admire, but cannot tread them all.
Where lies our path!—a poet, and inquire
What hills, what vales, what streams become the lyre!
See, there Parnassus lifts his head of snow;
See at his foot, the cool Cephissus flow;
There Ossa rises; there Olympus towers;
Between them, Tempè breathes in beds of flowers,
Forever verdant; and there Peneus glides
Through laurels whispering on his shady sides.
Your theme is Music:—Yonder rolls the wave,
Where dolphins snatch'd Arion from his grave,
Enchanted by his lyre:—Citheron's shade
Is yonder seen, where first Amphion play'd
Those potent airs, that, from the yielding earth,
Charm'd stones around him, and gave cities birth.
And fast by Hæmus, Thracian Hebrus creeps
O'er golden sands, and still for Orpheus weeps,
Whose gory head, borne by the stream along,
Was still melodious, and expired in song.
There Nereids sing, and Triton winds his shell;
There be thy path—for there the Muses dwell.
    No, no—a lonelier, lovelier path be mine:

63

Greece and her charms I leave, for Palestine.
There, purer streams through happier valleys flow,
And sweeter flowers on holier mountains blow.
I love to breathe where Gilead sheds her balm;
I love to walk on Jordan's banks of palm;
I love to wet my foot in Hermon's dews;
I love the promptings of Isaiah's muse:
In Carmel's holy grots, I'll court repose,
And deck my mossy couch, with Sharon's deathless rose.

lines 55–96

   Now, he recalls the lamentable wail,
That pierc'd the shades of Rama's palmy vale
When Murder struck, thron'd on an infant's bier,
A note, for Satan's, and for Herod's ear.
Now, on a bank, o'erhung with waving wood,
Whose falling leaves flit o'er Ohio's flood,
The pilgrim stands; and o'er his memory rushes
The mingled tide of tears, and blood, that gushes
Along the valleys, where his childhood stray'd,
And round the temples, where his fathers pray'd.
How fondly then, from all but Hope exil'd,
To Zion's woe recurs Religion's child!
He sees the tear of Judah's captive daughters
Mingle, in silent flow, with Babel's waters;
While Salem's harp, by patriot pride unstrung,
Wrapp'd in the mist, that o'er the river hung,
Felt but the breeze, that wanton'd o'er the billow,
And the long, sweeping fingers of the willow.

lines 515–532

   On Arno's bosom, as he calmly flows,
And his cool arms round Vallombrosa throws.
Rolling his crystal tide through classic vales,
Alone,—at night,—the Italian boatman sails.
High o'er Mont Alto, walks, in maiden pride,

Night's queen:—he sees her image on that tide,
Now, ride the wave that curls its infant crest,
Around his prow, then rippling sinks to rest;
Now, glittering dance around his eddying oar,
Whose every sweep is echoed from the shore;
Now, far before him, on a liquid bed
Of waveless water, rest her radiant head.
How mild the empire of that virgin queen!
How dark the mountain's shade! how still the scene!
Hush'd by her silver sceptre, zephyrs sleep
On dewy leaves, that overhang the deep,
Nor dare to whisper through the boughs, nor stir
The valley's willow, nor the mountain's fir,
Nor make the pale and breathless aspen quiver,
Nor brush, with ruffling wing, that glassy river.
    Hark!—'tis a convent's bell:—its midnight chime.
For music measures even the march of Time:—
O'er bending trees, that fringe the distant shore,
Gray turrets rise:—the eye can catch no more.
The boatman, listening to the tolling bell,
Suspends his oar:—a low and solemn swell,
From the deep shade, that round the cloister lies,
Rolls through the air, and on the water dies.
What melting song wakes the cold ear of Night?
A funeral dirge, that pale nuns, rob'd in white,
Chant round a sister's dark and narrow bed,
To charm the parting spirit of the dead.
Triumphant is the spell! with raptur'd ear,
That uncaged spirit hovering lingers near;—
Why should she mount? why pant for brighter bliss,
A lovelier scene, a sweeter song than this!

lines 569 – 604

    In what rich harmony, what polished lays,
Should man address thy throne, when Nature pays
Her wild, her tuneful tribute to the sky!
Yes, Lord, she sings thee, but she knows not why.
The fountain's gush, the long resounding shore,

The zephyr's whisper, and the tempest's roar,
The rustling leaf, in autumn's fading woods,
The wintry storm, the rush of vernal floods,
The summer bower, by cooling breezes fann'd,
The torrent's fall, by dancing rainbows spann'd,
The streamlet, gurgling through its rocky glen,
The long grass, sighing o'er the graves of men,
The bird that crests yon dew-bespangled tree,
Shakes his bright plumes, and trills his descant free,
The scorching bolt, that from thine armory hurl'd,
Burns its red path, and cleaves a shrinking world;
All these are music to Religion's ear; —
Music, thy hand awakes, for man to hear.
Thy hand invested in their azure robes,
Thy breath made buoyant yonder circling globes,
That bound and blaze along the elastic wires,
That viewless vibrate on celestial lyres,
And in that high and radiant concave tremble,
Beneath whose dome, adoring hosts assemble,
To catch the notes, from those bright spheres that flow,
Which mortals dream of, but which angels know.

lines 752–777

from *A Word from a Petitioner*

A weapon that comes down as still
    As snow-flakes fall upon the sod;
But executes a freeman's will
    As lightning does the will of God;
And from its force, nor doors nor locks
Can shield you; — 't is the ballot-box.

Black as your deed shall be the balls
    That from that box shall pour like hail!
And, when the storm upon you falls,
    How will your craven cheeks turn pale!
For, at its coming though ye laugh,
'T will sweep you from your hall, like chaff.

Not women, now,—the *people* pray.
   Hear us,—or *from* us ye will hear!
Beware!—a desperate game ye play!
   The men that thicken in your rear,—
Kings though ye be,—may not be scorned.
Look to your move! your stake!—YE 'RE WARNED!

The Fugitive Slave's Apostrophe to the North Star

Star of the North! though night winds drift
   The fleecy drapery of the sky
Between thy lamp and me, I lift,
   Yea, lift with hope, my sleepless eye
To the blue heights wherein thou dwellest,
And of a land of freedom tellest.

Star of the North! while blazing day
   Pours round me its full tide of light,
And hides thy pale but faithful ray,
   I, too, lie hid, and long for night:
For night;—I dare not walk at noon,
Nor dare I trust the faithless moon,—

Nor faithless man, whose burning lust
   For gold hath riveted my chain;
Nor other leader can I trust,
   But thee, of even the starry train;
For, all the host around thee burning,
Like faithless man, keep turning, turning.

I may not follow where they go:
   Star of the North, I look to thee
While on I press; for well I know
   Thy light and truth shall set me free;—
Thy light, that no poor slave deceiveth;
Thy truth, that all my soul believeth.

They of the East beheld the star
   That over Bethlehem's manger glowed;
With joy they hailed it from afar,
   And followed where it marked the road,
Till, where its rays directly fell,
They found the Hope of Israel.

Wise were the men who followed thus
   The star that sets man free from sin!
Star of the North! thou art to us,—
   Who 're slaves because we wear a skin
Dark as is night's protecting wing,—
Thou art to us a holy thing.

And we are wise to follow thee!
   I trust thy steady light alone:
Star of the North! thou seem'st to me
   To burn before the Almighty's throne,
To guide me, through these forests dim
And vast, to liberty and HIM.

Thy beam is on the glassy breast
   Of the still spring, upon whose brink
I lay my weary limbs to rest,
   And bow my parching lips to drink.
Guide of the friendless negro's way,
I bless thee for this quiet ray!

In the dark top of southern pines
   I nestled, when the driver's horn
Called to the field, in lengthening lines,
   My fellows at the break of morn.
And there I lay, till thy sweet face
Looked in upon "my hiding-place."

The tangled cane-brake,—where I crept
   For shelter from the heat of noon,
And where, while others toiled, I slept

Till wakened by the rising moon,—
As its stalks felt the night wind free,
Gave me to catch a glimpse of thee.

Star of the North! in bright array
    The constellations round thee sweep,
Each holding on its nightly way,
    Rising, or sinking in the deep,
And, as it hangs in mid heaven flaming,
The homage of some nation claiming.

This nation to the Eagle cowers;
    Fit ensign! she 's a bird of spoil;—
Like worships like! for each devours
    The earnings of another's toil.
I 've felt her talons and her beak,
And now the gentler Lion seek.

The Lion, at the Virgin's feet
    Crouches, and lays his mighty paw
Into her lap!—an emblem meet
    Of England's Queen and English law:—
Queen, that hath made her Islands free!
Law, that holds out its shield to me!

Star of the North! upon that shield
    Thou shinest!—O, for ever shine!
The negro, from the cotton-field,
    Shall then beneath its orb recline,
And feed the Lion couched before it,
Nor heed the Eagle screaming o'er it!

SAMUEL WOODWORTH

(1785–1842)

The Bucket

Air — The Flower of Dumblane

How dear to this heart are the scenes of my childhood,
  When fond recollection presents them to view!
The orchard, the meadow, the deep-tangled wild-wood,
  And every loved spot which my infancy knew!
The wide-spreading pond, and the mill that stood by it,
  The bridge, and the rock where the cataract fell,
The cot of my father, the dairy-house nigh it,
  And e'en the rude bucket that hung in the well—
The old oaken bucket, the iron-bound bucket,
The moss-covered bucket which hung in the well.

That moss-covered vessel I hail'd as a treasure,
  For often at noon, when return'd from the field,
I found it the source of an exquisite pleasure,
  The purest and sweetest that nature can yield.
How ardent I seized it, with hands that were glowing,
  And quick to the white-pebbled bottom it fell;
Then soon, with the emblem of truth overflowing,
  And dripping with coolness, it rose from the well—
The old oaken bucket, the iron-bound bucket,
The moss-covered bucket, arose from the well.

How sweet from the green mossy brim to receive it,
  As poised on the curb it inclined to my lips!
Not a full blushing goblet could tempt me to leave it,
  The brightest that beauty or revelry sips.
And now, far removed from the loved habitation,
  The tear of regret will intrusively swell,
As fancy reverts to my father's plantation,
  And sighs for the bucket that hangs in the well—
The old oaken bucket, the iron-bound bucket,
The moss-covered bucket that hangs in the well!

RICHARD HENRY DANA

(1787–1879)

The Dying Raven

Come to these lonely woods to die alone?
It seems not many days since thou wast heard,
From out the mists of spring, with thy shrill note,
Calling unto thy mates—and their clear answers.
The earth was brown, then; and the infant leaves
Had not put forth to warm them in the sun,
Or play in the fresh air of heaven. Thy voice,
Shouting in triumph, told of winter gone,
And prophesying life to the seal'd ground,
Did make me glad with thoughts of coming beauties.
And now they're all around us;—offspring bright
Of earth,—a mother, who, with constant care,
Doth feed and clothe them all.—Now o'er her fields,
In blessed bands, or single, they are gone,
Or by her brooks they stand, and sip the stream;
Or peering o'er it,—vanity well feign'd—
In quaint approval seem to glow and nod
At their reflected graces.—Morn to meet,
They in fantastic labours pass the night,
Catching its dews, and rounding silvery drops
To deck their bosoms.—There, on tall, bald trees,
From varnish'd cells some peep, and the old boughs
Make to rejoice and dance in the unseen winds.
Over my head the winds and they make music;
And grateful, in return for what they take,
Bright hues and odours to the air they give.

Thus mutual love brings mutual delight—
Brings beauty, life;—for love is life—hate, death.

Thou Prophet of so fair a revelation!
Thou who abod'st with us the winter long,
Enduring cold or rain, and shaking oft,

From thy dark mantle, falling sleet or snow—
Thou, who with purpose kind, when warmer days
Shone on the earth, midst thaw and steam, cam'st forth
From rocky nook, or wood, thy priestly cell,
To speak of comfort unto lonely man—
Didst say to him,—though seemingly alone
'Midst wastes and snows, and silent, lifeless trees,
Or the more silent ground—that 't was not death,
But nature's sleep and rest, her kind repair;—
That Thou, albeit unseen, did'st bear with him
The winter's night, and, patient of the day,
And cheer'd by hope, (instinct divine in Thee,)
Waitedst return of summer.

More Thou saidst,
Thou Priest of Nature, Priest of God, to man!
Thou spok'st of Faith, (than instinct no less sure,)
Of Spirits near him, though he saw them not:
Thou bad'st him ope his intellectual eye,
And see his solitude all populous:
Thou showd'st him Paradise, and deathless flowers;
And didst him pray to listen to the flow
Of living waters.

Preacher to man's spirit!
Emblem of Hope! Companion! Comforter!
Thou faithful one! is this thine end? 'T was thou,
When summer birds were gone, and no form seen
In the void air, who cam'st, living and strong,
On thy broad, balanced pennons, through the winds.
And of thy long enduring, this the close!
Thy kingly strength brought down, of storms
Thou Conqueror!

The year's mild, cheering dawn
Upon thee shone a momentary light.
The gales of spring upbore thee for a day,
And then forsook thee. Thou art fallen now;
And liest amongst thy hopes and promises—

Beautiful flowers, and freshly springing blades,
Gasping thy life out.—Here for thee the grass
Tenderly makes a bed; and the young buds
In silence open their fair, painted folds—
To ease thy pain, the one—to cheer thee, these.
But thou art restless; and thy once keen eye
Is dull and sightless now. New blooming boughs,
Needlessly kind, have spread a tent for thee.
Thy mate is calling to the white, piled clouds,
And asks for thee. No answer give they back.
As I look up to their bright angel faces,
Intelligent and capable of voice
They seem to me. Their silence to my soul
Comes ominous. The same to thee, doom'd bird,
Silence or sound. For thee there is no sound,
No silence.—Near thee stands the shadow, Death;—
And now he slowly draws his sable veil
Over thine eyes. Thy senses soft he lulls
Into unconscious slumbers. The airy call
Thou 'lt hear no longer. 'Neath sun-lighted clouds,
With beating wing, or steady poise aslant,
Thou 'lt sail no more. Around thy trembling claws
Droop thy wings' parting feathers. Spasms of death
Are on thee.

       Laid thus low by age? Or is 't
All-grudging man has brought thee to this end?
Perhaps the slender hair, so subtly wound
Around the grain God gives thee for thy food,
Has proved thy snare, and makes thine inward pain!

    I needs must mourn for thee. For I, who have
No fields, nor gather into garners—I
Bear thee both thanks and love, not fear nor hate.

    And now, farewell! The falling leaves ere long
Will give thee decent covering. Till then,
Thine own black plumage, which will now no more
Glance to the sun, nor flash upon my eyes,

Like armour of steel'd knight of Palestine,
Must be thy pall. Nor will it moult so soon
As sorrowing thoughts on those borne from him, fade
In living man.

              Who scoffs these sympathies,
Makes mock of the divinity within;
Nor feels he gently breathing through his soul
The universal spirit. — Hear it cry,
"How does thy pride abase thee, man, vain man!
How deaden thee to universal love,
And joy of kindred, with all humble things, —
God's creatures all!"

              And surely it is so.
He who the lily clothes in simple glory,
He who doth hear the ravens cry for food,
Hath on our hearts, with hand invisible,
In signs mysterious, written what alone
Our *hearts* may read. — Death bring thee rest, poor Bird.

The Pleasure Boat

I.

Come, hoist the sail, the fast let go!
They 're seated all aboard.
Wave chases wave in easy flow:
The bay is fair and broad.

II.

The ripples lightly tap the boat.
Loose! — Give her to the wind!
She flies ahead: — They 're all afloat:
The strand is far behind.

III.

No danger reach so fair a crew!
Thou goddess of the foam,
I 'll pay thee ever worship due,
If thou wilt bring them home.

IV.

Fair ladies, fairer than the spray
The prow is dashing wide,
Soft breezes take you on your way,
Soft flow the blessed tide!

V.

O, might I like those breezes be,
And touch that arching brow,
I 'd toil for ever on the sea
Where ye are floating now.

VI.

The boat goes tilting on the waves;
The waves go tilting by;
There dips the duck;—her back she laves;
O'er head the sea-gulls fly.

VII.

Now, like the gull that darts for prey,
The little vessel stoops;
Then, rising, shoots along her way,
Like gulls in easy swoops.

VIII.

The sun-light falling on her sheet,
It glitters like the drift,
Sparkling, in scorn of summer's heat,
High up some mountain rift.

IX.

The winds are fresh—she 's driving fast.
Upon the bending tide,
The crinkling sail, and crinkling mast,
Go with her side by side.

X.

Why dies the breeze away so soon?
Why hangs the pennant down?
The sea is glass—the sun at noon.—
—Nay, lady, do not frown;

XI.

For, see, the winged fisher's plume
Is painted on the sea.
Below 's a cheek of lovely bloom.
Whose eyes look up at thee?

XII.

She smiles; thou need'st must smile on her.
And, see, beside her face
A rich, white cloud that doth not stir.—
What beauty, and what grace!

XIII.

And pictured beach of yellow sand,
And peaked rock, and hill,
Change the smooth sea to fairy land.—
How lovely and how still!

XIV.

From yonder isle the thrasher's flail
Strikes close upon the ear;
The leaping fish, the swinging sail
Of that far sloop sound near.

XV.

The parting sun sends out a glow
Across the placid bay,
Touching with glory all the show.—
—A breeze!—Up helm!—Away!

XVI.

Careening to the wind, they reach,
With laugh and call, the shore.
They 've left their foot-prints on the beach.
And shall I see them more?

XVII.

Goddess of Beauty, must I now
Vow'd worship to thee pay?
Dear goddess, I grow old, I trow:—
My head is growing gray.

Daybreak

*"The Pilgrim they laid in a large upper chamber, whose window
opened towards the sun rising: the name of the chamber was Peace;
where he slept till break of day, and then he awoke and sang."*
THE PILGRIM'S PROGRESS.

I.

Now, brighter than the host that all night long,
In fiery armour, up the heavens high
Stood watch, thou com'st to wait the morning's song,
Thou com'st to tell me day again is nigh.
Star of the dawning, cheerful is thine eye;
And yet in the broad day it must grow dim.
Thou seem'st to look on me, as asking why
My mourning eyes with silent tears do swim;
Thou bid'st me turn to God, and seek my rest in Him.

II.

"Canst thou grow sad," thou say'st, "as earth grows bright?
And sigh, when little birds begin discourse
In quick, low voices, e'er the streaming light
Pours on their nests, as sprung from day's fresh source?
With creatures innocent thou must perforce
A sharer be, if that thine heart be pure.
And holy hour like this, save sharp remorse,
Of ills and pains of life must be the cure,
And breathe in kindred calm, and teach thee to endure."

III.

I feel its calm. But there's a sombrous hue
Along that eastern cloud of deep, dull red;
Nor glitters yet the cold and heavy dew;
And all the woods and hill-tops stand outspread
With dusky lights, which warmth nor comfort shed.
Still—save the bird that scarcely lifts its song—
The vast world seems the tomb of all the dead—
The silent city emptied of its throng,
And ended, all alike, grief, mirth, love, hate, and wrong.

IV.

But wrong, and hate, and love, and grief, and mirth
Will quicken soon; and hard, hot toil and strife,
With headlong purpose, shake this sleeping earth
With discord strange, and all that man calls life.
With thousand scatter'd beauties nature's rife;
And airs, and woods, and streams breathe harmonies:—
Man weds not these, but taketh art to wife;
Nor binds his heart with soft and kindly ties:—
He, feverish, blinded, lives, and, feverish, sated, dies.

V.

And 't is because man useth so amiss
Her dearest blessings, Nature seemeth sad;
Else why should she in such fresh hour as this

Not lift the veil, in revelation glad,
From her fair face?—It is that man is mad!
Then chide me not, clear star, that I repine,
When nature grieves; nor deem this heart is bad.
Thou look'st towards earth; but yet the heavens are thine;
While I to earth am bound:—When will the heavens be mine?

VI.

If man would but his finer nature learn,
And not in life fantastic lose the sense
Of simpler things; could nature's features stern
Teach him be thoughtful; then, with soul intense,
I should not yearn for God to take me hence,
But bear my lot, albeit in spirit bow'd,
Remembering humbly why it is, and whence:
But when I see cold man, of reason proud,
My solitude is sad—I'm lonely in the crowd.

VII.

But not for this alone, the silent tear
Steals to mine eyes, while looking on the morn,
Nor for this solemn hour:—fresh life is near,—
But all my joys!—they died when newly born.
Thousands will wake to joy; while I, forlorn,
And like the stricken deer, with sickly eye
Shall see them pass. Breathe calm—my spirit's torn;
Ye holy thoughts,—lift up my soul on high!—
Ye hopes of things unseen, the far-off world bring nigh.

VIII.

And when I grieve, O, rather let it be
That I—whom nature taught to sit with her
On her proud mountains, by her rolling sea—
Who when the winds are up, with mighty stir
Of woods and waters—feel the quick'ning spur
To my strong spirit;—who, as mine own child,
Do love the flower, and in the ragged bur
A beauty see—that I this mother mild
Should leave,—and go with care, and passions fierce and wild!

IX.

How suddenly that straight and glittering shaft,
Shot 'thwart the earth!—In crown of living fire
Up comes the Day!—As if they conscious quaft
The sunny flood, hill, forest, city, spire
Laugh in the wakening light.—Go, vain desire!
The dusky lights have gone; go thou thy way!
And pining discontent, like them, expire!
Be call'd my chamber, PEACE, when ends the day;
And let me with the dawn, like PILGRIM, sing and pray!

The Husband's and Wife's Grave

Husband and wife! No converse now ye hold,
As once ye did in your young day of love,
On its alarms, its anxious hours, delays,
Its silent meditations, its glad hopes,
Its fears, impatience, quiet sympathies;
Nor do ye speak of joy assured, and bliss
Full, certain, and possess'd. Domestic cares
Call you not now together. Earnest talk
On what your children may be, moves you not.
Ye lie in silence, and an awful silence;
'T is not like that in which ye rested once
Most happy—silence eloquent, when heart
With heart held speech, and your mysterious frames,
Harmonious, sensitive, at every beat
Touch'd the soft notes of love.

                              Stillness profound,
Insensible, unheeding, folds you round;
And darkness, as a stone, has seal'd you in.
Away from all the living, here ye rest:
In all the nearness of the narrow tomb,
Yet feel ye not each other's presence now.
Dread fellowship!—together, yet alone.

Is this thy prison-house, thy grave, then, Love?
And doth death cancel the great bond that holds
Commingling spirits? Are thoughts that know no bounds,
But self-inspired, rise upward, searching out
The eternal Mind—the Father of all thought—
Are they become mere tenants of a tomb?—
Dwellers in darkness, who th' illuminate realms
Of uncreated light have visited and lived?—
Lived in the dreadful splendour of that throne,
Which One, with gentle hand the veil of flesh
Lifting, that hung 'twixt man and it, reveal'd
In glory?—throne, before which even now
Our souls, moved by prophetic power, bow down
Rejoicing, yet at their own natures awed?—
Souls that Thee know by a mysterious sense,
Thou awful, unseen Presence—are they quench'd,
Or burn they on, hid from our mortal eyes
By that bright day which ends not; as the sun
His robe of light flings round the glittering stars?

And with our frames do perish all our loves?
Do those that took their root and put forth buds,
And their soft leaves unfolded in the warmth
Of mutual hearts, grow up and live in beauty,
Then fade and fall, like fair unconscious flowers?
Are thoughts and passions that to the tongue give speech,
And make it send forth winning harmonies,—
That to the cheek do give its living glow,
And vision in the eye the soul intense
With that for which there is no utterance—
Are these the body's accidents?—no more?—
To live in it, and when that dies, go out
Like the burnt taper's flame?

                              O, listen, man!
A voice within us speaks that startling word,
"Man, thou shalt never die!" Celestial voices
Hymn it unto our souls: according harps,
By angel fingers touch'd when the mild stars
Of morning sang together, sound forth still

The song of our great immortality:
Thick clustering orbs, and this our fair domain,
The tall, dark mountains, and the deep-toned seas,
Join in this solemn, universal song.
—O, listen, ye, our spirits; drink it in
From all the air! 'T is in the gentle moonlight;
'T is floating 'midst day's setting glories; Night,
Wrapt in her sable robe, with silent step
Comes to our bed and breathes it in our ears:
Night, and the dawn, bright day, and thoughtful eve,
All time, all bounds, the limitless expanse,
As one vast mystic instrument, are touch'd
By an unseen, living Hand, and conscious chords
Quiver with joy in this great jubilee.
—The dying hear it; and as sounds of earth
Grow dull and distant, wake their passing souls
To mingle in this heavenly harmony.

Why is it that I linger round this tomb?
What holds it? Dust that cumber'd those I mourn.
They shook it off, and laid aside earth's robes,
And put on those of light. They're gone to dwell
In love—their God's and angels'. Mutual love
That bound them here, no longer needs a speech
For full communion; nor sensations strong,
Within the breast, their prison, strive in vain
To be set free, and meet their kind in joy.
Changed to celestials, thoughts that rise in each,
By natures new, impart themselves though silent.
Each quick'ning sense, each throb of holy love,
Affections sanctified, and the full glow
Of being, which expand and gladden one,
By union all mysterious, thrill and live
In both immortal frames:—Sensation all,
And thought, pervading, mingling sense and thought!
Ye pair'd, yet one! wrapt in a consciousness
Twofold, yet single—this is love, this life!

Why call we then the square-built monument,
The upright column, and the low laid slab,
Tokens of death, memorials of decay?
Stand in this solemn, still assembly, man,
And learn thy proper nature; for thou see'st,
In these shaped stones and letter'd tables, figures
Of life: More are they to thy soul than those
Which he who talk'd on Sinai's mount with God,
Brought to the old Judeans—types are these,
Of thine eternity.

               I thank Thee, Father,
That at this simple grave, on which the dawn
Is breaking, emblem of that day which hath
No close, Thou kindly unto my dark mind
Hast sent a sacred light, and that away
From this green hillock, whither I had come
In sorrow, Thou art leading me in joy.

The Chanting Cherubs

I.

Whence came ye, Cherubs? from the moon?
   Or from a shining star?
Ye, sure, are sent, a blessed boon,
   From kinder worlds afar;
For while I look, my heart is all delight:
Earth has no creatures half so pure and bright.

II.

From moon, nor star, we hither flew;
   The moon doth wane away;
The stars—they pale at morning dew:
   We 're children of the day;
Nor change, nor night, was ever ours to bear;
Eternal light, and love, and joy, we share.

III.

Then, sons of light, from Heaven above,
   Some blessed news ye bring.
Come ye to chant eternal love,
   And tell how angels sing,
And in your breathing, conscious forms to show
How purer forms above live, breathe, and glow?

IV.

Our parent is a human mind;
   His winged thoughts are we;
To sun, nor stars, are we confined:
   We pierce the deepest sea.
Moved by a Brother's call, our Father bade
Us light on earth: and here our flight is stayed.

RICHARD HENRY WILDE

(1789–1847)

The Lament of the Captive

My life is like the summer rose
   That opens to the morning sky,
And, ere the shades of evening close,
   Is scattered on the ground to die:
Yet on that rose's humble bed
The softest dews of night are shed;
As if she wept such waste to see—
But none shall drop a tear for me!

My life is like the autumn leaf
   That trembles in the moon's pale ray,
Its hold is frail—its date is brief—
   Restless, and soon to pass away:
Yet when that leaf shall fall and fade,
The parent tree will mourn its shade,
The wind bewail the leafless tree,
But none shall breathe a sigh for me!

My life is like the print, which feet
   Have left on TAMPA's desert strand,
Soon as the rising tide shall beat,
   Their track will vanish from the sand:
Yet, as if grieving to efface
All vestige of the human race,
On that lone shore loud moans the sea,
But none shall thus lament for me!

To the Mocking-Bird

Winged mimic of the woods! thou motley fool,
Who shall thy gay buffoonery describe?
Thine ever-ready notes of ridicule
Pursue thy fellows still with jest and gibe;

Wit, sophist, songster, Yorick of thy tribe,
Thou sportive satirist of Nature's school,
To thee the palm of scoffing we ascribe,
Arch mocker, and mad abbot of misrule!
For such thou art by day; but all night long
Thou pour'st a soft, sweet, solemn, pensive strain,
As if thou didst, in this thy moonlight song,
Like to the melancholy Jaques complain,
Musing on falsehood, violence, and wrong,
And sighing for thy motley coat again!

from *Hesperia*

Saint Augustine, thy praise was sung by one
Who, though a jurist in his graver hours, —
Ay, and a politician, — had been won
To trifle with the Muses in thy bowers:
Relic of ancient prowess! past and gone,
What were his reveries 'mid thy falling towers,
Thy Spanish dances and Minorcan Graces,
Altars and orange groves, and Grecian faces?

Saint Anastasia's isle and single palm,
The ruined palace and the empty cell,
Thy rich, luxurious breezes, breathing balm,
The vacant convent and the silent bell,
Thy very air so mystical and calm,
The Constitution's column left to tell—
Alas! none other of the race remain—
How brief the date of liberty in Spain!

All these, and more than I can sing or say,
Court me in vain with their attractive charms;
I may no longer in these haunts delay,
Dreaming of festive scenes, or war's alarms,
In rapture bending over ladies gay,
Or burning as I list to feats of arms:
All I have heard, or feel, I may not tell, —
Much must die with me: Florida, farewell!

Farewell, sweet Florida! upon my dream
Too long I linger, for it is of thee;
Though unexhausted the delightful theme,
From its seductive loveliness I flee;
Leaving unsung full many a crystal stream,
Of most deceptive depth and purity,—
Saint Juan's orange-groves,—Dominga's smiles,—
Smyrna,—Lake George, and all his fairy isles.

Thy thousand silver lakes and shooting stars,
Thy boundless woods and ever-blooming vales,
Thy old invasions and religious wars,
Thine Indian legends and romantic tales,
Thine insurrections and domestic jars,
Thy nameless flowers and voluptuous gales,
All that will win some deathless poet's rhyme,
I leave,—bequeathing thee and them to TIME!

Canto I, stanzas 52–56

Change blots out change,—their very memory dies,
Yet dim traditions of extinguished years
Over oblivion's gloomy gulf arise,
A sky's first rainbow on the flood's last tears:
Glimpses of old creations greet our eyes,
Lost Pleiads' symphonies salute our ears,
With some Hesperian or Atlantic rhyme,
Shedding faint twilight on the depths of TIME!

This world now new was once perhaps the old,—
Oldest of all not utterly forgot,—
For giant Mammoths a luxuriant fold,
Monsters that were of earth, and now are not,—
Sauri, that both on land and ocean rolled,—
Leviathan, Hydrargos, Behemot,
Titanic tortoises, Cyclopean trees,—
All that Geology obscurely sees.

Enough!—too much—of this!—'t is but a dream
That might provoke the pity of the wise,
And cynic's sneer. Return we to our theme,
Our country's plains, lakes, rivers, woods, and skies;
Her mountain-cataract and ocean-stream,
And Nature's solitude, so dear to eyes
That, looking upon man too close and long,
Are sick of power, guilt, fraud, and force, and wrong.

Canto II, stanzas 21–23

Beyond Vermont's green hills, against the skies,
'Mid light clouds floating in the deepest blue,
New-Hampshire's distant, snow-clad mountains rise,
Lofty, distinct, and palpable to view:
Hill, dale, brook, forest, lake, or lawn supplies
The lovely landscape with a different hue,
Sunset and moonlight lending each their ray,
As into twilight melts the closing day.

The moon is high! how well her calm, cold beams
Light Art and Nature's desert wilds and walls!
Whether on Alpine heights her lustre gleams,
Or on the plundered Colosseum falls,
The chosen star of ruins still she seems:
In all she hides or shows—obscures—recalls—
Oblivion, memory, and fancy blend
As on the partial pages of a friend.

Canto III, stanzas 50–51

Mount Auburn! loveliest city of the dead,
No cemetery on earth with thee may vie
In native beauty. Wheresoe'er we tread,
Wood, water, rocks, turf, flowers, salute the eye:
Afar the ocean's bosom is outspread,
And naught distracts our meditations high
And holy reveries. Earth and air and wave
Are tranquil all, as man's best home, the Grave!

What obelisk arises on yon hill,
That overlooks a stately town and bay?
It is a scene to gaze on! Look thy fill!
Yet temples, islands, shipping, what are they?
All charms of art and nature, taste and skill,
Fail to withdraw us from that column gray:
The first great battle-ground our fathers prest,
It marks a Warren's glorious bed of rest!

Canto III, stanzas 101–102

Father of Rivers! standing by thy side,
Life's turbid eddies seem but little worth,
As Fancy traces thy all-conquering tide
To the far-distant regions of the North,
And marks how calm and pure its waters glide,
Till on their course Missouri rushes forth,
Like the Barbarian on his Roman prey,
Leaving behind the stain Time never wears away!

Beltrami, when with peril, toil, and pain
He trod the wilderness to seek thy spring,
And fondly deemed he had the fate to gain,
As he beheld thy new-born streamlet fling
Its drops in bubbles forth like falling rain,
Thought his a triumph worthy of a king,
Himself the Bruce of this the Western Nile: —
At travellers' vanity how woodsmen smile!

At thy true sources the red Indian drank,
Ay, and the weary hunter quenched his thirst,
Nor paused the Naiad of the fount to thank,
Nor thought what giant stream might there be nurst,
Cradled upon its green and mossy bank,
Till from their bed the swelling sources burst,
And to earth's mightiest river gathering, flow
To greet noon's sun above,—the Mexic gulf below!

Thy borders forests and thy stream an ocean,
Dark—fathomless—a torrent in its course;
Whirling and boiling, ceaseless in commotion,
And its own banks corroding by its force;
Image of those who live by deep emotion,—
Victims of love, hope, anger, fear, remorse,
And all the fearful passions that consume
Man's heart between the cradle and the tomb.

Foul are the tenants of thy waters,—all
Amphibious beasts or hideous fish of prey;
And art and nature's perils are not small,
That threat the snorting steam-barb on his way:
Yet whoso tastes thy tide will oft recall
The sweetness of that draught some sultry day,
Till the incredulous untravelled sneer,
And ask you if the stream is *always* clear?

Yet thou too hast thy spots of vernal green,
And leagues of villages thy banks to grace;
Where fields of cane, with orange-groves between
Embosoming white villas, interlace,
Making a bright and happy sylvan scene,
Viewed by its very serfs with laughing face,
The home of hospitality and ease,
Where all alike are pleased, and seek to please.

Canto IV, stanzas 64–69

If the romantic land whose soil I tread
Could give back all its passions—first and last—
Awaking from their dust her fiery dead,
And with them all the history of the past,
No light upon my visions could they shed,
No balm upon my wounded spirit cast:
For me there is no help, no hope, no cure,
I have but to dissemble and endure.

Those very dead—with whom I 've lived so long
That I might lose the living—all combined—
Told or untold their fate, in tale or song,
Could bring no new emotion to my mind;
All known, and all unknown, of right or wrong,
Might come and go, and leave no trace behind.
My heart is stagnant,—Life exhausted shrinks,
Earth fades, and even the flame ethereal sinks.

Canto IV, stanzas 74–75

Where dost thou lie, great Nimrod of the West!
Lord of the wilderness! unhouséd BOONE?
Upon what mountain dost thou take thy rest,
The starry sky thy tent, thy lamp the Moon?
Thou wouldst not sleep with so profound a zest
If thy prophetic dreams could tell how soon
Man and his arts thy forest haunts will spoil
With farms, roads, houses, cities, strife, and toil!

And where is he, the noble savage,—one
Who, had his nation annals, should not die,—
The native orator that called the Sun
"Father of Colors," blending Newton's eye
With Tully's pictured words?—His goal is won,
And now in hunting-grounds beyond the sky
The "Little Turtle" deer and elk pursues,
Nor dreams his fame inspires the white man's muse.

And thou, sophistic Volney! where art thou?
Whose page the Indian chief's bold figures bore
To the far Seine, where Mirabeau's scathed brow,
The Demosthenian laurel briefly wore:
To what Convention doth he thunder now?
What realms of chaos do thy steps explore?
What empires ruined—or to ruin—share
Thine eloquence and his,—if eloquence be there?

The earth we trample answers, Dust to dust!
With all before the flood, and since the fall,
Evil and good, ye sleep,—just and unjust,—
One mother's kindred breast receives us all:
For all beyond, who shall avouch man's trust?
And who refute? What bigot dare to call
For judgment on his fellow-mortal's head?
"What fool rush in where angels dare not tread"?

Marvels, Ohio, on thy soil abound,
Fragments it puzzles Science to explain,
Of mammoth, mastodon, and Indian mound,
Temple, tomb, fortress?—still discussed in vain!
Who may the history of those bones expound?
Where do the annals of that age remain?
What spell shall call both races from the deep
Where Earth's primeval forms and secrets sleep?

Gigantic Sauri, lizards, bats, and fern,
Embalmed in rock with tortoise, bird, and shell,
Wrecks of an old creation rude and stern,
Remain the story of our globe to tell:
Much from that lesson human pride may learn,
And even Philosophy, who reasons well,
By every new discovery might be taught
How limited at last is human thought!

From Nature's fragments some few truths we wrest;
But on these mortal relics endless gloom,
Like Etna on the rebel giant's breast,
Lies, with o'erwhelming weight, a living tomb!
Theirs is a mystery as yet unguessed.
When were they raised, and wherefore? How? By whom?
Whence came the workmen? Who destroyed them? Why?
The Echo of OBLIVION answers,—*I!*

Canto IV, stanzas 81–87

Across the Prairie's silent waste I stray,
A fertile, verdant, woodless, boundless plain;
Shadeless it lies beneath the glare of day,
But gentle breezes sweep the grassy main,
Over whose surface, as they rest or play,
The waving billows sink or rise again;
While some far distant lonely hut or tree
Looms like a solitary sail at sea!

What is yon rude and overhanging steep
That frowns on Illinois' unmurmuring tide,—
Fortress, or cliff, or Pharos of the deep?
Stern Nature's monument of savage pride,
The Sioux's tower of hunger!—Pisa's keep,
Amid whose horrors Ugolino died,
Before that rock of famine well might quail,
Did but an Indian Dante tell its tale.

Wouldst thou receive of Superstition's power
And man's credulity astounding proof,
Behold the modern saint and prophet's bower,
The city of Nauvoo. All grave reproof
Were lost upon such folly:—hour by hour,
Wall upon wall ascends, and roof on roof,
And soon the Impostor's temple will arise,
As if to flout the lightning of the skies.

This in the nineteenth century!—So blind
Are they who deem the mighty triumph wrought,
And point us boldly to "the march of mind,"
As though the world were near perfection brought,
And the Millennium reached, or left behind,
Because scarce worthy of a second thought:
Sages, Philosophers, and Sophists, you
Who praise all things as good, laud great NAUVOO!

Savage Leucadia! to thy steep repair
The pilgrims of a faith,—the bleeding heart;
Sacred thy shrine to Love and to Despair,
And wanting only Sappho's lyric art
To give imprisoned echoes to the air,
Till Oolaïtha's gentle ghost should start,
Wondering to see a pale-face at her grave,
Calling her name and spirit from the wave!

Hast thou forgot our Indian friend's abode,
Our welcome, and the scenes we witnessed there?
The wigwam floor with robes and peltry strewed,—
The calumet of Peace that all must share,—
The council-fire,—the conjurer's tricks it showed,—
The Medicine dance,—the wolf,—the moose,—the bear,—
And the great ball-play, with the dawn begun,
And hardly finished by the set of sun.

How keen, how active is the mimic strife!
What grace of form and motion they display!
Hundred of Grecian statues sprung to life
Would not have seemed of more immortal clay,
Or more Apollo-like. The angry knife
Is laid aside,—or sport might turn to fray,
So fierce the struggle between bands that watch
To stop or urge the ball, or turn, or catch.

Not Angelo's nor Donatello's skill
In folds more graceful human form could twine;
Nor his—my countryman—who, if he will,
May rival yet the artist called "Divine."
Sinews and muscles twist and swell,—veins fill,—
Hither and thither waving groups incline,
Till the live mass crashes confused to earth,
And the ball springs like Discord's apple forth!

Sons of the Forest!—yet not wholly rude,
Children of Nature, eloquent are they,
By their Great Spirit taught in solitude,
To boast o'er pain a more than stoic sway;

Their pastime war affords, the chase their food;
No foe they pardon, and no friend betray;
Admiring nothing,—men without a tear,—
Strangers to falsehood, pity, mirth, and fear.

Here Chastellux and Chateaubriand found
Matter to point a moral or a tale;
This was Atala's consecrated ground,
Ample the canvas—if the colors fail.
Yet should a trump of more exalted sound
The Christian genius and the Martyr hail:
To the fallen monarchs of the vainly free,
"Faithful among the faithless," only he!

Behold the sinking mountain! year by year,
Lower and lower still, the boatman thinks,
Its rudely castellated cliffs appear,
And he is sure that in the stream it sinks.
Gazing in wonder, not unmixed with fear
To see how fast its rocky basis shrinks,
He murmurs to himself in lower tone,
"What does the Devil do with all this stone?"

Superior! shall I call thee lake or sea?
Thou broad Atlantic of the Western waters,
Whose ocean-depths and spring-like purity,
Unstained by civilized or savage slaughters,
Proclaim thee worthiest of streams to be
The bath and mirror of Hesperia's daughters,
Their Caspian thou! alike to freeze or shine,
And every Caspian beauty matched by thine!

Beside thy beach stern Nature's tablets rise,
Her pictured rocks, eternal and sublime,
Mountains her canvass, framed in sea and skies,—
Her colors air and water, earth and time.
Fata Morgana's magic landscape flies,
Even with the mists that o'er Messina climb;
But this endures,—traced on creation's youth,
It will outlive all earthly things save TRUTH!

Colossal wall and column, arch and dome,
O'erhanging cliff and cavern, and cascade,
Ruins like those of Egypt, Greece, or Rome,
And towers that seem as if by giants made;
Surpassing beauty—overwhelming gloom—
Masses of dazzling light and blinding shade,—
All that can awe, delight, o'erpower, amaze,
Rises for leagues on leagues to our bewildered gaze!

Ozolapaida! Helen of the West,
Whose fatal beauty and adulterous joy
Two nations with the scourge of war opprest
Twice tenfold longer than the siege of Troy:
Assiniboin and Sioux both confessed
Such prize well worth the struggle to destroy
A kindred people; but no Homer kept
The memory of thy charms, and so they slept.

Canto IV, stanzas 91–105

FITZ-GREENE HALLECK

(1790–1867)

On the Death of Joseph Rodman Drake

Of New-York, Sept. 1820

Green be the turf above thee,
   Friend of my better days!
None knew thee but to love thee,
   Nor named thee but to praise.

Tears fell, when thou wert dying,
   From eyes unused to weep,
And long, where thou art lying,
   Will tears the cold turf steep.

When hearts, whose truth was proven,
   Like thine, are laid in earth,
There should a wreath be woven
   To tell the world their worth,

And I, who woke each morrow
   To clasp thy hand in mine,
Who shared thy joy and sorrow,
   Whose weal and woe were thine;

It should be mine to braid it
   Around thy faded brow,
But I've in vain essayed it,
   And feel I cannot now.

While memory bids me weep thee,
   Nor thoughts nor words are free,
The grief is fixed too deeply
   That mourns a man like thee.

Alnwick Castle

Home of the Percys' high-born race,
  Home of their beautiful and brave,
Alike their birth and burial place,
  Their cradle, and their grave!
Still sternly o'er the Castle gate
Their house's Lion stands in state,
  As in his proud departed hours;
And warriors frown in stone on high,
And feudal banners "flout the sky"
  Above his princely towers.

A gentle hill its side inclines,
  Lovely in England's fadeless green,
To meet the quiet stream which winds
  Through this romantic scene
As silently and sweetly still,
As when, at evening, on that hill,
  While summer's wind blew soft and low,
Seated by gallant Hotspur's side,
His Katherine was a happy bride,
  A thousand years ago.

Gaze on the Abbey's ruined pile:
  Does not the succouring Ivy, keeping
Her watch around it, seem to smile,
  As o'er a loved one sleeping?
One solitary turret gray
  Still tells, in melancholy glory,
The legend of the Cheviot day,
  The Percys' proudest border story.
That day its roof was triumph's arch;
  Then rang, from aisle to pictured dome,
The light step of the soldier's march,
  The music of the trump and drum;
And babe and sire, the old, the young,
And the monk's hymn, and minstrel's song,
And woman's pure kiss, sweet and long,
  Welcomed her warrior home.

Wild roses by the Abbey towers
   Are gay in their young bud and bloom:
They were born of a race of funeral flowers
That garlanded, in long-gone hours,
   A Templar's knightly tomb.
He died, the sword in his mailed hand,
On the holiest spot of the Blessed Land,
   Where the Cross was damped with his dying breath;
When blood ran free as festal wine,
And the sainted air of Palestine
   Was thick with the darts of death.

Wise with the lore of centuries,
What tales, if there be "tongues in trees,"
   Those giant oaks could tell,
Of beings born and buried here;
Tales of the peasant and the peer,
Tales of the bridal and the bier,
   The welcome and farewell,
Since on their boughs the startled bird
First, in her twilight slumbers, heard
   The Norman's curfew bell.

I wandered through the lofty halls
   Trod by the Percys of old fame,
And traced upon the chapel walls
   Each high, heroic name,
From him who once his standard set
Where now, o'er mosque and minaret,
   Glitter the Sultan's crescent moons;
To him who, when a younger son,
Fought for King George at Lexington,
   A Major of Dragoons.

    *   *   *   *

That last half stanza—it has dashed
   From my warm lip the sparkling cup;
The light that o'er my eye-beam flashed,
   The power that bore my spirit up
Above this bank-note world—is gone;
And Alnwick's but a market town,

And this, alas! its market day,
And beasts and borderers throng the way;
Oxen, and bleating lambs in lots,
Northumbrian boors, and plaided Scots;
    Men in the coal and cattle line,
From Teviot's bard and hero land,
From royal Berwick's beach of sand,
From Wooller, Morpeth, Hexham, and
    Newcastle-upon-Tyne.

These are not the romantic times
So beautiful in Spencer's rhymes,
    So dazzling to the dreaming boy:
Ours are the days of fact, not fable;
Of Knights, but not of the Round Table;
    Of Bailie Jarvie, not Rob Roy:
'Tis what "our President," Munro,
    Has called "the era of good feeling:"
The Highlander, the bitterest foe
To modern laws, has felt their blow,
Consented to be taxed, and vote,
And put on pantaloons and coat,
    And leave off cattle-stealing:
Lord Stafford mines for coal and salt,
The Duke of Norfolk deals in malt,
    The Douglas in red herrings;
And noble name, and cultured land,
Palace, and park, and vassal band
Are powerless to the notes of hand
    Of Rothschild, or the Barings.

The age of bargaining, said Burke,
    Has come: to-day the turbaned Turk,
(Sleep, Richard of the lion heart!
Sleep on, nor from your cearments start,)
    Is England's friend and fast ally;
The Moslem tramples on the Greek,
    And on the Cross and altar stone,
    And Christendom looks tamely on,
And hears the Christian maiden shriek,

And sees the Christian father die;
And not a sabre blow is given
For Greece and fame, for faith and heaven,
   By Europe's craven chivalry.

You'll ask if yet the Percy lives
   In the armed pomp of feudal state?
The present representatives
   Of Hotspur and his "gentle Kate,"
Are some half dozen serving men,
In the drab coat of William Penn;
   A chambermaid, whose lip and eye,
And cheek, and brown hair, bright and curling,
   Spoke Nature's aristocracy;
And one, half groom half Seneschal,
Who bowed me through court, bower, and hall,
From donjon keep to turret wall,
For ten-and-sixpence sterling.

Marco Bozzaris

At midnight, in his guarded tent,
   The Turk was dreaming of the hour
When Greece, her knee in suppliance bent,
   Should tremble at his power:
In dreams, through camp and court, he bore
The trophies of a conqueror;
   In dreams his song of triumph heard;
Then wore his monarch's signet ring:
Then pressed that monarch's throne—a king;
As wild his thoughts, and gay of wing,
   As Eden's garden bird.

At midnight, in the forest shades,
   Bozzaris ranged his Suliote band,
True as the steel of their tried blades,
   Heroes in heart and hand.
There had the Persian's thousands stood,
There had the glad earth drunk their blood

On old Platæa's day;
And now there breathed that haunted air
The sons of sires who conquered there,
With arm to strike, and soul to dare,
 As quick, as far as they.

An hour passed on—the Turk awoke;
 That bright dream was his last;
He woke—to hear his sentries shriek,
"To arms! they come! the Greek! the Greek!"
He woke—to die midst flame, and smoke,
And shout, and groan, and sabre stroke,
 And death shots falling thick and fast
As lightnings from the mountain cloud;
And heard, with voice as trumpet loud,
 Bozzaris cheer his band:
"Strike—till the last armed foe expires;
Strike—for your altars and your fires;
Strike—for the green graves of your sires;
 God—and your native land!"

They fought—like brave men, long and well;
 They piled that ground with Moslem slain,
They conquered—but Bozzaris fell,
 Bleeding at every vein.
His few surviving comrades saw
His smile when rang their proud hurrah,
 And the red field was won;
Then saw in death his eyelids close
Calmly, as to a night's repose,
 Like flowers at set of sun.

Come to the bridal chamber, Death!
 Come to the mother's, when she feels,
For the first time, her first-born's breath;
 Come when the blessed seals
That close the pestilence are broke,
And crowded cities wail its stroke;
Come in consumption's ghastly form,
The earthquake shock, the ocean storm;

Come when the heart beats high and warm,
  With banquet song, and dance, and wine;
And thou art terrible—the tear,
The groan, the knell, the pall, the bier;
And all we know, or dream, or fear
  Of agony, are thine.

But to the hero, when his sword
  Has won the battle for the free,
Thy voice sounds like a prophet's word;
And in its hollow tones are heard
  The thanks of millions yet to be.
Come, when his task of fame is wrought—
Come, with her laurel-leaf, blood-bought—
  Come in her crowning hour—and then
Thy sunken eye's unearthly light
To him is welcome as the sight
  Of sky and stars to prisoned men:
Thy grasp is welcome as the hand
Of brother in a foreign land;
Thy summons welcome as the cry
That told the Indian isles were nigh
  To the world-seeking Genoese,
When the land wind, from woods of palm,
And orange groves, and fields of balm,
  Blew o'er the Haytian seas.

Bozzaris! with the storied brave
  Greece nurtured in her glory's time,
Rest thee—there is no prouder grave,
  Even in her own proud clime.
She wore no funeral weeds for thee,
  Nor bade the dark hearse wave its plume,
Like torn branch from death's leafless tree
In sorrow's pomp and pageantry,
  The heartless luxury of the tomb:
But she remembers thee as one
Long loved, and for a season gone;
For thee her poet's lyre is wreathed,
Her marble wrought, her music breathed;

For thee she rings the birthday bells;
Of thee her babes' first lisping tells;
For thine her evening prayer is said
At palace couch and cottage bed;
Her soldier, closing with the foe,
Gives for thy sake a deadlier blow;
His plighted maiden, when she fears
For him, the joy of her young years,
Thinks of thy fate, and checks her tears:
   And she, the mother of thy boys,
Though in her eye and faded cheek
Is read the grief she will not speak,
   The memory of her buried joys,
And even she who gave thee birth,
Will, by their pilgrim-circled hearth,
   Talk of thy doom without a sigh:
For thou art Freedom's now, and Fame's;
One of the few, the immortal names,
   That were not born to die.

Red Jacket

*A Chief of the Indian Tribes, the Tuscaroras,
on Looking at His Portrait by Weir*

Cooper, whose name is with his country's woven,
   First in her files, her PIONEER of mind—
A wanderer now in other climes, has proven
   His love for the young land he left behind;

And throned her in the senate hall of nations,
   Robed like the deluge rainbow, heaven-wrought,
Magnificent as his own mind's creations,
   And beautiful as its green world of thought:

And faithful to the Act of Congress, quoted
   As law authority,—it passed nem. con.—
He writes that we are, as ourselves have voted,
   The most enlightened people ever known.

That all our week is happy as a Sunday
    In Paris, full of song and dance and laugh;
And that, from Orleans to the Bay of Fundy,
    There's not a bailiff, or an epitaph.

And furthermore— in fifty years, or sooner,
    We shall export our poetry and wine;
And our brave fleet, eight frigates and a schooner,
    Will sweep the seas from Zembla to the Line.

If he were with me, King of Tuscarora!
    Gazing, as I, upon thy portrait now,
In all its medalled, fringed, and beaded glory,
    Its eye's dark beauty, and its thoughtful brow—

Its brow, half martial, and half diplomatic,
    Its eye, upsoaring like an eagle's wings;
Well might he boast that we, the Democratic,
    Outrival Europe, even in our Kings!

For thou wast monarch born. Tradition's pages
    Tell not the planting of thy parent tree,
But that the forest tribes have bent for ages
    To thee, and to thy sires, the subject knee.

Thy name is princely,— if no poet's magic
    Could make RED JACKET grace an English rhyme,
Though some one with a genius for the tragic
    Hath introduced it in a pantomime,

Yet it is music in the language spoken
    Of thine own land; and on her herald roll;
As bravely fought for, and as proud a token
    As Cœur de Lion's, of a warrior's soul.

Thy garb—though Austria's bosom-star would frighten
    That medal pale, as diamonds the dark mine,
And George the Fourth wore, at his court at Brighton,
    A more becoming evening dress than thine;

Yet 'tis a brave one, scorning wind and weather,
   And fitted for thy couch, on field and flood,
As Rob Roy's tartan for the Highland heather,
   Or forest green for England's Robin Hood.

Is strength a monarch's merit, like a whaler's?
   Thou art as tall, as sinewy, and as strong
As earth's first kings—the Argo's gallant sailors,
   Heroes in history and gods in song.

Is beauty?—Thine has with thy youth departed;
   But the love-legends of thy manhood's years,
And she who perished, young and broken-hearted,
   Are—but I rhyme for smiles and not for tears.

Is eloquence?—Her spell is thine that reaches
   The heart, and makes the wisest head its sport;
And there's one rare, strange virtue in thy speeches,
   The secret of their mastery,—they are short.

The monarch mind, the mystery of commanding,
   The birth-hour gift, the art Napoleon,
Of winning, fettering, moulding, wielding, banding
   The hearts of millions till they move as one;

Thou hast it. At thy bidding men have crowded
   The road to death as to a festival;
And minstrels, at their sepulchres, have shrouded
   With banner-folds of glory the dark pall.

Who will believe? Not I—for in deceiving
   Lies the dear charm of life's delightful dream;
I cannot spare the luxury of believing
   That all things beautiful are what they seem.

Who will believe that, with a smile whose blessing
   Would, like the Patriarch's, sooth a dying hour,
With voice as low, as gentle, and caressing,
   As e'er won maiden's lip in moonlit bower;

With look, like patient Job's, eschewing evil;
   With motions graceful, as a bird's in air;
Thou art, in sober truth, the veriest devil
   That e'er clinched fingers in a captive's hair!

That in thy breast there springs a poison fountain,
   Deadlier than that where bathes the Upas tree;
And in thy wrath, a nursing cat-o'-mountain
   Is calm as her babe's sleep, compared with thee!

And underneath that face, like summer ocean's,
   Its lip as moveless, and its cheek as clear,
Slumbers a whirlwind of the heart's emotions,
   Love, hatred, pride, hope, sorrow,—all save fear.

Love—for thy land, as if she were thy daughter,
   Her pipe in peace, her tomahawk in wars;
Hatred—of missionaries and cold water;
   Pride—in thy rifle-trophies and thy scars;

Hope—that thy wrongs, may be by the Great Spirit,
   Remembered and revenged, when thou art gone;
Sorrow—that none are left thee to inherit
   Thy name, thy fame, thy passions, and thy throne!

from *Connecticut*

I.

They burnt their last witch in CONNECTICUT
   About a century and a half ago;
They made a school-house of her forfeit hut,
   And gave a pitying sweet-briar leave to grow
Above her thankless ashes; and they put
   A certified description of the show
Between two weeping willows, craped with black,
On the last page of that year's almanac.

II.

Some warning and well-meant remarks were made
　　Upon the subject by the weekly printers;
The people murmured at the taxes laid
　　To pay for jurymen and pitch-pine splinters,
And the sad story made the rose-leaf fade
　　Upon young listeners' cheeks for several winters,
When told at fire-side eves by those who saw
Executed—the lady and the law.

III.

She and the law found rest: years rose and set;
　　That generation, cottagers and kings,
Slept with their fathers, and the violet
　　Has mourned above their graves a hundred springs:
Few persons keep a file of the Gazette,
　　And almanacs are sublunary things,
So that her fame is almost lost to earth,
As if she ne'er had breathed; and of her birth,

IV.

And death, and lonely life's mysterious matters,
　　And how she played, in our forefathers' times,
The very devil with their sons and daughters;
　　And how those "delicate Ariels" of her crimes,
The spirits of the rocks, and woods, and waters,
　　Obeyed her bidding when, in charméd rhymes,
She muttered, at deep midnight, spells whose power
Woke from brief dream of dew the sleeping summer flower.

V.

And hushed the night-bird's solitary hymn,
　　And spoke in whispers to the forest-tree,
Till his awed branches trembled, leaf and limb,
　　And grouped her church-yard shapes of fantasie
Round merry moonlight's meadow-fountain's brim,

And, mocking for a space the dread decree,
Brought back to dead, cold lips the parted breath,
And changed to banquet-board the bier of death,

VI.

None knew—except a patient, precious few,
Who've read the folios of one COTTON MATHER,
A chronicler of tales more strange than true,
New-England's chaplain, and her history's father;
A second Monmouth's GEOFFRY, a new
HERODOTUS, their laurelled victor rather,
For in one art he soars above them high:
The Greek or Welshman does not always lie.

VII.

Know ye the venerable COTTON? He
Was the first publisher's tourist on this station;
The first who made, by libelling earth and sea,
A huge book, and a handsome speculation:
And ours was then a land of mystery,
Fit theme for poetry's exaggeration,
The wildest wonder of the month; and there
He wandered freely, like a bird or bear,

VIII.

And wove his forest dreams into quaint prose,
Our sires his heroes, where, in holy strife,
They treacherously war with friends and foes;
Where meek Religion wears the assassin's knife,
And 'bids the desert blossom like the rose,'
By sprinkling earth with blood of Indian life,
And rears her altars o'er the indignant bones
Of murdered maidens, wives, and little ones.

JOHN HOWARD PAYNE

(1791–1852)

Home, Sweet Home!

'Mid pleasures and palaces though we may roam,
Be it ever so humble, there's *no* place like home.
A charm from the sky seems to hallow us there,
Which, seek through the *world*, is ne'er met with elsewhere.
      Home! sweet home!
      There's no place like home!

An exile from home, splendour dazzles in vain!
Oh! give me my lowly thatch'd cottage again!
The birds singing gaily that came at my call,
Give me *them*, with the *peace of mind* DEARER than all!
      Home! sweet home!
      There's no place like home!

LYDIA HUNTLEY
SIGOURNEY
(1791–1865)

Indian Names

*"How can the red men be forgotten, while so many of
our states and territories, bays, lakes and rivers, are
indelibly stamped by names of their giving?"*

Ye say they all have passed away,
  That noble race and brave,
That their light canoes have vanished
  From off the crested wave;
That 'mid the forests where they roamed
  There rings no hunter shout,
But their names is on your waters,
  Ye may not wash it out.

'Tis where Ontario's billow
  Like Ocean's surge is curled,
Where strong Niagara's thunders wake
  The echo of the world.
Where red Missouri bringeth
  Rich tribute from the west,
And Rappahannock sweetly sleeps
  On green Virginia's breast.

Ye say their cone-like cabins,
  That clustered o'er the vale,
Have fled away like withered leaves
  Before the autumn gale,
But their memory liveth on your hills,
  Their baptism on your shore,
Your everlasting rivers speak
  Their dialect of yore.

Old Massachusetts wears it,
  Within her lordly crown,
And broad Ohio bears it,
  Amid his young renown;
Connecticut hath wreathed it
  Where her quiet foliage waves,
And bold Kentucky breathed it hoarse
  Through all her ancient caves.

Wachuset hides its lingering voice
  Within his rocky heart,
And Alleghany graves its tone
  Throughout his lofty chart;
Monadnock on his forehead hoar
  Doth seal the sacred trust,
Your mountains build their monument,
  Though ye destroy their dust.

Ye call these red-browed brethren
  The insects of an hour,
Crushed like the noteless worm amid
  The regions of their power;
Ye drive them from their father's lands,
  Ye break of faith the seal,
But can ye from the court of Heaven
  Exclude their last appeal?

Ye see their unresisting tribes,
  With toilsome step and slow,
On through the trackless desert pass,
  A caravan of woe;
Think ye the Eternal's ear is deaf?
  His sleepless vision dim?
Think ye the *soul's blood* may not cry
  From that far land to him?

JOHN NEAL

(1793–1876)

from *The Battle of Niagara*

There's a fierce gray Bird, with a bending beak,
With a glittering eye and a piercing shriek,
That nurses her brood where the cliff-flowers blow
On the precipice top—in perpetual snow—
Where the fountains are mute or in secrecy flow:
A BIRD that is first to worship the sun,
When he gallops in light—till the cloud-tides run
In billows of fire as his course is done:
Above where the torrent is forth in its might—
Above where the fountain is gushing in light—
Above where the silvery flashing is seen
Of streamlets that bend o'er the rich mossy green,
Emblazed with the tint of the young morning's eye—
Like ribbons of flame—or the bow of the sky:
Above that dark torrent—above that bright stream,
Her voice may be heard with its clear wild scream,
As she chants to her God and unfolds in his beam;
While her young are all laid in his rich red blaze,
And their winglets are fledged in his hottest rays:
Proud Bird of the Cliff! where the barren yew springs:
Where the sunshine stays, and the wind-harp sings;
And the heralds of battle are pluming their wings:
That BIRD is abroad over hill-top and flood—
Over valley and rock, over mountain and wood—
Sublimely she sails with her storm-cleaving brood!

Canto I, lines 1–25

O save thy children blue Ontario!—
Who, in the wilderness, can calmly go
To do their worship in a lonely place,
By altars reeking with the she-wolf's trace:
And gaze intrepidly upon the skies,

113

While the red lightning in its anger flies—
When white men, in their terrour, close their eyes:
For man is there sublime—he is a god!
Great Nature's master-piece! like him who trod
The banks of paradise, and stood alone,
The wonder of the skies—erect upon his throne.

   Not like the airy god of moulded light,
Just stepping from his chariot on the sight;
Poising his beauties on a rolling cloud,
With arm unstretched and bow-string twanging loud:
And arrows singing as they pierce the air,
With tinkling sandals and with golden hair;
As if he paused upon his bounding way,
And loosened his fierce arrows—but in play:
But like that angry god, in blazing light
Bursting from space! and standing in his might:
Revealed in his omnipotent array
Apollo of the skies! and Deity of Day!
In godlike wrath! piercing his myriad-foe
With quenchless shafts, that lighten as they go:
Not like that god, when up in air he springs,
With brightening mantle, and with sunny wings,
When heavenly musick murmurs from his strings—
A buoyant vision—an embodied dream
Of dainty Poesy—and boyishly supreme.

   Not the thin spirit waked by young Desire,
Gazing o'er heaven, till her thoughts take fire:
Panting and breathless in her heart's wild trance—
Bright, shapeless forms—the godlings of Romance.
Not that Apollo—not resembling him,
Of silver brow, and woman's nerveless limb:
But man!—all man!—the monarch of the wild!
Not the faint spirit—that corrupting smil'd
On soft voluptuous Greece—but Nature's child,
Arrested in the chase! with piercing eye
Fix'd in its airy light'ning on the sky,
Where some red Bird is languid, eddying, drooping,
Pierced by his arrows in her swiftest stooping.

Thus springing to the skies!—a boy will stand
With arms uplifted, and unconscious hand
Tracing its arrow in its loftiest flight—
And watch it kindling as it cleaves the light,
Of worlds unseen but by the Indian sight;
His robe and hair upon the wind at length,
A creature of the hills!—all grace and strength:
All muscle and all flame—his eager eye
Fixed on one spot as if he could descry
His bleeding victim nestling in the sky.
Not that Apollo!—not the heavenly one,
Voluptuous spirit of a setting sun,—
But this—the offspring of young Solitude,
Child of the holy spot, where none intrude
But genii of the torrent—cliff, and wood—
Nursling of cloud and storm—the desert's fiery brood.

     Great Nature's man!—and not a thing all light:
Etherial vision of distempered sight;
But mingled clouds and sunshine—flame and light.
With arrow not like his of sport—that go
In light of musick from a silver bow:
But barbed with flint—with feather—reeking red,
The heart-blood that some famished wolf hath shed!

     Ontario of the woods! may no broad sail
Ever unfold upon thy mountain gale!
Thy waters were thus spread—so fresh and blue
But for thy white fowl and the light canoe.
Should once the smooth dark lustre of thy breast
With mightier burthens, ever be oppressed—
Farewell to thee! and all thy loveliness!
Commerce will rear her arks—and Nature's dress
Be scattered to the winds: thy shores will bloom,
Like dying flow'rets sprinkled o'er a tomb;
The feverish, fleeting lustre of the flowers
Burst into life in Art's unnatural bowers;
Not the green—graceful—wild luxuriance
Of Nature's garlands, in their negligence:
The clambering jassimine, and flushing rose

That in the wilderness their hearts disclose:
The dewy violet, and the bud of gold,
Where drooping lilies on the wave unfold;
Where nameless flowers hang fainting on the air,
As if they breathed their lovely spirits there;
Where heaven itself is bluer, and the light
Is but a coloured fragrance—floating—bright;
Where the sharp note—and whistling song is heard,
Of many a golden beak, and sunny sparkling bird:

There the tame honeysuckle will arise;
The gaudy hot-house plant will spread its dyes,
In flaunting boldness to the sunny skies:
And sickly buds, as soon as blown, will shed
Their fainting leaves o'er their untimely bed;
Unnatural violets in the blaze appear—
With hearts unwet by youthful Flora's tear:
And the loose poppy with its sleepy death,
And flashy leaf: the warm and torpid breath
Of lazy garlands, over crawling vines;
The tawdry wreath that Fashion intertwines
To deck her languid brow: the streamy gold,
And purple flushing of the tulip's fold;
And velvet buds, of crimson, and of blue,
Unchangeable and lifeless, as the hue
Of Fashion's gaudy wreaths, that ne'er were wet with dew.

Canto II, lines 75–180

It is that hour when listening ones will weep
And know not why: when we would gladly sleep
The last still sleep; and feel no touch of fear,
Till we are startled by a falling tear,
That unexpected gathers in our eye,
While we were panting for yon blessed sky:
That hour of gratitude—of whispering prayer,
When we can hear a worship in the air:
When we are lifted from the earth, and feel
Light fanning wings around us faintly wheel,

And o'er our lids and brow a blessing steal:
And then—as if our sins were all forgiven—
And all our tears were wiped—and we in heaven!

It is that hour of quiet extacy,
When every ruffling wind, that passes by
The sleeping leaf, makes busiest minstrelsy:
When all at once! amid the quivering shade,
Millions of diamond sparklers, are betrayed!
When dry leaves rustle, and the whistling song
Of keen-tuned grass, comes piercingly along:
When windy pipes are heard—and many a lute,
Is touched amid the skies, and then is mute:
When even the foliage on the glittering steep,
Of feathery bloom—is whispering in its sleep:
When all the garlands of the precipice,
Shedding their blossoms, in their moonlight bliss,
Are floating loosely on the eddying air,
And breathing out their fragrant spirits there:
And all their braided tresses in their height,
Are talking faintly to the evening light:
When every cave and grot—and bower and lake,
And drooping flowret-bell, are all awake:
When starry eyes are burning on the cliff
Of many a crouching tyrant too, as if
Such melodies were grateful even to him:
When life is loveliest—and the blue skies swim
In lustre, warm as sunshine—but more dim:
When all the holy centinels of night
Step forth to watch in turn, and worship by their light.

Canto III, lines 31 – 69

Fresher and fresher comes the air. The blue
Of yonder high pavillion swims in dew.
The boundless hum that sunset waked in glee:
The dark wood's vesper-hymn to Liberty—
Hath died away. A deep outspreading hush
Is on the air. The heavy, watery rush

Of far off lake-tides, and the weighty roll
Of tumbling deeps, that fall upon the soul
Like the strong lulling of the ocean wave
In dying thunder o'er the sailor's grave:
And now and then a blueish flare is spread
Faint o'er the western heavens, as if 'twere shed
In dreadful omen to the coming dead.
As if—amid the skies, some warriour form
Revealed his armour thro' a robe of storm!

The shadows deepen. Now the leaden tramp
Of stationed sentry—far—and flat—and damp—
Sounds like the measured death-step, when it comes
With the deep minstrelsy of unstrung drums:
In heavy pomp—with pauses—o'er the grave
Where soldiers bury soldiers: where the wave
Of sable plumes—and darkened flags are seen—
And trailing steeds with funeral lights between:
And folded arms—and boding horns—and tread
Of martial feet descending to the bed,
Where Glory—Fame—Ambition lie in state,
To give the nuptial clasp, and wreath that Fate
Wove in the battle storm, their brows to decorate.

Listen!—there comes a distant, wandering shout,
A sound, as if a challenge passed about:
A gun is heard! O, can it be indeed
That on a night, like this, brave men may bleed!
Now comes,—all rushing—with a fiery start—
The struggling neigh of steeds, as if they part
Upon the mountain tops, where cloud-tides break,
And rear upon the winds! and plunge, and shake
Their voices proudly o'er a sleeping lake.
A heavy walk is heard. They come, indeed;
They come, the Star-troops! while the Eagle-breed
Flap loudly o'er each helm, and o'er each foaming steed.

Canto IV, lines 1–40

CARLOS WILCOX

(1794–1827)

from *The Age of Benevolence*

A sultry noon, not in the summer's prime
When all is fresh with life, and youth, and bloom,
But near its close when vegetation stops,
And fruits mature, stand ripening in the sun,
Sooths and enervates with its thousand charms,
Its images of silence and of rest,
The melancholy mind. The fields are still;
The husbandman has gone to his repast,
And, that partaken, on the coolest side
Of his abode, reclines, in sweet repose.
Deep in the shaded stream the cattle stand,
The flocks beside the fence, with heads all prone
And panting quick. The fields for harvest ripe,
No breezes bend in smooth and graceful waves,
While with their motion, dim and bright by turns,
The sun-shine seems to move; nor e'en a breath
Brushes along the surface with a shade,
Fleeting and thin, like that of flying smoke.
The slender stalks, their heavy bended heads
Support as motionless, as oaks their tops.
O'er all the woods the top-most leaves are still,
E'en the wild poplar leaves, that, pendant hung
By stems elastic, quiver at a breath,
Rest in the general calm. The thistle down
Seen high and thick, by gazing up beside
Some shading object, in a silver shower
Plumb down, and slower than the slowest snow,
Through all the sleepy atmosphere descends;
And where it lights, though on the steepest roof,
Or smallest spire of grass, remains unmoved.
White as a fleece, as dense and as distinct
From the resplendent sky, a single cloud
On the soft bosom of the air becalmed,

Drops a lone shadow as distinct and still,
On the bare plain, or sunny mountain's side;
Or in the polished mirror of the lake,
In which the deep reflected sky appears
A calm sublime immensity below.

*   *   *   *   *   *   Beneath a sun
That crowns the centre of the azure cope,
A blaze of light intense o'erspreads the whole
Of nature's face; and he that overlooks,
From some proud eminence, the champaign round,
Notes all the buildings, scattered far and near,
Both great and small, magnificent and mean,
By their smooth roofs of shining silver white,
Spangling with brighter spots the bright expanse.
No sound, nor motion, of a living thing
The stillness breaks, but such as serve to soothe
Or cause the soul to feel the stillness more.
The yellow-hammer by the way-side picks,
Mutely, the thistle's seed; but in her flight,
So smoothly serpentine, her wings outspread
To rise a little, closed to fall as far,
Moving like sea-fowl o'er the heaving waves,
With each new impulse chimes a feeble note.
The russet grasshopper, at times, is heard,
Snapping his many wings, as half he flies,
Half hovers in the air. Where strikes the sun
With sultriest beams, upon the sandy plain,
Or stony mount, or in the close deep vale,
The harmless locust of this western clime,
At intervals, amid the leaves unseen,
Is heard to sing with one unbroken sound,
As with a long-drawn breath, beginning low,
And rising to the midst with shriller swell,
Then in low cadence dying all away.
Beside the stream collected in a flock,
The noiseless butterflies, though on the ground,
Continue still to wave their open fans
Powder'd with gold; while on the jutting twigs
The spindling insects that frequent the banks,

Rest, with their thin transparent wings outspread
As when they fly. Oft times, though seldom seen,
The cuckoo, that in summer haunts our groves,
Is heard to moan, as if at every breath
Panting aloud. The hawk in mid-air high,
On his broad pinions sailing round and round,
With not a flutter, or but now and then,
As if his trembling balance to regain,
Utters a single scream but faintly heard,
And all again is still.

WILLIAM CULLEN BRYANT

(1794–1878)

Thanatopsis

To him who in the love of nature holds
Communion with her visible forms, she speaks
A various language; for his gayer hours
She has a voice of gladness, and a smile
And eloquence of beauty, and she glides
Into his darker musings, with a mild
And gentle sympathy, that steals away
Their sharpness, ere he is aware. When thoughts
Of the last bitter hour come like a blight
Over thy spirit, and sad images
Of the stern agony, and shroud, and pall,
And breathless darkness, and the narrow house,
Make thee to shudder, and grow sick at heart;—
Go forth, under the open sky, and list
To Nature's teachings, while from all around—
Earth and her waters, and the depths of air,—
Comes a still voice—Yet a few days, and thee
The all-beholding sun shall see no more
In all his course; nor yet in the cold ground,
Where thy pale form was laid, with many tears,
Nor in the embrace of ocean shall exist
Thy image. Earth, that nourished thee, shall claim
Thy growth, to be resolved to earth again;
And, lost each human trace, surrendering up
Thine individual being, shalt thou go
To mix forever with the elements,
To be a brother to the insensible rock
And to the sluggish clod, which the rude swain
Turns with his share, and treads upon. The oak
Shall send his roots abroad, and pierce thy mould.
Yet not to thy eternal resting place
Shalt thou retire alone—nor couldst thou wish
Couch more magnificent. Thou shalt lie down

With patriarchs of the infant world—with kings,
The powerful of the earth—the wise, the good,
Fair forms, and hoary seers of ages past,
All in one mighty sepulchre.—The hills
Rock-ribbed and ancient as the sun,—the vales
Stretching in pensive quietness between;
The venerable woods—rivers that move
In majesty, and the complaining brooks
That make the meadows green; and poured round all,
Old ocean's gray and melancholy waste,—
Are but the solemn decorations all
Of the great tomb of man. The golden sun,
The planets, all the infinite host of heaven,
Are shining on the sad abodes of death,
Through the still lapse of ages. All that tread
The globe are but a handful to the tribes
That slumber in its bosom.—Take the wings
Of morning—and the Barcan desert pierce,
Or lose thyself in the continuous woods
Where rolls the Oregan, and hears no sound,
Save his own dashings—yet—the dead are there,
And millions in those solitudes, since first
The flight of years began, have laid them down
In their last sleep—the dead reign there alone.
So shalt thou rest—and what if thou shalt fall
Unheeded by the living—and no friend
Take note of thy departure? All that breathe
Will share thy destiny. The gay will laugh
When thou art gone, the solemn brood of care
Plod on, and each one as before will chase
His favorite phantom; yet all these shall leave
Their mirth and their employments, and shall come,
And make their bed with thee. As the long train
Of ages glide away, the sons of men,
The youth in life's green spring, and he who goes
In the full strength of years, matron, and maid,
And the sweet babe, and the gray-headed man,—
Shall one by one be gathered to thy side,
By those, who in their turn shall follow them.
So live, that when thy summons comes to join

The innumerable caravan, that moves
To that mysterious realm, where each shall take
His chamber in the silent halls of death,
Thou go not, like the quarry-slave at night,
Scourged to his dungeon, but sustained and soothed
By an unfaltering trust, approach thy grave,
Like one who wraps the drapery of his couch
About him, and lies down to pleasant dreams.

"I Cannot Forget With What Fervid Devotion"

I cannot forget with what fervid devotion
    I worshipped the visions of verse and of fame:
Each gaze at the glories of earth, sky, and ocean,
    To my kindled emotions, was wind over flame.

And deep were my musings in life's early blossom,
    'Mid the twilight of mountain groves wandering long;
How thrilled my young veins, and how throbbed my
        full bosom,
    When o'er me descended the spirit of song.

'Mong the deep-cloven fells that for ages had listened
    To the rush of the pebble-paved river between,
Where the king-fisher screamed and gray precipice
        glistened,
    All breathless with awe have I gazed on the scene;

Till I felt the dark power, o'er my reveries stealing,
    From his throne in the depth of that stern solitude,
And he breathed through my lips, in that tempest
        of feeling,
    Strains warm with his spirit, though artless and rude.

Bright visions! I mixed with the world and ye faded;
    No longer your pure rural worshipper now;
In the haunts your continual presence pervaded,
    Ye shrink from the signet of care on my brow.

In the old mossy groves on the breast of the mountain,
  In deep lonely glens where the waters complain,
By the shade of the rock, by the gush of the fountain,
  I seek your loved footsteps, but seek them in vain.

Oh, leave not, forlorn and forever forsaken,
  Your pupil and victim, to life and its tears!
But sometimes return, and in mercy awaken
  The glories ye showed to his earlier years.

To a Waterfowl

Whither, 'midst falling dew,
While glow the heavens with the last steps of day
Far, through their rosy depths, dost thou pursue
    Thy solitary way?

    Vainly the fowler's eye
Might mark thy distant flight to do thee wrong,
As, darkly painted on the crimson sky,
    Thy figure floats along.

    Seek'st thou the plashy brink
Of weedy lake, or marge of river wide,
Or where the rocking billows rise and sink
    On the chafed ocean side?

    There is a Power whose care
Teaches thy way along that pathless coast,—
The desert and illimitable air,—
    Lone wandering, but not lost.

    All day thy wings have fanned,
At that far height, the cold thin atmosphere,
Yet stoop not, weary, to the welcome land,
    Though the dark night is near.

    And soon that toil shall end,
Soon shalt thou find a summer home, and rest,
And scream among thy fellows; reeds shall bend,
    Soon, o'er thy sheltered nest.

Thou'rt gone, the abyss of heaven
Hath swallow'd up thy form; yet, on my heart
Deeply hath sunk the lesson thou hast given,
    And shall not soon depart.

He, who, from zone to zone,
Guides through the boundless sky thy certain flight,
In the long way that I must tread alone,
    Will lead my steps aright.

Inscription for the Entrance to a Wood

Stranger, if thou hast learnt a truth which needs
No school of long experience, that the world
Is full of guilt and misery, and hast seen
Enough of all its sorrows, crimes, and cares,
To tire thee of it, enter this wild wood
And view the haunts of Nature. The calm shade
Shall bring a kindred calm, and the sweet breeze
That makes the green leaves dance, shall waft a balm
To thy sick heart. Thou wilt find nothing here
Of all that pained thee in the haunts of men
And made thee loathe thy life. The primal curse
Fell, it is true, upon the unsinning earth,
But not in vengeance. God hath yoked to guilt
Her pale tormentor, misery. Hence, these shades
Are still the abodes of gladness, the thick roof
Of green and stirring branches is alive
And musical with birds, that sing and sport
In wantonness of spirit; while below
The squirrel, with raised paws and form erect,
Chirps merrily. Throngs of insects in the shade
Try their thin wings and dance in the warm beam
That waked them into life. Even the green trees
Partake the deep contentment; as they bend
To the soft winds, the sun from the blue sky
Looks in and sheds a blessing on the scene.
Scarce less the cleft-born wild-flower seems to enjoy
Existence, than the winged plunderer

That sucks its sweets. The massy rocks themselves,
And the old and ponderous trunks of prostrate trees
That lead from knoll to knoll a causey rude
Or bridge the sunken brook, and their dark roots,
With all their earth upon them, twisting high,
Breathe fixed tranquillity. The rivulet
Sends forth glad sounds and tripping o'er its bed
Of pebbly sands, or leaping down the rocks,
Seems, with continuous laughter, to rejoice
In its own being. Softly tread the marge,
Lest from her midway perch thou scare the wren
That dips her bill in water. The cool wind,
That stirs the stream in play, shall come to thee,
Like one that loves thee nor will let thee pass
Ungreeted, and shall give its light embrace.

Green River

When breezes are soft and skies are fair,
I steal an hour from study and care,
And hie me away to the woodland scene,
Where wanders the stream with waters of green;
As if the bright fringe of herbs on its brink,
Had given their stain to the wave they drink;
And they, whose meadows it murmurs through,
Have named the stream from its own fair hue.

Yet pure its waters—its shallows are bright
With colored pebbles and sparkles of light,
And clear the depths where its eddies play,
And dimples deepen and whirl away,
And the plane-tree's speckled arms o'ershoot
The swifter current that mines its root,
Through whose shifting leaves, as you walk the hill,
The quivering glimmer of sun and rill,
With a sudden flash on the eye is thrown,
Like the ray that streams from the diamond stone.
Oh, loveliest there the spring days come,
With blossoms, and birds, and wild-bees' hum;

The flowers of summer are fairest there,
And freshest the breath of the summer air;
And sweetest the golden autumn day
In silence and sunshine glides away.

Yet fair as thou art, thou shun'st to glide,
Beautiful stream! by the village side;
But windest away from haunts of men,
To quiet valley and shaded glen;
And forest, and meadow, and slope of hill,
Around thee, are lonely, lovely, and still.
Lonely—save when, by thy rippling tides,
From thicket to thicket the angler glides;
Or the simpler comes with basket and book,
For herbs of power on thy banks to look;
Or haply, some idle dreamer, like me,
To wander, and muse, and gaze on thee.
Still—save the chirp of birds that feed
On the river cherry and seedy reed,
And thy own mild music gushing out
With mellow murmur and fairy shout,
From dawn, to the blush of another day,
Like traveller singing along his way.

That fairy music I never hear,
Nor gaze on those waters so green and clear,
And mark them winding away from sight,
Darkened with shade or flashing with light,
While o'er them the vine to its thicket clings,
And the zephyr stoops to freshen his wings,
But I wish that fate had left me free
To wander these quiet haunts with thee,
Till the eating cares of earth should depart,
And the peace of the scene pass into my heart;
And I envy thy stream, as it glides along,
Through its beautiful banks in a trance of song.

Though forced to drudge for the dregs of men,
And scrawl strange words with the barbarous pen,
And mingle among the jostling crowd,

Where the sons of strife are subtle and loud—
I often come to this quiet place,
To breathe the airs that ruffle thy face,
And gaze upon thee in silent dream,
For in thy lonely and lovely stream,
An image of that calm life appears,
That won my heart in my greener years.

A Winter Piece

The time has been that these wild solitudes,
Yet beautiful as wild—were trod by me
Oftener than now; and when the ills of life
Had chafed my spirit—when the unsteady pulse
Beat with strange flutterings—I would wander forth
And seek the woods. The sunshine on my path
Was to me as a friend. The swelling hills,
The quiet dells retiring far between,
With gentle invitation to explore
Their windings, were a calm society
That talked with me and soothed me. Then the chant
Of birds, and chime of brooks, and soft caress
Of the fresh sylvan air, made me forget
The thoughts that broke my peace, and I began
To gather simples by the fountain's brink,
And lose myself in day-dreams. While I stood
In nature's loneliness, I was with one
With whom I early grew familiar, one
Who never had a frown for me, whose voice
Never rebuked me for the hours I stole
From cares I loved not, but of which the world
Deems highest, to converse with her. When shrieked
The bleak November winds, and smote the woods,
And the brown fields were herbless, and the shades,
That met above the merry rivulet,
Were spoiled, I sought, I loved them still,—they seemed
Like old companions in adversity.
Still there was beauty in my walks; the brook,
Bordered with sparkling frost-work, was as gay

As with its fringe of summer flowers. Afar,
The village with its spires, the path of streams,
And dim receding valleys, hid before
By interposing trees, lay visible
Through the bare grove, and my familiar haunts
Seemed new to me. Nor was I slow to come
Among them, when the clouds, from their still skirts,
Had shaken down on earth the feathery snow,
And all was white. The pure keen air abroad,
Albeit it breathed no scent of herb, nor heard
Love call of bird nor merry hum of bee,
Was not the air of death. Bright mosses crept
Over the spotted trunks, and the close buds,
That lay along the boughs, instinct with life,
Patient, and waiting the soft breath of Spring,
Feared not the piercing spirit of the North.
The snow-bird twittered on the beechen bough,
And 'neath the hemlock, whose thick branches bent
Beneath its bright cold burden, and kept dry
A circle, on the earth, of withered leaves,
The partridge found a shelter. Through the snow
The rabbit sprang away. The lighter track
Of fox, and the racoon's broad path were there,
Crossing each other. From his hollow tree,
The squirrel was abroad, gathering the nuts
Just fallen, that asked the winter cold and sway
Of winter blast, to shake them from their hold.
     But winter has yet brighter scenes,—he boasts
Splendors beyond what gorgeous summer knows;
Or autumn, with his many fruits, and woods
All flushed with many hues. Come, when the rains
Have glazed the snow, and clothed the trees with ice;
While the slant sun of February pours
Into the bowers a flood of light. Approach!
The encrusted surface shall upbear thy steps,
And the broad arching portals of the grove
Welcome thy entering. Look! the massy trunks
Are cased in the pure chrystal, each light spray,
Nodding and tinkling in the breath of heaven,
Is studded with its trembling water-drops,

That stream with rainbow radiance as they move.
But round the parent stem the long low boughs
Bend, in a glittering ring, and arbors hide
The grassy floor. Oh! you might deem the spot,
The spacious cavern of the virgin mine,
Deep in the womb of earth—where the gems grow,
And diamonds put forth radiant rods and bud
With amethyst and topaz—and the place
Lit up, most royally, with the pure beam
That dwells in them. Or haply the vast hall
Of fairy palace, that outlasts the night,
And fades not in the glory of the sun;—
Where chrystal columns send forth slender shafts
And crossing arches; and fantastic aisles
Wind from the sight in brightness, and are lost
Among the crowded pillars. Raise thine eye,—
Thou seest no cavern roof, no palace vault;
There the blue sky and the white drifting cloud
Look in. Again the wildered fancy dreams
Of spouting fountains, frozen as they rose,
And fixed, with all their branching jets, in air,
And all their sluices sealed. All, all is light;
Light without shade. But all shall pass away
With the next sun. From numberless vast trunks,
Loosened, the crashing ice shall make a sound
Like the far roar of rivers, and the eve
Shall close o'er the brown woods as it was wont.

    And it is pleasant, when the noisy streams
Are just set free, and milder suns melt off
The plashy snow, save only the firm drift
In the deep glen or the close shade of pines,—
'Tis pleasant to behold the wreaths of smoke
Roll up among the maples of the hill,
Where the shrill sound of youthful voices wakes
The shriller echo, as the clear pure lymph,
That from the wounded trees, in twinkling drops,
Falls, 'mid the golden brightness of the morn,
Is gathered in with brimming pails, and oft,
Wielded by sturdy hands, the stroke of axe
Makes the woods ring. Along the quiet air,

Come and float calmly off the soft light clouds,
Such as you see in summer, and the winds
Scarce stir the branches. Lodged in sunny cleft,
Where the cold breezes come not, blooms alone
The little wind-flower, whose just opened eye
Is blue as the spring heaven it gazes at—
Startling the loiterer in the naked groves
With unexpected beauty, for the time
Of blossoms and green leaves is yet afar.
And ere it comes, the encountering winds shall oft
Muster their wrath again, and rapid clouds
Shade heaven, and bounding on the frozen earth
Shall fall their volleyed stores, rounded like hail,
And white like snow, and the loud North again
Shall buffet the vexed forests in his rage.

"Oh Fairest of the Rural Maids"

Oh fairest of the rural maids!
Thy birth was in the forest shades;
Green boughs, and glimpses of the sky,
Were all that met thy infant eye.

Thy sports, thy wanderings, when a child,
Were ever in the sylvan wild;
And all the beauty of the place
Is in thy heart and on thy face.

The twilight of the trees and rocks
Is in the light shade of thy locks;
Thy step is as the wind, that weaves
Its playful way among the leaves.

Thy eyes are springs, in whose serene
And silent waters heaven is seen;
Their lashes are the herbs that look
On their young figures in the brook.

The forest depths, by foot unprest,
Are not more sinless than thy breast;
The holy peace, that fills the air
Of those calm solitudes, is there.

The Ages

I.

When to the common rest that crowns our days,
Called in the noon of life, the good man goes,
Or full of years, and ripe in wisdom, lays
His silver temples in their last repose;
When, o'er the buds of youth the death-wind blows,
And blights the fairest; when our bitterest tears
Stream, as the eyes of those that love us close,
We think on what they were, with many fears
Lest Goodness die with them, and leave the coming years.

II.

And therefore, to our hearts, the days gone by,—
When lived the honored sage whose death we wept,
And the soft virtues beamed from many an eye,
And beat in many a heart that long has slept,—
Like spots of earth where angel-feet have stept—
Are holy; and high-dreaming bards have told
Of times when worth was crowned, and faith was kept,
Ere friendship grew a snare, or love waxed cold—
Those pure and happy times—the golden days of old.

III.

Peace to the just man's memory,—let it grow
Greener with years, and blossom through the flight
Of ages; let the mimic canvas show
His calm benevolent features; let the light
Stream on his deeds of love, that shunned the sight
Of all but heaven, and, in the book of fame,

The glorious record of his virtues write,
And hold it up to men, and bid them claim
A palm like his, and catch from him the hallowed flame.

IV.

But oh, despair not of their fate who rise
To dwell upon the earth when we withdraw;
Lo! the same shaft, by which the righteous dies,
Strikes through the wretch that scoffed at mercy's law,
And trode his brethren down, and felt no awe
Of him who will avenge them. Stainless worth,
Such as the sternest age of virtue saw,
Ripens, meanwhile, till time shall call it forth
From the low modest shade, to light and bless the earth.

V.

Has Nature, in her calm majestic march,
Faltered with age at last? does the bright sun
Grow dim in heaven? or, in their far blue arch,
Sparkle the crowd of stars, when day is done,
Less brightly? when the dew-lipped Spring comes on,
Breathes she with airs less soft, or scents the sky
With flowers less fair than when her reign begun?
Does prodigal Autumn, to our age, deny
The plenty that once swelled beneath his sober eye?

VI.

Look on this beautiful world, and read the truth
In her fair page; see, every season brings
New change, to her, of everlasting youth;
Still the green soil, with joyous living things,
Swarms, the wide air is full of joyous wings,
And myriads, still, are happy in the sleep
Of ocean's azure gulfs, and where he flings
The restless surge. Eternal Love doth keep
In his complacent arms, the earth, the air, the deep.

VII.

Will then the merciful One, who stamped our race
With his own image, and who gave them sway
O'er earth, and the glad dwellers on her face,
Now that our flourishing nations far away
Are spread, where'er the moist earth drinks the day,
Forget the ancient care that taught and nursed
His latest offspring? will he quench the ray
Infused by his own forming smile at first,
And leave a work so fair all blighted and accursed?

VIII.

Oh, no! a thousand cheerful omens give
Hope of yet happier days whose dawn is nigh.
He who has tamed the elements, shall not live
The slave of his own passions; he whose eye
Unwinds the eternal dances of the sky,
And in the abyss of brightness dares to span
The sun's broad circle, rising yet more high,
In God's magnificent works his will shall scan—
And love and peace shall make their paradise with man.

IX.

Sit at the feet of history—through the night
Of years the steps of virtue she shall trace,
And show the earlier ages, where her sight
Can pierce the eternal shadows o'er their face;—
When, from the genial cradle of our race,
Went forth the tribes of men, their pleasant lot
To choose, where palm-groves cooled their dwelling-place,
Or freshening rivers ran; and there forgot
The truth of heaven, and kneeled to gods that heard them not.

X.

Then waited not the murderer for the night,
But smote his brother down in the bright day,
And he who felt the wrong, and had the might,

His own avenger, girt himself to slay;
Beside the path the unburied carcass lay;
The shepherd, by the fountains of the glen,
Fled, while the robber swept his flock away,
And slew his babes. The sick, untended then,
Languished in the damp shade, and died afar from men.

XI.

But misery brought in love—in passion's strife
Man gave his heart to mercy pleading long,
And sought out gentle deeds to gladden life;
The weak, against the sons of spoil and wrong,
Banded, and watched their hamlets, and grew strong.
States rose, and, in the shadow of their might,
The timid rested. To the reverent throng,
Grave and time-wrinkled men, with locks all white,
Gave laws, and judged their strifes, and taught the way
    of right.

XII.

Till bolder spirits seized the rule, and nailed
On men the yoke that man should never bear,
And drove them forth to battle: Lo! unveiled
The scene of those stern ages! What is there?
A boundless sea of blood, and the wild air
Moans with the crimson surges that entomb
Cities and bannered armies; forms that wear
The kingly circlet, rise, amid the gloom,
O'er the dark wave, and straight are swallowed in
    its womb.

XIII.

Those ages have no memory—but they left
A record in the desert—columns strown
On the waste sands, and statues fall'n and cleft,
Heaped like a host in battle overthrown;
Vast ruins, where the mountain's ribs of stone
Were hewn into a city; streets that spread

In the dark earth, where never breath has blown
Of heaven's sweet air, nor foot of man dares tread
The long and perilous ways—the Cities of the Dead;

XIV.

And tombs of monarchs to the clouds up-piled—
They perished—but the eternal tombs remain—
And the black precipice, abrupt and wild,
Pierced by long toil and hollowed to a fane;—
Huge piers and frowning forms of gods sustain
The everlasting arches, dark and wide,
Like the night heaven when clouds are black with rain.
But idly skill was tasked, and strength was plied,
All was the work of slaves to swell a despot's pride.

XV.

And virtue cannot dwell with slaves, nor reign
O'er those who cower to take a tyrant's yoke;
She left the down-trod nations in disdain,
And flew to Greece, when liberty awoke,
New-born, amid those beautiful vales, and broke
Sceptre and chain with her fair youthful hands,
As the rock shivers in the thunder stroke.
And lo! in full-grown strength, an empire stands
Of leagued and rival states, the wonder of the lands.

XVI.

Oh, Greece! thy flourishing cities were a spoil
Unto each other; thy hard hand oppressed
And crushed the helpless; thou didst make thy soil
Drunk with the blood of those that loved thee best;
And thou didst drive, from thy unnatural breast,
Thy just and brave to die in distant climes;
Earth shuddered at thy deeds, and sighed for rest
From thine abominations; after times
That yet shall read thy tale, will tremble at thy crimes.

XVII.

Yet there was that within thee which has saved
Thy glory, and redeemed thy blotted name;
The story of thy better deeds, engraved
On fame's unmouldering pillar, puts to shame
Our chiller virtue; the high art to tame
The whirlwind of thy passions was thine own;
And the pure ray, that from thy bosom came,
Far over many a land and age has shone,
And mingles with the light that beams from God's own
        throne.

XVIII.

And Rome—thy sterner, younger sister, she
Who awed the world with her imperial frown—
Rome drew the spirit of her race from thee,—
The rival of thy shame and thy renown.
Yet her degenerate children sold the crown
Of earth's wide kingdoms to a line of slaves;
Guilt reigned, and wo with guilt, and plagues came down,
Till the North broke its flood-gates, and the waves
Whelmed the degraded race, and weltered o'er their graves.

XIX.

Vainly that ray of brightness from above,
That shone around the Galilean lake,
The light of hope, the leading star of love,
Struggled, the darkness of that day to break;
Even its own faithless guardians strove to slake,
In fogs of earth, the pure immortal flame;
And priestly hands, for Jesus' blessed sake,
Were red with blood, and charity became
In that stern war of forms, a mockery and a name.

XX.

They triumphed, and less bloody rites were kept
Within the quiet of the convent cell;
The well-fed inmates pattered prayer, and slept,
And sinned, and liked their easy penance well.

Where pleasant was the spot for men to dwell,
Amid its fair broad lands the abbey lay,
Sheltering dark orgies that were shame to tell,
And cowled and barefoot beggars swarmed the way,
All in their convent weeds, of black, and white, and gray.

XXI.

Oh, sweetly the returning muses' strain
Swelled over that famed stream, whose gentle tide
In their bright lap the Etrurian vales detain,
Sweet, as when winter storms have ceased to chide,
And all the new leaved woods, resounding wide,
Send out wild hymns upon the scented air.
Lo! to the smiling Arno's classic side
The emulous nations of the west repair,
And kindle their quenched urns, and drink fresh spirit
         there.

XXII.

Still, heaven deferred the hour ordained to rend
From saintly rottenness the sacred stole;
And cowl and worshipped shrine could still defend
The wretch with felon stains upon his soul;
And crimes were set to sale, and hard his dole
Who could not bribe a passage to the skies;
And vice beneath the mitre's kind control,
Sinned gaily on, and grew to giant size,
Shielded by priestly power; and watched by priestly eyes.

XXIII.

At last the earthquake came—the shock, that hurled
To dust, in many fragments dashed and strown,
The throne, whose roots were in another world,
And whose far-stretching shadow awed our own.
From many a proud monastic pile, o'erthrown,
Fear-struck, the hooded inmates rushed and fled;
The web, that for a thousand years had grown
O'er prostrate Europe, in that day of dread
Crumbled and fell, as fire dissolves the flaxen thread.

XXIV.

The spirit of that day is still awake,
And spreads himself, and shall not sleep again;
But through the idle mesh of power shall break,
Like billows o'er the Asian monarch's chain;
Till men are filled with him, and feel how vain,
Instead of the pure heart and innocent hands,
Are all the proud and pompous modes to gain
The smile of heaven;—till a new age expands
Its white and holy wings above the peaceful lands.

XXV.

For look again on the past years;—behold,
Flown, like the night-mare's hideous shapes, away
Full many a horrible worship, that, of old,
Held, o'er the shuddering realms, unquestioned sway:
See crimes that feared not once the eye of day,
Rooted from men, without a name or place:
See nations blotted out from earth, to pay
The forfeit of deep guilt;—with glad embrace
The fair disburdened lands welcome a nobler race.

XXVI.

Thus error's monstrous shapes from earth are driven;
They fade, they fly—but truth survives their flight;
Earth has no shades to quench that beam of heaven;
Each ray, that shone, in early time, to light
The faltering footsteps in the path of right,
Each gleam of clearer brightness, shed to aid
In man's maturer day his bolder sight,
All blended, like the rainbow's radiant braid,
Pour yet, and still shall pour, the blaze that cannot fade.

XXVII.

Late, from this western shore, that morning chased
The deep and ancient night, that threw its shroud
O'er the green land of groves, the beautiful waste,
Nurse of full streams, and lifter up of proud
Sky-mingling mountains that o'erlook the cloud.

Erewhile, where yon gay spires their brightness rear,
Trees waved, and the brown hunter's shouts were loud
Amid the forest; and the bounding deer
Fled at the glancing plume, and the gaunt wolf yelled near.

XXVIII.

And where his willing waves yon bright blue bay
Sends up, to kiss his decorated brim,
And cradles, in his soft embrace, the gay
Young group of grassy islands born of him,
And, crowding nigh, or in the distance dim,
Lifts the white throng of sails, that bear or bring
The commerce of the world; — with tawny limb,
And belt and beads in sunlight glistening,
The savage urged his skiff like wild bird on the wing.

XXIX.

Then, all this youthful paradise around,
And all the broad and boundless mainland, lay
Cooled by the interminable wood, that frowned
O'er mount and vale, where never summer ray
Glanced, till the strong tornado broke his way
Through the gray giants of the sylvan wild;
Yet many a sheltered glade, with blossoms gay,
Beneath the showery sky and sunshine mild,
Within the shaggy arms of that dark forest smiled.

XXX.

There stood the Indian hamlet, there the lake
Spread its blue sheet that flashed with many an oar,
Where the brown otter plunged him from the brake,
And the deer drank: as the light gale flew o'er,
The twinkling maize-field rustled on the shore;
And while that spot, so wild, and lone, and fair,
A look of glad and innocent beauty wore,
And peace was on the earth and in the air,
The warrior lit the pile, and bound his captive there:

XXXI.

Not unavenged—the foeman, from the wood,
Beheld the deed, and when the midnight shade
Was stillest, gorged his battle-axe with blood;
All died—the wailing babe—the shrieking maid—
And in the flood of fire that scathed the glade,
The roofs went down; but deep the silence grew,
When on the dewy woods the day-beam played;
No more the cabin smokes rose wreathed and blue,
And ever, by their lake, lay moored the light canoe.

XXXII.

Look now abroad—another race has filled
These populous borders—wide the wood recedes,
And towns shoot up, and fertile realms are tilled;
The land is full of harvests and green meads;
Streams numberless, that many a fountain feeds,
Shine, disembowered, and give to sun and breeze
Their virgin waters; the full region leads
New colonies forth, that toward the western seas
Spread, like a rapid flame among the autumnal trees.

XXXIII.

Here the free spirit of mankind, at length,
Throws its last fetters off; and who shall place
A limit to the giant's unchained strength,
Or curb his swiftness in the forward race?
Far, like the comet's way through infinite space,
Stretches the long untravelled path of light
Into the depths of ages: we may trace,
Distant, the brightening glory of its flight,
Till the receding rays are lost to human sight.

XXXIV.

Europe is given a prey to sterner fates,
And writhes in shackles; strong the arms that chain
To earth her struggling multitude of states;

She too is strong, and might not chafe in vain
Against them, but shake off the vampyre train
That batten on her blood, and break their net.
Yes, she shall look on brighter days, and gain
The meed of worthier deeds; the moment set
To rescue and raise up, draws near—but is not yet.

XXXV.

But thou, my country, thou shalt never fall,
But with thy children—thy maternal care,
Thy lavish love, thy blessings showered on all—
These are thy fetters—seas and stormy air
Are the wide barrier of thy borders, where
Among thy gallant sons that guard thee well,
Thou laugh'st at enemies: who shall then declare
The date of thy deep-founded strength, or tell
How happy, in thy lap, the sons of men shall dwell?

The Rivulet

This little rill that, from the springs
Of yonder grove, its current brings,
Plays on the slope awhile, and then
Goes prattling into groves again,
Oft to its warbling waters drew
My little feet, when life was new.
When woods in early green were drest,
And from the chambers of the west
The warmer breezes, travelling out,
Breathed the new scent of flowers about,
My truant steps from home would stray,
Upon its grassy side to play,
List the brown thrasher's vernal hymn,
And crop the violet on its brim,
With blooming cheek and open brow,
As young and gay, sweet rill, as thou.

And when the days of boyhood came,
And I had grown in love with fame,
Duly I sought thy banks, and tried
My first rude numbers by thy side.
Words cannot tell how bright and gay
The scenes of life before me lay.
Then glorious hopes, that now to speak
Would bring the blood into my cheek,
Passed o'er me; and I wrote on high
A name I deemed should never die.

Years change thee not. Upon yon hill
The tall old maples, verdant still,
Yet tell, grandeur of decay,
How swift the years have passed away,
Since first, a child, and half afraid,
I wandered in the forest shade.
Thou, ever joyous rivulet,
Dost dimple, leap, and prattle yet;
And sporting with the sands that pave
The windings of thy silver wave,
And dancing to thy own wild chime,
Thou laughest at the lapse of time.
The same sweet sounds are in my ear
My early childhood loved to hear;
As pure thy limpid waters run,
As bright they sparkle to the sun;
As fresh and thick the bending ranks
Of herbs that line thy oozy banks;
The violet there, in soft May dew,
Comes up, as modest and as blue;
As green amid thy current's stress,
Floats the scarce-rooted water cress;
And the brown ground bird, in thy glen,
Still chirps as merrily as then.

Thou changest not—but I am changed,
Since first thy pleasant banks I ranged;
And the grave stranger, come to see
The play-place of his infancy,

Has scarce a single trace of him
Who sported once upon thy brim.
The visions of my youth are past—
Too bright, too beautiful to last.
I've tried the world—it wears no more
The coloring of romance it wore.
Yet well has nature kept the truth
She promised to my earliest youth;
The radiant beauty, shed abroad
On all the glorious works of God,
Shows freshly, to my sobered eye,
Each charm it wore in days gone by.

A few brief years shall pass away,
And I, all trembling, weak, and gray,
Bowed to the earth, which waits to fold
My ashes in the embracing mould,
(If haply the dark will of fate
Indulge my life so long a date)
May come for the last time to look
Upon my childhood's favorite brook.
Then dimly on my eye shall gleam
The sparkle of thy dancing stream;
And faintly on my ear shall fall
Thy prattling current's merry call;
Yet shalt thou flow as glad and bright
As when thou met'st my infant sight.

And I shall sleep—and on thy side,
As ages after ages glide,
Children their early sports shall try,
And pass to hoary age and die.
But thou, unchanged from year to year,
Gaily shalt play and glitter here;
Amid young flowers and tender grass
Thy endless infancy shalt pass;
And, singing down thy narrow glen,
Shalt mock the fading race of men.

Summer Wind

It is a sultry day; the sun has drank
The dew that lay upon the morning grass,
There is no rustling in the lofty elm
That canopies my dwelling, and its shade
Scarce cools me. All is silent, save the faint
And interrupted murmur of the bee,
Settling on the sick flowers, and then again
Instantly on the wing. The plants around
Feel the too potent fervors; the tall maize
Rolls up its long green leaves; the clover droops
Its tender foliage, and declines its blooms.
But far in the fierce sunshine tower the hills,
With all their growth of woods, silent and stern,
As if the scorching heat and dazzling light
Were but an element they loved. Bright clouds,
Motionless pillars of the brazen heaven;—
Their bases on the mountains—their white tops
Shining in the far ether—fire the air
With a reflected radiance, and make turn
The gazer's eye away. For me, I lie
Languidly in the shade, where the thick turf,
Yet virgin from the kisses of the sun,
Retains some freshness, and I woo the wind
That still delays its coming. Why so slow,
Gentle and voluble spirit of the air?
Oh, come and breathe upon the fainting earth
Coolness and life. Is it that in his caves
He hears me? See, on yonder woody ridge,
The pine is bending his proud top, and now,
Among the nearer groves, chesnut and oak
Are tossing their green boughs about. He comes!
Lo, where the grassy meadow runs in waves!
The deep distressful silence of the scene
Breaks up with mingling of unnumbered sounds
And universal motion. He is come,
Shaking a shower of blossoms from the shrubs,
And bearing on their fragrance; and he brings
Music of birds, and rustling of young boughs,

And sound of swaying branches, and the voice
Of distant waterfalls. All the green herbs
Are stirring in his breath; a thousand flowers,
By the road-side and the borders of the brook,
Nod gaily to each other; glossy leaves
Are twinkling in the sun, as if the dew
Were on them yet, and silver waters break
Into small waves and sparkle as he comes.

An Indian at the Burying-Place
of His Fathers

It is the spot I came to seek,—
    My fathers' ancient burial-place,
Ere from these vales, ashamed and weak,
    Withdrew our wasted race.
It is the spot,—I know it well—
Of which our old traditions tell.

For here the upland bank sends out
    A ridge toward the river side;
I know the shaggy hills about,
    The meadows smooth and wide;
The plains, that, toward the southern sky,
Fenced east and west by mountains lie.

A white man, gazing on the scene,
    Would say a lovely spot was here,
And praise the lawns so fresh and green
    Between the hills so sheer.
I like it not—I would the plain
Lay in its tall old groves again.

The sheep are on the slopes around,
    The cattle in the meadows feed,
And laborers turn the crumbling ground,
    Or drop the yellow seed,
And prancing steeds, in trappings gay,
Whirl the bright chariot o'er the way.

Methinks it were a nobler sight
   To see these vales in woods arrayed,
Their summits in the golden light,
   Their trunks in grateful shade,
And herds of deer, that bounding go
O'er rills and prostrate trees below.

And then to mark the lord of all,
   The forest hero, trained to wars,
Quivered and plumed, and lithe and tall,
   And seamed with glorious scars,
Walk forth, amid his reign, to dare
The wolf, and grapple with the bear.

This bank, in which the dead were laid,
   Was sacred when its soil was ours;
Hither the silent Indian maid
   Brought wreaths of beads and flowers,
And the gray chief and gifted seer
Worshipped the god of thunders here.

But now the wheat is green and high
   On clods that hid the warrior's breast,
And scattered in the furrows lie
   The weapons of his rest,
And there, in the loose sand, is thrown
Of his large arm the mouldering bone.

Ah, little thought the strong and brave,
   Who bore their lifeless chieftain forth;
Or the young wife, that weeping gave
   Her first-born to the earth,
That the pale race, who waste us now,
Among their bones should guide the plough.

They waste us—aye—like April snow
   In the warm noon, we shrink away;
And fast they follow, as we go

Towards the setting day,—
Till they shall fill the land, and we
Are driven into the western sea.

But I behold a fearful sign,
    To which the white men's eyes are blind;
Their race may vanish hence, like mine,
    And leave no trace behind,
Save ruins o'er the region spread,
And the white stones above the dead.

Before these fields were shorn and tilled,
    Full to the brim our rivers flowed;
The melody of waters filled
    The fresh and boundless wood;
And torrents dashed and rivulets played,
And fountains spouted in the shade.

Those grateful sounds are heard no more,
    The springs are silent in the sun,
The rivers, by the blackened shore,
    With lessening current run;
The realm our tribes are crushed to get
May be a barren desert yet.

After a Tempest

The day had been a day of wind and storm;—
    The wind was laid, the storm was overpast,—
And stooping from the zenith, bright and warm
    Shone the great sun on the wide earth at last.
    I stood upon the upland slope and cast
My eye upon a broad and beauteous scene,
    Where the vast plain lay girt by mountains vast,
And hills o'er hills lifted their heads of green,
With pleasant vales scooped out and villages between.

The rain-drops glistened on the trees around,
　　Whose shadows on the tall grass were not stirred,
Save when a shower of diamonds, to the ground,
　　Was shaken by the flight of startled bird;
　　For birds were warbling round, and bees were heard
About the flowers; the cheerful rivulet sung
　　And gossiped, as he hastened ocean-ward;
To the gray oak the squirrel, chiding clung,
And chirping from the ground the grasshopper upsprung.

And from beneath the leaves that kept them dry
　　Flew many a glittering insect here and there,
And darted up and down the butterfly,
　　That seemed a living blossom of the air.
　　The flocks came scattering from the thicket, where
The violent rain had pent them; in the way
　　Strolled groups of damsels frolicksome and fair;
The farmer swung the scythe or turned the hay,
And 'twixt the heavy swaths his children were at play.

It was a scene of peace—and, like a spell,
　　Did that serene and golden sunlight fall
Upon the motionless wood that clothed the fell,
　　And precipice upspringing like a wall,
　　And glassy river and white waterfall,
And happy living things that trod the bright
　　And beauteous scene; while far beyond them all,
On many a lovely valley, out of sight,
Was poured from the blue heavens the same soft
　　　　golden light.

I looked, and thought the quiet of the scene
　　An emblem of the peace that yet shall be,
When, o'er earth's continents and isles between,
　　The noise of war shall cease from sea to sea,
　　And married nations dwell in harmony;
When millions, crouching in the dust to one,
　　No more shall beg their lives on bended knee,
Nor the black stake be dressed, nor in the sun
The o'erlabored captive toil, and wish his life were done.

Too long, at clash of arms amid her bowers
    And pools of blood, the earth has stood aghast,
The fair earth, that should only blush with flowers
    And ruddy fruits; but not for aye can last
    The storm, and sweet the sunshine when 'tis past.
Lo, the clouds roll away—they break—they fly,
    And, like the glorious light of summer, cast
O'er the wide landscape from the embracing sky,
On all the peaceful world the smile of heaven shall lie.

Autumn Woods

    Ere, in the northern gale,
The summer tresses of the trees are gone,
The woods of Autumn, all around our vale,
    Have put their glory on.

    The mountains that infold
In their wide sweep, the colored landscape round,
Seem groups of giant kings, in purple and gold,
    That guard the enchanted ground.

    I roam the woods that crown
The upland, where the mingled splendors glow,
Where the gay company of trees look down
    On the green fields below.

    My steps are not alone
In these bright walks; the sweet southwest, at play,
Flies, rustling, where the painted leaves are strown
    Along the winding way.

    And far in heaven, the while,
The sun, that sends that gale to wander here,
Pours out on the fair earth his quiet smile,—
    The sweetest of the year.

Where now the solemn shade,
Verdure and gloom where many branches meet;
So grateful, when the noon of summer made
    The valleys sick with heat?

Let in through all the trees
Come the strange rays; the forest depths are bright;
Their sunny-colored foliage, in the breeze,
    Twinkles, like beams of light.

The rivulet, late unseen,
Where bickering through the shrubs its waters run,
Shines with the image of its golden screen,
    And glimmerings of the sun.

But 'neath yon crimson tree,
Lover to listening maid might breathe his flame,
Nor mark, within its roseate canopy,
    Her blush of maiden shame.

Oh, Autumn! why so soon
Depart the hues that make thy forests glad;
Thy gentle wind and thy fair sunny noon,
    And leave thee wild and sad!

Ah! 'twere a lot too blest
Forever in thy colored shades to stray;
Amidst the kisses of the soft southwest
    To rove and dream for aye;

And leave the vain low strife
That makes men mad—the tug for wealth and power,
The passions and the cares that wither life,
    And waste its little hour.

November

Yet one smile more, departing distant sun!
   One mellow smile through the soft vapory air,
Ere, o'er the frozen earth, the loud winds run,
   Or snows are sifted o'er the meadows bare.
One smile on the brown hills and naked trees,
   And the dark rocks whose summer wreaths are cast,
And the blue Gentian flower, that, in the breeze,
   Nods lonely, of her beauteous race the last.
Yet a few sunny days, in which the bee
   Shall murmur by the hedge that skirts the way,
The cricket chirp upon the russet lea,
   And man delight to linger in thy ray.
Yet one rich smile, and we will try to bear
The piercing winter frost, and winds, and darkened air.

Forest Hymn

The groves were God's first temples. Ere man learned
To hew the shaft, and lay the architrave,
And spread the roof above them, — ere he framed
The lofty vault, to gather and roll back
The sound of anthems; in the darkling wood,
Amidst the cool and silence, he knelt down
And offered to the Mightiest, solemn thanks
And supplication. For his simple heart
Might not resist the sacred influences,
Which, from the stilly twilight of the place,
And from the gray old trunks that high in heaven
Mingled their mossy boughs, and from the sound
Of the invisible breath that swayed at once
All their green tops, stole over him, and bowed
His spirit with the thought of boundless power
And inaccessible majesty. Ah, why
Should we, in the world's riper years, neglect
God's ancient sanctuaries, and adore
Only among the crowd, and under roofs

That our frail hands have raised. Let me, at least,
Here, in the shadow of this aged wood,
Offer one hymn—thrice happy, if it find
Acceptance in his ear.

                              Father, thy hand
Hath reared these venerable columns, thou
Didst weave this verdant roof. Thou didst look down
Upon the naked earth, and, forthwith, rose
All these fair ranks of trees. They, in thy sun,
Budded, and shook their green leaves in thy breeze,
And shot towards heaven. The century-living crow
Whose birth was in their tops, grew old and died
Among their branches, till, at last, they stood,
As now they stand, massive and tall and dark,
Fit shrine for humble worshipper to hold
Communion with his Maker. Here are seen
No traces of man's pomp or pride;—no silks
Rustle, nor jewels shine, nor envious eyes
Encounter; no fantastic carvings show
The boast of our vain race to change the form
Of thy fair works. But thou art here—thou fill'st
The solitude. Thou art in the soft winds
That run along the summit of these trees
In music;—thou art in the cooler breath,
That from the inmost darkness of the place,
Comes, scarcely felt;—the barky trunks, the ground,
The fresh moist ground, are all instinct with thee.
Here is continual worship;—nature, here,
In the tranquillity that thou dost love,
Enjoys thy presence. Noiselessly, around,
From perch to perch, the solitary bird
Passes; and yon clear spring, that, 'midst its herbs,
Wells softly forth and visits the strong roots
Of half the mighty forest, tells no tale
Of all the good it does. Thou hast not left
Thyself without a witness, in these shades,
Of thy perfections. Grandeur, strength, and grace
Are here to speak of thee. This mighty oak—
By whose immoveable stem I stand and seem

Almost annihilated—not a prince,
In all that proud old world beyond the deep,
E'er wore his crown as loftily as he
Wears the green coronal of leaves with which
Thy hand has graced him. Nestled at his root
Is beauty, such as blooms not in the glare
Of the broad sun. That delicate forest flower,
With scented breath, and look so like a smile,
Seems, as it issues from the shapeless mould,
An emanation of the indwelling Life,
A visible token of the upholding Love,
That are the soul of this wide universe.

My heart is awed within me, when I think
Of the great miracle that still goes on,
In silence, round me—the perpetual work
Of thy creation, finished, yet renewed
Forever. Written on thy works I read
The lesson of thy own eternity.
Lo! all grow old and die—but see, again,
How on the faltering footsteps of decay
Youth presses—ever gay and beautiful youth
In all its beautiful forms. These lofty trees
Wave not less proudly that their ancestors
Moulder beneath them. Oh, there is not lost
One of earth's charms: upon her bosom yet,
After the flight of untold centuries,
The freshness of her far beginning lies
And yet shall lie. Life mocks the idle hate
Of his arch enemy Death—yea—seats himself
Upon the sepulchre, and blooms and smiles,
And of the triumphs of his ghastly foe
Makes his own nourishment. For he came forth
From thine own bosom, and shall have no end.

There have been holy men who hid themselves
Deep in the woody wilderness, and gave
Their lives to thought and prayer, till they outlived
The generation born with them, nor seemed
Less aged than the hoary trees and rocks

Around them;—and there have been holy men
Who deemed it were not well to pass life thus.
But let me often to these solitudes
Retire, and in thy presence re-assure
My feeble virtue. Here its enemies,
The passions, at thy plainer footsteps shrink
And tremble and are still. Oh, God! when thou
Dost scare the world with tempests, set on fire
The heavens with falling thunderbolts, or fill,
With all the waters of the firmament,
The swift dark whirlwind that uproots the woods
And drowns the villages; when, at thy call,
Uprises the great deep and throws himself
Upon the continent and overwhelms
Its cities—who forgets not, at the sight
Of these tremendous tokens of thy power,
His pride, and lays his strifes and follies by?
Oh, from these sterner aspects of thy face
Spare me and mine, nor let us need the wrath
Of the mad unchained elements to teach
Who rules them. Be it ours to meditate
In these calm shades thy milder majesty,
And, to the beautiful order of thy works,
Learn to conform the order of our lives.

The Conjunction of Jupiter and Venus

I would not always reason. The straight path
Wearies us with its never-varying lines,
And we grow melancholy. I would make
Reason my guide, but she should sometimes sit
Patiently by the way-side, while I traced
The mazes of the pleasant wilderness
Around me. She should be my counsellor,
But not my tyrant. For the spirit needs
Impulses from a deeper source than hers,
And there are motions, in the mind of man,
That she must look upon with awe. I bow
Reverently to her dictates, but not less

Hold to the fair illusions of old time—
Illusions that shed brightness over life,
And glory over nature. Look even now,
Where two bright planets in the twilight meet,
Upon the saffron heaven,—the imperial star
Of Jove, and she that from her radiant urn
Pours forth the light of love. Let me believe,
Awhile, that they are met for ends of good,
Amid the evening glory, to confer
Of men and their affairs, and to shed down
Kind influences. Lo! their orbs burn more bright,
And shake out softer fires! The great earth feels
The gladness and the quiet of the time.
Meekly the mighty river, that infolds
This mighty city, smooths his front, and far
Glitters and burns even to the rocky base
Of the dark heights that bound him to the west;
And a deep murmur, from the many streets,
Rises like a thanksgiving. Put we hence
Dark and sad thoughts awhile—there's time for them
Hereafter—on the morrow we will meet,
With melancholy looks, to tell our griefs,
And make each other wretched; this calm hour,
This balmy, blessed evening, we will give
To cheerful hopes and dreams of happy days,
Born of the meeting of those glorious stars.

Enough of drought has parched the year, and scared
The land with dread of famine. Autumn, yet,
Shall make men glad with unexpected fruits.
The dog-star shall shine harmless; genial days
Shall softly glide away into the keen
And wholesome cold of winter; he that fears
The pestilence, shall gaze on those pure beams,
And breathe, with confidence, the quiet air.

Emblems of Power and Beauty! well may they
Shine brightest on our borders, and withdraw
Towards the great Pacific, marking out
The path of empire. Thus, in our own land,

Ere long, the better Genius of our race,
Having encompassed earth, and tamed its tribes,
Shall sit him down beneath the farthest west,
By the shore of that calm ocean, and look back
On realms made happy.

                Light the nuptial torch,
And say the glad, yet solemn rite, that knits
The youth and maiden. Happy days to them
That wed this evening!—a long life of love,
And blooming sons and daughters! Happy they
Born at this hour,—for they shall see an age
Whiter and holier than the past, and go
Late to their graves. Men shall wear softer hearts,
And shudder at the butcheries of war,
As now at other murders.

                Hapless Greece!
Enough of blood has wet thy rocks, and stained
Thy rivers; deep enough thy chains have worn
Their links into thy flesh; the sacrifice
Of thy pure maidens, and thy innocent babes,
And reverend priests, has expiated all
Thy crimes of old. In yonder mingling lights
There is an omen of good days for thee.
Thou shalt arise from 'midst the dust and sit
Again among the nations. Thine own arm
Shall yet redeem thee. Not in wars like thine
The world takes part. Be it a strife of kings,—
Despot with despot battling for a throne,—
And Europe shall be stirred throughout her realms,
Nations shall put on harness, and shall fall
Upon each other, and in all their bounds
The wailing of the childless shall not cease.
Thine is a war for liberty, and thou
Must fight it single-handed. The old world
Looks coldly on the murderers of thy race,
And leaves thee to the struggle; and the new,—
I fear me thou could'st tell a shameful tale
Of fraud and lust of gain;—thy treasury drained,

And Missolonghi fallen. Yet thy wrongs
Shall put new strength into thy heart and hand,
And God and thy good sword shall yet work out,
For thee, a terrible deliverance.

October

Aye, thou art welcome, heaven's delicious breath!
    When woods begin to wear the crimson leaf,
    And suns grow meek, and the meek suns grow brief,
And the year smiles as it draws near its death.
Wind of the sunny south! oh, still delay
    In the gay woods and in the golden air,
    Like to a good old age released from care,
Journeying, in long serenity, away.
In such a bright, late quiet, would that I
    Might wear out life like thee, 'mid bowers and brooks,
    And dearer yet, the sunshine of kind looks,
And music of kind voices ever nigh;
And when my last sand twinkled in the glass,
Pass silently from men, as thou dost pass.

The Damsel of Peru

Where olive leaves were twinkling in every wind that blew,
There sat beneath the pleasant shade a damsel of Peru,
Betwixt the slender boughs, as they opened to the air,
Came glimpses of her ivory neck and of her glossy hair;
And sweetly rang her silver voice, within that shady nook,
As from the shrubby glen is heard the sound of hidden
        brook.

'Tis a song of love and valor, in the noble Spanish tongue,
That once upon the sunny plains of Old Castile was sung;
When, from their mountain holds, on the Moorish rout below,
Had rushed the Christians like a flood, and swept away the
        foe.
Awhile that melody is still, and then breaks forth anew,
A wilder rhyme, a livelier note, of freedom and Peru.

A white hand parts the branches, a lovely face looks forth,
And bright dark eyes gaze steadfastly and sadly towards the
     north.
Thou look'st in vain, sweet maiden, the sharpest sight would
     fail,
To spy a sign of human life abroad in all the vale;
For the noon is coming on, and the sunbeams fiercely beat,
And the silent hills and forest tops seem reeling in the heat.

That white hand is withdrawn, that fair sad face is gone,
But the music of that silver voice is flowing sweetly on,
Not as of late, in cheerful tones, but mournfully and low,—
A ballad of a tender maid heart broken long ago,
Of him who died in battle, the youthful and the brave,
And her who died of sorrow, upon his early grave.

But see, along that mountain's slope, a fiery horseman ride;
Mark his torn plume, his tarnished belt, the sabre at his side.
His spurs are buried rowel deep, he rides with loosened rein,
There's blood upon his charger's flank and foam upon his
     mane,
He speeds toward the olive grove, along that shaded hill,—
God shield the helpless maiden there, if he should mean her
     ill!

And suddenly that song has ceased, and suddenly I hear
A shriek sent up amid the shade, a shriek—but not of fear.
For tender accents follow, and tenderer pauses speak
The overflow of gladness, when words are all too weak:
"I lay my good sword at thy feet, for now Peru is free,
"And I am come to dwell beside the olive grove with thee."

To an American Painter Departing for Europe

Thine eyes shall see the light of distant skies:
     Yet, Cole! thy heart shall bear to Europe's strand
     A living image of thy native land,
Such as on thy own glorious canvass lies.
Lone lakes—savannahs where the bison roves—

Rocks rich with summer garlands—solemn streams—
Skies, where the desert eagle wheels and screams—
Spring bloom and autumn blaze of boundless groves.
Fair scenes shall greet thee where thou goest—fair,
But different—every where the trace of men,
Paths, homes, graves, ruins, from the lowest glen
To where life shrinks from the fierce Alpine air.
Gaze on them, till the tears shall dim thy sight,
But keep that earlier, wilder image bright.

To the Fringed Gentian

Thou blossom bright with autumn dew,
And colored with the heaven's own blue,
That openest, when the quiet light
Succeeds the keen and frosty night.

Thou comest not when violets lean
O'er wandering brooks and springs unseen,
Or columbines, in purple drest,
Nod o'er the ground bird's hidden nest.

Thou waitest late, and com'st alone,
When woods are bare and birds are flown,
And frosts and shortening days portend
The aged year is near its end.

Then doth thy sweet and quiet eye
Look through its fringes to the sky,
Blue—blue—as if that sky let fall
A flower from its cerulean wall.

I would that thus, when I shall see
The hour of death draw near to me,
Hope, blossoming within my heart,
May look to heaven as I depart.

The Prairies

These are the Gardens of the Desert, these
The unshorn fields, boundless and beautiful,
For which the speech of England has no name—
The Prairies. I behold them for the first,
And my heart swells, while the dilated sight
Takes in the encircling vastness. Lo! they stretch
In airy undulations, far away,
As if the ocean, in his gentlest swell,
Stood still, with all his rounded billows fixed,
And motionless for ever.—Motionless?—
No—they are all unchained again. The clouds
Sweep over with their shadows, and, beneath,
The surface rolls and fluctuates to the eye;
Dark hollows seem to glide along and chase
The sunny ridges. Breezes of the South!
Who toss the golden and the flame-like flowers,
And pass the prairie-hawk that, poised on high,
Flaps his broad wings, yet moves not—ye have played
Among the palms of Mexico and vines
Of Texas, and have crisped the limpid brooks
That from the fountains of Sonora glide
Into the calm Pacific—have ye fanned
A nobler or a lovelier scene than this?
Man hath no part in all this glorious work:
The hand that built the firmament hath heaved
And smoothed these verdant swells, and sown their slopes
With herbage, planted them with island groves,
And hedged them round with forests. Fitting floor
For this magnificent temple of the sky—
With flowers whose glory and whose multitude
Rival the constellations! The great heavens
Seem to stoop down upon the scene in love,—
A nearer vault, and of a tenderer blue,
Than that which bends above the eastern hills.
    As o'er the verdant waste I guide my steed,
Among the high rank grass that sweeps his sides,
The hollow beating of his footstep seems
A sacrilegious sound. I think of those

Upon whose rest he tramples. Are they here—
The dead of other days?—and did the dust
Of these fair solitudes once stir with life
And burn with passion? Let the mighty mounds
That overlook the rivers, or that rise
In the dim forest crowded with old oaks,
Answer. A race, that long has passed away,
Built them;—a disciplined and populous race
Heaped, with long toil, the earth, while yet the Greek
Was hewing the Pentelicus to forms
Of symmetry, and rearing on its rock
The glittering Parthenon. These ample fields
Nourished their harvests, here their herds were fed,
When haply by their stalls the bison lowed,
And bowed his maned shoulder to the yoke.
All day this desert murmured with their toils,
Till twilight blushed and lovers walked, and wooed
In a forgotten language, and old tunes,
From instruments of unremembered form,
Gave the soft winds a voice. The red man came—
The roaming hunter tribes, warlike and fierce,
And the mound-builders vanished from the earth.
The solitude of centuries untold
Has settled where they dwelt. The prairie wolf
Hunts in their meadows, and his fresh-dug den
Yawns by my path. The gopher mines the ground
Where stood their swarming cities. All is gone—
All—save the piles of earth that hold their bones—
The platforms where they worshipped unknown gods—
The barriers which they builded from the soil
To keep the foe at bay—till o'er the walls
The wild beleaguerers broke, and, one by one,
The strongholds of the plain were forced, and heaped
With corpses. The brown vultures of the wood
Flocked to those vast uncovered sepulchres,
And sat, unscared and silent, at their feast.
Haply some solitary fugitive,
Lurking in marsh and forest, till the sense
Of desolation and of fear became
Bitterer than death, yielded himself to die.

Man's better nature triumphed. Kindly words
Welcomed and soothed him; the rude conquerors
Seated the captive with their chiefs; he chose
A bride among their maidens, and at length
Seemed to forget,—yet ne'er forgot,—the wife
Of his first love, and her sweet little ones
Butchered, amid their shrieks, with all his race.
    Thus change the forms of being. Thus arise
Races of living things, glorious in strength,
And perish, as the quickening breath of God
Fills them, or is withdrawn. The red man too—
Has left the blooming wilds he ranged so long,
And, nearer to the Rocky Mountains, sought
A wider hunting-ground. The beaver builds
No longer by these streams, but far away,
On waters whose blue surface ne'er gave back
The white man's face—among Missouri's springs,
And pools whose issues swell the Oregan,
He rears his little Venice. In these plains
The bison feeds no more. Twice twenty leagues
Beyond remotest smoke of hunter's camp,
Roams the majestic brute, in herds that shake
The earth with thundering steps—yet here I meet
His ancient footprints stamped beside the pool.
    Still this great solitude is quick with life.
Myriads of insects, gaudy as the flowers
They flutter over, gentle quadrupeds,
And birds, that scarce have learned the fear of man,
Are here, and sliding reptiles of the ground,
Startlingly beautiful. The graceful deer
Bounds to the wood at my approach. The bee,
A more adventurous colonist than man,
With whom he came across the eastern deep,
Fills the savannas with his murmurings,
And hides his sweets, as in the golden age,
Within the hollow oak. I listen long
To his domestic hum, and think I hear
The sound of that advancing multitude
Which soon shall fill these deserts. From the ground
Comes up the laugh of children, the soft voice

Of maidens, and the sweet and solemn hymn
Of Sabbath worshippers. The low of herds
Blends with the rustling of the heavy grain
Over the dark-brown furrows. All at once
A fresher wind sweeps by, and breaks my dream,
And I am in the wilderness alone.

The Fountain

Fountain, that springest on this grassy slope,
Thy quick cool murmur mingles pleasantly,
With the cool sound of breezes in the beach,
Above me in the noontide. Thou dost wear
No stain of thy dark birthplace; gushing up
From the red mould and slimy roots of earth,
Thou flashest in the sun. The mountain air,
In winter, is not clearer, nor the dew
That shines on mountain blossom. Thus doth God
Bring, from the dark and foul, the pure and bright.

This tangled thicket on the bank above
Thy basin, how thy waters keep it green!
For thou dost feed the roots of the wild vine
That trails all over it, and to the twigs
Ties fast her clusters. There the spice-bush lifts
Her leafy lances; the viburnum there,
Paler of foliage, to the sun holds up
Her circlet of green berries. In and out
The chipping sparrow, in her coat of brown,
Steals silently, lest I should mark her nest.

Not such thou wert of yore, ere yet the axe
Had smitten the old woods. Then hoary trunks
Of oak, and plane, and hickory, o'er thee held
A mighty canopy. When April winds
Grew soft, the maple burst into a flush
Of scarlet flowers. The tulip-tree, high up,
Opened, in airs of June, her multitude
Of golden chalices to humming-birds
And silken-winged insects of the sky.

Frail wood-plants clustered round thy edge in Spring.
The liverleaf put forth her sister blooms
Of faintest blue. Here the quick-footed wolf,
Passing to lap thy waters, crushed the flower
Of sanguinaria, from whose brittle stem
The red drops fell like blood. The deer, too, left
Her delicate foot-print in the soft moist mould,
And on the fallen leaves. The slow-paced bear,
In such a sultry summer noon as this,
Stopped at thy stream, and drank, and leaped across.

But thou hast histories that stir the heart
With deeper feeling; while I look on thee
They rise before me. I behold the scene
Hoary again with forests; I behold
The Indian warrior, whom a hand unseen
Has smitten with his death-wound in the woods,
Creep slowly to thy well-known rivulet,
And slake his death-thirst. Hark, that quick fierce cry
That rends the utter silence; 'tis the whoop
Of battle, and a throng of savage men
With naked arms and faces stained like blood,
Fill the green wilderness; the long bare arms
Are heaved aloft, bows twang and arrows stream;
Each makes a tree his shield, and every tree
Sends forth its arrow. Fierce the fight and short,
As is the whirlwind. Soon the conquerors
And conquered vanish, and the dead remain
Mangled by tomahawks. The mighty woods
Are still again, the frighted bird comes back
And plumes her wings; but thy sweet waters run
Crimson with blood. Then, as the sun goes down,
Amid the deepening twilight I descry
Figures of men that crouch and creep unheard,
And bear away the dead. The next day's shower
Shall wash the tokens of the fight away.

I look again—a hunter's lodge is built,
With poles and boughs, beside thy crystal well,
While the meek autumn stains the woods with gold,

And sheds his golden sunshine. To the door
The red man slowly drags the enormous bear
Slain in the chestnut thicket, or flings down
The deer from his strong shoulders. Shaggy fells
Of wolf and cougar hang upon the walls,
And loud the black-eyed Indian maidens laugh,
That gather, from the rustling heaps of leaves,
The hickory's white nuts, and the dark fruit
That falls from the gray butternut's long boughs.

So centuries passed by, and still the woods
Blossomed in spring, and reddened when the year
Grew chill, and glistened in the frozen rains
Of winter, till the white man swung the axe
Beside thee—signal of a mighty change.
Then all around was heard the crash of trees,
Trembling awhile and rushing to the ground,
The low of ox, and shouts of men who fired
The brushwood, or who tore the earth with ploughs.
The grain sprang thick and tall, and hid in green
The blackened hill-side; ranks of spiky maize
Rose like a host embattled; the buckwheat
Whitened broad acres, sweetening with its flowers
The August wind. White cottages were seen
With rose-trees at the windows; barns from which
Came loud and shrill the crowing of the cock;
Pastures where rolled and neighed the lordly horse,
And white flocks browsed and bleated. A rich turf
Of grasses brought from far o'ercrept thy bank,
Spotted with the white clover. Blue-eyed girls
Brought pails, and dipped them in thy crystal pool;
And children, ruddy-cheeked and flaxen-haired,
Gathered the glistening cowslip from thy edge.

Since then, what steps have trod thy border! Here
On thy green bank, the woodman of the swamp
Has laid his axe, the reaper of the hill
His sickle, as they stooped to taste thy stream.
The sportsman, tired with wandering in the still
September noon, has bathed his heated brow

In thy cool current. Shouting boys, let loose
For a wild holiday, have quaintly shaped
Into a cup the folded linden leaf,
And dipped thy sliding crystal. From the wars
Returning, the plumed soldier by thy side
Has sat, and mused how pleasant 'twere to dwell
In such a spot, and be as free as thou,
And move for no man's bidding more. At eve,
When thou wert crimson with the crimson sky,
Lovers have gazed upon thee, and have thought
Their mingled lives should flow as peacefully
And brightly as thy waters. Here the sage,
Gazing into thy self-replenished depth,
Has seen eternal order circumscribe
And bind the motions of eternal change,
And from the gushing of thy simple fount
Has reasoned to the mighty universe.

Is there no other change for thee, that lurks
Among the future ages? Will not man
Seek out strange arts to wither and deform
The pleasant landscape which thou makest green?
Or shall the veins that feed thy constant stream
Be choked in middle earth, and flow no more
For ever, that the water-plants along
Thy channel perish, and the bird in vain
Alight to drink? Haply shall these green hills
Sink, with the lapse of years, into the gulf
Of ocean waters, and thy source be lost
Amidst the bitter brine? Or shall they rise,
Upheaved in broken cliffs and airy peaks,
Haunts of the eagle and the snake, and thou
Gush midway from the bare and barren steep?

The Painted Cup

The fresh savannas of the Sangamon
Here rise in gentle swells, and the long grass
Is mixed with rustling hazels. Scarlet tufts

Are glowing in the green, like flakes of fire;
The wanderers of the prairie know them well,
And call that brilliant flower the Painted Cup.

    Now, if thou art a poet, tell me not
That these bright chalices were tinted thus
To hold the dew for fairies, when they meet
On moonlight evenings in the hazel bowers,
And dance till they are thirsty. Call not up,
Amid this fresh and virgin solitude,
The faded fancies of an elder world;
But leave these scarlet cups to spotted moths
Of June, and glistening flies, and humming-birds,
To drink from, when on all these boundless lawns
The morning sun looks hot. Or let the wind
O'erturn in sport their ruddy brims, and pour
A sudden shower upon the strawberry plant,
To swell the reddening fruit that even now
Breathes a slight fragrance from the sunny slope.

    But thou art of a gayer fancy. Well—
Let then the gentle Manitou of flowers,
Lingering amid the bloomy waste he loves,
Though all his swarthy worshippers are gone—
Slender and small, his rounded cheek all brown
And ruddy with the sunshine; let him come
On summer mornings, when the blossoms wake,
And part with little hands the spiky grass;
And touching, with his cherry lips, the edge
Of these bright beakers, drain the gathered dew.

The Night Journey of a River

Oh River, gentle River! gliding on
In silence underneath this starless sky!
Thine is a ministry that never rests
Even while the living slumber. For a time
The meddler, man, hath left the elements
In peace; the ploughman breaks the clods no more;

The miner labors not, with steel and fire,
To rend the rock, and he that hews the stone,
And he that fells the forest, he that guides
The loaded wain, and the poor animal
That drags it, have forgotten, for a time,
Their toils, and share the quiet of the earth.
    Thou pausest not in thine allotted task,
Oh darkling River! Through the night I hear
Thy wavelets rippling on the pebbly beach;
I hear thy current stir the rustling sedge,
That skirts thy bed; thou intermittest not
Thine everlasting journey, drawing on
A silvery train from many a woodland spring
And mountain-brook. The dweller by thy side,
Who moored his little boat upon thy beach,
Though all the waters that upbore it then
Have slid away o'er night, shall find, at morn,
Thy channel filled with waters freshly drawn
From distant cliffs, and hollows where the rill
Comes up amid the water-flags. All night
Thou givest moisture to the thirsty roots
Of the lithe willow and o'erhanging plane,
And cherishest the herbage of thy bank,
Spotted with little flowers, and sendest up
Perpetually the vapors from thy face,
To steep the hills with dew, or darken heaven
With drifting clouds, that trail the shadowy shower.
    Oh River! darkling River! what a voice
Is that thou utterest while all else is still—
The ancient voice that, centuries ago,
Sounded between thy hills, while Rome was yet
A weedy solitude by Tiber's stream!
How many, at this hour, along thy course,
Slumber to thine eternal murmurings,
That mingle with the utterance of their dreams!
At dead of night the child awakes and hears
Thy soft, familiar dashings, and is soothed,
And sleeps again. An airy multitude
Of little echoes, all unheard by day,
Faintly repeat, till morning, after thee,

The story of thine endless goings forth.
    Yet there are those who lie beside thy bed
For whom thou once didst rear the bowers that screen
Thy margin, and didst water the green fields;
And now there is no night so still that they
Can hear thy lapse; their slumbers, were thy voice
Louder than Ocean's, it could never break.
For them the early violet no more
Opens upon thy bank, nor, for their eyes,
Glitter the crimson pictures of the clouds,
Upon thy bosom, when the sun goes down.
Their memories are abroad, the memories
Of those who last were gathered to the earth,
Lingering within the homes in which they sat,
Hovering above the paths in which they walked,
Haunting them like a presence. Even now
They visit many a dreamer in the forms
They walked in, ere at last they wore the shroud.
And eyes there are which will not close to dream,
For weeping and for thinking of the grave,
The new-made grave, and the pale one within.
These memories and these sorrows all shall fade,
And pass away, and fresher memories
And newer sorrows come and dwell awhile
Beside thy borders, and, in turn, depart.
    On glide thy waters, till at last they flow
Beneath the windows of the populous town,
And all night long give back the gleam of lamps,
And glimmer with the trains of light that stream
From halls where dancers whirl. A dimmer ray
Touches thy surface from the silent room
In which they tend the sick, or gather round
The dying; and a slender, steady beam
Comes from the little chamber, in the roof
Where, with a feverous crimson on her cheek,
The solitary damsel, dying, too,
Plies the quick needle till the stars grow pale.
There, close beside the haunts of revel, stand
The blank, unlighted windows, where the poor,
In hunger and in darkness, wake till morn.

There, drowsily, on the half-conscious ear
Of the dull watchman, pacing on the wharf,
Falls the soft ripple of the waves that strike
On the moored bark; but guiltier listeners
Are nigh, the prowlers of the night, who steal
From shadowy nook to shadowy nook, and start
If other sounds than thine are in the air.
 Oh, glide away from those abodes, that bring
Pollution to thy channel and make foul
Thy once clear current; summon thy quick waves
And dimpling eddies; linger not, but haste,
With all thy waters, haste thee to the deep,
There to be tossed by shifting winds and rocked
By that mysterious force which lives within
The sea's immensity, and wields the weight
Of its abysses, swaying to and fro
The billowy mass, until the stain, at length,
Shall wholly pass away, and thou regain
The crystal brightness of thy mountain-springs.

The Constellations

O Constellations of the early night,
That sparkled brighter as the twilight died,
And made the darkness glorious! I have seen
Your rays grow dim upon the horizon's edge,
And sink behind the mountains. I have seen
The great Orion, with his jewelled belt,
That large-limbed warrior of the skies, go down
Into the gloom. Beside him sank a crowd
Of shining ones. I look in vain to find
The group of sister-stars, which mothers love
To show their wondering babes, the gentle Seven.
Along the desert space mine eyes in vain
Seek the resplendent cressets which the Twins
Uplifted in their ever-youthful hands.
The streaming tresses of the Egyptian Queen
Spangle the heavens no more. The Virgin trails
No more her glittering garments through the blue.

Gone! all are gone! and the forsaken Night,
With all her winds, in all her dreary wastes,
Sighs that they shine upon her face no more.
    Now only here and there a little star
Looks forth alone. Ah me! I know them not,
Those dim successors of the numberless host
That filled the heavenly fields, and flung to earth
Their quivering fires. And now the middle watch
Betwixt the eve and morn is past, and still
The darkness gains upon the sky, and still
It closes round my way. Shall, then, the Night,
Grow starless in her later hours? Have these
No train of flaming watchers, that shall mark
Their coming and farewell? O Sons of Light!
Have ye then left me ere the dawn of day
To grope along my journey sad and faint?
    Thus I complained, and from the darkness round
A voice replied—was it indeed a voice,
Or seeming accents of a waking dream
Heard by the inner ear? But thus it said:
O Traveller of the Night! thine eyes are dim
With watching; and the mists, that chill the vale
Down which thy feet are passing, hide from view
The ever-burning stars. It is thy sight
That is so dark, and not the heavens. Thine eyes,
Were they but clear, would see a fiery host
Above thee; Hercules, with flashing mace,
The Lyre with silver chords, the Swan uppoised
On gleaming wings, the Dolphin gliding on
With glistening scales, and that poetic steed,
With beamy mane, whose hoof struck out from earth
The fount of Hippocrene, and many more,
Fair clustered splendors, with whose rays the Night
Shall close her march in glory, ere she yield,
To the young Day, the great earth steeped in dew.
    So spake the monitor, and I perceived
How vain were my repinings, and my thought
Went backward to the vanished years and all
The good and great who came and passed with them,
And knew that ever would the years to come

Bring with them, in their course, the good and great,
Lights of the world, though, to my clouded sight,
Their rays might seem but dim, or reach me not.

Dante

Who, mid the grasses of the field
    That spring beneath our careless feet,
First found the shining stems that yield
    The grains of life-sustaining wheat:

Who first, upon the furrowed land,
    Strewed the bright grains to sprout, and grow,
And ripen for the reaper's hand—
    We know not, and we cannot know.

But well we know the hand that brought
    And scattered, far as sight can reach,
The seeds of free and living thought
    On the broad field of modern speech.

Mid the white hills that round us lie,
    We cherish that Great Sower's fame,
And, as we pile the sheaves on high,
    With awe we utter Dante's name.

Six centuries, since the poet's birth,
    Have come and flitted o'er our sphere:
The richest harvest reaped on earth
    Crowns the last century's closing year.

MARIA GOWEN BROOKS

(1794? – 1845)

from *Zophiël, or the Bride of Seven*

Canto the Third: Palace of the Gnomes

I.

'Tis now the hour of mirth, the hour of love,
   The hour of melancholy: Night, as vain
Of her full beauty, seems to pause above,
   That all may look upon her ere it wane.

II.

The heavenly angel watched his subject star
   O'er all that's good and fair benignly smiling;
The sighs of wounded love he hears, from far;
   Weeps that he cannot heal, and wafts a hope beguiling.

III.

The nether earth looks beauteous as a gem;
   High o'er her groves in floods of moonlight laving,
The towering palm displays his silver stem,
   The while his plumy leaves scarce in the breeze are waving.

IV.

The nightingale among his roses sleeps;
   The soft-eyed doe in thicket deep is sleeping;
The dark green myrrh her tears of fragrance weeps,
   And, every odorous spike in limpid dew is steeping.

V.

Proud prickly cerea, now thy blossom 'scapes
   Its cell; brief cup of light; and seems to say,
"I am not for gross mortals: blood of grapes—
   And sleep for them! Come spirits, while ye may!"

VI.

A silent stream winds darkly through the shade,
   And slowly gains the Tigris, where 'tis lost;
By a forgotten prince, of old, 'twas made,
   And, in its course, full many a fragment crost

Of marble fairly carved; and by its side
   Her golden dust the flaunting lotos threw
O'er her white sisters, throned upon the tide,
   And queen of every flower that loves perpetual dew.

VII.

Gold-sprinkling lotos, theme of many a song
   By slender Indian warbled to his fair!
Still tastes the stream thy rosy kiss, though long
   Has been but dust the hand that placed thee there.

VIII.

The little temple where its relics rest,
   Long since has fallen; its broken columns lie
Beneath the lucid wave, and give its breast
   A whitened glimmer as 'tis stealing by.

IX.

Here, cerea, too, thy clasping mazes twine
   The only pillar time has left erect;
Thy serpent arms embrace it, as 'twere thine,
   And roughly mock the beam it should reflect.

X.

An ancient prince, in happy madness blest,
   Was wont to wander to this spot; and deem'd
A water nymph came to him, and carest
   And loved him well; haply he only dream'd;

But on the spot a little dome arose,
    And flowers were set that still in wildness bloom;
And the cold ashes that were him, repose,
    Carefully shrined in this lone ivory tomb.

XI.

It is a place so strangely wild and sweet,
    That spirits love to come; and now, upon
A moonlight fragment, Zophiël chose his seat,
    In converse close with soft Phraërion;

XII.

Who, on the moss, beside him lies reclining,
    O'erstrewn with leaves, from full-blown roses shaken,
By nightingales, that on their branches twining,
    The live-long night to love and music waken.

XIII.

Phraërion, gentle sprite! nor force nor fire
    He had to wake in others doubt or fear:
He'd hear a tale of bliss, and not aspire
    To taste himself; 'twas meet for his compeer.

XIV.

No soul-creative in this being born,
    Its restless, daring, fond, aspirings hid:
Within the vortex of rebellion drawn,
    He joined the shining ranks *as others did*.

XV.

Success but little had advanced; defeat,
    He thought so little, scarce, to him, were worse;
And, as he'd held, in heaven, inferior seat,
    Less was his bliss, and lighter was his curse.

XVI.

He formed no plans for happiness: content
    To curl the tendril, fold the bud; his pain
So light, he scarcely felt his banishment.
    Zophiël, perchance, had held him in disdain;

But, form'd for friendship, from his o'erfraught soul
    'Twas such relief his burning thoughts to pour
In other ears, that, oft the strong control
    Of pride he felt them burst, and could restrain no more.

Zophiël was soft, but yet all flame; by turns
    Love, grief, remorse, shame, pity, jealousy,
Each boundless in his breast, impels or burns:
    His joy was bliss, his pain was agony.

And mild Phraërion was of heaven, and *there*,
    Nothing imperfect in its kind can be:
There every form is fresh, soft, bright, and fair,
    Yet differing each, with that variety,

Not least of miracles, which *here* we trace;
    And wonder and admire the cause that form'd
So like, and yet so different every face,
    Though of the self-same clay by the same process warm'd.

XVII.

"Order is heaven's first law." But that obeyed,
    The planets fixed, the Eternal mind at leisure;
A vast profusion spread o'er all it made,
    As if in endless change were found eternal pleasure.

XVIII.

Harmless Phraërion form'd to dwell on high,
    Retain'd the looks that had been his above;
And his harmonious lip and sweet blue eye
    Sooth'd the fallen seraph's heart, and changed his scorn
        to love,

Who, when he saw him in some garden pleasant,
　　Happy, because too little thought had he
To place, in contrast, past delight with present,
　　Had given his soul of fire for that inanity.

XIX.

But oh! in him the Eternal had infused
　　The restless soul that doth itself devour,
Unless it can create; and fallen, misused,
　　But forms the vast design to mourn the feeble power.

XX.

In plenitude of love, the Power benign
　　Nearer itself some beings fain would lift;
To share its joys, assist its vast design
　　With high intelligence; oh, dangerous gift!

XXI.

Superior passion, knowledge, force, and fire,
　　The glorious creatures took; but each the slave
Of his own strength, soon burnt with wild desire,
　　And basely turn'd it 'gainst the hand that gave.

XXII.

But Zóphiël, fallen sufferer, now no more
　　Thought of the past; the aspiring voice was mute
That urged him on to meet his doom before,
　　And all dissolved to love each varied attribute.

XXIII.

"Come, my Phraërion, give me an embrace,"
　　He said. "I hope a respite of repose,
Like that respiring from thy sunny face;
　　Even the peace thy guileless bosom knows.

XXIV.

"Rememberest thou that cave of Tigris, where
    We went with fruits and flowers and meteor light,
And the fair creature, on the damp rock, there
    Shivering and trembling so? Ah! well she might!

"False were my words, infernal my intent;
    Then, as I knelt before her feet and sued;
Yet, still she blooms, uninjured, innocent,
    Though now, for seven long months, by Zóphiël watched
        and wooed.

XXV.

"Gentle Phraërion, 'tis for her I crave
    Assistance: what I could have blighted *then*,
'Tis *now* my only care to guard and save;
    Companion, then, my airy flight again.

XXVI.

"Conduct me to those hoards of sweets and dews,
    Treasured in haunts to all but thee unknown,
For favorite sprites: teach me their power and use,
    And whatsoe'er thou wilt, of Zóphiël, be it done!

XXVII.

"Throughout fair Ecbatane the deeds I've wrought
    Have cast such dread, that of all Sardius' train
I doubt if there be one, from tent or court,
    Who'll try what 'tis to thwart a Spirit's love again.

XXVIII.

"My Egla, left in her acacia grove,
    Has learnt to lay aside that piteous fear
That sorrow'd thee; and I but live to prove
    A love for her as harmless as sincere.

XXIX.

"Inspirer of the arts of Greece, I charm
　　Her ear with songs she never heard before;
And many an hour of thoughtfulness disarm
　　With stories cull'd from that vague, wondrous lore,

"But seldom told to mortals;—arts on gems
　　Inscribed that still exist; but hidden so
From fear of those who told that diadems
　　Have pass'd from brows that vainly ached to know:

"Nor glimpse had mortal, save that those fair things
　　Loved, ages past, like her I now adore,
Caught from their Angels some low whisperings,
　　Then told of them to such as dared not tell them more;

"But toil'd in lonely nooks far from the eye
　　Of shuddering, longing men; then, buried deep,
Till distant ages bade their secrets lie,
　　In hopes that time might tell what their dread oaths must
　　　　keep.

XXX.

"Egla looks on me doubtful but amused;
　　Admires, but trembling, dares not bid me stay;
Yet hour by hour her timid heart, more used,
　　Grows to my sight and words; and when a day

"I leave her, for my needful cares, at leisure
　　To muse upon and feel her lonely state;
At my returning, though restrain'd her pleasure,
　　There needs no Spirit's eye to see she does not hate.

XXXI.

"Oft have I look'd in mortal hearts, to know
　　How love, by slow advances, knows to twine
Each fibre with his wreaths; then overthrow
　　At once each stern resolve. The maiden's mine!

"Yet have I never press'd her ermine hand,
    Nor touch'd the living coral of her lip;
Though listening to its tones, so sweet, so bland,
    I've thought,—oh, impious thought!—who form'd
        might sip!

XXXII.

"Most impious thought! Soul, I would rein thee in
    E'en as the quick-eyed Parthian quells his steeds;
But thou wilt start, and rise, and plunge in sin,
    Till gratitude weeps out, and wounded reason bleeds!

XXXIII.

"Soul, what a mystery thou art! not one
    Admires, or loves, or worships virtue more
Than I; but passion hurls me on, till torn
    By keen remorse, I cool, to curse me and deplore.

XXXIV.

"But to my theme. Now, in the stilly night,
    I hover o'er her fragrant couch, and sprinkle
Sweet dews about her, as she slumbers light,
    Dews sought, with toil, beneath the pale star's twinkle,

"From plants of secret virtue. All for lust
    Too high and pure my bliss; her gentle breath
I hear, inhale, then weep; (for oh! she must:
    That form is mortal, and must sleep in death.)

XXXV.

"And oft, when nature pants, and the thick air,
    Charged with foul particles, weighs sluggish o'er,
I breathe them all; that deep disgust I bear
    To leave a fluid pure and sane for her.

XXXVI.

"How dear is this employ! how innocent!
    My soul's wild elements forbear their strife;
While, on these harmless cares, pleased and intent,
    I hope to save her beauty and her life,

"For many a rapturous year. But mortal ne'er
    Shall hold her to his heart! to me confined,
Her soul must glow; nor ever shall she bear
    That mortal fruit for which her form's designed.

XXXVII.

"No grosser blood, commingling with her own,
    Shall ever make her mother. Oh! that mild
Sad glance I love—that lip—that melting tone
    Shall ne'er be given to any mortal's child.

XXXVIII.

"But only for her Spirit shall she live;
    Unsoil'd by earth, fresh, chaste, and innocent!
And all a Spirit dares or can I'll give;
    And sure I thus can make her far more blest,

"Framed as she is, than mortal love could do;
    For more than mortal's to this creature given,
She's Spirit more than half; her beauty's hue
    Is of the sky, and speaks my native heaven.

XXXIX.

"But! the night wanes! while all is bright above,"
    He said, and round Phraërion, nearer drawn,
One beauteous arm he flung, "first to my love;
    We'll see her safe; then, to our task till dawn."

XL.

'Tis often thus with Spirits: when retired
    Afar from haunts of men; so they delight

To move in their own beauteous forms attired;
  Though like thin shades or air they mock dull mortals'
    sight.

XLI.

Well pleased Phraërion answered that embrace;
  All balmy he with thousand breathing sweets
From thousand dewy flowers. "But to what place,"
  He said, "will Zóphiël go? who danger greets

"As if 'twere peace. The Palace of the Gnome,
  Tahathyam, for our purpose most were meet;
But then the wave, so cold and fierce, the gloom,
  The whirlpools, rocks, that guard that deep retreat

"Yet, there are fountains which no sunny ray
  E'er danced upon, and drops come there at last
Which for whole ages, filtering all the way,
  Through all the veins of earth in winding maze have past.

XLII.

"These take from mortal beauty every stain,
  And smooth the unseemly lines of age and pain,
    With every wondrous efficacy rife;
  Nay once a spirit whispered of a draught,
Of which a drop, by any mortal quaft,
  Would save for terms of years his feeble flickering life.

XLIII.

"A Spirit told thee it would save from death
  The being who should taste that drop? Is't so?
Oh! dear Phraërion, for another breath
  We have not time! come, follow me! we'll go

"And take one look, then guide me to the track
  Of the Gnome's palace: there is not a blast
To stir the sea-flower! we will go and back
  Ere morn—nay come!—the night is wasting fast.

XLIV.

"My friend, O Zóphiël! only once I went,
　　Then, though bold Antreon bore me, such the pain,
I came back to the air, so rack'd and spent,
　　That for a whole sweet moon I had no joy again.

XLV.

"What sayst thou, back at morn?—the night, a day
　　And half the night that follows it, alas!
Were time too little for that fearful way;
　　And then such depths, such caverns we must pass"—

XLVI.

"Nothing! beloved Phraërion, I know how
　　To brave such risks; and first, the path will break,
As oft I've done in water depths; and thou
　　Need'st only follow through the way I make."

XLVII.

The soft Flower-Spirit shuddered; look'd on high,
　　And from his bolder brother would have fled;
But then the anger kindling in that eye
　　He could not bear. So to fair Egla's bed
Followed and looked; then shuddering all with dread,
　　To wondrous realms unknown to men he led;

Continuing long in sunset course his flight,
　　Until for flowery Sicily he bent;
Then, where Italia smiled upon the night,
　　Between their nearest shores chose midway his descent.

XLVIII.

The sea was calm, and the reflected moon
　　Still trembled on its surface; not a breath
Curl'd the broad mirror. Night had past her noon;
　　How soft the air! how cold the depths beneath!

XLIX.

The spirits hover o'er that surface smooth,
    Zóphiël's white arm around Phraërion's twined
In fond caress, his tender fears to sooth,
    While either's nearer wing the other's crossed behind.

L.

Well pleased, Phraërion half forgot his dread;
    And first, with foot as white as lotus leaf,
The sleepy surface of the waves essayed;
    But then his smile of love gave place to drops of grief.

LI.

How could he for that fluid dense and chill
    Change the sweet floods of air they floated on?
E'en at a touch his shrinking fibres thrill;
    But ardent Zóphiël, panting, hurries on;

And (catching his mild brother's tears, with lip
    That whisper'd courage 'twixt each glowing kiss,)
Persuades to plunge: limbs, wings, and locks they dip:
    Whate'er the other's pains, the lover felt but bliss.

LII.

Quickly he draws Phraërion on; his toil
    Even lighter than he hoped: some power benign
Seems to restrain the surges, while they boil
    Mid crags and caverns, as of his design

Respectful. That black, bitter element,
    As if obedient to his wish, gave way;
So, comforting Phraërion, on he went
    And a high craggy arch they reach, at dawn of day

Upon the upper world; and forced them through
    That arch the thick cold floods with such a roar
That the bold Sprite receded; and would view
    The cave before he ventured to explore.

LIII.

Then fearful lest his frighted guide might part
    And not be miss'd, amid such strife and din,
He strained him closer to his burning heart,
    And trusting to his strength rush'd fiercely in.

LIV.

On, on, for many a weary mile they fare;
    Till thinner grew the floods, long dark and dense,
From nearness to earth's core; and now a glare
    Of grateful light, relieved their piercing sense;

As when, above, the sun his genial streams
    Of warmth and light darts mingling with the waves
Whole fathoms down; while amorous of his beams
    Each scaly monstrous thing leaps from its slimy caves.

LV.

And now Phraërion, with a tender cry,
    Far sweeter than the land-bird's note, afar
Heard through the azure arches of the sky,
    By the long baffled storm-worn mariner:

"Hold, Zóphiël! rest thee now: our task is done,
    Tahathyam's realms alone can give this light!
Oh! though 'tis not the life-awakening sun,
    How sweet to see it break upon such fearful night!"

LVI.

Clear grew the wave, and thin; a substance white
    The wide expanding cavern floors and flanks;
Could one have look'd from high, how fair the sight!
    Like these the dolphin on Bahaman banks

Cleaves the warm fluid, in his rainbow tints,
    While even his shadow on the sands below
Is seen; as thro' the wave he glides and glints
    Where lies the polished shell and branching corals grow.

LVII.

No massive gate impedes; the wave in vain
    Might strive against the air to break or fall;
And, at the portal of that strange domain,
    A clear bright curtain seem'd, or crystal wall.

LVIII.

The Spirits pass its bounds, but would not far
    Tread the slant pavement, like unbidden guest;
The while, on either side, a bower of spar
    Gave invitation for a moment's rest.

LIX.

And, deep in either bower, a little throne
    Look'd so fantastic, it were hard to know
If busy Nature fashion'd it alone,
    Or found some curious artist here below.

LX.

Soon spoke Phraërion: "Come, Tahathyam, come,
    Thou know'st me well! I saw thee once to love;
And bring a guest to view thy sparkling dome
    Who comes full fraught with tidings from above."

LXI.

Those gentle tones, angelically clear,
    Past from his lips, in mazy depths retreating,
(As if that bower had been the cavern's ear),
    Full many a stadia far; and kept repeating,

As through the perforated rock they pass,
    Echo to echo guiding them; their tone
(As just from the sweet spirit's lip) at last
    Tahathyam heard; where, on a glittering throne

He solitary sat. 'Twas many a year
   Ere such delightful, grateful sound had blest
His pleasured sense; and with a starting tear,
   Half joy, half grief, he rose to greet his guest.

LXII.

First sending through the rock an answering strain
   To give both Spirits welcome, where they wait,
And bid them haste; for he might strive in vain
   Half mortal as he was, to reach that gate

For many a day. But in the bower they hear
   His bidding; and, from cumbrous matter free,
Arose; and to his princely home came near
   With such spiritual strange velocity,

They met him, just as by his palace door
   The Gnome appeared, with all his band, elate
In the display of his resplendent store,
   To such as knew his father's high estate.

LXIII.

His sire, a Seraph, framed to dwell above,
   Had lightly left his pure and blissful home
To taste the blandishments of mortal love;
   And from that lowly union sprang the Gnome,

Tahathyam, first of his compeers, and best,
   He look'd like heaven, fair semi-earthly thing!
The rest were born of many a maid carest
   After his birth, and chose him for their king.

LXIV.

He sat upon a car, (and the large pearl
   Once cradled in it glimmered, now, without)
Bound midway on two serpents' backs, that curl
   In silent swiftness as he glides about.

LXV.

A shell, 'twas first in liquid amber wet;
   Then ere the fragrant cement harden'd round,
All o'er with large and precious stones 'twas set
   By skillful Tsavaven or made or found.

LXVI.

The reins seem'd pliant crystal (but their strength
   Had match'd his earthly mother's silken band;)
And, fleck'd with rubies, flow'd in ample length,
   Like sparkles o'er Tahathyam's beauteous hand.

LXVII.

The reptiles, in their fearful beauty, drew
   As if from love, like steeds of Araby;
Like blood of lady's lip their scarlet hue;
   Their scales so bright and sleek, 'twas pleasure but to see.

LXVIII.

With open mouths, as proud to show the bit,
   They raise their heads, and arch their necks—(with eye
As bright as if with meteor fire 'twere lit);
   And dart their barbed tongues, 'twixt fangs of ivory.

LXIX.

These, when the quick-advancing Sprites they saw
   Furl their swift wings, and tread with angel grace
The smooth fair pavement, check'd their speed in awe,
   And glided far aside as if to give them space.

LXX.

Tahathyam, lighted with a pleasing pride,
   And in like guise, to meet the strangers bent
His courteous steps; the while on either side
   Fierce Aishalat and Pshaämayim went.

LXXI.

Bright Ramaöur followed on, in order meet;
   Then Nahalcoul and Zotzaraven, best
Beloved, save Rouämasak of perfume sweet;
   Then Talhazak and Marmorak; the rest

A crowd of various use and properties,
   Arranged to meet their monarch's wishes, vie
In seemly show to please the stranger's eyes,
   And show what could be wrought without or soil or sky.

LXXII.

And Zóphiël, though a spirit, ne'er had seen
   The like before; and, for he had to ask
A boon, almost as dear as heaven, his mien
   Was softness all; but 'twas a painful task

To his impatience thus the time to wait
   Due to such welcome: all his soul possest
With thoughts of her he'd left in lonely state,
   Unguarded, how he burnt to proffer his request!

LXXIII.

The fond Phraërion look'd on him, and knew
   How much it pain'd him here below to stay;
So towards the princely Gnome he gently drew
   To tell what purpose brought them down from day;

And said, "O! king, this humble offering take;
   How hard the task to bring I need not tell;
Receive the poor, poor gift, for friendship's sake!"
   Tahathyam took a yellow asphodel,

A deep-blue lotus, and a full moss-rose,
   And then spoke out, "My Talhazak, come hither,
Look at these flowers, cropt where the sun-beam glows;
   Crust them with diamond, never let them wither!"

LXXIV.

Then, soon, Phraërion: "Monarch, if 'tis truth,
   Thou hast (and that 'tis false sweet powers forfend!)
A draught whose power perpetuates life and youth,
   Wilt thou bestow one drop upon my friend?"

LXXV.

Then Zóphiël could no more withhold, but knelt
   And said, "Oh! sovereign! happier far than I!
Born as thou wert, and in earth's entrails pent,
   Though once I shared thy father's bliss on high.

LXXVI.

One only draught! and if its power I prove,
   By thy sweet mother, to an Angel dear,
Whate'er thou wilt, of all the world above,
   Down to these nether realms I'll bring thee every year.

LXXVII.

Thy tributary slave, I'll scorn the pain,
   Though storms and rocks my feeling substance tear!
Tahathyam, let me not implore in vain,
   Give me the draught, and save me from despair!

LXXVIII.

Tahathyam paused; as if the bold request
   He liked not to refuse, nor wish'd to grant;
Then (after much revolving in his breast),
   "What of this cup can an Immortal want?

LXXIX.

"My Angel sire, for many a year, endured
   The vilest toils, deep hidden in the ground,
To mix this drink; nor was't at last procured
   Till all he fear'd had happ'd: Death's sleep profound

"Seized my fair mother. I had shared her doom:
    Mortal, like her he held than heaven more dear;
But, by his chymic arts, he robb'd the tomb
    And fixed my solitary being here;

"As if to hide from the Life-giver's eye,
    Of his presumptuous task, untried before
The prized success, bidding the secret lie
    For ever here; I never saw him more,

"When this was done. Yet what avails to live,
    From age to age, thus hidden 'neath the wave?
Nor life nor being have I power *to give*,
    And here, alas! are no more lives to save!

LXXX.

"For my loved father's sight in vain I pine!
    Where is the bright Cephroniel? Spirit tell
But how he fares, and what thou ask'st is thine!"
    Fair hope from Zóphiël's look that moment fell.

LXXXI.

The anxious Gnome observed; and soon bethought
    How far his exile limited his will;
And half divining why he so besought
    Gift, worthless, save to man, continued still

His speech:—"Thou askest much: should I impart
    Spirit, to thee, what my great father fain
Would hide from heaven? and what with all his art
    Even the second power desires in vain?

LXXXII.

"All long but cannot touch: a sword of flame
    Guards the life-fruit once seen. Yet, Spirit, know
There is a service,—do what I shall name,
    And let the danger threaten,—I'll bestow.

LXXXIII.

"But first partake our humble banquet, spread
    Within these rude walls, and repose awhile;"
He said, and to the sparry portal led
    And usher'd his fair guests with hospitable smile.

LXXXIV.

High towered the palace and its massive pile,
    Made dubious if of nature or of art,
So wild and so uncouth; yet, all the while,
    Shaped to strange grace in every varying part.

LXXXV.

And groves adorn'd it, green in hue, and bright,
    As icicles about a laurel-tree;
And danced about their twigs a wonderous light;
    Whence came that light so far beneath the sea?

LXXXVI.

Zóphiël looked up to know, and to his view
    The vault scarce seem'd less vast than that of day;
No rocky roof was seen; a tender blue
    Appear'd, as of the sky, and clouds about it play:

LXXXVII.

And, in the midst, an orb look'd as 'twere meant
    To shame the sun, it mimick'd him so well.
But ah! no quickening, grateful warmth it sent;
    Cold as the rock beneath, the paly radiance fell.

LXXXVIII.

Within, from thousand lamps the lustre strays,
    Reflected back from gems about the wall;
And from twelve dolphin shapes a fountain plays,
    Just in the centre of the spacious hall;

LXXXIX.

But whether in the sunbeam form'd to sport,
　These shapes once lived in suppleness and pride,
And then, to decorate this wonderous court,
　Were stolen from the waves and petrified,

Or, moulded by some imitative Gnome,
　And scaled all o'er with gems, they were but stone,
Casting their showers and rainbows 'neath the dome,
　To man or angel's eye might not be known.

XC.

No snowy fleece in these sad realms was found,
　Nor silken ball, by maiden loved so well;
But ranged in lightest garniture around,
　In seemly folds, a shining tapestry fell.

XCI.

And fibres of asbestos, bleached in fire,
　And all with pearls and sparkling gems o'er-fleck'd,
Of that strange court composed the rich attire,
　And such the cold, fair form of sad Tahathyam deck'd.

XCII.

Of marble white the table they surround,
　And reddest coral deck'd each curious couch,
Which softly yielding to their forms was found,
　And of a surface smooth and wooing to the touch.

XCIII.

Of sunny gold and silver, like the moon,
　Here was no lack; but if the veins of earth,
Torn open by man's weaker race, so soon
　Supplied the alluring hoard, or here had birth

That baffling, maddening, fascinating art,
    Half told by Sprite most mischievous, that he
Might laugh to see men toil, then not impart,
    The guests left uninquired:—'tis still a mystery.

XCIV.

Here were no flowers, but a sweet odour breathed,
    Of amber pure; a glistening coronal,
Of various-coloured gems, each brow enwreathed,
    In form of garland, for the festival.

XCV.

All that the shell contains most delicate,
    Of vivid colours, ranged and drest with care,
Was spread for food, and still was in the state
    Of its first freshness:—if such creatures, rare
Among cold rocks, so far from upper air,
    By force of art, might live and propagate,
Or were in hoards preserved, the muse cannot declare.

XCVI.

But here, so low from the life-wakening sun,
    However humble, life was sought in vain;
But when by chance, or gift, or peril won,
    'Twas prized and guarded well in this domain.

XCVII.

Four dusky Spirits, by a secret art
    Taught by a father, thoughtful of his wants,
Tahathyam kept, for menial toil apart,
    But only deep in sea were their permitted haunts.

XCVIII.

The banquet-cups, of many a hue and shape,
    Boss'd o'er with gems, were beautiful to view;
But, for the madness of the vaunted grape,
    Their only draught was a pure limpid dew,

To Spirits sweet; but these half-mortal lips
   Long'd for the streams that once on earth they quaffed;
And, half in shame, Tahathyam coldly sips
   And craves excuses for the temperate draught.

XCIX.

"Man tastes," he said, "the grapes sweet blood that streams
   To steep his heart when pain'd; when sorrowing he
In wild delirium drowns the sense, and dreams
   Of bliss arise, to cheat his misery."

C.

Nor with their dews were any mingling sweets
   Save those, to mortal lip, of poison fell;
No murmuring bee, was heard in these retreats,
   The mineral clod alone supplied their hydromel.

CI.

The Spirits while they sat, in social guise,
   Pledging each goblet with an answering kiss,
Mark'd many a Gnome conceal his bursting sighs;
   And thought death happier than a life like this.

CII.

But they had music; at one ample side
   Of the vast area of that sparkling hall,
Fringed round with gems, that all the rest outvied;
   In form of canopy, was seen to fall

The stony tapestry, over what, at first,
   An altar to some deity appear'd;
But it had cost full many a year to adjust
   The limpid crystal tubes that 'neath uprear'd

Their different lucid lengths; and so complete
   Their wondrous rangement, that a tuneful Gnome
Drew from them sounds more varied, clear, and sweet,
   Than ever yet had rung in any earthly dome.

CIII.

Loud, shrilly, liquid, soft; at that quick touch
   Such modulation woo'd his angel ears
That Zóphiël wonder'd, started from his couch
   And thought upon the music of the spheres.

CIV.

Tahathyam mark'd; and casting down the board
   A wistful glance to one who shared his cheer,
"My Ragasycheon," said he; at his word
   A Gnome arose, and knew what strains he fain would hear.

CV.

More like the dawn of youth in form and face,
   And than his many pheres more lightly drest,
Yet unsurpass'd in beauty and in grace,
   Silken-haired Ragasycheon soon express'd

The feelings rising at his master's heart;
   Choosing such tones as when the breezes sigh
Through some lone portico; or far apart,
   From ruder sounds of mirth in the deep forest die.

CVI.

Preluding low, in notes that faint and tremble,
   Swelling, awakening, dying, plaining deep,
While such sensations in the soul assemble,
   As make it pleasure to the eyes to weep.

CVII.

Is there a heart that ever loved in vain,
   Though years have thrown their veil o'er all most dear,
That lives not each sensation o'er again
   In sympathy with sounds like those that mingle here?

CVIII.

Still the fair Gnome's light hands the chime prolong;
   And while his utmost art the strain employs,
Cephroniel's softened son in gushing song,
   Pour'd forth his sad, deep sense of long departed joys.

CIX.

SONG

Oh, my Phronema! how thy yellow hair
   Was fragrant, when, by looks alone carest,
I felt it, wafted by the pitying air,
   Float o'er my lips and touch my fervid breast!

How my least word lent colour to thy cheek!
   And how thy gentle form would heave and swell,
As if the love thy heart contained would break
   That warm pure shrine where nature bade it dwell.

We parted; years are past, and *thou* art dead:
   Never, Phronema, shall I see thee more!
One little ringlet of thy graceful head
   Lies next my heart; 'tis all I may adore.

Torn from thy sight, to save a life of gloom,
   Hopes unaccomplish'd warmest wishes crost—
How can I longer bear my weary doom?
   Alas! what have I gain'd for all I lost?

CX.

The music ceased; and from Tahathyam pass'd
   The mournful exstasy that lent it zest;
But tears adown his paly cheek fell fast,
   And sprinkled the asbestos o'er his breast.

CXI.

Then thus: "If but a being half so dear
   Could to these realms be brought, the slow distress
Of my long solitude were less severe,
   And I might learn to bear my weariness.

CXII.

"There's a nepenthic draught, which the warm breath
   Of mortals, when they quaff, keeps in suspense;
Giving the pale similitude of death,
   While thus chain'd up the quick perceptive sense.

"Haply 'twere possible. But to the shrine,
   Where like a god I guard Cephroniel's gift!"
Soon through the rock they wind; the draught divine
   Was hidden by a veil the king alone might lift.

CXIII.

Cephroniel's son, with half-averted face
   And faltering hand, that curtain drew, and show'd,
Of solid diamond formed, a lucid vase;
   And warm within the pure elixir glow'd;

CXIV.

Bright red, like flame and blood, (could they so meet)
   Ascending, sparkling, dancing, whirling, ever
In quick perpetual movement; and of heat
   So high, the rock was warm beneath their feet,
(Yet heat in its intenseness hurtful never),

Even to the entrance of the long arcade
   Which led to that deep shrine, in the rock's breast
As far as if the half-angel were afraid
   To know the secret he himself possessed.

CXV.

Tahathyam filled a slip of spar with dread,
   As if stood by and frown'd some power divine;
Then trembling, as he turned to Zóphiël said,
   "But for one service shalt thou call it thine.

CXVI.

"Bring me a wife; as I have named the way;
    (I will not risk destruction save for love!)
Fair-haired and beauteous like my mother; say—
    Plight me this pact; so shalt thou bear above,

"For thine own purpose, what has here been kept
    Since bloom'd the second age, to Angels dear.
Bursting from earth's dark womb the fierce wave swept
    Off every form that lived and loved, while here,
Deep hidden here, I still lived on and wept."

CXVII.

Then, Zóphiël, pitying his emotion: "So
    I promise; nay, unhappy prince, I swear
By what I dare not utter; I will go
    And search; and one of all the loveliest bear

"Away, the while she sleeps, to be thy wife:
    Give her nepenthic drink, and through the wave
Brave hell's worst pains to guard her gentle life.
    Monarch! 'tis said; now, give me what I crave!

CXVIII.

"Tahathyam Evanath, son of a sire
    Who knew how love burns in a breast divine,
If this thy gift sustain—one vital fire,
    Sigh not for things of earth, for all earth's best are thine."

CXIX.

He took the spar: the high-wrought hopes of both
    Forbad delay. So to the palace back
They came; Tahathyam faintly pressed; nor loth
    Saw his fair guests depart to wend their watery track.

Composed at the Request of a Lady, and Descriptive of Her Feelings

She Returned to the North, and Died Soon After

Adieu, fair isle! I love thy bowers,
   I love thy dark-eyed daughters there;
The cool pomegranate's scarlet flowers
   Look brighter in their jetty hair.

They praised my forehead's stainless white;
   And when I thirsted, gave a draught
From the full clustering cocoa's height,
   And smiling, blessed me as I quaff'd.

Well pleased, the kind return I gave,
   And, clasped in their embraces' twine,
Felt the soft breeze, like Lethe's wave,
   Becalm this beating heart of mine.

Why will my heart so wildly beat?
   Say, Seraphs, is my lot too blest,
That thus a fitful, feverish heat
   Must rifle me of health and rest?

Alas! I fear my native snows —
   A clime too cold, a heart too warm —
Alternate chills — alternate glows —
   Too fiercely threat my flower-like form.

The orange-tree has fruit and flowers;
   The grenadilla, in its bloom,
Hangs o'er its high, luxuriant bowers,
   Like fringes from a Tyrian loom.

When the white coffee-blossoms swell,
   The fair moon full, the evening long,
I love to hear the warbling bell,
   And sun-burnt peasant's wayward song.

Drive gently on, dark muleteer,
   And the light seguidilla frame;
Fain would I listen still, to hear
   At every close thy mistress' name.

Adieu, fair isle! the waving palm
   Is pencilled on thy purest sky;
Warm sleeps the bay, the air is balm,
   And, soothed to languor, scarce a sigh

Escapes for those I love so well,
   For those I've loved and left so long,
On me their fondest musings dwell,
   To them alone my sighs belong.

On, on, my bark! blow southern breeze!
   No longer would I lingering stay;
'Twere better far *to die* with these
   Than *live in pleasure* far away.

JOSEPH RODMAN DRAKE
(1795–1820)

The Mocking-Bird

Early on a pleasant day,
In the poets' month of May;
Field and forest look'd so fair,
So refreshing was the air,
That, despite of morning dew,
Forth I walk'd where, tangling grew,
Many a thorn and briery bush,
Where the red-breast and the thrush,
Gaily rais'd their early lay,
Thankful for returning day;
Every thicket, bush, and tree,
Swell'd the grateful harmony.
As it sweetly swept along,
Echo seem'd to catch the song;
But the plain was wide and clear,
Echo never whisper'd there.
From a neighb'ring mocking-bird
Came the answering note I heard;
Near a murmuring streamlet's side,
Perch'd on branch extending wide.
Low, and soft, the song began;
Scarce I caught it, as it ran
Through the ring-dove's plaintive wail,
Chattering jay, and whistling quail,
Twittering sparrow, cat-bird's cry,
Red-bird's whistle, robin's sigh,
Black-bird, blue-bird, swallow, lark;
Each his native note might mark.
Oft he tried the lesson o'er,
Each time louder than before;
Burst at length the finish'd song:
Loud and clear it pour'd along.
All the choir in silence heard,

Hush'd before the wondrous bird.
All transported and amaz'd,
Scarcely breathing, long I gaz'd.
Now it reach'd the loudest swell;
Lower, lower, now it fell;
Lower, lower, lower still,
Scarce it sounded o'er the rill.
Now the warbler ceas'd to sing;
And I saw him spread his wing;
And I saw him take his flight,
Other regions to delight.
Then, in most poetic wise,
I began to moralize.
   In this bird can fancy trace
An emblem of the rhyming race.
Ere with heaven's immortal fire,
Loud they strike the quivering wire;
Ere in high, majestic song,
Thundering wars the verse along;
Soft and low each note they sing,
Soft they try each varied string;
Till each power is tried and known;
Then the kindling spark is blown.
Thus, perchance, has Maro sung;
Thus, his harp has Milton strung;
Thus, immortal Avon's child;
Thus, O Scott! thy witch-notes wild;
Thus, has Pope's melodious lyre
Rung each note with Homer's fire;
Thus, did Campbell's war-blast roar
Round the cliffs of Elsinore;
Thus, he dug the soldier's grave,
Iser! by thy purpled wave.

The National Painting

Awake! ye forms of verse divine—
  Painting! descend on canvass wing,
And hover ov'r my head, Design!
  Your son, your glorious son, I sing!
At T*******'s name I break my sloth,
  To load him with poetic riches;
The Titian of a tablecloth!
  The Guido of a pair of breeches!

Come star-eyed maid—Equality!
  In thine adorers' praise I revel;
Who brings, so fierce, his love to thee—
  All forms and faces to a level:
Old, young—great, small—the grave, the gay;
  Each man might swear the next his brother;
And there they stand in dread array,
  To fire their votes at one another.

How bright their buttons shine! how straight
  Their coat-flaps fall in plaited grace;
How smooth the hair on every pate;
  How vacant each immortal face!
And then thy tints—the shade—the flush—
  (I wrong them with a strain too humble)
Not mighty S*****d's strength of brush
  Can match thy glowing hues, my T——l.

Go on, great painter! dare be dull;
  No longer after nature dangle;
Call rectilinear beautiful;
  Find grace and freedom in an angle:
Pour on the red—the green—the yellow—
  Paint till a horse may mire upon it,
And while I've strength to write or bellow,
  I'll sound your praises in a sonnet.

from *The Culprit Fay*

I.

'Tis the middle watch of a summer's night—
The earth is dark, but the heavens are bright;
Naught is seen in the vault on high
But the moon, and the stars, and the cloudless sky,
And the flood which rolls its milky hue,
A river of light on the welkin blue.
The moon looks down on old Cronest,
She mellows the shades on his shaggy breast,
And seems his huge grey form to throw
In a silver cone on the wave below;
His sides are broken by spots of shade,
By the walnut bough and the cedar made,
And through their clustering branches dark
Glimmers and dies the fire-fly's spark—
Like starry twinkles that momently break
Through the rifts of the gathering tempest's rack.

II.

The stars are on the moving stream,
    And fling, as its ripples gently flow,
A burnished length of wavy beam
    In an eel-like, spiral line below;
The winds are whist, and the owl is still,
    The bat in the shelvy rock is hid,
And naught is heard on the lonely hill
But the cricket's chirp and the answer shrill
    Of the gauze-winged katy-did;
And the plaint of the wailing whip-poor-will
    Who mourns unseen, and ceaseless sings,
Ever a note of wail and wo,
    Till morning spreads her rosy wings,
And earth and sky in her glances glow.

III.

'Tis the hour of fairy ban and spell:
The wood-tick has kept the minutes well;

He has counted them all with click and stroke,
Deep in the heart of the mountain oak,
And he has awakened the sentry elve
    Who sleeps with him in the haunted tree,
To bid him ring the hour of twelve,
    And call the fays to their revelry;
Twelve small strokes on his tinkling bell—
('Twas made of the white snail's pearly shell:—)
"Midnight comes, and all is well!
Hither, hither, wing your way!
'Tis the dawn of the fairy day."

IV.

They come from beds of lichen green,
They creep from the mullen's velvet screen;
    Some on the backs of beetles fly
From the silver tops of moon-touched trees,
    Where they swung in their cobweb hammocks high,
And rock'd about in the evening breeze;
    Some from the hum-bird's downy nest—
They had driven him out by elfin power,
    And pillowed on plumes of his rainbow breast,
Had slumbered there till the charmed hour;
    Some had lain in the scoop of the rock,
With glittering ising-stars inlaid;
    And some had opened the four-o'clock,
And stole within its purple shade.
    And now they throng the moonlight glade,
Above—below—on every side,
    Their little minim forms arrayed
In the tricksy pomp of fairy pride!

V.

They come not now to print the lea,
In freak and dance around the tree,
Or at the mushroom board to sup,
And drink the dew from the buttercup;—
A scene of sorrow waits them now,
For an Ouphe has broken his vestal vow;

He has loved an earthly maid,
And left for her his woodland shade;
He has lain upon her lip of dew,
And sunned him in her eye of blue,
Fann'd her cheek with his wing of air,
Played with the ringlets of her hair,
And, nestling on her snowy breast,
Forgot the lily-king's behest.
For this the shadowy tribes of air
    To the elfin court must haste away:—
And now they stand expectant there,
    To hear the doom of the Culprit Fay.

The American Flag

I.

When Freedom from her mountain height
    Unfurled her standard to the air,
She tore the azure robe of night,
    And set the stars of glory there.
She mingled with its gorgeous dyes
The milky baldric of the skies,
And striped its pure celestial white,
With streakings of the morning light;
Then from his mansion in the sun
She called her eagle bearer down,
And gave into his mighty hand,
    The symbol of her chosen land.

II.

Majestic monarch of the cloud,
    Who rear'st aloft thy regal form,
To hear the tempest trumpings loud
    And see the lightning lances driven,
When strike the warriors of the storm,
    And rolls the thunder-drum of heaven,
Child of the sun! to thee 'tis given

To guard the banner of the free,
To hover in the sulphur smoke,
To ward away the battle stroke,
And bid its blendings shine afar,
Like rainbows on the cloud of war,
    The harbingers of victory!

III.

Flag of the brave! thy folds shall fly,
    The sign of hope and triumph high,
When speaks the signal trumpet tone,
    And the long line comes gleaming on.
Ere yet the life-blood, warm and wet,
    Has dimm'd the glistening bayonet,
Each soldier eye shall brightly turn
    To where thy sky-born glories burn;
And as his springing steps advance,
    Catch war and vengeance from the glance.
And when the cannon-mouthings loud
    Heave in wild wreaths the battle shroud,
And gory sabres rise and fall
Like shoots of flame on midnight's pall;
    Then shall thy meteor glances glow,
And cowering foes shall shrink beneath
    Each gallant arm that strikes below
That lovely messenger of death.

IV.

Flag of the seas! on ocean wave
    Thy stars shall glitter o'er the brave;
When death, careering on the gale,
    Sweeps darkly round the bellied sail,
And frighted waves rush wildly back
    Before the broadside's reeling rack,
Each dying wanderer of the sea
    Shall look at once to heaven and thee,
    And smile to see thy splendours fly
    In triumph o'er his closing eye.

V.

Flag of the free heart's hope and home!
    By angel hands to valour given;
Thy stars have lit the welkin dome,
    And all thy hues were born in heaven.
Forever float that standard sheet!
    Where breathes the foe but falls before us,
With Freedom's soil beneath our feet,
    And Freedom's banner streaming o'er us?

Niagara

I.

Roar, raging torrent! and thou, mighty river,
Pour thy white foam on the valley below;
Frown, ye dark mountains! and shadow for ever
The deep rocky bed where the wild rapids flow.
The green sunny glade, and the smooth flowing fountain,
Brighten the home of the coward and slave;
The flood and the forest, the rock and the mountain,
Rear on their bosoms the free and the brave.

II.

Nurslings of nature, I mark your bold bearing,
Pride in each aspect and strength in each form,
Hearts of warm impulse, and souls of high daring,
Born in the battle and rear'd in the storm.
The red levin flash and the thunder's dread rattle,
The rock-riven wave and the war trumpet's breath,
The din of the tempest, the yell of the battle,
Nerve your steeled bosoms to danger and death.

III.

High on the brow of the Alps' snowy towers
The mountain Swiss measures his rock-breasted moors,
O'er his lone cottage the avalanche lowers,

Round its rude portal the spring-torrent pours.
Sweet is his sleep amid peril and danger,
Warm is his greeting to kindred and friends,
Open his hand to the poor and the stranger,
Stern on his foeman his sabre descends.

IV.

Lo! where the tempest the dark waters sunder
Slumbers the sailor boy, reckless and brave,
Warm'd by the lightning and lulled by the thunder,
Fann'd by the whirlwind and rock'd on the wave;
Wildly the winter wind howls round his pillow,
Cold on his bosom the spray showers fall;
Creaks the strained mast at the rush of the billow,
Peaceful he slumbers regardless of all.

V.

Mark how the cheek of the warrior flushes,
As the battle drum beats and the war torches glare;
Like a blast of the north to the onset he rushes,
And his wide-waving falchion gleams brightly in air.
Around him the death-shot of foemen are flying,
At his feet friends and comrades are yielding their breath;
He strikes to the groans of the wounded and dying,
But the war cry he strikes with is, 'conquest or death!'

VI.

Then pour thy broad wave like a flood from the heavens,
Each son that thou rearest, in the battle's wild shock,
When the death-speaking note of the trumpet is given,
Will charge like thy torrent or stand like thy rock.
Let his roof be the cloud and the rock be his pillow,
Let him stride the rough mountain, or toss on the foam,
He will strike fast and well on the field or the billow,
In triumph and glory, for God and his home!

To a Friend

"You damn me with faint praise."

I.

Yes, faint was my applause and cold my praise,
Though soul was glowing in each polished line;
But nobler subjects claim the poet's lays,
A brighter glory waits a muse like thine.
Let amorous fools in lovesick measure pine;
Let Strangford whimper on, in fancied pain,
And leave to Moore his rose leaves and his vine;
Be thine the task a higher crown to gain,
The envied wreath that decks the patriot's holy strain.

II.

Yet not in proud triumphal song alone,
Or martial ode, or sad sepulchral dirge,
There needs no voice to make our glories known;
There needs no voice the warrior's soul to urge
To tread the bounds of nature's stormy verge;
Columbia still shall win the battle's prize;
But be it thine to bid her mind emerge
To strike her harp, until its soul arise
From the neglected shade, where low in dust it lies.

III.

Are there no scenes to touch the poet's soul?
No deeds of arms to wake the lordly strain?
Shall Hudson's billows unregarded roll?
Has Warren, has Montgomery died in vain?
Shame! that while every mountain stream and plain
Hath theme for truth's proud voice or fancy's wand,
No native bard the patriot harp hath ta'en,
But left to minstrels of a foreign strand
To sing the beauteous scenes of nature's loveliest land.

IV.

Oh! for a seat on Appalachia's brow,
That I might scan the glorious prospect round,
Wild waving woods, and rolling floods below,
Smooth level glades and fields with grain embrown'd,
High heaving hills, with tufted forests crown'd,
Rearing their tall tops to the heaven's blue dome,
And emerald isles, like banners green unwound,
Floating along the lake, while round them roam
Bright helms of billowy blue and plumes of dancing foam.

V.

'Tis true no fairies haunt our verdant meads,
No grinning imps deform our blazing hearth;
Beneath the kelpie's fang no traveller bleeds,
Nor gory vampyre taints our holy earth,
Nor spectres stalk to frighten harmless mirth,
Nor tortured demon howls adown the gale;
Fair reason checks these monsters in their birth.
Yet have we lay of love and horrid tale
Would dim the manliest eye and make the bravest pale.

VI.

Where is the stony eye that hath not shed
Compassion's heart-drops o'er the sweet Mc Rea?
Through midnight's wilds by savage bandits led,
"Her heart is sad—her love is far away!"
Elate that lover waits the promised day
When he shall clasp his blooming bride again—
Shine on, sweet visions! dreams of rapture, play!
Soon the cold corse of her he loved in vain
Shall blight his withered heart and fire his frenzied brain.

VII.

Romantic Wyoming! could none be found
Of all that rove thy Eden groves among,
To wake a native harp's untutored sound,
And give thy tale of woe the voice of song?
Oh! if description's cold and nerveless tongue

From stranger harps such hallowed strains could call,
How doubly sweet the descant wild had rung,
From one who, lingering round thy ruined wall,
Had plucked thy mourning flowers and wept thy timeless
    fall.

VIII.

The Huron chief escaped from foemen nigh,
His frail bark launches on Niagara's tides,
"Pride in his port, defiance in his eye,"
Singing his song of death the warrior glides;
In vain they yell along the river sides,
In vain the arrow from its sheaf is torn,
Calm to his doom the willing victim rides,
And, till adown the roaring torrent borne,
Mocks them with gesture proud, and laughs their rage
    to scorn.

IX.

But if the charms of daisied hill and vale,
And rolling flood, and towering rock sublime,
If warrior deed or peasant's lowly tale
Of love or woe should fail to wake the rhyme,
If to the wildest heights of song you climb,
(Tho' some who know you less, might cry, beware!)
Onward! I say—your strains shall conquer time;
Give your bright genius wing, and hope to share
Imagination's worlds—the ocean, earth, and air.

X.

Arouse, my friend—let vivid fancy soar,
Look with creative eye on nature's face,
Bid airy sprites in wild Niagara roar,
And view in every field a fairy race.
Spur thy good Pacolet to speed apace,
And spread a train of nymphs on every shore;
Or if thy muse would woo a ruder grace,
The Indian's evil Manitou's explore,
And rear the wondrous tale of legendary lore.

XI.

Away! to Susquehannah's utmost springs,
Where, throned in mountain mist, Areouski reigns,
Shrouding in lurid clouds his plumeless wings,
And sternly sorrowing o'er his tribes remains;
His was the arm, like comet ere it wanes
That tore the streamy lightnings from the skies,
And smote the mammoth of the southern plains;
Wild with dismay the Creek affrighted flies,
While in triumphant pride Kanawa's eagles rise.

XII.

Or westward far, where dark Miami wends,
Seek that fair spot as yet to fame unknown;
Where, when the vesper dew of heaven descends,
Soft music breathes in many a melting tone,
At times so sadly sweet it seems the moan
Of some poor Ariel penanced in the rock;
Anon a louder burst—a scream! a groan!
And now amid the tempest's reeling shock,
Gibber, and shriek, and wail—and fiend-like laugh and mock.

XIII.

Or climb the Pallisado's lofty brows,
Where dark Omana waged the war of hell,
Till, waked to wrath, the mighty spirit rose
And pent the demons in their prison cell;
Full on their head the uprooted mountain fell,
Enclosing all within its horrid womb
Straight from the teeming earth the waters swell,
And pillared rocks arise in cheerless gloom
Around the drear abode—their last eternal tomb!

XIV.

Be these your future themes—no more resign
The soul of song to laud your lady's eyes;
Go! kneel a worshipper at nature's shrine!
For you her fields are green, and fair her skies!

For you her rivers flow, her hills arise!
And will you scorn them all, to pour forth tame
And heartless lays of feigned or fancied sighs?
Still will you cloud the muse? nor blush for shame
To cast away renown, and hide your head from fame?

Bronx

I sat me down upon a green bank-side,
   Skirting the smooth edge of a gentle river,
Whose waters seemed unwillingly to glide,
   Like parting friends who linger while they sever;
Enforced to go, yet seeming still unready,
   Backward they wind their way in many a wistful eddy.

Grey o'er my head the yellow-vested willow
   Ruffled its hoary top in the fresh breezes,
Glancing in light, like spray on a green billow,
   Or the fine frost-work which young winter freezes;
When first his power in infant pastime trying,
Congeals sad autumn's tears on the dead branches lying.

From rocks around hung the loose ivy dangling,
   And in the clefts sumach of liveliest green,
Bright ising-stars the little beach was spangling,
   The gold-cup sorrel from his gauzy screen
Shone like a fairy crown, enchased and beaded,
Left on some morn, when light flashed in their eyes
      unheeded.

The hum-bird shook his sun-touched wings around,
   The bluefinch caroll'd in the still retreat;
The antic squirrel capered on the ground
   Where lichens made a carpet for his feet:
Through the transparent waves, the ruddy minkle
Shot up in glimmering sparks his red fin's tiny twinkle.

There were dark cedars with loose mossy tresses,
   White powdered dog-trees, and stiff hollies flaunting
Gaudy as rustics in their May-day dresses,
   Blue pelloret from purple leaves upslanting
A modest gaze, like eyes of a young maiden
Shining beneath dropt lids the evening of her wedding.

The breeze fresh springing from the lips of morn,
   Kissing the leaves, and sighing so to lose 'em,
The winding of the merry locust's horn,
   The glad spring gushing from the rock's bare bosom:
Sweet sights, sweet sounds, all sights, all sounds excelling,
Oh! 'twas a ravishing spot formed for a poet's dwelling.

And did I leave thy loveliness, to stand
   Again in the dull world of earthly blindness?
Pained with the pressure of unfriendly hands,
   Sick of smooth looks, agued with icy kindness?
Left I for this thy shades, where none intrude,
To prison wandering thought and mar sweet solitude?

Yet I will look upon thy face again,
   My own romantic Bronx, and it will be
A face more pleasant than the face of men.
   Thy waves are old companions, I shall see
A well-remembered form in each old tree,
And hear a voice long loved in thy wild minstrelsy.

JAMES GATES
PERCIVAL
(1795–1856)

The Coral Grove

Deep in the wave is a coral grove,
Where the purple mullet, and gold-fish rove,
Where the sea-flower spreads its leaves of blue,
That never are wet with falling dew,
But in bright and changeful beauty shine,
Far down in the green and glassy brine.
The floor is of sand, like the mountain drift,
And the pearl shells spangle the flinty snow;
From coral rocks the sea plants lift
Their boughs, where the tides and billows flow;
The water is calm and still below,
For the winds and waves are absent there,
And the sands are bright as the stars that glow
In the motionless fields of upper air:
There with its waving blade of green,
The sea-flag streams through the silent water,
And the crimson leaf of the dulse is seen
To blush, like a banner bathed in slaughter:
There with a light and easy motion,
The fan-coral sweeps through the clear deep sea;
And the yellow and scarlet tufts of ocean,
Are bending like corn on the upland lea:
And life, in rare and beautiful forms,
Is sporting amid those bowers of stone,
And is safe, when the wrathful spirit of storms,
Has made the top of the wave his own:
And when the ship from his fury flies,
Where the myriad voices of ocean roar,
When the wind-god frowns in the murky skies,
And demons are waiting the wreck on shore;

219

Then far below in the peaceful sea,
The purple mullet, and gold-fish rove,
Where the waters murmur tranquilly,
Through the bending twigs of the coral grove.

GEORGE MOSES HORTON

(1798? – 1883?)

On Liberty and Slavery

Alas! and am I born for this,
  To wear this slavish chain?
Deprived of all created bliss,
  Through hardship, toil and pain!

How long have I in bondage lain,
  And languished to be free!
Alas! and must I still complain—
  Deprived of liberty.

Oh, Heaven! and is there no relief
  This side the silent grave—
To soothe the pain—to quell the grief
  And anguish of a slave?

Come Liberty, thou cheerful sound,
  Roll through my ravished ears!
Come, let my grief in joys be drowned,
  And drive away my fears.

Say unto foul oppression, Cease:
  Ye tyrants rage no more,
And let the joyful trump of peace,
  Now bid the vassal soar.

Soar on the pinions of that dove
  Which long has cooed for thee,
And breathed her notes from Afric's grove,
  The sound of Liberty.

Oh, Liberty! thou golden prize,
  So often sought by blood—
We crave thy sacred sun to rise,
  The gift of nature's God!

Bid Slavery hide her haggard face,
    And barbarism fly:
I scorn to see the sad disgrace
    In which enslaved I lie.

Dear Liberty! upon thy breast,
    I languish to respire;
And like the Swan unto her nest,
    I'd to thy smiles retire.

Oh, blest asylum—heavenly balm!
    Unto thy boughs I flee—
And in thy shades the storm shall calm,
    With songs of Liberty!

On Hearing of the Intention of a Gentleman to Purchase the Poet's Freedom

When on life's ocean first I spread my sail,
I then implored a mild auspicious gale;
And from the slippery strand I took my flight,
And sought the peaceful haven of delight.

Tyrannic storms arose upon my soul,
And dreadful did their mad'ning thunders roll;
The pensive muse was shaken from her sphere,
And hope, it vanish'd in the clouds of fear.

At length a golden sun broke thro' the gloom,
And from his smiles arose a sweet perfume—
A calm ensued, and birds began to sing,
And lo! the sacred muse resumed her wing.

With frantic joy she chaunted as she flew,
And kiss'd the clement hand that bore her thro'
Her envious foes did from her sight retreat,
Or prostrate fall beneath her burning feet.

'Twas like a proselyte, allied to Heaven—
Or rising spirits' boast of sins forgiven,
Whose shout dissolves the adamant away
Whose melting voice the stubborn rocks obey.

'Twas like the salutation of the dove,
Borne on the zephyr thro' some lonesome grove,
When Spring returns, and Winter's chill is past,
And vegetation smiles above the blast.

'Twas like the evening of a nuptial pair,
When love pervades the hour of sad despair—
'Twas like fair Helen's sweet return to Troy,
When every Grecian bosom swell'd with joy.

The silent harp which on the osiers hung,
Was then attuned, and manumission sung:
Away by hope the clouds of fear were driven,
And music breathed my gratitude to heaven.

Hard was the race to reach the distant goal,
The needle oft was shaken from the pole:
In such distress, who could forbear to weep?
Toss'd by the headlong billows of the deep!

The tantalizing beams which shone so plain,
Which turn'd my former pleasures into pain—
Which falsely promised all the joys of fame,
Gave way, and to a more substantial flame.

Some philanthropic souls as from afar,
With pity strove to break the slavish bar;
To whom my floods of gratitude shall roll,
And yield with pleasure to their soft control.

And sure of Providence this work begun—
He shod my feet this rugged race to run;
And in despite of all the swelling tide,
Along the dismal path will prove my guide.

Thus on the dusky verge of deep despair,
Eternal Providence was with me there;
When pleasure seemed to fade on life's gay dawn,
And the last beam of hope was almost gone.

SAMUEL HENRY DICKSON

(1798–1872)

Song—Written at the North

I sigh for the land of the Cypress and Pine,
Where the Jessamine blooms, and the gay Woodbine;
Where the moss droops low from the green Oak tree,
Oh! that sunbright land is the land for me.

The snowy flower of the Orange there,
Sheds its sweet fragrance through the air—
And the Indian rose delights to 'twine
Its branches with the laughing vine.

There the Humming-bird of rainbow plume,
Hangs over the scarlet creeper's bloom,
While midst the leaves his varying dies,
Sparkle like half-seen fairy eyes.

There the deer leaps light through the open glade,
Or hides him far in the forest shade,
When the woods resound in the dewy morn,
With the clang of the merry hunter's horn.

There the echoes ring through the livelong day,
With the Mockbird's changeful roundelay,
And at night when the scene is calm and still,
With the moan of the plaintive Whip-poor-Will.

Oh! I sigh for the land of the Cypress and Pine,
Of the Laurel, the Rose, and the gay Woodbine;
Where the long grey moss decks the rugged Oak tree,
That sunbright land is the land for me.

A. BRONSON ALCOTT

(1799–1888)

Sonnet XIV

"Ye blessed creatures, I have heard the call
Ye to each other make: I see
The heavens laugh with you in your jubilee;
My heart is at your festival,
My head hath its coronal,
The fulness of your bliss I feel—I feel it all."
WORDSWORTH.

Not Wordsworth's genius, Pestalozzi's love,
The stream have sounded of clear infancy.
Baptismal waters from the Head above
These babes I foster daily are to me;
I dip my pitcher in these living springs
And draw, from depths below, sincerity;
Unsealed, mine eyes behold all outward things
Arrayed in splendors of divinity.
What mount of vision can with mine compare?
Not Roman Jove nor yet Olympian Zeus
Darted from loftier ether through bright air
One spark of holier fire for human use.
Glad tidings thence these angels downward bring,
As at their birth the heavenly choirs do sing.

Sonnet XVIII

"Thus sing I to cragg'd clifts and hills,
To sighing winds, to murmuring rills,
To wasteful woods, to empty groves,
Such things as my dear mind most loves."
HENRY MORE.

Adventurous mariner! in whose gray skiff,
Dashing disastrous o'er the fretful wave,
The steersman, subject to each breeze's whiff,

Or blast capricious that o'er seas doth rave,
Scarce turns his rudder from the fatal cliff,—
Scorning his craft or e'en himself to save.
Ye Powers of air, that shift the seaman's grave,
Adjust the tackle of his right intent,
And bring him safely to the port he meant!
Long musing there on that divinity
Who to his hazard had assistance lent,
He verses cons, oft taken by surprise
In diverse meanings, and shrewd subtlety,
That pass quaint Donne, and even Shakespeare wise.

Sonnet XIX

"But else, in deep of night, when drowsiness
Hath locked up mortal sense, then listen I
To the celestial Syrens' harmony
That sit upon the nine infolded spheres,
And sing to those that hold the vital shears,
And turn the adamantine spindle round,
On which the fate of gods and men is wound."
MILTON.

Romancer, far more coy than that coy sex!
Perchance some stroke of magic thee befell,
Ere thy baronial keep the Muse did vex,
Nor grant deliverance from enchanted spell,
But tease thee all the while and sore perplex,
Till thou that wizard tale shouldst fairly tell,
Better than poets in thy own clear prose.
Painter of sin in its deep scarlet dyes,
Thy doomsday pencil Justice doth expose,
Hearing and judging at the dread assize;
New England's guilt blazoning before all eyes,
No other chronicler than thee she chose.
Magician deathless! dost thou vigil keep,
Whilst 'neath our pines thou feignest deathlike sleep?

THOMAS COLE

(1801–1848)

"I saw a Cave of sable depth profound"

I saw a Cave of sable depth profound
Oped 'neath a precipice whose awful height
Was lost mid clouds that darkly hung around
Forever hiding from the human sight
Its vast mysterious head—About the mouth
of the black Cavern grisly mosses hung
And clambering herbage in festoons uncouth
Did wildly wave like hair—The stray winds sung
With the rude rocks, the tangled growth, the Cavern these
Strains mingled deep—of Love, of Joy of dark Despair.

A Painter

I know 'tis vain ye mountains, and ye woods,
To strive to match your wild, and wondrous hues,
Ye rocks and lakes, and ever rolling floods,
Gold-cinctur'd eve, or morn begemm'd with dews—

Yes, day by day & year by year Ive toild
In the lone chamber, and the sunny field
To match your beauty; but I have been foil'd:
I cannot conquer; but I will not yield—

How oft have I, where spread the pictur'd scene
Wrought on the canvas with fond, anxious care,
Deem'd I had equalled Natures, forests green,
Her lakes, her rocks, and e'en the ambient air.

Vain unpious thought! such feverish fancies sweep
Swift from the brain—when Nature's landscapes break
Upon the thrilling sense—O I could weep
Not that *she* is so beautiful; but *I* so weak—

O! for a power to snatch the living light
From heaven, & darkness from some deep abyss,
Made palpable: with skill to mingle right
Their mystery of beauty! then mine would be bliss!

Lines Suggested by Hearing Music
on the Boston Common at Night

Music it was I heard, and music too
Of mortal utterance; but it did sound
Unto my Fancy's ear like that of spirits;
Spirits that dwell within the vasty caves
Near the earths center—
                              Silence dwelt around.
Then came soft sounds slowly, with pauses 'twixt
Like sighs of sleepers in deep distant caves
They sank and list'ning silence reign'd again.

Then rose a voice, a single voice but shrill
It rent the sable curtains of the gloom
And pierc'd the confines of each echoing cave,
And ev'ry spirit rais'd his sleepy head
From the cold pillow of the dripping rock—
Again the single voice, rung with a shriller tone,
Each spirit answer'd from his hidden nook—
Some voices came from distant winding clifts
And sought the ear like Angel whisperings.
From the deep arches of the rocky roof
Tones rich as those of heav'ns own trumpets burst.
From out the dark profound abysms arose
Sounds as of earthquake, thunder, or the roar
Of booming cataracts—Silence again—

Hark! they have met within the giant hall:
Whose roof is pillar'd by huge mountain tops,
And voices shrill, and deep in concord loudly join.
The heaving harmony sweeps to and fro
Surge over surge and fills the ample place.

Ocean of sound sublime!! The tides contend,
Augment, higher, yet higher; Earth cannot
Contain; it yields—tis riven—and falling rocks
And tottering pinnacles join their dread voices
In the tumultuous and astounding roar—

'Tis past. And nought now strikes the waiting ear
Save the soft echoes ling'ring on their way.
Soft! They have ceas'd to whisper, having found
The cave of silence their eternal tomb.

The Lament of the Forest

In joyous Summer, when the exulting earth
Flung fragrance from innumerable flowers
Through the wide wastes of heaven, as on she took
In solitude her everlasting way,
I stood among the mountain heights, alone!
The beauteous mountains, which the voyager
On Hudson's breast far in the purple west
Magnificent, beholds; the abutments broad
Whence springs the immeasurable dome of heaven.
A lake was spread before me, so serene
That I had deemed it heaven with silver clouds,
Had not the drowning butterfly, or wing
Of skimming swallow, ever and anon
Wrinkled its glorious face with spreading rings.
It was Earth's offering to the imperial sky
That in their rugged palms the mountains held
Aloft. Around it rose precipitous steeps,
With rock, and crag, and dell, and cavern dank;
Which seemed an amphitheatre hugely built
By mighty Titans when the world was young;
And though the Flood o'erwhelmed the builders, hurled
Downward its loftiest battlements, and crushed
The massive seats, columns and arches vast;
Silent and desolate, it rears on high
A thousand Colosseums heaped in one!
Forests of shadowy pine, hemlock and beech,

And oak and maple ever beautiful,
O'er every rent and boss of ruin spread,
Rank above rank arrayed: the topmost pines
Quivered among the clouds, and on the lake,
Peaceful and calm, the lower woods looked down,
A silent people through the lapsing years.

Beside that lake I lingered long, like one
Who gazes on the face of her he loves,
Entranced in thoughts too glad for utterance.
I watched the breeze upon the mountain's breast
Toss the green pine and birchen foliage gray;
The clouds, like angels on their heavenward flight,
Inhaled the perfume from the azalea's flower,
And small white violet, whose honied breath
Made the air sweet, and marked the wavelets break,
Casting the pollen of the rifled flowers
In mimic rage, like gold-dust, on the shores.
The sun descended, and the twilight spread
Its soft empurpled wings; and that blessed hour,
When spirits stooping from the crimson clouds
Commune with man, whose grovelling instincts now
Are laid aside as robes of earthliness
By Nature's pure and solitary fount.

                    .   .   .   .   .

Over my senses stole a sweet repose,
And dreams, which are but wakefulness of soul—
A brief exemption from encumbering clay.
I heard a sound! 'T was wild and strange; a voice
As of ten thousand! Musical it was
A gush of richest concord, deep and slow;
A song that filled the universal air!
It was the voice of the great Forest, sent
From every valley and dark mountain top
Within the bosom of this mighty land.

LAMENT.

Mortal, whose love for our umbrageous realms
Exceeds the love of all the race of man;
Whom we have loved; for whom have opened wide

With welcome our innumerable arms;
Open thine ears! The voice that ne'er before
Was heard by living man, is lifted up,
And fills the air—the voice of our complaint.
Thousands of years!—yea, they have passed away
As drops of dew upon the sunlit rose,
Or silver vapors of the summer sea;
Thousands of years! like wind-strains on the harp,
Or like forgotten thoughts, have passed away
Unto the bourne of unremembered things.
Thousands of years! When the fresh earth first broke
Through chaos, swift in new-born joy even then
The stars of heaven beheld us waving high
Upon the mountains, slumbering in the vales:
Or yet the race of man had seen their light,
Before the virgin breast of earth was scarred
By steel, or granite masses rent from rocks
To build vast Thebes or old Persepolis,
Our arms were clasped around the hills, our locks
Shaded the streams that loved us, our green tops
Were resting places for the weary clouds.
Then all was harmony and peace; but MAN
Arose—he who now vaunts antiquity—
He the destroyer—and in the sacred shades
Of the far East began destruction's work.
Echo, whose voice had answered to the call
Of thunder or of winds, or to the cry
Of cataracts—sound of sylvan habitants
Or song of birds—uttered responses sharp
And dissonant; the axe unresting smote
Our reverend ranks, and crashing branches lashed
The ground, and mighty trunks, the pride of years,
Rolled on the groaning earth with all their umbrage.
Stronger than wintry blasts, and gathering strength,
Swept that tornado, stayless, till the Earth,
Our ancient mother, blasted lay and bare
Beneath the burning sun. The little streams
That oft had raised their voices in the breeze
In joyful unison with ours, did waste
And pine as if in grief that we were not.

Our trackless shades, our dim ubiquity,
In solemn garb of the primeval world,
Our glory, our magnificence, were gone;
And but on difficult places, marsh or steep,
The remnants of our failing race were left,
Like scattered clouds upon the mountain-top.
The vast Hyrcanian wood, and Lebanon's
Dark ranks of cedar were cut down like grass;
And man, whose poets sang our happy shades,
Whose sages taught that Innocence and Peace,
Daughters of Solitude, sojourned in us,
Held not his arm, until Necessity,
Stern master e'en of him, seized it and bound,
And from extinction saved our scanty tribes.

'Seasons there were, when man, at war with man,
Left us to raze proud cities, desolate
Old empires, and pour out his blood on soil
That once was all our own. When death has made
All silent, all secure, we have returned,
Twisted our roots around the prostrate shafts
And broken capitals, or struck them deep
Into the mould made richer by man's blood.
Such seasons were but brief: so soon as earth
Was sanctified again by shade and art,
Again resolved to nature, man came back,
And once more swept our feeble hosts away.

'Yet was there one bright, virgin continent
Remote, that Roman name had never reached,
Nor ancient dreams, in all their universe;
As inaccessible in primal time
To human eye and thought, as Uranus
Far in his secret void. For round it rolled
A troubled deep, whose everlasting roar
Echoed in every zone; whose drear expanse
Spread dark and trackless as the midnight sky;
And stories of vast whirlpools, stagnant seas,
Terrible monsters, that with horror struck
The mariner's soul, these held aloof full long

The roving race of Europe from that land,
The land of beauty and of many climes,
The land of mighty cataracts, where now
Our own proud eagle flaps his chainless wing.

'Thus guarded through long centuries, untouched
By man, save him, our native child, whose foot
Disdained the bleak and sun-beat soil, who loved
Our shafted halls, the covert of the deer,
We flourished, we rejoiced. From mountain top
To mountain top we gazed, and over vales
And glimmering plains we saw our banners green
Wide waving yet untorn. Gladly the Spring
On bloomy wing shed fragrance over us;
And Summer laughed beneath our verdant roof,
And Autumn sighed to leave our golden courts;
And when the crimson leaves were strewn in showers
Upon the ample lap of Oregon,
Or the great Huron's lake of lazuli,
Winter upraised his rude and stormy songs,
And we in a wild chorus answered him.
O peace primeval! would thou hadst remained!
What moved thee to unbar thine emerald gates,
O mighty Deep! when the destroyer came?
Strayed then thy blasts upon Olympus' air,
Or were they lulled to breezes round the brow
Of rich Granada's crafty conqueror,
When with strong wing they should have rushed upon
Our enemy, and smitten him, as when
The fleet of Xerxes on the Grecian coast
Was cast like foam and weed upon the rocks!

'But impotent the voice of our complaint:
He came! Few were his numbers first, but soon
The work of desolation was begun
Close by the heaving main; then on the banks
Of rivers inland far, our strength was shorn,
And fire and steel performed their office well.
No stay was there—no rest. The tiny cloud
Oft seen in torrid climes, at first sends forth

A faint light breeze; but gathering, as it moves,
Darkness and bulk, it spans the spacious sky
With lurid palm, and sweeps stupendous o'er
The crashing world. And thus comes rushing on
This human hurricane, boundless as swift.
Our sanctuary, this secluded spot,
Which the stern rocks have guarded until now,
Our enemy has marked. This gentle lake
Shall lose our presence in its limpid breast,
And from the mountains we shall melt away,
Like wreaths of mist upon the winds of heaven.
Our doom is near: behold from east to west
The skies are darkened by ascending smoke;
Each hill and every valley is become
An altar unto Mammon, and the gods
Of man's idolatry—the victims we.
Missouri's floods are ruffled as by storm,
And Hudson's rugged hills at midnight glow
By light of man-projected meteors.
We feed ten thousand fires: in our short day
The woodland growth of centuries is consumed;
Our crackling limbs the ponderous hammer rouse
With fervent heat. Tormented by our flame,
Fierce vapors struggling hiss on every hand.
On Erie's shores, by dusky Arkansas,
Our ranks are falling like the heavy grain
In harvest-time on Wolga's distant banks.

'A few short years!—these valleys, greenly clad,
These slumbering mountains, resting in our arms,
Shall naked glare beneath the scorching sun,
And all their wimpling rivulets be dry.
No more the deer shall haunt these bosky glens,
Nor the pert squirrel chatter near his store.
A few short years!—our ancient race shall be,
Like Israels', scattered 'mong the tribes of men.'

The Voyage of Life, Part 2nd

As the broad mountain where the shadows flit
Of clouds dispersing in the summer-breeze;
Or like the eye of one who high does sit
On Taòrmìnas' antique height & sees
The fiery Mount afar, the Ruin near at hand,
The flowers, the purple waves that wash the golden strand.

So changed my thought from light to shade;
At times exulting in the glow of hope, at times
In darkness cast by what my soul had said;
'Till sunk in reverie her words seemed chimes
From some far tower, that tell of nuptial joy,
Or knell that fills the air as with a lingering sigh.

Again I raised my downcast eyes to look
Upon the scene so beautiful when lo!
The stream no longer from the cavern took
Its gentle way 'tween flowery banks & low
But through a landscape varied, rich & vast
Beneath a sky that dusky cloud had surely never passed.

Wide was the river; with majestic flow
And pomp & power it swept the curving banks
Like some great conqueror whose march is slow
Through tributary lands; while the abasèd ranks,
Shrinking give back on either hand o'erawed
As though their hearts confirmed the presence of a God.

And like some Wizard's mirror, that displays
The Macrocosm, it did reflect the sky,
Rocks, lawns & mountains with their purple haze,
And living things, the filmy butterfly,
The trembling fawn that drinks, the fluttering dove
And the triumphant eagle soaring far above.

And trees like those which spread their pleasant shade
Oer the green slopes of Eden, & the bowers

Of the once sinless pair, soft, intermingling made
Stood on each shore with branches lifted high
And caught eolian strains that wandered from the sky.

Far, far away the shining river sped
Towards the etherial mountains which did close
Fold beyond fold until they vanishèd
In the horizon's silver, whence uprose
A structure strangely beautiful & vast
Which every earthly fane Egyptian, Gothic, Greek,
    surpassed.

It seemed a gorgeous palace in the sky
Such as the glad sun builds above the Deep
On summer-eve & lighteth dazzlingly,
Where towering clouds climb up the azure steep
And pinnacles on pinnacles fantastic rise
And ever-changing charm the wondering eyes.

There, rank oer rank that climbed the crystal air
In horizontal majesty, were crossed
The multitudinous shafts, or ranged afar
Till in the blue perspective they were lost,
And arches linked with arches stretched along
Like to the mystic measures of an antique song.

An antique song whose half-discovered sense
Seems to spring forth from depths, as yet, unknown
And fills the heart with wonder & suspense
Until to thrilling rapture it is grown;
Breathless we listen to each wandering strain
And when the numbers cease we listen still again.

Above the columned pile sublimely rose
A Dome stupendous, like the moon it shone
When first upon the orient sky she glows
And moves along the Ocean's verge alone;
And yet beyond, above, another sphere
And yet another, vaster, dimly did appear.

As though the blue supernal space were filled
With towers & temples, which the eye intent
Piercing the filmy atmosphere that veiled,
From glorious dome to dome rejoicing went,
And the deep folds of ether were unfurled
To show the splendors of a higher world.

But from the vision of the upper air
My eye descended to the lucid stream;
The wingèd Boat—the Voyagers were there;
But the fair Infant of my earlier dream
Now stood a Youth on manhood's verge, his eye
Flashing with confidence & hot expectancy,

Was lifted toward the sky-encastled scene,
His hand had grasped the helm once gently held
By that Angelic figure so serene,
And eager stretching toward the scene beheld,
His bosom heaved as if with secret powers
Possessed to tread the deep—to outstrip the flying Hours.

With face benignant yet impinged by sorrow,
As oft the sky of eve by melancholy cloud
Which though it doth forbode a stormy morrow
Is not less beautiful, the Angel stood
Upon the bank as from the Boat just freed
And waved her graceful hand & bade the Youth "God
      Speed."

As one emerging from some misty vale
Meets the glad splendor of the rising sun;
Or mariner who the wintry sea doth sail
Through opening wrack beholds the harbor won,
So did I gaze upon the charming scene
And in my joy forgot the Vision Infantine.

When thus the Voice in plaintive accents mild:
"Ah simple mortal Earth has many a show
"That passes quickly—thou a credulous child,
"All men are children & they thoughtless go

Through life's strange vale lingering by every flower
"Forgetful life is labor and its term an hour.

"The scene before thee beautiful & bright
"Is but a phantasm of Youths heated brain
"And doomed to fade as day before the night;
"Fleeting its glory, transitory, vain;
"Save that it teaches the meek humble soul
"Earth's grandeur 'neer should be the spirit's Goal.

"Not that the earth foundationless is laid,
"An unsubstantial thing, a cloud, a mist;
"But 'tis a darkling soil wherein the seed
"Of Virtue planted, tended may subsist
"And washed by many tears may grow
"To more enduring beauty than these gauds below.

"But mark the Youth, how filled his eager eye
"With the bright exhalation. — See! he aims
"To reach the portal of the palace high
"Above whose cloudy arch resplendant flames
"The tempting semblance of a conqueror's crown
"And wreath to bind the brows of him who wins renown.

"And while he gazes greater glories rise
"Loftier still loftier; ardent young desire
"With telescopic vision fills the skies.
"Gay are the banks in verdurous attire
"And swift the river floweth toward his hope
"The palace stands beyond, reached by a gentle slope.

"Weak & deluded one! Dost thou not know
"Thy Bark is hasting down the Stream of Life
"And tarries not for any golden show
"In pleasure's bowers though with beauty rife!
"So doth the comet pass the planets by
"Nor rests; but speeds on its appointed destiny.

"Does not thine eye perceive that when yon towers
"Are well nigh gained with sudden sweep the stream

"And growing swiftness, shoots away & pours
"Impetuous, towards a shadowy ravine deep
"Cleft in the mountain's vast & misty side
"As though it eager sought its thwarted floods to hide."

The voice had paused: And is it thus I cried,
That Youth's fond hopes must ever pass away;
As empty dreams, untouched unsatisfied:
Why leaves the Angel on his dangerous way
The Voyager? That hand divine could steer
The willing Boat to where yon glittering domes uprear.

And lingering by these fresh & verdant shores
E'en youth might live a long long life of joy
And shun perchance the torrent where it pours
Adown yon dread descent. To which reply
Soon came, "Shrouded as now thou art in earth
"Thou canst not see the end for which came mortal birth.

"In the Almighty mind the secret cause is laid;
"This must thou learn, that our brief mortal life
"Nor rests nor lingers; nor is checked nor stayed
"By human skill or might howeer so rife;
"Nor is it in an Angel's godlike power
"To lengthen out its wasting thread one single hour.

"Through feeble Infancy is steered the Bark of Life
"By Angel hands; but growing man demands
"The helm in confidence & dares the strife
"Of the far-sweeping waves. The lurking sands,
"The rapids foaming through the channel dim,
"The roaring cataract are all unknown to him.

"Wisdom is born of sorrow & of care
"And from man's conflicts with the world arise
"A sense of weakness & of chilling fear
"And driven from earth his hopes ascend the skies;
"Thus is he left upon the stream alone
"To chasten pride & give young desire a purer, holier tone.

"He is alone; but still deserted never
"The Angel yet shall watch his perilous way,
"And though the clouds of earth may seem to sever,
"Still through the darkness shines the Angelic ray;
"And in the hour of midnight o'er the deep
"The Guardian Spirit kind will constant vigil keep."

The Dial

Gray hairs, unwelcome monitors, begin
To mingle with the locks that shade my brow
And sadly warn me that I stand within
That pale uncertain called the middle age.
Upon the billows head which soon must bow
I reel; and gaze into the depths where rage
No more the wars 'twixt Time & Life as now,
And gazing swift, descend towards that great Deep
Whose secrets the Almighty One doth keep.

I am as one on mighty errand bound
Uncertain is the distance—fixed the hour;
He stops to gaze upon the Dial's round
Trembling & earnest; when a rising cloud
Casts its oblivious shadow & no more
The gnomon tells what he would know and loud
Thunders are heard & gathering tempests lower.
Lamenting mispent time he hastes away
And treads again the dim & dubious way.

Lago Maggiore

O sky & earth! How ye are linked together
Upon the bosom of this gentle lake;
The wild & wandering breeze is doubtful whether
It may your calm & sweet communion break.
'Tis thus within my silent bosom mingle
The memory of distant scenes—my home
And these enchanting prospects; whilst I, single

And silently in pensive thought do roam.
　　The distant & the present sometimes meet
　　In dream-like hues; but dark thoughts quickly rise
　　And mar the mirror of the vision sweet,
　　And truth oerwhelmeth with a sad surprise;
　　'Twixt me & those I love an ocean lies
　　And all the glory of the landscape dies.

EDWARD COOTE PINKNEY

(1802–1828)

Italy

I.

Know'st thou the land which lovers ought to choose?
Like blessings there descend the sparkling dews;
In gleaming streams the chrystal rivers run,
The purple vintage clusters in the sun;
Odours of flowers haunt the balmy breeze,
Rich fruits hang high upon the vernant trees;
And vivid blossoms gem the shady groves,
Where bright-plumed birds discourse their careless loves.
Beloved!—speed we from this sullen strand
Until thy light feet press that green shore's yellow sand.

II.

Look seaward thence, and nought shall meet thine eye
But fairy isles like paintings on the sky;
And, flying fast and free before the gale,
The gaudy vessel with its glancing sail;
And waters glittering in the glare of noon,
Or touched with silver by the stars and moon,
Or flecked with broken lines of crimson light
When the far fisher's fire affronts the night.
Lovely as loved! towards that smiling shore
Bear we our household gods, to fix for evermore.

III.

It looks a dimple on the face of earth,
The seal of beauty, and the shrine of mirth;
Nature is delicate and graceful there,
The place's genius, feminine and fair:
The winds are awed, nor dare to breathe aloud;
The air seems never to have borne a cloud,

Save where volcanoes send to heav'n their curled
And solemn smokes, like altars of the world.
Thrice beautiful!—to that delightful spot
Carry our married hearts, and be all pain forgot.

IV.

There Art too shows, when Nature's beauty palls,
Her sculptured marbles, and her pictured walls;
And there are forms in which they both conspire
To whisper themes that know not how to tire:
The speaking ruins in that gentle clime
Have but been hallowed by the hand of Time,
And each can mutely prompt some thought of flame
—The meanest stone is not without a name.
Then come, beloved!—hasten o'er the sea
To build our happy hearth in blooming Italy.

The Voyager's Song

"A tradition prevailed among the natives of Puerto Rico, that in the Isle of Bimini, one of the Lucayos, there was a fountain of such wonderful virtue, as to renew the youth and recal the vigour of every person who bathed in its salutary waters. In hopes of finding this grand restorative, Ponce de Leon and his followers, ranged through the islands, searching with fruitless solicitude for the fountain, which was the chief object of the expedition."
—ROBERTSON'S AMERICA.

I.

Sound trumpets, ho!—weigh anchor—loosen sail—
The seaward flying banners chide delay;
As if 'twere heaven that breathes this kindly gale,
Our life-like bark beneath it speeds away.
Flit we, a gliding dream, with troublous motion,
Across the slumbers of uneasy ocean;
And furl our canvass by a happier land,
So fraught with emanations from the sun,
That potable gold streams through the sand
Where element should run.

II.

Onward, my friends, to that bright, florid isle,
The jewel of a smooth and silver sea,
With springs on which perennial summers smile
A power of causing immortality.
For Bimini;—in its enchanted ground,
The hallowed fountains we would seek, are found;
Bathed in the waters of those mystic wells,
The frame starts up in renovated truth,
And, freed from Time's deforming spells,
Resumes its proper youth.

III.

Hail, better birth!—once more my feelings all
A graven image to themselves shall make,
And, placed upon my heart for pedestal,
That glorious idol long will keep awake
Their natural religion, nor be cast
To earth by Age, the great Iconoclast.
As from Gadara's founts they once could come,
Charm-called, from these Love's genii shall arise,
And build their perdurable home,
Miranda, in thine eyes.

IV.

By Nature wisely gifted, not destroyed
With golden presents, like the Roman maid,—
A sublunary paradise enjoyed,
Shall teach thee bliss incapable of shade;—
An Eden ours, nor angry gods, nor men,
Nor star-clad Fates, can take from us again.
Superiour to animal decay,
Sun of that perfect heaven, thou'lt calmly see
Stag, raven, phenix, drop away
With *human* transiency.

V.

Thus rich in being,—beautiful,—adored,
Fear not exhausting pleasure's precious mine;
The wondrous waters we approach, when poured
On passion's lees, supply the wasted wine:
Then be thy bosom's tenant prodigal,
And confident of termless carnival.
Like idle yellow leaves afloat on time,
Let others lapse to death's pacific sea,—
We'll fade nor fall, but sport sublime
In green eternity.

VI.

The envious years, which steal our pleasures, thou
May'st call at once, like magic memory, back,
And, as they pass o'er thine unwithering brow,
Efface their footsteps ere they form a track.
Thy bloom with wilful weeping never stain,
Perpetual life must not belong to pain.
For me,—this world has not yet been a place
Conscious of joys so great as will be mine,
Because the light has kissed no face
Forever fair as thine.

To . . . .

'Twas eve; the broadly shining sun
Its long, celestial course, had run;
The twighlight heaven, so soft and blue,
Met earth in tender interview,
Ev'n as the angel met of yore
His gifted mortal paramour,
Woman, a child of morning then,—
A spirit still,—compared with men.
Like happy islands of the sky,
The gleaming clouds reposed on high,
Each fixed sublime, deprived of motion,
A Delos to the airy ocean.

Upon the stirless shore no breeze
Shook the green drapery of the trees,
Or, rebel to tranquillity,
Awoke a ripple on the sea.
Nor, in a more tumultuous sound,
Were the world's audible breathings drowned;
The low strange hum of herbage growing,
The voice of hidden waters flowing,
Made songs of nature, which the ear
Could scarcely be pronounced to hear;
But noise had furled its subtle wings,
And moved not through material things,
All which lay calm as they had been
Parts of the painter's mimic scene.
'Twas eve; my thoughts belong to thee,
Thou shape of separate memory!
When, like a stream to lands of flame,
Unto my mind a vision came.
Methought, from human haunts and strife
Remote, we lived a loving life;
Our wedded spirits seemed to blend
In harmony too sweet to end,
Such concord as the echoes cherish
Fondly, but leave at length to perish.
Wet rain-stars are thy lucid eyes,
The Hyades of earthly skies,
But then upon my heart they shone,
As shines on snow the fervid sun.
And fast went by those moments bright,
Like meteors shooting through the night;
But faster fleeted the wild dream,
That clothed them with their transient beam.
Yet love can years to days condense,
And long appeared that life intense;
It was,—to give a better measure
Than time,—a century of pleasure.

Serenade

Look out upon the stars, my love,
And shame them with thine eyes,
On which, than on the lights above,
There hang more destinies.
Night's beauty is the harmony
Of blending shades and light;
Then, Lady, up,—look out, and be
A sister to the night!—

Sleep not!—thine image wakes for aye,
Within my watching breast:
Sleep not!—from her soft sleep should fly,
Who robs all hearts of rest.
Nay, Lady, from thy slumbers break,
And make this darkness gay,
With looks, whose brightness well might make
Of darker nights a day.

A Health

I fill this cup to one made up of loveliness alone,
A woman, of her gentle sex the seeming paragon;
To whom the better elements and kindly stars have given,
A form so fair, that, like the air, 'tis less of earth than
        heaven.

Her every tone is music's own, like those of morning birds,
And something more than melody dwells ever in her words;
The coinage of her heart are they, and from her lips each
        flows
As one may see the burthened bee forth issue from the rose.

Affections are as thoughts to her, the measures of her hours;
Her feelings have the fragrancy, the freshness, of young
        flowers;
And lovely passions, changing oft, so fill her, she appears
The image of themselves by turns,—the idol of past years!

Of her bright face one glance will trace a picture on the
    brain,
And of her voice in echoing hearts a sound must long
    remain,
But memory such as mine of her so very much endears,
When death is nigh my latest sigh will not be life's but hers.

I filled this cup to one made up of loveliness alone,
A woman, of her gentle sex the seeming paragon—
Her health! and would on earth there stood some more of
    such a frame,
That life might be all poetry, and weariness a name.

On Parting

Alas! our pleasant moments fly
  On rapid wings away,
While those recorded with a sigh,
  Mock us by long delay.

Time,—envious time,—loves not to be
  In company with mirth,
But makes malignant pause to see
  The work of pain on earth.

The Widow's Song

I burn no incense, hang no wreath,
  On this, thine early tomb:
Such cannot cheer the place of death,
  But only mock its gloom.
Here odorous smoke and breathing flower
  No grateful influence shed;
They lose their perfume and their power,
  When offered to the dead.

And if, as is the Afghaun's creed,
    The spirit may return,
A disembodied sense to feed,
    On fragrance, near its urn—
It is enough, that she, whom thou
    Did'st love in living years,
Sits desolate beside it now,
    And falls these heavy tears.

GEORGE POPE MORRIS

(1802—1864)

The Oak

Woodman, spare that tree!
  Touch not a single bough!
In youth it sheltered me,
  And I'll protect it now.
'Twas my forefather's hand
  That placed it near his cot;
There, woodman, let it stand,
  Thy axe shall harm it not!

That old familiar tree,
  Whose glory and renown
Are spread o'er land and sea,
  And wouldst thou hack it down?
Woodman, forbear thy stroke!
  Cut not its earth-bound ties;
Oh, spare that aged oak,
  Now towering to the skies!

When but an idle boy
  I sought its grateful shade;
In all their gushing joy
  Here too my sisters played.
My mother kiss'd me here;
  My father press'd my hand—
Forgive this foolish tear,
  But let that old oak stand!

My heart-strings round thee cling,
  Close as thy bark, old friend!
Here shall the wild-bird sing,
  And still thy branches bend.
Old tree! the storm still brave!
  And, woodman, leave the spot;
While I've a hand to save,
  Thy axe shall harm it not.

LYDIA MARIA CHILD

(1802—1880)

The New-England Boy's Song
About Thanksgiving Day

Over the river, and through the wood,
  To grandfather's house we go;
    The horse knows the way,
    To carry the sleigh,
  Through the white and drifted snow.

Over the river, and through the wood,
  To grandfather's house away!
    We would not stop
    For doll or top,
  For 't is Thanksgiving day.

Over the river, and through the wood,
  Oh, how the wind does blow!
    It stings the toes,
    And bites the nose,
  As over the ground we go.

Over the river, and through the wood,
  With a clear blue winter sky,
    The dogs do bark,
    And children hark,
  As we go jingling by.

Over the river, and through the wood,
  To have a first-rate play—
    Hear the bells ring
    Ting a ling ding,
  Hurra for Thanksgiving day!

Over the river, and through the wood—
  No matter for winds that blow;

Or if we get
The sleigh upset,
Into a bank of snow.

Over the river, and through the wood,
To see little John and Ann;
We will kiss them all,
And play snow-ball,
And stay as long as we can.

Over the river, and through the wood,
Trot fast, my dapple grey!
Spring over the ground,
Like a hunting hound,
For 't is Thanksgiving day!

Over the river, and through the wood,
And straight through the barn-yard gate;
We seem to go
Extremely slow,
It is so hard to wait.

Over the river, and through the wood—
Old Jowler hears our bells;
He shakes his pow,
With a loud bow wow,
And thus the news he tells.

Over the river, and through the wood—
When grandmother sees us come,
She will say, Oh dear,
The children are here,
Bring a pie for every one.

Over the river, and through the wood—
Now grandmother's cap I spy!
Hurra for the fun!
Is the pudding done?
Hurra for the pumpkin pie!

RALPH WALDO EMERSON

(1803–1882)

The Sphinx

The Sphinx is drowsy,
    Her wings are furled;
Her ear is heavy,
    She broods on the world.
"Who'll tell me my secret,
    The ages have kept? —
I awaited the seer,
    While they slumbered and slept; —

"The fate of the man-child;
    The meaning of man;
Known fruit of the unknown;
    Dædalian plan;
Out of sleeping a waking,
    Out of waking a sleep;
Life death overtaking;
    Deep underneath deep?

"Erect as a sunbeam,
    Upspringeth the palm;
The elephant browses,
    Undaunted and calm;
In beautiful motion
    The thrush plies his wings;
Kind leaves of his covert,
    Your silence he sings.

"The waves, unashamed,
    In difference sweet,
Play glad with the breezes,
    Old playfellows meet;
The journeying atoms,

Primordial wholes,
  Firmly draw, firmly drive,
    By their animate poles.

"Sea, earth, air, sound, silence,
    Plant, quadruped, bird,
By one music enchanted,
    One deity stirred,—
Each the other adorning,
    Accompany still;
Night veileth the morning,
    The vapor the hill.

"The babe by its mother
    Lies bathed in joy;
Glide its hours uncounted,—
    The sun is its toy;
Shines the peace of all being,
    Without cloud, in its eyes;
And the sum of the world
    In soft miniature lies.

"But man crouches and blushes,
    Absconds and conceals;
He creepeth and peepeth,
    He palters and steals;
Infirm, melancholy,
    Jealous glancing around,
An oaf, an accomplice,
    He poisons the ground.

"Outspoke the great mother,
    Beholding his fear;—
At the sound of her accents
    Cold shuddered the sphere:—
'Who has drugged my boy's cup?
    Who has mixed my boy's bread?
Who, with sadness and madness,
    Has turned the man-child's head?' "

I heard a poet answer,
   Aloud and cheerfully,
"Say on, sweet Sphinx! thy dirges
   Are pleasant songs to me.
Deep love lieth under
   These pictures of time;
They fade in the light of
   Their meaning sublime.

"The fiend that man harries
   Is love of the Best;
Yawns the pit of the Dragon,
   Lit by rays from the Blest.
The Lethe of nature
   Can't trace him again,
Whose soul sees the perfect,
   Which his eyes seek in vain.

"Profounder, profounder,
   Man's spirit must dive;
To his aye-rolling orbit
   No goal will arrive;
The heavens that now draw him
   With sweetness untold,
Once found,—for new heavens
   He spurneth the old.

"Pride ruined the angels,
   Their shame them restores;
And the joy that is sweetest
   Lurks in stings of remorse.
Have I a lover
   Who is noble and free?—
I would he were nobler
   Than to love me.

"Eterne alternation
   Now follows, now flies;
And under pain, pleasure,—
   Under pleasure, pain lies.

Love works at the centre,
　　Heart-heaving alway;
Forth speed the strong pulses
　　To the borders of day.

"Dull Sphinx, Jove keep thy five wits!
　　Thy sight is growing blear;
Rue, myrrh, and cummin for the Sphinx—
　　Her muddy eyes to clear!"—
The old Sphinx bit her thick lip,—
　　Said, "Who taught thee me to name?
I am thy spirit, yoke-fellow,
　　Of thine eye I am eyebeam.

"Thou art the unanswered question;
　　Couldst see thy proper eye,
Alway it asketh, asketh;
　　And each answer is a lie.
So take thy quest through nature,
　　It through thousand natures ply;
Ask on, thou clothed eternity;
　　Time is the false reply."

Uprose the merry Sphinx,
　　And crouched no more in stone;
She melted into purple cloud,
　　She silvered in the moon;
She spired into a yellow flame;
　　She flowered in blossoms red;
She flowed into a foaming wave;
　　She stood Monadnoc's head.

Thorough a thousand voices
　　Spoke the universal dame:
"Who telleth one of my meanings,
　　Is master of all I am."

Each and All

Little thinks, in the field, yon red-cloaked clown,
Of thee from the hill-top looking down;
The heifer that lows in the upland farm,
Far-heard, lows not thine ear to charm;
The sexton, tolling his bell at noon,
Deems not that great Napoleon
Stops his horse, and lists with delight,
Whilst his files sweep round yon Alpine height;
Nor knowest thou what argument
Thy life to thy neighbor's creed has lent.
All are needed by each one;
Nothing is fair or good alone.
I thought the sparrow's note from heaven,
Singing at dawn on the alder bough;
I brought him home, in his nest, at even;
He sings the song, but it pleases not now,
For I did not bring home the river and sky;—
He sang to my ear,—they sang to my eye.
The delicate shells lay on the shore;
The bubbles of the latest wave
Fresh pearls to their enamel gave;
And the bellowing of the savage sea
Greeted their safe escape to me.
I wiped away the weeds and foam,
I fetched my sea-born treasures home;
But the poor, unsightly, noisome things
Had left their beauty on the shore,
With the sun, and the sand, and the wild uproar.
The lover watched his graceful maid,
As 'mid the virgin train she strayed,
Nor knew her beauty's best attire
Was woven still by the snow-white choir.
At last she came to his hermitage,
Like the bird from the woodlands to the cage;—
The gay enchantment was undone,
A gentle wife, but fairy none.
Then I said, 'I covet truth;
Beauty is unripe childhood's cheat;

I leave it behind with the games of youth.'—
As I spoke, beneath my feet
The ground-pine curled its pretty wreath,
Running over the club-moss burrs;
I inhaled the violet's breath;
Around me stood the oaks and firs;
Pine-cones and acorns lay on the ground,
Over me soared the eternal sky,
Full of light and of deity;
Again I saw, again I heard,
The rolling river, the morning bird;—
Beauty through my senses stole;
I yielded myself to the perfect whole.

The Problem

I like a church; I like a cowl;
I love a prophet of the soul;
And on my heart monastic aisles
Fall like sweet strains, or pensive smiles;
Yet not for all his faith can see
Would I that cowled churchman be.

Why should the vest on him allure,
Which I could not on me endure?

Not from a vain or shallow thought
His awful Jove young Phidias brought;
Never from lips of cunning fell
The thrilling Delphic oracle;
Out from the heart of nature rolled
The burdens of the Bible old;
The litanies of nations came,
Like the volcano's tongue of flame,
Up from the burning core below,—
The canticles of love and woe;
The hand that rounded Peter's dome,
And groined the aisles of Christian Rome,
Wrought in a sad sincerity;

Himself from God he could not free;
He builded better than he knew;—
The conscious stone to beauty grew.

Know'st thou what wove yon woodbird's nest
Of leaves, and feathers from her breast?
Or how the fish outbuilt her shell,
Painting with morn each annual cell?
Or how the sacred pine-tree adds
To her old leaves new myriads?
Such and so grew these holy piles,
Whilst love and terror laid the tiles.
Earth proudly wears the Parthenon,
As the best gem upon her zone;
And Morning opes with haste her lids,
To gaze upon the Pyramids;
O'er England's abbeys bends the sky,
As on its friends, with kindred eye;
For, out of Thought's interior sphere,
These wonders rose to upper air;
And Nature gladly gave them place,
Adopted them into her race,
And granted them an equal date
With Andes and with Ararat.

These temples grew as grows the grass;
Art might obey, but not surpass.
The passive Master lent his hand
To the vast soul that o'er him planned;
And the same power that reared the shrine,
Bestrode the tribes that knelt within.
Ever the fiery Pentecost
Girds with one flame the countless host,
Trances the heart through chanting choirs,
And through the priest the mind inspires.
The word unto the prophet spoken
Was writ on tables yet unbroken;
The word by seers or sibyls told,
In groves of oak, or fanes of gold,
Still floats upon the morning wind,

Still whispers to the willing mind.
One accent of the Holy Ghost
The heedless world hath never lost.
I know what say the fathers wise, —
The Book itself before me lies,
Old *Chrysostom*, best Augustine,
And he who blent both in his line,
The younger *Golden Lips* or mines,
Taylor, the Shakspeare of divines.
His words are music in my ear,
I see his cowled portrait dear;
And yet, for all his faith could see,
I would not the good bishop be.

To Rhea

Thee, dear friend, a brother soothes,
Not with flatteries, but truths,
Which tarnish not, but purify
To light which dims the morning's eye.
I have come from the spring-woods,
From the fragrant solitudes; —
Listen what the poplar-tree
And murmuring waters counselled me.

If with love thy heart has burned;
If thy love is unreturned;
Hide thy grief within thy breast,
Though it tear thee unexpressed;
For when love has once departed
From the eyes of the false-hearted,
And one by one has torn off quite
The bandages of purple light;
Though thou wert the loveliest
Form the soul had ever dressed,
Thou shalt seem, in each reply,
A vixen to his altered eye;
Thy softest pleadings seem too bold,

Thy praying lute will seem to scold;
Though thou kept the straightest road,
Yet thou errest far and broad.

But thou shalt do as do the gods
In their cloudless periods;
For of this lore be thou sure, —
Though thou forget, the gods, secure,
Forget never their command,
But make the statute of this land.
As they lead, so follow all,
Ever have done, ever shall.
Warning to the blind and deaf,
'Tis written on the iron leaf,
Who drinks of Cupid's nectar cup
Loveth downward, and not up;
Therefore, who loves, of gods or men,
Shall not by the same be loved again;
His sweetheart's idolatry
Falls, in turn, a new degree.
When a god is once beguiled
By beauty of a mortal child,
And by her radiant youth delighted,
He is not fooled, but warily knoweth
His love shall never be requited.
And thus the wise Immortal doeth. —
'Tis his study and delight
To bless that creature day and night;
From all evils to defend her;
In her lap to pour all splendor;
To ransack earth for riches rare,
And fetch her stars to deck her hair:
He mixes music with her thoughts,
And saddens her with heavenly doubts:
All grace, all good his great heart knows,
Profuse in love, the king bestows:
Saying, 'Hearken! Earth, Sea, Air!
This monument of my despair
Build I to the All-Good, All-Fair.
Not for a private good,

But I, from my beatitude,
Albeit scorned as none was scorned,
Adorn her as was none adorned.
I make this maiden an ensample
To Nature, through her kingdoms ample,
Whereby to model newer races,
Statelier forms, and fairer faces;
To carry man to new degrees
Of power, and of comeliness.
These presents be the hostages
Which I pawn for my release.
See to thyself, O Universe!
Thou art better, and not worse.'—
And the god, having given all,
Is freed forever from his thrall.

The Visit

Askest, 'How long thou shalt stay,'
Devastator of the day?
Know, each substance, and relation,
Thorough nature's operation,
Hath its unit, bound, and metre;
And every new compound
Is some product and repeater,—
Product of the early found.
But the unit of the visit,
The encounter of the wise,—
Say, what other metre is it
Than the meeting of the eyes?
Nature poureth into nature
Through the channels of that feature.
Riding on the ray of sight,
More fleet than waves or whirlwinds go,
Or for service, or delight,
Hearts to hearts their meaning show,
Sum their long experience,
And import intelligence.
Single look has drained the breast;

Single moment years confessed.
The duration of a glance
Is the term of convenance,
And, though thy rede be church or state,
Frugal multiples of that.
Speeding Saturn cannot halt;
Linger,—thou shalt rue the fault;
If Love his moment overstay,
Hatred's swift repulsions play.

Uriel

It fell in the ancient periods,
    Which the brooding soul surveys,
Or ever the wild Time coined itself
    Into calendar months and days.

This was the lapse of Uriel,
Which in Paradise befell.
Once, among the Pleiads walking,
SAID overheard the young gods talking;
And the treason, too long pent,
To his ears was evident.
The young deities discussed
Laws of form, and metre just,
Orb, quintessence, and sunbeams,
What subsisteth, and what seems.
One, with low tones that decide,
And doubt and reverend use defied,
With a look that solved the sphere,
And stirred the devils everywhere,
Gave his sentiment divine
Against the being of a line.
'Line in nature is not found;
Unit and universe are round;
In vain produced, all rays return;
Evil will bless, and ice will burn.'
As Uriel spoke with piercing eye,
A shudder ran around the sky;

The stern old war-gods shook their heads;
The seraphs frowned from myrtle-beds;
Seemed to the holy festival
The rash word boded ill to all;
The balance-beam of Fate was bent;
The bounds of good and ill were rent;
Strong Hades could not keep his own,
But all slid to confusion.
A sad self-knowledge, withering, fell
On the beauty of Uriel;
In heaven once eminent, the god
Withdrew, that hour, into his cloud;
Whether doomed to long gyration
In the sea of generation,
Or by knowledge grown too bright
To hit the nerve of feebler sight.
Straightway, a forgetting wind
Stole over the celestial kind,
And their lips the secret kept,
If in ashes the fire-seed slept.
But now and then, truth-speaking things
Shamed the angels' veiling wings;
And, shrilling from the solar course,
Or from fruit of chemic force,
Procession of a soul in matter,
Or the speeding change of water,
Or out of the good of evil born,
Came Uriel's voice of cherub scorn,
And a blush tinged the upper sky,
And the gods shook, they knew not why.

The World-Soul

Thanks to the morning light,
　　Thanks to the foaming sea,
To the uplands of New Hampshire,
　　To the green-haired forest free;
Thanks to each man of courage,

To the maids of holy mind;
To the boy with his games undaunted,
  Who never looks behind.

Cities of proud hotels,
  Houses of rich and great,
Vice nestles in your chambers,
  Beneath your roofs of slate.
It cannot conquer folly,
  Time-and-space-conquering steam
And the light-outspeeding telegraph
  Bears nothing on its beam.

The politics are base;
  The letters do not cheer;
And 'tis far in the deeps of history,
  The voice that speaketh clear.
Trade and the streets ensnare us,
  Our bodies are weak and worn;
We plot and corrupt each other,
  And we despoil the unborn.

Yet there in the parlor sits
  Some figure of noble guise,—
Our angel, in a stranger's form,
  Or woman's pleading eyes;
Or only a flashing sunbeam
  In at the window-pane;
Or Music pours on mortals
  Its beautiful disdain.

The inevitable morning
  Finds them who in cellars be;
And be sure the all-loving Nature
  Will smile in a factory.
Yon ridge of purple landscape,
  Yon sky between the walls,
Hold all the hidden wonders,
  In scanty intervals.

Alas! the Sprite that haunts us
   Deceives our rash desire;
It whispers of the glorious gods,
   And leaves us in the mire.
We cannot learn the cipher
   That's writ upon our cell;
Stars help us by a mystery
   Which we could never spell.

If but one hero knew it,
   The world would blush in flame;
The sage, till he hit the secret,
   Would hang his head for shame.
But our brothers have not read it,
   Not one has found the key;
And henceforth we are comforted, —
   We are but such as they.

Still, still the secret presses,
   The nearing clouds draw down;
The crimson morning flames into
   The fopperies of the town.
Within, without the idle earth,
   Stars weave eternal rings;
The sun himself shines heartily,
   And shares the joy he brings.

And what if Trade sow cities
   Like shells along the shore,
And thatch with towns the prairie broad,
   With railways ironed o'er? —
They are but sailing foam-bells
   Along Thought's cansing stream,
And take their shape and sun-color
   From him that sends the dream.

For Destiny does not like
   To yield to men the helm;
And shoots his thought, by hidden nerves,
   Throughout the solid realm.

The patient Dæmon sits,
    With roses and a shroud;
He has his way, and deals his gifts,—
    But ours is not allowed.

He is no churl nor trifler,
    And his viceroy is none,—
Love-without-weakness,—
    Of Genius sire and son.
And his will is not thwarted;
    The seeds of land and sea
Are the atoms of his body bright,
    And his behest obey.

He serveth the servant,
    The brave he loves amain;
He kills the cripple and the sick,
    And straight begins again.
For gods delight in gods,
    And thrust the weak aside;
To him who scorns their charities,
    Their arms fly open wide.

When the old world is sterile,
    And the ages are effete,
He will from wrecks and sediment
    The fairer world complete.
He forbids to despair;
    His cheeks mantle with mirth;
And the unimagined good of men
    Is yeaning at the birth.

Spring still makes spring in the mind,
    When sixty years are told;
Love wakes anew this throbbing heart,
    And we are never old.
Over the winter glaciers,
    I see the summer glow,
And, through the wild-piled snowdrift,
    The warm rosebuds below.

Mithridates

I cannot spare water or wine,
    Tobacco-leaf, or poppy, or rose;
From the earth-poles to the line,
    All between that works or grows,
Every thing is kin of mine.

Give me agates for my meat;
Give me cantharids to eat;
From air and ocean bring me foods,
From all zones and altitudes; —

From all natures, sharp and slimy,
    Salt and basalt, wild and tame:
Tree and lichen, ape, sea-lion,
    Bird, and reptile, be my game.

Ivy for my fillet band;
Blinding dog-wood in my hand;
Hemlock for my sherbet cull me,
And the prussic juice to lull me;
Swing me in the upas boughs,
Vampyre-fanned, when I carouse.

Too long shut in strait and few,
Thinly dieted on dew,
I will use the world, and sift it,
To a thousand humors shift it,
As you spin a cherry.
O doleful ghosts, and goblins merry!
O all you virtues, methods, mights,
Means, appliances, delights,
Reputed wrongs and braggart rights,
Smug routine, and things allowed,
Minorities, things under cloud!
Hither! take me, use me, fill me,
Vein and artery, though ye kill me!
God! I will not be an owl,
But sun me in the Capitol.

Hamatreya

Minott, Lee, Willard, Hosmer, Meriam, Flint
Possessed the land which rendered to their toil
Hay, corn, roots, hemp, flax, apples, wool, and wood.
Each of these landlords walked amidst his farm,
Saying, ' 'Tis mine, my children's, and my name's:
How sweet the west wind sounds in my own trees!
How graceful climb those shadows on my hill!
I fancy these pure waters and the flags
Know me, as does my dog: we sympathize;
And, I affirm, my actions smack of the soil.'
Where are these men? Asleep beneath their grounds;
And strangers, fond as they, their furrows plough.
Earth laughs in flowers, to see her boastful boys
Earth-proud, proud of the earth which is not theirs;
Who steer the plough, but cannot steer their feet
Clear of the grave.
They added ridge to valley, brook to pond,
And sighed for all that bounded their domain.
'This suits me for a pasture; that's my park;
We must have clay, lime, gravel, granite-ledge,
And misty lowland, where to go for peat.
The land is well,—lies fairly to the south.
'Tis good, when you have crossed the sea and back,
To find the sitfast acres where you left them.'
Ah! the hot owner sees not Death, who adds
Him to his land, a lump of mould the more.
Hear what the Earth says:—

EARTH-SONG.

'Mine and yours;
Mine, not yours.
Earth endures;
Stars abide—
Shine down in the old sea;
Old are the shores;
But where are old men?
I who have seen much,
Such have I never seen.

'The lawyer's deed
Ran sure,
In tail,
To them, and to their heirs
Who shall succeed,
Without fail,
Forevermore.

'Here is the land,
Shaggy with wood,
With its old valley,
Mound, and flood.
But the heritors?
Fled like the flood's foam,—
The lawyer, and the laws,
And the kingdom,
Clean swept herefrom.

'They called me theirs,
Who so controlled me;
Yet every one
Wished to stay, and is gone.
How am I theirs,
If they cannot hold me,
But I hold them?'

When I heard the Earth-song,
I was no longer brave;
My avarice cooled
Like lust in the chill of the grave.

The Rhodora:

On Being Asked, Whence Is the Flower?

In May, when sea-winds pierced our solitudes,
I found the fresh Rhodora in the woods,
Spreading its leafless blooms in a damp nook,
To please the desert and the sluggish brook.
The purple petals, fallen in the pool,
Made the black water with their beauty gay;
Here might the red-bird come his plumes to cool,
And court the flower that cheapens his array.
Rhodora! if the sages ask thee why
This charm is wasted on the earth and sky,
Tell them, dear, that if eyes were made for seeing,
Then Beauty is its own excuse for being:
Why thou wert there, O rival of the rose!
I never thought to ask, I never knew;
But, in my simple ignorance, suppose
The self-same Power that brought me there brought you.

The Humble-Bee

Burly, dozing, humble-bee,
Where thou art is clime for me.
Let them sail for Porto Rique,
Far-off heats through seas to seek;
I will follow thee alone,
Thou animated torrid-zone!
Zigzag steerer, desert cheerer,
Let me chase thy waving lines;
Keep me nearer, me thy hearer,
Singing over shrubs and vines.

Insect lover of the sun,
Joy of thy dominion!
Sailor of the atmosphere;
Swimmer through the waves of air;

Voyager of light and noon;
Epicurean of June;
Wait, I prithee, till I come
Within earshot of thy hum,—
All without is martyrdom.

When the south wind, in May days,
With a net of shining haze
Silvers the horizon wall,
And, with softness touching all,
Tints the human countenance
With a color of romance,
And, infusing subtle heats,
Turns the sod to violets,
Thou, in sunny solitudes,
Rover of the underwoods,
The green silence dost displace
With thy mellow, breezy bass.

Hot midsummer's petted crone,
Sweet to me thy drowsy tone
Tells of countless sunny hours,
Long days, and solid banks of flowers;
Of gulfs of sweetness without bound
In Indian wildernesses found;
Of Syrian peace, immortal leisure,
Firmest cheer, and bird-like pleasure.

Aught unsavory or unclean
Hath my insect never seen;
But violets and bilberry bells,
Maple-sap, and daffodels,
Grass with green flag half-mast high,
Succory to match the sky,
Columbine with horn of honey,
Scented fern, and agrimony,
Clover, catchfly, adder's tongue,
And brier roses, dwelt among;
All beside was unknown waste,
All was picture as he passed.

Wiser far than human seer,
Yellow-breeched philosopher!
Seeing only what is fair,
Sipping only what is sweet,
Thou dost mock at fate and care,
Leave the chaff, and take the wheat.
When the fierce north-western blast
Cools sea and land so far and fast,
Thou already slumberest deep;
Woe and want thou canst outsleep;
Want and woe, which torture us,
Thy sleep makes ridiculous.

The Snow-Storm

Announced by all the trumpets of the sky,
Arrives the snow, and, driving o'er the fields,
Seems nowhere to alight: the whited air
Hides hills and woods, the river, and the heaven,
And veils the farm-house at the garden's end.
The sled and traveller stopped, the courier's feet
Delayed, all friends shut out, the housemates sit
Around the radiant fireplace, enclosed
In a tumultuous privacy of storm.

Come see the north wind's masonry.
Out of an unseen quarry evermore
Furnished with tile, the fierce artificer
Curves his white bastions with projected roof
Round every windward stake, or tree, or door.
Speeding, the myriad-handed, his wild work
So fanciful, so savage, nought cares he
For number or proportion. Mockingly,
On coop or kennel he hangs Parian wreaths;
A swan-like form invests the hidden thorn;
Fills up the farmer's lane from wall to wall,
Maugre the farmer's sighs; and, at the gate,

A tapering turret overtops the work.
And when his hours are numbered, and the world
Is all his own, retiring, as he were not,
Leaves, when the sun appears, astonished Art
To mimic in slow structures, stone by stone,
Built in an age, the mad wind's night-work,
The frolic architecture of the snow.

from *Woodnotes II*

Once again the pine-tree sung: —
'Speak not thy speech my boughs among;
Put off thy years, wash in the breeze;
My hours are peaceful centuries.
Talk no more with feeble tongue;
No more the fool of space and time,
Come weave with mine a nobler rhyme.
Only thy Americans
Can read thy line, can meet thy glance,
But the runes that I rehearse
Understands the universe;
The least breath my boughs which tossed
Brings again the Pentecost,
To every soul it soundeth clear
In a voice of solemn cheer, —
"Am I not thine? Are not these thine?"
And they reply, "Forever mine!"
My branches speak Italian,
English, German, Basque, Castilian,
Mountain speech to Highlanders,
Ocean tongues to islanders,
To Fin, and Lap, and swart Malay,
To each his bosom secret say.
Come learn with me the fatal song
Which knits the world in music strong,
Whereto every bosom dances,

Kindled with courageous fancies.
Come lift thine eyes to lofty rhymes,
Of things with things, of times with times,
Primal chimes of sun and shade,
Of sound and echo, man and maid,
The land reflected in the flood,
Body with shadow still pursued.
For Nature beats in perfect tune,
And rounds with rhyme her every rune,
Whether she work in land or sea,
Or hide underground her alchemy.
Thou canst not wave thy staff in air,
Or dip thy paddle in the lake,
But it carves the bow of beauty there,
And the ripples in rhymes the oar forsake.
The wood is wiser far than thou;
The wood and wave each other know.
Not unrelated, unaffied,
But to each thought and thing allied,
Is perfect Nature's every part,
Rooted in the mighty Heart.
But thou, poor child! unbound, unrhymed,
Whence camest thou, misplaced, mistimed?
Whence, O thou orphan and defrauded?
Is thy land peeled, thy realm marauded?
Who thee divorced, deceived, and left?
Thee of thy faith who hath bereft,
And torn the ensigns from thy brow,
And sunk the immortal eye so low?
Thy cheek too white, thy form too slender,
Thy gait too slow, thy habits tender
For royal man;—they thee confess
An exile from the wilderness,—
The hills where health with health agrees,
And the wise soul expels disease.
Hark! in thy ear I will tell the sign
By which thy hurt thou may'st divine.
When thou shalt climb the mountain cliff,
Or see the wide shore from thy skiff,
To thee the horizon shall express

Only emptiness and emptiness;
There is no man of Nature's worth
In the circle of the earth;
And to thine eye the vast skies fall,
Dire and satirical,
On clucking hens, and prating fools,
On thieves, on drudges, and on dolls.
And thou shalt say to the Most High,
"Godhead! all this astronomy,
And fate, and practice, and invention,
Strong art, and beautiful pretension,
This radiant pomp of sun and star,
Throes that were, and worlds that are,
Behold! were in vain and in vain;—
It cannot be,—I will look again;
Surely now will the curtain rise,
And earth's fit tenant me surprise;—
But the curtain doth *not* rise,
And Nature has miscarried wholly
Into failure, into folly."

'Alas! thine is the bankruptcy,
Blessed Nature so to see.
Come, lay thee in my soothing shade,
And heal the hurts which sin has made.
I will teach the bright parable
Older than time,
Things undeclarable,
Visions sublime.
I see thee in the crowd alone;
I will be thy companion.
Let thy friends be as the dead in doom,
And build to them a final tomb;
Let the starred shade that nightly falls
Still celebrate their funerals,
And the bell of beetle and of bee
Knell their melodious memory.
Behind thee leave thy merchandise,
Thy churches, and thy charities;
And leave thy peacock wit behind;

Enough for thee the primal mind
That flows in streams, that breathes in wind.
Leave all thy pedant lore apart;
God hid the whole world in thy heart.
Love shuns the sage, the child it crowns,
And gives them all who all renounce.
The rain comes when the wind calls;
The river knows the way to the sea;
Without a pilot it runs and falls,
Blessing all lands with its charity;
The sea tosses and foams to find
Its way up to the cloud and wind;
The shadow sits close to the flying ball;
The date fails not on the palm-tree tall;
And thou,—go burn thy wormy pages,—
Shalt outsee seers, and outwit sages.
Oft didst thou thread the woods in vain
To find what bird had piped the strain;—
Seek not, and the little eremite
Flies gayly forth and sings in sight.

'Hearken once more!
I will tell thee the mundane lore.
Older am I than thy numbers wot;
Change I may, but I pass not.
Hitherto all things fast abide,
And anchored in the tempest ride.
Trenchant time behoves to hurry
All to yean and all to bury:
All the forms are fugitive,
But the substances survive.
Ever fresh the broad creation,
A divine improvisation,
From the heart of God proceeds,
A single will, a million deeds.
Once slept the world an egg of stone,
And pulse, and sound, and light was none;
And God said, "Throb!" and there was motion,
And the vast mass became vast ocean.
Onward and on, the eternal Pan,

Who layeth the world's incessant plan,
Halteth never in one shape,
But forever doth escape,
Like wave or flame, into new forms
Of gem, and air, of plants, and worms.
I, that to-day am a pine,
Yesterday was a bundle of grass.
He is free and libertine,
Pouring of his power the wine
To every age, to every race;
Unto every race and age
He emptieth the beverage;
Unto each, and unto all,
Maker and original.
The world is the ring of his spells,
And the play of his miracles.
As he giveth to all to drink,
Thus or thus they are and think.
He giveth little or giveth much,
To make them several or such.
With one drop sheds form and feature;
With the second a special nature;
The third adds heat's indulgent spark;
The fourth gives light which eats the dark;
In the fifth drop himself he flings,
And conscious Law is King of kings.
Pleaseth him, the Eternal Child,
To play his sweet will, glad and wild;
As the bee through the garden ranges,
From world to world the godhead changes;
As the sheep go feeding in the waste,
From form to form he maketh haste;
This vault which glows immense with light
Is the inn where he lodges for a night.
What recks such Traveller if the bowers
Which bloom and fade like meadow flowers
A bunch of fragrant lilies be,
Or the stars of eternity?
Alike to him the better, the worse,—
The glowing angel, the outcast corse.

Thou metest him by centuries,
And lo! he passes like the breeze;
Thou seek'st in globe and galaxy,
He hides in pure transparency;
Thou askest in fountains and in fires,
He is the essence that inquires.
He is the axis of the star;
He is the sparkle of the spar;
He is the heart of every creature;
He is the meaning of each feature;
And his mind is the sky,
Than all it holds more deep, more high.'

from *Monadnoc*

'Every morn I lift my head,
Gaze o'er New England underspread,
South from Saint Lawrence to the Sound,
From Katskill east to the sea-bound.
Anchored fast for many an age,
I await the bard and sage,
Who, in large thoughts, like fair pearl-seed,
Shall string Monadnoc like a bead.
Comes that cheerful troubadour,
This mound shall throb his face before,
As when, with inward fires and pain,
It rose a bubble from the plain.
When he cometh, I shall shed,
From this wellspring in my head,
Fountain drop of spicier worth
Than all vintage of the earth.
There's fruit upon my barren soil
Costlier far than wine or oil.
There's a berry blue and gold, —
Autumn-ripe, its juices hold
Sparta's stoutness, Bethlehem's heart,
Asia's rancor, Athens' art,
Slowsure Britain's secular might,
And the German's inward sight.

I will give my son to eat
Best of Pan's immortal meat,
Bread to eat, and juice to drink;
So the thoughts that he shall think
Shall not be forms of stars, but stars,
Nor pictures pale, but Jove and Mars.
He comes, but not of that race bred
Who daily climb my specular head.
Oft as morning wreathes my scarf,
Fled the last plumule of the Dark,
Pants up hither the spruce clerk
From South Cove and City Wharf.
I take him up my rugged sides,
Half-repentant, scant of breath,—
Bead-eyes my granite chaos show,
And my midsummer snow;
Open the daunting map beneath,—
All his county, sea and land,
Dwarfed to measure of his hand;
His day's ride is a furlong space,
His city tops a glimmering haze.
I plant his eyes on the sky-hoop bounding:
"See there the grim gray rounding
Of the bullet of the earth
Whereon ye sail,
Tumbling steep
In the uncontinented deep."
He looks on that, and he turns pale.
'Tis even so; this treacherous kite,
Farm-furrowed, town-incrusted sphere,
Thoughtless of its anxious freight,
Plunges eyeless on forever;
And he, poor parasite,
Cooped in a ship he cannot steer,—
Who is the captain he knows not,
Port or pilot trows not,—
Risk or ruin he must share.
I scowl on him with my cloud,
With my north wind chill his blood;
I lame him, clattering down the rocks;

And to live he is in fear.
Then, at last, I let him down
Once more into his dapper town,
To chatter, frightened, to his clan,
And forget me if he can.'

Fable

The mountain and the squirrel
Had a quarrel;
And the former called the latter 'Little Prig.'
Bun replied,
'You are doubtless very big;
But all sorts of things and weather
Must be taken in together,
To make up a year
And a sphere.
And I think it no disgrace
To occupy my place.
If I'm not so large as you,
You are not so small as I,
And not half so spry.
I'll not deny you make
A very pretty squirrel track;
Talents differ; all is well and wisely put;
If I cannot carry forests on my back,
Neither can you crack a nut.'

Ode, Inscribed to W. H. Channing

Though loath to grieve
The evil time's sole patriot,
I cannot leave
My honied thought
For the priest's cant,
Or statesman's rant.

If I refuse
My study for their politique,
Which at the best is trick,
The angry Muse
Puts confusion in my brain.

But who is he that prates
Of the culture of mankind,
Of better arts and life?
Go, blindworm, go,
Behold the famous States
Harrying Mexico
With rifle and with knife!

Or who, with accent bolder,
Dare praise the freedom-loving mountaineer?
I found by thee, O rushing Contoocook!
And in thy valleys, Agiochook!
The jackals of the negro-holder.

The God who made New Hampshire
Taunted the lofty land
With little men; —
Small bat and wren
House in the oak: —
If earth-fire cleave
The upheaved land, and bury the folk,
The southern crocodile would grieve.
Virtue palters; Right is hence;
Freedom praised, but hid;
Funeral eloquence
Rattles the coffin-lid.

What boots thy zeal,
O glowing friend,
That would indignant rend
The northland from the south?
Wherefore? to what good end?
Boston Bay and Bunker Hill
Would serve things still; —
Things are of the snake.

The horseman serves the horse,
The neatherd serves the neat,
The merchant serves the purse,
The eater serves his meat;
'Tis the day of the chattel,
Web to weave, and corn to grind;
Things are in the saddle,
And ride mankind.

There are two laws discrete,
Not reconciled,—
Law for man, and law for thing;
The last builds town and fleet,
But it runs wild,
And doth the man unking.

'Tis fit the forest fall,
The steep be graded,
The mountain tunnelled,
The sand shaded,
The orchard planted,
The glebe tilled,
The prairie granted,
The steamer built.

Let man serve law for man;
Live for friendship, live for love,
For truth's and harmony's behoof;
The state may follow how it can,
As Olympus follows Jove.

    Yet do not I invite
The wrinkled shopman to my sounding woods,
Nor bid the unwilling senator
Ask votes of thrushes in the solitudes.
Every one to his chosen work;—
Foolish hands may mix and mar;
Wise and sure the issues are.
Round they roll till dark is light,

Sex to sex, and even to odd;—
The over-god
Who marries Right to Might,
Who peoples, unpeoples,—
He who exterminates
Races by stronger races,
Black by white faces,—
Knows to bring honey
Out of the lion;
Grafts gentlest scion
On pirate and Turk.

The Cossack eats Poland,
Like stolen fruit;
Her last noble is ruined,
Her last poet mute:
Straight, into double band
The victors divide;
Half for freedom strike and stand;—
The astonished Muse finds thousands at her side.

Astræa

Himself it was who wrote
His rank, and quartered his own coat.
There is no king nor sovereign state
That can fix a hero's rate;
Each to all is venerable,
Cap-a-pie invulnerable,
Until he write, where all eyes rest,
Slave or master on his breast.

I saw men go up and down,
In the country and the town,
With this prayer upon their neck,—
'Judgment and a judge we seek.'
Not to monarchs they repair,
Nor to learned jurist's chair;

But they hurry to their peers,
To their kinsfolk and their dears;
Louder than with speech they pray, —
'What am I? companion, say.'
And the friend not hesitates
To assign just place and mates;
Answers not in word or letter,
Yet is understood the better;
Is to his friend a looking-glass,
Reflects his figure that doth pass.
Every wayfarer he meets
What himself declared repeats,
What himself confessed records,
Sentences him in his words;
The form is his own corporal form,
And his thought the penal worm.

Yet shine forever virgin minds,
Loved by stars and purest winds,
Which, o'er passion throned sedate,
Have not hazarded their state;
Disconcert the searching spy,
Rendering to a curious eye
The durance of a granite ledge
To those who gaze from the sea's edge.
It is there for benefit;
It is there for purging light;
There for purifying storms;
And its depths reflect all forms;
It cannot parley with the mean, —
Pure by impure is not seen.
For there's no sequestered grot,
Lone mountain tarn, or isle forgot,
But Justice, journeying in the sphere,
Daily stoops to harbor there.

Compensation

Why should I keep holiday
  When other men have none?
Why but because, when these are gay,
  I sit and mourn alone?

And why, when mirth unseals all tongues,
  Should mine alone be dumb?
Ah! late I spoke to silent throngs,
  And now their hour is come.

Forerunners

Long I followed happy guides,
I could never reach their sides;
Their step is forth, and, ere the day,
Breaks up their leaguer, and away.
Keen my sense, my heart was young,
Right good-will my sinews strung,
But no speed of mine avails
To hunt upon their shining trails.
On and away, their hasting feet
Make the morning proud and sweet;
Flowers they strew,—I catch the scent;
Or tone of silver instrument
Leaves on the wind melodious trace;
Yet I could never see their face.
On eastern hills I see their smokes,
Mixed with mist by distant lochs.
I met many travellers
Who the road had surely kept;
They saw not my fine revellers,—
These had crossed them while they slept.
Some had heard their fair report,
In the country or the court.
Fleetest couriers alive
Never yet could once arrive,
As they went or they returned,

At the house where these sojourned.
Sometimes their strong speed they slacken,
Though they are not overtaken;
In sleep their jubilant troop is near,—
I tuneful voices overhear;
It may be in wood or waste,—
At unawares 'tis come and past.
Their near camp my spirit knows
By signs gracious as rainbows.
I thenceforward, and long after,
Listen for their harp-like laughter,
And carry in my heart, for days,
Peace that hallows rudest ways.

Sursum Corda

Seek not the spirit, if it hide
Inexorable to thy zeal:
Baby, do not whine and chide:
Art thou not also real?
Why shouldst thou stoop to poor excuse?
Turn on the accuser roundly; say,
'Here am I, here will I remain
Forever to myself soothfast;
Go thou, sweet Heaven, or at thy pleasure stay!'
Already Heaven with thee its lot has cast,
For only it can absolutely deal.

Give All to Love

Give all to love;
Obey thy heart;
Friends, kindred, days,
Estate, good-fame,
Plans, credit, and the Muse,—
Nothing refuse.

'Tis a brave master;
Let it have scope:
Follow it utterly,
Hope beyond hope:
High and more high
It dives into noon,
With wing unspent,
Untold intent;
But it is a god,
Knows its own path,
And the outlets of the sky.

It was not for the mean;
It requireth courage stout,
Souls above doubt,
Valor unbending;
Such 'twill reward,—
They shall return
More than they were,
And ever ascending.

Leave all for love;
Yet, hear me, yet,
One word more thy heart behoved,
One pulse more of firm endeavor,—
Keep thee to-day,
To-morrow, forever,
Free as an Arab
Of thy beloved.

Cling with life to the maid;
But when the surprise,
First vague shadow of surmise
Flits across her bosom young
Of a joy apart from thee,
Free be she, fancy-free;
Nor thou detain her vesture's hem,
Nor the palest rose she flung
From her summer diadem.

Though thou loved her as thyself,
As a self of purer clay,
Though her parting dims the day,
Stealing grace from all alive;
Heartily know,
When half-gods go,
The gods arrive.

Eros

The sense of the world is short,—
Long and various the report,—
　　To love and be beloved;
Men and gods have not outlearned it;
And, how oft soe'er they've turned it,
　　'Tis not to be improved.

from *Initial, Dæmonic, and Celestial Love*

II.

The Dæmonic and the Celestial Love

Man was made of social earth,
Child and brother from his birth,
Tethered by a liquid cord
Of blood through veins of kindred poured.
Next his heart the fireside band
Of mother, father, sister, stand:
These, like strong amulets preferred,
Throbs of a wild religion stirred;—
Virtue, to love, to hate them, vice;
Till dangerous Beauty came, at last,
Till Beauty came to snap all ties;
The maid, abolishing the past,
With lotus wine obliterates
Dear memory's stone-incarved traits,
And, by herself, supplants alone

Friends year by year more inly known.
When her calm eyes opened bright,
All were foreign in their light.
It was ever the self-same tale,
The first experience will not fail;
Only two in the garden walked,
And with snake and seraph talked.

But God said,
'I will have a purer gift;
There is smoke in the flame;
New flowerets bring, new prayers uplift,
And love without a name.
Fond children, ye desire
To please each other well;
Another round, a higher,
Ye shall climb on the heavenly stair,
And selfish preference forbear;
And in right deserving,
And without a swerving
Each from your proper state,
Weave roses for your mate.

'Deep, deep are loving eyes,
Flowed with naphtha fiery sweet;
And the point is paradise,
Where their glances meet:
Their reach shall yet be more profound,
And a vision without bound;
The axis of those eyes sun-clear
Be the axis of the sphere:
So shall the lights ye pour amain
Go, without check or intervals,
Through from the empyrean walls
Unto the same again.'

Close, close to men,
Like undulating layer of air,
Right above their heads,
The potent plain of Dæmons spreads.

Stands to each human soul its own,
For watch, and ward, and furtherance,
In the snares of Nature's dance;
And the lustre and the grace
Which fascinate each youthful heart,
Beaming from its counterpart,
Translucent through the mortal covers,
Is the Dæmon's form and face.
To and fro the Genius hies,—
A gleam which plays and hovers
Over the maiden's head,
And dips sometimes as low as to her eyes.
Unknown, albeit lying near,
To men, the path to the Dæmon sphere;
And they that swiftly come and go
Leave no track on the heavenly snow.
Sometimes the airy synod bends,
And the mighty choir descends,
And the brains of men thenceforth,
In crowded and in still resorts,
Teem with unwonted thoughts:
As, when a shower of meteors
Cross the orbit of the earth,
And, lit by fringent air,
Blaze near and far,
Mortals deem the planets bright
Have slipped their sacred bars,
And the lone seaman all the night
Sails, astonished, amid stars.

Beauty of a richer vein,
Graces of a subtler strain,
Unto men these moonmen lend,
And our shrinking sky extend.
So is man's narrow path
By strength and terror skirted;
Also, (from the song the wrath
Of the Genii be averted!
The Muse the truth uncolored speaking,)
The Dæmons are self-seeking:

Their fierce and limitary will
Draws men to their likeness still.
The erring painter made Love blind,—
Highest Love who shines on all;
Him, radiant, sharpest-sighted god,
None can bewilder;
Whose eyes pierce
The universe,
Path-finder, road-builder,
Mediator, royal giver;
Rightly seeing, rightly seen,
Of joyful and transparent mien.
'Tis a sparkle passing
From each to each, from thee to me,
To and fro perpetually;
Sharing all, daring all,
Levelling, displacing
Each obstruction, it unites
Equals remote, and seeming opposites.
And ever and forever Love
Delights to build a road:
Unheeded Danger near him strides,
Love laughs, and on a lion rides.
But Cupid wears another face,
Born into Dæmons less divine:
His roses bleach apace,
His nectar smacks of wine.
The Dæmon ever builds a wall,
Himself encloses and includes,
Solitude in solitudes:
In like sort his love doth fall.
He is an oligarch;
He prizes wonder, fame, and mark;
He loveth crowns;
He scorneth drones;
He doth elect
The beautiful and fortunate,
And the sons of intellect,
And the souls of ample fate,
Who the Future's gates unbar,—

Minions of the Morning Star.
In his prowess he exults,
And the multitude insults.
His impatient looks devour
Oft the humble and the poor;
And, seeing his eye glare,
They drop their few pale flowers,
Gathered with hope to please,
Along the mountain towers,—
Lose courage, and despair.
He will never be gainsaid,—
Pitiless, will not be stayed;
His hot tyranny
Burns up every other tie.
Therefore comes an hour from Jove
Which his ruthless will defies,
And the dogs of Fate unties.
Shiver the palaces of glass;
Shrivel the rainbow-colored walls,
Where in bright Art each god and sibyl dwelt,
Secure as in the zodiac's belt;
And the galleries and halls,
Wherein every siren sung,
Like a meteor pass.
For this fortune wanted root
In the core of God's abysm,—
Was a weed of self and schism;
And ever the Dæmonic Love
Is the ancestor of wars,
And the parent of remorse.

Merlin I

Thy trivial harp will never please
Or fill my craving ear;
Its chords should ring as blows the breeze,
Free, peremptory, clear.
No jingling serenader's art,
Nor tinkle of piano strings,

Can make the wild blood start
In its mystic springs.
The kingly bard
Must smite the chords rudely and hard,
As with hammer or with mace;
That they may render back
Artful thunder, which conveys
Secrets of the solar track,
Sparks of the supersolar blaze.
Merlin's blows are strokes of fate,
Chiming with the forest tone,
When boughs buffet boughs in the wood;
Chiming with the gasp and moan
Of the ice-imprisoned flood;
With the pulse of manly hearts;
With the voice of orators;
With the din of city arts;
With the cannonade of wars;
With the marches of the brave;
And prayers of might from martyrs' cave.

Great is the art,
Great be the manners, of the bard.
He shall not his brain encumber
With the coil of rhythm and number;
But, leaving rule and pale forethought,
He shall aye climb
For his rhyme.
'Pass in, pass in,' the angels say,
In to the upper doors,
Nor count compartments of the floors,
But mount to paradise
By the stairway of surprise.

Blameless master of the games,
King of sport that never shames,
He shall daily joy dispense
Hid in song's sweet influence.
Things more cheerly live and go,
What time the subtle mind

Sings aloud the tune whereto
Their pulses beat,
And march their feet,
And their members are combined.

By Sybarites beguiled,
He shall no task decline;
Merlin's mighty line
Extremes of nature reconciled,—
Bereaved a tyrant of his will,
And made the lion mild.
Songs can the tempest still,
Scattered on the stormy air,
Mould the year to fair increase,
And bring in poetic peace.

He shall not seek to weave,
In weak, unhappy times,
Efficacious rhymes;
Wait his returning strength.
Bird, that from the nadir's floor
To the zenith's top can soar,
The soaring orbit of the muse exceeds that journey's length.
Nor profane affect to hit
Or compass that, by meddling wit,
Which only the propitious mind
Publishes when 'tis inclined.
There are open hours
When the God's will sallies free,
And the dull idiot might see
The flowing fortunes of a thousand years;—
Sudden, at unawares,
Self-moved, fly-to the doors
Nor sword of angels could reveal
What they conceal.

Merlin II

The rhyme of the poet
Modulates the king's affairs;
Balance-loving Nature
Made all things in pairs.
To every foot its antipode;
Each color with its counter glowed;
To every tone beat answering tones,
Higher or graver;
Flavor gladly blends with flavor;
Leaf answers leaf upon the bough;
And match the paired cotyledons.
Hands to hands, and feet to feet,
Coeval grooms and brides;
Eldest rite, two married sides
In every mortal meet.
Light's far furnace shines,
Smelting balls and bars,
Forging double stars,
Glittering twins and trines.
The animals are sick with love,
Lovesick with rhyme;
Each with all propitious time
Into chorus wove.

Like the dancers' ordered band,
Thoughts come also hand in hand;
In equal couples mated,
Or else alternated;
Adding by their mutual gage,
One to other, health and age.
Solitary fancies go
Short-lived wandering to and fro,
Most like to bachelors,
Or an ungiven maid,
Not ancestors,
With no posterity to make the lie afraid,
Or keep truth undecayed.
Perfect-paired as eagle's wings,

Justice is the rhyme of things;
Trade and counting use
The self-same tuneful muse;
And Nemesis,
Who with even matches odd,
Who athwart space redresses
The partial wrong,
Fills the just period,
And finishes the song.

Subtle rhymes, with ruin rife,
Murmur in the house of life,
Sung by the Sisters as they spin;
In perfect time and measure they
Build and unbuild our echoing clay,
As the two twilights of the day
Fold us music-drunken in.

Bacchus

Bring me wine, but wine which never grew
In the belly of the grape,
Or grew on vine whose tap-roots, reaching through
Under the Andes to the Cape,
Suffered no savor of the earth to scape.

Let its grapes the morn salute
From a nocturnal root,
Which feels the acrid juice
Of Styx and Erebus;
And turns the woe of Night,
By its own craft, to a more rich delight.

We buy ashes for bread;
We buy diluted wine;
Give me of the true,—
Whose ample leaves and tendrils curled
Among the silver hills of heaven,
Draw everlasting dew;

Wine of wine,
Blood of the world,
Form of forms, and mould of statures,
That I intoxicated,
And by the draught assimilated,
May float at pleasure through all natures;
The bird-language rightly spell,
And that which roses say so well.

Wine that is shed
Like the torrents of the sun
Up the horizon walls,
Or like the Atlantic streams, which run
When the South Sea calls.

Water and bread,
Food which needs no transmuting,
Rainbow-flowering, wisdom-fruiting
Wine which is already man,
Food which teach and reason can.

Wine which Music is,—
Music and wine are one,—
That I, drinking this,
Shall hear far Chaos talk with me;
Kings unborn shall walk with me;
And the poor grass shall plot and plan
What it will do when it is man.
Quickened so, will I unlock
Every crypt of every rock.

I thank the joyful juice
For all I know;—
Winds of remembering
Of the ancient being blow,
And seeming-solid walls of use
Open and flow.

Pour, Bacchus! the remembering wine;
Retrieve the loss of me and mine!

Vine for vine be antidote,
And the grape requite the lote!
Haste to cure the old despair, —
Reason in Nature's lotus drenched,
The memory of ages quenched;
Give them again to shine;
Let wine repair what this undid;
And where the infection slid,
A dazzling memory revive;
Refresh the faded tints,
Recut the aged prints,
And write my old adventures with the pen
Which on the first day drew,
Upon the tablets blue,
The dancing Pleiads and eternal men.

Merops

What care I, so they stand the same, —
    Things of the heavenly mind, —
How long the power to give them name
    Tarries yet behind?

Thus far to-day your favors reach,
    O fair, appeasing presences!
Ye taught my lips a single speech,
    And a thousand silences.

Space grants beyond his fated road
    No inch to the god of day;
And copious language still bestowed
    One word, no more, to say.

Saadi

Trees in groves,
Kine in droves,
In ocean sport the scaly herds,

Wedge-like cleave the air the birds,
To northern lakes fly wind-borne ducks,
Browse the mountain sheep in flocks,
Men consort in camp and town,
But the poet dwells alone.

God, who gave to him the lyre,
Of all mortals the desire,
For all breathing men's behoof,
Straitly charged him, 'Sit aloof;'
Annexed a warning, poets say,
To the bright premium,—
Ever, when twain together play,
Shall the harp be dumb.

Many may come,
But one shall sing;
Two touch the string,
The harp is dumb.
Though there come a million,
Wise Saadi dwells alone.

Yet Saadi loved the race of men,—
No churl, immured in cave or den;
In bower and hall
He wants them all,
Nor can dispense
With Persia for his audience;
They must give ear,
Grow red with joy and white with fear;
But he has no companion;
Come ten, or come a million,
Good Saadi dwells alone.

Be thou ware where Saadi dwells;
Wisdom of the gods is he,—
Entertain it reverently.
Gladly round that golden lamp
Sylvan deities encamp,
And simple maids and noble youth

Are welcome to the man of truth.
Most welcome, they who need him most,
They feed the spring which they exhaust;
For greater need
Draws better deed:
But, critic, spare thy vanity,
Nor show thy pompous parts,
To vex with odious subtlety
The cheerer of men's hearts.

Sad-eyed Fakirs swiftly say
Endless dirges to decay,
Never in the blaze of light
Lose the shudder of midnight;
Pale at overflowing noon
Hear wolves barking at the moon;
In the bower of dalliance sweet
Hear the far Avenger's feet;
And shake before those awful Powers,
Who in their pride forgive not ours.
Thus the sad-eyed Fakirs preach:
'Bard, when thee would Allah teach,
And lift thee to his holy mount,
He sends thee from his bitter fount
Wormwood,—saying, "Go thy ways,
Drink not the Malaga of praise,
But do the deed thy fellows hate,
And compromise thy peaceful state;
Smite the white breasts which thee fed;
Stuff sharp thorns beneath the head
Of them thou shouldst have comforted;
For out of woe and out of crime
Draws the heart a lore sublime." '
And yet it seemeth not to me
That the high gods love tragedy;
For Saadi sat in the sun,
And thanks was his contrition;
For haircloth and for bloody whips,
Had active hands and smiling lips;
And yet his runes he rightly read,

And to his folk his message sped.
Sunshine in his heart transferred
Lighted each transparent word,
And well could honoring Persia learn
What Saadi wished to say;
For Saadi's nightly stars did burn
Brighter than Dschami's day.

Whispered the Muse in Saadi's cot:
'O gentle Saadi, listen not,
Tempted by thy praise of wit,
Or by thirst and appetite
For the talents not thine own,
To sons of contradiction.
Never, son of eastern morning,
Follow falsehood, follow scorning.
Denounce who will, who will deny,
And pile the hills to scale the sky;
Let theist, atheist, pantheist,
Define and wrangle how they list,
Fierce conserver, fierce destroyer, —
But thou, joy-giver and enjoyer,
Unknowing war, unknowing crime,
Gentle Saadi, mind thy rhyme;
Heed not what the brawlers say,
Heed thou only Saadi's lay.

'Let the great world bustle on
With war and trade, with camp and town:
A thousand men shall dig and eat;
At forge and furnace thousands sweat;
And thousands sail the purple sea,
And give or take the stroke of war,
Or crowd the market and bazaar;
Oft shall war end, and peace return,
And cities rise where cities burn,
Ere one man my hill shall climb,
Who can turn the golden rhyme.
Let them manage how they may,
Heed thou only Saadi's lay.

Seek the living among the dead,—
Man in man is imprisoned;
Barefooted Dervish is not poor,
If fate unlock his bosom's door,
So that what his eye hath seen
His tongue can paint as bright, as keen;
And what his tender heart hath felt
With equal fire thy heart shall melt.
For, whom the Muses smile upon,
And touch with soft persuasion,
His words like a storm-wind can bring
Terror and beauty on their wing;
In his every syllable
Lurketh nature veritable;
And though he speak in midnight dark,—
In heaven no star, on earth no spark,—
Yet before the listener's eye
Swims the world in ecstasy,
The forest waves, the morning breaks,
The pastures sleep, ripple the lakes,
Leaves twinkle, flowers like persons be,
And life pulsates in rock or tree.
Saadi, so far thy words shall reach:
Suns rise and set in Saadi's speech!'

And thus to Saadi said the Muse:
'Eat thou the bread which men refuse;
Flee from the goods which from thee flee;
Seek nothing,—Fortune seeketh thee.
Nor mount, nor dive; all good things keep
The midway of the eternal deep.
Wish not to fill the isles with eyes
To fetch thee birds of paradise:
On thine orchard's edge belong
All the brags of plume and song;
Wise Ali's sunbright sayings pass
For proverbs in the market-place;
Through mountains bored by regal art,
Toil whistles as he drives his cart.
Nor scour the seas, nor sift mankind,

A poet or a friend to find:
Behold, he watches at the door!
Behold his shadow on the floor!
Open innumerable doors
The heaven where unveiled Allah pours
The flood of truth, the flood of good,
The Seraph's and the Cherub's food:
Those doors are men: the Pariah hind
Admits thee to the perfect Mind.
Seek not beyond thy cottage wall
Redeemers that can yield thee all:
While thou sittest at thy door
On the desert's yellow floor,
Listening to the gray-haired crones,
Foolish gossips, ancient drones,
Saadi, see! they rise in stature
To the height of mighty Nature,
And the secret stands revealed
Fraudulent Time in vain concealed,—
That blessed gods in servile masks
Plied for thee thy household tasks.'

Xenophanes

By fate, not option, frugal Nature gave
One scent to hyson and to wall-flower,
One sound to pine-groves and to waterfalls,
One aspect to the desert and the lake.
It was her stern necessity: all things
Are of one pattern made; bird, beast, and flower,
Song, picture, form, space, thought, and character,
Deceive us, seeming to be many things,
And are but one. Beheld far off, they differ
As God and devil; bring them to the mind,
They dull its edge with their monotony.
To know one element, explore another,
And in the second reappears the first.
The specious panorama of a year
But multiplies the image of a day,—

A belt of mirrors round a taper's flame;
And universal Nature, through her vast
And crowded whole, an infinite paroquet,
Repeats one note.

The Day's Ration

              When I was born,
From all the seas of strength Fate filled a chalice,
Saying, 'This be thy portion, child; this chalice,
Less than a lily's, thou shalt daily draw
From my great arteries,—nor less, nor more.'
All substances the cunning chemist Time
Melts down into that liquor of my life,—
Friends, foes, joys, fortunes, beauty, and disgust.
And whether I am angry or content,
Indebted or insulted, loved or hurt,
All he distils into sidereal wine
And brims my little cup; heedless, alas!
Of all he sheds how little it will hold,
How much runs over on the desert sands.
If a new Muse draw me with splendid ray,
And I uplift myself into its heaven,
The needs of the first sight absorb my blood,
And all the following hours of the day
Drag a ridiculous age.
To-day, when friends approach, and every hour
Brings book, or starbright scroll of genius,
The little cup will hold not a bead more,
And all the costly liquor runs to waste;
Nor gives the jealous lord one diamond drop
So to be husbanded for poorer days.
Why need I volumes, if one word suffice?
Why need I galleries, when a pupil's draught
After the master's sketch fills and o'erfills
My apprehension? why seek Italy,
Who cannot circumnavigate the sea
Of thoughts and things at home, but still adjourn
The nearest matters for a thousand days?

Blight

Give me truths;
For I am weary of the surfaces,
And die of inanition. If I knew
Only the herbs and simples of the wood,
Rue, cinquefoil, gill, vervain, and agrimony,
Blue-vetch, and trillium, hawkweed, sassafras,
Milkweeds, and murky brakes, quaint pipes, and sundew,
And rare and virtuous roots, which in these woods
Draw untold juices from the common earth,
Untold, unknown, and I could surely spell
Their fragrance, and their chemistry apply
By sweet affinities to human flesh,
Driving the foe and stablishing the friend,—
O, that were much, and I could be a part
Of the round day, related to the sun
And planted world, and full executor
Of their imperfect functions.
But these young scholars, who invade our hills,
Bold as the engineer who fells the wood,
And travelling often in the cut he makes,
Love not the flower they pluck, and know it not,
And all their botany is Latin names.
The old men studied magic in the flowers,
And human fortunes in astronomy,
And an omnipotence in chemistry,
Preferring things to names, for these were men,
Were unitarians of the united world,
And, wheresoever their clear eye-beams fell,
They caught the footsteps of the SAME. Our eyes
Are armed, but we are strangers to the stars,
And strangers to the mystic beast and bird,
And strangers to the plant and to the mine.
The injured elements say, 'Not in us;'
And night and day, ocean and continent,
Fire, plant, and mineral say, 'Not in us,'
And haughtily return us stare for stare.
For we invade them impiously for gain;
We devastate them unreligiously,

And coldly ask their pottage, not their love.
Therefore they shove us from them, yield to us
Only what to our griping toil is due;
But the sweet affluence of love and song,
The rich results of the divine consents
Of man and earth, of world beloved and lover,
The nectar and ambrosia, are withheld;
And in the midst of spoils and slaves, we thieves
And pirates of the universe, shut out
Daily to a more thin and outward rind,
Turn pale and starve. Therefore, to our sick eyes,
The stunted trees look sick, the summer short,
Clouds shade the sun, which will not tan our hay,
And nothing thrives to reach its natural term;
And life, shorn of its venerable length,
Even at its greatest space is a defeat,
And dies in anger that it was a dupe;
And, in its highest noon and wantonness,
Is early frugal, like a beggar's child;
With most unhandsome calculation taught,
Even in the hot pursuit of the best aims
And prizes of ambition, checks its hand,
Like Alpine cataracts frozen as they leaped,
Chilled with a miserly comparison
Of the toy's purchase with the length of life.

Musketaquid

Because I was content with these poor fields,
Low, open meads, slender and sluggish streams,
And found a home in haunts which others scorned,
The partial wood-gods overpaid my love.
And granted me the freedom of their state,
And in their secret senate have prevailed
With the dear, dangerous lords that rule our life,
Made moon and planets parties to their bond,
And through my rock-like, solitary wont
Shot million rays of thought and tenderness.

For me, in showers, in sweeping showers, the spring
Visits the valley;—break away the clouds,—
I bathe in the morn's soft and silvered air,
And loiter willing by yon loitering stream.
Sparrows far off, and nearer, April's bird,
Blue-coated,—flying before from tree to tree,
Courageous, sing a delicate overture
To lead the tardy concert of the year.
Onward and nearer rides the sun of May;
And wide around, the marriage of the plants
Is sweetly solemnized. Then flows amain
The surge of summer's beauty; dell and crag,
Hollow and lake, hill-side, and pine arcade,
Are touched with genius. Yonder ragged cliff
Has thousand faces in a thousand hours.

Beneath low hills, in the broad interval
Through which at will our Indian rivulet
Winds mindful still of sannup and of squaw,
Whose pipe and arrow oft the plough unburies,
Here in pine houses built of new fallen trees,
Supplanters of the tribe, the farmers dwell.
Traveller, to thee, perchance, a tedious road,
Or, it may be, a picture; to these men,
The landscape is an armory of powers,
Which, one by one, they know to draw and use.
They harness beast, bird, insect, to their work;
They prove the virtues of each bed of rock,
And, like the chemist mid his loaded jars,
Draw from each stratum its adapted use
To drug their crops or weapon their arts withal.
They turn the frost upon their chemic heap,
They set the wind to winnow pulse and grain,
They thank the spring-flood for its fertile slime,
And, on cheap summit-levels of the snow,
Slide with the sledge to inaccessible woods
O'er meadows bottomless. So, year by year,
They fight the elements with elements,
(That one would say, meadow and forest walked,

Transmuted in these men to rule their like,)
And by the order in the field disclose
The order regnant in the yeoman's brain.

What these strong masters wrote at large in miles,
I followed in small copy in my acre;
For there's no rood has not a star above it;
The cordial quality of pear or plum
Ascends as gladly in a single tree
As in broad orchards resonant with bees;
And every atom poises for itself,
And for the whole. The gentle deities
Showed me the lore of colors and of sounds,
The innumerable tenements of beauty,
The miracle of generative force,
Far-reaching concords of astronomy
Felt in the plants, and in the punctual birds;
Better, the linked purpose of the whole,
And, chiefest prize, found I true liberty
In the glad home plain-dealing nature gave.
The polite found me impolite; the great
Would mortify me, but in vain; for still
I am a willow of the wilderness,
Loving the wind that bent me. All my hurts
My garden spade can heal. A woodland walk,
A quest of river-grapes, a mocking thrush,
A wild-rose, or rock-loving columbine,
Salve my worst wounds.
For thus the wood-gods murmured in my ear:
'Dost love our manners? Canst thou silent lie?
Canst thou, thy pride forgot, like nature pass
Into the winter night's extinguished mood?
Canst thou shine now, then darkle,
And being latent feel thyself no less?
As, when the all-worshipped moon attracts the eye,
The river, hill, stems, foliage are obscure
Yet envies none, none are unenviable.'

Threnody

The South-wind brings
Life, sunshine, and desire,
And on every mount and meadow
Breathes aromatic fire;
But over the dead he has no power,
The lost, the lost, he cannot restore;
And, looking over the hills, I mourn
The darling who shall not return.

I see my empty house,
I see my trees repair their boughs;
And he, the wondrous child,
Whose silver warble wild
Outvalued every pulsing sound
Within the air's cerulean round,—
The hyacinthine boy, for whom
Morn well might break and April bloom,—
The gracious boy, who did adorn
The world whereinto he was born,
And by his countenance repay
The favor of the loving Day,—
Has disappeared from the Day's eye;
Far and wide she cannot find him;
My hopes pursue, they cannot bind him.
Returned this day, the south wind searches,
And finds young pines and budding birches;
But finds not the budding man;
Nature, who lost him, cannot remake him;
Fate let him fall, Fate can't retake him;
Nature, Fate, Men, him seek in vain.

And whither now, my truant wise and sweet,
O, whither tend thy feet?
I had the right, few days ago,
Thy steps to watch, thy place to know;
How have I forfeited the right?
Hast thou forgot me in a new delight?
I hearken for thy household cheer,

O eloquent child!
Whose voice, an equal messenger,
Conveyed thy meaning mild.
What though the pains and joys
Whereof it spoke were toys
Fitting his age and ken,
Yet fairest dames and bearded men,
Who heard the sweet request,
So gentle, wise, and grave,
Bended with joy to his behest,
And let the world's affairs go by,
Awhile to share his cordial game,
Or mend his wicker wagon-frame,
Still plotting how their hungry ear
That winsome voice again might hear;
For his lips could well pronounce
Words that were persuasions.

Gentlest guardians marked serene
His early hope, his liberal mien;
Took counsel from his guiding eyes
To make this wisdom earthly wise.
Ah, vainly do these eyes recall
The school-march, each day's festival,
When every morn my bosom glowed
To watch the convoy on the road;
The babe in willow wagon closed,
With rolling eyes and face composed;
With children forward and behind,
Like Cupids studiously inclined;
And he the chieftain paced beside,
The centre of the troop allied,
With sunny face of sweet repose,
To guard the babe from fancied foes.
The little captain innocent
Took the eye with him as he went;
Each village senior paused to scan
And speak the lovely caravan.
From the window I look out
To mark thy beautiful parade,

Stately marching in cap and coat
To some tune by fairies played;—
A music heard by thee alone
To works as noble led thee on.

Now Love and Pride, alas! in vain,
Up and down their glances strain.
The painted sled stands where it stood;
The kennel by the corded wood;
The gathered sticks to stanch the wall
Of the snow-tower, when snow should fall;
The ominous hole he dug in the sand,
And childhood's castles built or planned;
His daily haunts I well discern,—
The poultry-yard, the shed, the barn,—
And every inch of garden ground
Paced by the blessed feet around,
From the roadside to the brook
Whereinto he loved to look.
Step the meek birds where erst they ranged;
The wintry garden lies unchanged;
The brook into the stream runs on;
But the deep-eyed boy is gone.

On that shaded day,
Dark with more clouds than tempests are,
When thou didst yield thy innocent breath
In birdlike heavings unto death,
Night came, and Nature had not thee;
I said, 'We are mates in misery.'
The morrow dawned with needless glow;
Each snowbird chirped, each fowl must crow;
Each tramper started; but the feet
Of the most beautiful and sweet
Of human youth had left the hill
And garden,—they were bound and still.
There's not a sparrow or a wren,
There's not a blade of autumn grain,
Which the four seasons do not tend,
And tides of life and increase lend;

And every chick of every bird,
And weed and rock-moss is preferred.
O ostrich-like forgetfulness!
O loss of larger in the less!
Was there no star that could be sent,
No watcher in the firmament,
No angel from the countless host
That loiters round the crystal coast,
Could stoop to heal that only child,
Nature's sweet marvel undefiled,
And keep the blossom of the earth,
Which all her harvests were not worth?
Not mine,—I never called thee mine,
But Nature's heir,—if I repine,
And seeing rashly torn and moved
Not what I made, but what I loved,
Grow early old with grief that thou
Must to the wastes of Nature go,—
'Tis because a general hope
Was quenched, and all must doubt and grope.
For flattering planets seemed to say
This child should ills of ages stay,
By wondrous tongue, and guided pen,
Bring the flown Muses back to men.
Perchance not he but Nature ailed,
The world and not the infant failed.
It was not ripe yet to sustain
A genius of so fine a strain,
Who gazed upon the sun and moon
As if he came unto his own,
And, pregnant with his grander thought,
Brought the old order into doubt.
His beauty once their beauty tried;
They could not feed him, and he died,
And wandered backward as in scorn,
To wait an æon to be born.
Ill day which made this beauty waste,
Plight broken, this high face defaced!
Some went and came about the dead;
And some in books of solace read;

Some to their friends the tidings say;
Some went to write, some went to pray;
One tarried here, there hurried one;
But their heart abode with none.
Covetous death bereaved us all,
To aggrandize one funeral.
The eager fate which carried thee
Took the largest part of me:
For this losing is true dying;
This is lordly man's down-lying,
This his slow but sure reclining,
Star by star his world resigning.

O child of paradise,
Boy who made dear his father's home,
In whose deep eyes
Men read the welfare of the times to come,
I am too much bereft.
The world dishonored thou hast left.
O truth's and nature's costly lie!
O trusted broken prophecy!
O richest fortune sourly crossed!
Born for the future, to the future lost!

THE deep Heart answered, 'Weepest thou?
Worthier cause for passion wild
If I had not taken the child.
And deemest thou as those who pore,
With aged eyes, short way before,—
Think'st Beauty vanished from the coast
Of matter, and thy darling lost?
Taught he not thee—the man of eld,
Whose eyes within his eyes beheld
Heaven's numerous hierarchy span
The mystic gulf from God to man?
To be alone wilt thou begin
When worlds of lovers hem thee in?
To-morrow, when the masks shall fall
That dizen Nature's carnival,

The pure shall see by their own will,
Which overflowing Love shall fill,
'Tis not within the force of fate
The fate-conjoined to separate.
But thou, my votary, weepest thou?
I gave thee sight—where is it now?
I taught thy heart beyond the reach
Of ritual, bible, or of speech;
Wrote in thy mind's transparent table,
As far as the incommunicable;
Taught thee each private sign to raise,
Lit by the supersolar blaze.
Past utterance, and past belief,
And past the blasphemy of grief,
The mysteries of Nature's heart;
And though no Muse can these impart,
Throb thine with Nature's throbbing breast,
And all is clear from east to west.

'I came to thee as to a friend;
Dearest, to thee I did not send
Tutors, but a joyful eye,
Innocence that matched the sky,
Lovely locks, a form of wonder,
Laughter rich as woodland thunder,
That thou might'st entertain apart
The richest flowering of all art:
And, as the great all-loving Day
Through smallest chambers takes its way,
That thou might'st break thy daily bread
With prophet, Savior, and head;
That thou might'st cherish for thine own
The riches of sweet Mary's Son,
Boy-Rabbi, Israel's paragon.
And thoughtest thou such guest
Would in thy hall take up his rest?
Would rushing life forget her laws,
Fate's glowing revolution pause?
High omens ask diviner guess;
Not to be conned to tediousness.

And know my higher gifts unbind
The zone that girds the incarnate mind.
When the scanty shores are full
With Thought's perilous, whirling pool;
When frail Nature can no more,
Then the Spirit strikes the hour:
My servant Death, with solving rite,
Pours finite into infinite.

'Wilt thou freeze love's tidal flow,
Whose streams through nature circling go?
Nail the wild star to its track
On the half-climbed zodiac?
Light is light which radiates,
Blood is blood which circulates,
Life is life which generates,
And many-seeming life is one,—
Wilt thou transfix and make it none?
Its onward force too starkly pent
In figure, bone, and lineament?
Wilt thou, uncalled, interrogate,
Talker! the unreplying Fate?
Nor see the genius of the whole
Ascendant in the private soul,
Beckon it when to go and come,
Self-announced its hour of doom?
Fair the soul's recess and shrine,
Magic-built to last a season;
Masterpiece of love benign;
Fairer that expansive reason
Whose omen 'tis, and sign.
Wilt thou not ope thy heart to know
What rainbows teach, and sunsets show?
Verdict which accumulates
From lengthening scroll of human fates,
Voice of earth to earth returned,
Prayers of saints that inly burned,—
Saying, *What is excellent,*
As God lives, is permanent;
Hearts are dust, hearts' loves remain;

Heart's love will meet thee again.
Revere the Maker; fetch thine eye
Up to his style, and manners of the sky.
Not of adamant and gold
Built be heaven stark and cold;
No, but a nest of bending reeds,
Flowering grass, and scented weeds;
Or like a traveller's fleeing tent,
Or bow above the tempest bent;
Built of tears and sacred flames,
And virtue reaching to its aims;
Built of furtherance and pursuing,
Not of spent deeds, but of doing.
Silent rushes the swift Lord
Through ruined systems still restored,
Broadsowing, bleak and void to bless,
Plants with worlds the wilderness;
Waters with tears of ancient sorrow
Apples of Eden ripe to-morrow.
House and tenant go to ground,
Lost in God, in Godhead found.'

Hymn:
Sung at the Completion of the Concord Monument

April 19, 1836

By the rude bridge that arched the flood,
　Their flag to April's breeze unfurled,
Here once the embattled farmers stood,
　And fired the shot heard round the world.

The foe long since in silence slept;
　Alike the conqueror silent sleeps;
And Time the ruined bridge has swept
　Down the dark stream which seaward creeps.

On this green bank, by this soft stream,
 We set to-day a votive stone;
That memory may their deed redeem,
 When, like our sires, our sons are gone.

Spirit, that made those heroes dare
 To die, or leave their children free,
Bid Time and Nature gently spare
 The shaft we raise to them and thee.

Brahma

If the red slayer think he slays,
 Or if the slain think he is slain,
They know not well the subtle ways
 I keep, and pass, and turn again.

Far or forgot to me is near;
 Shadow and sunlight are the same;
The vanished gods to me appear;
 And one to me are shame and fame.

They reckon ill who leave me out;
 When me they fly, I am the wings;
I am the doubter and the doubt,
 And I the hymn the Brahmin sings.

The strong gods pine for my abode,
 And pine in vain the sacred Seven;
But thou, meek lover of the good!
 Find me, and turn thy back on heaven.

Freedom

Once I wished I might rehearse
Freedom's pæan in my verse,
That the slave who caught the strain
Should throb until he snapped his chain.
But the Spirit said, 'Not so;

Speak it not, or speak it low;
Name not lightly to be said,
Gift too precious to be prayed,
Passion not to be expressed
But by heaving of the breast:
Yet,—wouldst thou the mountain find
Where this deity is shrined,
Who gives to seas and sunset skies
Their unspent beauty of surprise,
And, when it lists him, waken can
Brute or savage into man;
Or, if in thy heart he shine,
Blends the starry fates with thine,
Draws angels nigh to dwell with thee,
And makes thy thoughts archangels be;
Freedom's secret wilt thou know?—
Counsel not with flesh and blood;
Loiter not for cloak or food;
Right thou feelest, rush to do.'

Voluntaries

I.

Low and mournful be the strain,
Haughty thought be far from me;
Tones of penitence and pain,
Moanings of the tropic sea;
Low and tender in the cell
Where a captive sits in chains,
Crooning ditties treasured well
From his Afric's torrid plains.
Sole estate his sire bequeathed—
Hapless sire to hapless son—
Was the wailing song he breathed,
And his chain when life was done.

What his fault, or what his crime?
Or what ill planet crossed his prime?

Heart too soft and will too weak
To front the fate that crouches near,—
Dove beneath the vulture's beak;—
Will song dissuade the thirsty spear?
Dragged from his mother's arms and breast,
Displaced, disfurnished here,
His wistful toil to do his best
Chilled by a ribald jeer.
Great men in the Senate sate,
Sage and hero, side by side,
Building for their sons the State,
Which they shall rule with pride.
They forbore to break the chain
Which bound the dusky tribe,
Checked by the owners' fierce disdain,
Lured by "Union" as the bribe.
Destiny sat by, and said,
'Pang for pang your seed shall pay,
Hide in false peace your coward head,
I bring round the harvest-day.'

II.

Freedom all winged expands,
Nor perches in a narrow place;
Her broad van seeks unplanted lands;
She loves a poor and virtuous race.
Clinging to a colder zone
Whose dark sky sheds the snow-flake down,
The snow-flake is her banner's star,
Her stripes the boreal streamers are.
Long she loved the Northman well;
Now the iron age is done,
She will not refuse to dwell
With the offspring of the Sun;
Foundling of the desert far,
Where palms plume, siroccos blaze,
He roves unhurt the burning ways
In climates of the summer star.
He has avenues to God

Hid from men of Northern brain,
Far beholding, without cloud,
What these with slowest steps attain.
If once the generous chief arrive
To lead him willing to be led,
For freedom he will strike and strive,
And drain his heart till he be dead.

III.

In an age of fops and toys,
Wanting wisdom, void of right,
Who shall nerve heroic boys
To hazard all in Freedom's fight,—
Break sharply off their jolly games,
Forsake their comrades gay,
And quit proud homes and youthful dames,
For famine, toil, and fray?
Yet on the nimble air benign
Speed nimbler messages,
That waft the breath of grace divine
To hearts in sloth and ease.
So nigh is grandeur to our dust,
So near is God to man,
When Duty whispers low, *Thou must*,
The youth replies, *I can*.

IV.

O, well for the fortunate soul
Which Music's wings infold,
Stealing away the memory
Of sorrows new and old!
Yet happier he whose inward sight,
Stayed on his subtile thought,
Shuts his sense on toys of time,
To vacant bosoms brought.
But best befriended of the God
He who, in evil times,
Warned by an inward voice,
Heeds not the darkness and the dread,

Biding by his rule and choice,
Feeling only the fiery thread
Leading over heroic ground,
Walled with mortal terror round,
To the aim which him allures,
And the sweet heaven his deed secures.

Stainless soldier on the walls,
Knowing this,—and knows no more,—
Whoever fights, whoever falls,
Justice conquers evermore,
Justice after as before,—
And he who battles on her side,
God, though he were ten times slain,
Crowns him victor glorified,
Victor over death and pain;
Forever: but his erring foe,
Self-assured that he prevails,
Looks from his victim lying low,
And sees aloft the red right arm
Redress the eternal scales.
He, the poor foe, whom angels foil,
Blind with pride, and fooled by hate,
Writhes within the dragon coil,
Reserved to a speechless fate.

v.

Blooms the laurel which belongs
To the valiant chief who fights;
I see the wreath, I hear the songs
Lauding the Eternal Rights,
Victors over daily wrongs:
Awful victors, they misguide
Whom they will destroy,
And their coming triumph hide
In our downfall, or our joy:
They reach no term, they never sleep,
In equal strength through space abide;
Though, feigning dwarfs, they crouch and creep,

The strong they slay, the swift outstride:
Fate's grass grows rank in valley clods,
And rankly on the castled steep,—
Speak it firmly, these are gods,
All are ghosts beside.

Days

Daughters of Time, the hypocritic Days,
Muffled and dumb like barefoot dervishes,
And marching single in an endless file,
Bring diadems and fagots in their hands.
To each they offer gifts after his will,
Bread, kingdoms, stars, and sky that holds them all.
I, in my pleachéd garden, watched the pomp,
Forgot my morning wishes, hastily
Took a few herbs and apples, and the Day
Turned and departed silent. I, too late,
Under her solemn fillet saw the scorn.

Sea-Shore

I heard or seemed to hear the chiding Sea
Say, Pilgrim, why so late and slow to come?
Am I not always here, thy summer home?
Is not my voice thy music, morn and eve?
My breath thy healthful climate in the heats,
My touch thy antidote, my bay thy bath?
Was ever building like my terraces?
Was ever couch magnificent as mine?
Lie on the warm rock-ledges, and there learn
A little hut suffices like a town.
I make your sculptured architecture vain,
Vain beside mine. I drive my wedges home,
And carve the coastwise mountain into caves.
Lo! here is Rome, and Nineveh, and Thebes,
Karnak, and Pyramid, and Giant's Stairs,
Half piled or prostrate; and my newest slab
Older than all thy race.

Behold the Sea,
The opaline, the plentiful and strong,
Yet beautiful as is the rose in June,
Fresh as the trickling rainbow of July;
Sea full of food, the nourisher of kinds,
Purger of earth, and medicine of men;
Creating a sweet climate by my breath,
Washing out harms and griefs from memory,
And, in my mathematic ebb and flow,
Giving a hint of that which changes not.
Rich are the sea-gods:—who gives gifts but they?
They grope the sea for pearls, but more than pearls:
They pluck Force thence, and give it to the wise.
For every wave is wealth to Dædalus,
Wealth to the cunning artist who can work
This matchless strength. Where shall he find, O waves!
A load your Atlas shoulders cannot lift?

I with my hammer pounding evermore
The rocky coast, smite Andes into dust,
Strewing my bed, and, in another age,
Rebuild a continent of better men.
Then I unbar the doors: my paths lead out
The exodus of nations: I disperse
Men to all shores that front the hoary main.

I too have arts and sorceries;
Illusion dwells forever with the wave.
I know what spells are laid. Leave me to deal
With credulous and imaginative man;
For, though he scoop my water in his palm,
A few rods off he deems it gems and clouds.
Planting strange fruits and sunshine on the shore,
I make some coast alluring, some lone isle,
To distant men, who must go there, or die.

Song of Nature

Mine are the night and morning,
The pits of air, the gulf of space,
The sportive sun, the gibbous moon,
The innumerable days.

I hide in the solar glory,
I am dumb in the pealing song,
I rest on the pitch of the torrent,
In slumber I am strong.

No numbers have counted my tallies,
No tribes my house can fill,
I sit by the shining Fount of Life,
And pour the deluge still;

And ever by delicate powers
Gathering along the centuries
From race on race the rarest flowers,
My wreath shall nothing miss.

And many a thousand summers
My apples ripened well,
And light from meliorating stars
With firmer glory fell.

I wrote the past in characters
Of rock and fire the scroll,
The building in the coral sea,
The planting of the coal.

And thefts from satellites and rings
And broken stars I drew,
And out of spent and aged things
I formed the world anew;

What time the gods kept carnival,
Tricked out in star and flower,
And in cramp elf and saurian forms
They swathed their too much power.

Time and Thought were my surveyors,
They laid their courses well,
They boiled the sea, and baked the layers
Of granite, marl, and shell.

But he, the man-child glorious,—
Where tarries he the while?
The rainbow shines his harbinger,
The sunset gleams his smile.

My boreal lights leap upward,
Forthright my planets roll,
And still the man-child is not born,
The summit of the whole.

Must time and tide forever run?
Will never my winds go sleep in the west?
Will never my wheels which whirl the sun
And satellites have rest?

Too much of donning and doffing,
Too slow the rainbow fades,
I weary of my robe of snow,
My leaves and my cascades;

I tire of globes and races,
Too long the game is played;
What without him is summer's pomp,
Or winter's frozen shade?

I travail in pain for him,
My creatures travail and wait;
His couriers come by squadrons,
He comes not to the gate.

Twice I have moulded an image,
And thrice outstretched my hand,
Made one of day, and one of night,
And one of the salt sea-sand.

One in a Judæan manger,
And one by Avon stream,
One over against the mouths of Nile,
And one in the Academe.

I moulded kings and saviours,
And bards o'er kings to rule;—
But fell the starry influence short,
The cup was never full.

Yet whirl the glowing wheels once more,
And mix the bowl again;
Seethe, Fate! the ancient elements,
Heat, cold, wet, dry, and peace, and pain.

Let war and trade and creeds and song
Blend, ripen race on race,
The sunburnt world a man shall breed
Of all the zones, and countless days.

No ray is dimmed, no atom worn,
My oldest force is good as new,
And the fresh rose on yonder thorn
Gives back the bending heavens in dew.

Two Rivers

Thy summer voice, Musketaquit,
Repeats the music of the rain;
But sweeter rivers pulsing flit
Through thee, as thou through Concord Plain.

Thou in thy narrow banks art pent:
The stream I love unbounded goes
Through flood and sea and firmament;
Through light, through life, it forward flows.

I see the inundation sweet,
I hear the spending of the stream
Through years, through men, through nature fleet,
Through passion, thought, through power and dream.

Musketaquit, a goblin strong,
Of shard and flint makes jewels gay;
They lose their grief who hear his song,
And where he winds is the day of day.

So forth and brighter fares my stream,—
Who drink it shall not thirst again;
No darkness stains its equal gleam,
And ages drop in it like rain.

Waldeinsamkeit

I do not count the hours I spend
In wandering by the sea;
The forest is my loyal friend,
Like God it useth me.

In plains that room for shadows make
Of skirting hills to lie,
Bound in by streams which give and take
Their colors from the sky;

Or on the mountain-crest sublime,
Or down the oaken glade,
O what have I to do with time?
For this the day was made.

Cities of mortals woe-begone
Fantastic care derides,
But in the serious landscape lone
Stern benefit abides.

Sheen will tarnish, honey cloy,
And merry is only a mask of sad,
But, sober on a fund of joy,
The woods at heart are glad.

There the great Planter plants
Of fruitful worlds the grain,
And with a million spells enchants
The souls that walk in pain.

Still on the seeds of all he made
The rose of beauty burns;
Through times that wear, and forms that fade,
Immortal youth returns.

The black ducks mounting from the lake,
The pigeon in the pines,
The bittern's boom, a desert make
Which no false art refines.

Down in yon watery nook,
Where bearded mists divide,
The gray old gods whom Chaos knew,
The sires of Nature, hide.

Aloft, in secret veins of air,
Blows the sweet breath of song,
O, few to scale those uplands dare,
Though they to all belong!

See thou bring not to field or stone
The fancies found in books;
Leave authors' eyes, and fetch your own,
To brave the landscape's looks.

And if, amid this dear delight,
My thoughts did home rebound,
I well might reckon it a slight
To the high cheer I found.

Oblivion here thy wisdom is,
Thy thrift, the sleep of cares;
For a proud idleness like this
Crowns all thy mean affairs.

Terminus

It is time to be old,
To take in sail:—
The god of bounds,
Who sets to seas a shore,
Came to me in his fatal rounds,
And said: 'No more!
No farther spread
Thy broad ambitious branches, and thy root.
Fancy departs: no more invent,
Contract thy firmament
To compass of a tent.
There's not enough for this and that,
Make thy option which of two;
Economize the failing river,
Not the less revere the Giver,
Leave the many and hold the few.
Timely wise accept the terms,
Soften the fall with wary foot;
A little while
Still plan and smile,
And, fault of novel germs,
Mature the unfallen fruit.

Curse, if thou wilt, thy sires,
Bad husbands of their fires,
Who, when they gave thee breath,
Failed to bequeath
The needful sinew stark as once,
The Baresark marrow to thy bones,
But left a legacy of ebbing veins,
Inconstant heat and nerveless reins, —
Amid the Muses, left thee deaf and dumb,
Amid the gladiators, halt and numb.'

As the bird trims her to the gale,
I trim myself to the storm of time,
I man the rudder, reef the sail,
Obey the voice at eve obeyed at prime:
'Lowly faithful, banish fear,
Right onward drive unharmed;
The port, well worth the cruise, is near,
And every wave is charmed.'

Suum Cuique

Wilt thou seal up the avenues of ill?
Pay every debt, as if God wrote the bill.

Memory

Night-dreams trace on Memory's wall
Shadows of the thoughts of day,
And thy fortunes, as they fall,
The bias of the will betray.

The Harp

One musician is sure,
His wisdom will not fail,
He has not tasted wine impure,
Nor bent to passion frail.
Age cannot cloud his memory,
Nor grief untune his voice,
Ranging down the ruled scale
From tone of joy to inward wail,
Tempering the pitch of all
In his windy cave.
He all the fables knows,
And in their causes tells,—
Knows Nature's rarest moods,
Ever on her secret broods.
The Muse of men is coy,
Oft courted will not come;
In palaces and market-squares
Entreated, she is dumb;
But my minstrel knows and tells
The counsel of the gods,
Knows of Holy Book the spells,
Knows the law of Night and Day,
And the heart of girl and boy,
The tragic and the gay,
And what is writ on Table Round
Of Arthur and his peers,
What sea and land discoursing say
In sidereal years.
He renders all his lore
In numbers wild as dreams,
Modulating all extremes,—
What the spangled meadow saith
To the children who have faith;
Only to children children sing,
Only to youth will spring be spring.

Who is the Bard thus magnified?
When did he sing? and where abide?

Chief of song where poets feast
In the wind-harp which thou seest
In the casement at my side.

Æolian harp,
How strangely wise thy strain!
Gay for youth, gay for youth,
(Sweet is art, but sweeter truth,)
In the hall at summer eve
Fate and Beauty skilled to weave.
From the eager opening strings
Rung loud and bold the song.
Who but loved the wind-harp's note?
How should not the poet dote
On its mystic tongue,
With its primeval memory,
Reporting what old minstrels told
Of Merlin locked the harp within,—
Merlin paying the pain of sin,
Pent in a dungeon made of air,—
And some attain his voice to hear,—
Words of pain and cries of fear,
But pillowed all on melody,
As fits the griefs of bards to be.
And what if that all-echoing shell,
Which thus the buried Past can tell,
Should rive the Future, and reveal
What his dread folds would fain conceal?
It shares the secret of the earth,
And of the kinds that owe her birth.
Speaks not of self that mystic tone,
But of the Overgods alone:
It trembles to the cosmic breath,—
As it heareth, so it saith;
Obeying meek the primal Cause,
It is the tongue of mundane laws.
And this, at least, I dare affirm,
Since genius too has bound and term,
There is no bard in all the choir,
Not Homer's self, the poet sire,

Wise Milton's odes of pensive pleasure,
Or Shakspeare, whom no mind can measure,
Nor Collins' verse of tender pain,
Nor Byron's clarion of disdain,
Scott, the delight of generous boys,
Or Wordsworth, Pan's recording voice,—
Not one of all can put in verse,
Or to this presence could rehearse,
The sights and voices ravishing
The boy knew on the hills in spring,
When pacing through the oaks he heard
Sharp queries of the sentry-bird,
The heavy grouse's sudden whir,
The rattle of the kingfisher;
Saw bonfires of the harlot flies
In the lowland, when day dies;
Or marked, benighted and forlorn,
The first far signal-fire of morn.
These syllables that Nature spoke,
And the thoughts that in him woke,
Can adequately utter none
Save to his ear the wind-harp lone.
Therein I hear the Parcæ reel
The threads of man at their humming-wheel,
The threads of life, and power, and pain,
So sweet and mournful falls the strain.
And best can teach its Delphian chord
How Nature to the soul is moored,
If once again that silent string,
As erst it wont, would thrill and ring.

Not long ago, at eventide,
It seemed, so listening, at my side
A window rose, and, to say sooth,
I looked forth on the fields of youth:
I saw fair boys bestriding steeds,
I knew their forms in fancy weeds,
Long, long concealed by sundering fates,
Mates of my youth,—yet not my mates,
Stronger and bolder far than I,

With grace, with genius, well attired,
And then as now from far admired,
Followed with love
They knew not of,
With passion cold and shy.
O joy, for what recoveries rare!
Renewed, I breathe Elysian air,
See youth's glad mates in earliest bloom,—
Break not my dream, obtrusive tomb!
Or teach thou, Spring! the grand recoil
Of life resurgent from the soil
Wherein was dropped the mortal spoil.

Grace

How much, Preventing God! how much I owe
To the defences thou hast round me set:
Example, custom, fear, occasion slow;—
These scorned bondmen were my parapet.
I dare not peep over this parapet,
To gauge with glance the roaring gulf below,
The depths of sin to which I had descended,
Had not these me against myself defended.

Mottoes from the Essays

Nature (1836)

A subtle chain of countless rings
The next unto the farthest brings;
The eye reads omens where it goes,
And speaks all languages the rose;
And, striving to be man, the worm
Mounts through all the spires of form.

Compensation

I.

The wings of Time are black and white,
Pied with morning and with night.
Mountain tall and ocean deep
Trembling balance duly keep.
In changing moon and tidal wave
Glows the feud of Want and Have.
Gauge of more and less through space,
Electric star or pencil plays,
The lonely Earth amid the balls
That hurry through the eternal halls,
A makeweight flying to the void,
Supplemental asteroid,
Or compensatory spark,
Shoots across the neutral Dark.

II.

Man's the elm, and Wealth the vine;
Stanch and strong the tendrils twine:
Though the frail ringlets thee deceive,
None from its stock that vine can reave.
Fear not, then, thou child infirm,
There's no god dare wrong a worm;
Laurel crowns cleave to deserts,
And power to him who power exerts.
Hast not thy share? On winged feet,
Lo! it rushes thee to meet;
And all that Nature made thy own,
Floating in air or pent in stone,
Will rive the hills and swim the sea,
And, like thy shadow, follow thee.

Spiritual Laws

The living Heaven thy prayers respect,
House at once and architect,
Quarrying man's rejected hours,
Builds therewith eternal towers;
Sole and self-commanded works,
Fears not undermining days,
Grows by decays,
And, by the famous might that lurks
In reaction and recoil,
Makes flame to freeze, and ice to boil;
Forging, through swart arms of Offence,
The silver seat of Innocence.

History

There is no great and no small
To the Soul that maketh all:
And where it cometh, all things are;
And it cometh everywhere.

———

I am owner of the sphere,
Of the seven stars and the solar year,
Of Cæsar's hand, and Plato's brain,
Of Lord Christ's heart, and Shakspeare's strain.

Self-Reliance

Cast the bantling on the rocks,
Suckle him with the she-wolf's teat,
Wintered with the hawk and fox,
Power and speed be hands and feet.

Circles

Nature centres into balls,
And her proud ephemerals,
Fast to surface and outside,
Scan the profile of the sphere;
Knew they what that signified,
A new genesis were here.

Art

Give to barrows, trays, and pans
Grace and glimmer of romance;
Bring the moonlight into noon
Hid in gleaming piles of stone;
On the city's paved street
Plant gardens lined with lilacs sweet;
Let spouting fountains cool the air,
Singing in the sun-baked square;
Let statue, picture, park, and hall,
Ballad, flag, and festival,
The past restore, the day adorn,
And make to-morrow a new morn.
So shall the drudge in dusty frock
Spy behind the city clock
Retinues of airy kings,
Skirts of angels, starry wings,
His fathers shining in bright fables,
His children fed at heavenly tables.
'Tis the privilege of Art
Thus to play its cheerful part,
Man on earth to acclimate,
And bend the exile to his fate,
And, moulded of one element
With the days and firmament,
Teach him on these as stairs to climb,
And live on even terms with Time;
Whilst upper life the slender rill
Of human sense doth overfill.

Experience

The lords of life, the lords of life, —
I saw them pass,
In their own guise,
Like and unlike,
Portly and grim, —
Use and Surprise,
Surface and Dream,
Succession swift and spectral Wrong,
Temperament without a tongue,
And the inventor of the game
Omnipresent without name; —
Some to see, some to be guessed,
They marched from east to west:
Little man, least of all,
Among the legs of his guardians tall,
Walked about with puzzled look.
Him by the hand dear Nature took,
Dearest Nature, strong and kind,
Whispered, 'Darling, never mind!
To-morrow they will wear another face,
The founder thou; these are thy race!'

Nature (1844)

The rounded world is fair to see,
Nine times folded in mystery:
Though baffled seers cannot impart
The secret of its laboring heart,
Throb thine with Nature's throbbing breast,
And all is clear from east to west.
Spirit that lurks each form within
Beckons to spirit of its kin;
Self-kindled every atom glows,
And hints the future which it owes.

Nominalist and Realist

In countless upward-striving waves
The moon-drawn tide-wave strives;
In thousand far-transplanted grafts
The parent fruit survives;
So, in the new-born millions,
The perfect Adam lives.
Not less are summer-mornings dear
To every child they wake,
And each with novel life his sphere
Fills for his proper sake.

Fate

Her planted eye to-day controls,
Is in the morrow most at home,
And sternly calls to being souls
That curse her when they come.

Wealth

Who shall tell what did befall,
Far away in time, when once,
Over the lifeless ball,
Hung idle stars and suns?
What god the element obeyed?
Wings of what wind the lichen bore,
Wafting the puny seeds of power,
Which, lodged in rock, the rock abrade?
And well the primal pioneer
Knew the strong task to it assigned,
Patient through Heaven's enormous year
To build in matter home for mind.
From air the creeping centuries drew
The matted thicket low and wide,
This must the leaves of ages strew
The granite slab to clothe and hide,
Ere wheat can wave its golden pride.

What smiths, and in what furnace, rolled
(In dizzy æons dim and mute
The reeling brain can ill compute)
Copper and iron, lead and gold?
What oldest star the fame can save
Of races perishing to pave
The planet with a floor of lime?
Dust is their pyramid and mole:
Who saw what ferns and palms were pressed
Under the tumbling mountain's breast,
In the safe herbal of the coal?
But when the quarried means were piled,
All is waste and worthless, till
Arrives the wise selecting will,
And, out of slime and chaos, Wit
Draws the threads of fair and fit.
Then temples rose, and towns, and marts,
The shop of toil, the hall of arts;
Then flew the sail across the seas
To feed the North from tropic trees;
The storm-wind wove, the torrent span,
Where they were bid the rivers ran;
New slaves fulfilled the poet's dream,
Galvanic wire, strong-shouldered steam.
Then docks were built, and crops were stored,
And ingots added to the hoard.
But, though light-headed man forget,
Remembering Matter pays her debt:
Still, through her motes and masses, draw
Electric thrills and ties of Law,
Which bind the strength of Nature wild
To the conscience of a child.

Worship

This is he, who, felled by foes,
Sprung harmless up, refreshed by blows:
He to captivity was sold,
But him no prison-bars would hold:

Though they sealed him in a rock,
Mountain chains he can unlock:
Thrown to lions for their meat,
The crouching lion kissed his feet:
Bound to the stake, no flames appalled,
But arched o'er him an honoring vault.
This is he men miscall Fate,
Threading dark ways, arriving late,
But ever coming in time to crown
The truth, and hurl wrong-doers down.
He is the oldest, and best known,
More near than aught thou call'st thy own,
Yet, greeted in another's eyes,
Disconcerts with glad surprise.
This is Jove, who, deaf to prayers,
Floods with blessings unawares.
Draw, if thou canst, the mystic line
Severing rightly his from thine,
Which is human, which divine.

Illusions

Flow, flow the waves hated,
Accursed, adored,
The waves of mutation:
No anchorage is.
Sleep is not, death is not;
Who seem to die live.
House you were born in,
Friends of your spring-time,
Old man and young maid,
Day's toil and its guerdon,
They are all vanishing,
Fleeing to fables,
Cannot be moored.
See the stars through them,
Through treacherous marbles.
Know, the stars yonder,

The stars everlasting,
Are fugitive also,
And emulate, vaulted,
The lambent heat-lightning,
And fire-fly's flight.

When thou dost return
On the wave's circulation,
Beholding the shimmer,
The wild dissipation,
And, out of endeavor
To change and to flow,
The gas become solid,
And phantoms and nothings
Return to be things,
And endless imbroglio
Is law and the world, —
Then first shalt thou know,
That in the wild turmoil,
Horsed on the Proteus,
Thou ridest to power,
And to endurance.

"Awed I behold once more"

Awed I behold once more
My old familiar haunts; here the blue river
The same blue wonder that my infant eye
Admired, sage doubting whence the traveller came, —
Whence brought his sunny bubbles ere he washed
The fragrant flag roots in my father's fields,
And where thereafter in the world he went.
Look, here he is unaltered, save that now
He hath broke his banks & flooded all the vales
With his redundant waves.

Here is the rock where yet a simple child
I caught with bended pin my earliest fish,
Much triumphing, — And these the fields

Over whose flowers I chased the butterfly,
A blooming hunter of a fairy fine.
And hark! where overhead the ancient crows
Hold their sour conversation in the sky.
   These are the same, but I am not the same
But wiser than I was, & wise enough
Not to regret the changes, tho' they cost
Me many a sigh. Oh call not Nature dumb;
These trees & stones are audible to me,
These idle flowers, that tremble in the wind,
I understand their faery syllables,
And all their sad significance. This wind,
That rustles down the well-known forest road—
It hath a sound more eloquent than speech.
The stream, the trees, the grass, the sighing wind,
All of them utter sounds of admonishment
And grave parental love.

They are not of our race, they seem to say,
And yet have knowledge of our moral race,
And somewhat of majestic sympathy,
Something of pity for the puny clay,
That holds & boasts the immeasureable mind.

I feel as I were welcome to these trees
After long months of weary wandering,
Acknowledged by their hospitable boughs;
They know me as their son, for side by side,
They were coeval with my ancestors,
Adorned with them my country's primitive times,
And soon may give my dust their funeral shade.

"Dear brother, would you know the life"

Dear brother, would you know the life
Please God, that I would lead?
On the first wheels that quit this weary town
Over yon western bridges I would ride
And with a cheerful benison forsake

Each street & spire & roof incontinent.
Then would I seek where God might guide my steps,
Deep in a woodland tract, a sunny farm,
Amid the mountain counties, Hants Franklin Berks,
Where down the rock ravine a river roars,
Even from a brook, & where old woods
Not tamed & cleared, cumber the ample ground
With their centennial wrecks.
Find me a slope where I can feel the sun
And mark the rising of the early stars.
There will I bring my books, my household gods,
The reliquaires of my dead saint, & dwell
In the sweet odor of her memory.
There, in the uncouth solitude, unlock
My stock of art, plant dials, in the grass,
Hang in the air a bright thermometer,
And aim a telescope at the inviolate Sun.

"*Who knows this or that*"

Who knows this or that
Hark in the wall to the rat
Since the world was, he has gnawed;
Of his wisdom of his fraud
What dost thou know
In the wretched little beast
Is life & heart
Child & parent
Not without relation
To fruitful field & sun & moon
What art thou? his wicked eye
Is cruel to thy cruelty

Intellect

Rule which by obeying grows
Knowledge not its fountain knows
Wave removing whom it bears
From the shores which he compares
Adding wings thro things to range
Makes him to his own blood strange

"The patient Pan"

The patient Pan,
Drunken with nectar
Sleeps or feigns slumber
Drowsily humming
Music to the march of Time.
This poor tooting creaking cricket,
Pan half asleep, rolling over
His great body in the grass,
Tooting, creaking,
Feigns to sleep, sleeping never:
Tis his manner,
Well he knows his own affair,
Piling mountain-chains of phlegm
On the nervous brain of man,
As he holds down central fires
Under Alps & Andes cold.
Haply else we could not live

Maia

Illusion works impenetrable,
Weaving webs innumerable,
Her gay pictures never fail,
Crowds each on other, veil on veil,
A charmer who will be believed
By Man who thirsts to be deceived.

SARAH HELEN WHITMAN

(1803–1878)

To ——

Vainly my heart had with thy sorceries striven:
It had no refuge from thy love,—no Heaven
But in thy fatal presence;—from afar
It owned thy power and trembled like a star
O'erfraught with light and splendor. Could I deem
How dark a shadow should obscure its beam?—
Could I believe that pain could ever dwell
Where thy bright presence cast its blissful spell?
Thou wert my proud palladium;—could I fear
The avenging Destinies when thou wert near?—
Thou wert my Destiny;—thy song, thy fame,
The wild enchantments clustering round thy name,
Were my soul's heritage, its royal dower;
Its glory and its kingdom and its power!

NATHANIEL HAWTHORNE
(1804–1864)

"I left my low and humble home"

I left my low and humble home,
Far from my Father's fields to roam.
My peaceful cot no more had charms,
My only joy was War's alarms.
I panted for the field of fight,
I gaz'd upon the deathless light,
Which o'er the Hero's grave is shed,
The glorious memory of the dead.
Ambition show'd a distant star,
That shed its radience bright and far,
And pointed to a path which led
O'er heaps of dying and of dead;
Onward I press'd with eager feet,
And War's dread thunder still would greet
My reckless ears. Where'er I trod,
I saw the green and verdant sod,
Turn red with blood of slaughter'd foes,
And Fury veil'd in smoke arose.
I gain'd the envied height, and there,
I sigh'd for that lone cottage, where
The early hours of life flew by,
On wings of youthful ecstacy.
Too late I found that Glory's ray,
Could never bring one happy day.

"Oh could I raise the darken'd veil"

Oh could I raise the darken'd veil,
Which hides my future life from me,
Could unborn ages slowly sail,
Before my view—and could I see
My every action painted there,
To cast one look I would not dare.
There poverty and grief might stand,
And dark Despair's corroding hand,
Would make me seek the lonely tomb
To slumber in its endless gloom.
Then let me never cast a look,
Within Fate's fix'd mysterious book.

The Ocean

The Ocean has its silent caves,
Deep, quiet and alone;
Though there be fury on the waves,
Beneath them there is none.
The awful spirits of the deep
Hold their communion there;
And there are those for whom we weep,
The young, the bright, the fair.

Calmly the wearied seamen rest
Beneath their own blue sea.
The ocean solitudes are blest,
For there is purity.
The earth has guilt, the earth has care,
Unquiet are its graves;
But peaceful sleep is ever there,
Beneath the dark blue waves.

NATHANIEL PARKER WILLIS

(1806–1867)

January 1, 1829

Winter is come again. The sweet south west
Is a forgotten wind, and the strong earth
Has laid aside its mantle to be bound
By the frost fetter. There is not a sound
Save of the skaiter's heel, and there is laid
An icy finger on the lip of streams,
And the clear icicle hangs cold and still,
And the snow-fall is noiseless as a thought.
Spring has a rushing sound, and Summer sends
Many sweet voices with its odors out,
And Autumn rustleth its decaying robe
With a complaining whisper. Winter's dumb!
God made his ministry a silent one,
And he has given him a foot of steel
And an unlovely aspect, and a breath
Sharp to the senses—and we know that He
Tempereth well, and hath a meaning hid
Under the shadow of his hand. Look up!
And it shall be interpreted—Your home
Hath a temptation now. There is no voice
Of waters with beguiling for your ear,
And the cool forest and the meadows green
Witch not your feet away; and in the dells
There are no violets, and upon the hills
There are no sunny places to lie down.
You must go in, and by your cheerful fire
Wait for the offices of love, and hear
Accents of human tenderness, and feast
Your eye upon the beauty of the young.
It is a season for the quiet thought,
And the still reckoning with thyself. The year
Gives back the spirits of its dead, and time
Whispers the history of its vanished hours;

351

And the heart, calling its affections up,
Counteth its wasted ingots. Life stands still
And settles like a fountain, and the eye
Sees clearly through its depths, and noteth all
That stirred its troubled waters. It is well
That Winter with the dying year should come!

Psyche,
Before the Tribunal of Venus

Lift up thine eyes, sweet Psyche! What is she
That those soft fringes timidly should fall
Before her, and thy spiritual brow
Be shadowed as her presence were a cloud?
A loftier gift is thine than she can give—
That queen of beauty. She may mould the brow
To perfectness, and give unto the form
A beautiful proportion; she may stain
The eye with a celestial blue—the cheek
With carmine of the sunset; she may breathe
Grace into every motion, like the play
Of the least visible tissue of a cloud;
She may give all that is within her own
Bright cestus—and one silent look of thine,
Like stronger magic, will outcharm it all.

Ay, for the soul is better than its frame,
The spirit than its temple. What's the brow,
Or the eye's lustre, or the step of air,
Or color, but the beautiful links that chain
The mind from its rare element? There lies
A talisman in intellect which yields
Celestial music, when the master hand
Touches it cunningly. It sleeps beneath
The outward semblance, and to common sight
Is an invisible and hidden thing;
But when the lip is faded, and the cheek

Robbed of its daintiness, and when the form
Witches the sense no more, and human love
Falters in its idolatry, this spell
Will hold its strength unbroken, and go on
Stealing anew the affections.
                      Marvel not
That Love leans sadly on his bended bow.
He hath found out the loveliness of mind,
And he is spoilt for beauty. So 'twill be
Ever—the glory of the human form
Is but a perishing thing, and Love will droop
When its brief grace hath faded; but the mind
Perisheth not, and when the outward charm
Hath had its brief existence, it awakes,
And is the lovelier that it slept so long—
Like wells that by the wasting of their flow
Have had their deeper fountains broken up.

from *Melanie*

IV

A calm and lovely paradise
   Is Italy, for minds at ease.
The sadness of its sunny skies
   Weighs not upon the lives of these.
The ruin'd aisle, the crumbling fane,
   The broken column, vast and prone,
It may be joy—it may be pain—
   Amid such wrecks to walk alone!
The saddest man will sadder be,
   The gentlest lover gentler there,
As if, whate'er the spirit's key,
   It strengthened in that solemn air.

The heart soon grows to mournful things,
   And Italy has not a breeze
But comes on melancholy wings;
   And even her majestic trees
Stand ghost-like in the Cæsar's home,
   As if their conscious roots were set
In the old graves of giant Rome,
   And drew their sap all kingly yet!
And every stone your feet beneath
   Is broken from some mighty thought,
And sculptures in the dust still breathe
   The fire with which their lines were wrought,
And sunder'd arch, and plunder'd tomb
Still thunder back the echo, "Rome!"

Yet gaily o'er Egeria's fount
   The ivy flings its emerald veil,
And flowers grow fair on Numa's mount,
   And light-sprung arches span the dale,
And soft, from Caracalla's Baths,
   The herdsman's song comes down the breeze,
While climb his goats the giddy paths
   To grass-grown architrave and frieze;
And gracefully Albano's hill
   Curves into the horizon's line,
And sweetly sings that classic rill,
   And fairly stands that nameless shrine,
And here, oh, many a sultry noon
And starry eve, that happy June,
   Came Angelo and Melanie,
And earth for us was all in tune—
For while Love talk'd with them, Hope walked
      apart with me!

The Confessional

"When thou hast met with careless hearts and cold,
Hearts that young love may touch, but never hold,
Not changeless, as the loved and left of old—
Remember me—remember me—
I passionately pray of thee!"
                                    LADY E. S. WORTLEY.

I thought of thee—I thought of thee,
    On ocean—many a weary night—
When heaved the long and sullen sea,
    With only waves and stars in sight.
We stole along by isles of balm,
    We furl'd before the coming gale,
We slept amid the breathless calm,
    We flew beneath the straining sail—
But thou wert lost for years to me,
And, day and night, I thought of thee!

I thought of thee—I thought of thee,
    In France—amid the gay saloon,
Where eyes as dark as eyes may be
    Are many as the leaves in June—
Where life is love, and ev'n the air
    Is pregnant with impassion'd thought,
And song and dance and music are
    With one warm meaning only fraught—
My half-snar'd heart broke lightly free,
And, with a blush, I thought of thee!

I thought of thee—I thought of thee,
    In Florence,—where the fiery hearts
Of Italy are breathed away
    In wonders of the deathless arts;
Where strays the Contadina down
    Val d'Arno with a song of old;
Where clime and woman seldom frown,
    And life runs over sands of gold;
I stray'd to lone Fiesolé
On many an eve, and thought of thee.

I thought of thee—I thought of thee,
   In Rome,—when on the Palatine
Night left the Cæsar's palace free
   To Time's forgetful foot and mine;
Or, on the Coliseum's wall,
   When moonlight touch'd the ivied stone,
Reclining, with a thought of all
   That o'er this scene has come and gone—
The shades of Rome would start and flee
Unconsciously—I thought of thee.

I thought of thee—I thought of thee,
   In Vallombrosa's holy shade,
Where nobles born the friars be,
   By life's rude changes humbler made.
Here Milton fram'd his Paradise;
   I slept within his very cell;
And, as I clos'd my weary eyes,
   I thought the cowl would fit me well—
The cloisters breath'd, it seem'd to me,
Of heart's-ease—but I thought of thee.

I thought of thee—I thought of thee,
   In Venice,—on a night in June;
When, through the city of the sea,
   Like dust of silver slept the moon.
Slow turn'd his oar the gondolier,
   And, as the black barks glided by,
The water to my leaning ear
   Bore back the lover's passing sigh—
It was no place alone to be—
I thought of thee—I thought of thee.

I thought of thee—I thought of thee,
   In the Ionian Isles—when straying
With wise Ulysses by the sea—
   Old Homer's songs around me playing;
Or, watching the bewitched caique,
   That o'er the star-lit waters flew,
I listen'd to the helmsman Greek,

Who sung the song that Sappho knew—
The poet's spell, the bark, the sea,
All vanished—as I thought of thee.

I thought of thee—I thought of thee,
    In Greece—when rose the Parthenon
Majestic o'er the Egean sea,
    And heroes with it, one by one;
When, in the grove of Academe,
    Where Lais and Leontium stray'd
Discussing Plato's mystic theme,
    I lay at noontide in the shade—
The Egean wind, the whispering tree,
Had voices—and I thought of thee.

I thought of thee—I thought of thee,
    In Asia—on the Dardanelles;
Where, swiftly as the waters flee,
    Each wave some sweet old story tells;
And, seated by the marble tank
    Which sleeps by Ilium's ruins old,
(The fount where peerless Helen drank,
    And Venus lav'd her locks of gold,)
I thrill'd such classic haunts to see,
Yet even here—I thought of thee.

I thought of thee—I thought of thee,
    Where glide the Bosphor's lovely waters,
All palace-lined, from sea to sea;
    And ever on its shores the daughters
Of the delicious East are seen,
    Printing the brink with slipper'd feet,
And oh, those snowy folds between,
    What eyes of heaven your glances meet!
Peris of light no fairer be—
Yet—in Stamboul—I thought of thee.

I've thought of thee—I've thought of thee,
    Through change that teaches to forget;
Thy face looks up from every sea,

In every star thine eyes are set,
Though roving beneath Orient skies,
   Whose golden beauty breathes of rest,
I envy every bird that flies
   Into the far and clouded West:
I think of thee—I think of thee!
Oh, dearest! hast thou thought of me?

Unseen Spirits

The shadows lay along Broadway,
   'Twas near the twilight-tide—
And slowly there a lady fair
   Was walking in her pride.
Alone walk'd she; but, viewlessly,
   Walk'd spirits at her side.

Peace charm'd the street beneath her feet,
   And Honor charm'd the air;
And all astir look'd kind on her,
   And call'd her good as fair—
For all God ever gave to her
   She kept with chary care.

She kept with care her beauties rare
   From lovers warm and true—
For her heart was cold to all but gold,
   And the rich came not to woo—
But honor'd well are charms to sell
   If priests the selling do.

Now walking there was one more fair—
   A slight girl, lily-pale;
And she had unseen company
   To make the spirit quail—
'Twixt Want and Scorn she walk'd forlorn,
   And nothing could avail.

No mercy now can clear her brow
　　For this world's peace to pray;
For, as love's wild prayer dissolved in air,
　　Her woman's heart gave way!—
But the sin forgiven by Christ in heaven
　　By man is cursed alway!

City Lyrics

Argument.—The poet starts from the Bowling Green to take his sweet-heart up to Thompson's for an ice, or (if she is inclined for more) ices. He confines his muse to matters which any every-day man and young woman may see in taking the same promenade for the same innocent refreshment.

Come out, love—the night is enchanting!
　　The moon hangs just over Broadway;
The stars are all lighted and panting—
　　(Hot weather up there, I dare say!)
'Tis seldom that "coolness" entices,
　　And love is no better for chilling—
But come up to Thompson's for ices,
　　And cool your warm heart for a shilling!

What perfume comes balmily o'er us?
　　Mint juleps from City Hotel!
A loafer is smoking before us—
　　(A nasty cigar, by the smell!)
Oh Woman! thou secret past knowing!
　　Like lilachs that grow by the wall,
You breathe every air that is going,
　　Yet gather but sweetness from all!

On, on! by St. Paul's, and the Astor!
　　Religion seems very ill-plann'd!
For one day we list to the pastor,
　　For six days we list to the band!
The sermon may dwell on the future,
　　The organ your pulses may calm—
When—pest!—that remember'd cachucha
　　Upsets both the sermon and psalm!

Oh, pity the love that must utter
    While goes a swift omnibus by!
(Though sweet is *I scream** when the flutter
    Of fans shows thermometers high)—
But if what I bawl, or I mutter,
    Falls into your ear but to die,
Oh, the dew that falls into the gutter
    Is not more unhappy than I!

*Query. —Should this be *Ice cream*, or *I scream?*—*Printer's Devil.*

The Lady in the White Dress, Whom I Helped Into the Omnibus

I know her not! Her hand has been in mine,
And the warm pressure of her taper arm
Has thrill'd upon my fingers, and the hem
Of her white dress has lain upon my feet,
Till my hush'd pulse, by the caressing folds,
Was kindled to a fever! I, to her,
Am but the undistinguishable leaf
Blown by upon the breeze—yet I have sat,
And in the blue depths of her stainless eyes,
(Close as a lover in his hour of bliss,
And steadfastly as look the twin stars down
Into unfathomable wells,) have gazed!
And I have felt from out its gate of pearl
Her warm breath on my cheek, and while she sat
Dreaming away the moments, I have tried
To count the long dark lashes in the fringe
Of her bewildering eyes! The kerchief sweet
That enviably visits her red lip
Has slumber'd, while she held it, on my knee,—
And her small foot has crept between mine own—
And yet, she knows me not!

> Now, thanks to heaven
For blessings chainless in the rich man's keeping—
Wealth that the miser cannot hide away!
Buy, if they will, the invaluable flower—
They cannot store its fragrance from the breeze!
Wear, if they will, the costliest gem of Ind—
It pours its light on every passing eye!
And he who on this beauty sets his name—
Who dreams, perhaps, that for his use alone
Such loveliness was first of angels born—
Tell him, oh whisperer at his dreaming ear,
That I too, in her beauty, sun my eye,
And, unrebuked, may worship her in song—
Tell him that heaven, along our darkling way,
Hath set bright lamps with loveliness alight—
And all may in their guiding beams rejoice;
But he—as 'twere a watcher by a lamp—
Guards but this bright one's shining.

To Charles Roux, of Switzerland

*Written in His Album When He Was the Author's
Teacher in Modern Languages
Yale College, 1827*

I would not leave that land, if I were thou—
That glorious land of mountain and of flood,
  Whereon is graven GOD.
As if its hills were chosen for Earth's brow,
And its loud torrents gave the words he spoke,
  Leaping from rock to rock.

I would not leave it—for its children gave
Their blood like water, for a word, "be FREE!"
  Their last breath, "LIBERTY!"
Till Switzerland was made a mighty grave—
A land where heroes like a harvest fell—
  The land of WILLIAM TELL.

I would not leave it:—yet the holy wing
Of Freedom shadoweth this land, as thine!
    And when I call it "mine,"
I make myself a greater than a king.
We welcome freemen—and we welcome thee—
    Dwell with us, and BE FREE!

WILLIAM GILMORE SIMMS

(1806–1870)

The Lost Pleiad

I.

Not in the sky,
Where it was seen—
Nor, on the white tops of the glistering wave—
Nor in the mansions of the hidden deep—
However green,
In its enamell'd caves of mystery—
Shall the bright watcher have
A place—nor once again proud station keep!

II.

Gone, gone!
O! never more, to cheer
The mariner, who hold his course alone,
On the Atlantic, thro' the weary night,
When the waves turn to watchers, and do sleep—
Shall it appear—
With the sweet fixedness of certain light,
Shining upon the shut eye of the blue deep!

III.

O! when the shepherd on Chaldea's hills,
Watching his flocks;
Looks forth, in vain for thy first light to come,
Warning him home—
From his deep sleep, among the sky-kiss'd rocks—
How shall he wake, when dewy silence fills
The scene, to wonder at the weight of night,
Without the one strong beam, whose blessed light,
As to the wandering child, his native rills,
Was natural to his sight!

IV.

Vain, vain!
O! less than vain, shall he look forth—
The sailor from his barque—
(Howe'er the North,
Doth raise his certain lamp, when tempests lower)
To catch the light of the lost star again—
The weary hour,
To him, shall be more weary, when the dark
Displays not the lost planet on her tower.

V.

And lone
Where its first splendor, shone—
Shall be that pleasant company of stars:—
How should they know that death,
The happy glory of the immortal, mars,
When like the Earth, and all its common breath,
Extinguish'd are the pure beams of the sky,
Fallen from on high—
And their concerted springs of harmony
Snapt rudely, and all pleasant music, gone.

VI.

A strain—a mellow strain,
Of parting music, fill'd the earth and sky—
The stars lamenting, in unborrowed pain,
That one of the selectest one's, must die—
The brightest of their train!
Alas! it is the destiny—
The dearest hope is that which first is lost,
The tenderest flower is soonest nipt by frost—
Are not the shortest-lived, the loveliest—
And like the wandering orb that leaves the sky,
Look they not brightest, when about to fly,
The desolate spot they blest?

By the Swanannoa

Is it not lovely, while the day flows on
    Like some unnoticed water through the vale,
    Sun-sprinkled,—and, across the fields, a gale,
    Ausonian, murmurs out an idle tale,
Of groves deserted late, but lately won.
How calm the silent mountains, that, around,
    Bend their blue summits, as if grouped to hear
Some high ambassador from foreign ground,—
To hearken, and, most probably confound!
    While, leaping onward, with a voice of cheer,
Glad as some schoolboy ever on the bound,
    The lively Swanannoa sparkles near;—
A flash and murmur mark him as he roves,
Now foaming white o'er rocks, now glimpsing soft
      through groves.

from *The City of the Silent*

  With ruder pomp, in more barbaric taste,
His burial rites the Abyssinian grac'd;
Like the Egyptian, striving 'gainst the worm,
With costly balms preserved the mortal form;
But not with numerous swathings wrapt the dead,
His fancy counsell'd to unveil instead;
Most heedless, in his vanity, of shame,
Transparent amber clothed the naked frame;
Thus, to all eyes reveal'd, his farther rite,
Raised on high pillars, placed the corse in sight;
Thus, mocking Life with Death, and Time with Fate,
He left the loved one in his hideous state,
The sun still daily shining, but in vain,
On eyes that never smile on sun again!

  In better taste, with tribute more refin'd,
The Etrurian chief his sepulchre designed;
That wondrous race, of whom the little shown,
Reveals such promise in the vast unknown;

Kin to the Egyptian, father to the Greek—
If true the legend and conjecture speak—
In arts and arms that gloriously achiev'd,
And still survive the worship they believed;
That left to Rome their gods, without their faith,
And live in marble though they sleep in death;
A night of twenty centuries, like a spell,
Oppressing Genius that achieved so well,
Denying History, curious still to pierce
The purple pall that hangs about her hearse,
And, hush'd on every theme that might have taught,
Still speaking vaguely, wondrously, to Thought!

How, as with pick and axe, exploring deep
In vaults that shelter well their ancient sleep,
We break through caves of marble that reveal
What pride hath wrought, and Time would still conceal—
How do we start, as on our vision rise,
Perfect as when their children closed their eyes,
Stately in helm and armour, robes and gold,
Their Lucumones as they sway'd of old!—
Princes and chiefs, whose deeds of answering fame,
Thrill'd through their world, yet have for ours no name!
The weight of earth, for near three thousand years,
Press'd on the marble vault that hides their biers,
Preserving well from touch, and rude decay,
The haughty forms of manhood and of sway.

There, he reclines, as when he sought the strife,
Clad in bright armour, looking as in life,
The proud Lucumo!—They have scarcely gone,—
'Twould seem—who laid and seal'd him up in stone!
What awe pervades the soul as thus we gaze,
On this life-seeming state of ancient days;
No cunning effigy, the work of art,
Wrought in the marble, wanting sense and heart,
But the once powerful chieftain as he shone,
By nations honor'd and to thousands known;—
Himself, at length, his limbs composed, his breast
Expanding, as with happiest slumbers bless'd.

Even as we gaze, life seems to stir beneath,
The bosom heaves as with returning breath;
We look to see him rise,—we pause to hear
His trumpet peal of battle from the bier!
But death is in the movement;—'tis the light
That heaves the frame and stirs him to the sight;
Smote by the insidious air, the unwelcome day,
The crumbling corse sinks sudden to decay;
Time, mock'd so long, upon his subject darts,
The clay dissolves, the linkéd armour parts;—
The sceptre-grasping hand, the helméd brow,
And the mail'd breast that perfect seemed but now,
Subside to dust, and mock the fond surprize,
That hail'd the vision late with awe-struck eyes.

We glide below: with curious search we gaze
On these proud mansions of ancestral days;
Here wealth and care have vainly striven to prove
How proud their homage and how fond their love;
What toils they used, what precious unguents brought,
With what sad skill the funeral garments wrought;
What sacrifice of gold and pomp was made,
For the great chief whose relics here they laid!
Art spared no service! On the walls behold,
How fresh the colours twenty centuries old;
How rich the painting—with what free design,
Warm in each tint and bold in every line;
A wondrous story, which reveals a faith
That sees the soul escaped, surviving death;
Shows the group'd forms, in long procession led,
Surrounding fond, or following slow, the dead.—
There, stately still, the enfranchised ghost survey,
Led, by the rival Genii, into day—
The day that lets in judgment on the past,
Bright with great joys, or dread with clouds o'ercast,
There the good Angel, seeking still to save,
Receives and guides the freed one from the grave;
Beckons with smiling hope that soothes the fear,
And shows his "Esar" merciful and near.
Not so the Evil Genii, who withstand

The gentle guidance of his guardian hand;
They bar the way to mercy, and, with thirst
Of eager malice, hoping still the worst,
Declare, of evil deeds, the dark account,
That should deny the ambitious soul to mount.
The painter leaves in doubt the fearful strife,
Whose issue broods with doom or glorious life,
But, of his aim and hope enough are shown,
To prove his promise not unlike our own,
Show that his faith still sought an upward goal,
And challenged wings for the immortal soul!

The New Moon

"Bend thy bow, Dian! shoot thy silver shaft
  Through the dark bosom of yon murky cloud,
    That, like a shroud,
  Hangs heavy o'er the dwelling of sweet night!"

And the sky laugh'd,
Even as I spake the words; and, in the west,
The columns of her mansion shone out bright!
A glory hung above Eve's visible brow,
The maiden empress!—and she glided forth
In beauty, looking down on the tranced earth,
So fondly, that its rivulets below
Gush'd out to hail her, as if then first blest
With the soft motion of their voiceless birth.
A sudden burst of brightness o'er me broke—
The rugged crags of the dull cloud were cleft
By her sharp arrow, and the edges left,—
How sweetly wounded!—silver'd with the stroke;
Thus making a fit pathway for her march
Through the blue arch!

HENRY WADSWORTH LONGFELLOW

(1807–1882)

The Spirit of Poetry

There is a quiet spirit in these woods,
That dwells where'er the gentle south wind blows,
Where, underneath the white-thorn, in the glade,
The wild flowers bloom, or, kissing the soft air,
The leaves above their sunny palms outspread.
With what a tender and impassioned voice
It fills the nice and delicate ear of thought,
When the fast-ushering star of morning comes
O'er-riding the gray hills with golden scarf;
Or when the cowled and dusky-sandaled Eve,
In mourning weeds, from out the western gate,
Departs with silent pace! That spirit moves
In the green valley, where the silver brook,
From its full laver, pours the white cascade;
And, babbling low amid the tangled woods,
Slips down through moss-grown stones with endless laughter.
And frequent, on the everlasting hills,
Its feet go forth, when it doth wrap itself
In all the dark embroidery of the storm,
And shouts the stern, strong wind. And here, amid
The silent majesty of these deep woods,
Its presence shall uplift thy thoughts from earth,
As to the sunshine, and the pure bright air,
Their tops the green trees lift. Hence gifted bards
Have ever loved the calm and quiet shades.
For them there was an eloquent voice in all
The sylvan pomp of woods, the golden sun,
The flowers, the leaves, the river on its way,
Blue skies, and silver clouds, and gentle winds,—
The swelling upland, where the sidelong sun
Aslant the wooded slope, at evening, goes,—

Groves, through whose broken roof the sky looks in,
Mountain, and shattered cliff, and sunny vale,
The distant lake, fountains,—and mighty trees,
In many a lazy syllable, repeating
Their old poetic legends to the wind.

   And this is the sweet spirit, that doth fill
The world; and, in these wayward days of youth,
My busy fancy oft embodies it,
As a bright image of the light and beauty
That dwell in nature,—of the heavenly forms
We worship in our dreams, and the soft hues
That stain the wild bird's wing, and flush the clouds
When the sun sets. Within her eye
The heaven of April, with its changing light,
And when it wears the blue of May, is hung,
And on her lip the rich, red rose. Her hair
Is like the summer tresses of the trees,
When twilight makes them brown, and on her cheek
Blushes the richness of an autumn sky,
With ever-shifting beauty. Then her breath,
It is so like the gentle air of Spring,
As, from the morning's dewy flowers, it comes
Full of their fragrance, that it is a joy
To have it round us,—and her silver voice
Is the rich music of a summer bird,
Heard in the still night, with its passionate cadence.

A Psalm of Life

What the Heart of the Young Man Said to the Psalmist

   Tell me not, in mournful numbers,
     Life is but an empty dream!
For the soul is dead that slumbers,
     And things are not what they seem.

Life is real! Life is earnest!
 And the grave is not its goal;
Dust thou art, to dust returnest,
 Was not spoken of the soul.

Not enjoyment, and not sorrow,
 Is our destined end or way;
But to act, that each to-morrow
 Find us farther than to-day.

Art is long, and Time is fleeting,
 And our hearts, though stout and brave,
Still, like muffled drums, are beating
 Funeral marches to the grave.

In the world's broad field of battle,
 In the bivouac of Life,
Be not like dumb, driven cattle!
 Be a hero in the strife!

Trust no Future, howe'er pleasant!
 Let the dead Past bury its dead!
Act,—act in the living Present!
 Heart within, and God o'erhead!

Lives of great men all remind us
 We can make our lives sublime,
And, departing, leave behind us
 Footprints on the sands of time;

Footprints, that perhaps another,
 Sailing o'er life's solemn main,
A forlorn and shipwrecked brother,
 Seeing, shall take heart again.

Let us, then, be up and doing,
 With a heart for any fate;
Still achieving, still pursuing,
 Learn to labor and to wait.

Hymn to the Night

'Ασπασίη, τρίλλιστος.

I heard the trailing garments of the Night
    Sweep through her marble halls!
I saw her sable skirts all fringed with light
    From the celestial walls!

I felt her presence, by its spell of might,
    Stoop o'er me from above;
The calm, majestic presence of the Night,
    As of the one I love.

I heard the sounds of sorrow and delight,
    The manifold, soft chimes,
That fill the haunted chambers of the Night,
    Like some old poet's rhymes.

From the cool cisterns of the midnight air
    My spirit drank repose;
The fountain of perpetual peace flows there,—
    From those deep cisterns flows.

O holy Night! from thee I learn to bear
    What man has borne before!
Thou layest thy finger on the lips of Care,
    And they complain no more.

Peace! Peace! Orestes-like I breathe this prayer!
    Descend with broad-winged flight,
The welcome! the thrice-prayed for! the most fair!
    The best-beloved Night!

The Wreck of the Hesperus

It was the schooner Hesperus,
    That sailed the wintry sea;
And the skipper had taken his little daughtèr,
    To bear him company.

Blue were her eyes as the fairy-flax,
    Her cheeks like the dawn of day,
And her bosom white as the hawthorn buds,
    That ope in the month of May.

The skipper he stood beside the helm,
    His pipe was in his mouth,
And he watched how the veering flaw did blow
    The smoke now West, now South.

Then up and spake an old Sailòr,
    Had sailed the Spanish Main,
"I pray thee, put into yonder port,
    For I fear a hurricane.

"Last night, the moon had a golden ring,
    And to-night no moon we see!"
The skipper, he blew a whiff from his pipe,
    And a scornful laugh laughed he.

Colder and louder blew the wind,
    A gale from the Northeast;
The snow fell hissing in the brine,
    And the billows frothed like yeast.

Down came the storm, and smote amain,
    The vessel in its strength;
She shuddered and paused, like a frighted steed,
    Then leaped her cable's length.

"Come hither! come hither! my little daughtèr,
    And do not tremble so;
For I can weather the roughest gale,
    That ever wind did blow."

He wrapped her warm in his seaman's coat
    Against the stinging blast;
He cut a rope from a broken spar,
    And bound her to the mast.

"O father! I hear the church-bells ring,
    O say, what may it be?"
" 'T is a fog-bell on a rock-bound coast!"—
    And he steered for the open sea.

"O father! I hear the sound of guns,
    O say, what may it be?"
"Some ship in distress, that cannot live
    In such an angry sea!"

"O father! I see a gleaming light,
    O say, what may it be?"
But the father answered never a word,
    A frozen corpse was he.

Lashed to the helm, all stiff and stark,
    With his face turned to the skies,
The lantern gleamed through the gleaming snow
    On his fixed and glassy eyes.

Then the maiden clasped her hands and prayed
    That savèd she might be;
And she thought of Christ, who stilled the wave
    On the Lake of Galilee.

And fast through the midnight dark and drear,
    Through the whistling sleet and snow,
Like a sheeted ghost, the vessel swept
    Towards the reef of Norman's Woe.

And ever the fitful gusts between
    A sound came from the land;
It was the sound of the trampling surf,
    On the rocks and the hard sea-sand.

The breakers were right beneath her bows,
 She drifted a dreary wreck,
And a whooping billow swept the crew
 Like icicles from her deck.

She struck where the white and fleecy waves
 Looked soft as carded wool,
But the cruel rocks, they gored her side
 Like the horns of an angry bull.

Her rattling shrouds, all sheathed in ice,
 With the masts went by the board;
Like a vessel of glass, she stove and sank,
 Ho! ho! the breakers roared!

At daybreak, on the bleak sea-beach,
 A fisherman stood aghast,
To see the form of a maiden fair,
 Lashed close to a drifting mast.

The salt-sea was frozen on her breast,
 The salt tears in her eyes;
And he saw her hair, like the brown sea-weed,
 On the billows fall and rise.

Such was the wreck of the Hesperus,
 In the midnight and the snow!
Christ save us all from a death like this,
 On the reef of Norman's Woe!

The Village Blacksmith

Under a spreading chestnut tree
 The village smithy stands;
The smith, a mighty man is he,
 With large and sinewy hands;
And the muscles of his brawny arms
 Are strong as iron bands.

His hair is crisp, and black, and long,
　　His face is like the tan;
His brow is wet with honest sweat,
　　He earns whate'er he can,
And looks the whole world in the face,
　　For he owes not any man.

Week in, week out, from morn till night,
　　You can hear his bellows blow;
You can hear him swing his heavy sledge,
　　With measured beat and slow,
Like a sexton ringing the village bell,
　　When the evening sun is low.

And children coming home from school
　　Look in at the open door;
They love to see the flaming forge,
　　And hear the bellows roar,
And catch the burning sparks that fly
　　Like chaff from a threshing floor.

He goes on Sunday to the church,
　　And sits among his boys;
He hears the parson pray and preach,
　　He hears his daughter's voice,
Singing in the village choir,
　　And it makes his heart rejoice.

It sounds to him like her mother's voice,
　　Singing in Paradise!
He needs must think of her once more,
　　How in the grave she lies;
And with his hard, rough hand he wipes
　　A tear out of his eyes.

Toiling,—rejoicing,—sorrowing,
　　Onward through life he goes;
Each morning sees some task begin,
　　Each evening sees it close;
Something attempted, something done,
　　Has earned a night's repose.

Thanks, thanks to thee, my worthy friend,
   For the lesson thou hast taught!
Thus at the flaming forge of life
   Our fortunes must be wrought;
Thus on its sounding anvil shaped
   Each burning deed and thought!

The Skeleton in Armour

"Speak! speak! thou fearful guest!
   Who, with thy hollow breast
   Still in rude armour drest,
      Comest to daunt me!
Wrapt not in Eastern balms,
But with they fleshless palms
Stretched, as if asking alms,
      Why dost thou haunt me?"

Then, from those cavernous eyes
Pale flashes seemed to rise,
As when the Northern skies
      Gleam in December;
And, like the water's flow
Under December's snow,
Came a dull voice of woe
      From the heart's chamber.

"I was a Viking old!
My deeds, though manifold,
No Skald in song has told,
      No Saga taught thee!
Take heed, that in thy verse
Thou dost the tale rehearse,
Else dread a dead man's curse!
      For this I sought thee.

"Far in the Northern Land,
 By the wild Baltic's strand,
 I, with my childish hand,
     Tamed the ger-falcon;
 And, with my skates fast-bound,
 Skimmed the half-frozen Sound,
 That the poor whimpering hound
     Trembled to walk on.

"Oft to his frozen lair
 Tracked I the grisly bear,
 While from my path the hare
     Fled like a shadow;
 Oft through the forest dark
 Followed the were-wolf's bark,
 Until the soaring lark
     Sang from the meadow.

"But when I older grew,
 Joining a corsair's crew,
 O'er the dark sea I flew
     With the marauders.
 Wild was the life we led;
 Many the souls that sped,
 Many the hearts that bled,
     By our stern orders.

"Many a wassail-bout
 Wore the long Winter out;
 Often our midnight shout
     Set the cocks crowing,
 As we the Berserk's tale
 Measured in cups of ale,
 Draining the oaken pail,
     Filled to o'erflowing.

"Once as I told in glee
 Tales of the stormy sea,
 Soft eyes did gaze on me,
     Burning yet tender;

And as the white stars shine
On the dark Norway pine,
On that dark heart of mine
    Fell their soft splendor.

"I wooed the blue-eyed maid,
  Yielding, yet half afraid,
And in the forest's shade
    Our vows were plighted.
Under its loosened vest
Fluttered her little breast,
Like birds within their nest
    By the hawk frighted.

"Bright in her father's hall
  Shields gleamed upon the wall,
Loud sang the minstrels all,
    Chaunting his glory;
When of Old Hildebrand
I asked his daughter's hand,
Mute did the minstrels stand
    To hear my story.

"While the brown ale he quaffed,
  Loud then the champion laughed,
And as the wind-gusts waft
    The sea-foam brightly,
So the loud laugh of scorn,
Out of those lips unshorn,
From the deep drinking-horn
    Blew the foam lightly.

"She was a Prince's child,
  I but a Viking wild,
And though she blushed and smiled,
    I was discarded!
Should not the dove so white
Follow the sea-mew's flight,
Why did they leave that night
    Her nest unguarded?

"Scarce had I put to sea,
  Bearing the maid with me,—
  Fairest of all was she
      Among the Norsemen!—
  When on the white sea-strand,
  Waving his armèd hand,
  Saw we old Hildebrand,
      With twenty horsemen.

"Then launched they to the blast,
  Bent like a reed each mast,
  Yet we were gaining fast,
      When the wind failed us;
  And with a sudden flaw
  Came round the gusty Skaw,
  So that our foe we saw
      Laugh as he hailed us.

"And as to catch the gale
  Round veered the flapping sail,
  Death! was the helmsman's hail,
      Death without quarter!
  Mid-ships with iron keel
  Struck we her ribs of steel;
  Down her black hulk did reel
      Through the black water!

"As with his wings aslant,
  Sails the fierce cormorant,
  Seeking some rocky haunt,
      With his prey laden,
  So toward the open main,
  Beating to sea again,
  Through the wild hurricane,
      Bore I the maiden.

"Three weeks we westward bore,
  And when the storm was o'er,
  Cloud-like we saw the shore
      Stretching to lea-ward;

There for my lady's bower
Built I the lofty tower,
Which, to this very hour,
    Stands looking sea-ward.

"There lived we many years;
  Time dried the maiden's tears;
  She had forgot her fears,
    She was a mother;
Death closed her mild blue eyes,
Under that tower she lies;
Ne'er shall the sun arise
    On such another!

"Still grew my bosom then,
  Still as a stagnant fen!
  Hateful to me were men,
    The sun-light hateful!
In the vast forest here,
Clad in my warlike gear,
Fell I upon my spear,
    O, death was grateful!

"Thus, seamed with many scars
  Bursting these prison bars,
  Up to its native stars
    My soul ascended!
There from the flowing bowl
Deep drinks the warrior's soul,
Skoal! to the Northland! *skoal!*"
    —Thus the tale ended.

The Warning

Beware! The Israelite of old, who tore
  The lion in his path,—when, poor and blind,
He saw the blessed light of heaven no more,
  Shorn of his noble strength and forced to grind

In prison, and at last led forth to be
A pander to Philistine revelry,—

Upon the pillars of the temple laid
    His desperate hands, and in its overthrow
Destroyed himself, and with him those who made
    A cruel mockery of his sightless woe;
The poor, blind Slave, the scoff and jest of all,
Expired, and thousands perished in the fall!

There is a poor, blind Samson in this land,
    Shorn of his strength, and bound in bonds of steel,
Who may, in some grim revel, raise his hand,
    And shake the pillars of this Commonweal,
Till the vast Temple of our liberties
A shapeless mass of wreck and rubbish lies.

Mezzo Cammin

Boppard on the Rhine. August 25, 1842.

Half of my life is gone, and I have let
    The years slip from me and have not fulfilled
    The aspiration of my youth, to build
    Some tower of song with lofty parapet.
Not indolence, nor pleasure, nor the fret
    Of restless passions that would not be stilled,
    But sorrow, and a care that almost killed,
    Kept me from what I may accomplish yet;
Though, half-way up the hill, I see the Past
    Lying beneath me with its sounds and sights,—
    A city in the twilight dim and vast,
With smoking roofs, soft bells, and gleaming lights,—
    And hear above me on the autumnal blast
    The cataract of Death far thundering from the heights.

The Day Is Done

The day is done, and the darkness
  Falls from the wings of Night,
As a feather is wafted downward
  From an eagle in his flight.

I see the lights of the village
  Gleam through the rain and the mist,
And a feeling of sadness comes o'er me,
  That my soul cannot resist:

A feeling of sadness and longing,
  That is not akin to pain,
And resembles sorrow only
  As the mist resembles the rain.

Come, read to me some poem,
  Some simple and heartfelt lay,
That shall soothe this restless feeling,
  And banish the thoughts of day.

Not from the grand old masters,
  Not from the bards sublime,
Whose distant footsteps echo
  Through the corridors of Time.

For, like strains of martial music,
  Their mighty thoughts suggest
Life's endless toil and endeavour;
  And to-night I long for rest.

Read from some humbler poet,
  Whose songs gushed from his heart,
As showers from the clouds of summer,
  Or tears from the eyelids start;

Who, through long days of labor,
  And nights devoid of ease,
Still heard in his soul the music
  Of wonderful melodies.

Such songs have power to quiet
    The restless pulse of care,
And come like the benediction
    That follows after prayer.

Then read from the treasured volume
    The poem of thy choice,
And lend to the rhyme of the poet
    The beauty of thy voice.

And the night shall be filled with music,
    And the cares, that infest the day,
Shall fold their tents, like the Arabs,
    And as silently steal away.

Seaweed

When descends on the Atlantic
    The gigantic
Storm-wind of the equinox,
Landward in his wrath he scourges
    The toiling surges,
Laden with seaweed from the rocks:

From Bermuda's reefs; from edges
    Of sunken ledges,
In some far-off, bright Azore;
From Bahama, and the dashing,
    Silver-flashing
Surges of San Salvador;

From the tumbling surf, that buries
    The Orkneyan skerries,
Answering the hoarse Hebrides;
And from wrecks of ships, and drifting
    Spars, uplifting
On the desolate, rainy seas; —

Ever drifting, drifting, drifting
　　On the shifting
Currents of the restless main;
Till in sheltered coves, and reaches
　　Of sandy beaches,
All have found repose again.

So when storms of wild emotion
　　Strike the ocean
Of the poet's soul, ere long
From each cave and rocky fastness,
　　In its vastness,
Floats some fragment of a song:

From the far-off isles enchanted,
　　Heaven has planted
With the golden fruit of Truth;
From the flashing surf whose vision
　　Gleams Elysian
In the tropic clime of Youth;

From the strong Will, and the Endeavour
　　That for ever
Wrestles with the tides of Fate;
From the wreck of Hopes far-scattered,
　　Tempest-shattered,
Floating waste and desolate; —

Ever drifting, drifting, drifting
　　On the shifting
Currents of the restless heart;
Till at length in books recorded,
　　They, like hoarded
Household words, no more depart.

Afternoon in February

The day is ending,
The night is descending;
The marsh is frozen,
  The river dead.

Through clouds like ashes,
The red sun flashes
On village windows
  That glimmer red.

The snow recommences;
The buried fences
Mark no longer
  The road o'er the plain;

While through the meadows,
Like fearful shadows,
Slowly passes
  A funeral train.

The bell is pealing,
And every feeling
Within me responds
  To the dismal knell;

Shadows are trailing,
My heart is bewailing
And tolling within
  Like a funeral bell.

The Bridge

I stood on the bridge at midnight,
  As the clocks were striking the hour,
And the moon rose o'er the city,
  Behind the dark church-tower.

I saw her bright reflection
  In the waters under me,
Like a golden goblet falling
  And sinking into the sea.

And far in the hazy distance
  Of that lovely night in June,
The blaze of the flaming furnace
  Gleamed redder than the moon.

Among the long, black rafters
  The wavering shadows lay,
And the current that came from the ocean
  Seemed to lift and bear them away;

As, sweeping and eddying through them,
  Rose the belated tide,
And, streaming into the moonlight,
  The seaweed floated wide.

And like those waters rushing
  Among the wooden piers,
A flood of thoughts came o'er me
  That filled my eyes with tears.

How often, O, how often,
  In the days that had gone by,
I had stood on that bridge at midnight
  And gazed on that wave and sky!

How often, O, how often,
  I had wished that the ebbing tide
Would bear me away on its bosom
  O'er the ocean wild and wide!

For my heart was hot and restless,
  And my life was full of care,
And the burden laid upon me
  Seemed greater than I could bear.

But now it has fallen from me,
   It is buried in the sea;
And only the sorrow of others
   Throws its shadow over me.

Yet whenever I cross the river
   On its bridge with wooden piers,
Like the odor of brine from the ocean
   Comes the thought of other years.

And I think how many thousands
   Of care-encumbered men,
Each bearing his burden of sorrow,
   Have crossed the bridge since then.

I see the long procession
   Still passing to and fro,
The young heart hot and restless,
   And the old subdued and slow!

And forever and forever,
   As long as the river flows,
As long as the heart has passions,
   As long as life has woes;

The moon and its broken reflection
   And its shadows shall appear,
As the symbol of love in heaven,
   And its wavering image here.

Curfew

I.

Solemnly, mournfully,
   Dealing its dole,
The Curfew Bell
   Is beginning to toll.

Cover the embers,
　And put out the light;
Toil comes with the morning,
　And rest with the night.

Dark grow the windows,
　And quenched is the fire;
Sound fades into silence,
　All footsteps retire.

No voice in the chambers,
　No sound in the hall!
Sleep and oblivion
　Reign over all!

II.

The book is completed,
　And closed, like the day;
And the hand that has written it
　Lays it away.

Dim grow its fancies;
　Forgotten they lie;
Like coals in the ashes,
　They darken and die.

Song sinks into silence,
　The story is told,
The windows are darkened,
　The hearth-stone is cold.

Darker and darker
　The black shadows fall;
Sleep and oblivion
　Reign over all.

The Evening Star

Lo! in the painted oriel of the West,
Whose panes the sunken sun incarnadines,
Like a fair lady at her casement, shines
The evening star, the star of love and rest!
And then anon she doth herself divest
Of all her radiant garments, and reclines
Behind the sombre screen of yonder pines,
With slumber and soft dreams of love oppressed.

O my beloved, my sweet Hesperus!
My morning and my evening star of love!
My best and gentlest lady! even thus,
As that fair planet in the sky above,
Dost thou retire unto thy rest at night,
And from thy darkened window fades the light.

Autumn

Thou comest, Autumn, heralded by the rain,
With banners, by great gales incessant fanned,
Brighter than brightest silks of Samarcand,
And stately oxen harnessed to thy wain!
Thou standest, like imperial Charlemagne,
Upon thy bridge of gold; thy royal hand
Outstretched with benedictions o'er the land,
Blessing the farms through all thy vast domain!

Thy shield is the red harvest moon, suspended
So long beneath the heaven's o'erhanging eaves;
Thy steps are by the farmer's prayers attended;
Like flames upon an altar shine the sheaves;
And, following thee, in thy ovation splendid,
Thine almoner, the wind, scatters the golden leaves!

Couplet: February 24, 1847

In Hexameter sings serenely a Harvard Professor;
In Pentameter him damns censorious Poe.

Fragment: December 18, 1847

Soft through the silent air descend the feathery snow-flakes;
White are the distant hills, white are the neighboring fields;
Only the marshes are brown, and the river rolling among
    them
Weareth the leaden hue seen in the eyes of the blind.

The Fire of Drift-Wood

We sat within the farm-house old,
    Whose windows, looking o'er the bay,
Gave to the sea-breeze, damp and cold,
    An easy entrance, night and day.

Not far away we saw the port,—
    The strange, old-fashioned, silent town,—
The light-house,—the dismantled fort,—
    The wooden houses, quaint and brown.

We sat and talked until the night,
    Descending, filled the little room;
Our faces faded from the sight,
    Our voices only broke the gloom.

We spake of many a vanished scene,
    Of what we once had thought and said,
Of what had been, and might have been,
    And who was changed, and who was dead;

And all that fills the hearts of friends,
    When first they feel, with secret pain,
Their lives thenceforth have separate ends,
    And never can be one again;

The first slight swerving of the heart,
    That words are powerless to express,
And leave it still unsaid in part,
    Or say it in too great excess.

The very tones in which we spake
    Had something strange, I could but mark;
The leaves of memory seemed to make
    A mournful rustling in the dark.

Oft died the words upon our lips,
    As suddenly, from out the fire
Built of the wreck of stranded ships,
    The flames would leap and then expire.

And, as their splendor flashed and failed,
    We thought of wrecks upon the main,—
Of ships dismasted, that were hailed
    And sent no answer back again.

The windows, rattling in their frames,—
    The ocean, roaring up the beach,—
The gusty blast,—the bickering flames,—
    All mingled vaguely in our speech;

Until they made themselves a part
    Of fancies floating through the brain,—
The long-lost ventures of the heart,
    That send no answers back again.

O flames that glowed! O hearts that yearned!
    They were indeed too much akin,
The drift-wood fire without that burned,
    The thoughts that burned and glowed within.

from *Evangeline*

This is the forest primeval. The murmuring pines and the
 hemlocks,
Bearded with moss, and in garments green, indistinct in the
 twilight,
Stand like Druids of eld, with voices sad and prophetic,
Stand like harpers hoar, with beards that rest on their
 bosoms.
Loud from its rocky caverns, the deep-voiced neighbouring
 ocean
Speaks, and in accents disconsolate answers the wail of the
 forest.

 This is the forest primeval; but where are the hearts that
 beneath it
Leaped like the roe, when he hears in the woodland the
 voice of the huntsman?
Where is the thatch-roofed village, the home of Acadian
 farmers, —
Men whose lives glided on like rivers that water the
 woodlands,
Darkened by shadows of earth, but reflecting an image of
 heaven?
Waste are those pleasant farms, and the farmers forever
 departed!
Scattered like dust and leaves, when the mighty blasts of
 October
Seize them, and whirl them aloft, and sprinkle them far
 o'er the ocean.
Naught but tradition remains of the beautiful village
 of Grand-Pré.

lines 1–15

 In-doors, warm by the wide-mouthed fireplace, idly the
 farmer
Sat in his elbow-chair, and watched how the flames and the
 smoke-wreaths
Struggled together like foes in a burning city. Behind him,

Nodding and mocking along the wall, with gestures fantastic,
Darted his own huge shadow, and vanished away into
    darkness.
Faces, clumsily carved in oak, on the back of his arm-chair
Laughed in the flickering light, and the pewter plates on the
    dresser
Caught and reflected the flame, as shields of armies the
    sunshine.
Fragments of song the old man sang, and carols of
    Christmas,
Such as at home, in the olden time, his fathers before him
Sang in their Norman orchards and bright Burgundian
    vineyards.
Close at her father's side was the gentle Evangeline seated,
Spinning flax for the loom, that stood in the corner behind
    her.
Silent awhile were its treadles, at rest was its diligent shuttle,
While the monotonous drone of the wheel, like the drone of
    a bagpipe,
Followed the old man's song, and united the fragments
    together.
As in a church, when the chant of the choir at intervals
    ceases,
Footfalls are heard in the aisles, or words of the priest at the
    altar,
So, in each pause of the song, with measured motion the
    clock clicked.

Part I, ii, lines 52–70

Softly the evening came. The sun from the western horizon
Like a magician extended his golden wand o'er the
    landscape;
Twinkling vapors arose; and sky and water and forest
Seemed all on fire at the touch, and melted and mingled
    together.
Hanging between two skies, a cloud with edges of silver,
Floated the boat, with its dripping oars, on the motionless
    water.

Filled was Evangeline's heart with inexpressible sweetness.
Touched by the magic spell, the sacred fountains of feeling
Glowed with the light of love, as the skies and waters
    around her.
Then from a neighbouring thicket the mocking-bird, wildest
    of singers,
Swinging aloft on a willow spray that hung o'er the water,
Shook from his little throat such floods of delirious music,
That the whole air and the woods and the waves seemed
    silent to listen.
Plaintive at first were the tones and sad; then soaring to
    madness
Seemed they to follow or guide the revel of frenzied
    Bacchantes.
Then single notes were heard, in sorrowful, low lamentation;
Till, having gathered them all, he flung them abroad in
    derision,
As when, after a storm, a gust of wind through the tree-tops
Shakes down the rattling rain in a crystal shower on the
    branches.
With such a prelude as this, and hearts that throbbed with
    emotion,
Slowly they entered the Têche, where it flows through the
    green Opelousas,
And through the amber air, above the crest of the
    woodland,
Saw the column of smoke that arose from a neighbouring
    dwelling;—
Sounds of a horn they heard, and the distant lowing of
    cattle.

Part II, ii, lines 124–147

Far in the West there lies a desert land, where the mountains
Lift, through perpetual snows, their lofty and luminous
    summits.
Down from their desolate, deep ravines, where the gorge,
    like a gateway,
Opens a passage rude to the wheels of the emigrant's
    wagon,

Westward the Oregon flows and the Walleway and Owyhee.
Eastward, with devious course, among the Wind-river
      Mountains,
Through the Sweet-water Valley precipitate leaps the
      Nebraska;
And to the south, from Fontaine-qui-bout and the Spanish
      sierras,
Fretted with sands and rocks, and swept by the wind of the
      desert,
Numberless torrents, with ceaseless sound, descend to the
      ocean,
Like the great chords of a harp, in loud and solemn
      vibrations.
Spreading between these streams are the wondrous, beautiful
      prairies,
Billowy bays of grass ever rolling in shadow and sunshine,
Bright with luxuriant clusters of roses and purple amorphas.
Over them wander the buffalo herds, and the elk and the
      roebuck;
Over them wander the wolves, and herds of riderless horses;
Fires that blast and blight, and winds that are weary with
      travel;
Over them wander the scattered tribes of Ishmael's children,
Staining the desert with blood; and above their terrible war-
      trails
Circles and sails aloft, on pinions majestic, the vulture,
Like the implacable soul of a chieftain slaughtered in battle,
By invisible stairs ascending and scaling the heavens.
Here and there rise smokes from the camps of these savage
      marauders;
Here and there rise groves from the margins of swift-
      running rivers;
And the grim, taciturn bear, the anchorite monk of the
      desert,
Climbs down their dark ravines to dig for roots by the
      brook-side,
And over all is the sky, the clear and crystalline heaven,
Like the protecting hand of God inverted above them.

Part II, iv, lines 1–28

The Jewish Cemetery at Newport

How strange it seems! These Hebrews in their graves,
   Close by the street of this fair seaport town,
Silent beside the never-silent waves,
   At rest in all this moving up and down!

The trees are white with dust, that o'er their sleep
   Wave their broad curtains in the south-wind's breath,
While underneath such leafy tents they keep
   The long, mysterious Exodus of Death.

And these sepulchral stones, so old and brown,
   That pave with level flags their burial-place,
Seem like the tablets of the Law, thrown down
   And broken by Moses at the mountain's base.

The very names recorded here are strange,
   Of foreign accent, and of different climes;
Alvares and Rivera interchange
   With Abraham and Jacob of old times.

"Blessed be God! for he created Death!"
   The mourners said, "and Death is rest and peace";
Then added, in the certainty of faith,
   "And giveth Life that never more shall cease."

Closed are the portals of their Synagogue,
   No Psalms of David now the silence break,
No Rabbi reads the ancient Decalogue
   In the grand dialect the Prophets spake.

Gone are the living, but the dead remain,
   And not neglected; for a hand unseen,
Scattering its bounty, like a summer rain,
   Still keeps their graves and their remembrance green.

How came they here? What burst of Christian hate,
　　What persecution, merciless and blind,
Drove o'er the sea—that desert desolate—
　　These Ishmaels and Hagars of mankind?

They lived in narrow streets and lanes obscure,
　　Ghetto and Judenstrass, in mirk and mire;
Taught in the school of patience to endure
　　The life of anguish and the death of fire.

All their lives long, with the unleavened bread
　　And bitter herbs of exile and its fears,
The wasting famine of the heart they fed,
　　And slaked its thirst with marah of their tears.

Anathema maranatha! was the cry
　　That rang from town to town, from street to street;
At every gate the accursed Mordecai
　　Was mocked and jeered, and spurned by Christian feet.

Pride and humiliation hand in hand
　　Walked with them through the world where'er they went;
Trampled and beaten were they as the sand,
　　And yet unshaken as the continent.

For in the background figures vague and vast
　　Of patriarchs and of prophets rose sublime,
And all the great traditions of the Past
　　They saw reflected in the coming time.

And thus for ever with reverted look
　　The mystic volume of the world they read,
Spelling it backward, like a Hebrew book,
　　Till life became a Legend of the Dead.

But ah! what once has been shall be no more!
　　The groaning earth in travail and in pain
Brings forth its races, but does not restore,
　　And the dead nations never rise again.

from *The Song of Hiawatha*

XIV: PICTURE-WRITING.

In those days said Hiawatha,
"Lo! how all things fade and perish!
From the memory of the old men
Fade away the great traditions,
The achievements of the warriors,
The adventures of the hunters,
All the wisdom of the Medas,
All the craft of the Wabenos,
All the marvellous dreams and visions
Of the Jossakeeds, the Prophets!

    "Great men die and are forgotten,
Wise men speak; their words of wisdom
Perish in the ears that hear them,
Do not reach the generations
That, as yet unborn, are waiting
In the great, mysterious darkness
Of the speechless days that shall be!

    "On the grave-posts of our fathers
Are no signs, no figures painted;
Who are in those graves we know not,
Only know they are our fathers.
Of what kith they are and kindred,
From what old, ancestral Totem,
Be it Eagle, Bear, or Beaver,
They descended, this we know not,
Only know they are our fathers.

    "Face to face we speak together,
But we cannot speak when absent,
Cannot send our voices from us
To the friends that dwell afar off;
Cannot send a secret message,
But the bearer learns our secret,
May pervert it, may betray it,
May reveal it unto others."

    Thus said Hiawatha, walking

In the solitary forest,
Pondering, musing in the forest,
On the welfare of his people.
  From his pouch he took his colors,
Took his paints of different colors,
On the smooth bark of a birch-tree
Painted many shapes and figures,
Wonderful and mystic figures,
And each figure had a meaning,
Each some word or thought suggested.
  Gitche Manito the Mighty,
He, the Master of Life, was painted
As an egg, with points projecting
To the four winds of the heavens.
Everywhere is the Great Spirit,
Was the meaning of this symbol.
  Mitche Manito the Mighty,
He the dreadful Spirit of Evil,
As a serpent was depicted,
As Kenabeek, the great serpent.
Very crafty, very cunning,
Is the creeping Spirit of Evil,
Was the meaning of this symbol.
  Life and Death he drew as circles,
Life was white, but Death was darkened;
Sun and moon and stars he painted,
Man and beast, and fish and reptile,
Forests, mountains, lakes, and rivers.
  For the earth he drew a straight line,
For the sky a bow above it;
White the space between for day-time,
Filled with little stars for night-time;
On the left a point for sunrise,
On the right a point for sunset,
On the top a point for noon-tide,
And for rain and cloudy weather
Waving lines descending from it.
  Footprints pointing towards a wigwam
Were a sign of invitation,
Were a sign of guests assembling;

Bloody hands with palms uplifted
Were a symbol of destruction,
Were a hostile sign and symbol.

All these things did Hiawatha
Show unto his wondering people,
And interpreted their meaning,
And he said: "Behold, your grave-posts
Have no mark, no sign, nor symbol.
Go and paint them all with figures;
Each one with its household symbol,
With its own ancestral Totem;
So that those who follow after
May distinguish them and know them."

And they painted on the grave-posts
Of the graves yet unforgotten,
Each his own ancestral Totem,
Each the symbol of his household;
Figures of the Bear and Reindeer,
Of the Turtle, Crane, and Beaver,
Each inverted as a token
That the owner was departed,
That the chief who bore the symbol
Lay beneath in dust and ashes.

And the Jossakeeds, the Prophets,
The Wabenos, the Magicians,
And the Medicine-men, the Medas,
Painted upon bark and deer-skin
Figures for the songs they chanted,
For each song a separate symbol,
Figures mystical and awful,
Figures strange and brightly colored;
And each figure had its meaning,
Each some magic song suggested.

The Great Spirit, the Creator,
Flashing light through all the heaven;
The Great Serpent, the Kenabeek,
With his bloody crest erected,
Creeping, looking into heaven;
In the sky the sun, that listens,
And the moon eclipsed and dying;

Owl and eagle, crane and hen-hawk,
And the cormorant, bird of magic;
Headless men, that walk the heavens,
Bodies lying pierced with arrows,
Bloody hands of death uplifted,
Flags on graves, and great war-captains
Grasping both the earth and heaven!

Such as these the shapes they painted
On the birch-bark and the deer-skin;
Songs of war and songs of hunting,
Songs of medicine and of magic,
All were written in these figures,
For each figure had its meaning,
Each its separate song recorded.

Nor forgotten was the Love-Song,
The most subtle of all medicines,
The most potent spell of magic,
Dangerous more than war or hunting!
Thus the Love-Song was recorded,
Symbol and interpretation.

First a human figure standing,
Painted in the brightest scarlet;
'T is the lover, the musician,
And the meaning is, "My painting
Makes me powerful over others."

Then the figure seated, singing,
Playing on a drum of magic,
And the interpretation, "Listen!
'T is my voice you hear, my singing!"

Then the same red figure seated
In the shelter of a wigwam,
And the meaning of the symbol,
"I will come and sit beside you
In the mystery of my passion!"

Then two figures, man and woman,
Standing hand in hand together,
With their hands so clasped together
That they seem in one united,
And the words thus represented
Are, "I see your heart within you,

And your cheeks are red with blushes!"
　Next the maiden on an island,
In the centre of an island;
And the song this shape suggested
Was, "Though you were at a distance,
Were upon some far-off island,
Such the spell I cast upon you,
Such the magic power of passion,
I could straightway draw you to me!"
　Then the figure of the maiden
Sleeping, and the lover near her,
Whispering to her in her slumbers,
Saying, "Though you were far from me
In the land of Sleep and Silence,
Still the voice of love would reach you!"
　And the last of all the figures
Was a heart within a circle,
Drawn within a magic circle;
And the image had this meaning:
"Naked lies your heart before me,
To your naked heart I whisper!"
　Thus it was that Hiawatha,
In his wisdom, taught the people
All the mysteries of painting,
All the art of Picture-Writing,
On the smooth bark of the birch-tree,
On the white skin of the reindeer,
On the grave-posts of the village.

from XXII: HIAWATHA'S DEPARTURE

　Heavy with the heat and silence
Grew the afternoon of Summer;
With a drowsy sound the forest
Whispered round the sultry wigwam,
With a sound of sleep the water
Rippled on the beach below it;
From the corn-fields shrill and ceaseless
Sang the grasshopper, Pah-puk-keena;

And the guests of Hiawatha,
Weary with the heat of Summer,
Slumbered in the sultry wigwam.

Slowly o'er the simmering landscape
Fell the evening's dusk and coolness,
And the long and level sunbeams
Shot their spears into the forest,
Breaking through its shields of shadow,
Rushed into each secret ambush,
Searched each thicket, dingle, hollow;
Still the guests of Hiawatha
Slumbered in the silent wigwam.

From his place rose Hiawatha,
Bade farewell to old Nokomis,
Spake in whispers, spake in this wise,
Did not wake the guests, that slumbered:

"I am going, O Nokomis,
On a long and distant journey,
To the portals of the Sunset,
To the regions of the home-wind,
Of the Northwest wind, Keewaydin.
But these guests I leave behind me,
In your watch and ward I leave them;
See that never harm comes near them,
See that never fear molests them,
Never danger nor suspicion,
Never want of food or shelter,
In the lodge of Hiawatha!"

Forth into the village went he,
Bade farewell to all the warriors,
Bade farewell to all the young men,
Spake persuading, spake in this wise:

"I am going, O my people,
On a long and distant journey;
Many moons and many winters
Will have come, and will have vanished,
Ere I come again to see you.
But my guests I leave behind me;
Listen to their words of wisdom,
Listen to the truth they tell you,

For the Master of Life has sent them
From the land of light and morning!"
   On the shore stood Hiawatha,
Turned and waved his hand at parting;
On the clear and luminous water
Launched his birch canoe for sailing,
From the pebbles of the margin
Shoved it forth into the water;
Whispered to it, "Westward! westward!"
And with speed it darted forward.

   And the evening sun descending
Set the clouds on fire with redness,
Burned the broad sky, like a prairie,
Left upon the level water
One long track and trail of splendor,
Down whose stream, as down a river,
Westward, westward Hiawatha
Sailed into the fiery sunset,
Sailed into the purple vapors,
Sailed into the dusk of evening.

   And the people from the margin
Watched him floating, rising, sinking,
Till the birch canoe seemed lifted
High into that sea of splendor,
Till it sank into the vapors
Like the new moon slowly, slowly
Sinking in the purple distance.

   And they said, "Farewell for ever!"
Said, "Farewell, O Hiawatha!"
And the forests, dark and lonely,
Moved through all their depths of darkness,
Sighed, "Farewell, O Hiawatha!"
And the waves upon the margin
Rising, rippling on the pebbles,
Sobbed, "Farewell, O Hiawatha!"
And the heron, the Shuh-shuh-gah,
From her haunts among the fen-lands,
Screamed, "Farewell, O Hiawatha!"

   Thus departed Hiawatha,
Hiawatha the Beloved,

In the glory of the sunset,
In the purple mists of evening,
To the regions of the home-wind,
Of the Northwest wind Keewaydin,
To the Islands of the Blessed,
To the kingdom of Ponemah,
To the land of the Hereafter!

My Lost Youth

Often I think of the beautiful town
  That is seated by the sea;
Often in thought go up and down
The pleasant streets of that dear old town,
  And my youth comes back to me.
    And a verse of a Lapland song
    Is haunting my memory still:
  "A boy's will is the wind's will,
And the thoughts of youth are long, long thoughts."

I can see the shadowy lines of its trees,
  And catch, in sudden gleams,
The sheen of the far-surrounding seas,
And islands that were the Hesperides
  Of all my boyish dreams.
    And the burden of that old song,
    It murmurs and whispers still:
  "A boy's will is the wind's will,
And the thoughts of youth are long, long thoughts."

I remember the black wharves and the slips,
  And the sea-tides tossing free;
And Spanish sailors with bearded lips,
And the beauty and mystery of the ships,
  And the magic of the sea.
    And the voice of that wayward song
    Is singing and saying still:
  "A boy's will is the wind's will,
And the thoughts of youth are long, long thoughts."

I remember the bulwarks by the shore,
 And the fort upon the hill;
The sun-rise gun, with its hollow roar,
The drum-beat repeated o'er and o'er,
 And the bugle wild and shrill.
  And the music of that old song
  Throbs in my memory still:
"A boy's will is the wind's will,
And the thoughts of youth are long, long thoughts."

I remember the sea-fight far away,
 How it thundered o'er the tide!
And the dead captains, as they lay
In their graves, o'erlooking the tranquil bay,
 Where they in battle died.
  And the sound of that mournful song
  Goes through me with a thrill:
"A boy's will is the wind's will,
And the thoughts of youth are long, long thoughts."

I can see the breezy dome of groves,
 The shadows of Deering's Woods;
And the friendships old and the early loves
Come back with a sabbath sound, as of doves
 In quiet neighborhoods.
  And the verse of that sweet old song,
  It flutters and murmurs still:
"A boy's will is the wind's will,
And the thoughts of youth are long, long thoughts."

I remember the gleams and glooms that dart
 Across the schoolboy's brain;
The song and the silence in the heart,
That in part are prophecies, and in part
 Are longings wild and vain.
  And the voice of that fitful song
  Sings on, and is never still:
"A boy's will is the wind's will,
And the thoughts of youth are long, long thoughts."

There are things of which I may not speak;
  There are dreams that cannot die;
There are thoughts that make the strong heart weak,
And bring a pallor into the cheek,
  And a mist before the eye.
    And the words of that fatal song
    Come over me like a chill:
  "A boy's will is the wind's will,
And the thoughts of youth are long, long thoughts."

Strange to me now are the forms I meet
  When I visit the dear old town;
But the native air is pure and sweet,
And the trees that o'ershadow each well-known
      street,
  As they balance up and down,
    Are singing the beautiful song,
    Are sighing and whispering still:
  "A boy's will is the wind's will,
And the thoughts of youth are long, long thoughts."

And Deering's Woods are fresh and fair,
  And with joy that is almost pain
My heart goes back to wander there,
And among the dreams of the days that were,
  I find my lost youth again.
    And the strange and beautiful song,
    The groves are repeating it still:
  "A boy's will is the wind's will,
And the thoughts of youth are long, long thoughts."

The Children's Hour

Between the dark and the daylight,
  When the night is beginning to lower,
Comes a pause in the day's occupations,
  That is known as the Children's Hour.

I hear in the chamber above me
  The patter of little feet,
The sound of a door that is opened,
  And voices soft and sweet.

From my study I see in the lamplight,
  Descending the broad hall stair,
Grave Alice, and laughing Allegra,
  And Edith with golden hair.

A whisper, and then a silence:
  Yet I know by their merry eyes
They are plotting and planning together
  To take me by surprise.

A sudden rush from the stairway,
  A sudden raid from the hall!
By three doors left unguarded
  They enter my castle wall!

They climb up into my turret
  O'er the arms and back of my chair;
If I try to escape, they surround me;
  They seem to be everywhere.

They almost devour me with kisses,
  Their arms about me entwine,
Till I think of the Bishop of Bingen
  In his Mouse-Tower on the Rhine!

Do you think, O blue-eyed banditti,
  Because you have scaled the wall,
Such an old moustache as I am
  Is not a match for you all!

I have you fast in my fortress,
    And will not let you depart,
But put you down into the dungeon
    In the round-tower of my heart.

And there will I keep you forever,
    Yes, forever and a day,
Till the walls shall crumble to ruin,
    And moulder in dust away!

from *Tales of a Wayside Inn*

Prelude: The Wayside Inn

One Autumn night, in Sudbury town,
Across the meadows bare and brown,
The windows of the wayside inn
Gleamed red with fire-light through the leaves
Of woodbine, hanging from the eaves
Their crimson curtains rent and thin.

As ancient is this hostelry
As any in the land may be,
Built in the old Colonial day,
When men lived in a grander way,
With ampler hospitality;
A kind of old Hobgoblin Hall,
Now somewhat fallen to decay,
With weather-stains upon the wall,
And stairways worn, and crazy doors,
And creaking and uneven floors,
And chimneys huge, and tiled and tall.

A region of repose it seems,
A place of slumber and of dreams,
Remote among the wooded hills!
For there no noisy railway speeds,
Its torch-race scattering smoke and gleeds;

But noon and night, the panting teams
Stop under the great oaks, that throw
Tangles of light and shade below,
On roofs and doors and window-sills.
Across the road the barns display
Their lines of stalls, their mows of hay,
Through the wide doors the breezes blow,
The wattled cocks strut to and fro,
And, half effaced by rain and shine,
The Red Horse prances on the sign.
Round this old-fashioned, quaint abode
Deep silence reigned, save when a gust
Went rushing down the county road,
And skeletons of leaves, and dust,
A moment quickened by its breath,
Shuddered and danced their dance of death,
And through the ancient oaks o'erhead
Mysterious voices moaned and fled.

But from the parlor of the inn
A pleasant murmur smote the ear,
Like water rushing through a weir;
Oft interrupted by the din
Of laughter and of loud applause,
And, in each intervening pause,
The music of a violin.
The fire-light, shedding over all
The splendor of its ruddy glow,
Filled the whole parlor large and low;
It gleamed on wainscot and on wall,
It touched with more than wonted grace
Fair Princess Mary's pictured face;
It bronzed the rafters overhead,
On the old spinet's ivory keys
It played inaudible melodies,
It crowned the sombre clock with flame,
The hands, the hours, the maker's name,
And painted with a livelier red
The Landlord's coat-of-arms again;

And, flashing on the window-pane,
Emblazoned with its light and shade
The jovial rhymes, that still remain,
Writ near a century ago,
By the great Major Molineaux,
Whom Hawthorne has immortal made.

Before the blazing fire of wood
Erect the rapt musician stood;
And ever and anon he bent
His head upon his instrument,
And seemed to listen, till he caught
Confessions of its secret thought, —
The joy, the triumph, the lament,
The exultation and the pain;
Then, by the magic of his art,
He soothed the throbbings of its heart,
And lulled it into peace again.

Around the fireside at their ease
There sat a group of friends, entranced
With the delicious melodies;
Who from the far-off noisy town
Had to the wayside inn come down,
To rest beneath its old oak-trees.
The fire-light on their faces glanced,
Their shadows on the wainscot danced,
And, though of different lands and speech,
Each had his tale to tell, and each
Was anxious to be pleased and please.
And while the sweet musician plays,
Let me in outline sketch them all,
Perchance uncouthly as the blaze
With its uncertain touch portrays
Their shadowy semblance on the wall.

But first the Landlord will I trace;
Grave in his aspect and attire;
A man of ancient pedigree,
A Justice of the Peace was he,

Known in all Sudbury as "The Squire."
Proud was he of his name and race,
Of old Sir William and Sir Hugh,
And in the parlor, full in view,
His coat-of-arms, well framed and glazed,
Upon the walls in colors blazed;
He beareth gules upon his shield,
A chevron argent in the field,
With three wolf's heads, and for the crest
A Wyvern part-per-pale addressed
Upon a helmet barred; below
The scroll reads, "By the name of Howe."
And over this, no longer bright,
Though glimmering with a latent light,
Was hung the sword his grandsire bore,
In the rebellious days of yore,
Down there at Concord in the fight.

A youth was there, of quiet ways,
A Student of old books and days,
To whom all tongues and lands were known,
And yet a lover of his own;
With many a social virtue graced,
And yet a friend of solitude;
A man of such a genial mood
The heart of all things he embraced,
And yet of such fastidious taste,
He never found the best too good.
Books were his passion and delight,
And in his upper room at home
Stood many a rare and sumptuous tome,
In vellum bound, with gold bedight,
Great volumes garmented in white,
Recalling Florence, Pisa, Rome.
He loved the twilight that surrounds
The border-land of old romance;
Where glitter hauberk, helm, and lance,
And banner waves, and trumpet sounds,
And ladies ride with hawk on wrist,
And mighty warriors sweep along,

Magnified by the purple mist,
The dusk of centuries and of song.
The chronicles of Charlemagne,
Of Merlin and the Mort d'Arthure,
Mingled together in his brain
With tales of Flores and Blanchefleur,
Sir Ferumbras, Sir Eglamour,
Sir Launcelot, Sir Morgadour,
Sir Guy, Sir Bevis, Sir Gawain.

A young Sicilian, too, was there;—
In sight of Etna born and bred,
Some breath of its volcanic air
Was glowing in his heart and brain,
And, being rebellious to his liege,
After Palermo's fatal siege,
Across the western seas he fled,
In good King Bomba's happy reign.
His face was like a summer night,
All flooded with a dusky light;
His hands were small; his teeth shone white
As sea-shells, when he smiled or spoke;
His sinews supple and strong as oak;
Clean shaven was he as a priest,
Who at the mass on Sunday sings,
Save that upon his upper lip
His beard, a good palm's length at least,
Level and pointed at the tip,
Shot sideways, like a swallow's wings.
The poets read he o'er and o'er,
And most of all the Immortal Four
Of Italy; and next to those,
The story-telling bard of prose,
Who wrote the joyous Tuscan tales
Of the Decameron, that make
Fiesole's green hills and vales
Remembered for Boccaccio's sake.
Much too of music was his thought;
The melodies and measures fraught
With sunshine and the open air,

Of vineyards and the singing sea
Of his beloved Sicily;
And much it pleased him to peruse
The songs of the Sicilian muse, —
Bucolic songs by Meli sung
In the familiar peasant tongue,
That made men say, "Behold! once more
The pitying gods to earth restore
Theocritus of Syracuse!"

A Spanish Jew from Alicant
With aspect grand and grave was there;
Vender of silks and fabrics rare,
And attar of rose from the Levant.
Like an old Patriarch he appeared,
Abraham or Isaac, or at least
Some later Prophet or High-Priest;
With lustrous eyes, and olive skin,
And, wildly tossed from cheeks and chin,
The tumbling cataract of his beard.
His garments breathed a spicy scent
Of cinnamon and sandal blent,
Like the soft aromatic gales
That meet the mariner, who sails
Through the Moluccas, and the seas
That wash the shores of Celebes.
All stories that recorded are
By Pierre Alphonse he knew by heart,
And it was rumored he could say
The Parables of Sandabar,
And all the Fables of Pilpay,
Or if not all, the greater part!
Well versed was he in Hebrew books,
Talmud and Targum, and the lore
Of Kabala; and evermore
There was a mystery in his looks;
His eyes seemed gazing far away,
As if in vision or in trance
He heard the solemn sackbut play,
And saw the Jewish maidens dance.

A Theologian, from the school
Of Cambridge on the Charles, was there;
Skilful alike with tongue and pen,
He preached to all men everywhere
The Gospel of the Golden Rule,
The New Commandment given to men,
Thinking the deed, and not the creed,
Would help us in our utmost need.
With reverent feet the earth he trod,
Nor banished nature from his plan,
But studied still with deep research
To build the Universal Church,
Lofty as is the love of God,
And ample as the wants of man.

A Poet, too, was there, whose verse
Was tender, musical, and terse;
The inspiration, the delight,
The gleam, the glory, the swift flight,
Of thoughts so sudden, that they seem
The revelations of a dream,
All these were his; but with them came
No envy of another's fame;
He did not find his sleep less sweet
For music in some neighboring street,
Nor rustling hear in every breeze
The laurels of Miltiades.
Honor and blessings on his head
While living, good report when dead,
Who, not too eager for renown,
Accepts, but does not clutch, the crown!

Last the Musician, as he stood
Illumined by that fire of wood;
Fair-haired, blue-eyed, his aspect blithe,
His figure tall and straight and lithe,
And every feature of his face
Revealing his Norwegian race;
A radiance, streaming from within,

Around his eyes and forehead beamed,
The Angel with the violin,
Painted by Raphael, he seemed.
He lived in that ideal world
Whose language is not speech, but song;
Around him evermore the throng
Of elves and sprites their dances whirled;
The Strömkarl sang, the cataract hurled
Its headlong waters from the height;
And mingled in the wild delight
The scream of sea-birds in their flight,
The rumor of the forest trees,
The plunge of the implacable seas,
The tumult of the wind at night,
Voices of eld, like trumpets blowing,
Old ballads, and wild melodies
Through mist and darkness pouring forth,
Like Elivagar's river flowing
Out of the glaciers of the North.

The instrument on which he played
Was in Cremona's workshops made,
By a great master of the past,
Ere yet was lost the art divine;
Fashioned of maple and of pine,
That in Tyrolian forests vast
Had rocked and wrestled with the blast:
Exquisite was it in design,
Perfect in each minutest part,
A marvel of the lutist's art;
And in its hollow chamber, thus,
The maker from whose hands it came
Had written his unrivalled name,—
"Antonius Stradivarius."

And when he played, the atmosphere
Was filled with magic, and the ear
Caught echoes of that Harp of Gold,
Whose music had so weird a sound,

The hunted stag forgot to bound,
The leaping rivulet backward rolled,
The birds came down from bush and tree,
The dead came from beneath the sea,
The maiden to the harper's knee!

The music ceased; the applause was loud,
The pleased musician smiled and bowed;
The wood-fire clapped its hands of flame,
The shadows on the wainscot stirred,
And from the harpsichord there came
A ghostly murmur of acclaim,
A sound like that sent down at night
By birds of passage in their flight,
From the remotest distance heard.

Then silence followed; then began
A clamor for the Landlord's tale,—
The story promised them of old,
They said, but always left untold;
And he, although a bashful man,
And all his courage seemed to fail,
Finding excuse of no avail,
Yielded; and thus the story ran.

The Landlord's Tale: Paul Revere's Ride

Listen, my children, and you shall hear
Of the midnight ride of Paul Revere,
On the eighteenth of April, in Seventy-five;
Hardly a man is now alive
Who remembers that famous day and year.

He said to his friend, "If the British march
By land or sea from the town to-night,
Hang a lantern aloft in the belfry arch
Of the North Church tower as a signal light,—
One, if by land, and two, if by sea;

And I on the opposite shore will be,
Ready to ride and spread the alarm
Through every Middlesex village and farm,
For the country-folk to be up and to arm."

Then he said, "Good night!" and with muffled oar
Silently rowed to the Charlestown shore,
Just as the moon rose over the bay,
Where swinging wide at her moorings lay
The Somerset, British man-of-war;
A phantom ship, with each mast and spar
Across the moon like a prison bar,
And a huge black hulk, that was magnified
By its own reflection in the tide.

Meanwhile, his friend, through alley and street,
Wanders and watches with eager ears,
Till in the silence around him he hears
The muster of men at the barrack door,
The sound of arms, and the tramp of feet,
And the measured tread of the grenadiers,
Marching down to their boats on the shore.

Then he climbed the tower of the Old North Church,
By the wooden stairs, with stealthy tread,
To the belfry-chamber overhead,
And startled the pigeons from their perch
On the sombre rafters, that round him made
Masses and moving shapes of shade, —
By the trembling ladder, steep and tall,
To the highest window in the wall,
Where he paused to listen and look down
A moment on the roofs of the town,
And the moonlight flowing over all.

Beneath, in the churchyard, lay the dead,
In their night-encampment on the hill,
Wrapped in silence so deep and still
That he could hear, like a sentinel's tread,
The watchful night-wind, as it went

Creeping along from tent to tent,
And seeming to whisper, "All is well!"
A moment only he feels the spell
Of the place and the hour, and the secret dread
Of the lonely belfry and the dead;
For suddenly all his thoughts are bent
On a shadowy something far away,
Where the river widens to meet the bay,—
A line of black that bends and floats
On the rising tide, like a bridge of boats.

Meanwhile, impatient to mount and ride,
Booted and spurred, with a heavy stride
On the opposite shore walked Paul Revere.
Now he patted his horse's side,
Now gazed at the landscape far and near,
Then, impetuous, stamped the earth,
And turned and tightened his saddle-girth;
But mostly he watched with eager search
The belfry-tower of the Old North Church,
As it rose above the graves on the hill,
Lonely and spectral and sombre and still.
And lo! as he looks, on the belfry's height
A glimmer, and then a gleam of light!
He springs to the saddle, the bridle he turns,
But lingers and gazes, till full on his sight
A second lamp in the belfry burns!

A hurry of hoofs in a village street,
A shape in the moonlight, a bulk in the dark,
And beneath, from the pebbles, in passing, a spark
Struck out by a steed flying fearless and fleet:
That was all! And yet, through the gloom and the light,
The fate of a nation was riding that night;
And the spark struck out by that steed, in his flight,
Kindled the land into flame with its heat.

He has left the village and mounted the steep,
And beneath him, tranquil and broad and deep,
Is the Mystic, meeting the ocean tides;

And under the alders, that skirt its edge,
Now soft on the sand, now loud on the ledge,
Is heard the tramp of his steed as he rides.

It was twelve by the village clock
When he crossed the bridge into Medford town.
He heard the crowing of the cock,
And the barking of the farmer's dog,
And felt the damp of the river fog,
That rises after the sun goes down.

It was one by the village clock,
When he galloped into Lexington.
He saw the gilded weathercock
Swim in the moonlight as he passed,
And the meeting-house windows, blank and bare,
Gaze at him with a spectral glare,
As if they already stood aghast
At the bloody work they would look upon.

It was two by the village clock,
When he came to the bridge in Concord town.
He heard the bleating of the flock,
And the twitter of birds among the trees,
And felt the breath of the morning breeze
Blowing over the meadows brown.
And one was safe and asleep in his bed
Who at the bridge would be first to fall,
Who that day would be lying dead,
Pierced by a British musket-ball.

You know the rest. In the books you have read,
How the British Regulars fired and fled, —
How the farmers gave them ball for ball,
From behind each fence and farm-yard wall,
Chasing the red-coats down the lane,
Then crossing the fields to emerge again
Under the trees at the turn of the road,
And only pausing to fire and load.

So through the night rode Paul Revere;
And so through the night went his cry of alarm
To every Middlesex village and farm,—
A cry of defiance and not of fear,
A voice in the darkness, a knock at the door,
And a word that shall echo forevermore!
For, borne on the night-wind of the Past,
Through all our history, to the last,
In the hour of darkness and peril and need,
The people will waken and listen to hear
The hurrying hoof-beats of that steed,
And the midnight message of Paul Revere.

The Spanish Jew's Tale: Azrael

King Solomon, before his palace gate
At evening, on the pavement tesselate
Was walking with a stranger from the East,
Arrayed in rich attire as for a feast,
The mighty Runjeet-Sing, a learned man,
And Rajah of the realms of Hindostan.
And as they walked the guest became aware
Of a white figure in the twilight air,
Gazing intent, as one who with surprise
His form and features seemed to recognize;
And in a whisper to the king he said:
"What is yon shape, that, pallid as the dead,
Is watching me, as if he sought to trace
In the dim light the features of my face?"

The king looked, and replied: "I know him well;
It is the Angel men call Azrael,
'T is the Death Angel; what hast thou to fear?"
And the guest answered: "Lest he should come near,
And speak to me, and take away my breath!
Save me from Azrael, save me from death!
O king, that hast dominion o'er the wind,
Bid it arise and bear me hence to Ind."

The king gazed upward at the cloudless sky,
Whispered a word, and raised his hand on high,
And lo! the signet-ring of chrysoprase
On his uplifted finger seemed to blaze
With hidden fire, and rushing from the west
There came a mighty wind, and seized the guest
And lifted him from earth, and on they passed,
His shining garments streaming in the blast,
A silken banner o'er the walls upreared,
A purple cloud, that gleamed and disappeared.
Then said the Angel, smiling: "If this man
Be Rajah Runjeet-Sing of Hindostan,
Thou hast done well in listening to his prayer;
I was upon my way to seek him there."

Snow-Flakes

Out of the bosom of the Air,
    Out of the cloud-folds of her garments shaken,
Over the woodlands brown and bare
    Over the harvest-fields forsaken,
        Silent, and soft, and slow
        Descends the snow.

Even as our cloudy fancies take
    Suddenly shape in some divine expression,
Even as the troubled heart doth make
    In the white countenance confession,
        The troubled sky reveals
        The grief it feels.

This is the poem of the air,
    Slowly in silent syllables recorded;
This is the secret of despair,
    Long in its cloudy bosom hoarded,
        Now whispered and revealed
        To wood and field.

Divina Commedia

I.

Oft have I seen at some cathedral door
　　A laborer, pausing in the dust and heat,
　　Lay down his burden, and with reverent feet
　　Enter, and cross himself, and on the floor
Kneel to repeat his paternoster o'er;
　　Far off the noises of the world retreat;
　　The loud vociferations of the street
　　Become an undistinguishable roar.
So, as I enter here from day to day,
　　And leave my burden at this minster gate,
　　Kneeling in prayer, and not ashamed to pray,
The tumult of the time disconsolate
　　To inarticulate murmurs dies away,
　　While the eternal ages watch and wait.

II.

How strange the sculptures that adorn these towers!
　　This crowd of statues, in whose folded sleeves
　　Birds build their nests; while canopied with leaves
　　Parvis and portal bloom like trellised bowers,
And the vast minster seems a cross of flowers!
　　But fiends and dragons on the gargoyled eaves
　　Watch the dead Christ between the living thieves,
　　And, underneath, the traitor Judas lowers!
Ah! from what agonies of heart and brain,
　　What exultations trampling on despair,
　　What tenderness, what tears, what hate of wrong,
What passionate outcry of a soul in pain,
　　Uprose this poem of the earth and air,
　　This mediæval miracle of song!

III.

I enter, and I see thee in the gloom
　　Of the long aisles, O poet saturnine!
　　And strive to make my steps keep pace with thine.

The air is filled with some unknown perfume;
The congregation of the dead make room
    For thee to pass; the votive tapers shine;
    Like rooks that haunt Ravenna's groves of pine
    The hovering echoes fly from tomb to tomb.
From the confessionals I hear arise
    Rehearsals of forgotten tragedies,
    And lamentations from the crypts below;
And then a voice celestial, that begins
    With the pathetic words, "Although your sins
    As scarlet be," and ends with "as the snow."

IV.

With snow-white veil and garments as of flame,
    She stands before thee, who so long ago
    Filled thy young heart with passion and the woe
    From which thy song and all its splendors came;
And while with stern rebuke she speaks thy name,
    The ice about thy heart melts as the snow
    On mountain heights, and in swift overflow
    Comes gushing from thy lips in sobs of shame.
Thou makest full confession; and a gleam,
    As of the dawn on some dark forest cast,
    Seems on thy lifted forehead to increase;
Lethe and Eunoe—the remembered dream
    And the forgotten sorrow—bring at last
    That perfect pardon which is perfect peace.

V.

I lift mine eyes, and all the windows blaze
    With forms of saints and holy men who died,
    Here martyred and hereafter glorified;
    And the great Rose upon its leaves displays
Christ's Triumph, and the angelic roundelays,
    With splendor upon splendor multiplied;
    And Beatrice again at Dante's side
    No more rebukes, but smiles her words of praise.
And then the organ sounds, and unseen choirs
    Sing the old Latin hymns of peace and love,

And benedictions of the Holy Ghost;
And the melodious bells among the spires
O'er all the house-tops and through heaven above
Proclaim the elevation of the Host!

VI.

O star of morning and of liberty!
O bringer of the light, whose splendor shines
Above the darkness of the Apennines,
Forerunner of the day that is to be!
The voices of the city and the sea,
The voices of the mountains and the pines,
Repeat thy song, till the familiar lines
Are footpaths for the thought of Italy!
Thy fame is blown abroad from all the heights,
Through all the nations, and a sound is heard,
As of a mighty wind, and men devout,
Strangers of Rome, and the new proselytes,
In their own language hear thy wondrous word,
And many are amazed and many doubt.

Aftermath

When the Summer fields are mown,
When the birds are fledged and flown,
And the dry leaves strew the path;
With the falling of the snow,
With the cawing of the crow,
Once again the fields we mow
And gather in the aftermath.

Not the sweet, new grass with flowers
Is this harvesting of ours;
Not the upland clover bloom;
But the rowen mixed with weeds,
Tangled tufts from marsh and meads,
Where the poppy drops its seeds
In the silence and the gloom.

Belisarius

I am poor and old and blind;
The sun burns me, and the wind
    Blows through the city gate
And covers me with dust
From the wheels of the august
    Justinian the Great.

It was for him I chased
The Persians o'er wild and waste,
    As General of the East;
Night after night I lay
In their camps of yesterday;
    Their forage was my feast.

For him, with sails of red,
And torches at mast-head,
    Piloting the great fleet,
I swept the Afric coasts
And scattered the Vandal hosts,
    Like dust in a windy street.

For him I won again
The Ausonian realm and reign,
    Rome and Parthenope;
And all the land was mine
From the summits of Apennine
    To the shores of either sea.

    For him, in my feeble age,
I dared the battle's rage,
    To save Byzantium's state,
When the tents of Zabergan,
Like snow-drifts overran
    The road to the Golden Gate.

And for this, for this, behold!
Infirm and blind and old,
    With gray, uncovered head,
Beneath the very arch
Of my triumphal march,
    I stand and beg my bread!

Methinks I still can hear,
Sounding distinct and near,
 The Vandal monarch's cry,
As, captive and disgraced,
With majestic step he paced, —
 "All, all is Vanity!"

Ah! vainest of all things
Is the gratitude of kings;
 The plaudits of the crowd
Are but the clatter of feet
At midnight in the street,
 Hollow and restless and loud.

But the bitterest disgrace
Is to see forever the face
 Of the Monk of Ephesus!
The unconquerable will
This, too, can bear; — I still
 Am Belisarius!

Chaucer

An old man in a lodge within a park;
 The chamber walls depicted all around
 With portraitures of huntsman, hawk, and hound,
And the hurt deer. He listeneth to the lark,
Whose song comes with the sunshine through the dark
 Of painted glass in leaden lattice bound;
 He listeneth and he laugheth at the sound,
Then writeth in a book like any clerk.
He is the poet of the dawn, who wrote
 The Canterbury Tales, and his old age
 Made beautiful with song; and as I read
I hear the crowing cock, I hear the note
 Of lark and linnet, and from every page
 Rise odors of ploughed field or flowery mead.

Kéramos

Turn, turn, my wheel! Turn round and round
Without a pause, without a sound:
  So spins the flying world away!
This clay, well mixed with marl and sand,
Follows the motion of my hand;
For some must follow, and some command,
  Though all are made of clay!

Thus sang the Potter at his task
Beneath the blossoming hawthorn-tree,
While o'er his features, like a mask,
The quilted sunshine and leaf-shade
Moved, as the boughs above him swayed,
And clothed him, till he seemed to be
A figure woven in tapestry,
So sumptuously was he arrayed
In that magnificent attire
Of sable tissue flaked with fire.
Like a magician he appeared,
A conjurer without book or beard;
And while he plied his magic art—
For it was magical to me—
I stood in silence and apart,
And wondered more and more to see
That shapeless, lifeless mass of clay
Rise up to meet the master's hand,
And now contract and now expand,
And even his slightest touch obey;
While ever in a thoughtful mood
He sang his ditty, and at times
Whistled a tune between the rhymes,
As a melodious interlude.

Turn, turn, my wheel! All things must change
To something new, to something strange;
  Nothing that is can pause or stay;

The moon will wax, the moon will wane,
The mist and cloud will turn to rain,
The rain to mist and cloud again,
    To-morrow be to-day.

Thus still the Potter sang, and still,
By some unconscious act of will,
The melody and even the words
Were intermingled with my thought,
As bits of colored thread are caught
And woven into nests of birds.
And thus to regions far remote,
Beyond the ocean's vast expanse,
This wizard in the motley coat
Transported me on wings of song,
And by the northern shores of France
Bore me with restless speed along.

What land is this that seems to be
A mingling of the land and sea?
This land of sluices, dikes, and dunes?
This water-net, that tessellates
The landscape? this unending maze
Of gardens, through whose latticed gates
The imprisoned pinks and tulips gaze;
Where in long summer afternoons
The sunshine, softened by the haze,
Comes streaming down as through a screen;
Where over fields and pastures green
The painted ships float high in air,
And over all and everywhere
The sails of windmills sink and soar
Like wings of sea-gulls on the shore?

What land is this? Yon pretty town
Is Delft, with all its wares displayed;
The pride, the market-place, the crown
And centre of the Potter's trade.
See! every house and room is bright
With glimmers of reflected light

From plates that on the dresser shine;
Flagons to foam with Flemish beer,
Or sparkle with the Rhenish wine,
And pilgrim flasks with fleurs-de-lis,
And ships upon a rolling sea,
And tankards pewter topped, and queer
With comic mask and musketeer!
Each hospitable chimney smiles
A welcome from its painted tiles;
The parlor walls, the chamber floors,
The stairways and the corridors,
The borders of the garden walks,
Are beautiful with fadeless flowers,
That never droop in winds or showers,
And never wither on their stalks.

Turn, turn, my wheel! All life is brief;
What now is bud will soon be leaf,
    What now is leaf will soon decay;
The wind blows east, the wind blows west;
The blue eggs in the robin's nest
Will soon have wings and beak and breast,
    And flutter and fly away.

Now southward through the air I glide,
The song my only pursuivant,
And see across the landscape wide
The blue Charente, upon whose tide
The belfries and the spires of Saintes
Ripple and rock from side to side,
As, when an earthquake rends its walls,
A crumbling city reels and falls.

Who is it in the suburbs here,
This Potter, working with such cheer,
In this mean house, this mean attire,
His manly features bronzed with fire,
Whose figulines and rustic wares
Scarce find him bread from day to day?
This madman, as the people say,

Who breaks his tables and his chairs
To feed his furnace fires, nor cares
Who goes unfed if they are fed,
Nor who may live if they are dead?
This alchemist with hollow cheeks
And sunken, searching eyes, who seeks,
By mingled earths and ores combined
With potency of fire, to find
Some new enamel, hard and bright,
His dream, his passion, his delight?

O Palissy! within thy breast
Burned the hot fever of unrest;
Thine was the prophet's vision, thine
The exultation, the divine
Insanity of noble minds,
That never falters nor abates,
But labors and endures and waits,
Till all that it foresees it finds,
Or what it cannot find creates!

Turn, turn, my wheel! This earthen jar
A touch can make, a touch can mar;
*   And shall it to the Potter say,*
What makest thou? Thou hast no hand?
As men who think to understand
A world by their Creator planned,
*   Who wiser is than they.*

Still guided by the dreamy song,
As in a trance I float along
Above the Pyrenean chain,
Above the fields and farms of Spain,
Above the bright Majorcan isle
That lends its softened name to art,—
A spot, a dot upon the chart,
Whose little towns, red-roofed with tile,
Are ruby-lustred with the light
Of blazing furnaces by night,
And crowned by day with wreaths of smoke.

Then eastward, wafted in my flight
On my enchanter's magic cloak,
I sail across the Tyrrhene Sea
Into the land of Italy,
And o'er the windy Apennines,
Mantled and musical with pines.

The palaces, the princely halls,
The doors of houses and the walls
Of churches and of belfry towers,
Cloister and castle, street and mart,
Are garlanded and gay with flowers
That blossom in the fields of art.
Here Gubbio's workshops gleam and glow
With brilliant, iridescent dyes,
The dazzling whiteness of the snow,
The cobalt blue of summer skies;
And vase and scutcheon, cup and plate,
In perfect finish emulate
Faenza, Florence, Pesaro.

Forth from Urbino's gate there came
A youth with the angelic name
Of Raphael, in form and face
Himself angelic, and divine
In arts of color and design.
From him Francesco Xanto caught
Something of his transcendent grace,
And into fictile fabrics wrought
Suggestions of the master's thought.
Nor less Maestro Giorgio shines
With madre-perl and golden lines
Of arabesques, and interweaves
His birds and fruits and flowers and leaves
About some landscape, shaded brown,
With olive tints on rock and town.

Behold this cup within whose bowl,
Upon a ground of deepest blue
With yellow-lustred stars o'erlaid,

Colors of every tint and hue
Mingle in one harmonious whole!
With large blue eyes and steadfast gaze,
Her yellow hair in net and braid,
Necklace and ear-rings all ablaze
With golden lustre o'er the glaze,
A woman's portrait; on the scroll,
Cana, the Beautiful! A name
Forgotten save for such brief fame
As this memorial can bestow,—
A gift some lover long ago
Gave with his heart to this fair dame.

A nobler title to renown
Is thine, O pleasant Tuscan town,
Seated beside the Arno's stream;
For Lucca della Robbia there
Created forms so wondrous fair,
They made thy sovereignty supreme.
These choristers with lips of stone,
Whose music is not heard, but seen,
Still chant, as from their organ-screen,
Their Maker's praise; nor these alone,
But the more fragile forms of clay,
Hardly less beautiful than they,
These saints and angels that adorn
The walls of hospitals, and tell
The story of good deeds so well
That poverty seems less forlorn,
And life more like a holiday.

Here in this old neglected church,
That long eludes the traveller's search,
Lies the dead bishop on his tomb;
Earth upon earth he slumbering lies,
Life-like and death-like in the gloom;
Garlands of fruit and flowers in bloom
And foliage deck his resting-place;
A shadow in the sightless eyes,
A pallor on the patient face,

Made perfect by the furnace heat;
All earthly passions and desires
Burnt out by purgatorial fires;
Seeming to say, "Our years are fleet,
And to the weary death is sweet."

But the most wonderful of all
The ornaments on tomb or wall
That grace the fair Ausonian shores
Are those the faithful earth restores,
Near some Apulian town concealed,
In vineyard or in harvest field,—
Vases and urns and bas-reliefs,
Memorials of forgotten griefs,
Or records of heroic deeds
Of demigods and mighty chiefs:
Figures that almost move and speak,
And, buried amid mould and weeds,
Still in their attitudes attest
The presence of the graceful Greek,—
Achilles in his armor dressed,
Alcides with the Cretan bull,
And Aphrodite with her boy,
Or lovely Helena of Troy,
Still living and still beautiful.

Turn, turn, my wheel! 'T is nature's plan
The child should grow into the man,
*   The man grow wrinkled, old, and gray;*
In youth the heart exults and sings,
The pulses leap, the feet have wings;
In age the cricket chirps, and brings
*   The harvest home of day.*

And now the winds that southward blow,
And cool the hot Sicilian isle,
Bear me away. I see below
The long line of the Libyan Nile,
Flooding and feeding the parched lands
With annual ebb and overflow,

A fallen palm whose branches lie
Beneath the Abyssinian sky,
Whose roots are in Egyptian sands.
On either bank huge water-wheels,
Belted with jars and dripping weeds,
Send forth their melancholy moans,
As if, in their gray mantles hid,
Dead anchorites of the Thebaid
Knelt on the shore and told their beads,
Beating their breasts with loud appeals
And penitential tears and groans.

This city, walled and thickly set
With glittering mosque and minaret,
Is Cairo, in whose gay bazaars
The dreaming traveller first inhales
The perfume of Arabian gales,
And sees the fabulous earthen jars,
Huge as were those wherein the maid
Morgiana found the Forty Thieves
Concealed in midnight ambuscade;
And seeing, more than half believes
The fascinating tales that run
Through all the Thousand Nights and One,
Told by the fair Scheherezade.

More strange and wonderful than these
Are the Egyptian deities,
Ammon, and Emoth, and the grand
Osiris, holding in his hand
The lotus; Isis, crowned and veiled;
The sacred Ibis, and the Sphinx;
Bracelets with blue enamelled links;
The Scarabee in emerald mailed,
Or spreading wide his funeral wings;
Lamps that perchance their night-watch kept
O'er Cleopatra while she slept,—
All plundered from the tombs of kings.

Turn, turn, my wheel! The human race,
Of every tongue, of every place,
    Caucasian, Coptic, or Malay,
All that inhabit this great earth,
Whatever be their rank or worth,
Are kindred and allied by birth,
    And made of the same clay.

O'er desert sands, o'er gulf and bay,
O'er Ganges and o'er Himalay,
Bird-like I fly, and flying sing,
To flowery kingdoms of Cathay,
And bird-like poise on balanced wing
Above the town of King-te-tching,
A burning town, or seeming so,—
Three thousand furnaces that glow
Incessantly, and fill the air
With smoke uprising, gyre on gyre,
And painted by the lurid glare,
Of jets and flashes of red fire.

As leaves that in the autumn fall,
Spotted and veined with various hues,
Are swept along the avenues,
And lie in heaps by hedge and wall,
So from this grove of chimneys whirled
To all the markets of the world,
These porcelain leaves are wafted on,—
Light yellow leaves with spots and stains
Of violet and of crimson dye,
Or tender azure of a sky
Just washed by gentle April rains,
And beautiful with celadon.

Nor less the coarser household wares,—
The willow pattern, that we knew
In childhood, with its bridge of blue
Leading to unknown thoroughfares;
The solitary man who stares
At the white river flowing through

Its arches, the fantastic trees
And wild perspective of the view;
And intermingled among these
The tiles that in our nurseries
Filled us with wonder and delight,
Or haunted us in dreams at night.

And yonder by Nankin, behold!
The Tower of Porcelain, strange and old,
Uplifting to the astonished skies
Its ninefold painted balconies,
With balustrades of twining leaves,
And roofs of tile, beneath whose eaves
Hang porcelain bells that all the time
Ring with a soft, melodious chime;
While the whole fabric is ablaze
With varied tints, all fused in one
Great mass of color, like a maze
Of flowers illumined by the sun.

Turn, turn, my wheel! What is begun
At daybreak must at dark be done,
To-morrow will be another day;
To-morrow the hot furnace flame
Will search the heart and try the frame,
And stamp with honor or with shame
These vessels made of clay.

Cradled and rocked in Eastern seas,
The islands of the Japanese
Beneath me lie; o'er lake and plain
The stork, the heron, and the crane
Through the clear realms of azure drift,
And on the hillside I can see
The villages of Imari,
Whose thronged and flaming workshops lift
Their twisted columns of smoke on high,
Cloud cloisters that in ruins lie,
With sunshine streaming through each rift,
And broken arches of blue sky.

All the bright flowers that fill the land,
Ripple of waves on rock or sand,
The snow on Fusiyama's cone,
The midnight heaven so thickly sown
With constellations of bright stars,
The leaves that rustle, the reeds that make
A whisper by each stream and lake,
The saffron dawn, the sunset red,
Are painted on these lovely jars;
Again the skylark sings, again
The stork, the heron, and the crane
Float through the azure overhead,
The counterfeit and counterpart
Of Nature reproduced in Art.

Art is the child of Nature; yes,
Her darling child, in whom we trace
The features of the mother's face,
Her aspect and her attitude,
All her majestic loveliness
Chastened and softened and subdued
Into a more attractive grace,
And with a human sense imbued.
He is the greatest artist, then,
Whether of pencil or of pen,
Who follows Nature. Never man,
As artist or as artisan,
Pursuing his own fantasies,
Can touch the human heart, or please,
Or satisfy our nobler needs,
As he who sets his willing feet
In Nature's footprints, light and fleet,
And follows fearless where she leads.

Thus mused I on that morn in May,
Wrapped in my visions like the Seer,
Whose eyes behold not what is near,
But only what is far away,
When, suddenly sounding peal on peal,
The church-bell from the neighboring town

Proclaimed the welcome hour of noon.
The Potter heard, and stopped his wheel,
His apron on the grass threw down,
Whistled his quiet little tune,
Not overloud nor overlong,
And ended thus his simple song:

Stop, stop, my wheel! Too soon, too soon
The noon will be the afternoon,
*   Too soon to-day be yesterday;*
Behind us in our path we cast
The broken potsherds of the past,
And all are ground to dust at last,
*   And trodden into clay!*

Venice

White swan of cities, slumbering in thy nest
    So wonderfully built among the reeds
    Of the lagoon, that fences thee and feeds,
    As sayeth thy old historian and thy guest!
White water-lily, cradled and caressed
    By ocean streams, and from the silt and weeds
    Lifting thy golden filaments and seeds,
    Thy sun-illumined spires, thy crown and crest!
White phantom city, whose untrodden streets
    Are rivers, and whose pavements are the shifting
    Shadows of palaces and strips of sky;
I wait to see thee vanish like the fleets
    Seen in mirage, or towers of cloud uplifting
    In air their unsubstantial masonry.

The Harvest Moon

It is the Harvest Moon! On gilded vanes
    And roofs of villages, on woodland crests
    And their aerial neighborhoods of nests
    Deserted, on the curtained window-panes
Of rooms where children sleep, on country lanes
    And harvest-fields, its mystic splendor rests!
    Gone are the birds that were our summer guests,
    With the last sheaves return the laboring wains!
All things are symbols: the external shows
    Of Nature have their image in the mind,
    As flowers and fruits and falling of the leaves;
The song-birds leave us at the summer's close,
    Only the empty nests are left behind,
    And pipings of the quail among the sheaves.

The Cross of Snow

In the long, sleepless watches of the night,
    A gentle face—the face of one long dead—
    Looks at me from the wall, where round its head
    The night-lamp casts a halo of pale light.
Here in this room she died; and soul more white
    Never through martyrdom of fire was led
    To its repose; nor can in books be read
    The legend of a life more benedight.
There is a mountain in the distant West
    That, sun-defying, in its deep ravines
    Displays a cross of snow upon its side.
Such is the cross I wear upon my breast
    These eighteen years, through all the changing scenes
    And seasons, changeless since the day she died.

The Tide Rises, the Tide Falls

The tide rises, the tide falls,
The twilight darkens, the curlew calls;
Along the sea-sands damp and brown
The traveller hastens toward the town,
   And the tide rises, the tide falls.

Darkness settles on roofs and walls,
But the sea, the sea in the darkness calls;
The little waves, with their soft, white hands,
Efface the footprints in the sands,
   And the tide rises, the tide falls.

The morning breaks; the steeds in their stalls
Stamp and neigh, as the hostler calls;
The day returns, but nevermore
Returns the traveller to the shore,
   And the tide rises, the tide falls.

Night

Into the darkness and the hush of night
   Slowly the landscape sinks, and fades away,
   And with it fade the phantoms of the day,
   The ghosts of men and things, that haunt the light.
The crowd, the clamor, the pursuit, the flight,
   The unprofitable splendor and display,
   The agitations, and the cares that prey
   Upon our hearts, all vanish out of sight.
The better life begins; the world no more
   Molests us; all its records we erase
   From the dull common-place book of our lives,
That like a palimpsest is written o'er
   With trivial incidents of time and place,
   And lo! the ideal, hidden beneath, revives.

The Poet's Calendar

January.

I.

Janus am I; oldest of potentates;
    Forward I look, and backward, and below,
I count, as god of avenues and gates,
    The years that through my portals come and go.

II.

I block the roads, and drift the fields with snow;
    I chase the wild-fowl from the frozen fen;
My frosts congeal the rivers in their flow,
    My fires light up the hearths and hearts of men.

February.

I am lustration; and the sea is mine!
    I wash the sands and headlands with my tide;
My brow is crowned with branches of the pine;
    Before my chariot-wheels the fishes glide.
By me all things unclean are purified,
    By me the souls of men washed white again;
E'en the unlovely tombs of those who died
    Without a dirge, I cleanse from every stain.

March.

I Martius am! Once first, and now the third!
    To lead the Year was my appointed place;
A mortal dispossessed me by a word,
    And set there Janus with the double face.
Hence I make war on all the human race;
    I shake the cities with my hurricanes;
I flood the rivers and their banks efface,
    And drown the farms and hamlets with my rains.

April.

I open wide the portals of the Spring
    To welcome the procession of the flowers,
With their gay banners, and the birds that sing
    Their song of songs from their aerial towers.
I soften with my sunshine and my showers
    The heart of earth; with thoughts of love I glide
Into the hearts of men; and with the hours
    Upon the Bull with wreathèd horns I ride.

May.

Hark! The sea-faring wild-fowl loud proclaim
    My coming, and the swarming of the bees.
These are my heralds, and behold! my name
    Is written in blossoms on the hawthorn-trees.
I tell the mariner when to sail the seas;
    I waft o'er all the land from far away
The breath and bloom of the Hesperides,
    My birthplace. I am Maia. I am May.

June.

Mine is the Month of Roses; yes, and mine
    The Month of Marriages! All pleasant sights
And scents, the fragrance of the blossoming vine,
    The foliage of the valleys and the heights.
Mine are the longest days, the loveliest nights;
    The mower's scythe makes music to my ear;
I am the mother of all dear delights;
    I am the fairest daughter of the year.

July.

My emblem is the Lion, and I breathe
    The breath of Libyan deserts o'er the land;
My sickle as a sabre I unsheathe,
    And bent before me the pale harvests stand.

The lakes and rivers shrink at my command,
    And there is thirst and fever in the air;
The sky is changed to brass, the earth to sand;
    I am the Emperor whose name I bear.

August.

The Emperor Octavian, called the August,
    I being his favorite, bestowed his name
Upon me, and I hold it still in trust,
    In memory of him and of his fame.
I am the Virgin, and my vestal flame
    Burns less intensely than the Lion's rage;
Sheaves are my only garlands, and I claim
    The golden Harvests as my heritage.

September.

I bear the Scales, where hang in equipoise
    The night and day; and when unto my lips
I put my trumpet, with its stress and noise
    Fly the white clouds like tattered sails of ships;
The tree-tops lash the air with sounding whips;
    Southward the clamorous sea-fowl wing their flight;
The hedges are all red with haws and hips,
    The Hunter's Moon reigns empress of the night.

October.

My ornaments are fruits; my garments leaves,
    Woven like cloth of gold, and crimson dyed;
I do not boast the harvesting of sheaves,
    O'er orchards and o'er vineyards I preside.
Though on the frigid Scorpion I ride,
    The dreamy air is full, and overflows
With tender memories of the summer-tide,
    And mingled voices of the doves and crows.

November.

The Centaur, Sagittarius, am I,
　Born of Ixion's and the cloud's embrace;
With sounding hoofs across the earth I fly,
　A steed Thessalian with a human face.
Sharp winds the arrows are with which I chase
　The leaves, half dead already with affright;
I shroud myself in gloom; and to the race
　Of mortals bring nor comfort nor delight.

December.

Riding upon the Goat, with snow-white hair,
　I come, the last of all. This crown of mine
Is of the holly; in my hand I bear
　The thyrsus, tipped with fragrant cones of pine.
I celebrate the birth of the Divine,
　And the return of the Saturnian reign;—
My songs are carols sung at every shrine,
　Proclaiming "Peace on earth, good will to men."

from *Elegiac Verse*

Peradventure of old, some bard in Ionian Islands,
　Walking alone by the sea, hearing the wash of the waves,
Learned the secret from them of the beautiful verse elegiac,
　Breathing into his song motion and sound of the sea.

For as a wave of the sea, upheaving in long undulations,
　Plunges loud on the sands, pauses, and turns, and retreats,
So the Hexameter, rising and sinking, with cadence
　　sonorous,
　Falls; and in refluent rhythm back the Pentameter flows.

Wisely the Hebrews admit no Present tense in their
      language:
  While we are speaking the word, it is already the Past.

———————

In the twilight of age all things seem strange and
      phantasmal,
  As between daylight and dark ghost-like the landscape
    appears.

The Bells of San Blas

What say the Bells of San Blas
To the ships that southward pass
    From the harbor of Mazatlan?
To them it is nothing more
Than the sound of surf on the shore,—
    Nothing more to master or man.

But to me, a dreamer of dreams,
To whom what is and what seems
    Are often one and the same,—
The Bells of San Blas to me
Have a strange, wild melody,
    And are something more than a name.

For bells are the voice of the church;
They have tones that touch and search
    The hearts of young and old;
One sound to all, yet each
Lends a meaning to their speech,
    And the meaning is manifold.

They are a voice of the Past,
Of an age that is fading fast,
    Of a power austere and grand;
When the flag of Spain unfurled
Its folds o'er this western world,
    And the Priest was lord of the land.

The chapel that once looked down
On the little seaport town
　　Has crumbled into the dust;

And on oaken beams below
The bells swing to and fro,
　　And are green with mould and rust.

"Is, then, the old faith dead,"
　They say, "and in its stead
　　　Is some new faith proclaimed,
That we are forced to remain
Naked to sun and rain,
　　Unsheltered and ashamed?

"Once in our tower aloof
　We rang over wall and roof
　　　Our warnings and our complaints;
And round about us there
The white doves filled the air,
　　Like the white souls of the saints.

"The saints! Ah, have they grown
　Forgetful of their own?
　　　Are they asleep, or dead,
That open to the sky
Their ruined Missions lie,
　　No longer tenanted?

"Oh, bring us back once more
　The vanished days of yore,
　　　When the world with faith was filled;
Bring back the fervid zeal,
The hearts of fire and steel,
　　The hands that believe and build.

"Then from our tower again
We will send over land and main
        Our voices of command,
Like exiled kings who return
To their thrones, and the people learn
        That the Priest is lord of the land!"

O Bells of San Blas, in vain
Ye call back the Past again!
        The Past is deaf to your prayer:
Out of the shadows of night
The world rolls into light;
        It is daybreak everywhere.

JOHN GREENLEAF WHITTIER

(1807–1892)

Proem

I love the old melodious lays
Which softly melt the ages through,
    The songs of Spenser's golden days,
    Arcadian Sidney's silvery phrase,
Sprinkling our noon of time with freshest morning dew.

    Yet, vainly in my quiet hours
To breathe their marvellous notes I try;
    I feel them, as the leaves and flowers
    In silence feel the dewy showers,
And drink with glad still lips the blessing of the sky.

    The rigor of a frozen clime,
The harshness of an untaught ear,
    The jarring words of one whose rhyme
    Beat often Labor's hurried time,
Or Duty's rugged march through storm and strife, are here.

    Of mystic beauty, dreamy grace,
No rounded art the lack supplies;
    Unskilled the subtle lines to trace
    Or softer shades of Nature's face,
I view her common forms with unanointed eyes.

    Nor mine the seer-like power to show
The secrets of the heart and mind;
    To drop the plummet-line below
    Our common world of joy and woe,
A more intense despair or brighter hope to find.

Yet here at least an earnest sense
Of human right and weal is shown;
   A hate of tyranny intense,
   And hearty in its vehemence,
As if my brother's pain and sorrow were my own.

   Oh Freedom! if to me belong
Nor mighty Milton's gift divine,
   Nor Marvel's wit and graceful song,
   Still with a love as deep and strong
As theirs, I lay, like them, my best gifts on thy shrine!

Song of Slaves in the Desert

   Where are we going? where are we going,
     Where are we going, Rubee?

Lord of peoples, lord of lands,
Look across these shining sands,
Through the furnace of the noon,
Through the white light of the moon.
Strong the Ghiblee wind is blowing,
Strange and large the world is growing!
Speak and tell us where we are going,
     Where are we going, Rubee?

Bornou land was rich and good,
Wells of water, fields of food,
Dourra fields, and bloom of bean,
And the palm-tree cool and green:
Bornou land we see no longer,
Here we thirst and here we hunger,
Here the Moor-man smites in anger:
     Where are we going, Rubee?

When we went from Bornou land,
We were like the leaves and sand,—
We were many, we are few;
Life has one, and death has two:

Whitened bones our path are showing,
Thou All-seeing, thou All-knowing!
Hear us, tell us where are we going,
    Where are we going, Rubee?

Moons of marches from our eyes
Bornou land behind us lies;
Stranger round us day by day
Bends the desert circle gray;
Wild the waves of sand are flowing,
Hot the winds above them blowing,—
Lord of all things!—where are we going?
    Where are we going, Rubee?

We are weak, but Thou art strong;
Short our lives, but Thine is long;
We are blind, but Thou hast eyes;
We are fools, but Thou art wise!
Thou, our morrow's pathway knowing
Through the strange world round us growing,
Hear us, tell us where are we going,
    Where are we going, Rubee?

from *Songs of Labor*

Dedication

I would the gift I offer here
    Might graces from thy favor take,
And, seen through Friendship's atmosphere,
On softened lines and coloring, wear
The unaccustomed light of beauty, for thy sake.

Few leaves of Fancy's spring remain:
    But what I have I give to thee,—
The o'er-sunned bloom of summer's plain,
And paler flowers, the latter rain
Calls from the westering slope of life's autumnal lea.

Above the fallen groves of green,
    Where youth's enchanted forest stood,
The dry and wasting roots between,
A sober after-growth is seen,
As springs the pine where falls the gay-leafed maple wood!

Yet birds will sing, and breezes play
    Their leaf-harps in the sombre tree;
And through the bleak and wintry day
It keeps its steady green alway, —
So, even my after-thoughts may have a charm for thee.

Art's perfect forms no moral need,
    And beauty is its own excuse;
But for the dull and flowerless weed
Some healing virtue still must plead,
And the rough ore must find its honors in its use.

So haply these, my simple lays
    Of homely toil, may serve to show
The orchard bloom and tasselled maize
That skirt and gladden duty's ways,
The unsung beauty hid life's common things below!

Haply from them the toiler, bent
    Above his forge or plough, may gain
A manlier spirit of content,
And feel that life is wisest spent
Where the strong working hand makes strong the working
    brain: —

The doom which to the guilty pair
    Without the walls of Eden came,
Transforming sinless ease to care
And rugged toil, no more shall bear
The burden of old crime, or mark of primal shame.

A blessing now—a curse no more;
　　Since He, whose name we breathe with awe,
The coarse mechanic vesture wore,—
　　A poor man toiling with the poor,
In labor, as in prayer, fulfilling the same law.

Ichabod!

So fallen! so lost! the light withdrawn
　　Which once he wore!
The glory from his gray hairs gone
　　Forevermore!

Revile him not—the Tempter hath
　　A snare for all;
And pitying tears, not scorn and wrath,
　　Befit his fall!

Oh! dumb be passion's stormy rage,
　　When he who might
Have lighted up and led his age,
　　Falls back in night.

Scorn! would the angels laugh, to mark
　　A bright soul driven,
Fiend-goaded, down the endless dark,
　　From hope and heaven!

Let not the land, once proud of him,
　　Insult him now,
Nor brand with deeper shame his dim,
　　Dishonored brow.

But let its humbled sons, instead,
　　From sea to lake,
A long lament, as for the dead,
　　In sadness make.

Of all we loved and honored, nought
   Save power remains—
A fallen angel's pride of thought,
   Still strong in chains.

All else is gone; from those great eyes
   The soul has fled:
When faith is lost, when honor dies,
   The man is dead!

Then, pay the reverence of old days
   To his dead fame;
Walk backward, with averted gaze,
   And hide the shame!

Astræa

——"Jove means to settle
Astrea in her seat again,
And let down from his golden chain
An age of better metal."
              BEN JONSON, 1615.

O poet rare and old!
   Thy words are prophecies;
Forward the age of gold,
   The new Saturnian lies.

The universal prayer
   And hope are not in vain;
Rise, brothers! and prepare
   The way for Saturn's reign.

Perish shall all which takes
   From labor's board and can;
Perish shall all which makes
   A spaniel of the man!

Free from its bonds the mind,
  The body from the rod;
Broken all chains that bind
  The image of our God.

Just men no longer pine
  Behind their prison-bars;
Through the rent dungeon shine
  The free sun and the stars.

Earth own, at last, untrod
  By sect, or caste, or clan,
The fatherhood of God,
  The brotherhood of man!

Fraud fail, craft perish, forth
  The money-changers driven,
And God's will done on earth,
  As now in heaven!

First-Day Thoughts

In calm and cool and silence, once again
  I find my old accustomed place among
  My brethren, where, perchance, no human tongue
  Shall utter words; where never hymn is sung,
  Nor deep-toned organ blown, nor censer swung,
Nor dim light falling through the pictured pane!
There, syllabled by silence, let me hear
The still small voice which reached the prophet's ear;
Read in my heart a still diviner law
Than Israel's leader on his tables saw!
There let me strive with each besetting sin,
  Recall my wandering fancies, and restrain
  The sore disquiet of a restless brain;
  And, as the path of duty is made plain,
May grace be given that I may walk therein,
  Not like the hireling, for his selfish gain,

With backward glances and reluctant tread,
Making a merit of his coward dread,—
But, cheerful, in the light around me thrown,
Walking as one to pleasant service led;
Doing God's will as if it were my own,
Yet trusting not in mine, but in His strength alone!

The Haschish

Of all that Orient lands can vaunt
    Of marvels with our own competing,
The strangest is the Haschish plant,
    And what will follow on its eating.

What pictures to the taster rise,
    Of Dervish or of Almeh dances!
Of Eblis, or of Paradise,
    Set all aglow with Houri glances!

The poppy visions of Cathay,
    The heavy beer-trance of the Suabian;
The wizard lights and demon play
    Of nights Walpurgis and Arabian!

The Mollah and the Christian dog
    Change place in mad metempsychosis;
The Muezzin climbs the synagogue,
    The Rabbi shakes his beard at Moses!

The Arab by his desert well
    Sits choosing from some Caliph's daughters,
And hears his single camel's bell
    Sound welcome to his regal quarters.

The Koran's reader makes complaint
    Of Shitan dancing on and off it;
The robber offers alms, the saint
    Drinks Tokay and blasphemes the Prophet!

Such scenes that Eastern plant awakes;
    But we have one ordained to beat it,
The Haschish of the West, which makes
    Or fools or knaves of all who eat it.

The preacher eats, and straight appears
    His Bible in a new translation;
Its angels negro overseers,
    And Heaven itself a snug plantation!

The man of peace, about whose dreams
    The sweet millennial angels cluster,
Tastes the mad weed, and plots and schemes,
    A raving Cuban filibuster!

The noisiest Democrat, with ease,
    It turns to Slavery's parish beadle;
The shrewdest statesman eats and sees
    Due southward point the polar needle.

The Judge partakes, and sits ere long
    Upon his bench a railing blackguard;
Decides off-hand that right is wrong,
    And reads the ten commandments backward!

O, potent plant! so rare a taste
    Has never Turk or Gentoo gotten;
The hempen Haschish of the East
    Is powerless to our Western Cotton!

Maud Muller

Maud Muller, on a summer's day,
Raked the meadow sweet with hay.

Beneath her torn hat glowed the wealth
Of simple beauty and rustic health.

Singing, she wrought, and her merry glee
The mock-bird echoed from his tree.

But, when she glanced to the far-off town,
White from its hill-slope looking down,

The sweet song died, and a vague unrest
And a nameless longing filled her breast—

A wish, that she hardly dared to own,
For something better than she had known.

The Judge rode slowly down the lane,
Smoothing his horse's chestnut mane.

He drew his bridle in the shade
Of the apple-trees, to greet the maid,

And ask a draught from the spring that flowed
Through the meadow, across the road.

She stooped where the cool spring bubbled up,
And filled for him her small tin cup,

And blushed as she gave it, looking down
On her feet so bare, and her tattered gown.

"Thanks!" said the Judge, "a sweeter draught
From a fairer hand was never quaffed."

He spoke of the grass and flowers and trees,
Of the singing birds and the humming bees;

Then talked of the haying, and wondered whether
The cloud in the west would bring foul weather.

And Maud forgot her brier-torn gown,
And her graceful ankles bare and brown;

And listened, while a pleased surprise
Looked from her long-lashed hazel eyes.

At last, like one who for delay
Seeks a vain excuse, he rode away.

Maud Muller looked and sighed: "Ah, me!
That I the Judge's bride might be!

"He would dress me up in silks so fine,
And praise and toast me at his wine.

"My father should wear a broadcloth coat;
My brother should sail a painted boat.

"I'd dress my mother so grand and gay,
And the baby should have a new toy each day.

"And I'd feed the hungry and clothe the poor,
And all should bless me who left our door."

The Judge looked back as he climbed the hill,
And saw Maud Muller standing still.

"A form more fair, a face more sweet,
Ne'er hath it been my lot to meet.

"And her modest answer and graceful air
Show her wise and good as she is fair.

"Would she were mine, and I to-day,
Like her, a harvester of hay:

"No doubtful balance of rights and wrongs,
Nor weary lawyers with endless tongues,

"But low of cattle and song of birds,
And health and quiet and loving words."

But he thought of his sisters proud and cold,
And his mother vain of her rank and gold.

So, closing his heart, the Judge rode on,
And Maud was left in the field alone.

But the lawyers smiled that afternoon,
When he hummed in court an old love-tune;

And the young girl mused beside the well,
Till the rain on the unraked clover fell.

He wedded a wife of richest dower,
Who lived for fashion, as he for power.

Yet oft, in his marble hearth's bright glow,
He watched a picture come and go:

And sweet Maud Muller's hazel eyes
Looked out in their innocent surprise.

Oft, when the wine in his glass was red,
He longed for the wayside well instead;

And closed his eyes on his garnished rooms,
To dream of meadows and clover-blooms.

And the proud man sighed, with a secret pain:
"Ah, that I were free again!

"Free as when I rode that day,
Where the barefoot maiden raked her hay."

She wedded a man unlearned and poor,
And many children played round her door.

But care and sorrow, and child-birth pain,
Left their traces on heart and brain.

And oft, when the summer sun shone hot
On the new-mown hay in the meadow lot,

And she heard the little spring brook fall
Over the roadside, through the wall,

In the shade of the apple-tree again
She saw a rider draw his rein.

And, gazing down with timid grace,
She felt his pleased eyes read her face.

Sometimes her narrow kitchen walls
Stretched away into stately halls;

The weary wheel to a spinnet turned,
The tallow candle an astral burned,

And for him who sat by the chimney-lug,
Dozing and grumbling o'er pipe and mug,

A manly form at her side she saw,
And joy was duty and love was law.

Then she took up her burden of life again,
Saying only, "It might have been."

Alas for maiden, alas for Judge,
For rich repiner and household drudge!

God pity them both! and pity us all,
Who vainly the dreams of youth recall.

For of all sad words of tongue or pen,
The saddest are these: "It might have been!"

Ah, well! for us all some sweet hope lies
Deeply buried from human eyes;

And, in the hereafter, angels may
Roll the stone from its grave away!

The Barefoot Boy

Blessings on thee, little man,
Barefoot boy, with cheek of tan!
With thy turned-up pantaloons,
And thy merry whistled tunes;
With thy red lip, redder still
Kissed by strawberries on the hill;
With the sunshine on thy face,

Through thy torn brim's jaunty grace:
From my heart I give thee joy—
I was once a barefoot boy!
Prince thou art—the grown-up man
Only is republican.
Let the million-dollared ride!
Barefoot, trudging at his side,
Thou hast more than he can buy,
In the reach of ear and eye—
Outward sunshine, inward joy:
Blessings on thee, barefoot boy!

O, for boyhood's painless play,
Sleep that wakes in laughing day,
Health that mocks the doctor's rules,
Knowledge never learned of schools,
Of the wild bee's morning chase,
Of the wild-flower's time and place,
Flight of fowl, and habitude
Of the tenants of the wood;
How the tortoise bears his shell,
How the woodchuck digs his cell,
And the ground-mole sinks his well;
How the robin feeds her young,
How the oriole's nest is hung;
Where the whitest lilies blow,
Where the freshest berries grow,
Where the ground-nut trails its vine,
Where the wood-grape's clusters shine;
Of the black wasp's cunning way,
Mason of his walls of clay,
And the architectural plans
Of gray, hornet artisans!—
For, eschewing books and tasks,
Nature answers all he asks;
Hand in hand with her he walks,
Face to face with her he talks,
Part and parcel of her joy,—
Blessings on the barefoot boy!

O, for boyhood's time of June,
Crowding years in one brief moon,
When all things I heard or saw
Me, their master, waited for.
I was rich in flowers and trees,
Humming-birds and honey-bees;
For my sport the squirrel played,
Plied the snouted mole his spade;
For my taste the blackberry cone
Purpled over hedge and stone;
Laughed the brook for my delight
Through the day and through the night,
Whispering at the garden wall,
Talked with me from fall to fall;
Mine the sand-rimmed pickerel pond,
Mine the walnut slopes beyond,
Mine, on bending orchard trees,
Apples of Hesperides!
Still, as my horizon grew,
Larger grew my riches too;
All the world I saw or knew
Seemed a complex Chinese toy,
Fashioned for a barefoot boy!

O, for festal dainties spread,
Like my bowl of milk and bread,—
Pewter spoon and bowl of wood,
On the door-stone, gray and rude!
O'er me, like a regal tent,
Cloudy-ribbed, the sunset bent,
Purple-curtained, fringed with gold,
Looped in many a wind-swung fold;
While for music came the play
Of the pied frogs' orchestra;
And, to light the noisy choir,
Lit the fly his lamp of fire.
I was monarch: pomp and joy
Waited on the barefoot boy!

Cheerily, then, my little man,
Live and laugh, as boyhood can!
Though the flinty slopes be hard,
Stubble-speared the new-mown sward,
Every morn shall lead thee through
Fresh baptisms of the dew;
Every evening from thy feet
Shall the cool wind kiss the heat:
All too soon these feet must hide
In the prison cells of pride,
Lose the freedom of the sod,
Like a colt's for work be shod,
Made to tread the mills of toil,
Up and down in ceaseless moil:
Happy if their track be found
Never on forbidden ground;
Happy if they sink not in
Quick and treacherous sands of sin.
Ah! that thou couldst know thy joy,
Ere it passes, barefoot boy!

Skipper Ireson's Ride

Of all the rides since the birth of time,
Told in story or sung in rhyme,—
On Apuleius's Golden Ass,
Or one-eyed Calendar's horse of brass,
Witch astride of a human hack,
Islam's prophet on Al-Borák,—
The strangest ride that ever was sped
Was Ireson's, out from Marblehead!
      Old Floyd Ireson, for his hard heart,
        Tarred and feathered and carried in a cart
          By the women of Marblehead!

Body of turkey, head of owl,
Wings a-droop like a rained-on fowl,
Feathered and ruffled in every part,
Skipper Ireson stood in the cart.

Scores of women, old and young,
Strong of muscle, and glib of tongue,
Pushed and pulled up the rocky lane,
Shouting and singing the shrill refrain:
    "Here's Flud Oirson, fur his horrd horrt,
    Torr'd an' futherr'd an' corr'd in a corrt
      By the women o' Morble'ead!"

Wrinkled scolds with hands on hips,
Girls in bloom of cheek and lips,
Wild-eyed, free-limbed, such as chase
Bacchus round some antique vase,
Brief of skirt, with ankles bare,
Loose of kerchief and loose of hair,
With couch-shells blowing and fish-horns' twang,
Over and over the Mænads sang:
    "Here's Flud Oirson, fur his horrd horrt,
    Torr'd an' futherr'd an' corr'd in a corrt
      By the women o' Morble'ead!"

Small pity for him!—He sailed away
From a leaking ship, in Chaleur Bay,—
Sailed away from a sinking wreck,
With his own town's-people on her deck!
"Lay by! lay by!" they called to him.
Back he answered, "Sink or swim!
Brag of your catch of fish again!"
And off he sailed through the fog and rain!
    Old Floyd Ireson, for his hard heart,
    Tarred and feathered and carried in a cart
      By the women of Marblehead!

Fathoms deep in dark Chaleur
That wreck shall lie forevermore.
Mother and sister, wife and maid,
Looked from the rocks of Marblehead
Over the moaning and rainy sea,—
Looked for the coming that might not be!
What did the winds and the sea-birds say
Of the cruel captain who sailed away?—

Old Floyd Ireson, for his hard heart,
Tarred and feathered and carried in a cart
By the women of Marblehead!

Through the street, on either side,
Up flew windows, doors swung wide;
Sharp-tongued spinsters, old wives gray,
Treble lent the fish-horn's bray.
Sea-worn grandsires, cripple-bound,
Hulks of old sailors run aground,
Shook head, and fist, and hat, and cane,
And cracked with curses the hoarse refrain:
"Here's Flud Oirson, fur his horrd horrt,
Torr'd an' futherr'd an' corr'd in a corrt
By the women o' Morble'ead!"

Sweetly along the Salem road
Bloom of orchard and lilac showed.
Little the wicked skipper knew
Of the fields so green and the sky so blue.
Riding there in his sorry trim,
Like an Indian idol glum and grim,
Scarcely he seemed the sound to hear
Of voices shouting far and near:
"Here's Flud Oirson, fur his horrd horrt,
Torr'd an' futherr'd an' corr'd in a corrt
By the women o' Morble'ead!"

"Hear me, neighbors!" at last he cried, —
"What to me is this noisy ride?
What is the shame that clothes the skin
To the nameless horror that lives within?
Waking or sleeping, I see a wreck,
And hear a cry from a reeling deck!
Hate me and curse me, — I only dread
The hand of God and the face of the dead!"
Said old Floyd Ireson, for his hard heart,
Tarred and feathered and carried in a cart
By the women of Marblehead!

Then the wife of the skipper lost at sea
Said, "God has touched him!—why should we?"
Said an old wife mourning her only son,
"Cut the rogue's tether and let him run!"
So with soft relentings and rude excuse,
Half scorn, half pity, they cut him loose,
And gave him a cloak to hide him in,
And left him alone with his shame and sin.
   Poor Floyd Ireson, for his hard heart,
   Tarred and feathered and carried in a cart
   By the women of Marblehead!

Telling the Bees

Here is the place; right over the hill
 Runs the path I took;
You can see the gap in the old wall still,
 And the stepping-stones in the shallow brook.

There is the house, with the gate red-barred,
 And the poplars tall;
And the barn's brown length, and the cattle-yard,
 And the white horns tossing above the wall.

There are the bee-hives ranged in the sun;
 And down by the brink
Of the brook are her poor flowers, weed-o'errun,
 Pansy and daffodil, rose and pink.

A year has gone, as the tortoise goes,
 Heavy and slow;
And the same rose blows, and the same sun glows,
 And the same brook sings of a year ago.

There's the same sweet clover-smell in the breeze;
 And the June sun warm
Tangles his wings of fire in the trees,
 Setting, as then, over Fernside farm.

I mind me how with a lover's care
   From my Sunday coat
I brushed off the burs, and smoothed my hair,
   And cooled at the brook-side my brow and throat.

Since we parted, a month had passed,—
   To love, a year;
Down through the beeches I looked at last
   On the little red gate and the well-sweep near.

I can see it all now,—the slantwise rain
   Of light through the leaves,
The sundown's blaze on her window-pane,
   The bloom of her roses under the eaves.

Just the same as a month before,—
   The house and the trees,
The barn's brown gable, the vine by the door,—
   Nothing changed but the hives of bees.

Before them, under the garden wall,
   Forward and back,
Went drearily singing the chore-girl small,
   Draping each hive with a shred of black.

Trembling, I listened: the summer sun
   Had the chill of snow;
For I knew she was telling the bees of one
   Gone on the journey we all must go!

Then I said to myself, "My Mary weeps
   For the dead to-day:
Haply her blind old grandsire sleeps
   The fret and the pain of his age away."

But her dog whined low; on the doorway sill,
   With his cane to his chin,
The old man sat; and the chore-girl still
   Sung to the bees stealing out and in.

And the song she was singing ever since
  In my ear sounds on: —
"Stay at home, pretty bees, fly not hence!
  Mistress Mary is dead and gone!"

My Playmate

The pines were dark on Ramoth hill,
  Their song was soft and low;
The blossoms in the sweet May wind
  Were falling like the snow.

The blossoms drifted at our feet,
  The orchard birds sang clear;
The sweetest and the saddest day
  It seemed of all the year.

For, more to me than birds or flowers,
  My playmate left her home,
And took with her the laughing spring,
  The music and the bloom.

She kissed the lips of kith and kin,
  She laid her hand in mine:
What more could ask the bashful boy
  Who fed her father's kine?

She left us in the bloom of May:
  The constant years told o'er
Their seasons with as sweet May morns,
  But she came back no more.

I walk, with noiseless feet, the round
  Of uneventful years;
Still o'er and o'er I sow the spring
  And reap the autumn ears.

She lives where all the golden year
  Her summer roses blow;
The dusky children of the sun
  Before her come and go.

There haply with her jewelled hands
   She smooths her silken gown,—
No more the homespun lap wherein
   I shook the walnuts down.

The wild grapes wait us by the brook,
   The brown nuts on the hill,
And still the May-day flowers make sweet
   The woods of Follymill.

The lilies blossom in the pond,
   The bird builds in the tree,
The dark pines sing on Ramoth hill
   The slow song of the sea.

I wonder if she thinks of them,
   And how the old time seems,—
If ever the pines of Ramoth wood
   Are sounding in her dreams.

I see her face, I hear her voice:
   Does she remember mine?
And what to her is now the boy
   Who fed her father's kine?

What cares she that the orioles build
   For other eyes than ours,—
That other hands with nuts are filled,
   And other laps with flowers?

O playmate in the golden time!
   Our mossy seat is green,
Its fringing violets blossom yet,
   The old trees o'er it lean.

The winds so sweet with birch and fern
   A sweeter memory blow;
And there in spring the veeries sing
   The song of long ago.

And still the pines of Ramoth wood
   Are moaning like the sea,—
The moaning of the sea of change
   Between myself and thee!

Barbara Frietchie

Up from the meadows rich with corn,
Clear in the cool September morn,

The clustered spires of Frederick stand
Green-walled by the hills of Maryland.

Round about them orchards sweep,
Apple- and peach-tree fruited deep,

Fair as a garden of the Lord
To the eyes of the famished rebel horde,

On that pleasant morn of the early fall
When Lee marched over the mountain wall,—

Over the mountains winding down,
Horse and foot, into Frederick town.

Forty flags with their silver stars,
Forty flags with their crimson bars,

Flapped in the morning wind: the sun
Of noon looked down, and saw not one.

Up rose old Barbara Frietchie then,
Bowed with her fourscore years and ten;

Bravest of all in Frederick town,
She took up the flag the men hauled down;

In her attic-window the staff she set,
To show that one heart was loyal yet.

Up the street came the rebel tread,
Stonewall Jackson riding ahead.

Under his slouched hat left and right
He glanced: the old flag met his sight.

"Halt!"—the dust-brown ranks stood fast.
"Fire!"—out blazed the rifle-blast.

It shivered the window, pane and sash;
It rent the banner with seam and gash.

Quick, as it fell, from the broken staff
Dame Barbara snatched the silken scarf;

She leaned far out on the window-sill,
And shook it forth with a royal will.

"Shoot, if you must, this old gray head,
But spare your country's flag," she said.

A shade of sadness, a blush of shame,
Over the face of the leader came;

The nobler nature within him stirred
To life at that woman's deed and word:

"Who touches a hair of yon gray head
Dies like a dog! March on!" he said.

All day long through Frederick street
Sounded the tread of marching feet:

All day long that free flag tost
Over the heads of the rebel host.

Ever its torn folds rose and fell
On the loyal winds that loved it well;

And through the hill-gaps sunset light
Shone over it with a warm good-night.

Barbara Frietchie's work is o'er,
And the Rebel rides on his raids no more.

Honor to her! and let a tear
Fall, for her sake, on Stonewall's bier.

Over Barbara Frietchie's grave
Flag of Freedom and Union, wave!

Peace and order and beauty draw
Round thy symbol of light and law;

And ever the stars above look down
On thy stars below in Frederick town!

What the Birds Said

The birds against the April wind
    Flew northward, singing as they flew;
They sang, "The land we leave behind
    Has swords for corn-blades, blood for dew."

"O wild-birds, flying from the South,
    What saw and heard ye, gazing down?"
"We saw the mortar's upturned mouth,
    The sickened camp, the blazing town!

"Beneath the bivouac's starry lamps,
    We saw your march-worn children die;
In shrouds of moss, in cypress swamps,
    We saw your dead uncoffined lie.

"We heard the starving prisoner's sighs,
    And saw, from line and trench, your sons
Follow our flight with home-sick eyes
    Beyond the battery's smoking guns."

"And heard and saw ye only wrong
    And pain," I cried, "O wing-worn flocks?"
"We heard," they sang, "the freedman's song,
    The crash of Slavery's broken locks!

"We saw from new, uprising States
    The treason-nursing mischief spurned,
As, crowding Freedom's ample gates,
    The long-estranged and lost returned.

"O'er dusky faces, seamed and old,
    And hands horn-hard with unpaid toil,
With hope in every rustling fold,
    We saw your star-dropt flag uncoil.

"And struggling up through sounds accursed,
    A grateful murmur clomb the air;
A whisper scarcely heard at first,
    It filled the listening heavens with prayer.

"And sweet and far, as from a star,
    Replied a voice which shall not cease,
Till, drowning all the noise of war,
    It sings the blessed song of peace!"

So to me, in a doubtful day
    Of chill and slowly greening spring,
Low stooping from the cloudy gray,
    The wild-birds sang or seemed to sing.

They vanished in the misty air,
    The song went with them in their flight;
But lo! they left the sunset fair,
    And in the evening there was light.

Snow-Bound

The sun that brief December day
Rose cheerless over hills of gray,
And, darkly circled, gave at noon
A sadder light than waning moon.
Slow tracing down the thickening sky
Its mute and ominous prophecy,
A portent seeming less than threat,
It sank from sight before it set.
A chill no coat, however stout,
Of homespun stuff could quite shut out,
A hard, dull bitterness of cold,
    That checked, mid-vein, the circling race
    Of life-blood in the sharpened face,
The coming of the snow-storm told.
The wind blew east: we heard the roar
Of Ocean on his wintry shore,
And felt the strong pulse throbbing there
Beat with low rhythm our inland air.

Meanwhile we did our nightly chores, —
Brought in the wood from out of doors,
Littered the stalls, and from the mows
Raked down the herd's-grass for the cows;
Heard the horse whinnying for his corn;
And, sharply clashing horn on horn,
Impatient down the stanchion rows
The cattle shake their walnut bows;
While, peering from his early perch
Upon the scaffold's pole of birch,
The cock his crested helmet bent
And down his querulous challenge sent.

Unwarmed by any sunset light
The gray day darkened into night,
A night made hoary with the swarm
And whirl-dance of the blinding storm,
As zigzag wavering to and fro
Crossed and recrossed the wingéd snow:

And ere the early bed-time came
The white drift piled the window-frame,
And through the glass the clothes-line posts
Looked in like tall and sheeted ghosts.

So all night long the storm roared on:
The morning broke without a sun;
In tiny spherule traced with lines
Of Nature's geometric signs,
In starry flake, and pellicle,
All day the hoary meteor fell;
And, when the second morning shone,
We looked upon a world unknown,
On nothing we could call our own.
Around the glistening wonder bent
The blue walls of the firmament,
No cloud above, no earth below, —
A universe of sky and snow!
The old familiar sights of ours
Took marvellous shapes; strange domes and towers
Rose up where sty or corn-crib stood,
Or garden wall, or belt of wood;
A smooth white mound the brush-pile showed,
A fenceless drift what once was road;
The bridle-post an old man sat
With loose-flung coat and high cocked hat;
The well-curb had a Chinese roof;
And even the long sweep, high aloof,
In its slant splendor, seemed to tell
Of Pisa's leaning miracle.

A prompt, decisive man, no breath
Our father wasted: "Boys, a path!"
Well pleased, (for when did farmer boy
Count such a summons less than joy?)
Our buskins on our feet we drew;
    With mittened hands, and caps drawn low,
    To guard our necks and ears from snow,
We cut the solid whiteness through.
And, where the drift was deepest, made

A tunnel walled and overlaid
With dazzling crystal: we had read
Of rare Aladdin's wondrous cave,
And to our own his name we gave,
With many a wish the luck were ours
To test his lamp's supernal powers.
We reached the barn with merry din,
And roused the prisoned brutes within.
The old horse thrust his long head out,
And grave with wonder gazed about;
The cock his lusty greeting said,
And forth his speckled harem led;
The oxen lashed their tails, and hooked,
And mild reproach of hunger looked;
The hornéd patriarch of the sheep,
Like Egypt's Amun roused from sleep,
Shook his sage head with gesture mute,
And emphasized with stamp of foot.

All day the gusty north-wind bore
The loosening drift its breath before;
Low circling round its southern zone,
The sun through dazzling snow-mist shone.
No church-bell lent its Christian tone
To the savage air, no social smoke
Curled over woods of snow-hung oak.
A solitude made more intense
By dreary voicéd elements,
The shrieking of the mindless wind,
The moaning tree-boughs swaying blind,
And on the glass the unmeaning beat
Of ghostly finger-tips of sleet.
Beyond the circle of our hearth
No welcome sound of toil or mirth
Unbound the spell, and testified
Of human life and thought outside.
We minded that the sharpest ear
The buried brooklet could not hear,
The music of whose liquid lip
Had been to us companionship,

And, in our lonely life, had grown
To have an almost human tone.

As night drew on, and, from the crest
Of wooded knolls that ridged the west,
The sun, a snow-blown traveller, sank
From sight beneath the smothering bank,
We piled, with care, our nightly stack
Of wood against the chimney-back,—
The oaken log, green, huge, and thick,
And on its top the stout back-stick;
The knotty forestick laid apart,
And filled between with curious art
The ragged brush; then, hovering near,
We watched the first red blaze appear,
Heard the sharp crackle, caught the gleam
On whitewashed wall and sagging beam,
Until the old, rude-furnished room
Burst, flower-like, into rosy bloom;
While radiant with a mimic flame
Outside the sparkling drift became,
And through the bare-boughed lilac-tree
Our own warm hearth seemed blazing free.
The crane and pendent trammels showed,
The Turks' heads on the andirons glowed;
While childish fancy, prompt to tell
The meaning of the miracle,
Whispered the old rhyme: *"Under the tree,*
When fire outdoors burns merrily,
There the witches are making tea."

The moon above the eastern wood
Shone at its full; the hill-range stood
Transfigured in the silver flood,
Its blown snows flashing cold and keen,
Dead white, save where some sharp ravine
Took shadow, or the sombre green
Of hemlocks turned to pitchy black
Against the whiteness at their back.
For such a world and such a night

Most fitting that unwarming light,
Which only seemed where'er it fell
To make the coldness visible.

Shut in from all the world without,
We sat the clean-winged hearth about,
Content to let the north-wind roar
In baffled rage at pane and door,
While the red logs before us beat
The frost-line back with tropic heat;
And ever, when a louder blast
Shook beam and rafter as it passed,
The merrier up its roaring draught
The great throat of the chimney laughed.
The house-dog on his paws outspread
Laid to the fire his drowsy head,
The cat's dark silhouette on the wall
A couchant tiger's seemed to fall;
And, for the winter fireside meet,
Between the andirons' straddling feet,
The mug of cider simmered slow,
The apples sputtered in a row,
And, close at hand, the basket stood
With nuts from brown October's wood.

What matter how the night behaved?
What matter how the north-wind raved?
Blow high, blow low, not all its snow
Could quench our hearth-fire's ruddy glow.
O Time and Change!—with hair as gray
As was my sire's that winter day,
How strange it seems, with so much gone
Of life and love, to still live on!
Ah, brother! only I and thou
Are left of all that circle now,—
The dear home faces whereupon
That fitful firelight paled and shone.
Henceforward, listen as we will,
The voices of that hearth are still;
Look where we may, the wide earth o'er,

Those lighted faces smile no more.
We tread the paths their feet have worn,
    We sit beneath their orchard-trees,
    We hear, like them, the hum of bees
And rustle of the bladed corn;
We turn the pages that they read,
    Their written words we linger o'er,
But in the sun they cast no shade,
No voice is heard, no sign is made,
    No step is on the conscious floor!
Yet Love will dream, and Faith will trust,
(Since He who knows our need is just,)
That somehow, somewhere, meet we must.
Alas for him who never sees
The stars shine through his cypress-trees!
Who, hopeless, lays his dead away,
Nor looks to see the breaking day
Across the mournful marbles play!
Who hath not learned, in hours of faith,
    The truth to flesh and sense unknown,
That Life is ever lord of Death,
    And Love can never lose its own!

We sped the time with stories old,
    Wrought puzzles out, and riddles told,
    Or stammered from our school-book lore
"The Chief of Gambia's golden shore."
    How often since, when all the land
    Was clay in Slavery's shaping hand,
    As if a trumpet called, I've heard
    Dame Mercy Warren's rousing word:
"Does not the voice of reason cry,
    Claim the first right which Nature gave,
From the red scourge of bondage fly,
    Nor deign to live a burdened slave!"
    Our father rode again his ride
    On Memphremagog's wooded side;
    Sat down again to moose and samp
    In trapper's hut and Indian camp;
    Lived o'er the old idyllic ease

Beneath St. François' hemlock-trees;
Again for him the moonlight shone
On Norman cap and bodiced zone;
Again he heard the violin play
Which led the village dance away,
And mingled in its merry whirl
The grandam and the laughing girl.
Or, nearer home, our steps he led
Where Salisbury's level marshes spread
   Mile-wide as flies the laden bee;
Where merry mowers, hale and strong,
Swept, scythe on scythe, their swaths along
   The low green prairies of the sea.
We shared the fishing off Boar's Head,
   And round the rocky Isles of Shoals
   The hake-broil on the drift-wood coals;
The chowder on the sand-beach made,
Dipped by the hungry, steaming hot,
With spoons of clam-shell from the pot.
We heard the tales of witchcraft old,
And dream and sign and marvel told
To sleepy listeners as they lay
Stretched idly on the salted hay,
Adrift along the winding shores,
When favoring breezes designed to blow
The square sail of the gundalow
And idle lay the useless oars.
Our mother, while she turned her wheel
Or run the new-knit stocking-heel,
Told how the Indian hordes came down
At midnight on Cochecho town,
And how her own great-uncle bore
His cruel scalp-mark to fourscore.
Recalling, in her fitting phrase,
   So rich and picturesque and free,
   (The common unrhymed poetry
Of simple life and country ways,)
The story of her early days, —
She made us welcome to her home;
Old hearths grew wide to give us room;

We stole with her a frightened look
At the gray wizard's conjuring-book,
The fame whereof went far and wide
Through all the simple country side;
We heard the hawks at twilight play,
The boat-horn on Piscataqua,
The loon's weird laughter far away;
We fished her little trout-brook, knew
What flowers in wood and meadow grew,
What sunny hillsides autumn-brown
She climbed to shake the ripe nuts down,
Saw where in sheltered cove and bay
The ducks' black squadron anchored lay,
And heard the wild-geese calling loud
Beneath the gray November cloud.

Then, haply, with a look more grave,
And soberer tone, some tale she gave
From painful Sewell's ancient tome,
Beloved in every Quaker home,
Of faith fire-winged by martyrdom,
Or Chalkley's Journal, old and quaint,—
Gentlest of skippers, rare sea-saint!—
Who, when the dreary calms prevailed,
And water-butt and bread-cask failed,
And cruel, hungry eyes pursued
His portly presence mad for food,
With dark hints muttered under breath
Of casting lots for life or death,
Offered, if Heaven withheld supplies,
To be himself the sacrifice.
Then, suddenly, as if to save
The good man from his living grave,
A ripple on the water grew,
A school of porpoise flashed in view.
"Take, eat," he said, "and be content;
These fishes in my stead are sent
By Him who gave the tangled ram
To spare the child of Abraham."

Our uncle, innocent of books,
Was rich in lore of fields and brooks,
The ancient teachers never dumb
Of Nature's unhoused lyceum.
In moons and tides and weather wise,
He read the clouds as prophecies,
And foul or fair could well divine,
By many an occult hint and sign,
Holding the cunning-warded keys
To all the woodcraft mysteries;
Himself to Nature's heart so near
That all her voices in his ear
Of beast or bird had meanings clear,
Like Apollonius of old,
Who knew the tales the sparrows told,
Or Hermes, who interpreted
What the sage cranes of Nilus said;
A simple, guileless, childlike man,
Content to live where life began;
Strong only on his native grounds,
The little world of sights and sounds
Whose girdle was the parish bounds,
Whereof his fondly partial pride
The common features magnified,
As Surrey hills to mountains grew
In White of Selborne's loving view,—
He told how teal and loon he shot,
And how the eagle's eggs he got,
The feats on pond and river done,
The prodigies of rod and gun;
Till, warming with the tales he told,
Forgotten was the outside cold,
The bitter wind unheeded blew,
From ripening corn the pigeons flew,
The partridge drummed i' the wood, the mink
Went fishing down the river-brink.
In fields with bean or clover gay,
The woodchuck, like a hermit gray,
Peered from the doorway of his cell;
The muskrat plied the mason's trade,

And tier by tier his mud-walls laid;
And from the shagbark overhead
The grizzled squirrel dropped his shell.

Next, the dear aunt, whose smile of cheer
And voice in dreams I see and hear, —
The sweetest woman ever Fate
Perverse denied a household mate,
Who, lonely, homeless, not the less
Found peace in love's unselfishness,
And welcome wheresoe'er she went,
A calm and gracious element,
Whose presence seemed the sweet income
And womanly atmosphere of home, —
Called up her girlhood memories,
The huskings and the apple-bees,
The sleigh-rides and the summer sails,
Weaving through all the poor details
And homespun warp of circumstance
A golden woof-thread of romance.
For well she kept her genial mood
And simple faith of maidenhood;
Before her still a cloud-land lay,
The mirage loomed across her way;
The morning dew, that dries so soon
With others, glistened at her noon;
Through years of toil and soil and care
From glossy tress to thin gray hair,
All unprofaned she held apart
The virgin fancies of the heart.
Be shame to him of woman born
Who hath for such but thought of scorn.

There, too, our elder sister plied
Her evening task the stand beside;
A full, rich nature, free to trust,
Truthful and almost sternly just,
Impulsive, earnest, prompt to act,
And make her generous thought a fact,

Keeping with many a light disguise
The secret of self-sacrifice.
O heart sore-tried! thou hast the best
That Heaven itself could give thee, — rest,
Rest from all bitter thoughts and things!
    How many a poor one's blessing went
    With thee beneath the low green tent
Whose curtain never outward swings!

As one who held herself a part
Of all she saw, and let her heart
    Against the household bosom lean,
Upon the motley-braided mat
Our youngest and our dearest sat,
Lifting her large, sweet, asking eyes,
    Now bathed within the fadeless green
And holy peace of Paradise.
O, looking from some heavenly hill,
    Or from the shade of saintly palms,
    Or silver reach of river calms,
Do those large eyes behold me still?
With me one little year ago: —
The chill weight of the winter snow
    For months upon her grave has lain;
And now, when summer south-winds blow
    And brier and harebell bloom again,
I tread the pleasant paths we trod,
I see the violet-sprinkled sod
Whereon she leaned, too frail and weak
The hillside flowers she loved to seek,
Yet following me where'er I went
With dark eyes full of love's content.
The birds are glad; the brier-rose fills
The air with sweetness; all the hills
Stretch green to June's unclouded sky;
But still I wait with ear and eye
For something gone which should be nigh,
A loss in all familiar things,
In flower that blooms, and bird that sings.
And yet, dear heart! remembering thee,

Am I not richer than of old?
Safe in thy immortality,
    What change can reach the wealth I hold?
    What chance can mar the pearl and gold
Thy love hath left in trust with me?
And while in life's late afternoon,
    Where cool and long the shadows grow,
I walk to meet the night that soon
    Shall shape and shadow overflow,
I cannot feel that thou art far,
Since near at need the angels are;
And when the sunset gates unbar,
    Shall I not see thee waiting stand,
And, white against the evening star,
    The welcome of thy beckoning hand?

Brisk wielder of the birch and rule,
The master of the district school
Held at the fire his favored place,
Its warm glow lit a laughing face
Fresh-hued and fair, where scarce appeared
The uncertain prophecy of beard.
He teased the mitten-blinded cat,
Played cross-pins on my uncle's hat,
Sang songs, and told us what befalls
In classic Dartmouth's college halls.
Born the wild Northern hills among,
From whence his yeoman father wrung
By patient toil subsistence scant,
Not competence and yet not want,
He early gained the power to pay
His cheerful, self-reliant way;
Could doff at ease his scholar's gown
To peddle wares from town to town;
Or through the long vacation's reach
In lonely lowland districts teach,
Where all the droll experience found
At stranger hearths in boarding round,
The moonlit skater's keen delight,
The sleigh-drive through the frosty night,

The rustic party, with its rough
Accompaniment of blind-man's-buff,
And whirling plate, and forfeits paid,
His winter task a pastime made.
Happy the snow-locked homes wherein
He tuned his merry violin,
Or played the athlete in the barn,
Or held the good dame's winding yarn,
Or mirth-provoking versions told
Of classic legends rare and old,
Wherein the scenes of Greece and Rome
Had all the commonplace of home,
And little seemed at best the odds
'Twixt Yankee pedlers and old gods;
Where Pindus-born Araxes took
The guise of any grist-mill brook,
And dread Olympus at his will
Became a huckleberry hill.

A careless boy that night he seemed;
    But at his desk he had the look
And air of one who wisely schemed,
    And hostage from the future took
    In trainéd thought and lore of book.
Large-brained, clear-eyed, — of such as he
Shall Freedom's young apostles be,
Who, following in War's bloody trail,
Shall every lingering wrong assail;
All chains from limb and spirit strike,
Uplift the black and white alike;
Scatter before their swift advance
The darkness and the ignorance,
The pride, the lust, the squalid sloth,
Which nurtured Treason's monstrous growth,
Made murder pastime, and the hell
Of prison-torture possible;
The cruel lie of caste refute,
Old forms remould, and substitute
For Slavery's lash the freeman's will,
For blind routine, wise-handed skill;

A school-house plant on every hill,
Stretching in radiate nerve-lines thence
The quick wires of intelligence;
Till North and South together brought
Shall own the same electric thought,
In peace a common flag salute,
And, side by side in labor's free
And unresentful rivalry,
Harvest the fields wherein they fought.

Another guest that winter night
Flashed back from lustrous eyes the light.
Unmarked by time, and yet not young,
The honeyed music of her tongue
And words of meekness scarcely told
A nature passionate and bold,
Strong, self-concentred, spurning guide,
Its milder features dwarfed beside
Her unbent will's majestic pride.
She sat among us, at the best,
A not unfeared, half-welcome guest,
Rebuking with her cultured phrase
Our homeliness of words and ways.
A certain pard-like, treacherous grace
    Swayed the lithe limbs and drooped the lash,
    Lent the white teeth their dazzling flash;
    And under low brows, black with night,
    Rayed out at times a dangerous light;
The sharp heat-lightnings of her face
Presaging ill to him whom Fate
Condemned to share her love or hate.
A woman tropical, intense
In thought and act, in soul and sense,
She blended in a like degree
The vixen and the devotee,
Revealing with each freak or feint
    The temper of Petruchio's Kate,
The raptures of Siena's saint.
Her tapering hand and rounded wrist
Had facile power to form a fist;

The warm, dark languish of her eyes
Was never safe from wrath's surprise.
Brows saintly calm and lips devout
Knew every change of scowl and pout;
And the sweet voice had notes more high
And shrill for social battle-cry.

Since then what old cathedral town
Has missed her pilgrim staff and gown,
What convent-gate has held its lock
Against the challenge of her knock!
Through Smyrna's plague-hushed thoroughfares,
Up sea-set Malta's rocky stairs,
Gray olive slopes of hills that hem
Thy tombs and shrines, Jerusalem,
Or startling on her desert throne
The crazy Queen of Lebanon
With claims fantastic as her own,
Her tireless feet have held their way;
And still, unrestful, bowed, and gray,
She watches under Eastern skies,
    With hope each day renewed and fresh,
    The Lord's quick coming in the flesh,
Whereof she dreams and prophesies!

Where'er her troubled path may be,
    The Lord's sweet pity with her go!
The outward wayward life we see,
    The hidden springs we may not know.
Nor is it given us to discern
    What threads the fatal sisters spun,
    Through what ancestral years has run
The sorrow with the woman born,
What forged her cruel chain of moods,
What set her feet in solitudes,
    And held the love within her mute,
What mingled madness in the blood,
    A life-long discord and annoy,
    Water of tears with oil of joy,
And hid within the folded bud

Perversities of flower and fruit.
It is not ours to separate
The tangled skein of will and fate,
To show what metes and bounds should stand
Upon the soul's debatable land,
And between choice and Providence
Divide the circle of events;
But He who knows our frame is just,
Merciful, and compassionate,
And full of sweet assurances
And hope for all the language is,
That He remembereth we are dust!

At last the great logs, crumbling low,
Sent out a dull and duller glow,
The bull's-eye watch that hung in view,
Ticking its weary circuit through,
Pointed with mutely-warning sign
Its black hand to the hour of nine.
That sign the pleasant circle broke:
My uncle ceased his pipe to smoke,
Knocked from its bowl the refuse gray
And laid it tenderly away,
Then roused himself to safely cover
The dull red brands with ashes over.
And while, with care, our mother laid
The work aside, her steps she stayed
One moment, seeking to express
Her grateful sense of happiness
For food and shelter, warmth and health,
And love's contentment more than wealth,
With simple wishes (not the weak,
Vain prayers which no fulfilment seek,
But such as warm the generous heart,
O'er-prompt to do with Heaven its part)
That none might lack, that bitter night,
For bread and clothing, warmth and light.

Within our beds awhile we heard
The wind that round the gables roared,

With now and then a ruder shock,
Which made our very bedsteads rock.
We heard the loosened clapboards tost,
The board-nails snapping in the frost;
And on us, through the unplastered wall,
Felt the light sifted snow-flakes fall.
But sleep stole on, as sleep will do
When hearts are light and life is new;
Faint and more faint the murmurs grew,
Till in the summer-land of dreams
They softened to the sound of streams,
Low stir of leaves, and dip of oars,
And lapsing waves on quiet shores.

Next morn we wakened with the shout
Of merry voices high and clear;
And saw the teamsters drawing near
To break the drifted highways out.
Down the long hillside treading slow
We saw the half-buried oxen go,
Shaking the snow from heads uptost,
Their straining nostrils white with frost.
Before our door the straggling train
Drew up, an added team to gain.
The elders threshed their hands a-cold,
    Passed, with the cider-mug, their jokes
    From lip to lip; the younger folks
Down the loose snow-banks, wrestling, rolled,
Then toiled again the cavalcade
    O'er windy hill, through clogged ravine,
    And woodland paths that wound between
Low drooping pine-boughs winter-weighed.
From every barn a team afoot,
At every house a new recruit,
Where, drawn by Nature's subtlest law,
Haply the watchful young men saw
Sweet doorway pictures of the curls
And curious eyes of merry girls,
Lifting their hands in mock defence
Against the snow-ball's compliments,

And reading in each missive tost
The charm with Eden never lost.

We heard once more the sleigh-bells' sound;
    And, following where the teamsters led,
The wise old Doctor went his round,
Just pausing at our door to say,
In the brief autocratic way
Of one who, prompt at Duty's call,
Was free to urge her claim on all,
    That some poor neighbor sick abed
At night our mother's aid would need.
For, one in generous thought and deed,
    What mattered in the sufferer's sight
    The Quaker matron's inward light,
The Doctor's mail of Calvin's creed?
All hearts confess the saints elect
    Who, twain in faith, in love agree,
And melt not in an acid sect
    The Christian pearl of charity!

So days went on: a week had passed
Since the great world was heard from last.
The Almanac we studied o'er,
Read and reread our little store,
Of books and pamphlets, scarce a score;
One harmless novel, mostly hid
From younger eyes, a book forbid,
And poetry, (or good or bad,
A single book was all we had,)
Where Ellwood's meek, drab-skirted Muse,
    A stranger to the heathen Nine,
    Sang, with a somewhat nasal whine,
The wars of David and the Jews.
At last the floundering carrier bore
The village paper to our door.
Lo! broadening outward as we read,
To warmer zones the horizon spread;
In panoramic length unrolled
We saw the marvels that it told.

Before us passed the painted Creeks,
   And daft McGregor on his raids
   In Costa Rica's everglades.
And up Taygetos winding slow
Rode Ypsilanti's Mainote Greeks,
A Turk's head at each saddle-bow!
Welcome to us its week-old news,
Its corner for the rustic Muse,
   Its monthly gauge of snow and rain,
Its record, mingling in a breath
The wedding bell and dirge of death;
Jest, anecdote, and love-lorn tale,
The latest culprit sent to jail;
Its hue and cry of stolen and lost,
Its vendue sales and goods at cost,
   And traffic calling loud for gain.
We felt the stir of hall and street,
The pulse of life that round us beat;
The chill embargo of the snow
Was melted in the genial glow;
Wide swung again our ice-locked door,
And all the world was ours once more!

Clasp, Angel of the backward look
   And folded wings of ashen gray
   And voice of echoes far away,
The brazen covers of thy book;
The weird palimpsest old and vast,
Wherein thou hid'st the spectral past;
Where, closely mingling, pale and glow
The characters of joy and woe;
The monographs of outlived years,
Or smile-illumed or dim with tears,
   Green hills of life that slope to death,
And haunts of home, whose vistaed trees
Shade off to mournful cypresses
   With the white amaranths underneath.
Even while I look, I can but heed
   The restless sands' incessant fall,

Importunate hours that hours succeed,
Each clamorous with its own sharp need,
    And duty keeping pace with all.
Shut down and clasp the heavy lids;
I hear again the voice that bids
The dreamer leave his dream midway
For larger hopes and graver fears:
Life greatens in these later years,
The century's aloe flowers to-day!

Yet, haply, in some lull of life,
Some Truce of God which breaks its strife,
The worldling's eyes shall gather dew,
    Dreaming in throngful city ways
Of winter joys his boyhood knew;
And dear and early friends—the few
Who yet remain—shall pause to view
    These Flemish pictures of old days;
Sit with me by the homestead hearth,
And stretch the hands of memory forth
    To warm them at the wood-fire's blaze!
And thanks untraced to lips unknown
Shall greet me like the odors blown
From unseen meadows newly mown,
Or lilies floating in some pond,
Wood-fringed, the wayside gaze beyond;
The traveller owns the grateful sense
Of sweetness near, he knows not whence,
And, pausing, takes with forehead bare
The benediction of the air.

from *Among the Hills*

Prelude

Along the roadside, like the flowers of gold
That tawny Incas for their gardens wrought,
Heavy with sunshine droops the golden-rod,

And the red pennons of the cardinal-flowers
Hang motionless upon their upright staves.
The sky is hot and hazy, and the wind,
Wing-weary with its long flight from the south,
Unfelt; yet, closely scanned, yon maple leaf
With faintest motion, as one stirs in dreams,
Confesses it. The locust by the wall
Stabs the noon-silence with his sharp alarm.
A single hay-cart down the dusty road
Creaks slowly, with its driver fast asleep
On the load's top. Against the neighboring hill,
Huddled along the stone wall's shady side,
The sheep show white, as if a snow-drift still
Defied the dog-star. Through the open door
A drowsy smell of flowers—gray heliotrope,
And white sweet-clover, and shy mignonette—
Comes faintly in, and silent chorus lends
To the pervading symphony of peace.

No time is this for hands long overworn
To task their strength; and (unto Him be praise
Who giveth quietness!) the stress and strain
Of years that did the work of centuries
Have ceased, and we can draw our breath once more
Freely and full. So, as yon harvesters
Make glad their nooning underneath the elms
With tale and riddle and old snatch of song,
I lay aside grave themes, and idly turn
The leaves of Memory's sketch-book, dreaming o'er
Old summer pictures of the quiet hills,
And human life, as quiet, at their feet.

And yet not idly all. A farmer's son,
Proud of field-lore and harvest craft, and feeling
All their fine possibilities, how rich
And restful even poverty and toil
Become when beauty, harmony, and love
Sit at their humble hearth as angels sat
At evening in the patriarch's tent, when man
Makes labor noble, and his farmer's frock

The symbol of a Christian chivalry
Tender and just and generous to her
Who clothes with grace all duty; still, I know
Too well the picture has another side,—
How wearily the grind of toil goes on
Where love is wanting, how the eye and ear
And heart are starved amidst the plenitude
Of nature, and how hard and colorless
Is life without an atmosphere. I look
Across the lapse of half a century,
And call to mind old homesteads, where no flower
Told that the spring had come, but evil weeds,
Nightshade and rough-leaved burdock in the place
Of the sweet doorway greeting of the rose
And honeysuckle, where the house walls seemed
Blistering in sun, without a tree or vine
To cast the tremulous shadow of its leaves
Across the curtainless windows from whose panes
Fluttered the signal rags of shiftlessness;
Within, the cluttered kitchen-floor, unwashed
(Broom-clean I think they called it); the best room
Stifling with cellar damp, shut from the air
In hot midsummer, bookless, pictureless
Save the inevitable sampler hung
Over the fireplace, or a mourning-piece,
A green-haired woman, peony-cheeked, beneath
Impossible willows; the wide-throated hearth
Bristling with faded pine-boughs half concealing
The piled-up rubbish at the chimney's back;
And, in sad keeping with all things about them,
Shrill, querulous women, sour and sullen men,
Untidy, loveless, old before their time,
With scarce a human interest save their own
Monotonous round of small economies,
Or the poor scandal of the neighborhood;
Blind to the beauty everywhere revealed,
Treading the May-flowers with regardless feet;
For them the song-sparrow and the bobolink
Sang not, nor winds made music in the leaves;
For them in vain October's holocaust

Burned, gold and crimson, over all the hills,
The sacramental mystery of the woods.
Church-goers, fearful of the unseen Powers,
But grumbling over pulpit-tax and pew-rent,
Saving, as shrewd economists, their souls
And winter pork with the least possible outlay
Of salt and sanctity; in daily life
Showing as little actual comprehension
Of Christian charity and love and duty,
As if the Sermon on the Mount had been
Outdated like a last year's almanac:
Rich in broad woodlands and in half-tilled fields,
And yet so pinched and bare and comfortless,
The veriest straggler limping on his rounds,
The sun and air his sole inheritance,
Laughed at a poverty that paid its taxes,
And hugged his rags in self-complacency!

Not such should be the homesteads of a land
Where whoso wisely wills and acts may dwell
As king and lawgiver, in broad-acred state,
With beauty, art, taste, culture, books, to make
His hour of leisure richer than a life
Of fourscore to the barons of old time,
Our yeoman should be equal to his home
Set in the fair, green valleys, purple walled,
A man to match his mountains, not to creep
Dwarfed and abased below them. I would fain
In this light way (of which I needs must own
With the knife-grinder of whom Canning sings,
"Story, God bless you! I have none to tell you!")
Invite the eye to see and heart to feel
The beauty and the joy within their reach, —
Home, and home loves, and the beatitudes
Of nature free to all. Haply in years
That wait to take the places of our own,
Heard where some breezy balcony looks down
On happy homes, or where the lake in the moon
Sleeps dreaming of the mountains, fair as Ruth,
In the old Hebrew pastoral, at the feet

Of Boaz, even this simple lay of mine
May seem the burden of a prophecy,
Finding its late fulfilment in a change
Slow as the oak's growth, lifting manhood up
Through broader culture, finer manners, love,
And reverence, to the level of the hills.

O Golden Age, whose light is of the dawn,
And not of sunset, forward, not behind,
Flood the new heavens and earth, and with thee bring
All the old virtues, whatsoever things
Are pure and honest and of good repute,
But add thereto whatever bard has sung
Or seer has told of when in trance and dream
They saw the Happy Isles of prophecy!
Let Justice hold her scale, and Truth divide
Between the right and wrong; but give the heart
The freedom of its fair inheritance;
Let the poor prisoner, cramped and starved so long,
At Nature's table feast his ear and eye
With joy and wonder; let all harmonies
Of sound, form, color, motion, wait upon
The princely guest, whether in soft attire
Of leisure clad, or the coarse frock of toil.
And, lending life to the dead form of faith,
Give human nature reverence for the sake
Of One who bore it, making it divine
With the ineffable tenderness of God;
Let common need, the brotherhood of prayer,
The heirship of an unknown destiny,
The unsolved mystery round about us, make
A man more precious than the gold of Ophir.
Sacred, inviolate, unto whom all things
Should minister, as outward types and signs
Of the eternal beauty which fulfils
The one great purpose of creation, Love,
The sole necessity of Earth and Heaven!

My Triumph

The autumn-time has come;
On woods that dream of bloom,
And over purpling vines,
The low sun fainter shines.

The aster-flower is failing,
The hazel's gold is paling;
Yet overhead more near
The eternal stars appear!

And present gratitude
Insures the future's good,
And for the things I see
I trust the things to be;

That in the paths untrod,
And the long days of God,
My feet shall still be led,
My heart be comforted.

O living friends who love me!
O dear ones gone above me!
Careless of other fame,
I leave to you my name.

Hide it from idle praises,
Save it from evil phrases:
Why, when dear lips that spake it
Are dumb, should strangers wake it?

Let the thick curtain fall;
I better know than all
How little I have gained,
How vast the unattained.

Not by the page word-painted
Let life be banned or sainted:
Deeper than written scroll
The colors of the soul.

Sweeter than any sung
My songs that found no tongue;
Nobler than any fact
My wish that failed of act.

Others shall sing the song,
Others shall right the wrong,—
Finish what I begin,
And all I fail of win.

What matter, I or they?
Mine or another's day,
So the right word be said
And life the sweeter made?

Hail to the coming singers!
Hail to the brave light-bringers!
Forward I reach and share
All that they sing and dare.

The airs of heaven blow o'er me;
A glory shines before me
Of what mankind shall be,—
Pure, generous, brave, and free.

A dream of man and woman
Diviner but still human,
Solving the riddle old,
Shaping the Age of Gold!

The love of God and neighbor;
An equal-handed labor;
The richer life, where beauty
Walks hand in hand with duty.

Ring, bells in unreared steeples,
The joy of unborn peoples!
Sound, trumpets far off blown,
Your triumph is my own!

Parcel and part of all,
I keep the festival,
Fore-reach the good to be,
And share the victory.

I feel the earth move sunward,
I join the great march onward,
And take, by faith, while living,
My freehold of thanksgiving.

Burning Drift-Wood

Before my drift-wood fire I sit,
 And see, with every waif I burn,
Old dreams and fancies coloring it,
 And folly's unlaid ghosts return.

O ships of mine, whose swift keels cleft
 The enchanted sea on which they sailed,
Are these poor fragments only left
 Of vain desires and hopes that failed?

Did I not watch from them the light
 Of sunset on my towers in Spain,
And see, far off, uploom in sight
 The Fortunate Isles I might not gain?

Did sudden lift of fog reveal
 Arcadia's vales of song and spring,
And did I pass, with grazing keel,
 The rocks whereon the sirens sing?

Have I not drifted hard upon
 The unmapped regions lost to man,
The cloud-pitched tents of Prester John,
 The palace domes of Kubla Khan?

Did land winds blow from jasmine flowers,
   Where Youth the ageless Fountain fills?
Did Love make sign from rose blown bowers,
   And gold from Eldorado's hills?

Alas! the gallant ships, that sailed
   On blind Adventure's errand sent,
Howe'er they laid their courses, failed
   To reach the haven of Content.

And of my ventures, those alone
   Which Love had freighted, safely sped,
Seeking a good beyond my own,
   By clear-eyed Duty piloted.

O mariners, hoping still to meet
   The luck Arabian voyagers met,
And find in Bagdad's moonlit street
   Haroun al Raschid walking yet,

Take with you, on your Sea of Dreams,
   The fair, fond fancies dear to youth.
I turn from all that only seems,
   And seek the sober grounds of truth.

What matter that it is not May,
   That birds have flown, and trees are bare,
That darker grows the shortening day,
   And colder blows the wintry air!

The wrecks of passion and desire,
   The castles I no more rebuild,
May fitly feed my drift-wood fire,
   And warm the hands that age has chilled.

Whatever perished with my ships,
   I only know the best remains;
A song of praise is on my lips
   For losses which are now my gains.

Heap high my hearth! No worth is lost;
  No wisdom with the folly dies.
Burn on, poor shreds, your holocaust
  Shall be my evening sacrifice!

Far more than all I dared to dream,
  Unsought before my door I see;
On wings of fire and steeds of steam
  The world's great wonders come to me,

And holier signs, unmarked before,
  Of Love to seek and Power to save,—
The righting of the wronged and poor,
  The man evolving from the slave;

And life, no longer chance or fate,
  Safe in the gracious Fatherhood.
I fold o'er-wearied hands and wait,
  In full assurance of the good.

And well the waiting time must be,
  Though brief or long its granted days,
If Faith and Hope and Charity
  Sit by my evening hearth-fire's blaze.

And with them, friends whom Heaven has spared,
  Whose love my heart has comforted,
And, sharing all my joys, has shared
  My tender memories of the dead,—

Dear souls who left us lonely here,
  Bound on their last, long voyage, to whom
We, day by day, are drawing near,
  Where every bark has sailing room.

I know the solemn monotone
  Of waters calling unto me;
I know from whence the airs have blown
  That whisper of the Eternal Sea.

As low my fires of drift-wood burn,
  I hear that sea's deep sounds increase,
And, fair in sunset light, discern
  Its mirage-lifted Isles of Peace.

EDGAR ALLAN POE

(1809–1849)

"Stanzas"

How often we forget all time, when lone
Admiring Nature's universal throne;
Her woods—her wilds—her mountains—the intense
Reply of HERS *to* OUR *intelligence!*

I

In youth have I known one with whom the Earth
In secret communing held—as he with it,
In day light, and in beauty from his birth:
Whose fervid, flick'ring torch of life was lit
From the sun and stars, whence he had drawn forth
A passionate light—such for his spirit was fit—
And yet that spirit knew—not in the hour
Of its own fervor—what had o'er it power.

2

Perhaps it may be that my mind is wrought
To a ferver by the moon beam that hangs o'er,
But I will half believe that wild light fraught
With more of sov'reignty than ancient lore
Hath ever told—or is it of a thought
The unembodied essence, and no more
That with a quick'ning spell doth o'er us pass
As dew of the night-time, o'er the summer grass?

3

Doth o'er us pass, when, as th' expanding eye
To the lov'd object—so the tear to the lid
Will start, which lately slept in apathy?
And yet it need not be—(that object) hid
From us in life—but common—which doth lie
Each hour before us—but *then* only bid
With a strange sound, as of a harp-string broken
T' awake us—'Tis a symbol and a token.

506

4

Of what in other worlds shall be — and giv'n
In beauty by our God, to those alone
Who otherwise would fall from life and Heav'n
Drawn by their heart's passion, and that tone,
That high tone of the spirit which hath striv'n
Tho' not with Faith — with godliness — whose throne
With desp'rate energy 't hath beaten down;
Wearing its own deep feeling as a crown.

The Lake — To ——

In spring of youth it was my lot
To haunt of the wide world a spot
The which I could not love the less —
So lovely was the loneliness
Of a wild lake, with black rock bound,
And the tall pines that towered around.

But when the Night had thrown her pall
Upon that spot, as upon all,
And the mystic wind went by
Murmuring in melody —
Then — ah then I would awake
To the terror of the lone lake.

Yet that terror was not fright,
But a tremulous delight —
A feeling not the jewelled mine
Could teach or bribe me to define —
Nor Love — although the Love were thine.

Death was in that poisonous wave,
And in its gulf a fitting grave
For him who thence could solace bring
To his lone imagining —
Whose solitary soul could make
An Eden of that dim lake.

To Science

Science! true daughter of Old Time thou art!
   Who alterest all things with thy peering eyes.
Why preyest thou thus upon the poet's heart,
   Vulture, whose wings are dull realities?
How should he love thee? or how deem thee wise,
   Who wouldst not leave him in his wandering
To seek for treasure in the jewelled skies,
   Albeit he soared with an undaunted wing?
Hast thou not dragged Diana from her car?
   And driven the Hamadryad from the wood
To seek a shelter in some happier star?
   Hast thou not torn the Naiad from her flood,
The Elfin from the green grass, and from me
The summer dream beneath the tamarind tree?

Al Aaraaf

PART I

O! nothing earthly save the ray
(Thrown back from flowers) of Beauty's eye,
As in those gardens where the day
Springs from the gems of Circassy—
O! nothing earthly save the thrill
Of melody in woodland rill—
Or (music of the passion-hearted)
Joy's voice so peacefully departed
That like the murmur in the shell,
Its echo dwelleth and will dwell—
Oh, nothing of the dross of ours—
Yet all the beauty—all the flowers
That list our Love, and deck our bowers—
Adorn yon world afar, afar—
The wandering star.

'Twas a sweet time for Nesace—for there
Her world lay lolling on the golden air,
Near four bright suns—a temporary rest—
An oasis in desert of the blest.
Away—away—'mid seas of rays that roll
Empyrean splendor o'er th' unchained soul—
The soul that scarce (the billows are so dense)
Can struggle to its destin'd eminence—
To distant spheres, from time to time, she rode,
And late to ours, the favour'd one of God—
But, now, the ruler of an anchor'd realm,
She throws aside the sceptre—leaves the helm,
And, amid incense and high spiritual hymns,
Laves in quadruple light her angel limbs.

Now happiest, loveliest in yon lovely Earth,
Whence sprang the "Idea of Beauty" into birth,
(Falling in wreaths thro' many a startled star,
Like woman's hair 'mid pearls, until, afar,
It lit on hills Achaian, and there dwelt)
She look'd into Infinity—and knelt.
Rich clouds, for canopies, about her curled—
Fit emblems of the model of her world—
Seen but in beauty—not impeding sight
Of other beauty glittering thro' the light—
A wreath that twined each starry form around,
And all the opal'd air in color bound.

All hurriedly she knelt upon a bed
Of flowers: of lilies such as rear'd the head
On the fair Capo Deucato, and sprang
So eagerly around about to hang
Upon the flying footsteps of——deep pride—
Of her who lov'd a mortal—and so died.
The Sephalica, budding with young bees,
Uprear'd its purple stem around her knees:
And gemmy flower, of Trebizond misnam'd—

Inmate of highest stars, where erst it sham'd
All other loveliness: its honied dew
(The fabled nectar that the heathen knew)
Deliriously sweet, was dropp'd from Heaven,
And fell on gardens of the unforgiven
In Trebizond—and on a sunny flower
So like its own above that, to this hour,
It still remaineth, torturing the bee
With madness, and unwonted reverie:
In Heaven, and all its environs, the leaf
And blossom of the fairy plant, in grief
Disconsolate linger—grief that hangs her head,
Repenting follies that full long have fled,
Heaving her white breast to the balmy air,
Like guilty beauty, chasten'd, and more fair:
Nyctanthes too, as sacred as the light
She fears to perfume, perfuming the night:
And Clytia pondering between many a sun,
While pettish tears adown her petals run:
And that aspiring flower that sprang on Earth—
And died, ere scarce exalted into birth,
Bursting its odorous heart in spirit to wing
Its way to Heaven, from garden of a king:
And Valisnerian lotus thither flown
From struggling with the waters of the Rhone:
And thy most lovely purple perfume, Zante!
Isola d'oro!—Fior di Levante!
And the Nelumbo bud that floats for ever
With Indian Cupid down the holy river—
Fair flowers, and fairy! to whose care is given
To bear the Goddess' song, in odors, up to Heaven:

> "Spirit! that dwellest where,
>   In the deep sky,
>   The terrible and fair,
>   In beauty vie!
>   Beyond the line of blue—
>   The boundary of the star
>   Which turneth at the view
>   Of thy barrier and thy bar—

Of the barrier overgone
   By the comets who were cast
From their pride, and from their throne
   To be drudges till the last—
To be carriers of fire
   (The red fire of their heart)
With speed that may not tire
   And with pain that shall not part—
Who livest—*that* we know—
   In Eternity—we feel—
But the shadow of whose brow
   What spirit shall reveal?
Tho' the beings whom thy Nesace,
   Thy messenger hath known
Have dream'd for thy Infinity
   A model of their own—
Thy will is done, Oh, God!
   The star hath ridden high
Thro' many a tempest, but she rode
   Beneath thy burning eye;
And here, in thought, to thee—
   In thought that can alone
Ascend thy empire and so be
   A partner of thy throne—
By winged Fantasy,
   My embassy is given,
Till secrecy shall knowledge be
   In the environs of Heaven."

She ceas'd—and buried then her burning cheek
Abash'd, amid the lilies there, to seek
A shelter from the fervour of His eye;
For the stars trembled at the Deity.
She stirr'd not—breath'd not—for a voice was there
How solemnly pervading the calm air!
A sound of silence on the startled ear
Which dreamy poets name "the music of the sphere."
Ours is a world of words: Quiet we call
"Silence"—which is the merest word of all.
All Nature speaks, and ev'n ideal things

Flap shadowy sounds from visionary wings—
But ah! not so when, thus, in realms on high
The eternal voice of God is passing by,
And the red winds are withering in the sky!

   "What tho' in worlds which sightless cycles run,
Link'd to a little system, and one sun—
Where all my love is folly and the crowd
Still think my terrors but the thunder cloud,
The storm, the earthquake, and the ocean-wrath—
(Ah! will they cross me in my angrier path?)
What tho' in worlds which own a single sun
The sands of Time grow dimmer as they run,
Yet thine is my resplendency, so given
To bear my secrets thro' the upper Heaven.
Leave tenantless thy crystal home, and fly,
With all thy train, athwart the moony sky—
Apart—like fire-flies in Sicilian night,
And wing to other worlds another light!
Divulge the secrets of thy embassy
To the proud orbs that twinkle—and so be
To ev'ry heart a barrier and a ban
Lest the stars totter in the guilt of man!"

   Up rose the maiden in the yellow night,
The single-mooned eve!—on Earth we plight
Our faith to one love—and one moon adore—
The birth-place of young Beauty had no more.
As sprang that yellow star from downy hours
Up rose the maiden from her shrine of flowers,
And bent o'er sheeny mountain and dim plain
Her way—but left not yet her Therasæan reign.

PART II

High on a mountain of enamell'd head—
Such as the drowsy shepherd on his bed
Of giant pasturage lying at his ease,
Raising his heavy eyelid, starts and sees

With many a mutter'd "hope to be forgiven"
What time the moon is quadrated in Heaven—
Of rosy head, that towering far away
Into the sunlit ether, caught the ray
Of sunken suns at eve—at noon of night,
While the moon danc'd with the fair stranger light—
Uprear'd upon such height arose a pile
Of gorgeous columns on th' unburthen'd air,
Flashing from Parian marble that twin smile
Far down upon the wave that sparkled there,
And nursled the young mountain in its lair.
Of molten stars their pavement, such as fall
Thro' the ebon air, besilvering the pall
Of their own dissolution, while they die—
Adorning then the dwellings of the sky.
A dome, by linked light from Heaven let down,
Sat gently on these columns as a crown—
A window of one circular diamond, there,
Look'd out above into the purple air,
And rays from God shot down that meteor chain
And hallow'd all the beauty twice again,
Save when, between th' Empyrean and that ring,
Some eager spirit flapp'd his dusky wing.
But on the pillars Seraph eyes have seen
The dimness of this world: that greyish green
That Nature loves the best for Beauty's grave
Lurk'd in each cornice, round each architrave—
And every sculptur'd cherub thereabout
That from his marble dwelling peeréd out,
Seem'd earthly in the shadow of his niche—
Achaian statues in a world so rich?
Friezes from Tadmor and Persepolis—
From Balbec, and the stilly, clear abyss
Of beautiful Gomorrah! O, the wave
Is now upon thee—but too late to save!

Sound loves to revel in a summer night:
Witness the murmur of the grey twilight
That stole upon the ear, in Eyraco,
Of many a wild star-gazer long ago—

That stealeth ever on the ear of him
Who, musing, gazeth on the distance dim,
And sees the darkness coming as a cloud—
Is not its form—its voice—most palpable and loud?

But what is this?—it cometh—and it brings
A music with it—'tis the rush of wings—
A pause—and then a sweeping, falling strain
And Nesace is in her halls again.
From the wild energy of wanton haste
   Her cheeks were flushing, and her lips apart;
And zone that clung around her gentle waist
   Had burst beneath the heaving of her heart.
Within the centre of that hall to breathe
She paus'd and panted, Zanthe! all beneath,
The fairy light that kiss'd her golden hair
And long'd to rest, yet could but sparkle there!

   Young flowers were whispering in melody
To happy flowers that night—and tree to tree;
Fountains were gushing music as they fell
In many a star-lit grove, or moon-lit dell;
Yet silence came upon material things—
Fair flowers, bright waterfalls and angel wings—
And sound alone that from the spirit sprang
Bore burthen to the charm the maiden sang:

     " 'Neath blue-bell or streamer—
       Or tufted wild spray
    That keeps, from the dreamer,
       The moonbeam away—
    Bright beings! that ponder,
       With half closing eyes,
    On the stars which your wonder
       Hath drawn from the skies,
    Till they glance thro' the shade, and
       Come down to your brow
    Like——eyes of the maiden
       Who calls on you now—

Arise! from your dreaming
    In violet bowers,
To duty beseeming
    These star-litten hours—
And shake from your tresses
    Encumber'd with dew
The breath of those kisses
    That cumber them too—
(O! how, without you, Love!
    Could angels be blest?)
Those kisses of true love
    That lull'd ye to rest!
Up!—shake from your wing
    Each hindering thing:
The dew of the night—
    It would weigh down your flight;
And true love caresses—
    O! leave them apart!
They are light on the tresses,
    But lead on the heart.

Ligeia! Ligeia!
    My beautiful one!
Whose harshest idea
    Will to melody run,
O! is it thy will
    On the breezes to toss?
Or, capriciously still,
    Like the lone Albatross,
Incumbent on night
    (As she on the air)
To keep watch with delight
    On the harmony there?

Ligeia! wherever
    Thy image may be,
No magic shall sever
    Thy music from thee.

Thou hast bound many eyes
   In a dreamy sleep—
But the strains still arise
   Which *thy* vigilance keep—
The sound of the rain
   Which leaps down to the flower,
And dances again
   In the rhythm of the shower—
The murmur that springs
   From the growing of grass
Are the music of things—
   But are modell'd, alas!—
Away, then my dearest,
   O! hie thee away
To springs that lie clearest
   Beneath the moon-ray—
To lone lake that smiles,
   In its dream of deep rest,
At the many star-isles
   That enjewel its breast—
Where wild flowers, creeping,
   Have mingled their shade,
On its margin is sleeping
   Full many a maid—
Some have left the cool glade, and
   Have slept with the bee—
Arouse them my maiden,
   On moorland and lea—
Go! breathe on their slumber,
   All softly in ear,
The musical number
   They slumber'd to hear—
For what can awaken
   An angel so soon
Whose sleep hath been taken
   Beneath the cold moon,
As the spell which no slumber
   Of witchery may test,
The rhythmical number
   Which lull'd him to rest?"

Spirits in wing, and angels to the view,
A thousand seraphs burst th' Empyrean thro',
Young dreams still hovering on their drowsy flight —
Seraphs in all but "Knowledge," the keen light
That fell, refracted, thro' thy bounds, afar
O Death! from eye of God upon that star:
Sweet was that error — sweeter still that death —
Sweet was that error — ev'n with *us* the breath
Of Science dims the mirror of our joy —
To them 'twere the Simoom, and would destroy —
For what (to them) availeth it to know
That Truth is Falsehood — or that Bliss is Woe?
Sweet was their death — with them to die was rife
With the last ecstasy of satiate life —
Beyond that death no immortality —
But sleep that pondereth and is not "to be" —
And there — oh! may my weary spirit dwell —
Apart from Heaven's Eternity — and yet how far from Hell!

What guilty spirit, in what shrubbery dim,
Heard not the stirring summons of that hymn?
But two: they fell: for Heaven no grace imparts
To those who hear not for their beating hearts.
A maiden-angel and her seraph-lover —
O! where (and ye may seek the wide skies over)
Was Love, the blind, near sober Duty known?
Unguided Love hath fallen — 'mid "tears of perfect moan."

He was a goodly spirit — he who fell:
A wanderer by moss-y-mantled well —
A gazer on the lights that shine above —
A dreamer in the moonbeam by his love:
What wonder? for each star is eye-like there,
And looks so sweetly down on Beauty's hair —
And they, and ev'ry mossy spring were holy
To his love-haunted heart and melancholy.
The night had found (to him a night of wo)
Upon a mountain crag, young Angelo —
Beetling it bends athwart the solemn sky,
And scowls on starry worlds that down beneath it lie.

Here sate he with his love—his dark eye bent
With eagle gaze along the firmament:
Now turn'd it upon her—but ever then
It trembled to the orb of EARTH again.

"Ianthe, dearest, see! how dim that ray!
How lovely 'tis to look so far away!
She seem'd not thus upon that autumn eve
I left her gorgeous halls—nor mourn'd to leave.
That eve—that eve—I should remember well—
The sun-ray dropp'd, in Lemnos, with a spell
On th' Arabesque carving of a gilded hall
Wherein I sate, and on the draperied wall—
And on my eye-lids—O the heavy light!
How drowsily it weigh'd them into night!
On flowers, before, and mist, and love they ran
With Persian Saadi in his Gulistan:
But O that light!—I slumber'd—Death, the while,
Stole o'er my senses in that lovely isle
So softly that no single silken hair
Awoke that slept—or knew that he was there.

The last spot of Earth's orb I trod upon
Was a proud temple call'd the Parthenon—
More beauty clung around her column'd wall
Than ev'n thy glowing bosom beats withal,
And when old Time my wing did disenthral
Thence sprang I—as the eagle from his tower,
And years I left behind me in an hour.
What time upon her airy bounds I hung
One half the garden of her globe was flung
Unrolling as a chart unto my view—
Tenantless cities of the desert too!
Ianthe, beauty crowded on me then,
And half I wish'd to be again of men."

"My Angelo! and why of them to be?
A brighter dwelling-place is here for thee—
And greener fields than in yon world above,
And woman's loveliness—and passionate love."

"But, list, Ianthe! when the air so soft
  Fail'd, as my pennon'd spirit leapt aloft,
  Perhaps my brain grew dizzy—but the world
  I left so late was into chaos hurl'd—
  Sprang from her station, on the winds apart,
  And roll'd, a flame, the fiery Heaven athwart.
  Methought, my sweet one, then I ceased to soar
  And fell—not swiftly as I rose before,
  But with a downward, tremulous motion thro'
  Light, brazen rays, this golden star unto!
  Nor long the measure of my falling hours,
  For nearest of all stars was thine to ours—
  Dread star! that came, amid a night of mirth,
  A red Dædalion on the timid Earth."

"We came—and to thy Earth—but not to us
  Be given our lady's bidding to discuss:
  We came, my love; around, above, below,
  Gay fire-fly of the night we come and go,
  Nor ask a reason save the angel-nod
  She grants to us, as granted by her God—
  But, Angelo, than thine grey Time unfurl'd
  Never his fairy wing o'er fairier world!
  Dim was its little disk, and angel eyes
  Alone could see the phantom in the skies,
  When first Al Aaraaf knew her course to be
  Headlong thitherward o'er the starry sea—
  But when its glory swell'd upon the sky,
  As glowing Beauty's bust beneath man's eye,
  We paus'd before the heritage of men,
  And thy star trembled—as doth Beauty then!"

Thus, in discourse, the lovers whiled away
The night that waned and waned and brought no day.
They fell: for Heaven to them no hope imparts,
Who hear not for the beating of their hearts.

Romance

Romance, who loves to nod and sing,
With drowsy head and folded wing,
Among the green leaves as they shake
Far down within some shadowy lake,
To me a painted paroquet
Hath been—a most familiar bird—
Taught me my alphabet to say—
To lisp my very earliest word
While in the wild wood I did lie,
A child—with a most knowing eye.

Of late, eternal Condor years
So shake the very Heaven on high
With tumult as they thunder by,
I have no time for idle cares
Through gazing on the unquiet sky.
And when an hour with calmer wings
Its down upon my spirit flings—
That little time with lyre and rhyme
To while away—forbidden things!
My heart would feel to be a crime
Unless it trembled with the strings.

Fairy-Land

Dim vales—and shadowy floods—
And cloudy-looking woods,
Whose forms we can't discover
For the tears that drip all over
Huge moons there wax and wane—
Again—again—again—
Every moment of the night—
Forever changing places—
And they put out the star-light
With the breath from their pale faces.
About twelve by the moon-dial
One more filmy than the rest

(A kind which, upon trial,
They have found to be the best)
Comes down—still down—and down
With its centre on the crown
Of a mountain's eminence,
While its wide circumference
In easy drapery falls
Over hamlets, over halls,
Wherever they may be—
O'er the strange woods—o'er the sea—
Over spirits on the wing—
Over every drowsy thing—
And buries them up quite
In a labyrinth of light—
And then, how deep!—O, deep!
Is the passion of their sleep.
In the morning they arise,
And their moony covering
Is soaring in the skies,
With the tempests as they toss,
Like——almost any thing—
Or a yellow Albatross.
They use that moon no more
For the same end as before—
Videlicet a tent—
Which I think extravagant:
Its atomies, however,
Into a shower dissever,
Of which those butterflies,
Of Earth, who seek the skies,
And so come down again
(Never-contented things!)
Have brought a specimen
Upon their quivering wings.

"Alone"

From childhood's hour I have not been
As others were—I have not seen
As others saw—I could not bring
My passions from a common spring—
From the same source I have not taken
My sorrow—I could not awaken
My heart to joy at the same tone—
And all I lov'd—*I* lov'd alone—
Then—in my childhood—in the dawn
Of a most stormy life—was drawn
From ev'ry depth of good and ill
The mystery which binds me still—
From the torrent, or the fountain—
From the red cliff of the mountain—
From the sun that 'round me roll'd
In its autumn tint of gold—
From the lightning in the sky
As it pass'd me flying by—
From the thunder, and the storm—
And the cloud that took the form
(When the rest of Heaven was blue)
Of a demon in my view—

To Helen

Helen, thy beauty is to me
  Like those Nicéan barks of yore,
That gently, o'er a perfumed sea,
  The weary, way-worn wanderer bore
  To his own native shore.

On desperate seas long wont to roam,
  Thy hyacinth hair, thy classic face,
Thy Naiad airs have brought me home
  To the glory that was Greece,
  And the grandeur that was Rome.

Lo! in yon brilliant window-niche
    How statue-like I see thee stand,
The agate lamp within thy hand!
    Ah, Psyche, from the regions which
Are Holy-Land!

Israfel

In Heaven a spirit doth dwell
    "Whose heart-strings are a lute;"
None sing so wildly well
As the angel Israfel,
And the giddy stars (so legends tell)
Ceasing their hymns, attend the spell
    Of his voice, all mute.

Tottering above
    In her highest noon,
    The enamoured moon
Blushes with love,
    While, to listen, the red levin
    (With the rapid Pleiads, even,
    Which were seven,)
    Pauses in Heaven.

And they say (the starry choir
    And the other listening things)
That Israfeli's fire
Is owing to that lyre
    By which he sits and sings—
The trembling living wire
Of those unusual strings.

But the skies that angel trod,
    Where deep thoughts are a duty—
Where Love's a grown-up God—
    Where the Houri glances are
Imbued with all the beauty
    Which we worship in a star.

Therefore, thou art not wrong,
    Israfeli, who despisest
An unimpassioned song;
To thee the laurels belong,
    Best bard, because the wisest!
Merrily live, and long!

The ecstasies above
    With thy burning measures suit—
Thy grief, thy joy, thy hate, thy love,
With the fervour of thy lute—
Well may the stars be mute!

Yes, Heaven is thine; but this
    Is a world of sweets and sours;
    Our flowers are merely—flowers,
And the shadow of thy perfect bliss
    Is the sunshine of ours.

If I could dwell
Where Israfel
    Hath dwelt, and he where I,
He might not sing so wildly well
    A mortal melody,
While a bolder note than this might swell
    From my lyre within the sky.

The Valley of Unrest

Once it smiled a silent dell
Where the people did not dwell;
They had gone unto the wars,
Trusting to the mild-eyed stars,
Nightly, from their azure towers,
To keep watch above the flowers,
In the midst of which all day
The red sun-light lazily lay.
Now each visitor shall confess
The sad valley's restlessness.

Nothing there is motionless—
Nothing save the airs that brood
Over the magic solitude.
Ah, by no wind are stirred those trees
That palpitate like the chill seas
Around the misty Hebrides!
Ah, by no wind those clouds are driven
That rustle through the unquiet Heaven
Uneasily, from morn till even,
Over the violets there that lie
In myriad types of the human eye—
Over the lilies there that wave
And weep above a nameless grave!
They wave:—from out their fragrant tops
Eternal dews come down in drops.
They weep:—from off their delicate stems
Perennial tears descend in gems.

The City in the Sea

Lo! Death has reared himself a throne
In a strange city lying alone
Far down within the dim West,
Where the good and the bad and the worst and the best
Have gone to their eternal rest.
There shrines and palaces and towers
(Time-eaten towers that tremble not!)
Resemble nothing that is ours.
Around, by lifting winds forgot,
Resignedly beneath the sky
The melancholy waters lie.

No rays from the holy heaven come down
On the long night-time of that town;
But light from out the lurid sea
Streams up the turrets silently—
Gleams up the pinnacles far and free—
Up domes—up spires—up kingly halls—
Up fanes—up Babylon-like walls—

Up shadowy long-forgotten bowers
Of sculptured ivy and stone flowers—
Up many and many a marvellous shrine
Whose wreathéd friezes intertwine
The viol, the violet, and the vine.

Resignedly beneath the sky
The melancholy waters lie.
So blend the turrets and shadows there
That all seem pendulous in air,
While from a proud tower in the town
Death looks gigantically down.

There open fanes and gaping graves
Yawn level with the luminous waves;
But not the riches there that lie
In each idol's diamond eye—
Not the gaily-jewelled dead
Tempt the waters from their bed;
For no ripples curl, alas!
Along that wilderness of glass—
No swellings tell that winds may be
Upon some far-off happier sea—
No heavings hint that winds have been
On seas less hideously serene.

But lo, a stir is in the air!
The wave—there is a movement there!
As if the towers had thrust aside,
In slightly sinking, the dull tide—
As if their tops had feebly given
A void within the filmy Heaven.
The waves have now a redder glow—
The hours are breathing faint and low—
And when, amid no earthly moans,
Down, down that town shall settle hence.
Hell, rising from a thousand thrones,
Shall do it reverence.

To F——

Beloved! amid the earnest woes
   That crowd around my earthly path—
(Drear path, alas! where grows
Not even one lonely rose)—
   My soul at least a solace hath
In dreams of thee, and therein knows
An Eden of bland repose.

And thus thy memory is to me
   Like some enchanted far-off isle
In some tumultuous sea—
Some ocean throbbing far and free
   With storms—but where meanwhile
Serenest skies continually
   Just o'er that one bright island smile.

The Coliseum

Type of the antique Rome! Rich reliquary
Of lofty contemplation left to Time
By buried centuries of pomp and power!
At length—at length—after so many days
Of weary pilgrimage and burning thirst,
(Thirst for the springs of lore that in thee lie,)
I kneel, an altered and an humble man,
Amid thy shadows, and so drink within
My very soul thy grandeur, gloom, and glory!

Vastness! and Age! and Memories of Eld!
Silence! and Desolation! and dim Night!
I feel ye now—I feel ye in your strength—
O spells more sure than e'er Judæan king
Taught in the gardens of Gethsemane!
O charms more potent than the rapt Chaldee
Ever drew down from out the quiet stars!

Here, where a hero fell, a column falls!
Here, where the mimic eagle glared in gold,
A midnight vigil holds the swarthy bat!
Here, where the dames of Rome their gilded hair
Waved to the wind, now wave the reed and thistle!
Here, where on golden throne the monarch lolled,
Glides, spectre-like, unto his marble home,
Lit by the wan light of the horned moon,
The swift and silent lizard of the stones!

But stay! these walls—these ivy-clad arcades—
These mouldering plinths—these sad and blackened shafts—
These vague entablatures—this crumbling frieze—
These shattered cornices—this wreck—this ruin—
These stones—alas! these gray stones—are they all—
All of the famed, and the colossal left
By the corrosive Hours to Fate and me?

"Not all"—the Echoes answer me—"not all!
Prophetic sounds and loud, arise forever
From us, and from all Ruin, unto the wise,
As melody from Memnon to the Sun.
We rule the hearts of mightiest men—we rule
With a despotic sway all giant minds.
We are not impotent—we pallid stones.
Not all our power is gone—not all our fame—
Not all the magic of our high renown—
Not all the wonder that encircles us—
Not all the mysteries that in us lie—
Not all the memories that hang upon
And cling around about us as a garment,
Clothing us in a robe of more than glory."

The Haunted Palace

In the greenest of our valleys
  By good angels tenanted,
Once a fair and stately palace—
  Radiant palace—reared its head.
In the monarch Thought's dominion—
  It stood there!
Never seraph spread a pinion
  Over fabric half so fair!

Banners yellow, glorious, golden,
  On its roof did float and flow—
(This—all this—was in the olden
  Time long ago)
And every gentle air that dallied,
  In that sweet day,
Along the ramparts plumed and pallid,
  A wingéd odor went away.

Wanderers in that happy valley,
  Through two luminous windows, saw
Spirits moving musically,
  To a lute's well-tunéd law,
Round about a throne where, sitting,
  Porphyrogene,
In state his glory well befitting
  The ruler of the realm was seen.

And all with pearl and ruby glowing
  Was the fair palace door,
Through which came flowing, flowing, flowing,
  And sparkling evermore,
A troop of Echoes whose sweet duty
  Was but to sing,
In voices of surpassing beauty,
  The wit and wisdom of their king.

But evil things, in robes of sorrow,
    Assailed the monarch's high estate.
(Ah, let us mourn!—for never morrow
    Shall dawn upon him, desolate!)
And round about his home the glory
    That blushed and bloomed,
Is but a dim-remembered story
    Of the old-time entombed.

And travellers, now, within that valley,
    Through the encrimsoned windows see
Vast forms that move fantastically
    To a discordant melody,
While, like a ghastly rapid river,
    Through the pale door
A hideous throng rush out forever
    And laugh—but smile no more.

Silence

There are some qualities—some incorporate things,
    That have a double life, which thus is made
A type of that twin entity which springs
    From matter and light, evinced in solid and shade.
There is a two-fold *Silence*—sea and shore—
    Body and soul. One dwells in lonely places,
    Newly with grass o'ergrown; some solemn graces,
Some human memories and tearful lore,
Render him terrorless: his name's "No More."
He is the corporate Silence: dread him not!
    No power hath he of evil in himself;
But should some urgent fate (untimely lot!)
    Bring thee to meet his shadow (nameless elf,
That haunteth the lone regions where hath trod
No foot of man,) commend thyself to God!

The Conqueror Worm

Lo! 'tis a gala night
   Within the lonesome latter years!
An angel throng, bewinged, bedight
   In veils, and drowned in tears,
Sit in a theatre, to see
   A play of hopes and fears,
While the orchestra breathes fitfully
   The music of the spheres.

Mimes, in the form of God on high,
   Mutter and mumble low,
And hither and thither fly—
   Mere puppets they, who come and go
At bidding of vast formless things
   That shift the scenery to and fro,
Flapping from out their Condor wings
   Invisible Wo!

That motley drama—oh, be sure
   It shall not be forgot!
With its Phantom chased for evermore,
   By a crowd that seize it not,
Through a circle that ever returneth in
   To the self-same spot,
And much of Madness, and more of Sin,
   And Horror the soul of the plot.

But see, amid the mimic rout
   A crawling shape intrude!
A blood-red thing that writhes from out
   The scenic solitude!
It writhes!—it writhes!—with mortal pangs
   The mimes become its food,
And seraphs sob at vermin fangs
   In human gore imbued.

Out—out are the lights—out all!
   And, over each quivering form,
The curtain, a funeral pall,
   Comes down with the rush of a storm,
While the angels, all pallid and wan,
   Uprising, unveiling, affirm
That the play is the tragedy, "Man,"
   And its hero the Conqueror Worm.

Lenore

Ah, broken is the golden bowl!—the spirit flown forever!
Let the bell toll!—a saintly soul floats on the Stygian
   river:—
And, Guy De Vere, hast *thou* no tear?—weep now or never
   more!
See! on yon drear and rigid bier low lies thy love, Lenore!
Come, let the burial rite be read—the funeral song be
   sung!—
An anthem for the queenliest dead that ever died so young—
A dirge for her the doubly dead in that she died so young.

"Wretches! ye loved her for her wealth and ye hated her for
   her pride;
And, when she fell in feeble health, ye blessed her—that she
   died:—
How *shall* the ritual then be read—the requiem how be
   sung
By you—by yours, the evil eye—by yours the slanderous
   tongue
That did to death the innocence that died and died so
   young?"

Peccavimus:—yet rave not thus! but let a Sabbath song
Go up to God so solemnly the dead may feel no wrong!
The sweet Lenore hath gone before, with Hope that flew
   beside,
Leaving thee wild for the dear child that should have been
   thy bride—

For her, the fair and debonair, that now so lowly lies,
The life upon her yellow hair, but not within her eyes—
The life still there upon her hair, the death upon her eyes.

"Avaunt!—avaunt! to friends from fiends the indignant ghost
    is riven—
From Hell unto a high estate within the utmost Heaven—
From moan and groan to a golden throne beside the King
    of Heaven:—
Let *no* bell toll, then, lest her soul, amid its hallowed mirth
Should catch the note as it doth float up from the damnéd
    Earth!
And I—tonight my heart is light:—no dirge will I upraise,
But waft the angel on her flight with a Pæan of old days!"

Dream-Land

By a route obscure and lonely,
Haunted by ill angels only,
Where an Eidolon, named NIGHT,
On a black throne reigns upright,
I have reached these lands but newly
From an ultimate dim Thule—
From a wild weird clime that lieth, sublime,
    Out of SPACE—out of TIME.

Bottomless vales and boundless floods,
And chasms, and caves, and Titan woods,
With forms that no man can discover
For the tears that drip all over;
Mountains toppling evermore
Into seas without a shore;
Seas that restlessly aspire,
Surging, unto skies of fire;
Lakes that endlessly outspread
Their lone waters—lone and dead,—
Their still waters—still and chilly
With the snows of the lolling lily.

By the lakes that thus outspread
Their lone waters, lone and dead,—
Their sad waters, sad and chilly
With the snows of the lolling lily,—
By the mountains—near the river
Murmuring lowly, murmuring ever,—
By the grey woods,—by the swamp
Where the toad and the newt encamp,—
By the dismal tarns and pools
  Where dwell the Ghouls,—
By each spot the most unholy—
In each nook most melancholy,—
There the traveller meets, aghast,
Sheeted Memories of the Past—
Shrouded forms that start and sigh
As they pass the wanderer by—
White-robed forms of friends long given,
In agony, to the Earth—and Heaven.

For the heart whose woes are legion
'Tis a peaceful, soothing region—
For the spirit that walks in shadow
'Tis—oh 'tis an Eldorado!
But the traveller, travelling through it,
May not—dare not openly view it;
Never its mysteries are exposed
To the weak human eye unclosed;
So wills its King, who hath forbid
The uplifting of the fringéd lid;
And thus the sad Soul that here passes
Beholds it but through darkened glasses.

By a route obscure and lonely,
Haunted by ill angels only,
Where an Eidolon, named NIGHT,
On a black throne reigns upright,
I have wandered home but newly
From this ultimate dim Thule.

The Raven

Once upon a midnight dreary, while I pondered, weak and
    weary,
Over many a quaint and curious volume of forgotten lore—
While I nodded, nearly napping, suddenly there came a
    tapping,
As of some one gently rapping, rapping at my chamber
    door.
" 'Tis some visiter," I muttered, "tapping at my chamber
    door—
                    Only this and nothing more."

Ah, distinctly I remember it was in the bleak December;
And each separate dying ember wrought its ghost upon the
    floor.
Eagerly I wished the morrow;—vainly I had sought to
    borrow
From my books surcease of sorrow—sorrow for the lost
    Lenore—
For the rare and radiant maiden whom the angels name
    Lenore—
                    Nameless *here* for evermore.

And the silken, sad, uncertain rustling of each purple
    curtain
Thrilled me—filled me with fantastic terrors never felt
    before;
So that now, to still the beating of my heart, I stood
    repeating
" 'Tis some visiter entreating entrance at my chamber
    door—
Some late visiter entreating entrance at my chamber
    door;—
                    This it is and nothing more."

Presently my soul grew stronger; hesitating then no longer,
"Sir," said I, "or Madam, truly your forgiveness I implore;
But the fact is I was napping, and so gently you came
          rapping,
And so faintly you came tapping, tapping at my chamber
          door,
That I scarce was sure I heard you"—here I opened wide
          the door;——
                    Darkness there and nothing more.

Deep into that darkness peering, long I stood there
          wondering, fearing,
Doubting, dreaming dreams no mortal ever dared to dream
          before;
But the silence was unbroken, and the stillness gave no
          token,
And the only word there spoken was the whispered word,
          "Lenore?"
This I whispered, and an echo murmured back the word,
          "Lenore!"
                    Merely this and nothing more.

Back into the chamber turning, all my soul within me
          burning,
Soon again I heard a tapping somewhat louder than before.
"Surely," said I, "surely that is something at my window
          lattice;
Let me see, then, what thereat is, and this mystery explore—
Let my heart be still a moment and this mystery explore;—
                    'Tis the wind and nothing more!"

Open here I flung the shutter, when, with many a flirt and
          flutter,
In there stepped a stately Raven of the saintly days of yore;
Not the least obeisance made he; not a minute stopped or
          stayed he;
But, with mien of lord or lady, perched above my chamber
          door—
Perched upon a bust of Pallas just above my chamber door—
                    Perched, and sat, and nothing more.

Then this ebony bird beguiling my sad fancy into smiling,
  By the grave and stern decorum of the countenance it
      wore,
"Though thy crest be shorn and shaven, thou," I said, "art
      sure no craven,
Ghastly grim and ancient Raven wandering from the
      Nightly shore—
Tell me what thy lordly name is on the Night's Plutonian
      shore!"
                    Quoth the Raven "Nevermore."

Much I marvelled this ungainly fowl to hear discourse so
      plainly,
Though its answer little meaning—little relevancy bore;
For we cannot help agreeing that no living human being
Ever yet was blessed with seeing bird above his chamber
      door—
Bird or beast upon the sculptured bust above his chamber
      door,
                    With such name as "Nevermore."

But the Raven, sitting lonely on the placid bust, spoke only
That one word, as if his soul in that one word he did
      outpour.
Nothing farther then he uttered—not a feather then he
      fluttered—
Till I scarcely more than muttered "Other friends have
      flown before—
On the morrow *he* will leave me, as my Hopes have flown
      before."
                    Then the bird said "Nevermore."

Startled at the stillness broken by reply so aptly spoken,
"Doubtless," said I, "what it utters is its only stock and store
Caught from some unhappy master whom unmerciful
      Disaster
Followed fast and followed faster till his songs one burden
      bore—
Till the dirges of his Hope that melancholy burden bore
                Of 'Never—nevermore.' "

But the Raven still beguiling my sad fancy into smiling,
Straight I wheeled a cushioned seat in front of bird, and
        bust and door;
Then, upon the velvet sinking, I betook myself to linking
Fancy unto fancy, thinking what this ominous bird of yore—
What this grim, ungainly, ghastly, gaunt, and ominous bird
        of yore
                        Meant in croaking "Nevermore."

This I sat engaged in guessing, but no syllable expressing
To the fowl whose fiery eyes now burned into my bosom's
        core;
This and more I sat divining, with my head at ease reclining
On the cushion's velvet lining that the lamp-light gloated
        o'er,
But whose velvet-violet lining with the lamp-light gloating
        o'er,
                        She shall press, ah, nevermore!

Then, methought, the air grew denser, perfumed from an
        unseen censer
Swung by seraphim whose foot-falls tinkled on the tufted
        floor.
"Wretch," I cried, "thy God hath lent thee—by these angels
        he hath sent thee
Respite—respite and nepenthe from thy memories of Lenore;
Quaff, oh quaff this kind nepenthe and forget this lost
        Lenore!"
                        Quoth the Raven "Nevermore."

"Prophet!" said I, "thing of evil!—prophet still, if bird or
        devil!—
Whether Tempter sent, or whether tempest tossed thee here
        ashore,
Desolate yet all undaunted, on this desert land enchanted—
On this home by Horror haunted—tell me truly, I implore—
Is there—*is* there balm in Gilead?—tell me—tell me, I
        implore!"
                        Quoth the Raven "Nevermore."

"Prophet!" said I, "thing of evil!—prophet still, if bird or
    devil!
By that Heaven that bends above us—by that God we both
    adore—
Tell this soul with sorrow laden if, within the distant
    Aidenn,
It shall clasp a sainted maiden whom the angels name
    Lenore—
Clasp a rare and radiant maiden whom the angels name
    Lenore."
                Quoth the Raven "Nevermore."

"Be that word our sign of parting, bird or fiend!" I shrieked,
    upstarting—
"Get thee back into the tempest and the Night's Plutonian
    shore!
Leave no black plume as a token of that lie thy soul hath
    spoken!
Leave my loneliness unbroken!—quit the bust above my
    door!
Take thy beak from out my heart, and take thy form from
    off my door!"
                Quoth the Raven "Nevermore."

And the Raven, never flitting, still is sitting, *still* is sitting
On the pallid bust of Pallas just above my chamber door;
And his eyes have all the seeming of a demon's that is
    dreaming,
And the lamp-light o'er him streaming throws his shadow
    on the floor;
And my soul from out that shadow that lies floating on the
    floor
                Shall be lifted—nevermore!

Ulalume—A Ballad

The skies they were ashen and sober;
    The leaves they were crispéd and sere—
    The leaves they were withering and sere:
It was night, in the lonesome October
    Of my most immemorial year:
It was hard by the dim lake of Auber,
    In the misty mid region of Weir:—
It was down by the dank tarn of Auber,
    In the ghoul-haunted woodland of Weir.

Here once, through an alley Titanic,
    Of cypress, I roamed with my Soul—
    Of cypress, with Psyche, my Soul.
These were days when my heart was volcanic
    As the scoriac rivers that roll—
    As the lavas that restlessly roll
Their sulphurous currents down Yaanek,
    In the ultimate climes of the Pole—
That groan as they roll down Mount Yaanek,
    In the realms of the Boreal Pole.

Our talk had been serious and sober,
    But our thoughts they were palsied and sere—
    Our memories were treacherous and sere;
For we knew not the month was October,
    And we marked not the night of the year—
    (Ah, night of all nights in the year!)
We noted not the dim lake of Auber,
    (Though once we had journeyed down here)
We remembered not the dank tarn of Auber,
    Nor the ghoul-haunted woodland of Weir.

And now, as the night was senescent,
    And star-dials pointed to morn—
    As the star-dials hinted of morn—
At the end of our path a liquescent
    And nebulous lustre was born,
Out of which a miraculous crescent

Arose with a duplicate horn—
Astarte's bediamonded crescent,
    Distinct with its duplicate horn.

And I said—"She is warmer than Dian;
    She rolls through an ether of sighs—
    She revels in a region of sighs.
She has seen that the tears are not dry on
    These cheeks where the worm never dies,
And has come past the stars of the Lion,
    To point us the path to the skies—
    To the Lethean peace of the skies—
Come up, in despite of the Lion,
    To shine on us with her bright eyes—
Come up, through the lair of the Lion,
    With love in her luminous eyes."

But Psyche, uplifting her finger,
    Said—"Sadly this star I mistrust—
    Her pallor I strangely mistrust—
Ah, hasten!—ah, let us not linger!
    Ah, fly!—let us fly!—for we must."
In terror she spoke; letting sink her
    Wings till they trailed in the dust—
In agony sobbed; letting sink her
    Plumes till they trailed in the dust—
    Till they sorrowfully trailed in the dust.

I replied—"This is nothing but dreaming.
    Let us on, by this tremulous light!
    Let us bathe in this crystalline light!
Its Sibyllic splendor is beaming
    With Hope and in Beauty to-night—
    See!—it flickers up the sky through the night!
Ah, we safely may trust to its gleaming
    And be sure it will lead us aright—
We surely may trust to a gleaming
    That cannot but guide us aright
Since it flickers up to Heaven through the night."

Thus I pacified Psyche and kissed her,
   And tempted her out of her gloom—
   And conquered her scruples and gloom;
And we passed to the end of the vista—
   But were stopped by the door of a tomb—
   By the door of a legended tomb:—
And I said—"What is written, sweet sister,
   On the door of this legended tomb?"
   She replied—"Ulalume—Ulalume!—
   'T is the vault of thy lost Ulalume!"

Then my heart it grew ashen and sober
   As the leaves that were crispéd and sere—
   As the leaves that were withering and sere—
And I cried—"It was surely October,
   On *this* very night of last year,
   That I journeyed—I journeyed down here!—
   That I brought a dread burden down here—
   On this night, of all nights in the year,
   Ah; what demon hath tempted me here?
Well I know, now, this dim lake of Auber—
   This misty mid region of Weir:—
Well I know, now, this dank tarn of Auber—
   This ghoul-haunted woodland of Weir."

Said we, then—the two, then—"Ah, can it
   Have been that the woodlandish ghouls—
   The pitiful, the merciful ghouls,
To bar up our way and to ban it
   From the secret that lies in these wolds—
   From the thing that lies hidden in these wolds—
Have drawn up the spectre of a planet
   From the limbo of lunary souls—
This sinfully scintillant planet
   From the Hell of the planetary souls?"

The Bells

1

Hear the sledges with the bells—
    Silver bells!
What a world of merriment their melody foretells!
    How they tinkle, tinkle, tinkle,
        In the icy air of night!
    While the stars that oversprinkle
    All the Heavens, seem to twinkle
        With a crystalline delight;
    Keeping time, time, time,
    In a sort of Runic rhyme,
To the tintinabulation that so musically wells
    From the bells, bells, bells, bells,
        Bells, bells, bells—
        From the jingling and the tinkling of the bells.

2

Hear the mellow wedding bells—
    Golden bells!
What a world of happiness their harmony foretells!
    Through the balmy air of night
    How they ring out their delight!—
        From the molten-golden notes
        And all in tune,
    What a liquid ditty floats
To the turtle-dove that listens while she gloats
        On the moon!
    Oh, from out the sounding cells
What a gush of euphony voluminously wells!
        How it swells!
        How it dwells
    On the Future!—how it tells
    Of the rapture that impels
To the swinging and the ringing
    Of the bells, bells, bells!—

Of the bells, bells, bells, bells,
   Bells, bells, bells —
To the rhyming and the chiming of the bells!

3

Hear the loud alarum bells —
   Brazen bells!
What tale of terror, now, their turbulency tells!
   In the startled ear of Night
   How they scream out their affright!
    Too much horrified to speak,
    They can only shriek, shriek,
     Out of tune,
In a clamorous appealing to the mercy of the fire —
In a mad expostulation with the deaf and frantic fire,
    Leaping higher, higher, higher,
    With a desperate desire
   And a resolute endeavor
   Now — now to sit, or never,
By the side of the pale-faced moon.
    Oh, the bells, bells, bells!
   What a tale their terror tells
    Of despair!
  How they clang and clash and roar!
  What a horror they outpour
In the bosom of the palpitating air!
    Yet the ear, it fully knows,
    By the twanging
    And the clanging,
  How the danger ebbs and flows: —
  Yes, the ear distinctly tells,
    In the jangling
    And the wrangling,
  How the danger sinks and swells,
By the sinking or the swelling in the anger of the bells —
    Of the bells —
  Of the bells, bells, bells, bells,
   Bells, bells, bells —
  In the clamor and the clangor of the bells.

4

Hear the tolling of the bells—
              Iron bells!
What a world of solemn thought their monody compels!
              In the silence of the night
              How we shiver with affright
          At the melancholy meaning of the tone!
              For every sound that floats
              From the rust within their throats
                  Is a groan.
                  And the people—ah, the people
                  They that dwell up in the steeple
                      All alone,
              And who, tolling, tolling, tolling,
                  In that muffled monotone,
              Feel a glory in so rolling
                  On the human heart a stone—
          They are neither man nor woman—
          They are neither brute nor human,
                  They are Ghouls:—
          And their king it is who tolls:—
          And he rolls, rolls, rolls, rolls
                  A Pæan from the bells!
              And his merry bosom swells
                  With the Pæan of the bells!
              And he dances and he yells;
          Keeping time, time, time,
          In a sort of Runic rhyme,
                  To the Pæan of the bells—
                  Of the bells:—
          Keeping time, time, time,
          In a sort of Runic rhyme,
                  To the throbbing of the bells—
          Of the bells, bells, bells—
                  To the sobbing of the bells:—
          Keeping time, time, time,
                  As he knells, knells, knells,
          In a happy Runic rhyme,
                  To the rolling of the bells—

Of the bells, bells, bells:—
   To the tolling of the bells—
Of the bells, bells, bells, bells,
   Bells, bells, bells—
To the moaning and the groaning of the bells.

For Annie

Thank Heaven! the crisis—
   The danger is past,
And the lingering illness
   Is over at last—
And the fever called "Living"
   Is conquered at last.

Sadly, I know
   I am shorn of my strength,
And no muscle I move
   As I lie at full length—
But no matter!—I feel
   I am better at length.

And I rest so composedly,
   Now, in my bed,
That any beholder
   Might fancy me dead—
Might start at beholding me,
   Thinking me dead.

The moaning and groaning,
   The sighing and sobbing,
Are quieted now,
   With that horrible throbbing
At heart:—ah, that horrible,
   Horrible throbbing!

The sickness—the nausea—
  The pitiless pain—
Have ceased, with the fever
  That maddened my brain—
With the fever called "Living"
  That burned in my brain.

And oh! of all tortures
  That torture the worst
Has abated—the terrible
  Torture of thirst
For the napthaline river
  Of Passion accurst:—
I have drank of a water
  That quenches all thirst:—

Of a water that flows,
  With a lullaby sound,
From a spring but a very few
  Feet under ground—
From a cavern not very far
  Down under ground.

And ah! let it never
  Be foolishly said
That my room it is gloomy
  And narrow my bed;
For man never slept
  In a different bed—
And, to *sleep*, you must slumber
  In just such a bed.

My tantalized spirit
  Here blandly reposes,
Forgetting, or never
  Regretting its roses—
Its old agitations
  Of myrtles and roses:

For now, while so quietly
   Lying, it fancies
A holier odor
   About it, of pansies—
A rosemary odor,
   Commingled with pansies—
With rue and the beautiful
   Puritan pansies.

And so it lies happily,
   Bathing in many
A dream of the truth
   And the beauty of Annie—
Drowned in a bath
   Of the tresses of Annie.

She tenderly kissed me,
   She fondly caressed,
And then I fell gently
   To sleep on her breast—
Deeply to sleep
   From the heaven of her breast.

When the light was extinguished,
   She covered me warm,
And she prayed to the angels
   To keep me from harm—
To the queen of the angels
   To shield me from harm.

And I lie so composedly,
   Now, in my bed,
(Knowing her love)
   That you fancy me dead—
And I rest so contentedly,
   Now in my bed,
(With her love at my breast)
   That you fancy me dead—
That you shudder to look at me,
   Thinking me dead:—

But my heart it is brighter
　　Than all of the many
Stars in the sky,
　　For it sparkles with Annie—
It glows with the light
　　Of the love of my Annie—
With the thought of the light
　　Of the eyes of my Annie.

Eldorado

　　Gaily bedight,
　　A gallant knight,
In sunshine and in shadow,
　　Had journeyed long,
　　Singing a song,
In search of Eldorado.

　　But he grew old—
　　This knight so bold—
And o'er his heart a shadow
　　Fell, as he found
　　No spot of ground
That looked like Eldorado.

　　And, as his strength
　　Failed him at length,
He met a pilgrim shadow—
　　'Shadow,' said he,
　　'Where can it be—
This land of Eldorado?'

　　'Over the Mountains
　　Of the Moon,
Down the Valley of the Shadow,
　　Ride, boldly ride,'
　　The shade replied,—
'If you seek for Eldorado!'

Annabel Lee

It was many and many a year ago,
   In a kingdom by the sea,
That a maiden there lived whom you may know
   By the name of Annabel Lee; —
And this maiden she lived with no other thought
   Than to love and be loved by me.

She was a child and *I* was a child,
   In this kingdom by the sea,
But we loved with a love that was more than love —
   I and my Annabel Lee —
With a love that the wingéd seraphs of Heaven
   Coveted her and me.

And this was the reason that, long ago,
   In this kingdom by the sea,
A wind blew out of a cloud by night
   Chilling my Annabel Lee;
So that her high-born kinsmen came
   And bore her away from me,
To shut her up in a sepulchre
   In this kingdom by the sea.

The angels, not half so happy in Heaven,
   Went envying her and me;
Yes! that was the reason (as all men know,
   In this kingdom by the sea)
That the wind came out of the cloud, chilling
   And killing my Annabel Lee.

But our love it was stronger by far than the love
   Of those who were older than we —
   Of many far wiser than we —
And neither the angels in Heaven above
   Nor the demons down under the sea
Can ever dissever my soul from the soul
   Of the beautiful Annabel Lee: —

For the moon never beams without bringing me dreams
 Of the beautiful Annabel Lee;
And the stars never rise but I see the bright eyes
 Of the beautiful Annabel Lee;
And so, all the night-tide, I lie down by the side
Of my darling, my darling, my life and my bride
 In her sepulchre there by the sea—
 In her tomb by the side of the sea.

ABRAHAM LINCOLN

(1809–1865)

My Childhood-Home I See Again

My childhood-home I see again,
   And gladden with the view;
And still as mem'ries crowd my brain,
   There's sadness in it too.

O memory! thou mid-way world
   'Twixt Earth and Paradise,
Where things decayed, and loved ones lost
   In dreamy shadows rise.

And freed from all that's gross or vile,
   Seem hallowed, pure, and bright,
Like scenes in some enchanted isle,
   All bathed in liquid light.

As distant mountains please the eye,
   When twilight chases day—
As bugle-tones, that, passing by,
   In distance die away—

As leaving some grand water-fall
   We ling'ring, list it's roar,
So memory will hallow all
   We've known, but know no more.

Now twenty years have passed away,
   Since here I bid farewell
To woods, and fields, and scenes of play
   And school-mates loved so well.

Where many were, how few remain
   Of old familiar things!

But seeing these to mind again
    The lost and absent brings.

The friends I left that parting day—
    How changed, as time has sped!
Young childhood grown, strong manhood grey,
    And half of all are dead.

I hear the lone survivors tell
    How nought from death could save,
Till every sound appears a knell,
    And every spot a grave.

I range the fields with pensive tread,
    And pace the hollow rooms;
And feel (companions of the dead)
    I'm living in the tombs.

And here's an object more of dread,
    Than ought the grave contains—
A human-form, with reason fled,
    While wretched life remains.

Poor Matthew! Once of genius bright,—
    A fortune-favored child—
Now locked for aye, in mental night,
    A haggard mad-man wild.

Poor Matthew! I have ne'er forgot
    When first with maddened will,
Yourself you maimed, your father fought,
    And mother strove to kill;

And terror spread, and neighbours ran,
    Your dang'rous strength to bind;
And soon a howling crazy man,
    Your limbs were fast confined.

How then you writhed and shrieked aloud,
    Your bones and sinnews bared;
And fiendish on the gaping crowd,
    With burning eye-balls glared.

And begged, and swore, and wept, and prayed,
    With maniac laughter joined—
How fearful are the signs displayed,
    By pangs that kill the mind!

And when at length, tho' drear and long,
    Time soothed your fiercer woes—
How plaintively your mournful song,
    Upon the still night rose.

I've heard it oft, as if I dreamed,
    Far-distant, sweet, and lone;
The funeral dirge it ever seemed
    Of reason dead and gone.

To drink it's strains, I've stole away,
    All silently and still,
Ere yet the rising god of day
    Had streaked the Eastern hill.

Air held his breath; the trees all still
    Seemed sorr'wing angels round.
Their swelling tears in dew-drops fell
    Upon the list'ning ground.

But this is past, and nought remains
    That raised you o'er the brute.
Your mad'ning shrieks and soothing strains
    Are like forever mute.

Now fare thee well: more thou the cause
    Than subject now of woe.
All mental pangs, but time's kind laws,
    Hast lost the power to know.

And now away to seek some scene
   Less painful than the last—
With less of horror mingled in
   The present and the past.

The very spot where grew the bread
   That formed my bones, I see.
How strange, old field, on thee to tread,
   And feel I'm part of thee!

OLIVER WENDELL HOLMES

(1809–1894)

Old Ironsides

Ay, tear her tattered ensign down!
    Long has it waved on high,
And many an eye has danced to see
    That banner in the sky;
Beneath it rung the battle shout,
    And burst the cannon's roar;—
The meteor of the ocean air
    Shall sweep the clouds no more!

Her deck, once red with heroes' blood
    Where knelt the vanquished foe,
When winds were hurrying o'er the flood
    And waves were white below,
No more shall feel the victor's tread,
    Or know the conquered knee;—
The harpies of the shore shall pluck
    The eagle of the sea!

O better that her shattered hulk
    Should sink beneath the wave;
Her thunders shook the mighty deep,
    And there should be her grave;
Nail to the mast her holy flag,
    Set every thread-bare sail,
And give her to the god of storms,—
    The lightning and the gale!

The Chambered Nautilus

This is the ship of pearl, which, poets feign,
 Sails the unshadowed main,—
 The venturous bark that flings
On the sweet summer wind its purpled wings
In gulfs enchanted, where the siren sings,
 And coral reefs lie bare,
Where the cold sea-maids rise to sun their streaming hair.

Its webs of living gauze no more unfurl;
 Wrecked is the ship of pearl!
 And every chambered cell,
Where its dim dreaming life was wont to dwell,
As the frail tenant shaped his growing shell,
 Before thee lies revealed,—
Its irised ceiling rent, its sunless crypt unsealed!

Year after year beheld the silent toil
 That spread his lustrous coil;
 Still, as the spiral grew,
He left the past year's dwelling for the new,
Stole with soft step its shining archway through,
 Built up its idle door,
Stretched in his last-found home, and knew the old no
  more.

Thanks for the heavenly message brought by thee,
 Child of the wandering sea,
 Cast from her lap forlorn!
From thy dead lips a clearer note is born
Than ever Triton blew from wreathèd horn!
 While on mine ear it rings,
Through the deep caves of thought I hear a voice that
  sings:—

Build thee more stately mansions, O my soul,
    As the swift seasons roll!
    Leave thy low-vaulted past!
Let each new temple, nobler than the last,
Shut thee from heaven with a dome more vast,
    Till thou at length art free,
Leaving thine outgrown shell by life's unresting sea!

The Living Temple

Not in the world of light alone,
Where God has built his blazing throne,
Nor yet alone in earth below,
With belted seas that come and go,
And endless isles of sunlit green,
Is all thy Maker's glory seen:
Look in upon thy wondrous frame,—
Eternal wisdom still the same!

The smooth, soft air with pulse-like waves
Flows murmuring through its hidden caves,
Whose streams of brightening purple rush
Fired with a new and livelier blush,
While all their burden of decay
The ebbing current steals away,
And red with Nature's flame they start
From the warm fountains of the heart.

No rest that throbbing slave may ask,
Forever quivering o'er his task,
While far and wide a crimson jet
Leaps forth to fill the woven net
Which in unnumbered crossing tides
The flood of burning life divides,
Then kindling each decaying part
Creeps back to find the throbbing heart.

But warmed with that unchanging flame
Behold the outward moving frame,
Its living marbles jointed strong
With glistening band and silvery thong,
And linked to reason's guiding reins
By myriad rings in trembling chains,
Each graven with the threaded zone
Which claims it as the master's own.

See how yon beam of seeming white
Is braided out of seven-hued light,
Yet in those lucid globes no ray
By any chance shall break astray.
Hark how the rolling surge of sound,
Arches and spirals circling round,
Wakes the hushed spirit through thine ear
With music it is heaven to hear.

Then mark the cloven sphere that holds
All thought in its mysterious folds,
That feels sensation's faintest thrill
And flashes forth the sovereign will;
Think on the stormy world that dwells
Locked in its dim and clustering cells!
The lightning gleams of power it sheds
Along its hollow glassy threads!

O Father! grant thy love divine
To make these mystic temples thine!
When wasting age and wearying strife
Have sapped the leaning walls of life,
When darkness gathers over all,
And the last tottering pillars fall,
Take the poor dust thy mercy warms
And mould it into heavenly forms!

The Deacon's Masterpiece:
or the Wonderful "One-Hoss-Shay"

A Logical Story

Have you heard of the wonderful one-hoss-shay,
That was built in such a logical way
It ran a hundred years to a day,
And then, of a sudden, it——ah, but stay,
I'll tell you what happened without delay,
Scaring the parson into fits,
Frightening people out of their wits,—
Have you ever heard of that, I say?

Seventeen hundred and fifty-five.
Georgius Secundus was then alive,—
Snuffy old drone from the German hive!
That was the year when Lisbon-town
Saw the earth open and gulp her down,
And Braddock's army was done so brown,
Left without a scalp to its crown.
It was on the terrible Earthquake-day
That the Deacon finished the one-hoss-shay.

Now in building of chaises, I tell you what,
There is always *somewhere* a weakest spot,—
In hub, tire, felloe, in spring or thill,
In panel, or crossbar, or floor, or sill,
In screw, bolt, thoroughbrace,—lurking still
Find it somewhere you must and will,—
Above or below, or within or without,—
And that's the reason, beyond a doubt,
A chaise *breaks down*, but doesn't *wear out*.

But the Deacon swore (as Deacons do,
With an "I dew vum," or an "I tell *yeou*,")
He would build one shay to beat the taown
'n' the keounty 'n' all the kentry raoun';
It should be so built that it *couldn'* break daown:
—"Fur," said the Deacon, "'t's mighty plain

Thut the weakes' place mus' stan the strain;
'n' the way t' fix it, uz I maintain,
          Is only jest
T' make that place uz strong uz the rest."

So the Deacon inquired of the village folk
Where he could find the strongest oak,
That couldn't be split nor bent nor broke,—
That was for spokes and floor and sills;
He sent for lancewood to make the thills;
The crossbars were ash, from the straightest trees;
The panels of white-wood, that cuts like cheese,
But lasts like iron for things like these;
The hubs of logs from the "Settler's ellum,"—
Last of its timber,—they couldn't sell 'em,
Never an axe had seen their chips,
And the wedges flew from between their lips,
Their blunt ends frizzled like celery-tips;
Step and prop-iron, bolt and screw,
Spring, tire, axle, and linchpin too,
Steel of the finest, bright and blue;
Thoroughbrace bison-skin, thick and wide;
Boot, top, dasher, from tough old hide
Found in the pit when the tanner died.
That was the way he "put her through."—
"There!" said the Deacon, "naow she'll dew!"

Do! I tell you, I rather guess
She was a wonder, and nothing less!
Colts grew horses, beards turned gray,
Deacon and deaconess dropped away,
Children and grand-children—where were they?
But there stood the stout old one-hoss-shay
As fresh as on Lisbon-earthquake-day!

EIGHTEEN HUNDRED;—it came and found
The Deacon's Masterpiece strong and sound.
Eighteen hundred increased by ten;—
"Hahnsum kerridge" they called it then.
Eighteen hundred and twenty came;—

Running as usual; much the same.
Thirty and forty at last arrive,
And then come fifty, and FIFTY-FIVE.

Little of all we value here
Wakes on the morn of its hundredth year
Without both feeling and looking queer.
In fact, there's nothing that keeps its youth,
So far as I know, but a tree and truth.
(This is a moral that runs at large;
Take it.—You're welcome.—No extra charge.)

FIRST OF NOVEMBER,—the Earthquake-day.—
There are traces of age in the one-hoss-shay,
A general flavor of mild decay,
But nothing local, as one may say.
There couldn't be,—for the Deacon's art
Had made it so like in every part
That there wasn't a chance for one to start.
For the wheels were just as strong as the thills,
And the floor was just as strong as the sills,
And the panels just as strong as the floor,
And the whippletree neither less nor more,
And the back-crossbar as strong as the fore,
And spring and axle and hub *encore*.
And yet, *as a whole*, it is past a doubt
In another hour it will be *worn out!*

First of November, 'Fifty-five!
This morning the parson takes a drive.
Now, small boys, get out of the way!
Here comes the wonderful one-horse-shay,
Drawn by a rat-tailed, ewe-necked bay.
"Huddup!" said the parson.—Off went they.

The parson was working his Sunday's text,—
Had got to *fifthly*, and stopped perplexed
At what the—Moses—was coming next.
All at once the horse stood still,

Close by the meet'n'-house on the hill.
—First a shiver, and then a thrill,
Then something decidedly like a spill,—
And the parson was sitting upon a rock,
At half-past nine by the meet'n-house clock,—
Just the hour of the Earthquake shock!
—What do you think the parson found,
When he got up and stared around?
The poor old chaise in a heap or mound,
As if it had been to the mill and ground!
You see, of course, if you're not a dunce,
How it went to pieces all at once,—
All at once, and nothing first,—
Just as bubbles do when they burst.

End of the wonderful one-hoss-shay.
Logic is logic. That's all I say.

Contentment

"Man wants but little here below."

Little I ask; my wants are few;
  I only wish a hut of stone,
(A *very plain* brown stone will do,)
      That I may call my own;—
And close at hand is such a one,
In yonder street that fronts the sun.

Plain food is quite enough for me;
  Three courses are as good as ten;—
If Nature can subsist on three,
      Thank Heaven for three. Amen!
I always thought cold victual nice;—
My *choice* would be vanilla-ice.

I care not much for gold or land;—
  Give me a mortgage here and there,—

Some good bank-stock,—some note of hand,
    Or trifling railroad share;—
I only ask that Fortune send
A *little* more than I shall spend.

Honors are silly toys, I know,
    And titles are but empty names;—
I would, *perhaps*, be Plenipo,—
        But only near St. James;—
I'm very sure I should not care
To fill our Gubernator's chair.

Jewels are baubles; 'tis a sin
    To care for such unfruitful things;—
One good-sized diamond in a pin,—
        Some, *not so large*, in rings,—
A ruby, and a pearl, or so,
Will do for me;—I laugh at show.

My dame should dress in cheap attire;
    (Good, heavy silks are never dear;)—
I own perhaps I *might* desire
        Some shawls of true cashmere,—
Some marrowy crapes of China silk,
Like wrinkled skins on scalded milk.

I would not have the horse I drive
    So fast that folks must stop and stare;
An easy gait—two, forty-five—
        Suits me; I do not care;—
Perhaps, for just a *single spurt*,
Some seconds less would do no hurt.

Of pictures, I should like to own
    Titians and Raphaels three or four,—
I love so much their style and tone,—
        One Turner, and no more,—
(A landscape,—foreground golden dirt;
The sunshine painted with a squirt.)

Of books but few,—some fifty score
   For daily use, and bound for wear;
The rest upon an upper floor;—
      Some *little* luxury *there*
Of red morocco's gilded gleam,
And vellum rich as country cream.

Busts, cameos, gems,—such things as these,
   Which others often show for pride,
I value for their power to please,
      And selfish churls deride;—
One Stradivarius, I confess,
Two Meerschaums, I would fain possess.

Wealth's wasteful tricks I will not learn,
   Nor ape the glittering upstart fool;—
Shall not carved tables serve my turn,
      But *all* must be of buhl?
Give grasping pomp its double share,—
I ask but *one* recumbent chair.

Thus humble let me live and die,
   Nor long for Midas' golden touch,
If Heaven more generous gifts deny,
      I shall not miss them *much*,—
Too grateful for the blessing lent
Of simple tastes and mind content!

The Voiceless

We count the broken lyres that rest
   Where the sweet wailing singers slumber,—
But o'er their silent sister's breast
   The wild flowers who will stoop to number?
A few can touch the magic string,
   And noisy Fame is proud to win them;—
Alas for those that never sing,
   But die with all their music in them!

Nay, grieve not for the dead alone
    Whose song has told their hearts' sad story,—
Weep for the voiceless, who have known
    The cross without the crown of glory!
Not where Leucadian breezes sweep
    O'er Sappho's memory-haunted billow,
But where the glistening night-dews weep
    On nameless sorrow's churchyard pillow.

O hearts that break and give no sign
    Save whitening lip and fading tresses,
Till Death pours out his cordial wine
    Slow-dropped from Misery's crushing presses,—
If singing breath or echoing chord
    To every hidden pang were given,
What endless melodies were poured,
    As sad as earth, as sweet as heaven!

The Two Streams

Behold the rocky wall
    That down its sloping sides
Pours the swift rain-drops, blending, as they fall,
    In rushing river-tides!

Yon stream, whose sources run
    Turned by a pebble's edge,
Is Athabasca, rolling toward the sun
    Through the cleft mountain-ledge.

The slender rill had strayed,
    But for the slanting stone,
To evening's ocean, with the tangled braid
    Of foam-flecked Oregon,

So from the heights of Will
    Life's parting stream descends,
And, as a moment turns its slender rill,
    Each widening torrent bends,—

From the same cradle's side,
From the same mother's knee,—
One to long darkness and the frozen tide,
One to the Peaceful Sea!

from *Wind-Clouds and Star-Drifts*

III
SYMPATHIES

The snows that glittered on the disk of Mars
Have melted, and the planet's fiery orb
Rolls in the crimson summer of its year;
But what to me the summer or the snow
Of worlds that throb with life in forms unknown,
If life indeed be theirs; I heed not these.
My heart is simply human; all my care
For them whose dust is fashioned like mine own;
These ache with cold and hunger, live in pain,
And shake with fear of worlds more full of woe;
There may be others worthier of my love,
But such I know not save through these I know.

There are two veils of language, hid beneath
Whose sheltering folds, we dare to be ourselves;
And not that other self which nods and smiles
And babbles in our name; the one is Prayer,
Lending its licensed freedom to the tongue
That tells our sorrows and our sins to Heaven;
The other, Verse, that throws its spangled web
Around our naked speech and makes it bold.
I, whose best prayer is silence; sitting dumb
In the great temple where I nightly serve
Him who is throned in light, have dared to claim
The poet's franchise, though I may not hope
To wear his garland; hear me while I tell
My story in such form as poets use,
But breathed in fitful whispers, as the wind
Sighs and then slumbers, wakes and sighs again.

Thou Vision, floating in the breathless air
Between me and the fairest of the stars,
I tell my lonely thoughts as unto thee.
Look not for marvels of the scholar's pen
In my rude measure; I can only show
A slender-margined, unillumined page,
And trust its meaning to the flattering eye
That reads it in the gracious light of love.
Ah, would thou clothe thyself in breathing shape
And nestle at my side, my voice should lend
Whate'er my verse may lack of tender rhythm
To make thee listen.
            I have stood entrancéd
When, with her fingers wandering o'er the keys,
The white enchantress with the golden hair
Breathed all her soul through some unvalued rhyme;
Some flower of song that long had lost its bloom;
Lo! its dead summer kindled as she sang!
The sweet contralto, like the ringdove's coo,
Thrilled it with brooding, fond, caressing tones,
And the pale minstrel's passion lived again,
Tearful and trembling as a dewy rose
The wind has shaken till it fills the air
With light and fragrance. Such the wondrous charm
A song can borrow when the bosom throbs
That lends it breath.
            So from the poet's lips
His verse sounds doubly sweet, for none like him
Feels every cadence of its wave-like flow;
He lives the passion over, while he reads,
That shook him as he sang his lofty strain,
And pours his life through each resounding line,
As ocean, when the stormy winds are hushed,
Still rolls and thunders through his billowy caves.

Nearing the Snow-Line

Slow toiling upward from the misty vale,
   I leave the bright enamelled zones below;
   No more for me their beauteous bloom shall glow,
Their lingering sweetness load the morning gale;
Few are the slender flowerets, scentless, pale,
   That on their ice-clad stems all trembling blow
   Along the margin of unmelting snow;
Yet with unsaddened voice thy verge I hail,
   White realm of peace above the flowering line;
Welcome thy frozen domes, thy rocky spires!
   O'er thee undimmed the moon-girt planets shine,
On thy majestic altars fade the fires
That filled the air with smoke of vain desires,
   And all the unclouded blue of heaven is thine!

The Flaneur

Boston Common, December 6, 1882.

During the Transit of Venus

I love all sights of earth and skies,
From flowers that glow to stars that shine;
The comet and the penny show,
All curious things, above, below,
Hold each in turn my wandering eyes:
I claim the Christian Pagan's line,
Humani nihil, — even so, —
And is not human life divine?

When soft the western breezes blow,
And strolling youths meet sauntering maids,
I love to watch the stirring trades
Beneath the Vallombrosa shades
Our much-enduring elms bestow;
The vender and his rhetoric's flow,
That lambent stream of liquid lies;
The bait he dangles from his line,

The gudgeon and his gold-washed prize.
I halt before the blazoned sign
That bids me linger to admire
The drama time can never tire,
The little hero of the hunch,
With iron arm and soul of fire,
And will that works his fierce desire,—
Untamed, unscared, unconquered Punch!
My ear a pleasing torture finds
In tones the withered sibyl grinds,—
The *dame sans merci's* broken strain,
Whom I erewhile, perchance, have known,
When Orleans filled the Bourbon throne,
A siren singing by the Seine.

But most I love the tube that spies
The orbs celestial in their march;
That shows the comet as it whisks
Its tail across the planets' disks,
As if to blind their blood-shot eyes;
Or wheels so close against the sun
We tremble at the thought of risks
Our little spinning ball may run,
To pop like corn that children parch,
From summer something overdone,
And roll, a cinder, through the skies.

Grudge not to-day the scanty fee
To him who farms the firmament,
To whom the milky way is free;
Who holds the wondrous crystal key,
The silent Open Sesame
That Science to her sons has lent;
Who takes his toll, and lifts the bar
That shuts the road to sun and star.

If Venus only comes to time,
(And prophets say she must and shall,)
To-day will hear the tinkling chime
Of many a ringing silver dime,

For him whose optic glass supplies
The crowd with astronomic eyes,—
The Galileo of the Mall.

Dimly the transit morning broke;
The sun seemed doubting what to do,
As one who questions how to dress,
And takes his doublets from the press,
And halts between the old and new.
Please Heaven he wear his suit of blue,
Or don, at least, his ragged cloak,
With rents that show the azure through!

I go the patient crowd to join
That round the tube my eyes discern,
The last new-comer of the file,
And wait, and wait, a weary while,
And gape, and stretch, and shrug, and smile,
(For each his place must fairly earn,
Hindmost and foremost, in his turn,)
Till hitching onward, pace by pace,
I gain at last the envied place,
And pay the white exiguous coin:
The sun and I are face to face;
He glares at me, I stare at him;
And lo! my straining eye has found
A little spot that, black and round,
Lies near the crimsoned fire-orb's rim.
O blessed, beauteous evening star,
Well named for her whom earth adores,—
The Lady of the dove-drawn car,—
I know thee in thy white simar;
But veiled in black, a rayless spot,
Blank as a careless scribbler's blot,
Stripped of thy robe of silvery flame,—
The stolen robe that Night restores
When Day has shut his golden doors,—
I see thee, yet I know thee not;
And canst thou call thyself the same?

A black, round spot,—and that is all;
And such a speck our earth would be
If he who looks upon the stars
Through the red atmosphere of Mars
Could see our little creeping ball
Across the disk of crimson crawl
As I our sister planet see.

And art thou, then, a world like ours,
Flung from the orb that whirled our own
A molten pebble from its zone?
How must thy burning sands absorb
The fire-waves of the blazing orb,
Thy chain so short, thy path so near,
Thy flame-defying creatures hear
The maelstroms of the photosphere!
And is thy bosom decked with flowers
That steal their bloom from scalding showers?
And hast thou cities, domes, and towers,
And life, and love that makes it dear,
And death that fills thy tribes with fear?

Lost in my dream, my spirit soars
Through paths the wandering angels know;
My all-pervading thought explores
The azure ocean's lucent shores;
I leave my mortal self below,
As up the star-lit stairs I climb,
And still the widening view reveals
In endless rounds the circling wheels
That build the horologe of time.
New spheres, new suns, new systems gleam;
The voice no earth-born echo hears
Steals softly on my ravished ears:
I hear them "singing as they shine"—
—A mortal's voice dissolves my dream:
My patient neighbor, next in line,
Hints gently there are those who wait.
O guardian of the starry gate,
What coin shall pay this debt of mine?
Too slight thy claim, too small the fee

That bids thee turn the potent key
The Tuscan's hand has placed in thine.
Forgive my own the small affront,
The insult of the proffered dime;
Take it, O friend, since this thy wont,
But still shall faithful memory be
A bankrupt debtor unto thee,
And pay thee with a grateful rhyme.

Prelude to a Volume Printed in Raised Letters for the Blind

Dear friends, left darkling in the long eclipse
That veils the noonday,—you whose finger-tips
A meaning in these ridgy leaves can find
Where ours go stumbling, senseless, helpless, blind,
This wreath of verse how dare I offer you
To whom the garden's choicest gifts are due?
The hues of all its glowing beds are ours,—
Shall you not claim its sweetest-smelling flowers?

Nay, those I have I bring you,—at their birth
Life's cheerful sunshine warmed the grateful earth;
If my rash boyhood dropped some idle seeds,
And here and there you light on saucy weeds
Among the fairer growths, remember still
Song comes of grace, and not of human will:
We get a jarring note when most we try,
Then strike the chord we know not how or why;
Our stately verse with too aspiring art
Oft overshoots and fails to reach the heart,
While the rude rhyme one human throb endears
Turns grief to smiles, and softens mirth to tears.

Kindest of critics, ye whose fingers read,
From Nature's lesson learn the poet's creed;
The queenly tulip flaunts in robes of flame,
The wayside seedling scarce a tint may claim,
Yet may the lowliest leaflets that unfold
A dewdrop fresh from heaven's own chalice hold.

THOMAS HOLLEY CHIVERS

(1809–1858)

To Isa Sleeping

"Sleep on, and dream of Heaven awhile!"
ROGERS.

As graceful as the Babylonian willow
Bending, at noontide, over some clear stream
In Palestine, in beauty did she seem
Upon the cygnet-down of her soft pillow;
And now her breast heaved like some gentle billow
Swayed by the presence of the full round moon—
Voluptuous as the summer South at noon—
Her cheeks as rosy as the radiant dawn,
When heaven is cloudless! When she breathed, the air
Around was perfume! Timid as the fawn,
And meeker than the dove, her soft words were
Like gentle music heard at night, when all
Around is still—until the soul of care
Was soothed, as noontide by some waterfall.

Avalon

"I will open my dark saying upon the Harp." —DAVID.

*"All thy waves and billows are gone over me. I sink
in deep mire where there is no standing!"* —PSALMS.

*"There be tears of perfect moan
Wept for thee in Helicon."* —MILTON.

I

Death's pale cold orb has turned to an eclipse
    My Son of Love!
The worms are feeding on thy lily-lips,
    My milk-white Dove!
Pale purple tinges thy soft finger-tips!

574

While nectar thy pure soul in glory sips,
As Death's cold frost mine own forever nips!
    Where thou art lying
    Beside the beautiful undying
  In the Valley of the pausing of the Moon,
  Oh! AVALON! my son! my son!

II

Wake up, oh! AVALON! my son! my son!
    And come from Death!
Heave off the clod that lies so heavy on
    Thy breast beneath
In that cold grave, my more than Precious One!
And come to me! for I am here alone—
With none to comfort me!—my hopes are gone
    Where thou art lying
    Beside the beautiful undying
  In the Valley of the pausing of the Moon,
  Oh! AVALON! my son! my son!

III

Forever more must I, on this damp sod,
    Renew and keep
My Covenant of Sorrows with my God,
    And weep, weep, weep!
Writhing in pain beneath Death's iron rod!
Till I shall go to that DIVINE ABODE—
Treading the path that thy dear feet have trod—
    Where thou art lying
    Beside the beautiful undying
  In the Valley of the pausing of the Moon,
  Oh! AVALON! my son! my son!

IV

Oh! precious Saviour! gracious heavenly Lord!
    Refresh my soul!
Here, with the healings of thy heavenly Word,
    Make my heart whole!

My little Lambs are scattered now abroad
In Death's dark Valley, where they bleat unheard!
Dear Shepherd! give their Shepherd his reward
  Where they are lying
  Beside the beautiful undying
 In the Valley of the pausing of the Moon,
With AVALON! my son! my son!

     V

For thou didst tread with fire-ensandaled feet,
  Star-crowned, forgiven,
The burning diapason of the stars so sweet,
  To God in Heaven!
And, walking on the sapphire-paven street,
Didst take upon the highest Sill thy seat—
Waiting in glory there my soul to meet,
  When I am lying
  Beside the beautiful undying
 In the Valley of the pausing of the Moon,
Oh! AVALON! my son! my son!

     VI

Thou wert my Micro-Uranos below—
  My Little Heaven!
My Micro-Cosmos in this world of wo,
  From morn till even!
A living Lyre of God who charmed me so
With thy sweet songs, that I did seem to go
Out of this world where thou art shining now,
  But without lying
  Beside the beautiful undying
 In the Valley of the pausing of the Moon,
Oh! AVALON! my son! my son!

VII

Thou wert my son of Melody alway,
  Oh! Child Divine!
Whose golden radiance filled the world with Day!
  For thou didst shine
A lustrous Diadem of Song for aye,
Whose Divertisments, through Heaven's Holyday,
  Now ravish Angel's ears—as well they may—
      While I am crying
      Beside the beautiful undying
    In the Valley of the pausing of the Moon,
    Oh! AVALON! my son! my son!

VIII

Thy soul did soar up to the Gates of God,
  Oh! Lark-like Child!
And through Heaven's Bowers of Bliss, by Angels trod,
  Poured Wood-notes wild!
In emulation of that Bird, which stood,
In solemn silence, listening to thy flood
Of golden Melody deluge the wood
      Where thou art lying
      Beside the beautiful undying
    In the Valley of the pausing of the Moon,
    Oh! AVALON! my son! my son!

IX

Throughout the Spring-time of Eternity,
  Oh! AVALON!
Paeans of thy selectest melody
  Pour forth, dear Son!
Clapping thy snow-white hands incessantly,
Amid Heaven's Bowers of Bliss in ecstasy—
The odor of thy song inviting me
      Where thou art lying
      Beside the beautiful undying
    In the Valley of the pausing of the Moon,
    Oh! AVALON! my son! my son!

X

The redolent quintessence of thy tongue,
    Oh! AVALON!
Embowered by Angels Heaven's sweet Bowers among—
    Many in one—
Is gathered from the choicest of the throng,
In an Æonian Hymn forever young,
Thou Philomelian Eclecticist of Song!
      While I am sighing
      Beside the beautiful undying
    In the Valley of the pausing of the Moon,
    For AVALON! my son! my son!

XI

Here lies dear Florence with her golden hair,
    And violet eyes;
Whom God, because she was for earth too fair,
    Took to the skies!
With whom my Zilly only could compare—
Or Eugene Percy, who was debonair,
And rivaled each in every thing most rare!
      These now are lying
      Beside the beautiful undying
    In the Valley of the pausing of the Moon,
    With AVALON! my son! my son!

XII

Her eyes were like two Violets bathed in dew
    From morn till even—
The modest Myrtle's blossom-Angel blue,
    And full of Heaven.
Up to the golden gates of God she flew,
To grow in glory as on earth she grew,
Heaven's own primeval joys again to view—
      While I am crying
      Beside the beautiful undying
    In the Valley of the pausing of the Moon,
    Oh! AVALON! my son! my son!

XIII

The Violet of her soul-suffused eyes
   Was like that flower
Which blows its purple trumpet at the skies
   For Dawn's first hour—
The Morning-glory at the first sunrise,
Nipt by Death's frost with all her glorious dyes!
For Florence rests where my dear Lily lies—
    Where thou art lying
    Beside the beautiful undying
  In the Valley of the pausing of the Moon,
Oh! AVALON! my son! my son!

XIV

Four little Angels killed by one cold Death
   To make God glad!
Four Cherubs gone to God, the best he hath—
   And all I had!
Taken together, as if in His wrath,
While walking, singing, on Hope's flowery path—
Breathing out gladness at each odorous breath—
    Now they are lying
    Beside the beautiful undying
  In the Valley of the pausing of the Moon,
Oh! AVALON! my son! my son!

XV

Thou wert like Taleisin, "full of eyes,"
   Bardling of Love!
My beautiful Divine Eumenides!
   My gentle Dove!
Thou silver Swan of Golden Elegies!
Whose Mendelsohnian Songs now fill the skies!
While I am weeping where my Lily lies!
    Where thou art lying
    Beside the beautiful undying
  In the Valley of the pausing of the Moon,
Oh! AVALON! my son! my son!

XVI

Kindling the high-uplifted stars at even
   With thy sweet song,
The Angels, on the Sapphire Sills of Heaven,
   In rapturous throng,
Melted to milder meekness, with the Seven
Bright Lamps of God to glory given,
Leant down to hear thy voice roll up the leven,
     Where thou art lying
     Beside the beautiful undying
   In the valley of the pausing of the Moon,
   Oh! AVALON! my son! my son!

XVII

Can any thing that Christ has ever said,
   Make my heart whole?
Can less than bringing back the early dead,
   Restore my soul?
No! this alone can make my Heavenly bread—
Christ's Bread of Life brought down from Heaven, instead
Of this sad Song, on which my soul has fed,
     Where thou art lying
     Beside the beautiful undying
   In the Valley of the pausing of the Moon,
   Oh! AVALON! my son! my son!

XVIII

Have I not need to weep from Morn till Even,
   Far bitterer tears
Than cruel Earth, the unforgiven,
   Through his long years—
Inquisitorial Hell, or strictest Heaven,
Wrung from Christ's bleeding heart when riven?
Thus from one grief unto another driven,
     Where thou art lying
     Beside the beautiful undying
   In the Valley of the pausing of the Moon,
   Oh! AVALON! my son! my son!

XIX

Yes! I have need to weep, to groan, to cry,
   And never faint,
Till, battering down God's Golden Gates on high,
   With my complaint,
I soften his great heart to make reply,
By sending my dear son from Heaven on high—
Or causing me in this dark grave to lie,
    Where thou art lying
    Beside the beautiful undying
  In the Valley of the pausing of the Moon,
Oh! AVALON! my son! my son!

XX

I see the BRIDEGROOM of the Heavenly Bride,
   In robes of light!
My little ONES now stand his form beside,
   In linen white!
Embowered by Angels, star-crowned, in their pride,
Singing Æonian songs in joyful tide—
Although much larger grown than when they died—
    While I am sighing
    Beside the beautiful undying
  In the Valley of the pausing of the Moon,
Oh! AVALON! my son! my son!

Apollo

What are stars, but hieroglyphics of God's glory writ in
    lightning
  On the wide-unfolded pages of the azure scroll above?
But the quenchless apotheoses of thoughts forever
    brightening
  In the mighty Mind immortal of the God, whose name is
    LOVE?
Diamond letters sculptured, rising, on the azure ether pages,
  That now sing to one another—unto one another shine—

God's eternal Scripture talking, through the midnight, to the
        Ages,
    Of the life that is immortal, of the life that is divine—
    Life that *cannot* be immortal, but the life that is divine.

Like some deep, impetuous river from the fountains
        everlasting,
    Down the serpentine soft valley of the vistas of all Time,
Over cataracts of adamant uplifted into mountains,
    Soared his soul to God in thunder on the wings of
        thought sublime,
With the rising golden glory of the sun in ministrations,
    Making oceans metropolitan of splendor for the dawn—
Piling pyramid on pyramid of music for the nations—
    Sings the Angel who sits shining everlasting in the sun,
    For the stars, which are the echoes of the shining of the
        sun.

Like the lightnings piled on lightnings, ever rising, never
        reaching,
    In one monument of glory towards the golden gates of
        God—
Voicing out themselves in thunder upon thunder in their
        preaching,
    Piled this Cyclop up his Epic where the Angels never
        trod.
Like the fountains everlasting that forever more are flowing
    From the throne within the centre of the City built on
        high,
With their genial irrigation life forever more bestowing—
    Flows his lucid, liquid river through the gardens of the
        sky,
    For the stars forever blooming in the gardens of the sky.

Lily Adair

On the beryl-rimmed rebecs of Ruby,
    Brought fresh from the hyaline streams,
She played, on the banks of the Yuba,
    Such songs as she heard in her dreams.
Like the heavens, when the stars from their eyries
    Look down through the ebon night air,
Were the groves by the Ouphantic Fairies
    Lit up for my Lily Adair—
    For my child-like Lily Adair—
    For my heaven-born Lily Adair—
For my beautiful, dutiful Lily Adair.

Like two rose-leaves in sunshine when blowing,
    Just curled softly, gently apart,
Were her lips by her passion, while growing
    In perfume on the stalk of her heart.
As mild as the sweet influences
    Of the Pleiades 'pregning the air—
More mild than the throned Excellencies
    Up in heaven, was my Lily Adair—
    Was my Christ-like Lily Adair—
    Was my lamb-like Lily Adair—
Was my beautiful, dutiful Lily Adair.

At the birth of this fair virgin Vestal,
    She was taken for Venus' child;
And her voice, though like diamond in crystal,
    Was not more melodious than mild.
Like the moon in her soft silver splendor,
    She was shrined in her own, past compare,
For no Angel in heaven was more tender
    Than my beautiful Lily Adair—
    Than my dove-like Lily Adair—
    Than my saint-like Lily Adair—
Than my beautiful, dutiful Lily Adair.

Thus she stood on the arabesque borders
   Of the beautiful blossoms that blew
On the banks of the crystalline waters,
   Every morn, in the diaphane dew.
The flowers, they were radiant with glory,
   And shed such perfume on the air,
That my soul, now to want them, feels sorry,
   And bleeds for my Lily Adair—
   For my much-loved Lily Adair—
   For my long-lost Lily Adair—
For my beautiful, dutiful Lily Adair.

The Wind

Thou wringest, with thy invisible hand, the foam
   Out of the emerald drapery of the sea,
Beneath whose foldings lies the Sea-Nymph's home—
   Lifted, to make it visible, by thee;
Till thou art exiled, earthward, from the maine,
To cool the parched tongue of the Earth with rain.

Thy viewless wing sweeps, with its tireless flight,
   Whole Navies from their boundings on the waves—
Wrapping the canvas, pregnant with thy might,
   Around the seamen in their watery graves!
Till thou dost fall asleep upon the grass,
And then the ocean is as smooth as glass.

Thou art the Gardner of the flowery earth—
   The Sower in the spring-time of the year—
Clearing plantations, in thy goings forth,
   Amid the wilderness, where all is drear—
Scattering ten thousand giant oaks around,
Like playthings, on the dark, opprobrious ground.

FANNY KEMBLE
(1809–1893)

To the Wissahiccon

My feet shall tread no more thy mossy side,
　When once they turn away, thou *Pleasant Water*,
Nor ever more, reflected in thy tide,
　Will shine the eyes of the White Island's daughter.
But often in my dreams, when I am gone
　Beyond the sea that parts thy home and mine,
　Upon thy banks the evening sun will shine,
And I shall hear thy low, still flowing on.
And when the burden of existence lies
　Upon my soul, darkly and heavily,
I'll clasp my hands over my weary eyes,
　Thou *Pleasant Water*, and thy clear waves see.
Bright be thy course for ever and for ever,
　Child of pure mountain springs, and mountain snow;
And as thou wanderest on to meet the river,
　Oh, still in light and music mayst thou flow!
I never shall come back to thee again,
When once my sail is shadowed on the main,
Nor ever shall I hear thy laughing voice
As on their rippling way thy waves rejoice,
Nor ever see the dark green cedar throw
Its gloomy shade o'er the clear depths below,
Never, from stony rifts of granite gray
Sparkling like diamond rocks in the sun's ray,
Shall I look down on thee, thou pleasant stream,
Beneath whose crystal folds the gold sands gleam;
Wherefore, farewell! but whensoe'er again
　The wintry spell melts from the earth and air;
And the young Spring comes dancing through thy glen,
　With fragrant, flowery breath, and sunny hair;
When through the snow the scarlet berries gleam,
Like jewels strewn upon thy banks, fair stream,
My spirit shall through many a summer's day
Return, among thy peaceful woods to stray.

Impromptu

You say you're glad I write—oh, say not so!
　My fount of song, dear friend, 's a bitter well;
And when the numbers freely from it flow,
　'Tis that my heart, and eyes, o'erflow as well.

Castalia, fam'd of yore,—the spring divine,
　Apollo's smile upon its current wears:
Moore and Anacreon, found its waves were wine,
　To me, it flows a sullen stream of tears.

MARGARET FULLER

(1810–1850)

Sistrum

Triune, shaping, restless power,
Life-flow from life's natal hour,
No music chords are in thy sound;
By some thou'rt but a rattle found;
Yet, without thy ceaseless motion,
To ice would turn their dead devotion.
Life-flow of my natal hour,
I will not weary of thy power,
Till in the changes of thy sound
A chord's three parts distinct are found.
I will faithful move with thee,
God-ordered, self-fed energy,
Nature in eternity.

Flaxman

We deemed the secret lost, the spirit gone,
Which spake in Greek simplicity of thought,
And in the forms of gods and heroes wrought
Eternal beauty from the sculptured stone,—
A higher charm than modern culture won
With all the wealth of metaphysic lore,
Gifted to analyze, dissect, explore.
A many-colored light flows from one sun;
Art, 'neath its beams, a motley thread has spun;
The prism modifies the perfect day;
But thou hast known such mediums to shun,
And cast once more on life a pure, white ray.
Absorbed in the creations of thy mind,
Forgetting daily self, my truest self I find.

EDMUND HAMILTON SEARS

(1810–1876)

"It came upon the midnight clear"

It came upon the midnight clear,
   That glorious song of old,
From angels bending near the earth
   To touch their harps of gold;
"Peace on the earth, good will to men
   From heaven's all-gracious King"—
The world in solemn stillness lay
   To hear the angels sing.

Still through the cloven skies they come
   With peaceful wings unfurled,
And still their heavenly music floats
   O'er all the weary world;
Above its sad and lowly plains
   They bend on hovering wing,
And ever o'er its Babel-sounds
   The blessed angels sing.

But with the woes of sin and strife
   The world has suffered long;
Beneath the angel-strain have rolled
   Two thousand years of wrong;
And man, at war with man, hears not
   The love-song which they bring;—
Oh hush the noise, ye men of strife,
   And hear the angels sing!

And ye, beneath life's crushing load,
   Whose forms are bending low,
Who toil along the climbing way
   With painful steps and slow,

Look now! for glad and golden hours
    Come swiftly on the wing;—
Oh, rest beside the weary road
    And hear the angels sing!

For lo! the days are hastening on
    By prophet bards foretold,
When with the ever circling years
    Comes round the age of gold;
When Peace shall over all the earth
    Its ancient splendors fling,
And the whole world give back the song
    Which now the angels sing.

CHRISTOPHER PEARSE CRANCH

(1813–1892)

Correspondences

All things in nature are beautiful types to the soul that can
    read them;
Nothing exists upon earth, but for unspeakable ends,
Every object that speaks to the senses was meant for the
    spirit;
Nature is but a scroll; God's handwriting thereon.
Ages ago when man was pure, ere the flood overwhelmed
    him,
While in the image of God every soul yet lived,
Every thing stood as a letter or word of a language familiar,
Telling of truths which now only the angels can read.
Lost to man was the key of those sacred hieroglyphics,
Stolen away by sin, till by heaven restored.
Now with infinite pains we here and there spell out a letter,
Here and there will the sense feebly shine through the dark.
When we perceive the light that breaks through the visible
    symbol,
What exultation is ours! *We* the discovery have made!
Yet is the meaning the same as when Adam lived sinless in
    Eden,
Only long hidden it slept, and now again is revealed.
Man unconsciously uses figures of speech every moment,
Little dreaming the cause why to such terms he is prone,
Little dreaming that every thing here has its own
    correspondence
Folded within its form, as in the body the soul.
Gleams of the mystery fall on us still, though much is
    forgotten,
And through our commonest speech, illumine the path of
    our thoughts.

Thus doth the lordly sun shine forth a type of the Godhead;
Wisdom and love the beams that stream on a darkened
world.
Thus do the sparkling waters flow, giving joy to the desert,
And the fountain of life opens itself to the thirst.
Thus doth the word of God distil like the rain and the
dew-drops;
Thus doth the warm wind breathe like to the Spirit of God;
And the green grass and the flowers are signs of the
regeneration.

O thou Spirit of Truth, visit our minds once more,
Give us to read in letters of light the language celestial
Written all over the earth, written all over the sky—
Thus may we bring our hearts once more to know our
Creator,
Seeing in all things around, types of the Infinite Mind.

Gnosis

Thought is deeper than all speech,
    Feeling deeper than all thought;
Souls to souls can never teach
    What unto themselves was taught.

We are spirits clad in veils;
    Man by man was never seen;
All our deep communing fails
    To remove the shadowy screen.

Heart to heart was never known;
    Mind with mind did never meet;
We are columns left alone,
    Of a temple once complete.

Like the stars that gem the sky,
    Far apart, though seeming near,
In our light we scattered lie;
    All is thus but starlight here.

What is social company
　　But a babbling summer stream?
What our wise philosophy
　　But the glancing of a dream?

Only when the sun of love
　　Melts the scattered stars of thought;
Only when we live above
　　What the dim-eyed world hath taught;

Only when our souls are fed
　　By the Fount which gave them birth,
And by inspiration led,
　　Which they never drew from earth,

We like parted drops of rain
　　Swelling till they meet and run,
Shall be all absorbed again,
　　Melting, flowing into one.

The Bird and the Bell

I.

'T was earliest morning in the early spring,
In Florence. Winter, dark and damp and chill,
Had yielded to the fruit-trees' blossoming,
Though sullen rains swept from the mountains still.
The tender green scarce seemed to have a will
To peep above the sod and greet the sky,—
Like an o'er-timid child who dreads a stranger's eye.

II.

The city slumbered in the dawning day;—
Old towers and domes and roof-tiles looming dim,
Bridges and narrow streets and cloisters gray,
And sculptured churches, where the Latin hymn
By lamplight called to mass. As o'er a limb
The spells of witchcraft strong but noiseless full,
The shadows of the Past reigned silent over all.

III.

Waking from sleep, I heard, but knew not where,
A bird, that sang alone its early song.
The quick, clear warble leaping through the air,—
The voice of spring, that all the winter long
Had slept,—now burst in melodies as strong
And tremulous as Love's first pure delight;—
I could not choose but bless a song so warm and bright.

IV.

Sweet bird! the fresh, clear sprinkle of thy voice
Came quickening all the springs of trust and love.
What heart could hear such joy, and not rejoice?
Thou blithe remembrancer of field and grove,
Dropping thy fairy flute-notes from above,
Fresh message from the Beauty Infinite
That clasps the world around and fills it with delight!

V.

It bore me to the breeze-swept banks of bloom,
To trees and falling waters, and the rush
Of south-winds sifting through the pine-grove's gloom;
Home-gardens filled with roses, and the gush
Of insect-trills in grass and roadside bush;
And apple-orchards flushed with blossoms sweet;
And all that makes the round of nature most complete.

VI.

It sang of freedom, dimmed by no alloy;
Peace, unpossessed upon our troubled sphere;
Some long Arcadian day of love and joy,
Unsoiled by fogs of superstitious fear;
A world of noble beings born to cheer
The wilderness of life, and prove the fact
Of human grandeur in each thought and word and act.

VII.

What was it jarred the vision and the spell,
And brought the reflux of the day and place?
Athwart the bird's song clanged a brazen bell.
Nature's improvisations could not face
That domineering voice; and in the race
Of rival tongues the Bell outrang the Bird,—
The swinging, clamoring brass which all the city heard.

VIII.

Santa Maria Novella's Church, hard by,
Calling its worshippers to morning prayer,
From its old *Campanile* lifted high
In the dull dampness of the clouded air,
Poured out its monotones, and did not spare
Its ringing shocks of unremitting sound,
That soon my warbler's notes were swept away and drowned.

IX.

Down from the time-stained belfry clanged the bell,
Joined in a moment by a hundred more.
Had I not heard the bird, I might have well
Floated on that sonorous flood that bore
Away all living voices, as with roar
Of deep vibrations, grand, monastic, bold,
Through street and stately square the metal music rolled.

X.

Oft have I listened in the dead of night,
When all those towers like chanting priests have prayed;
And the weird tones seemed tangled in the height
Of palaces,—as though all Florence made
One great ghost-organ, and the pipes that played
Were the dark channelled streets, pouring along
In beats and muffled swells the deep resounding song.

XI.

So now the incessant peal filled all the air,
And the sweet bird-voice, utterly forced away,
Ceased. And it seemed as if some spirit fair
Were hurled into oblivion; and the day
Grew suddenly more darkly, grimly gray,
Like a vast mort-cloth stretched from south to north,
While that tyrannic voice still rang its mandates forth.

XII.

And so I mused upon the things that were,
And those that should be, or that might have been;
And felt a life and freedom in the air,
And in the sprouting of the early green,
I could not match with man, who builds his screen
Darkening the sun, and in his own light stands,
And casts the shadow of himself along the lands.

XIII.

For him who haunts the temples of the Past,
And shapes his fond ideals by its rules;
Whose creed, whose labors, are but thoughts recast
In worn and shrunken moulds of antique schools, —
Copies of copies, wrought with others' tools;
For whom law stands for justice, Church for God,
Symbol for fact, for right divine the tyrant's rod; —

XIV.

Who fears to utter what his reason bids,
Unless it wears the colors of a sect;
Who hardly dares to lift his heavy lids,
And greet the coming Day with head erect,
But apes each general posture and defect
Entailed by time, — alert in others' tracks,
Like owls that build in some time-mantled ruin's cracks; —

XV.

For him yon clanging Bell a symbol bears,
That deadens every natural voice of spring.
Fitter for him the croaking chant, the prayers,
The torch, the cross, the censer's golden swing,
The organ-fugue,—a prisoned eagle's wing
Beating the frescoed dome,—the empty feast
Where at his tinselled altar stands the gay-robed priest.

XVI.

O mighty Church! who, old, but still adorned
With jewels of thy youth,—a wrinkled bride
Affianced to the blind,—so long hast scorned
The rising of the inevitable tide
That swells and surges up against thy pride,—
Thou, less the artist's than the tyrant's nurse,
Blight of philosophy, false star of poet's verse!—

XVII.

What though thy forms be picturesque and old,
And, clustered round thee, works of noblest art
Hallow thy temples! Once they may have told
Profound emotions of the inmost heart;
Now shadowed by a faith that stands apart,
And scowls against the sunlight shared abroad,
Burning in altar-nooks its candles to its god!

XVIII.

The saints who toiled to help the world's distress;
The noble lords of thought and speech divine;
The prophets crying through Time's wilderness;
The vast discoveries, the inventions fine
That stamped upon the centuries a sign
Of grandeur,—all, like music thundered down
By stern cathedral bells, were silenced by thy frown.

XIX.

Chained to Madonnas and ascetic saints,
Even Art itself felt thy all-narrowing force.
The painter saw thee peeping o'er his paints;
The sculptor's thought was fettered from its source;
Thy gloomy cloisters shaped the builder's course;
Thy organ drowned the shepherd's festive flute
With penitential groans, as though God's love were mute.

XX.

And yet, because there lurked some element
Of truth within the doctrine,—to man's need
Some fitness in the form; since more was meant
And more expressed than in the accepted creed,—
The artist's genius giving far less heed
To formulas than to his own ideal,—
The hand and heart wrought works the world has stamped
    as real.

XXI.

What didst thou for the already teeming soil
Of souls like Dante, Raphael, Angelo,
Save to suggest a theme or pay their toil?
While they o'erlooked their prison walls, and so
Caught from the skies above and earth below
Splendors wherewith they lit thy tarnished crown,
And clothed thee with a robe thou claimest as thine own.

XXII.

Names that in any age would have been great,
Works that to all time speak, and so belong,
Claim not as thine; nor subsidize the fate
That gave them to the nations for a long,
Unceasing heritage. Amid a throng
Of starry lights they live. Thy clanging bells
Can never drown their song, nor break their mighty spells.

XXIII.

No mother thou of Genius, but the nurse.
Seek not to stamp a vulgar name upon
The sons of Morning. Take the Poet's verse,
But not the Poet. He is not thy son.
Enough for thee, if sometimes he hath gone
Into thy narrow fold from pastures wide,
Where through immortal flowers God pours the living tide.

XXIV.

Enough if he hath decked thee with the wealth
Of his heaven-nurtured spirit,—showering gems
Of thought and fancy, coining youth and health
To gild with fame thy papal diadems;
Plucking life's roses with their roots and stems
To wreathe an altar which returned him naught
But the poor patronage of some suspected thought.

XXV.

What didst thou for the studious sage who saw
Through nature's veils the great organic force,—
Who sought and found the all-pervading law
That holds the rolling planets in their course?
When didst thou fail to check the flowing source
Of truths whose waters needs must inundate
The theologic dikes that guarded thy estate?

XXVI.

Is there a daring thought thou hast not crushed?
Is there a generous faith thou hast not cursed?
Is there a whisper, howe'er low and hushed,
Breathed for the future, but thou wast the first
To silence with thy tortures,—thou the worst
Of antichrists, and cunningest of foes
That ever against God and man's great progress rose?

XXVII.

Yet life was in thee once. Thy earlier youth
Was flushed with blossoms of a heavenly bloom.
Thy blight began, when o'er God's common truth
And man's nobility thou didst assume
The dread prerogative of life and doom;
And creeds which served as swaddling-bands were bound
Like grave-clothes round the limbs laid living under ground.

XXVIII.

When man grows wiser than his creed allows,
And nobler than the church he has outgrown;
When that which was his old familiar house
No longer is a home, but all alone,
Alone with God, he dares to lift the stone
From off the skylight between heaven and him,—
Then shines a grander day, then fade the spectres grim.

XXIX.

And never yet was growth, save when it broke
The letter of the dead scholastic form.
The bark drops off, and leaves the expanding oak
To stretch his giant arms through sun and storm.
The idols that upon his breast lay warm
The sage throws down, and breaks their hallowed shrine,
And follows the great hand that points to light divine.

XXX.

But thou, O Church! didst steal the mother's mask,
The counterfeit of Heaven,—so to enfold
Thy flock around thee. None looked near, to ask
"Art thou our mother, truly?" None so bold
As lift thy veils, and show how hard and cold
Those eyes of tyranny, that mouth of guile,
That low and narrow brow, the witchcraft of that smile,—

XXXI.

That subtle smile, deluding while it warmed;
That arrogant, inquisitorial nod;
That hand that stabbed, like Herod, the new-formed
And childlike life which drew its breath from God,
And, for that star by which the Magi trod
The road to Bethlehem, the Good Shepherd's home,
Lit lurid idol-fires on thy seven hills of Rome.

XXXII.

Rome, paralyzed and dumb,—who sat a queen
Among the nations, now thy abject slave;
Yet muttering in her cell, where gaunt and lean
Thy priests have kept her pining! Who shall save
And lift the captive from her living grave?
Is there no justice left to avert her doom,
Where monarchs sit and play their chess-games on her
    tomb?

XXXIII.

And thou, too, Venice, moaning by the sea,
Which moans and chafes with thee, on Lido's beach,—
Thou, almost in despair lest there should be
In Europe's life no life within thy reach,
No respite from thy tyrant,—thou shalt teach
Thy Austrian despot yet what hoarded hate
And sudden strength can do to change thy sad estate!

XXXIV.

For, lo, the fires are kindled. Hark! afar,
At last the thunders mutter under ground,
The northern lights flash cimeters of war,
Sardinia's trumpets to the battle sound.
See Florence, Parma, Modena, unbound,
Leap to their feet,—and stout Romagna brave
The Cardinal's frown, and swear to cower no more a slave!

XXXV.

See Sicily, whose blood is Ætna's veins
Of sleepless fire, heave with volcanic pants,
Seething, a restless surge of hearts and brains,
Till Garibaldi's quick Ithuriel lance
Wakes the whole South from its long, troubled trance,
And Naples, catching the contagious flame,
Welcomes her hero in with blessings on his name!

XXXVI.

The nations that in darkness sat have seen
The light. The blind receive their sight again.
The querulous old man who stands between
His children and their hopes, with threats insane,
Trembles, as though an earthquake split in twain
The crumbling rock beneath Saint Peter's dome;
And the last hiding-place of tyranny—is Rome.

XXXVII.

For Italy, long pining, sad, and crushed,
Has hurled her royal despots from the land.
Back to her wasted heart the blood has gushed.
Her wan cheek blooms, and her once nerveless hand
Guides with firm touch the purpose she has planned.
Thank God! thank generous France! the battle smoke
Lifts from her bloody fields. See, at her feet her yoke!

XXXVIII.

Not like a maddened anarch does she rise:
The torch she holds is no destroying flame,
But a clear beacon,—like her own clear eyes
Straining across the war-clouds; and the shame
Of wild misrule has never stained her name.
Calm and determined, politic yet bold,
She comes to take her place,—the Italy of old.

XXXIX.

She asks no boon, except to stand enrolled
Among the nations. Give her space and air,
Our Sister. She has pined in dungeons cold.
A little sunshine for our Sister fair,
A little hope to cover past despair.
God's blessing on the long-lost, the unbound!
The earth has waited long; the heavens now answer—
    "Found!"

XL.

The nations greet her as some lovely guest
Arriving late, where friends pour out the wine.
Ay, press around, and pledge her in the best
Your table yields, and in her praise combine!
And ye who love her most, press near, and twine
Her locks with wreaths, and in her large dark eyes
See all her sorrowing past, and her great future rise!

XLI.

But thou who claim'st the keys of God's own heaven,
And who wouldst fain usurp the keys of earth,—
Thou, leagued with priests and tyrants who have given
Their hands, and pledged their oaths to blight the birth
Of thine own children's rights,—for scorn and mirth
One day shalt stand, thy juggling falsehoods named,
Thy plots and wiles unmasked, thy heaven-high titles
    shamed!

XLII.

Look to the proud tiara on thy brow!
Its gems shall crush thee down like leaden weights.
Thy alchemy is dead; and wouldst thou now
Thunder anathemas against the states
Whose powers are Time's irrefragable fates?
Look to thy glories! they must shrink away,—
With meaner pomp must fall, and sink into decay.

XLIII.

Lo, thou art numbered with the things that were,
Soon to be laid upon the dusty shelves
Of antiquaries,—once so strong and fair,
Now classed with spells of magic, midnight elves,
And all half-lies, that pass away themselves
   When once a people rises to the light
Of primal truths and comprehends its heaven-born right.

XLIV.

Toil on; but little canst thou do to-day.
The sun is risen. The daylight dims thy shrines.
The age outstrips thee, marching on its way,
And overflowing all thy boundary lines.
How art thou fallen, O star! How lurid shines
   Thy taper underneath the glowing sky!
How feeble grows thy voice, how lustreless thine eye!

XLV.

Like some huge shell left by the ebbing tide,
In which once dwelt some wonder of the sea,
Thou liest, and men know not that thy pride
Of place outlives thy earlier potency,
But, coming nearer to thy mystery,
   Might call thee lovely, did not thy decay
And death-like odor drive them in contempt away.

XLVI.

So perish like thee all lies stereotyped
By human power or devilish artifice,—
Dark blot on Christ's pure shield, soon to be wiped
Away, and leave it fair for Heaven's free kiss;
So perish like thee, drowned in Time's abyss,
   All that hath robbed strong Genius of its youth,
All that hath ever barred the struggling soul from truth!

XLVII.

And yet we need not boast our larger scope
In this broad land, if creeds of later stamp
Still cast their gloom o'er manhood's dearest hope,
Still quench the heavenward flame of Reason's lamp,
And dogmas shamed by science still can cramp
The aspiring soul in dungeons scarce less drear
Than those of older times, when faith was one with fear.

XLVIII.

Nor dream that here the inquisitorial chair
Is but a byword, though we flush and weep
In honest indignation, when we hear
Chains clank in Rome, and wonder how the cheap
And common truth of Heaven must cringe, and creep,
And mask its face, lest Mother Church disown
The rebel thought that flouts the apostolic throne!

XLIX.

If we indeed are sure our faith is best,
Then may we dare to leave it large and free,
Nor fear to bring the creed to reason's test;
For best is strongest, fearing not to see
As well as feel. Then welcome, Liberty!
Down with the scaffolding the priest demands!
Let Truth stand free, alone, a house not built with hands!

L.

Down with the useless and the rotting props
That only cumber and deface each wall!
Off with the antiquated cloth that drops
Moth-eaten draperies round the columns tall.
Nor needs the heavenly Architect our small
Superfluous tricks of ornament and gilt,
To deck the royal courts his wisdom planned and built.

LI.

He wills a temple beautiful and wide
As man and nature,—not a cloister dim,
Nor strange pagoda of barbaric pride
Scrawled o'er with hieroglyph and picture grim
Of saint and fiend. Why seek to honor him
By crusting o'er with gold of Palestine
The simple, stainless dome whose builder is divine?

LII.

Thanks to the Central Good, the inflowing Power,
The Primal Life in which we live and move,—
The aroma of the soul, the passion-flower
We bear upon our hearts, the deathless love
Of right, outlives device, and floats above
All human creeds, though armed with power to brave
The scholar's daring thought, and make the world their
        slave.

LIII.

The music of the soul can ne'er be mute.
What though the brazen clang of antique form
Stop for a hundred years the angel's lute,
The angel smiles, and when the deafening storm
Has pealed along the ages, with the warm
Touch the immortals own, he sings again,
Clearer and sweeter, like the sunshine after rain.

LIV.

He sings the song no tyrant long resists;
He sings the song the world perforce must join,
Though ages stand as notes. For he insists
With such sweet emphasis, such chords divine,
That, soon or late, along the living line
Of hearts that form Humanity, there thrills
A sympathetic nerve no time or custom kills.

LV.

Humanity must answer when God speaks,
As sure as echo to the human voice.
And every grand o'ertopping lie which breaks
With furious flood and century-deafening noise
In the eternal symphony that joys
Along, is but some baser pipe or chord
That shall be tuned again when Reason sits as lord.

LVI.

Eternal Truth shines on o'er Error's cloud,
Which, for a little, veils the living light.
Therefore, though the true bard may sing aloud
His soul-song in the unreceptive night,
His words—swift, arrowy fires—must fly and light,
Sooner or later, kindling south and north,
Till skulking Falsehood from her den be hunted forth.

LVII.

Work on, O fainting hearts! Through storm and drouth,
Somewhere your wingéd heart-seeds will be blown,
And plant a living grove;—from mouth to mouth,
O'er oceans, into speech and lands unknown,
Even till the long-foreseen result be grown
To ripeness, filled like fruit with other seed,
Which Time shall sow anew, and reap when men shall need.

LVIII.

There is no death, but only change on change.
The life-force of all forms, in tree and flower,
In rocks and rivers, and in clouds that range
Through heaven, in grazing beasts, and in the power
Of mind, goes forth forever, an unspent dower,
Glowing and flashing through the universe,
Kindling the light of stars, and joy of poet's verse!

LIX.

Each hour and second is the marriage-morn
Of spirit-life and matter; as when kings
Wed peasants, and their simple charms adorn
With Oriental gems and sparkling rings
And diadems, and with all royal things
  Making their eyes familiar,—so, with tones
Sweet and unheard before, conduct them to their thrones.

LX.

One mighty circle God in heaven hath set,
Woven of myriad links,—lives, deaths unknown,—
Where all beginnings and all ends are met
To follow and serve each other,—Nature's zone
And zodiac, round whose seamless arc are strewn
  A million and a million hues of light
That blend and glow and burn, beyond our realm of night.

LXI.

O ye who pined in dungeons for the sake
Of truths which tyrants shadowed with their hate;
Whose only crime was that ye were awake
Too soon, or that your brothers slept too late,—
Mountainous minds! upon whose tops the great
  Sunrise of knowledge came, long ere its glance
Fell on the foggy swamps of fear and ignorance,—

LXII.

The time shall come when from your heights serene
Beyond the dark, ye will look back and smile
To see the sterile earth all growing green,
Where Science, Art, and Love repeat Heaven's style
In crowded city and on desert isle,
  Till Eden blooms where martyr-fires have burned,
And to the Lord of Life all hearts and minds are turned.

LXIII.

The seeds are planted, and the spring is near.
Ages of blight are but a fleeting frost.
Truth circles into truth. Each mote is dear
To God. No drop of ocean e'er is lost,
No leaf forever dry and tempest-tossed.
Life centres deathless underneath decay,
And no true word or deed can ever pass away.

LXIV.

And ye, O Seraphs in the morn of time!
Birds whose entrancing voices in the spring
Of primal Truth and Beauty, were the chime
Of heaven and earth! still we may hear you sing.
No clang of hierarchal bells shall ring,
To drown your carol, in the airs that move
And stir the dawning age of Liberty and Love!

LXV.

Light,—light breaks on the century's farthest round;
Light in the sky, light in the humblest home.
The unebbing tides of God, where errors drowned
Sink down to fathomless destruction, come
Swelling amain. Truth builds her eternal dome
Vast as the sky. Nations are linked in one.
Light, Love, henceforth shall reign forever and alone!

The Cataract Isle

I wandered through the ancient wood
  That crowns the cataract isle.
I heard the roaring of the flood
  And saw its wild, fierce smile.

Through tall tree-tops the sunshine flecked
  The huge trunks and the ground,
And the pomp of fullest summer decked
  The island all around.

And winding paths led all along
  Where friends and lovers strayed,
And voices rose with laugh and song
  From sheltered nooks of shade.

Through opening forest vistas whirled
  The rapids' foamy flash,
As they boiled along and plunged and swirled,
  And neared the last long dash.

I crept to the island's outer verge,
  Where the grand, broad river fell,—
Fell sheer down mid foam and surge
  In a white and blinding hell.

The steady rainbow gayly shone
  Above the precipice,
And the deep low tone of a thunder groan
  Rolled up from the drear abyss.

And all the day sprang up the spray
  Where the broad white sheets were poured,
And fell around in showery play,
  Or upward curled and soared.

And all the night those sheets of white
  Gleamed through the spectral mist,
When o'er the isle the broad moonlight
  The wintry foam-flakes kissed.

Mirrored within my dreamy thought,
    I see it, feel it all,—
That island with sweet visions fraught,
    That awful waterfall.

With sunflecked trees, and birds and flowers,
    The Isle of Life is fair;
But one deep voice thrills through its hours,
    One spectral form is there,—

A power no mortal can resist,
    Rolling forever on,—
A floating cloud, a shadowy mist,
    Eternal undertone.

And through the sunny vistas gleam
    The fate, the solemn smile.
Life is Niagara's rushing stream;
    Its dreams—that peaceful isle!

In the Palais Royal Garden

In the Palais Royal Garden I stood listening to-day,
Just at sunset, in the crowd that flaunted up and down so gay
As the strains of "Casta Diva" rose and fell and died away.

Lonely in the crowd of French I stood and listened to the
    strain,
And the breath of happier hours came blowing from the past
    again;
But the music brought a pleasure that was near akin to pain.

Italy, dear Italy, came back, with all her orange flowers,
With her sapphire skies and ocean, with her shrines and
    crumbling towers,
And her dark-eyed women sitting under their vine-shaded
    bowers.

And the rich and brilliant concerts in my own far distant
    land,
Where the world-renownéd singers, circled by the orchestral
    band
Poured their music on the crowds like costly wine upon the
    sand.

All the aroma of the best and brightest hours of love and
    song
Mingled with the yearning music, floated to me o'er the
    throng.
But it died as died the sunset. Ah, it could not linger long!

Through the streets the carriages are rolling with a heavy jar,
Feebly o'er the staring gas-lamps glimmers here and there a
    star.
Night looks down through narrow spaces; men are near, the
    skies are far.

Far too are my friends, the cherished,—north and south and
    o'er the sea.
And to-night I pant for music and for life that cannot be,
For the foreign city's crowd is naught but solitude to me.

Cornucopia

There's a lodger lives on the first floor;
    (My lodgings are up in the garret;)
At night and at morn he taketh a horn,
    And calleth his neighbors to share it,—
A horn so long and a horn so strong,
    I wonder how they can bear it.

I don't mean to say that he drinks,—
    I might be indicted for scandal.
But every one knows it, he night and day blows it,
    (I wish he'd blow out like a candle!)
His horn is so long, and he blows it so strong,
    He would make Handel fly off the handle.

By taking a horn I don't hint
      That he swigs either rum, gin, or whiskey.
It 's we, I am thinking, condemned to be drinking
      His strains that attempt to be frisky,
But are grievously sad. A donkey, I add,
      Is as musical, braying in *his* key.

It 's a puzzle to know what he 's at.
      I could pity him if it were madness.
I never yet knew him to play a tune through;
      And it gives me more anger than sadness
To hear his horn stutter and stammer in utter
      Confusion of musical badness.

At his wide-open window he stands,
      Overlooking his bit of a garden.
One can see the great ass at one end of his brass
      Blaring out, never asking your pardon.
Our nerves though he shatter, to him it 's no matter,
      As long as his tympanums harden.

He thinks, I 've no doubt, it is sweet,—
      While time, tune, and breath are all straying.
The little house-sparrows feel all through their marrows
      The jar and the fuss of his playing;
The windows are shaking, the babies are waking,
      The very dogs howling and baying.

One note out of twenty he hits;
      Blows all his *pianos* like *fortes*.
His time is his own. He goes sounding alone,
      A sort of Columbus or Cortes,
On a perilous ocean, without any notion
      Whereabouts in the dim deep his port is.

If he gets to his haven at last,
      He must needs be a desperate swimmer.
He has plenty of wind, but no compass, I find;
      And being a veteran trimmer,
He veers and he tacks, and returns on his tracks;
      And his prospects grow dimmer and dimmer.

Like a man late from club, he has lost
  His key, and around stumbles, moping,
Touching this, trying that,—now a sharp, now a flat,—
  Till he strikes on the note he is hoping;
And a terrible blare at the end of his air
  Shows he's got through at last with his groping.

There, he's finished,—at least for a while;
  He is tired, or come to his senses;
And out of his horn shakes the drops that were borne
  By the winds of his musical frenzies.
There's a rest, thank our stars! of ninety-nine bars,
  Ere the tempest of sound recommences.

When all the bad players are sent
  Where all the false notes are protested,
I'm sure that Old Nick will there play him a trick,
  When his bad trump and he are arrested;
And down in the regions of discord's mad legions
  His head with two French horns be crested!

The Spirit of the Age

A wondrous light is filling the air,
And rimming the clouds of the old despair;
And hopeful eyes look up to see
Truth's mighty electricity,—
Auroral shimmerings swift and bright,
That wave and flash in the silent night,—
Magnetic billows travelling fast,
And flooding all the spaces vast
From dim horizon to farthest cope
Of heaven, in streams of gathering hope.
Silent they mount and spread apace,
And the watchers see old Europe's face
Lit with expression new and strange,—
The prophecy of coming change.

Meantime, while thousands, wrapt in dreams,
Sleep heedless of the electric gleams,
Or ply their wonted work and strife,
Or plot their pitiful games of life;
While the emperor bows in his formal halls,
And the clerk whirls on at the masking balls;
While the lawyer sits at his dreary files,
And the banker fingers his glittering piles,
And the priest kneels down at his lighted shrine,
And the fop flits by with his mistress fine,—
The diplomat works at his telegraph wires:
His back is turned to the heavenly fires.
Over him flows the magnetic tide,
And the candles are dimmed by the glow outside.
Mysterious forces overawe,
Absorb, suspend the usual law.
The needle stood northward an hour ago;
Now it veers like a weathercock to and fro.
The message he sends flies not as once;
The unwilling wires yield no response.
Those iron veins that pulsed but late
From a tyrant's will to a people's fate,
Flowing and ebbing with feverish strength,
Are seized by a Power whose breadth and length,
Whose height and depth, defy all gauge
Save the great spirit of the age.
The mute machine is moved by a law
That knows no accident or flaw,
And the iron thrills to a different chime
Than that which rang in the dead old time.
For Heaven is taking the matter in hand,
And baffling the tricks of the tyrant band.
The sky above and the earth beneath
Heave with a supermundane breath.
Half-truths, for centuries kept and prized,
By higher truths are polarized.
Like gamesters on a railroad train,
Careless of stoppage, sun or rain,
We juggle, plot, combine, arrange,
And are swept along by the rapid change.

And some who from their windows mark
The unwonted lights that flood the dark,
Little by little, in slow surprise
Lift into space their sleepy eyes;
Little by little are made aware
That a spirit of power is passing there,—
That a spirit is passing, strong and free,—
The soul of the nineteenth century.

An Old Cat's Confessions

I am a very old pussy,
    My name is Tabitha Jane;
I have had about fifty kittens,
    So I think that I mustn't complain.

Yet I've had my full share of cat's troubles:
    I was run over once by a cart;
And they drowned seventeen of my babies,
    Which came near breaking my heart.

A gentleman once singed my whiskers,—
    I shall never forgive him for that!
And once I was bit by a mad dog,
    And once was deceived by a rat.

I was tied by some boys in a meal-bag,
    And pelted and pounded with stones;
They thought I was mashed to a jelly,
    But it didn't break one of my bones.

For cats that have good constitutions
    Have eight more lives than a man;
Which proves we are better than humans
    To my mind, if anything can.

One night, as I wandered with Thomas,—
   We were singing a lovely duet,—
I was shot in the back by a bullet;
   When you stroke me, I feel it there yet.

A terrier once threatened my kittens;
   O, it gave me a terrible fright!
But I scratched him, and sent him off howling,
   And I think that I served him just right.

But I've failed to fulfill all my duties:
   I have purred half my life in a dream;
And I never devoured the canary,
   And I never lapped half enough cream.

But I've been a pretty good mouser,
   (What squirrels and birds I have caught!)
And have brought up my frolicsome kittens
   As a dutiful mother-cat ought.

Now I think I've a right, being aged,
   To take an old tabby's repose;
To have a good breakfast and dinner,
   And sit by the fire and doze.

I don't care much for the people
   Who are living with me in this house,
But I own that I love a good fire,
   And occasional herring and mouse.

The Evening Primrose

"What are you looking at?" the farmer said;
    "That's nothing but a yellow flowering weed."
We turned, and saw our neighbor's grizzled head
    Above the fence, but took of him no heed.

There stood the simple man, and wondered much
    At us, who wondered at the twilight flowers
Bursting to life, as if a spirit's touch
    Awoke their slumbering souls to answer ours.

"It grows all o'er the island, wild," said he;
    "There are plenty in my field: I root 'em out.
But, for my life, it puzzles me to see
    What you make such a wonderment about."

The good man turned and to his supper went;
    While, kneeling on the grass with mute delight
Or whispered words, around the plant we bent,
    To watch the opening buds that love the night.

Slowly the rosy dusk of eve departed,
    And one by one the pale stars bloomed on high;
And one by one each folded calyx started,
    And bared its golden petals to the sky.

One throb from star to flower seemed pulsing through
    The night,—one living spirit blending all
In beauty and in mystery ever new,—
    One harmony divine through great and small.

E'en our plain neighbor, as he sips his tea,
    I doubt not, through his window feels the sky
Of evening bring a sweet and tender plea
    That links him even to dreamers such as I.

So through the symbol-alphabet that glows
    Through all creation, higher still and higher
The spirit builds its faith, and ever grows
    Beyond the rude form of its first desire.

O boundless Beauty and Beneficence!
  O deathless Soul that breathest in the weeds
And in a starlit sky!—e'en through the rents
  Of accident thou serv'st all human needs;

Nor stoopest idly to our petty cares;
  Nor knowest great or small, since folded in
By universal Love, all being shares
  The life that ever shall be or hath been.

December

No more the scarlet maples flash and burn
  Their beacon-fires from hilltop and from plain;
The meadow-grasses and the woodland fern
  In the bleak woods lie withered once again.

The trees stand bare, and bare each stony scar
  Upon the cliffs; half frozen glide the rills;
The steel-blue river like a scimitar
  Lies cold and curved between the dusky hills.

Over the upland farm I take my walk,
  And miss the flaunting flocks of golden-rod;
Each autumn flower a dry and leafless stalk,
  Each mossy field a track of frozen sod.

I hear no more the robin's summer song
  Through the gray network of the wintry woods;
Only the cawing crows that all day long
  Clamor about the windy solitudes.

Like agate stones upon earth's frozen breast,
  The little pools of ice lie round and still;
While sullen clouds shut downward east and west
  In marble ridges stretched from hill to hill.

Come once again, O southern wind,—once more
   Come with thy wet wings flapping at my pane;
Ere snow-drifts pile their mounds about my door,
   One parting dream of summer bring again.

Ah, no! I hear the windows rattle fast;
   I see the first flakes of the gathering snow,
That dance and whirl before the northern blast.
   No countermand the march of days can know.

December drops no weak, relenting tear,
   By our fond summer sympathies ensnared;
Nor from the perfect circle of the year
   Can even winter's crystal gems be spared.

My Old Palette

Many a year has fled away
   Since this old palette was new,
As may be seen by the spots of green
   And yellow and red and blue.

Many a picture was painted from this,
   While many were only dreamed;
And shadow and light like the black and white
   Across my life have streamed.

Accept, my friend, this plain old board
   All plastered and imbrowned,
Where the pleasure and strife of a painter's life
   Have left a mosaic ground.

The color that went to the picture's soul
   Has left but its body behind;
Yet strive to trace on its cloudy face
   Some gleam of the artist's mind.

And think of the friend upon whose thumb
    This brown old tablet hung,
And the baffled aim, where visions came
    Unpainted and unsung.

Mine be the records all obscure
    Upon the surface blent;
Be yours the love that seeks to prove
    My deed by my intent.

Music

*Read at the Annual Dinner of the Harvard Musical Association,
Boston, January 28, 1874.*

When "Music, Heavenly Maid," was *very* young,
She did not sing as poets say she sung.
Unlike the mermaids of the fairy tales,
She paid but slight attention to her scales.
Besides, poor thing! she had no instruments
But such as rude barbaric art invents.
There were no Steinways then, no Chickerings,
No spinnets, harpsichords, or metal strings;
No hundred-handed orchestras, no schools
To corset her in contrapuntal rules.
Some rude half-octave of a shepherd's song,
Some childish strumming all the summer long
On sinews stretched across a tortoise-shell,
Such as they say Apollo loved so well;
Some squeaking flageolet or scrannel pipe,
Some lyre poetic of the banjo type,—
Such were the means she summoned to her aid,
Prized as divine; on these she sang or played.

Music was then an infant, while she saw
Her sister arts full grown. Greece stood in awe
Before the Phidian Jove. Apelles drew
And Zeuxis painted. Marble temples "grew
As grows the grass"; and never saw the sun
A statelier vision than the Parthenon.

But she, the Muse who in these latter days
Lifts us and floats us in the golden haze
Of melodies and harmonies divine,
And steeps our souls and senses in such wine
As never Ganymede nor Hebe poured
For gods, when quaffing at the Olympian board,—
She, Heavenly Maid, must ply her music thin,
And sit and thrum her tinkling mandolin,
Chant her rude staves, and only prophesy
Her far-off days of immortality.

E'en so poor Cinderella, when she cowered
Beside her hearth, and saw her sisters, dowered
With grace and wealth, go forth to accomplish all
Their haughty triumphs at the Prince's ball,
While she in russet gown sat mournfully
Singing her "Once a king there chanced to be,"
Yet knows her prince will come; her splendid days
Are all foreshadowed in her dreaming gaze.

Then, as the years and centuries rolled on,
Like Santa-Clauses they have come and gone,
Bringing all means of utterance to the Muse.
No penny-trumpets, such as children use,
No barbarous Indian drums, no twanging lutes,
No buzzing Jews-harps, no Pandean flutes,
Were stuffed into her stockings, though they hung
On Time's great chimney, as when she was young;
But every rare and costly instrument
That skill can fabricate or art invent,—
Pianos, organs, viols, horns, trombones,
Hautboys, and clarinets with reedy tones,
Boehm-flutes and cornets, bugles, harps, bassoons,
Huge double-basses, kettle-drum half-moons,
And every queer contrivance made for tunes.

Through these the master-spirits round her throng,
And Europe rings with instruments and song.
Through these she breathes her wondrous symphonies,
Enchanting airs, and choral litanies.
Through these she speaks the word that never dies,
The universal language of the skies.
Around her gather those who held their art
To be of life the dearest, noblest part.
Bach, Handel, Haydn, and Mozart are there;
Beethoven, chief of all. The southern air
Is ringing with Rossini's birdlike notes;
About the north more earnest music floats,
Where Weber, Schumann, Schubert, Mendelssohn,
And long processions of the lords of Tone
All come to attend her. Like a queen enthroned
She sits and rules the realms she long has owned,
And sways the willing sense, the aspiring soul,
Where thousands bow before her sweet control.

Ah! greater than all words of mine can say,
The heights, the depths, the glories, of that sway.
No mortal tongue can bring authentic speech
Of that enchanted world beyond its reach;
No tongue but hers, when, lifted on the waves
Of Tone and Harmony, beyond the graves
Of all we lose, we drift entranced away
Out of the discords of the common day;
And she, the immortal goddess, on her breast
Lulls us to visions of a sweet unrest,
Smiles at the tyrannies of time and space,
And folds us in a mother's fond embrace,
Till, sailing on upon that mystic sea,
We feel that Life is Immortality.

Bird Language

One day in the bluest of summer weather,
  Sketching under a whispering oak,
I heard five bobolinks laughing together
  Over some ornithological joke.

What the fun was I could n't discover.
  Language of birds is a riddle on earth.
What could they find in whiteweed and clover
  To split their sides with such musical mirth?

Was it some prank of the prodigal summer,
  Face in the cloud or voice in the breeze,
Querulous catbird, woodpecker drummer,
  Cawing of crows high over the trees?

Was it some chipmunk's chatter, or weasel
  Under the stone-wall stealthy and sly?
Or was the joke about me at my easel,
  Trying to catch the tints of the sky?

Still they flew tipsily, shaking all over,
  Bubbling with jollity, brimful of glee,
While I sat listening deep in the clover,
  Wondering what their jargon could be.

'T was but the voice of a morning the brightest
  That ever dawned over yon shadowy hills;
'T was but the song of all joy that is lightest, —
  Sunshine breaking in laughter and trills.

Vain to conjecture the words they are singing;
  Only by tones can we follow the tune
In the full heart of the summer fields ringing,
  Ringing the rhythmical gladness of June!

from *Seven Wonders of the World*

The Printing-Press

In boyhood's days we read with keen delight
How young Aladdin rubbed his lamp and raised
The towering Djin whose form his soul amazed,
Yet who was pledged to serve him day and night.
But Gutenberg evoked a giant sprite
Of vaster power, when Europe stood and gazed
To see him rub his types with ink. Then blazed
Across the lands a glorious shape of light,
Who stripped the cowl from priests, the crown from kings,
And hand in hand with Faith and Science wrought
To free the struggling spirit's limèd wings,
And guard the ancestral throne of sovereign Thought.
The world was dumb. Then first it found its tongue
And spake—and heaven and earth in answer rung.

The Locomotive

Whirling along its living freight, it came,
Hot, panting, fierce, yet docile to command—
The roaring monster, blazing through the land
Athwart the night, with crest of smoke and flame;
Like those weird bulls Medea learned to tame
By sorcery, yoked to plough the Colchian strand
In forced obedience under Jason's hand.
Yet modern skill outstripped this antique fame,
When o'er our plains and through the rocky bar
Of hills it pushed its ever-lengthening line
Of iron roads, with gain far more divine
Than when the daring Argonauts from far
Came for the golden fleece, which like a star
Hung clouded in the dragon-guarded shrine.

The Photograph

Phœbus Apollo, from Olympus driven,
Lived with Admetus, tending herds and flocks:
And strolling o'er the pastures and the rocks
He found his life much duller than in Heaven.
For he had left his bow, his songs, his lyre,
His divinations and his healing skill,
And as a serf obeyed his master's will.
One day a new thought waked an old desire.
He took to painting, with his colors seven,
The sheep, the cows, the faces of the swains,
All shapes and hues in forests and on plains.
These old sun-pictures all are lost, or given
Away among the gods. Man owns but half
The Sun-god's secret—in the Photograph.

CHARLES TIMOTHY BROOKS

(1813–1883)

Our Island Home

Though here no towering mountain-steep
   Leaps, forest-crowned, to meet the sky;
Nor prairie, with majestic sweep,
   Enchants the gazer's roaming eye,—

Yet ocean's glittering garden-bed,
   Summer and winter, cheers the sight:
Its rose, the sun, at noon flames red;
   The moon, its lily, blooms by night.

The white-winged ships, in fleet career,
   Like sea-birds o'er the ocean skim;
They rise, glide on, and disappear
   Behind the horizon's shadowy rim.

So sail the fleets of clouds; and so
   Stars rise, and climb the heavens, and set,
Like human thoughts, that come and go—
   Whence—whither—no man knoweth yet.

Far onward sweeps the billowy main;
   To meet it bends th' o'erarching sky:
Of God's vast being emblems twain;
   Deep unto deep gives glad reply.

These open, each, a broad highway;
   To endless realms the soul invite:
The trackless ocean-floor by day,
   The star-lit stairs of heaven by night.

Oh, enviable lot! to dwell
   Surrounded by the great-voiced sea,
Whose waves intone, with trumpet-swell,
   The hymn of Law and Liberty!

Lines:
Composed at the Old Temples of Maralipoor

Speak out your secret, bellowing waves,
   That thunder round this temple's door,
And when the lashing tempest raves,
   Leap in, and wash the sand-heaped floor!

What hide ye in your watery tomb?
   What treasures snatched ye from the shore,
Ye sullen, restless waves that boom
   And thunder round this temple's door?

Say, is it true, as legends tell,
   That, ages since, great Bali's town,
O'erwhelmed by your encroaching swell,
   With tower and temple, all went down?

Speak out, thou stern old sentinel,
   That lingerest on the outer rock,
That brav'st the undermining swell,
   Defiest the overwhelming shock!

Lies there a city at thy feet,
   Far down beneath the moaning tide?
Say (for thou know'st), the tale repeat:
   What secret do these waters hide?

Ye all are voiceless,—silent stone,
   And sounding sea: no word ye speak,—
Nor sculptured shape nor billow's moan
   Can give the answer that I seek.

Old Ocean rolls as first he rolled
   Majestic on creation's day;
And still their course the waters hold,
   While man and all his works decay.

Yon grim old shapes—not one of all
　　Wears terror on his stony brow:
Dead sculptures line that rock-hewn wall,
　　The four-armed god is harmless now.

Yet can I, as I gaze, revere
　　The faith that thus, though dimly, bore
Its witness to the power that here
　　Rolls in the billows on the shore.

And this, too, is the self-same sea
　　That wets my native coast with spray;
And like a child it welcomes me,
　　As round my feet its waters play.

Oh! could I here to idols turn,
　　No human pile should be my shrine;
But, Ocean! how my heart would yearn
　　To come and be a child of thine!

JONES VERY

(1813–1880)

The New Birth

'Tis a new life—thoughts move not as they did
With slow uncertain steps across my mind,
In thronging haste fast pressing on they bid
The portals open to the viewless wind;
That comes not, save when in the dust is laid
The crown of pride that gilds each mortal brow,
And from before man's vision melting fade
The heavens and earth—Their walls are falling now—
Fast crowding on each thought claims utterance strong,
Storm-lifted waves swift rushing to the shore
On from the sea they send their shouts along,
Back through the cave-worn rocks their thunders roar,
And I a child of God by Christ made free
Start from death's slumbers to eternity.

"In Him we live, & move, & have our being"

Father! I bless thy name that I do live
And in each motion am made rich with thee
That when a glance is all that I can give
It is a kingdom's wealth, if I but see;
This stately body cannot move, save I
Will to its nobleness my little bring,
My voice its measured cadence will not try
Save I with every note consent to sing;
I cannot raise my hands to hurt or bless
But I with every action must conspire;
To show me there how little I possess
And yet that little more than I desire;
May each new act my new allegiance prove
Till in thy perfect love I ever live & move.

The Morning Watch

'Tis near the morning watch, the dim lamp burns
But scarcely shows how dark the slumbering street;
No sound of life the silent mart returns;
No friends from house to house their neighbors greet;
It is the sleep of death; a deeper sleep
Than e'er before on mortal eyelids fell;
No stars above the gloom their places keep;
No faithful watchmen of the morning tell;
Yet still they slumber on, though rising day
Hath through their windows poured the awakening light;
Or, turning in their sluggard trances, say—
"There yet are many hours to fill the night;"
They rise not yet; while on the bridegroom goes
'Till he the day's bright gates forever on them close!

The Garden

I saw the spot where our first parents dwelt;
And yet it wore to me no face of change,
For while amid its fields and groves I felt
As if I had not sinned, nor thought it strange;
My eye seemed but a part of every sight,
My ear heard music in each sound that rose,
Each sense forever found a new delight,
Such as the spirit's vision only knows;
Each act some new and ever-varying joy
Did by my Father's love for me prepare;
To dress the spot my ever fresh employ,
And in the glorious whole with Him to share;
No more without the flaming gate to stray,
No more for sin's dark stain the debt of death to pay.

The Song

When I would sing of crooked streams and fields,
On, on from me they stretch too far and wide,
And at their look my song all powerless yields,
And down the river bears me with its tide;
Amid the fields I am a child again,
The spots that then I loved I love the more,
My fingers drop the strangely-scrawling pen,
And I remember nought but nature's lore;
I plunge me in the river's cooling wave,
Or on the embroidered bank admiring lean,
Now some endangered insect life to save,
Now watch the pictured flowers and grasses green;
Forever playing where a boy I played,
By hill and grove, by field and stream delayed.

The Latter Rain

The latter rain, it falls in anxious haste
Upon the sun-dried fields and branches bare,
Loosening with searching drops the rigid waste
As if it would each root's lost strength repair;
But not a blade grows green as in the spring,
No swelling twig puts forth its thickening leaves;
The robins only mid the harvests sing
Pecking the grain that scatters from the sheaves;
The rain falls still—the fruit all ripened drops,
It pierces chestnut burr and walnut shell,
The furrowed fields disclose the yellow crops,
Each bursting pod of talents used can tell,
And all that once received the early rain
Declare to man it was not sent in vain.

The Dead

I see them crowd on crowd they walk the earth
Dry, leafless trees no Autumn wind laid bare;
And in their nakedness find cause for mirth,
And all unclad would winter's rudeness dare;
No sap doth through their clattering branches flow,
Whence springing leaves and blossoms bright appear;
Their hearts the living God have ceased to know,
Who gives the spring time to th'expectant year;
They mimic life, as if from him to steal
His glow of health to paint the livid cheek;
They borrow words for thoughts they cannot feel,
That with a seeming heart their tongue may speak;
And in their show of life more dead they live
Than those that to the earth with many tears they give.

Thy Brother's Blood

I have no Brother—they who meet me now
Offer a hand with their own wills defiled,
And while they wear a smooth unwrinkled brow
Know not that Truth can never be beguiled;
Go wash the hand that still betrays thy guilt;
Before the spirit's gaze what stain can hide?
Abel's red blood upon the earth is spilt,
And by thy tongue it cannot be denied;
I hear not with the ear—the heart doth tell
Its secret deeds to me untold before;
Go, all its hidden plunder quickly sell,
Then shalt thou cleanse thee from thy brother's gore;
Then will I take thy gift—that bloody stain
Shall not be seen upon thy hand again.

The Earth

I would lie low, the ground on which men tread,
Swept by thy spirit like the wind of heaven;
An earth where gushing springs and corn for bread
By me at every season should be given;
Yet not the water and the bread that now
Supplies their tables with its daily food;
But Thou wouldst give me fruit for every bough,
Such as Thou givest me, and call'st it good;
And water from the stream of life should flow,
By every dwelling that thy love has built;
Whose taste the ransomed of thy son shall know,
Whose robes are washed from every stain of guilt;
And men would own it was thy hand that blest,
And from my bosom find a surer rest.

The Cup

The bitterness of death is on me now,
Before me stands its dark unclosing door;
Yet to thy will submissive still I bow,
And follow him who for me went before;
The tomb cannot contain me though I die,
For his strong love awakes its sleeping dead;
And bids them through himself ascend on high,
To Him who is of all the living Head;
I gladly enter through the gloomy walls,
Where they have passed who loved their master here;
The voice they heard, to me it onward calls,
And can when faint my sinking spirit cheer;
And from the joy on earth it now has given,
Lead on to joy eternal in the heaven.

The New World

The night that has no star lit up by God,
The day that round men shines who still are blind,
The earth their grave-turned feet for ages trod,
And sea swept over by His mighty wind;
All these have passed away; the melting dream
That flitted o'er the sleeper's half-shut eye,
When touched by morning's golden-darting beam;
And he beholds around the earth and sky
That ever real stands; the rolling spheres,
And heaving billows of the boundless main,
That show though time is past no trace of years,
And earth restored he sees as his again;
The earth that fades not, and the heavens that stand;
Their strong foundations laid by God's right hand!

The New Man

The hands must touch and handle many things,
The eyes long waste their glances all in vain;
The feet course still in idle, mazy rings,
E'er man himself, the lost, shall back regain;
The hand that ever moves, the eyes that see,
While day holds out his shining lamp on high,
And strait as flies the honey-seeking bee,
Direct the feet to unseen flowers they spy,
These, when they come, the man revealed from heaven,
Shall labor all the day in quiet rest,
And find at eve the covert duly given,
Where with the bird they find sweet sleep and rest;
That shall their wasted strength to health restore,
And bid them seek the morn the hills and fields once more.

The Created

There is nought for thee by thy haste to gain;
'Tis not the swift with Me that win the race;
Through long endurance of delaying pain,
Thine opened eye shall see thy Father's face;
Nor here nor there, where now thy feet would turn,
Thou wilt find Him who ever seeks for thee;
But let obedience quench desires that burn,
And where thou art, thy Father too will be!
Behold! as day by day the spirit grows,
Thou see'st by inward light things hid before;
Till what God is, thyself, his image, shows;
And thou dost wear the robe that first thou wore,
When bright with radiance from his forming hand,
He saw thee Lord of all his creatures stand.

Autumn Leaves

The leaves though thick are falling; one by one
Decayed they drop from off their parent tree;
Their work with autumn's latest day is done,
Thou see'st them borne upon its breezes free;
They lie strown here and there, their many dyes
That yesterday so caught thy passing eye;
Soiled by the rain each leaf neglected lies,
Upon the path where now thou hurriest by;
Yet think thee not their beauteous tints less fair,
Than when they hung so gaily o'er thy head;
But rather find thee eyes, and look thee there
Where now thy feet so heedless o'er them tread;
And thou shalt see where wasting now they lie,
The unseen hues of immortality.

The Hand and the Foot

The hand and foot that stir not, they shall find
Sooner than all the rightful place to go;
Now in their motion free as roving wind,
Though first no snail so limited and slow;
I mark them full of labor all the day,
Each active motion made in perfect rest;
They cannot from their path mistaken stray,
Though 'tis not theirs, yet in it they are blest;
The bird has not their hidden track found out,
Nor cunning fox though full of art he be;
It is the way unseen, the certain route,
Where ever bound, yet thou art ever free;
The path of Him, whose perfect law of love
Bids spheres and atoms in just order move.

The Eye and Ear

Thou readest, but each lettered word can give
Thee but the sound that thou first gave to it;
Thou lookest on the page, things move and live
In light thine eye and thine alone has lit;
Ears are there yet unstopped, and eyes unclosed,
That see and hear as in one common day;
When they which present see have long reposed,
And he who hears has mouldered too to clay;
These ever see and hear; they are in Him,
Who speaks, and all is light; how dark before!
Each object throws aside its mantle dim,
That hid the starry robe that once it wore;
And shines full-born disclosing all that is,
Itself by all things seen and owned as His.

Yourself

'Tis to yourself I speak; you cannot know
Him whom I call in speaking such an one,
For thou beneath the earth liest buried low,
Which he alone as living walks upon;
Thou mayst at times have heard him speak to you,
And often wished perchance that you were he;
And I must ever wish that it were true,
For then thou couldst hold fellowship with me;
But now thou hearst us talk as strangers, met
Above the room wherein thou liest abed;
A word perhaps loud spoken thou mayst get,
Or hear our feet when heavily they tread;
But he who speaks, or him who's spoken to,
Must both remain as strangers still to you.

The Lost

The fairest day that ever yet has shone,
Will be when thou the day within shalt see;
The fairest rose that ever yet has blown,
When thou the flower thou lookest on shalt be.
But thou art far away among Time's toys;
Thyself the day thou lookest for in them,
Thyself the flower that now thine eye enjoys,
But wilted now thou hang'st upon thy stem.
The bird thou hearest on the budding tree,
Thou hast made sing with thy forgotten voice;
But when it swells again to melody,
The song is thine in which thou wilt rejoice;
And thou new risen 'midst these wonders live,
That now to them dost all thy substance give.

The Prayer

Wilt Thou not visit me?
The plant beside me feels thy gentle dew;
    And every blade of grass I see,
From thy deep earth its quickening moisture drew.

Wilt Thou not visit me?
Thy morning calls on me with cheering tone;
    And every hill and tree
Lend but one voice, the voice of Thee alone.

Come, for I need thy love;
More than the flower the dew, or grass the rain,
    Come, gently as thy holy dove;
And let me in thy sight rejoice to live again.

I will not hide from them,
When thy storms come, though fierce may be their wrath;
    But bow with leafy stem,
And strengthened follow on thy chosen path.

Yes, Thou wilt visit me:
Nor plant nor tree thy parent eye delight so well;
    As when from sin set free
My spirit loves with thine in peace to dwell.

The Cottage

The house my earthly parent left,
My heavenly Father e'er throws down;
For 'tis of air and sun bereft,
Nor stars its roof in beauty crown.

He gave it me, yet gave it not,
As one whose gifts are wise and good:
'Twas but a poor and clay-built cot,
And for a time the storms withstood;

But lengthening years, and frequent rain,
O'ercame its strength, it tottered, fell;
And left me homeless here again,
And where to go I could not tell.

But soon the light and open air,
Received me as a wandering child;
And I soon thought their house more fair,
And was from all my grief beguiled.

Mine was the grove, the pleasant field,
Where dwelt the flowers I daily trod;
And there beside them too I kneeled,
And called their friend, my Father, God.

The Strangers

Each care-worn face is but a book
    To tell of houses bought or sold;
Or filled with words that men have took
    From those who lived and spoke of old.

I see none whom I know, for they
    See other things than him they meet;
And though they stop me by the way,
    'Tis still some other one to greet.

There are no words that reach my ear,
    Those speak who tell of other things
Than what they mean for me to hear,
    For in their speech the counter rings.

I would be where each word is true,
    Each eye sees what it looks upon;
For here my eye has seen but few,
    Who in each act that act have done.

The Wild Rose of Plymouth

Upon the Plymouth shore the wild rose blooms
As when the Pilgrims lived beside the bay
And scents the morning air with sweet perfumes,
Though new this hour more ancient far than they;
More ancient than the wild, yet friendly race,
That roved the land before the Pilgrims came;
And here for ages found a dwelling-place
Of whom our histories tell us but the name!
Though new this hour out from the Past it springs
Telling this summer morning of earth's prime;
And happy visions of the Future brings
That reach beyond, e'en to the verge of time;
Wreathing earth's children in one flowery chain
Of Love and Beauty ever to remain.

The Lament of the Flowers

I looked to find Spring's early flowers,
    In spots where they were wont to bloom;
But they had perished in their bowers,
    The haunts they loved had proved their tomb!

The alder and the laurel green,
    Which sheltered them, had shared their fate;
And but the blackened ground was seen,
    Where hid their swelling buds of late.

From the bewildered, homeless bird,
    Whose half-built nest the flame destroys;
A low complaint of wrong I heard,
    Against the thoughtless, ruthless boys.

Sadly I heard its notes complain,
    And ask the young its haunts to spare;
Prophetic seemed the sorrowing strain,
    Sung o'er its home, but late so fair!

"No more, with hues like ocean shell,
    The delicate wind-flower here shall blow;
The spot that loved its form so well
    Shall ne'er again its beauty know."

"Or, if it bloom, like some pale ghost,
    Twill haunt the black and shadeless dell,
Where once it bloomed a numerous host,
    Of its once pleasant bowers to tell."

"And coming years no more shall find
    The laurel green upon the hills;
The frequent fire leaves naught behind,
    But e'en the very roots it kills."

"No more, upon the turnpike's side,
    The rose shall shed its sweet perfume;
The traveller's joy, the summer's pride,
    Will share with them a common doom."

"No more shall these, returning, fling
    Round Childhood's home a heavenly charm;
With song of bird, in early Spring,
    To glad the heart, and save from harm."

Autumn Flowers

Still blooming on, when Summer-flowers all fade,
    The golden rods and asters fill the glade;
The tokens they of an Exhaustless Love,
    That ever to the end doth constant prove.

To one fair tribe another still succeeds,
    As still the heart new forms of beauty needs;
Till these, bright children of the waning year!
    Its latest born have come our souls to cheer.

They glance upon us from their fringed eyes,
  And to their look our own in love replies;
Within our hearts we find for them a place,
  As for the flowers, which early Spring-time grace.

Despond not traveller! on life's lengthened way,
  When all thy early friends have passed away;
Say not, "No more the beautiful doth live,
  And to the earth a bloom and fragrance give."

To every season has our Father given
  Some tokens of his love to us from heaven;
Nor leaves us here, uncheered, to walk alone,
  When all we loved and prized, in youth, has gone.

Let but thy heart go forth to all around,
  Still by thy side the beautiful is found;
Along thy path the Autumn flowers shall smile,
  And to its close life's pilgrimage beguile.

The Origin of Man, I

Man has forgot his Origin; in vain
He searches for the record of his race
In ancient books, or seeks with toil to gain
From the deep cave, or rocks some primal trace.
And some have fancied, from a higher sphere,
Forgetful of his origin he came;
To dwell awhile a wandering exile here
Subject to sense, another, yet the same.
With mind bewildered, weak how should he know
The Source Divine from whom his being springs?
The darkened spirit does its shadow throw
On written record, and on outward things;
That else might plainly to his thought reveal
The wondrous truths, which now they but conceal.

EPES SARGENT
(1813–1880)

The Planet Jupiter

Ever at night have I looked up for thee,
   O'er thy sidereal sisterhood supreme!
Ever at night have scanned the purple sea
   For the reflection of thy quivering beam!
When the white cloud thy diamond radiance screened,
   And the Bahama breeze began to wail,
How on the plunging bows for hours I've leaned,
   And watched the gradual lifting of thy veil!
Bright planet! lustrous effluence! thou ray
   From the Eternal Source of life and light!
Gleam on the track where Truth shall lead the way,
   And gild the inward as the outward night!
Shine but as now upon my dying eyes,
And Hope, from earth to thee, from thee to Heaven,
     shall rise!

The Sea-Breeze at Matanzas

After a night of languor without rest,—
   Striving to sleep, yet wishing morn might come,
By the pent, scorching atmosphere oppressed,
   Impatient of the vile mosquito's hum,—
With what reviving freshness from the sea,
   Its airy plumage glittering with the spray,
Comes the strong day-breeze, rushing joyously
   Into the bright arms of the encircling bay!
It tempers the keen ardor of the sun;
   The drooping frame with life renewed it fills;
It lashes the green waters as they run;
   It sways the graceful palm-tree on the hills;
It breathes of ocean solitudes, and caves,
Luminous, vast, and cool, far down beneath the waves.

Rockall

Pale ocean rock! that, like a phantom shape,
Or some mysterious spirit's tenement,
Risest amid this weltering waste of waves,
Lonely and desolate, thy spreading base
Is planted in the sea's unmeasured depths,
Where rolls the huge leviathan o'er sands
Glistening with shipwrecked treasures. The strong wind
Flings up thy sides a veil of feathery spray
With sunbeams interwoven, and the hues
Which mingle in the rainbow. From thy top
The sea-birds rise, and sweep with sidelong flight
Downward upon their prey; or, with poised wings,
Skim to the horizon o'er the glittering deep.

Our bark, careening to the welcome breeze,
With white sails filled and streamers all afloat,
Shakes from her dipping prow the foam, while we
Gaze on thy outline mingling in the void,
And draw our breath like men who see, amazed,
Some mighty pageant passing. What had been
Our fate last night, if, when the aspiring waves
Were toppling o'er our mainmast, and the stars
Were shrouded in black vapors, we had struck
Full on thy sea-bound pinnacles, Rockall!

But now another prospect greets our sight,
And hope elate is rising with our hearts:
Intensely blue, the sky's resplendent arch
Bends over all serenely; not a cloud
Mars its pure radiance; not a shadow dims
The flashing billows. The refreshing air
It is a luxury to feel and breathe;
The senses are made keener, and drink in
The life, the joy, the beauty of the scene.

Repeller of the wild and thundering surge!
For ages has the baffled tempest howled
By thee with all its fury, and piled up
The massive waters like a falling tower
To dash thee down; but there thou risest yet,

As calm amid the roar of storms, the shock
Of waves uptorn, and hurled against thy front,
As when, on summer eves, the crimsoned main,
In lingering undulations, girds thee round!
    O, might I stand as steadfast and as free
'Mid the fierce strife and tumult of the world,
The crush of all the elements of woe,—
Unshaken by their terrors, looking forth
With placid eye on life's uncertain sea,
Whether its waves were darkly swelling high
Or dancing in the sunshine,—then might frown
The clouds of fate around me! Firm in faith,
Pointing serenely to that better world,
Where there is peace, would I abide the storm,
Unmindful of its rage and of its end.

DANIEL DECATUR EMMETT

(1815–1904)

Dixie's Land

I wish I was in de land ob cotton,
Old times dar am not forgotten,
    Look away! Look away! Look away! Dixie Land.
In Dixie Land whar I was born in,
Early on one frosty mornin,
    Look away! Look away! Look away! Dixie Land.

> *Den I wish I was in Dixie,*
> *Hooray! Hooray!*
> *In Dixie Land, I'll took my stand,*
> *To lib an die in Dixie,*
> *Away, Away, Away down south in Dixie,*
> *Away, Away, Away down south in Dixie.*

Old Missus marry "Will-de-weaber,"
Willium was a gay deceaber;
    Look away! Look away! Look away! Dixie Land.
But when he put his arm around 'er,
He smiled as fierce as a forty pounder.
    Look away! Look away! Look away! Dixie Land.

    Chorus.

His face was sharp as a butcher's cleaber,
But dat did not seem to greab 'er;
    Look away! Look away! Look away! Dixie Land.
Old Missus acted de foolish part,
And died for a man dat broke her heart.
    Look away! Look away! Look away! Dixie Land.

    Chorus.

Now here's a health to the next old Missus,
An all de gals dat want to kiss us;
    Look away! Look away! Look away! Dixie Land.
But if you want to drive 'way sorrow,
Come and hear dis song to-morrow.
    Look away! Look away! Look away! Dixie Land.

    Chorus.

Dar's buck-wheat cakes an Ingen' batter,
Makes you fat or a little fatter;
    Look away! Look away! Look away! Dixie Land.
Den hoe it down an scratch your grabble,
To Dixie land I'm bound to trabble.
    Look away! Look away! Look away! Dixie Land.

    Chorus.

Boatman's Dance

Ober de mountains, slick as an eel,
De boatman slide down on his heel;
He hop in de long boat brisk as a flea,
Den hoist up Anchor and put to sea

    O, dance de boatman dance;
    O, dance de boatman dance;
    Dance all night,
    Till de broad daylight,
Den go home wid de gals in de morning.

De boatman dance, de boatman sing,
De boatman up to ebery ting;
When de boatman gets on shore,
He spends his money an works for more.

    Chorus.

De Osyter boat should keep to de shore,
De fishin smack should venture more,
De Schoner sails before de wind,
De Steamboat leabes a streak behind.

Chorus.

I went on board de odder day,
To see what de boatmen had to say;
Dare I let my passion loose
Dey cram me in de Callaboose.

Chorus.

I've come dis time, I'll come no more;
Let me loose I'll go on shore;
Sez dey ole hoss we're a bully crew,
Wid a hoosier Mate and Captain too.

Chorus.

When you go to de boatman's ball,
Dance wid my wife or don't dance at all;
Sky blue jacket an tarpolin hat,
Look out my boys for de nine-tail cat.

Chorus.

De boatman is a thrifty man,
Dar's none can do as de boatman can;
I nebber see a putty gal in my life,
But dat she was a boatman's wife.

Chorus.

When de boatman blows his horn,
Look out old man, your hog is gone;
He cotched my sheep, he cotched my shoat,
Den put 'em in de bag an toat 'em to de boat.

Chorus.

PHILIP PENDLETON COOKE

(1816–1850)

Florence Vane

I loved thee long and dearly,
 Florence Vane;
My life's bright dream, and early,
 Hath come again;
I renew, in my fond vision,
 My heart's dear pain,
My hope, and thy derision,
 Florence Vane.

The ruin lone and hoary,
 The ruin old,
Where thou didst hark my story,
 At even told,—
That spot—the hues Elysian
 Of sky and plain—
I treasure in my vision,
 Florence Vane.

Thou wast lovelier than the roses
 In their prime;
Thy voice excelled the closes
 Of sweetest rhyme;
Thy heart was as a river
 Without a main.
Would I had loved thee never,
 Florence Vane!

But, fairest, coldest wonder!
 Thy glorious clay
Lieth the green sod under—
 Alas the day!

And it boots not to remember
 Thy disdain—
To quicken love's pale ember,
 Florence Vane.

The lilies of the valley
 By young graves weep,
The pansies love to dally
 Where maidens sleep;
May their bloom, in beauty vying,
 Never wane
Where thine earthly part is lying,
 Florence Vane!

Orthone

It was the Bastot Maulion
 Who told this tale to me,
At Ortaise, by an ingle side,
 In gossip frank and free,
At the good hostel of the Moon,
 Where I sometime attended
The will of Gaston Earl of Foix,
 That potent lord, and splendid.

The Lord Corasse—the Bastot said—
 Had taken on his hands
Feud with a Catalonian clerk,
 Who sought to tithe his lands;
And dealt so rudely by the priest
 That he was fain to fly—
For the lord's wrath had put his life,
 He deemed, in jeopardy.

But ere the priest went forth, he came
 And yielded to the lord,
In formal wise, the cause of feud;
 And then, at parting word,

Quoth he, "Corasse, your greater strength
    Has robbed me of my right:
I yield not to your argument,
    But only to your might."

"Ah, Master Martin!" said the lord,
    "I care not for your rage;
Free living shall you never have
    From my fair heritage."
"So much I know;" the clerk replied,
    "You violate the laws;
But, swift as may be, I will send
    A champion of my cause.

"And he shall deal so by your peace,
    That you will sorely rue
That you have borne against the right,
    And robbed me of my due."
And, with such words, the angry clerk
    Departed on his way:
The baron never saw him more
    From forth that summer day.

Three nights thereafter, Lord Corasse
    Lay quietly abed,
When, suddenly, the castle rung
    With wondrous sounds and dread;
A clatter in the kitchens—
    A thunder on the stair—
And shrillest voices screaming
    Around it in the air.

The Lord Corasse sate up, and stared,
    And seemed in trouble sore;
Then heard unmannered knocking
    All at his chamber door.
His lady drew the curtains
    In fear about her head,
But to his sword, reached forth the lord,
    And, full of courage, said—

"Now who be ye who thunder so?
     Pray let your names be shown."
And at the word, reply he heard,
     "They call my name Orthone."
"Orthone," replied the baron,
     "Who sent you here to me?"
"Your enemy, the Spanish clerk,
     Whose work I do"—quoth he.

"Orthone," said on the baron stout,
     "A beggar like the clerk
Will give you little thanks, or wage,
     For moiling at his work:
I pray you be my servant!"—
     With this the clamour ceased,
And Orthone said, "So let it be—
     I weary of the priest."

Thereafter Orthone served the lord,
     Invisible to him;
Would seek his chamber nightly,
     When lights were burning dim,
And bring him news of distant lands,
     Of battle-field, and court;
Did never post so little cost,
     Or bear such swift report.

One day the baron came to join
     A banquet at Ortaise,
And some loose speech of his did strike
     Earl Gaston with amaze.
"Brother!" quoth he, "how may it be—
     This thing thou dost declare—
Unless thou hast a messenger
     To fly upon the air?"

And then the baron answer made,
     For he was glad with wine,
And told the earl the story—
     Who thereof did opine

As of a marvel deep, and said,
    "If ever thou hast seen
This messenger, in any shape,
    Pray tell me of his mien."

"I have not seen him," said Corasse,
    "Small use it were to see;
Sufficient that he comes, and goes,
    And serves me faithfully."
Then said the earl, "When next he comes,
    I pray thee bid him show
What look he wears—what shape he bears—
    So much I fain would know."

The Lord Corasse is now abed,
    And merry Orthone seeks
His side again, and plucks his ear,
    And toys upon his cheeks.
"Orthone—Orthone!" said Lord Corasse—
    "Good servant, prithee, show
What look you wear—what shape you bear—
    So much I fain would know."

"Sir," said Orthone, "I plainly see
    That you are bent to lose
A willing servant: but, for once,
    I grant the thing you choose.
Whatever, when you leave this bed,
    Your eyes first rest upon—
Observe it well, for certainly
    That thing will be Orthone."

The sun is shining yellowly,
    And dazzles on the bed;
And Lord Corasse laughs loud to see
    His lady hide her head.
He sits upright, and laughs, and peers
    Around him everywhere,
But he may mark no living thing,
    No matter how he stare.

Uprose he then, and placed his foot
   Out on the rushes, strewn
So soft upon his chamber floor—
   Nor saw he yet Orthone.
But as he puts his foot abroad,
   A quick keen tickle goes,
Athwart the sole, and tingles
   Betwixt the wincing toes.

And as his foot he lifted,
   A single straw fell down,
And rested not, but skipped about,
   Over the rushes brown,
With somersets, and other feats—
   The like, man never saw,
And Lord Corasse looked on, and said,
   "The devil is in the straw."

But never deemed the Lord Corasse
   That he had seen Orthone;
That day went by, he sought his bed
   When as its toils were done;
And, at the middle watch of night,
   Orthone drew nigh again,
And plucked the baron by the ear,
   And plucked the counterpane.

"Orthone—Orthone!" his master said,
   "You err in coming here;
You broke that promise made to me—
   So much is surely clear."
"I made a promise," said Orthone,
   "And truly held thereby:
The tumbling straw, whose feats you saw,
   That little straw was I."

"Ah!" quoth the lord, "I deemed the straw
   Was surely out of nature:
But prithee take some other form
   Of greater bulk and stature."

And so, again, the voice has said,
    "What first you look upon,
Observe it well, for certainly
    That thing will be Orthone."

The baron rose up with the sun,
    And looking up and down—
Now here, now there—and everywhere—
    Saw but the rushes brown,
And oaken stools, and cabinets—
    The room's appurtenances:
No semblance of his servant met
    His shrewd and roving glances.

Then to a lattice broad, he stept,
    And cast it open wide;
And, looking down upon the court,
    He presently espied
A gaunt wild-sow, with ears, I trow,
    As long as of a hound,
And bristled back, and loathly dugs
    That trailed upon the ground.

The baron shouted to his men—
    It moved him so to see
That loathly beast—and bade them loose
    His bandogs speedily.
The mastiffs came out ramping,
    But eager-eyed and mute,
They snuffed the air, and flew to tear,
    And yell around the brute.

The wild-sow never tarried
    For bay, or roaring chace,
But gave a cry unearthly,
    And vanished from the place.
And then the baron knew the beast
    Was certainly Orthone,
And turned within, lamenting
    The thing that he had done.

Quoth he, "It would be merely just
   If Orthone left me now—
But certainly I deemed the beast
   Was but a loathly sow."
That night Corasse lay long awake,
   But lay awake in vain:
Orthone came not, and truly,
   He never came again.

So said the Bastot Maulion,
   And I have given his story
Fair place amongst my braver tales,
   Of policy and glory.
If it be true, or haply false,
   So much I cannot say:
But mysteries as great surround
   Our life by night and day.

JOSIAH D. CANNING

(1816–1892)

The Indian Gone!

By night I saw the *Hunter's moon*
    Slow gliding in the placid sky;
Her lustre mocked the sun at noon—
    I asked myself the reason why?
And straightway came the sad reply:
    She shines as she was wont to do
To aid the Indian's aiming eye,
      When by her light he strung his bow,
        But where is he?

Beside the ancient flood I strayed,
    Where dark traditions mark the shore;
With wizzard vision I essayed
    Into the misty past to pore.
I heard a mournful voice deplore
    The perfidy that slew his race;
'T was in a dialect of yore,
      And of a long-departed race.
        It answered me!

I wrought with ardor at the plough
    One smoky Indian-summer day;
The dank locks swept my heated brow,
    I bade the panting oxen stay.
Beneath me in the furrow lay
    A relic of the chase, full low;
I brushed the crumbling soil away—
      The Indian fashioned it, I know,
        But where is he?

When pheasants drumming in the wood
    Allured me forth my aim to try,
Amid the forest lone I stood,

And the dead leaves went rustling by.
The breeze played in the branches high;
    Slow music filled my listening ear;
It was a wailing funeral cry,
    For Nature mourned her children dear.
        It answered me!

HENRY DAVID THOREAU

(1817–1862)

"They who prepare my evening meal below"

They who prepare my evening meal below
Carelessly hit the kettle as they go
With tongs or shovel,
And ringing round and round,
Out of this hovel
It makes an eastern temple by the sound.

At first I thought a cow bell right at hand
Mid birches sounded o'er the open land,
Where I plucked flowers
Many years ago,
Spending midsummer hours
With such secure delight they hardly seemed to flow.

"On fields oer which the reaper's hand has passd"

On fields oer which the reaper's hand has passd
Lit by the harvest moon and autumn sun,
My thoughts like stubble floating in the wind
And of such fineness as October airs,
There after harvest could I glean my life
A richer harvest reaping without toil,
And weaving gorgeous fancies at my will
In subtler webs than finest summer haze.

Fog

Dull water spirit—and Protean god
Descended cloud fast anchored to the earth
That drawest too much air for shallow coasts
Thou ocean branch that flowest to the sun
Incense of earth, perfumed with flowers—

Spirit of lakes and rivers—seas and rills
Come to revisit now thy native scenes
Night thoughts of earth—dream drapery
Dew cloth—and fairy napkin
Thou wind-blown meadow of the air

"Dong, sounds the brass in the east"

Dong, sounds the brass in the east,
As if to a funeral feast,
But I like that sound the best
Out of the fluttering west.

The steeple ringeth a knell,
But the fairies' silvery bell
Is the voice of that gentle folk,
Or else the horizon that spoke.

Its metal is not of brass,
But air, and water, and glass,
And under a cloud it is swung,
And by the wind it is rung.

When the steeple tolleth the noon,
It soundeth not so soon,
Yet it rings a far earlier hour,
And the sun has not reached its tower.

Rumors from an Æolian Harp

There is a vale which none hath seen,
Where foot of man has never been,
Such as here lives with toil and strife,
An anxious and a sinful life.

There every virtue has its birth,
Ere it descends upon the earth,
And thither every deed returns,
Which in the generous bosom burns.

There love is warm, and youth is young,
And poetry is yet unsung,
For Virtue still adventures there,
And freely breathes her native air.

And ever, if you hearken well,
You still may hear its vesper bell,
And tread of high-souled men go by,
Their thoughts conversing with the sky.

"My life has been the poem I would have writ"

My life has been the poem I would have writ,
But I could not both live and utter it.

"I am a parcel of vain strivings tied"

I am a parcel of vain strivings tied
    By a chance bond together,
  Dangling this way and that, their links
      Were made so loose and wide,
              Methinks,
          For milder weather.

A bunch of violets without their roots,
    And sorrel intermixed,
  Encircled by a wisp of straw
      Once coiled about their shoots,
              The law
          By which I'm fixed.

A nosegay which Time clutched from out
    Those fair Elysian fields,
  With weeds and broken stems, in haste,
      Doth make the rabble rout
              That waste
          The day he yields.

And here I bloom for a short hour unseen,
    Drinking my juices up,
  With no root in the land
    To keep my branches green,
        But stand
    In a bare cup.

Some tender buds were left upon my stem
    In mimicry of life,
  But ah! the children will not know,
    Till time has withered them,
        The woe
    With which they're rife.

But now I see I was not plucked for naught,
    And after in life's vase
  Of glass set while I might survive,
    But by a kind hand brought
        Alive
    To a strange place.

That stock thus thinned will soon redeem its hours,
    And by another year,
  Such as God knows, with freer air,
  More fruits and fairer flowers
       Will bear,
    While I droop here.

"Light-winged Smoke, Icarian bird"

Light-winged Smoke, Icarian bird,
Melting thy pinions in thy upward flight,
Lark without song, and messenger of dawn,
Circling above the hamlets as thy nest;
Or else, departing dream, and shadowy form
Of midnight vision, gathering up thy skirts;
By night star-veiling, and by day
Darkening the light and blotting out the sun;
Go thou my incense upward from this hearth,
And ask the gods to pardon this clear flame.

Guido's Aurora

The God of day rolls his car up the slopes,
Reining his prancing steeds with steady hand,
The moon's pale orb through western shadows gropes,
While morning sheds its light o'er sea and land.

Castles and cities by the sounding main
Resound with all the busy din of life,
The fisherman unfurls his sails again
And the recruited warrior bides the strife.

The early breeze ruffles the poplar leaves,
The curling waves reflect the washed light,
The slumbering sea with the day's impulse heaves,
While o'er the western hills retires the drowsy night.

The sea birds dip their bills in ocean's foam,
Far circling out over the frothy waves—

Music

Far from this atmosphere that music sounds
Piercing some azure chink in the dull clouds
Of sense that overarch my recent years,
And steal his freshness from the noonday sun.
Ah, I have wandered many ways and lost
The boyant step, the whole responsive life
That stood with joy to hear what seemed then
Its echo, its own harmony borne back
Upon its ear. This tells of better space,
Far far beyond the hills the woods the clouds
That bound my low and plodding valley life,
Far from my sin, remote from my distrust,
Where first my healthy morning life perchance
Trod lightly as on clouds, and not as yet
My weary and faint hearted noon had sunk
Upon the clod while the bright day went by.
   Lately, I feared my life was empty, now

I know though a frail tenement that it still
Is worth repair, if yet its hollowness
Doth entertain so fine a guest within, and through
Its empty aisles there still doth ring
Though but the echo of so high a strain;
It shall be swept again and cleansed from sin
To be a thoroughfare for celestial airs;
Perchance the God who is proprietor
Will pity take on his poor tenant here
And countenance his efforts to improve
His property and make it worthy to revert,
At some late day Unto himself again.

Inspiration

Whate'er we leave to God, God does,
   And blesses us;
The work we choose should be our own,
   God lets alone.

If with light head erect I sing,
   Though all the muses lend their force,
From my poor love of anything,
   The verse is weak and shallow as its source.

But if with bended neck I grope,
   Listening behind me for my wit,
With faith superior to hope,
   More anxious to keep back than forward it,

Making my soul accomplice there
   Unto the flame my heart hath lit,
Then will the verse forever wear,
   Time cannot bend the line which God hath writ.

Always the general show of things
   Floats in review before my mind,
And such true love and reverence brings,
   That sometimes I forget that I am blind.

But soon there comes unsought, unseen,
  Some clear divine electuary,
And I, who had but sensual been,
  Grow sensible, and as God is am wary.

I hearing get who had but ears,
  And sight who had but eyes before,
I moments live who lived but years,
  And truth discern who knew but learning's lore.

I hear beyond the range of sound,
  I see beyond the verge of sight,
New earths—and skies—and seas—around,
  And in my day the sun doth pale his light.

A clear and ancient harmony
  Pierces my soul through all the din,
As through its utmost melody,
  Further behind than they, further within.

More swift its bolt than lightning is,
  Its voice than thunder is more loud,
It doth expand my privacies
  To all, and leave me single in the crowd.

It speaks with such authority,
  With so serene and lofty tone,
That idle Time runs gadding by,
  And leaves me with Eternity alone.

Then chiefly is my natal hour,
  And only then my prime of life,
Of manhood's strength it is the flower,
  'Tis peace's end and war's beginning strife.

'T hath come in summer's broadest noon,
  By a grey wall or some chance place,
Unseasoned time, insulted June,
  And vexed the day with its presuming face.

Such fragrance round my couch it makes,
  More rich than are Arabian drugs,
That my soul scents its life, and wakes
  The body up—from 'neath its perfumed rugs.

Such is the Muse—the heavenly maid,
  The star that guides our mortal course,
Which shows where life's true kernel's laid,
  Its wheat's fine flower, and its undying force.

She with one breath attunes the spheres,
  And also my poor human heart,
With one impulse propels the years
  Around, and gives my throbbing pulse its start.

I will not doubt forever more,
  Nor falter from a steadfast faith,
For though the system be turned oer,
  God takes not back the word which once he saith.

I will then trust the love untold,
  Which not my worth nor want hath bought
Which wooed me young and woos me old,
  And call the stars to witness now my thought.

My memory I'll educate
  To know the one historic truth,
Remembering to the latest date
  The only true, and sole immortal youth.

Be but thy inspiration given,
  No matter through what dangers sought,
I'll fathom hell or climb to heaven,
  And yet esteem that cheap which love has bought.

        Fame cannot tempt the bard
          Who's famous with his God,
          Nor laurel him reward,
          Who hath his maker's nod.

CORNELIUS MATHEWS

(1817–1889)

from *Poems on Man in His Various Aspects Under the American Republic*

The Sculptor

Leap up into the light, ye living Forms!
   And plant amid men your birthright feet;
Angry and fierce as the maned thunder's storms,
   And as the lightning beautiful and fleet.
Of quick and thoughtful souls the truest thoughts,
   Born of the marble at Heaven's happy hour—
Ye blessed Realities! who strike the doubts
   Begot of speech, dumb, with your better power.

   Human and life-like with no sense of pain,
Come forth, crowned heroes of the early age,
Chieftain and soldier, senator and sage—
   Benignant, wise and brave again!
Would the soul clothe itself in elder gloom—
   Let stand upon the cliff and in the shadowy grove,
The tawny ancient of the warrior race,
With dusky limb and flushing face,
Diffusing Autumn through the stilly place—
   For battle stern, or soothed for love.

Or should a spirit of a larger scope
   Seek to express itself in sacred stone:
Cast, life-long, on the mountain-slope
   Or seat upon the starry mountain-cone,
Colossal and resigned, the gloomy gods
Eying at large their lost abodes,
Towering and swart and knit in every limb,
   With brows on which the tempest lives,
   With eyes wherein the past survives;
Gloomy and battailous and grim.

Think not too much what other climes have done,
   What other ages: with painful following, weary—
Each step thou takest darkens thy natural sun,
   And makes thy coming course, thy by-gone, dreary.
Let the soul in thee lift its awful front,
   Facing the Universe that stands before it;
Beaten by day and night and tempests' brunt,
   All shapes—all glorious passions shall cross o'er it.
Forth from their midst some forms will leap
   That other souls have never disencumbered,
And up shall spring through all the broad-set land,
   The fair white people of thy love unnumbered.

The Journalist

As shakes the canvass of a thousand ships,
   Struck by a heavy land-breeze, far at sea—
Ruffle the thousand broad-sheets of the land,
   Filled with the people's breath of potency

A thousand images the hour will take,
   From him who strikes, who rules, who speaks, who sings;
Many within the hour their grave to make—
   Many to live, far in the heart of things.

A dark-dyed spirit he who coins the time,
   To virtue's wrong, in base disloyal lies—
Who makes the morning's breath, the evening's tide,
   The utterer of his blighting forgeries.

How beautiful who scatters, wide and free,
   The gold-bright seeds of loved and loving truth!
By whose perpetual hand, each day, supplied—
   Leaps to new life the empire's heart of youth.

To know the instant and to speak it true,
   Its passing lights of joy, its dark, sad cloud,
To fix upon the unnumbered gazers' view,
   Is to thy ready hand's broad strength allowed.

There is an in-wrought life in every hour,
   Fit to be chronicled at large and told—
'Tis thine to pluck to light its secret power,
   And on the air its many-colored heart unfold.

The angel that in sand-dropped minutes lives,
   Demands a message cautious as the ages—
Who stuns, with dusk-red words of hate, his ear,
   That mighty power to boundless wrath enrages.

Hell not the quiet of a Chosen Land,
   Thou grimy man over thine engine bending;
The spirit pent that breathes the life into its limbs,
   Docile for love is tyrannous in rending.

Obey, Rhinoceros! an infant's hand,
   Leviathan! obey the fisher mild and young,
Vexed Ocean! smile, for on thy broad-beat sand
   The little curlew pipes his shrilly song.

The Masses

When, wild and high, the uproar swells
   From crowds that gather at the set of day;
   When square and market roar in stormy play,
And fields of men, like lions, shake their fells
Of savage hair; when, quick and deep, call out the bells
     Through all the lower Heaven ringing,
       As if an earthquake's shock
       The city's base should rock,
     And set its troubled turrets singing:—

Remember, Men! on massy strength relying,
       There is a heart of right
       Not always open to the light,
Secret and still and force-defying.
In vast assemblies calm, let order rule,
   And, every shout a cadence owning,
   Make musical the vexed wind's moaning,
And be as little children at a singing-school.

But, when, thick as night, the sky is crusted o'er,
    Stifling life's pulse and making Heaven an idle dream,
Arise! and cry, up through the dark, to God's own throne:
    Your faces in a furnace glow,
    Your arms uplifted for the death-ward blow—
    Fiery and prompt as angry angels show:
Then draw the brand and fire the thunder-gun!
Be nothing said and all things done!
    Till every cobwebbed corner of the common-weal
    Is shaken free, and, creeping to its scabbard back the steel,
Let's shine again God's rightful sun!

WILLIAM ELLERY CHANNING

(1818–1901)

The Harbor

No more I seek, the prize is found,
  I furl my sails, my voyage is o'er;
The treacherous waves no longer sound
  But sing thy praise along the shore.

I steal from all I hoped of old,
  To throw more beauty round thy way;
The dross I part, and melt the gold,
  And stamp it with thy every-day.

I did not dream to welcome thee;
  Like all I have thou camest unknown,
An island in a misty sea,
  With stars, and flowers, and harvests strown.

A well is in the desert sand
  With purest water cold and clear,
Where overjoyed at rest I stand,
  And drink the sound I hoped to hear.

Hymn of the Earth

My highway is unfeatured air,
My consorts are the sleepless Stars,
And men, my giant arms upbear,
My arms unstained and free from scars.

I rest forever on my way,
Rolling around the happy Sun,
My children love the sunny day,
But noon and night to me are one.

My heart has pulses like their own,
I am their Mother, and my veins
Though built of the enduring stone,
Thrill as do theirs with godlike pains.

The forests and the mountains high,
The foaming ocean and the springs,
The plains,—O pleasant Company,
My voice through all your anthem rings.

Ye are so cheerful in your minds,
Content to smile, content to share,
My being in your Chorus finds
The echo of the spheral air.

No leaf may fall, no pebble roll,
No drop of water lose the road,
The issues of the general Soul
Are mirrored in its round abode.

The Barren Moors

On your bare rocks, O barren moors,
On your bare rocks I love to lie,—
They stand like crags upon the shores,
Or clouds upon a placid sky.

Across those spaces desolate,
The fox pursues his lonely way,
Those solitudes can fairly sate
The passage of my loneliest day.

Like desert Islands far at sea
Where not a ship can ever land,
Those dim uncertainties to me,
For something veritable stand.

A serious place distinct from all
Which busy Life delights to feel,
I stand in this deserted hall,
And thus the wounds of time conceal.

No friend's cold eye, or sad delay,
Shall vex me now where not a sound
Falls on the ear, and every day
Is soft as silence most profound.

No more upon these distant wolds
The agitating world can come,
A single pensive thought upholds
The arches of this dreamy home.

Within the sky above, one thought
Replies to you, O barren Moors,
Between, I stand, a creature taught
To stand between two silent floors.

Walden

It is not far beyond the Village church,
After we pass the wood that skirts the road,
A Lake, — the blue-eyed Walden, that doth smile
Most tenderly upon its neighbor Pines,
And they as if to recompense this love,
In double beauty spread their branches forth.
This Lake had tranquil loveliness and breadth,
And of late years has added to its charms,
For one attracted to its pleasant edge,
Has built himself a little Hermitage,
Where with much piety he passes life.

More fitting place I cannot fancy now,
For such a man to let the line run off
The mortal reel, such patience hath the lake,
Such gratitude and cheer is in the Pines.

But more than either lake or forest's depths,
This man has in himself; a tranquil man,
With sunny sides where well the fruit is ripe,
Good front, and resolute bearing to this life,
And some serener virtues, which control
This rich exterior prudence, virtues high,
That in the principles of Things are set,
Great by their nature and consigned to him,
Who, like a faithful Merchant, does account
To God for what he spends, and in what way.
Thrice happy art thou, Walden! in thyself,
Such purity is in thy limpid springs;
In those green shores which do reflect in thee,
And in this man who dwells upon thy edge,
A holy man within a Hermitage.
May all good showers fall gently into thee,
May thy surrounding forests long be spared,
And may the Dweller on thy tranquil shores,
There lead a life of deep tranquillity
Pure as thy Waters, handsome as thy Shores
And with those virtues which are like the Stars.

Murillo's Magdalen

Her eyes are fixed; they seek the skies.
   Was earth so low? Was life so vain?
Was Time such weary sacrifice?
   This hopeless task, this eating pain?

Smooth, smooth the tresses of thy hair;
   Release that cold, contracted brow!
I have not lived without despair;
   Look down on me—some mercy show!

I cannot bear those silent skies;
   The weight is pressing in my heart;
Life is eternal sacrifice,
   The livelong hour, the selfish smart.

I wake to tears, in tears I close
   The weary eyes so fixed above;
I cannot see the skies of rose,
   My heavy tresses will not move.

Hope cannot heal my breaking heart,
   Heaven will not lift my dread despair;
I need another soul to part
   These brows of steel and join in prayer.

Sails there no bark on life's wild sea
   That bears a soul whose faith has set,
Who may renew my light in me,
   And both shall thus the past forget?

WILLIAM WETMORE STORY

(1819–1895)

Cleopatra

[Dedicated to J. L. M.]

Here, Charmian, take my bracelets,
   They bar with a purple stain
My arms; turn over my pillows—
   They are hot where I have lain:
Open the lattice wider,
   A gauze o'er my bosom throw,
And let me inhale the odours
   That over the garden blow.

I dreamed I was with my Antony,
   And in his arms I lay;
Ah, me! the vision has vanished—
   The music has died away.
The flame and the perfume have perished—
   As this spiced aromatic pastille
That wound the blue smoke of its odour
   Is now but an ashy hill.

Scatter upon me rose-leaves,
   They cool me after my sleep,
And with sandal odours fan me
   Till into my veins they creep;
Reach down the lute, and play me
   A melancholy tune,
To rhyme with the dream that has vanished,
   And the slumbering afternoon.

There, drowsing in golden sunlight,
   Loiters the slow smooth Nile,
Through slender papyri, that cover
   The wary crocodile.

The lotus lolls on the water,
   And opens its heart of gold,
And over its broad leaf-pavement
   Never a ripple is rolled.
The twilight breeze is too lazy
   Those feathery palms to wave,
And yon little cloud is as motionless
   As a stone above a grave.

Ah, me! this lifeless nature
   Oppresses my heart and brain!
Oh! for a storm and thunder—
   For lightning and wild fierce rain!
Fling down that lute—I hate it!
   Take rather his buckler and sword,
And crash them and clash them together
   Till this sleeping world is stirred.

Hark! to my Indian beauty—
   My cockatoo, creamy white,
With roses under his feathers—
   That flashes across the light.
Look! listen! as backward and forward
   To his hoop of gold he clings,
How he trembles, with crest uplifted,
   And shrieks as he madly swings!
Oh, cockatoo, shriek for Antony!
   Cry, "Come, my love, come home!"
Shriek, "Antony! Antony! Antony!"
   Till he hears you even in Rome.

There—leave me, and take from my chamber
   That stupid little gazelle,
With its bright black eyes so meaningless,
   And its silly tinkling bell!
Take him,—my nerves he vexes—
   The thing without blood or brain,—
Or, by the body of Isis,
   I'll snap his thin neck in twain!

Leave me to gaze at the landscape
 Mistily stretching away,
Where the afternoon's opaline tremors
 O'er the mountains quivering play;
Till the fiercer splendour of sunset
 Pours from the west its fire,
And melted, as in a crucible,
 Their earthy forms expire;
And the bald blear skull of the desert
 With glowing mountains is crowned,
That burning like molten jewels
 Circle its temples round.

I will lie and dream of the past time,
 Æons of thought away,
And through the jungle of memory
 Loosen my fancy to play;
When, a smooth and velvety tiger,
 Ribbed with yellow and black,
Supple and cushion-footed
 I wandered, where never the track
Of a human creature had rustled
 The silence of mighty woods,
And, fierce in a tyrannous freedom,
 I knew but the law of my moods.
The elephant, trumpeting, started,
 When he heard my footstep near,
And the spotted giraffes fled wildly
 In a yellow cloud of fear.

I sucked in the noontide splendour,
 Quivering along the glade,
Or yawning, panting, and dreaming,
 Basked in the tamarisk shade,
Till I heard my wild mate roaring,
 As the shadows of night came on,
To brood in the trees' thick branches
 And the shadow of sleep was gone;
Then I roused, and roared in answer,

And unsheathed from my cushioned feet
My curving claws, and stretched me,
    And wandered my mate to greet.
We toyed in the amber moonlight,
    Upon the warm flat sand,
And struck at each other our massive arms—
    How powerful he was and grand!
His yellow eyes flashed fiercely
    As he crouched and gazed at me,
And his quivering tail, like a serpent,
    Twitched curving nervously.
Then like a storm he seized me,
    With a wild triumphant cry,
And we met, as two clouds in heaven
    When the thunders before them fly.
We grappled and struggled together,
    For his love like his rage was rude;
And his teeth in the swelling folds of my neck
    At times, in our play, drew blood.

Often another suitor—
    For I was flexile and fair—
Fought for me in the moonlight,
    While I lay couching there,
Till his blood was drained by the desert;
    And, ruffled with triumph and power,
He licked me and lay beside me
    To breathe him a vast half-hour.
Then down to the fountain we loitered,
    Where the antelopes came to drink;
Like a bolt we sprang upon them,
    Ere they had time to shrink.
We drank their blood and crushed them,
    And tore them limb from limb,
And the hungriest lion doubted
    Ere he disputed with him.
That was a life to live for!
    Not this weak human life,
With its frivolous bloodless passions,
    Its poor and petty strife!

Come to my arms, my hero,
   The shadows of twilight grow,
And the tiger's ancient fierceness
   In my veins begins to flow.
Come not cringing to sue me!
   Take me with triumph and power,
As a warrior storms a fortress!
   I will not shrink or cower.
Come, as you came in the desert,
   Ere we were women and men,
When the tiger passions were in us,
   And love as you loved me then!

from *A Contemporary Criticism*

He thanked me for my kindness, disagreed
With my conclusions in a modest way
(He's modest, *that* 't is only just to say);
But in a letter that he sends to-day
Here is his answer. Listen, while I read.

"Most noble sir,"—and so on, and so on,—
"A thousand thanks,"—hem—hem,—"in one so high,"
"Learned in art,"—et cetera,—"I shall try"—
Oh! that's about his picture,—"critic's eye;"
"Patron,"—pho, pho—where *has* the passage gone?
Ah! here we come to it at last: "You thought,"
He says, "that in too many arts I wrought;
And you advised me to stick close to one.
Thanks for your gracious counsel, all too kind;
And answering, if I chance to speak my mind
Too boldly, pardon. Yet it seems to me
All arts are one,—all branches on one tree;
All fingers, as it were, upon one hand.
You ask me to be thumb alone; but pray,
Reft of the answering fingers Nature planned,
Is not the hand deformed for work or play?
Or rather take, to illustrate my thought,
Music, the only art to science wrought,

The ideal art, that underlies the whole,
Interprets all, and is of all the soul.
Each art is, so to speak, a separate tone;
The perfect chord results from all in one.
Strike one, and as its last vibrations die,
Listen,—from all the other tones a cry
Wails forth, half-longing and half-prophecy.
So does the complement, the hint, the germ
Of every art within the others lie,
And in their inner essence all unite;
For what is melody but fluid form,
Or form, but fixed and stationed melody?
Colours are but the silent chords of light,
Touched by the painter into tone and key,
And harmonized in every changeful hue.
So colours live in sound,—the trumpet blows
Its scarlet, and the flute its tender blue;
The perfect statue, in its pale repose,
Has for the soul a melody divine,
That lingers dreaming round each subtle line,
And stills the gazer lest its charm he lose.
So rhythmic words, strung by the poet, own
Music and form and colour—every sense
Rhymes with the rest;—'t is in the means alone
The various arts receive their difference."

JAMES RUSSELL LOWELL

(1819–1891)

from *The Present Crisis*

Once to every man and nation comes the moment to
   decide,
In the strife of Truth with Falsehood, for the good or evil
   side;
Some great cause, God's new Messiah, offering each the
   bloom or blight,
Parts the goats upon the left hand, and the sheep upon the
   right,
And the choice goes by for ever 'twixt that darkness and
   that light.

Hast thou chosen, O my people, on whose party thou shalt
   stand,
Ere the Doom from its worn sandals shakes the dust
   against our land?
Though the cause of Evil prosper, yet 't is Truth alone is
   strong,
And, albeit she wander outcast now, I see around her
   throng
Troops of beautiful, tall angels, to enshield her from all
   wrong.

Backward look across the ages and the beacon-moments
   see,
That, like peaks of some sunk continent, jut through
   Oblivion's sea;
Not an ear in court or market for the low foreboding cry
Of those Crises, God's stern winnowers, from whose feet
   earth's chaff must fly;
Never shows the choice momentous till the judgment hath
   passed by.

Careless seems the great Avenger; history's pages but
    record
One death-grapple in the darkness 'twixt old systems and
    the Word;
Truth for ever on the scaffold, Wrong for ever on the
    throne, —
Yet that scaffold sways the future, and, behind the dim
    unknown,
Standeth God within the shadow, keeping watch above his
    own.

We see dimly in the Present what is small and what is great,
Slow of faith how weak an arm may turn the iron helm of
    fate,
But the soul is still oracular; amid the market's din,
List the ominous stern whisper from the Delphic cave
    within, —
"They enslave their children's children who make
    compromise with sin."

from *A Fable for Critics*

"There comes Emerson first . . ."

There comes Emerson first, whose rich words, every one
Are like gold nails in temples to hang trophies on,
Whose prose is grand verse, while his verse, the Lord
    knows,
Is some of it pr——No, 'tis not even prose;
I'm speaking of metres; some poems have welled
From those rare depths of soul that have ne'er been excelled;
They're not epics, but that doesn't matter a pin,
In creating, the only hard thing's to begin;
A grass-blade's no easier to make than an oak,
If you've once found the way, you've achieved the grand
    stroke;
In the worst of his poems are mines of rich matter,
But thrown in a heap with a crush and a clatter;
Now it is not one thing nor another alone

Makes a poem, but rather the general tone,
The something pervading, uniting the whole,
The before unconceived, unconceivable soul,
So that just in removing this trifle or that, you
Take away, as it were, a chief limb of the statue;
Roots, wood, bark, and leaves, singly perfect may be,
But, clapt hodge-podge together, they don't make a tree.

But, to come back to Emerson, (whom, by the way,
I believe we left waiting,)—his is, we may say,
A Greek head on right Yankee shoulders, whose range
Has Olympus for one pole, for t'other the Exchange;
He seems, to my thinking, (although I'm afraid
The comparison must, long ere this, have been made,)
A Plotinus-Montaigne, where the Egyptian's gold mist
And the Gascon's shrewd wit cheek-by-jowl co-exist;
All admire, and yet scarcely six converts he's got
To I don't (nor they either) exactly know what;
For though he builds glorious temples, 'tis odd
He leaves never a doorway to get in a god.
'Tis refreshing to old-fashioned people like me,
To meet such a primitive Pagan as he,
In whose mind all creation is duly respected
As parts of himself—just a little projected;
And who's willing to worship the stars and the sun,
A convert to—nothing but Emerson.
So perfect a balance there is in his head,
That he talks of things sometimes as if they were dead;
Life, nature, love, God, and affairs of that sort,
He looks at as merely ideas; in short,
As if they were fossils stuck round in a cabinet,
Of such vast extent that our earth's a mere dab in it;
Composed just as he is inclined to conjecture her,
Namely, one part pure earth, ninety-nine parts pure lecturer;
You are filled with delight at his clear demonstration,
Each figure, word, gesture, just fits the occasion,
With the quiet precision of science he'll sort 'em,
But you can't help suspecting the whole a *post mortem*.

There are persons, mole-blind to the soul's make and style,
Who insist on a likeness 'twixt him and Carlyle;
To compare him with Plato would be vastly fairer,
Carlyle's the more burly, but E. is the rarer;
He sees fewer objects, but clearlier, truelier,
If C.'s as original, E.'s more peculiar;
That he's more of a man you might say of the one,
Of the other he's more of an Emerson;
C.'s the Titan, as shaggy of mind as of limb,—
E. the clear-eyed Olympian, rapid and slim;
The one's two-thirds Norseman, the other half Greek,
Where the one's most abounding, the other's to seek;
C.'s generals require to be seen in the mass,—
E.'s specialties gain if enlarged by the glass;
C. gives nature and God his own fits of the blues,
And rims common-sense things with mystical hues,—
E. sits in a mystery calm and intense,
And looks coolly around him with sharp common-sense;
C. shows you how every-day matters unite
With the dim transdiurnal recesses of night,—
While E., in a plain, preternatural way,
Makes mysteries matters of mere every day;
C. draws all his characters quite *à la* Fuseli,—
He don't sketch their bundles of muscles and thews illy,
But he paints with a brush so untamed and profuse,
They seem nothing but bundles of muscles and thews;
E. is rather like Flaxman, lines strait and severe,
And a colorless outline, but full, round, and clear;—
To the men he thinks worthy he frankly accords
The design of a white marble statue in words.
C. labors to get at the centre, and then
Take a reckoning from there of his actions and men;
E. calmly assumes the said centre as granted,
And, given himself, has whatever is wanted.

He has imitators in scores, who omit
No part of the man but his wisdom and wit,—
Who go carefully o'er the sky-blue of his brain,
And when he has skimmed it once, skim it again;
If at all they resemble him, you may be sure it is

Because their shoals mirror his mists and obscurities,
As a mud-puddle seems deep as heaven for a minute,
While a cloud that floats o'er is reflected within it.

There comes ——, for instance; to see him 's rare sport,
Tread in Emerson's tracks with legs painfully short;
How he jumps, how he strains, and gets red in the face,
To keep step with the mystagogue's natural pace!
He follows as close as a stick to a rocket,
His fingers exploring the prophet's each pocket.
Fie, for shame, brother bard; with good fruit of your own,
Can't you let neighbor Emerson's orchards alone?
Besides, 'tis no use, you'll not find e'en a core,—
—— has picked up all the windfalls before.
They might strip every tree, and E. never would catch 'em,
His Hesperides have no rude dragon to watch 'em;
When they send him a dishfull, and ask him to try 'em,
He never suspects how the sly rogues came by 'em;
He wonders why 'tis there are none such his trees on,
And thinks 'em the best he has tasted this season.

"There is Hawthorne . . ."

There is Hawthorne, with genius so shrinking and rare
That you hardly at first see the strength that is there;
A frame so robust, with a nature so sweet,
So earnest, so graceful, so solid, so fleet,
Is worth a descent from Olympus to meet;
'Tis as if a rough oak that for ages had stood,
With his gnarled bony branches like ribs of the wood,
Should bloom, after cycles of struggle and scathe,
With a single anemone trembly and rathe;
His strength is so tender, his wildness so meek,
That a suitable parallel sets one to seek,—
He's a John Bunyan Fouqué, a Puritan Tieck;
When Nature was shaping him, clay was not granted
For making so full-sized a man as she wanted,
So, to fill out her model, a little she spared
From some finer-grained stuff for a woman prepared,
And she could not have hit a more excellent plan

For making him fully and perfectly man.
The success of her scheme gave her so much delight,
That she tried it again, shortly after, in Dwight;
Only, while she was kneading and shaping the clay,
She sang to her work in her sweet childish way,
And found, when she'd put the last touch to his soul,
That the music had somehow got mixed with the whole.

"There comes Poe with his raven . . ."

There comes Poe with his raven, like Barnaby Rudge,
Three-fifths of him genius and two-fifths sheer fudge,
Who talks like a book of iambs and pentameters,
In a way to make people of common-sense damn metres,
Who has written some things quite the best of their kind,
But the heart somehow seems all squeezed out by the mind,
Who—but hey-day! What's this? Messieurs Mathews and
      Poe,
You mustn't fling mud-balls at Longfellow so,
Does it make a man worse that his character 's such
As to make his friends love him (as you think) too much?
Why, there is not a bard at this moment alive
More willing than he that his fellows should thrive;
While you are abusing him thus, even now
He would help either one of you out of a slough;
You may say that he's smooth and all that till you're hoarse,
But remember that elegance also is force;
After polishing granite as much as you will,
The heart keeps its tough old persistency still;
Deduct all you can that still keeps you at bay,—
Why, he'll live till men weary of Collins and Gray;
I'm not over-fond of Greek metres in English,
To me rhyme 's a gain, so it be not too jinglish,
And your modern hexameter verses are no more
Like Greek ones than sleek Mr. Pope is like Homer;
As the roar of the sea to the coo of a pigeon is,
So, compared to your moderns, sounds old Melesigenes;
I may be too partial, the reason, perhaps, o't is
That I've heard the old blind man recite his own rhapsodies,

And my ear with that music impregnate may be,
Like the poor exiled shell with the soul of the sea,
Or as one can't bear Strauss when his nature is cloven
To its deeps within deeps by the stroke of Beethoven;
But, set that aside, and 'tis truth that I speak,
Had Theocritus written in English, not Greek,
I believe that his exquisite sense would scarce change a line
In that rare, tender, virgin-like pastoral Evangeline.
That's not ancient nor modern, its place is apart
Where time has no sway, in the realm of pure Art,
'Tis a shrine of retreat from Earth's hubbub and strife
As quiet and chaste as the author's own life.

from *The Biglow Papers*

Letter Six — The Pious Editor's Creed

I du believe in Freedom's cause,
    Ez fur away ez Paris is;
I love to see her stick her claws
    In them infarnal Pharisees;
It 's wal enough agin a king
    To dror resolves an' triggers, —
But libbaty 's a kind o' thing
    Thet don't agree with niggers.

I du believe the people want
    A tax on teas an' coffees,
Thet nothin' aint extravygunt, —
    Purvidin' I 'm in office;
Fer I hev loved my country sence
    My eye-teeth filled their sockets,
An' Uncle Sam I reverence,
    Partic'larly his pockets.

I du believe in *any* plan
    O' levyin' the taxes,
Ez long ez, like a lumberman,
    I git jest wut I axes:

I go free-trade thru thick an' thin,
 Because it kind o' rouses
The folks to vote,—an' keeps us in
 Our quiet custom-houses.

I du believe it 's wise an' good
 To sen' out furrin missions,
Thet is, on sartin understood
 An' orthydox conditions;—
I mean nine thousan' dolls. per ann.,
 Nine thousan' more fer outfit,
An' me to recommend a man
 The place 'ould jest about fit.

I du believe in special ways
 O' prayin' an' convartin';
The bread comes back in many days,
 An' buttered, tu, fer sartin;—
I mean in preyin' till one busts
 On wut the party chooses,
An' in convartin' public trusts
 To very privit uses.

I du believe hard coin the stuff
 Fer 'lectioneers to spout on;
The people 's ollers soft enough
 To make hard money out on;
Dear Uncle Sam pervides fer his,
 An' gives a good-sized junk to all,—
I don't care *how* hard money is,
 Ez long ez mine 's paid punctooal.

I du believe with all my soul
 In the gret Press's freedom,
To pint the people to the goal
 An' in the traces lead 'em;
Palsied the arm thet forges yokes
 At my fat contracts squintin',
An' withered be the nose thet pokes
 Inter the gov'ment printin'!

I du believe thet I should give
   Wut 's his'n unto Cæsar,
Fer it 's by him I move an' live,
   Frum him my bread an' cheese air;
I du believe thet all o' me
   Doth bear his souperscription,—
Will, conscience, honor, honesty,
   An' things o' thet description.

I du believe in prayer an' praise
   To him thet hez the grantin'
O' jobs,—in every thin' thet pays,
   But most of all in CANTIN';
This doth my cup with marcies fill,
   This lays all thought o' sin to rest,—
I *don't* believe in princerple,
   But, O, I *du* in interest.

I du believe in bein' this
   Or thet, ez it may happen
One way or t'other hendiest is
   To ketch the people nappin';
It aint by princerples nor men
   My preudunt course is steadied,—
I scent wich pays the best, an' then
   Go into it baldheaded.

I du believe thet holdin' slaves
   Comes nat'ral tu a Presidunt,
Let 'lone the rowdedow it saves
   To hev a wal-broke precedunt;
Fer any office, small or gret,
   I could n't ax with no face,
Without I 'd ben, thru dry an' wet,
   Th' unrizzest kind o' doughface.

I du believe wutever trash
   'll keep the people in blindness,—
Thet we the Mexicuns can thrash
   Right inter brotherly kindness,

Thet bombshells, grape, an' powder 'n' ball
 Air good-will's strongest magnets,
Thet peace, to make it stick at all,
 Must be druv in with bagnets.

In short, I firmly du believe
 In Humbug generally,
Fer it 's a thing thet I perceive
 To hev a solid vally;
This heth my faithful shepherd ben,
 In pasturs sweet heth led me,
An' this 'll keep the people green
 To feed ez they hev fed me.

from *The Vision of Sir Launfal*

Prelude to Part the First

Over his keys the musing organist,
 Beginning doubtfully and far away,
First lets his fingers wander as they list,
 And builds a bridge from Dreamland for his lay:
Then, as the touch of his loved instrument
 Gives hope and fervor, nearer draws his theme,
First guessed by faint auroral flushes sent
 Along the wavering vista of his dream.

———

 Not only around our infancy
 Doth heaven with all its splendors lie;
 Daily, with souls that cringe and plot,
 We Sinais climb and know it not;
Over our manhood bend the skies;
 Against our fallen and traitor lives
The great winds utter prophecies;
 With our faint hearts the mountain strives;
Its arms outstretched, the druid wood

Waits with its benedicite;
And to our age's drowsy blood
   Still shouts the inspiring sea.

Earth gets its price for what Earth gives us;
   The beggar is taxed for a corner to die in,
The priest hath his fee who comes and shrives us,
   We bargain for the graves we lie in;
At the Devil's booth are all things sold,
Each ounce of dross costs its ounce of gold;
   For a cap and bells our lives we pay,
Bubbles we earn with a whole soul's tasking:
   'T is heaven alone that is given away,
'T is only God may be had for the asking;
There is no price set on the lavish summer,
And June may be had by the poorest comer.
And what is so rare as a day in June?
   Then, if ever, come perfect days;
Then Heaven tries the earth if it be in tune,
   And over it softly her warm ear lays:
Whether we look, or whether we listen,
We hear life murmur, or see it glisten;
Every clod feels a stir of might,
   An instinct within it that reaches and towers,
And, grasping blindly above it for light,
   Climbs to a soul in grass and flowers;
The flush of life may well be seen
   Thrilling back over hills and valleys;
The cowslip startles in meadows green,
   The buttercup catches the sun in its chalice,
And there 's never a leaf or a blade too mean
   To be some happy creature's palace;
The little bird sits at his door in the sun,
   Atilt like a blossom among the leaves,
And lets his illumined being o'errun
   With the deluge of summer it receives;
His mate feels the eggs beneath her wings,
And the heart in her dumb breast flutters and sings;
He sings to the wide world, and she to her nest, —
In the nice ear of Nature which song is the best?

Now is the high-tide of the year,
   And whatever of life hath ebbed away
Comes flooding back, with a ripply cheer,
   Into every bare inlet and creek and bay;
Now the heart is so full that a drop overfills it,
We are happy now because God so wills it;
No matter how barren the past may have been,
'T is enough for us now that the leaves are green;
We sit in the warm shade and feel right well
How the sap creeps up and the blossoms swell;
We may shut our eyes, but we cannot help knowing
That skies are clear and grass is growing;
The breeze comes whispering in our ear,
That dandelions are blossoming near,
   That maize has sprouted, that streams are flowing,
That the river is bluer than the sky,
That the robin is plastering his house hard by;
And if the breeze kept the good news back,
For other couriers we should not lack;
   We could guess it all by yon heifer's lowing,—
And hark! how clear bold chanticleer,
Warmed with the new wine of the year,
   Tells all in his lusty crowing!

Joy comes, grief goes, we know not how;
Every thing is happy now,
   Every thing is upward striving;
'T is as easy now for the heart to be true
As for grass to be green or skies to be blue,—
   'T is the natural way of living:
Who knows whither the clouds have fled?
   In the unscarred heaven they leave no wake;
And the eyes forget the tears they have shed,
   The heart forgets its sorrow and ache;
The soul partakes the season's youth,
   And the sulphurous rifts of passion and woe
Lie deep 'neath a silence pure and smooth,
   Like burnt-out craters healed with snow.
What wonder if Sir Launfal now
Remembered the keeping of his vow?

Remembered Music

A Fragment

Thick-rushing, like an ocean vast
   Of bisons the far prairie shaking,
The notes crowd heavily and fast
As surfs, one plunging while the last
   Draws seaward from its foamy breaking.

Or in low murmurs they began,
   Rising and rising momently,
As o'er a harp Æolian
A fitful breeze, until they ran
   Up to a sudden ecstasy.

And then, like minute-drops of rain
   Ringing in water silverly,
They lingering dropped and dropped again,
Till it was almost like a pain
   To listen when the next would be.

from *Under the Willows*

May is a pious fraud of the almanac,
A ghastly parody of real Spring
Shaped out of snow and breathed with eastern wind;
Or if, o'er-confident, she trust the date,
And, with her handful of anemones,
Herself as shivery, steal into the sun,
The season need but turn his hourglass round,
And Winter suddenly, like crazy Lear,
Reels back, and brings the dead May in his arms,
Her budding breasts and wan dislustred front
With frosty streaks and drifts of his white beard
All overblown. Then, warmly walled with books,
While my wood-fire supplies the sun's defect,
Whispering old forest-sagas in its dreams,
I take my May down from the happy shelf

Where perch the world's rare song-birds in a row,
Waiting my choice to open with full breast,
And beg an alms of spring-time, ne'er denied
Indoors by vernal Chaucer, whose fresh woods
Throb thick with merle and mavis all the year.

July breathes hot, sallows the crispy fields,
Curls up the wan leaves of the lilac-hedge,
And every eve cheats us with show of clouds
That braze the horizon's western rim, or hang
Motionless, with heaped canvas drooping idly,
Like a dim fleet by starving men besieged,
Conjectured half, and half descried afar,
Helpless of wind, and seeming to slip back
Adown the smooth curve of the oily sea.

Ode Recited at the Harvard Commemoration

July 21, 1865

I.

Weak-winged is song,
    Nor aims at that clear-ethered height
Whither the brave deed climbs for light:
    We seem to do them wrong,
Bringing our robin's-leaf to deck their hearse
Who in warm life-blood wrote their nobler verse,
Our trivial song to honor those who come
With ears attuned to strenuous trump and drum,
And shaped in squadron-strophes their desire,
Live battle-odes whose lines were steel and fire:
    Yet sometimes feathered words are strong,
A gracious memory to buoy up and save
From Lethe's dreamless ooze, the common grave
    Of the unventurous throng.

II.

To-day our Reverend Mother welcomes back
  Her wisest Scholars, those who understood
The deeper teaching of her mystic tome,
    And offered their fresh lives to make it good:
        No lore of Greece or Rome,
No science peddling with the names of things,
Or reading stars to find inglorious fates,
      Can lift our life with wings
Far from Death's idle gulf that for the many waits,
      And lengthen out our dates
With that clear fame whose memory sings
In manly hearts to come, and nerves them and dilates:
Nor such thy teaching, Mother of us all!
      Not such the trumpet-call
      Of thy diviner mood,
      That could thy sons entice
From happy homes and toils, the fruitful nest
Of those half-virtues which the world calls best,
      Into War's tumult rude;
      But rather far that stern device
The sponsors chose that round thy cradle stood
      In the dim, unventured wood,
      The VERITAS that lurks beneath
      The letter's unprolific sheath,
  Life of whate'er makes life worth living,
Seed-grain of high emprise, immortal food,
  One heavenly thing whereof earth hath the giving.

III.

Many loved Truth, and lavished life's best oil
  Amid the dust of books to find her,
Content at last, for guerdon of their toil,
    With the cast mantle she hath left behind her.
      Many in sad faith sought for her,
      Many with crossed hands sighed for her;
      But these, our brothers, fought for her,
      At life's dear peril wrought for her,
      So loved her that they died for her,

Tasting the raptured fleetness
Of her divine completeness:
    Their higher instinct knew
Those love her best who to themselves are true,
And what they dare to dream of dare to do;
    They followed her and found her
    Where all may hope to find,
Not in the ashes of the burnt-out mind,
But beautiful, with danger's sweetness round her;
    Where faith made whole with deed
    Breathes its awakening breath
    Into the lifeless creed,
    They saw her plumed and mailed,
    With sweet stern face unveiled,
And all-repaying eyes, look proud on them in death.

IV.

    Our slender life runs rippling by, and glides
    Into the silent hollow of the past;
        What is there that abides
    To make the next age better for the last?
        Is earth too poor to give us
    Something to live for here that shall outlive us?
        Some more substantial boon
Than such as flows and ebbs with Fortune's fickle moon?
        The little that we see
        From doubt is never free;
        The little that we do
        Is but half-nobly true;
        With our laborious hiving
What men call treasure, and the gods call dross,
    Life seems a jest of Fate's contriving,
    Only secure in every one's conniving,
A long account of nothings paid with loss,
Where we poor puppets, jerked by unseen wires,
    After our little hour of strut and rave,
With all our pasteboard passions and desires,
Loves, hates, ambitions, and immortal fires,
    Are tossed pell-mell together in the grave.

But stay! no age was e'er degenerate,
Unless men held it at too cheap a rate,
For in our likeness still we shape our fate;
 Ah, there is something here
Unfathomed by the cynic's sneer,
Something that gives our feeble light
A high immunity from Night,
Something that leaps life's narrow bars
To claim its birthright with the hosts of heaven;
 A seed of sunshine that doth leaven
Our earthly dulness with the beams of stars,
  And glorify our clay
With light from fountains elder than the Day;
 A conscience more divine than we,
 A gladness fed with secret tears,
 A vexing, forward-reaching sense
 Of some more noble permanence;
  A light across the sea,
Which haunts the soul and will not let it be,
Still glimmering from the heights of undegenerate years.

v.

  Whither leads the path
  To ampler fates that leads?
  Not down through flowery meads,
  To reap an aftermath
  Of youth's vainglorious weeds,
  But up the steep, amid the wrath
 And shock of deadly-hostile creeds,
 Where the world's best hope and stay
By battle's flashes gropes a desperate way,
And every turf the fierce foot clings-to bleeds.
 Peace hath her not ignoble wreath,
 Ere yet the sharp, decisive word
Light the black lips of cannon, and the sword
 Dreams in its easeful sheath;
But some day the live coal behind the thought,
  Whether from Baäl's stone obscene,
  Or from the shrine serene
  Of God's pure altar brought,

Bursts up in flame; the war of tongue and pen
Learns with what deadly purpose it was fraught,
And, helpless in the fiery passion caught,
Shakes all the pillared state with shock of men:
Some day the soft Ideal that we wooed
Confronts us fiercely, foe-beset, pursued,
And cries reproachful: "Was it, then, my praise,
And not myself was loved? Prove now thy truth;
I claim of thee the promise of thy youth;
Give me thy life, or cower in empty phrase,
The victim of thy genius, not its mate!"
   Life may be given in many ways,
   And loyalty to Truth be sealed
As bravely in the closet as the field,
      So bountiful is Fate;
      But then to stand beside her,
      When craven churls deride her,
To front a lie in arms and not to yield,
      This shows, methinks, God's plan
      And measure of a stalwart man,
      Limbed like the old heroic breeds,
      Who stands self-poised on manhood's solid earth,
   Not forced to frame excuses for his birth,
Fed from within with all the strength he needs.

VI.

Such was he, our Martyr-Chief,
      Whom late the Nation he had led,
      With ashes on her head,
Wept with the passion of an angry grief:
Forgive me, if from present things I turn
To speak what in my heart will beat and burn,
And hang my wreath on his world-honored urn.
      Nature, they say, doth dote,
      And cannot make a man
      Save on some worn-out plan,
      Repeating us by rote:
For him her Old World moulds aside she threw,
      And, choosing sweet clay from the breast

Of the unexhausted West,
With stuff untainted shaped a hero new,
Wise, steadfast in the strength of God, and true.
How beautiful to see
Once more a shepherd of mankind indeed,
Who loved his charge, but never loved to lead;
One whose meek flock the people joyed to be,
Not lured by any cheat of birth,
But by his clear-grained human worth,
And brave old wisdom of sincerity!
They knew that outward grace is dust;
They could not choose but trust
In that sure-footed mind's unfaltering skill,
And supple-tempered will
That bent like perfect steel to spring again and thrust.
His was no lonely mountain-peak of mind,
Thrusting to thin air o'er our cloudy bars,
A sea-mark now, now lost in vapors blind;
Broad prairie rather, genial, level-lined,
Fruitful and friendly for all human kind,
Yet also nigh to Heaven and loved of loftiest stars.
Nothing of Europe here,
Or, then, of Europe fronting mornward still,
Ere any names of Serf and Peer
Could Nature's equal scheme deface;
Here was a type of the true elder race,
And one of Plutarch's men talked with us face to face.
I praise him not; it were too late;
And some innative weakness there must be
In him who condescends to victory
Such as the Present gives, and cannot wait,
Safe in himself as in a fate.
So always firmly he:
He knew to bide his time,
And can his fame abide,
Still patient in his simple faith sublime,
Till the wise years decide.
Great captains, with their guns and drums,
Disturb our judgment for the hour,
But at last silence comes;

These all are gone, and, standing like a tower,
Our children shall behold his fame,
   The kindly-earnest, brave, foreseeing man,
Sagacious, patient, dreading praise, not blame,
   New birth of our new soil, the first American.

VII.

Long as man's hope insatiate can discern
   Or only guess some more inspiring goal
   Outside of Self, enduring as the pole,
Along whose course the flying axles burn
Of spirits bravely-pitched, earth's manlier brood;
   Long as below we cannot find
The meed that stills the inexorable mind;
So long this faith to some ideal Good,
   Under whatever mortal names it masks,
   Freedom, Law, Country, this ethereal mood
That thanks the Fates for their severer tasks,
   Feeling its challenged pulses leap,
   While others skulk in subterfuges cheap,
And, set in Danger's van, has all the boon it asks,
   Shall win man's praise and woman's love,
   Shall be a wisdom that we set above
All other skills and gifts to culture dear,
   A virtue round whose forehead we inwreathe
   Laurels that with a living passion breathe
When other crowns grow, while we twine them, sear.
   What brings us thronging these high rites to pay,
And seal these hours the noblest of our year,
   Save that our brothers found this better way?

VIII.

We sit here in the Promised Land
   That flows with Freedom's honey and milk;
   But 't was they won it, sword in hand,
Making the nettle danger soft for us as silk.
   We welcome back our bravest and our best; —
   Ah me! not all! some come not with the rest,
Who went forth brave and bright as any here!

I strive to mix some gladness with my strain,
But the sad strings complain,
And will not please the ear;
I sweep them for a pæan, but they wane
Again and yet again
Into a dirge, and die away in pain.
In these brave ranks I only see the gaps,
Thinking of dear ones whom the dumb turf wraps,
Dark to the triumph which they died to gain:
Fitlier may others greet the living,
For me the past is unforgiving;
I with uncovered head
Salute the sacred dead,
Who went, and who return not.—Say not so!
'T is not the grapes of Canaan that repay,
But the high faith that failed not by the way;
Virtue treads paths that end not in the grave;
No ban of endless night exiles the brave;
And to the saner mind
We rather seem the dead that stayed behind.
Blow, trumpets, all your exultations blow!
For never shall their aureoled presence lack:
I see them muster in a gleaming row,
With ever-youthful brows that nobler show;
We find in our dull road their shining track;
In every nobler mood
We feel the orient of their spirit glow,
Part of our life's unalterable good,
Of all our saintlier aspiration;
They come transfigured back,
Secure from change in their high-hearted ways,
Beautiful evermore, and with the rays
Of morn on their white Shields of Expectation!

IX.

But is there hope to save
Even this ethereal essence from the grave?
What ever 'scaped Oblivion's subtle wrong
Save a few clarion names, or golden threads of song?

Before my musing eye
The mighty ones of old sweep by,
Disvoicëd now and insubstantial things,
As noisy once as we; poor ghosts of kings,
Shadows of empire wholly gone to dust,
And many races, nameless long ago,
To darkness driven by that imperious gust
Of ever-rushing Time that here doth blow:
O visionary world, condition strange,
Where naught abiding is but only Change,
Where the deep-bolted stars themselves still shift and range!
Shall we to more continuance make pretence?
Renown builds tombs; a life-estate is Wit;
      And, bit by bit,
The cunning years steal all from us but woe;
Leaves are we, whose decays no harvest sow.
      But, when we vanish hence,
Shall they lie forceless in the dark below,
Save to make green their little length of sods,
Or deepen pansies for a year or two,
Who now to us are shining-sweet as gods?
Was dying all they had the skill to do?
That were not fruitless: but the Soul resents
Such short-lived service, as if blind events
Ruled without her, or earth could so endure;
She claims a more divine investiture
Of longer tenure than Fame's airy rents;
Whate'er she touches doth her nature share;
Her inspiration haunts the ennobled air,
      Gives eyes to mountains blind,
Ears to the deaf earth, voices to the wind,
And her clear trump sings succor everywhere
By lonely bivouacs to the wakeful mind;
For soul inherits all that soul could dare:
      Yea, Manhood hath a wider span
And larger privilege of life than man.
The single deed, the private sacrifice,
So radiant now through proudly-hidden tears,
Is covered up erelong from mortal eyes
With thoughtless drift of the deciduous years;

But that high privilege that makes all men peers,
That leap of heart whereby a people rise
  Up to a noble anger's height,
And, flamed on by the Fates, not shrink, but grow more
  bright,
  That swift validity in noble veins,
  Of choosing danger and disdaining shame,
   Of being set on flame
  By the pure fire that flies all contact base,
But wraps its chosen with angelic might,
   These are imperishable gains,
  Sure as the sun, medicinal as light,
  These hold great futures in their lusty reins
And certify to earth a new imperial race.

X.

  Who now shall sneer?
  Who dare again to say we trace
  Our lines to a plebeian race?
   Roundhead and Cavalier!
Dumb are those names erewhile in battle loud;
Dream-footed as the shadow of a cloud,
  They flit across the ear:
That is best blood that hath most iron in 't
To edge resolve with, pouring without stint
  For what makes manhood dear.
  Tell us not of Plantagenets,
Hapsburgs, and Guelfs, whose thin bloods crawl
Down from some victor in a border-brawl!
  How poor their outworn coronets,
Matched with one leaf of that plain civic wreath
Our brave for honor's blazon shall bequeath,
  Through whose desert a rescued Nation sets
Her heel on treason, and the trumpet hears
Shout victory, tingling Europe's sullen ears
  With vain resentments and more vain regrets!

XI.

  Not in anger, not in pride,
  Pure from passion's mixture rude

Ever to base earth allied,
But with far-heard gratitude,
Still with heart and voice renewed,
To heroes living and dear martyrs dead,
The strain should close that consecrates our brave.
Lift the heart and lift the head!
Lofty be its mood and grave,
Not without a martial ring,
Not without a prouder tread
And a peal of exultation:
Little right has he to sing
Through whose heart in such an hour
Beats no march of conscious power,
Sweeps no tumult of elation!
'T is no Man we celebrate,
By his country's victories great,
A hero half, and half the whim of Fate,
But the pith and marrow of a Nation
Drawing force from all her men,
Highest, humblest, weakest, all,
For her time of need, and then
Pulsing it again through them,
Till the basest can no longer cower,
Feeling his soul spring up divinely tall,
Touched but in passing by her mantle-hem.
Come back, then, noble pride, for 't is her dower!
How could poet ever tower,
If his passions, hopes, and fears,
If his triumphs and his tears,
Kept not measure with his people?
Boom, cannon, boom to all the winds and waves!
Clash out, glad bells, from every rocking steeple!
Banners, adance with triumph, bend your staves!
And from every mountain-peak
Let beacon-fire to answering beacon speak,
Katahdin tell Monadnock, Whiteface he,
And so leap on in light from sea to sea,
Till the glad news be sent
Across a kindling continent,

Making earth feel more firm and air breathe braver:
"Be proud! for she is saved, and all have helped to save her!
 She that lifts up the manhood of the poor,
 She of the open soul and open door,
 With room about her hearth for all mankind!
 The fire is dreadful in her eyes no more;
 From her bold front the helm she doth unbind,
 Sends all her handmaid armies back to spin,
 And bids her navies, that so lately hurled
 Their crashing battle, hold their thunders in,
 Swimming like birds of calm along the unharmful shore.
 No challenge sends she to the elder world,
 That looked askance and hated; a light scorn
 Plays o'er her mouth, as round her mighty knees
 She calls her children back, and waits the morn
Of nobler day, enthroned between her subject seas."

XII.

Bow down, dear Land, for thou hast found release!
 Thy God, in these distempered days,
 Hath taught thee the sure wisdom of His ways,
And through thine enemies hath wrought thy peace!
  Bow down in prayer and praise!
No poorest in thy borders but may now
Lift to the juster skies a man's enfranchised brow
O Beautiful! my Country! ours once more!
Smoothing thy gold of war-dishevelled hair
O'er such sweet brows as never other wore,
  And letting thy set lips,
  Freed from wrath's pale eclipse,
The rosy edges of their smile lay bare,
What words divine of lover or of poet
Could tell our love and make thee know it,
Among the Nations bright beyond compare?
  What were our lives without thee?
  What all our lives to save thee?
  We reck not what we gave thee;
  We will not dare to doubt thee,
But ask whatever else, and we will dare!

JULIA WARD HOWE

(1819–1910)

My Last Dance

The shell of objects inwardly consumed
Will stand till some convulsive wind awakes;
Such sense hath Fire to waste the heart of things,
Nature such love to hold the form she makes.

Thus wasted joys will show their early bloom,
Yet crumble at the breath of a caress;
The golden fruitage hides the scathèd bough;
Snatch it, thou scatterest wide its emptiness.

For pleasure bidden, I went forth last night
To where, thick hung, the festal torches gleamed;
Here were the flowers, the music, as of old;
Almost the very olden time it seemed.

For one with cheek unfaded (though he brings
My buried brothers to me in his look)
Said, 'Will you dance?' At the accustomed words
I gave my hand, the old position took.

Sound, gladsome measure! at whose bidding once
I felt the flush of pleasure to my brow,
While my soul shook the burthen of the flesh,
And in its young pride said, 'Lie lightly, thou!'

Then, like a gallant swimmer, flinging high
My breast against the golden waves of sound,
I rode the madd'ning tumult of the dance,
Mocking fatigue, that never could be found.

Chide not—it was not vanity, nor sense,
(The brutish scorn such vaporous delight,)
But Nature, cadencing her joy of strength
To the harmonious limits of her right.

708

She gave her impulse to the dancing Hours,
To winds that weep, to stars that noiseless turn;
She marked the measure rapid hearts must keep,
Devised each pace that glancing feet should learn.

And sure, that prodigal o'erflow of life,
Unvowed as yet to family or state,
Sweet sounds, white garments, flowery coronals
Make holy in the pageant of our fate.

Sound, measure! but to stir my heart no more—
For, as I moved to join the dizzy race,
My youth fell from me; all its blooms were gone,
And others showed them, smiling, in my face.

Faintly I met the shock of circling forms
Linked each to other, Fashion's galley-slaves,
Dream-wondering, like an unaccustomed ghost
That starts, surprised, to stumble over graves.

For graves were 'neath my feet, whose placid masks
Smiled out upon my folly mournfully,
While all the host of the departed said,
'Tread lightly—thou art ashes, even as we.'

Battle-Hymn of the Republic

Mine eyes have seen the glory of the coming of the Lord:
He is trampling out the vintage where the grapes of wrath
    are stored;
He hath loosed the fateful lightning of his terrible swift
    sword:
        His truth is marching on.

I have seen Him in the watch-fires of a hundred circling
    camps;
They have builded Him an altar in the evening dews and
    damps;

I can read His righteous sentence by the dim and flaring
    lamps.
           His day is marching on.

I have read a fiery gospel, writ in burnished rows of steel:
"As ye deal with my contemners, so with you my grace shall
    deal;
Let the Hero, born of woman, crush the serpent with his
    heel,
           Since God is marching on."

He has sounded forth the trumpet that shall never call
    retreat;
He is sifting out the hearts of men before his judgment-seat:
Oh! be swift, my soul, to answer Him! be jubilant, my feet!
           Our God is marching on.

In the beauty of the lilies Christ was born across the sea,
With a glory in his bosom that transfigures you and me:
As he died to make men holy, let us die to make men free,
           While God is marching on.

JOSIAH GILBERT HOLLAND

(1819–1881)

from *The Marble Prophecy*

Laocöon! thou great embodiment
Of human life and human history!
Thou record of the past, thou prophecy
Of the sad future, thou majestic voice,
Pealing along the ages from old time!
Thou wail of agonized humanity!
There lives no thought in marble like to thee!
Thou hast no kindred in the Vatican,
But standest separate among the dreams
Of old mythologies—alone—alone!
The beautiful Apollo at thy side
Is but a marble dream, and dreams are all
The gods and goddesses and fauns and fates
That populate these wondrous halls; but thou,
Standing among them, liftest up thyself
In majesty of meaning, till they sink
Far from the sight, no more significant
Than the poor toys of children. For thou art
A voice from out the world's experience,
Speaking of all the generations past
To all the generations yet to come
Of the long struggle, the sublime despair,
The wild and weary agony of man!

Ay, Adam and his offspring, in the toils
Of the twin serpents Sin and Suffering,
Thou dost impersonate; and as I gaze
Upon the twining monsters that enfold
In unrelaxing, unrelenting coils,
Thy awful energies, and plant their fangs
Deep in thy quivering flesh, while still thy might
In fierce convulsion foils the fateful wrench
That would destroy thee, I am overwhelmed

With a strange sympathy of kindred pain,
And see through gathering tears the tragedy,
The curse and conflict of a ruined race!
Those Rhodian sculptors were gigantic men,
Whose inspirations came from other source
Than their religion, though they chose to speak
Through its familiar language,—men who saw,
And, seeing quite divinely, felt how weak
To cure the world's great woe were all the powers
Whose reign their age acknowledged. So they sat—
The immortal three—and pondered long and well
What one great work should speak the truth for them,—
What one great work should rise and testify
That they had found the topmost fact of life,
Above the reach of all philosophies
And all religions—every scheme of man
To placate or dethrone. That fact they found,
And moulded into form. The silly priest
Whose desecrations of the altar stirred
The vengeance of his God, and summoned forth
The wreathed gorgons of the slimy deep
To crush him and his children, was the word
By which they spoke to their own age and race,
That listened and applauded, knowing not
That high above the small significance
They apprehended, rose the grand intent
That mourned their doom and breathed a world's
          despair!

Be sure it was no fable that inspired
So grand an utterance. Perchance some leaf
From an old Hebrew record had conveyed
A knowledge of the genesis of man.
Perchance some fine conception rose in them
Of unity of nature and of race,
Springing from one beginning. Nay, perchance
Some vision flashed before their thoughtful eyes
Inspired by God, which showed the mighty man,
Who, unbegotten, had begot a race
That to his lot was linked through countless time

By living chains, from which in vain it strove
To wrest its tortured limbs and leap amain
To freedom and to rest! It matters not:
The double word—the fable and the fact,
The childish figment and the mighty truth,
Are blent in one. The first was for a day
And dying Rome; the last for later time
And all mankind.

       These sculptors spoke their word
And then they died; and Rome—imperial Rome—
The mistress of the world—debauched by blood
And foul with harlotries—fell prone at length
Among the trophies of her crimes and slept.
Down toppling one by one her helpless gods
Fell to the earth, and hid their shattered forms
Within the dust that bore them, and among
The ruined shrines and crumbling masonry
Of their old temples. Still this wondrous group,
From its long home upon the Esquiline,
Beheld the centuries of change, and stood,
Impersonating in its conscious stone
The unavailing struggle to crowd back
The closing folds of doom. It paused to hear
A strange New Name proclaimed among the streets,
And catch the dying shrieks of martyred men,
And see the light of hope and heroism
Kindling in many eyes; and then it fell;
And in the ashes of an empire swathed
Its aching sense, and hid its tortured forms.

The old life went, the new life came; and Rome
That slew the prophets built their sepulchres,
And filled her heathen temples with the shrines
Of Christian saints whom she had tossed to beasts,
Or crucified, or left to die in chains
Within her dungeons. Ay, the old life went
But came again. The primitive, true age—
The simple, earnest age—when Jesus Christ
The Crucified was only known and preached,

Struck hands with paganism and passed away.
Rome built new temples and installed new names;
Set up her graven images, and gave
To Pope and priests the keeping of her gods.
Again she grasped at power no longer hers
By right of Roman prowess, and stretched out
Her hand upon the consciences of men.
The godlike liberty with which the Christ
Had made his people free she stole from them,
And bound them slaves to new observances.
Her times, her days, her ceremonials
Imposed a burden grievous to be borne,
And millions groaned beneath it. Nay, she grew
The vengeful persecutor of the free
Who would not bear her yoke, and bathed her hands
In blood as sweet as ever burst from hearts
Torn from the bosoms of the early saints
Within her Coliseum. She assumed
To be the arbiter of destiny.

Those whom she bound or loosed upon the earth,
Were bound or loosed in heaven! In God's own place,
She sat as God—supreme, infallible!
She shut the door of knowledge to mankind,
And bound the Word Divine. She sucked the juice
Of all prosperities within her realms,
Until her gaudy temples blazed with gold,
And from a thousand altars flashed the fire
Of priceless gems. To win her countless wealth
She sold as merchandise the gift of God.
She took the burden which the cross had borne,
And bound it fast to scourged and writhing loins
In thriftless Penance, till her devotees
Fled from their kind to find the boon of peace,
And died in banishment. Beneath her sway,
The proud old Roman blood grew thin and mean
Till virtue was the name it gave to fear,
Till heroism and brigandage were one,
And neither slaves nor beggars knew their shame!

What marvel that a shadow fell, world-wide,
And brooded o'er the ages? Was it strange
That in those dim and drowsy centuries,
When the dumb earth had ceased to quake beneath
The sounding wheels of progress, and the life
That erst had flamed so high had sunk so low
In cold monastic glooms and forms as cold,
The buried gods should listen in their sleep
And dream of resurrection? Was it strange
That listening well they should at length awake,
And struggle from their pillows? Was it strange
That men whose vision grovelled should perceive
The dust in motion, and with rapture greet
Each ancient deity with loud acclaim,
As if he brought with him the good old days
Of manly art and poetry and power?
Nay, was it strange that as they raised themselves,
And cleaned their drowsy eyelids of the dust,
And took their godlike attitudes again,
The grand old forms should feel themselves at home—
Saving perhaps a painful sense that men
Had dwindled somewhat? Was it strange, at last,
That all these gods should be installed anew,
And share the palace with His Holiness,
And that the Pope and Christian Rome can show
No art that equals that which had its birth
In pagan inspiration? Ah, what shame!
That after two millenniums of Christ,
Rome calls to her the thirsty tribes of earth,
And smites the heathen marble with her rod,
And bids them drink the best she has to give!

And when the gods were on their feet again
It was thy time to rise, Laocöon!
Those Rhodian sculptors had foreseen it all.
Their word was true: thou hadst the right to live.

In the quick sunlight on the Esquiline,
Where thou didst sleep, De Fredis kept his vines;
And long above thee grew the grapes whose blood

Ran wild in Christian arteries, and fed
The fire of Christian revels. Ah what fruit
Sucked up the marrow of thy marble there!
What fierce, mad dreams were those that scared the souls
Of men who drank, nor guessed what ichor stung
Their crimson lips, and tingled in their veins!
Strange growths were those that sprang above thy sleep:
Vines that were serpents; huge and ugly trunks
That took the forms of human agony—
Contorted, gnarled and grim—and leaves that bore
The semblance of a thousand tortured hands,
And snaky tendrils that entwined themselves
Around all forms of life within their reach,
And crushed or blighted them!

                At last the spade
Slid down to find the secret of the vines,
And touched thee with a thrill that startled Rome,
And swiftly called a shouting multitude
To witness thy unveiling.

                Ah what joy
Greeted the rising from thy long repose!
And one, the mighty master of his time,
The king of Christian art, with strong, sad face
Looked on, and wondered with the giddy crowd,—
Looked on and learned (too late, alas! for him),
That his humanity and God's own truth
Were more than Christian Rome, and spoke in words
Of larger import. Humbled Angelo
Bowed to the masters of the early days,
Grasped their strong hands across the centuries,
And went his way despairing!

                Thou, meantime,
Didst find thyself installed among the gods
Here in the Vatican; and thou, to-day,
Hast the same word for those who read thee well
As when thou wast created. Rome has failed:
Humanity is writhing in the toils

Of the old monsters as it writhed of old,
And there is neither help nor hope in her.
Her priests, her shrines, her rites, her mummeries,
Her pictures and her pageants, are as weak
To break the hold of Sin and Suffering
As those her reign displaced. Her iron hand
Shrivels the manhood it presumes to bless,
Drives to disgust or infidelity
The strong and free who dare to think and judge,
And wins a kiss from coward lips alone.
She does not preach the Gospel to the poor,
But takes it from their hands. The men who tread
The footsteps of the Master, and bow down
Alone to Him, she brands as heretics
Or hunts as fiends. She drives beyond her gates
The Christian worshippers of other climes,
And other folds and faiths, as if their brows
Were white with leprosy, and grants them there
With haughty scorn the privilege to kneel
In humble worship of the common Lord!

Is this the Christ, or look we still for Him?
Is the old problem solved, or lingers yet
The grand solution? Ay Laocöon!
Thy word is true, for Christian Rome has failed,
And I behold humanity in thee
As those who shaped thee saw it, when old Rome
In that far pagan evening fell asleep.

lines 145 – 392

THOMAS DUNN ENGLISH

(1819–1902)

Ben Bolt

Don't you remember sweet Alice, Ben Bolt—
　Sweet Alice whose hair was so brown,
Who wept with delight when you gave her a smile,
　And trembled with fear at your frown?
In the old church-yard in the valley, Ben Bolt,
　In a corner obscure and alone,
They have fitted a slab of the granite so grey,
　And Alice lies under the stone.

Under the hickory-tree, Ben Bolt,
　Which stood at the foot of the hill,
Together we've lain in the noonday shade,
　And listened to Appleton's mill.
The mill-wheel has fallen to pieces, Ben Bolt,
　The rafters have tumbled in,
And a quiet which crawls round the walls as you gaze
　Has followed the olden din.

Do you mind of the cabin of logs, Ben Bolt,
　At the edge of the pathless wood,
And the button-ball tree with its motley limbs,
　Which nigh by the door-step stood?
The cabin to ruin has gone, Ben Bolt,
　The tree you would seek for in vain;
And where once the lords of the forest waved
　Are grass and the golden grain.

And don't you remember the school, Ben Bolt,
　With the master so cruel and grim,
And the shaded nook in the running brook
　Where the children went to swim?

Grass grows on the master's grave, Ben Bolt,
    The spring of the brook is dry,
And of all the boys who were schoolmates then
    There are only you and I.

There is change in the things I loved, Ben Bolt,
    They have changed from the old to the new;
But I feel in the deeps of my spirit the truth,
    There never was change in you.
Twelvemonths twenty have past, Ben Bolt,
    Since first we were friends—yet I hail
Your presence a blessing, your friendship a truth,
    Ben Bolt of the salt-sea gale.

WALT WHITMAN

(1819–1892)

Leaves of Grass (1855)

I celebrate myself,
And what I assume you shall assume,
For every atom belonging to me as good belongs to you.

I loafe and invite my soul,
I lean and loafe at my ease . . . . observing a spear of
    summer grass.

Houses and rooms are full of perfumes . . . . the shelves are
    crowded with perfumes,
I breathe the fragrance myself, and know it and like it,
The distillation would intoxicate me also, but I shall not let it.

The atmosphere is not a perfume . . . . it has no taste of the
    distillation . . . . it is odorless,
It is for my mouth forever . . . . I am in love with it,
I will go to the bank by the wood and become undisguised
    and naked,
I am mad for it to be in contact with me.

The smoke of my own breath,
Echos, ripples, and buzzed whispers . . . . loveroot,
    silkthread, crotch and vine,
My respiration and inspiration . . . . the beating of my heart
    . . . . the passing of blood and air through my lungs,
The sniff of green leaves and dry leaves, and of the shore and
    darkcolored sea-rocks, and of hay in the barn,
The sound of the belched words of my voice . . . . words
    loosed to the eddies of the wind,
A few light kisses . . . . a few embraces . . . . a reaching
    around of arms,
The play of shine and shade on the trees as the supple
    boughs wag,

The delight alone or in the rush of the streets, or along the
    fields and hillsides,
The feeling of health . . . . the full-noon trill . . . . the
    song of me rising from bed and meeting the sun.

Have you reckoned a thousand acres much? Have you
    reckoned the earth much?
Have you practiced so long to learn to read?
Have you felt so proud to get at the meaning of poems?

Stop this day and night with me and you shall possess the
    origin of all poems,
You shall possess the good of the earth and sun . . . . there
    are millions of suns left,
You shall no longer take things at second or third hand
    . . . . nor look through the eyes of the dead . . . . nor
    feed on the spectres in books,
You shall not look through my eyes either, nor take things
    from me,
You shall listen to all sides and filter them from yourself.

I have heard what the talkers were talking . . . . the talk of
    the beginning and the end,
But I do not talk of the beginning or the end.

There was never any more inception than there is now,
Nor any more youth or age than there is now;
And will never be any more perfection than there is now,
Nor any more heaven or hell than there is now.

Urge and urge and urge,
Always the procreant urge of the world.

Out of the dimness opposite equals advance . . . . Always
    substance and increase,
Always a knit of identity . . . . always distinction . . . .
    always a breed of life.

To elaborate is no avail . . . . Learned and unlearned feel
    that it is so.

Sure as the most certain sure . . . . plumb in the uprights,
    well entretied, braced in the beams,
Stout as a horse, affectionate, haughty, electrical,
I and this mystery here we stand.

Clear and sweet is my soul . . . . and clear and sweet is all
    that is not my soul.

Lack one lacks both . . . . and the unseen is proved by the
    seen,
Till that becomes unseen and receives proof in its turn.

Showing the best and dividing it from the worst, age vexes
    age,
Knowing the perfect fitness and equanimity of things, while
    they discuss I am silent, and go bathe and admire
    myself.

Welcome is every organ and attribute of me, and of any man
    hearty and clean,
Not an inch nor a particle of an inch is vile, and none shall
    be less familiar than the rest.

I am satisfied . . . . I see, dance, laugh, sing;
As God comes a loving bedfellow and sleeps at my side all
    night and close on the peep of the day,
And leaves for me baskets covered with white towels bulging
    the house with their plenty,
Shall I postpone my acceptation and realization and scream
    at my eyes,
That they turn from gazing after and down the road,
And forthwith cipher and show me to a cent,
Exactly the contents of one, and exactly the contents of two,
    and which is ahead?

Trippers and askers surround me,
People I meet . . . . . the effect upon me of my early life
    . . . . of the ward and city I live in . . . . of the nation,
The latest news . . . . discoveries, inventions, societies
    . . . . authors old and new,

My dinner, dress, associates, looks, business, compliments,
    dues,
The real or fancied indifference of some man or woman I
    love,
The sickness of one of my folks—or of myself . . . . or ill-
    doing . . . . or loss or lack of money . . . . or
    depressions or exaltations,
They come to me days and nights and go from me again,
But they are not the Me myself.

Apart from the pulling and hauling stands what I am,
Stands amused, complacent, compassionating, idle, unitary,
Looks down, is erect, bends an arm on an impalpable certain
    rest,
Looks with its sidecurved head curious what will come next,
Both in and out of the game, and watching and wondering
    at it.

Backward I see in my own days where I sweated through
    fog with linguists and contenders,
I have no mockings or arguments . . . . I witness and wait.

I believe in you my soul . . . . the other I am must not
    abase itself to you,
And you must not be abased to the other.

Loafe with me on the grass . . . . loose the stop from your
    throat,
Not words, not music or rhyme I want . . . . not custom or
    lecture, not even the best,
Only the lull I like, the hum of your valved voice.

I mind how we lay in June, such a transparent summer
    morning;
You settled your head athwart my hips and gently turned
    over upon me,
And parted the shirt from my bosom-bone, and plunged
    your tongue to my barestript heart,
And reached till you felt my beard, and reached till you held
    my feet.

Swiftly arose and spread around me the peace and joy and
knowledge that pass all the art and argument of the
earth;
And I know that the hand of God is the elderhand of my
own,
And I know that the spirit of God is the eldest brother of
my own,
And that all the men ever born are also my brothers . . . .
and the women my sisters and lovers,
And that a kelson of the creation is love;
And limitless are leaves stiff or drooping in the fields,
And brown ants in the little wells beneath them,
And mossy scabs of the wormfence, and heaped stones, and
elder and mullen and pokeweed.

A child said, What is the grass? fetching it to me with full
hands;
How could I answer the child? . . . . I do not know what it
is any more than he.

I guess it must be the flag of my disposition, out of hopeful
green stuff woven.

Or I guess it is the handkerchief of the Lord,
A scented gift and remembrancer designedly dropped,
Bearing the owner's name someway in the corners, that we
may see and remark, and say Whose?

Or I guess the grass is itself a child . . . . the produced
babe of the vegetation.

Or I guess it is a uniform hieroglyphic,
And it means, Sprouting alike in broad zones and narrow
zones,
Growing among black folks as among white,
Kanuck, Tuckahoe, Congressman, Cuff, I give them the
same, I receive them the same.

And now it seems to me the beautiful uncut hair of
graves.

Tenderly will I use you curling grass,
It may be you transpire from the breasts of young men,
It may be if I had known them I would have loved them;
It may be you are from old people and from women,
and from offspring taken soon out of their mothers'
laps,
And here you are the mothers' laps.

This grass is very dark to be from the white heads of old
mothers,
Darker than the colorless beards of old men,
Dark to come from under the faint red roofs of mouths.

O I perceive after all so many uttering tongues!
And I perceive they do not come from the roofs of mouths
for nothing.

I wish I could translate the hints about the dead young men
and women,
And the hints about old men and mothers, and the offspring
taken soon out of their laps.

What do you think has become of the young and old men?
And what do you think has become of the women and
children?

They are alive and well somewhere;
The smallest sprout shows there is really no death,
And if ever there was it led forward life, and does not wait
at the end to arrest it,
And ceased the moment life appeared.

All goes onward and outward . . . . and nothing collapses,
And to die is different from what any one supposed, and
luckier.

Has any one supposed it lucky to be born?
I hasten to inform him or her it is just as lucky to die, and I
know it.

I pass death with the dying, and birth with the new-washed
    babe . . . . and am not contained between my hat and
    boots,
And peruse manifold objects, no two alike, and every one
    good,
The earth good, and the stars good, and their adjuncts all
    good.

I am not an earth nor an adjunct of an earth,
I am the mate and companion of people, all just as immortal
    and fathomless as myself;
They do not know how immortal, but I know.

Every kind for itself and its own . . . . for me mine male
    and female,
For me all that have been boys and that love women,
For me the man that is proud and feels how it stings to be
    slighted,
For me the sweetheart and the old maid . . . . for me
    mothers and the mothers of mothers,
For me lips that have smiled, eyes that have shed tears,
For me children and the begetters of children.

Who need be afraid of the merge?
Undrape . . . . you are not guilty to me, nor stale nor
    discarded,
I see through the broadcloth and gingham whether
    or no,
And am around, tenacious, acquisitive, tireless . . . . and
    can never be shaken away.

The little one sleeps in its cradle,
I lift the gauze and look a long time, and silently brush away
    flies with my hand.

The youngster and the redfaced girl turn aside up the bushy
    hill,
I peeringly view them from the top.

The suicide sprawls on the bloody floor of the bedroom.
It is so . . . . I witnessed the corpse . . . . there the pistol
    had fallen.

The blab of the pave . . . . the tires of carts and sluff of
    bootsoles and talk of the promenaders,
The heavy omnibus, the driver with his interrogating thumb,
    the clank of the shod horses on the granite floor,
The carnival of sleighs, the clinking and shouted jokes and
    pelts of snowballs;
The hurrahs for popular favorites . . . . the fury of roused
    mobs,
The flap of the curtained litter—the sick man inside, borne
    to the hospital,
The meeting of enemies, the sudden oath, the blows and fall,
The excited crowd—the policeman with his star quickly
    working his passage to the centre of the crowd;
The impassive stones that receive and return so many echoes,
The souls moving along . . . . are they invisible while the
    least atom of the stones is visible?
What groans of overfed or half-starved who fall on the flags
    sunstruck or in fits,
What exclamations of women taken suddenly, who hurry
    home and give birth to babes,
What living and buried speech is always vibrating here
    . . . . what howls restrained by decorum,
Arrests of criminals, slights, adulterous offers made,
    acceptances, rejections with convex lips,
I mind them or the resonance of them . . . . I come again
    and again.

The big doors of the country-barn stand open and ready,
The dried grass of the harvest-time loads the slow-drawn
    wagon,
The clear light plays on the brown gray and green intertinged,
The armfuls are packed to the sagging mow:
I am there . . . . I help . . . . I came stretched atop of the
    load,
I felt its soft jolts . . . . one leg reclined on the other,

I jump from the crossbeams, and seize the clover and timothy,
And roll head over heels, and tangle my hair full of wisps.

Alone far in the wilds and mountains I hunt,
Wandering amazed at my own lightness and glee,
In the late afternoon choosing a safe spot to pass the night,
Kindling a fire and broiling the freshkilled game,
Soundly falling asleep on the gathered leaves, my dog and
     gun by my side.

The Yankee clipper is under her three skysails . . . . she cuts
     the sparkle and scud,
My eyes settle the land . . . . I bend at her prow or shout
     joyously from the deck.

The boatmen and clamdiggers arose early and stopped for me,
I tucked my trowser-ends in my boots and went and had a
     good time,
You should have been with us that day round the chowder-
     kettle.

I saw the marriage of the trapper in the open air in the far-
     west . . . . the bride was a red girl,
Her father and his friends sat near by crosslegged and
     dumbly smoking . . . . they had moccasins to their feet
     and large thick blankets hanging from their shoulders;
On a bank lounged the trapper . . . . he was dressed mostly
     in skins . . . . his luxuriant beard and curls protected
     his neck,
One hand rested on his rifle . . . . the other hand held
     firmly the wrist of the red girl,
She had long eyelashes . . . . her head was bare . . . . her
     coarse straight locks descended upon her voluptuous
     limbs and reached to her feet.

The runaway slave came to my house and stopped outside,
I heard his motions crackling the twigs of the woodpile,
Through the swung half-door of the kitchen I saw him
     limpsey and weak,

And went where he sat on a log, and led him in and assured
    him,
And brought water and filled a tub for his sweated body and
    bruised feet,
And gave him a room that entered from my own, and gave
    him some coarse clean clothes,
And remember perfectly well his revolving eyes and his
    awkwardness,
And remember putting plasters on the galls of his neck and
    ankles;
He staid with me a week before he was recuperated and
    passed north,
I had him sit next me at table . . . . my firelock leaned in
    the corner.

Twenty-eight young men bathe by the shore,
Twenty-eight young men, and all so friendly,
Twenty-eight years of womanly life, and all so lonesome.

She owns the fine house by the rise of the bank,
She hides handsome and richly drest aft the blinds of the
    window.

Which of the young men does she like the best?
Ah the homeliest of them is beautiful to her.

Where are you off to, lady? for I see you,
You splash in the water there, yet stay stock still in your room.

Dancing and laughing along the beach came the twenty-
    ninth bather,
The rest did not see her, but she saw them and loved them.

The beards of the young men glistened with wet, it ran from
    their long hair,
Little streams passed all over their bodies.

An unseen hand also passed over their bodies,
It descended tremblingly from their temples and ribs.

The young men float on their backs, their white bellies swell
    to the sun . . . . they do not ask who seizes fast to them,
They do not know who puffs and declines with pendant and
    bending arch,
They do not think whom they souse with spray.

The butcher-boy puts off his killing-clothes, or sharpens his
    knife at the stall in the market,
I loiter enjoying his repartee and his shuffle and breakdown.

Blacksmiths with grimed and hairy chests environ the anvil,
Each has his main-sledge . . . . they are all out . . . . there
    is a great heat in the fire.

From the cinder-strewed threshold I follow their movements,
The lithe sheer of their waists plays even with their massive
    arms,
Overhand the hammers roll—overhand so slow—overhand
    so sure,
They do not hasten, each man hits in his place.

The negro holds firmly the reins of his four horses . . . . the
    block swags underneath on its tied-over chain,
The negro that drives the huge dray of the stoneyard . . . .
    steady and tall he stands poised on one leg on the
    stringpiece,
His blue shirt exposes his ample neck and breast and loosens
    over his hipband,
His glance is calm and commanding . . . . he tosses the
    slouch of his hat away from his forehead,
The sun falls on his crispy hair and moustache . . . . falls on
    the black of his polish'd and perfect limbs.

I behold the picturesque giant and love him . . . . and I do
    not stop there,
I go with the team also.

In me the caresser of life wherever moving . . . . backward
    as well as forward slueing,
To niches aside and junior bending.

Oxen that rattle the yoke or halt in the shade, what is that
    you express in your eyes?
It seems to me more than all the print I have read in my life.

My tread scares the wood-drake and wood-duck on my
    distant and daylong ramble,
They rise together, they slowly circle around.
. . . . I believe in those winged purposes,
And acknowledge the red yellow and white playing within
    me,
And consider the green and violet and the tufted crown
    intentional;
And do not call the tortoise unworthy because she is not
    something else,
And the mockingbird in the swamp never studied the
    gamut, yet trills pretty well to me,
And the look of the bay mare shames silliness out of me.

The wild gander leads his flock through the cool night,
Ya-honk! he says, and sounds it down to me like an invitation;
The pert may suppose it meaningless, but I listen closer,
I find its purpose and place up there toward the November
    sky.

The sharphoofed moose of the north, the cat on the
    housesill, the chickadee, the prairie-dog,
The litter of the grunting sow as they tug at her teats,
The brood of the turkeyhen, and she with her halfspread
    wings,
I see in them and myself the same old law.

The press of my foot to the earth springs a hundred
    affections,
They scorn the best I can do to relate them.

I am enamoured of growing outdoors,
Of men that live among cattle or taste of the ocean or woods,
Of the builders and steerers of ships, of the wielders of axes
    and mauls, of the drivers of horses,
I can eat and sleep with them week in and week out.

What is commonest and cheapest and nearest and easiest
    is Me,
Me going in for my chances, spending for vast returns,
Adorning myself to bestow myself on the first that will
    take me,
Not asking the sky to come down to my goodwill,
Scattering it freely forever.

The pure contralto sings in the organloft,
The carpenter dresses his plank . . . . the tongue of his
    foreplane whistles its wild ascending lisp,
The married and unmarried children ride home to their
    thanksgiving dinner,
The pilot seizes the king-pin, he heaves down with a strong
    arm,
The mate stands braced in the whaleboat, lance and harpoon
    are ready,
The duck-shooter walks by silent and cautious stretches,
The deacons are ordained with crossed hands at the altar,
The spinning-girl retreats and advances to the hum of the
    big wheel,
The farmer stops by the bars of a Sunday and looks at the
    oats and rye,
The lunatic is carried at last to the asylum a confirmed case,
He will never sleep any more as he did in the cot in his
    mother's bedroom;
The jour printer with gray head and gaunt jaws works at
    his case,
He turns his quid of tobacco, his eyes get blurred with the
    manuscript;
The malformed limbs are tied to the anatomist's table,
What is removed drops horribly in a pail;
The quadroon girl is sold at the stand . . . . the drunkard
    nods by the barroom stove,
The machinist rolls up his sleeves . . . . the policeman
    travels his beat . . . . the gate-keeper marks who pass,
The young fellow drives the express-wagon . . . . I love him
    though I do not know him;
The half-breed straps on his light boots to compete in
    the race,

The western turkey-shooting draws old and young . . . .
    some lean on their rifles, some sit on logs,
Out from the crowd steps the marksman and takes his
    position and levels his piece;
The groups of newly-come immigrants cover the wharf
    or levee,
The woollypates hoe in the sugarfield, the overseer views
    them from his saddle;
The bugle calls in the ballroom, the gentlemen run for their
    partners, the dancers bow to each other;
The youth lies awake in the cedar-roofed garret and harks to
    the musical rain,
The Wolverine sets traps on the creek that helps fill the
    Huron,
The reformer ascends the platform, he spouts with his
    mouth and nose,
The company returns from its excursion, the darkey brings
    up the rear and bears the well-riddled target,
The squaw wrapt in her yellow-hemmed cloth is offering
    moccasins and beadbags for sale,
The connoisseur peers along the exhibition-gallery with
    halfshut eyes bent sideways,
The deckhands make fast the steamboat, the plank is thrown
    for the shoregoing passengers,
The young sister holds out the skein, the elder sister
    winds it off in a ball and stops now and then for the
    knots,
The one-year wife is recovering and happy, a week ago she
    bore her first child,
The cleanhaired Yankee girl works with her sewing-machine
    or in the factory or mill,
The nine months' gone is in the parturition chamber, her
    faintness and pains are advancing;
The pavingman leans on his twohanded rammer—the
    reporter's lead flies swiftly over the notebook—the
    signpainter is lettering with red and gold,
The canal-boy trots on the towpath—the bookkeeper counts
    at his desk—the shoemaker waxes his thread,
The conductor beats time for the band and all the performers
    follow him,

The child is baptised—the convert is making the first
    professions,
The regatta is spread on the bay . . . . how the white sails
    sparkle!
The drover watches his drove, he sings out to them that
    would stray,
The pedlar sweats with his pack on his back—the purchaser
    higgles about the odd cent,
The camera and plate are prepared, the lady must sit for her
    daguerreotype,
The bride unrumples her white dress, the minutehand of the
    clock moves slowly,
The opium eater reclines with rigid head and just-opened lips,
The prostitute draggles her shawl, her bonnet bobs on her
    tipsy and pimpled neck,
The crowd laugh at her blackguard oaths, the men jeer and
    wink to each other,
(Miserable! I do not laugh at your oaths nor jeer you,)
The President holds a cabinet council, he is surrounded by
    the great secretaries,
On the piazza walk five friendly matrons with twined arms;
The crew of the fish-smack pack repeated layers of halibut in
    the hold,
The Missourian crosses the plains toting his wares and his
    cattle,
The fare-collector goes through the train—he gives notice
    by the jingling of loose change,
The floormen are laying the floor—the tinners are tinning
    the roof—the masons are calling for mortar,
In single file each shouldering his hod pass onward the
    laborers;
Seasons pursuing each other the indescribable crowd is
    gathered . . . . it is the Fourth of July . . . . what
    salutes of cannon and small arms!
Seasons pursuing each other the plougher ploughs and the
    mower mows and the wintergrain falls in the ground;
Off on the lakes the pikefisher watches and waits by the hole
    in the frozen surface,
The stumps stand thick round the clearing, the squatter
    strikes deep with his axe,

The flatboatmen make fast toward dusk near the cottonwood
    or pekantrees,
The coon-seekers go now through the regions of the Red
    river, or through those drained by the Tennessee, or
    through those of the Arkansas,
The torches shine in the dark that hangs on the
    Chattahoochee or Altamahaw;
Patriarchs sit at supper with sons and grandsons and great
    grandsons around them,
In walls of adobe, in canvass tents, rest hunters and trappers
    after their day's sport.
The city sleeps and the country sleeps,
The living sleep for their time . . . . the dead sleep
    for their time,
The old husband sleeps by his wife and the young husband
    sleeps by his wife;
And these one and all tend inward to me, and I tend
    outward to them,
And such as it is to be of these more or less I am.

I am of old and young, of the foolish as much as the wise,
Regardless of others, ever regardful of others,
Maternal as well as paternal, a child as well as a man,
Stuffed with the stuff that is coarse, and stuffed with the
    stuff that is fine,
One of the great nation, the nation of many nations—the
    smallest the same and the largest the same,
A southerner soon as a northerner, a planter nonchalant and
    hospitable,
A Yankee bound my own way . . . . ready for trade . . . .
    my joints the limberest joints on earth and the sternest
    joints on earth,
A Kentuckian walking the vale of the Elkhorn in my
    deerskin leggings,
A boatman over the lakes or bays or along coasts . . . . a
    Hoosier, a Badger, a Buckeye,
A Louisianian or Georgian, a poke-easy from sandhills and
    pines,
At home on Canadian snowshoes or up in the bush, or with
    fishermen off Newfoundland,

At home in the fleet of iceboats, sailing with the rest and
    tacking,
At home on the hills of Vermont or in the woods of Maine
    or the Texan ranch,
Comrade of Californians . . . . comrade of free
    northwesterners, loving their big proportions,
Comrade of raftsmen and coalmen—comrade of all who
    shake hands and welcome to drink and meat;
A learner with the simplest, a teacher of the thoughtfulest,
A novice beginning experient of myriads of seasons,
Of every hue and trade and rank, of every caste and religion,
Not merely of the New World but of Africa Europe or Asia
    . . . . a wandering savage,
A farmer, mechanic, or artist . . . . a gentleman, sailor,
    lover or quaker,
A prisoner, fancy-man, rowdy, lawyer, physician or priest.

I resist anything better than my own diversity,
And breathe the air and leave plenty after me,
And am not stuck up, and am in my place.

The moth and the fisheggs are in their place,
The suns I see and the suns I cannot see are in their place,
The palpable is in its place and the impalpable is in its
    place.

These are the thoughts of all men in all ages and lands, they
    are not original with me,
If they are not yours as much as mine they are nothing or
    next to nothing,
If they do not enclose everything they are next to nothing,
If they are not the riddle and the untying of the riddle they
    are nothing,
If they are not just as close as they are distant they are
    nothing.

This is the grass that grows wherever the land is and the
    water is,
This is the common air that bathes the globe.

This is the breath of laws and songs and behaviour,
This is the tasteless water of souls . . . . this is the true
    sustenance,
It is for the illiterate . . . . it is for the judges of the supreme
    court . . . . it is for the federal capitol and the state
    capitols,
It is for the admirable communes of literary men and
    composers and singers and lecturers and engineers and
    savans,
It is for the endless races of working people and farmers and
    seamen.

This is the trill of a thousand clear cornets and scream of the
    octave flute and strike of triangles.

I play not a march for victors only . . . . I play great marches
    for conquered and slain persons.

Have you heard that it was good to gain the day?
I also say it is good to fall . . . . battles are lost in the same
    spirit in which they are won.

I sound triumphal drums for the dead . . . . I fling through
    my embouchures the loudest and gayest music to them,
Vivas to those who have failed, and to those whose war-
    vessels sank in the sea, and those themselves who sank
    in the sea,
And to all generals that lost engagements, and all overcome
    heroes, and the numberless unknown heroes equal to
    the greatest heroes known.

This is the meal pleasantly set . . . . this is the meat and
    drink for natural hunger,
It is for the wicked just the same as the righteous I
    make appointments with all,
I will not have a single person slighted or left away,
The keptwoman and sponger and thief are hereby invited
    . . . . the heavy-lipped slave is invited . . . . the
    venerealee is invited,
There shall be no difference between them and the rest.

This is the press of a bashful hand . . . . this is the float and
    odor of hair,
This is the touch of my lips to yours . . . . this is the
    murmur of yearning,
This is the far-off depth and height reflecting my own
    face,
This is the thoughtful merge of myself and the outlet
    again.

Do you guess I have some intricate purpose?
Well I have . . . . for the April rain has, and the mica on the
    side of a rock has.

Do you take it I would astonish?
Does the daylight astonish? or the early redstart twittering
    through the woods?
Do I astonish more than they?

This hour I tell things in confidence,
I might not tell everybody but I will tell you.

Who goes there! hankering, gross, mystical, nude?
How is it I extract strength from the beef I eat?

What is a man anyhow? What am I? and what are you?
All I mark as my own you shall offset it with your own,
Else it were time lost listening to me.

I do not snivel that snivel the world over,
That months are vacuums and the ground but wallow
    and filth,
That life is a suck and a sell, and nothing remains at the end
    but threadbare crape and tears.

Whimpering and truckling fold with powders for invalids
    . . . . conformity goes to the fourth-removed,
I cock my hat as I please indoors or out.

Shall I pray? Shall I venerate and be ceremonious?

I have pried through the strata and analyzed to a hair,
And counselled with doctors and calculated close and found
    no sweeter fat than sticks to my own bones.

In all people I see myself, none more and not one a
    barleycorn less,
And the good or bad I say of myself I say of them.

And I know I am solid and sound,
To me the converging objects of the universe perpetually
    flow,
All are written to me, and I must get what the writing means.

And I know I am deathless,
I know this orbit of mine cannot be swept by a carpenter's
    compass,
I know I shall not pass like a child's carlacue cut with a burnt
    stick at night.

I know I am august,
I do not trouble my spirit to vindicate itself or be understood,
I see that the elementary laws never apologize,
I reckon I behave no prouder than the level I plant my house
    by after all.

I exist as I am, that is enough,
If no other in the world be aware I sit content,
And if each and all be aware I sit content.

One world is aware, and by far the largest to me, and that is
    myself,
And whether I come to my own today or in ten thousand or
    ten million years,
I can cheerfully take it now, or with equal cheerfulness I
    can wait.

My foothold is tenoned and mortised in granite,
I laugh at what you call dissolution,
And I know the amplitude of time.

I am the poet of the body,
And I am the poet of the soul.

The pleasures of heaven are with me, and the pains of hell
    are with me,
The first I graft and increase upon myself . . . . the latter I
    translate into a new tongue.

I am the poet of the woman the same as the man,
And I say it is as great to be a woman as to be a man,
And I say there is nothing greater than the mother of
    men.

I chant a new chant of dilation or pride,
We have had ducking and deprecating about enough,
I show that size is only developement.

Have you outstript the rest? Are you the President?
It is a trifle . . . . they will more than arrive there every
    one, and still pass on.

I am he that walks with the tender and growing night;
I call to the earth and sea half-held by the night.

Press close barebosomed night! Press close magnetic
    nourishing night!
Night of south winds! Night of the large few stars!
Still nodding night! Mad naked summer night!

Smile O voluptuous coolbreathed earth!
Earth of the slumbering and liquid trees!
Earth of departed sunset! Earth of the mountains misty-
    topt!
Earth of the vitreous pour of the full moon just tinged
    with blue!
Earth of shine and dark mottling the tide of the river!
Earth of the limpid gray of clouds brighter and clearer for
    my sake!
Far-swooping elbowed earth! Rich apple-blossomed earth!
Smile, for your lover comes!

Prodigal! you have given me love! . . . . therefore I to you
     give love!
O unspeakable passionate love!

Thruster holding me tight and that I hold tight!
We hurt each other as the bridegroom and the bride hurt
     each other.

You sea! I resign myself to you also . . . . I guess what
     you mean,
I behold from the beach your crooked inviting fingers,
I believe you refuse to go back without feeling of me;
We must have a turn together . . . . I undress . . . . hurry
     me out of sight of the land,
Cushion me soft . . . . rock me in billowy drowse,
Dash me with amorous wet . . . . I can repay you.

Sea of stretched ground-swells!
Sea breathing broad and convulsive breaths!
Sea of the brine of life! Sea of unshovelled and always-ready
     graves!
Howler and scooper of storms! Capricious and dainty sea!
I am integral with you . . . . I too am of one phase and of
     all phases.

Partaker of influx and efflux . . . . extoler of hate and
     conciliation,
Extoler of amies and those that sleep in each others' arms.

I am he attesting sympathy;
Shall I make my list of things in the house and skip the
     house that supports them?

I am the poet of commonsense and of the demonstrable and
     of immortality;
And am not the poet of goodness only . . . . I do not
     decline to be the poet of wickedness also.

Washes and razors for foofoos . . . . for me freckles and a
     bristling beard.

What blurt is it about virtue and about vice?
Evil propels me, and reform of evil propels me . . . . I stand
     indifferent,
My gait is no faultfinder's or rejecter's gait,
I moisten the roots of all that has grown.

Did you fear some scrofula out of the unflagging pregnancy?
Did you guess the celestial laws are yet to be worked over
     and rectified?

I step up to say that what we do is right and what we affirm
     is right . . . . and some is only the ore of right,
Witnesses of us . . . . one side a balance and the antipodal
     side a balance,
Soft doctrine as steady help as stable doctrine,
Thoughts and deeds of the present our rouse and early start.

This minute that comes to me over the past decillions,
There is no better than it and now.

What behaved well in the past or behaves well today is not
     such a wonder,
The wonder is always and always how there can be a mean
     man or an infidel.

Endless unfolding of words of ages!
And mine a word of the modern . . . . a word en masse.

A word of the faith that never balks,
One time as good as another time . . . . here or
     henceforward it is all the same to me.

A word of reality . . . . materialism first and last imbueing.

Hurrah for positive science! Long live exact demonstration!
Fetch stonecrop and mix it with cedar and branches of lilac;
This is the lexicographer or chemist . . . . this made a
     grammar of the old cartouches,
These mariners put the ship through dangerous unknown
     seas,

This is the geologist, and this works with the scalpel, and
    this is a mathematician.

Gentlemen I receive you, and attach and clasp hands with
    you,
The facts are useful and real . . . . they are not my dwelling
    . . . . I enter by them to an area of the dwelling.

I am less the reminder of property or qualities, and more the
    reminder of life,
And go on the square for my own sake and for others' sakes,
And make short account of neuters and geldings, and favor
    men and women fully equipped,
And beat the gong of revolt, and stop with fugitives and
    them that plot and conspire.

Walt Whitman, an American, one of the roughs, a kosmos,
Disorderly fleshy and sensual . . . . eating drinking and
    breeding,
No sentimentalist . . . . no stander above men and women or
    apart from them . . . . no more modest than immodest.

Unscrew the locks from the doors!
Unscrew the doors themselves from their jambs!

Whoever degrades another degrades me . . . . and whatever
    is done or said returns at last to me,
And whatever I do or say I also return.

Through me the afflatus surging and surging . . . . through
    me the current and index.

I speak the password primeval . . . . I give the sign of
    democracy;
By God! I will accept nothing which all cannot have their
    counterpart of on the same terms.

Through me many long dumb voices,
Voices of the interminable generations of slaves,
Voices of prostitutes and of deformed persons,

Voices of the diseased and despairing, and of thieves and
    dwarfs,
Voices of cycles of preparation and accretion,
And of the threads that connect the stars—and of wombs,
    and of the fatherstuff,
And of the rights of them the others are down upon,
Of the trivial and flat and foolish and despised,
Of fog in the air and beetles rolling balls of dung.

Through me forbidden voices,
Voices of sexes and lusts . . . . voices veiled, and I remove
    the veil,
Voices indecent by me clarified and transfigured.

I do not press my finger across my mouth,
I keep as delicate around the bowels as around the head and
    heart,
Copulation is no more rank to me than death is.

I believe in the flesh and the appetites,
Seeing hearing and feeling are miracles, and each part and
    tag of me is a miracle.

Divine am I inside and out, and I make holy whatever I
    touch or am touched from;
The scent of these arm-pits is aroma finer than prayer,
This head is more than churches or bibles or creeds.

If I worship any particular thing it shall be some of the
    spread of my body;
Translucent mould of me it shall be you,
Shaded ledges and rests, firm masculine coulter, it shall be you,
Whatever goes to the tilth of me it shall be you,
You my rich blood, your milky stream pale strippings of my
    life;
Breast that presses against other breasts it shall be you,
My brain it shall be your occult convolutions,
Root of washed sweet-flag, timorous pond-snipe, nest of
    guarded duplicate eggs, it shall be you,
Mixed tussled hay of head and beard and brawn it shall be you,

Trickling sap of maple, fibre of manly wheat, it shall be you;
Sun so generous it shall be you,
Vapors lighting and shading my face it shall be you,
You sweaty brooks and dews it shall be you,
Winds whose soft-tickling genitals rub against me it shall
    be you,
Broad muscular fields, branches of liveoak, loving lounger in
    my winding paths, it shall be you,
Hands I have taken, face I have kissed, mortal I have ever
    touched, it shall be you.

I dote on myself . . . . there is that lot of me, and all so
    luscious,
Each moment and whatever happens thrills me with joy.

I cannot tell how my ankles bend . . . . nor whence the
    cause of my faintest wish,
Nor the cause of the friendship I emit . . . . nor the cause
    of the friendship I take again.

To walk up my stoop is unaccountable . . . . I pause to
    consider if it really be,
That I eat and drink is spectacle enough for the great
    authors and schools,
A morning-glory at my window satisfies me more than the
    metaphysics of books.

To behold the daybreak!
The little light fades the immense and diaphanous shadows,
The air tastes good to my palate.

Hefts of the moving world at innocent gambols, silently
    rising, freshly exuding,
Scooting obliquely high and low.

Something I cannot see puts upward libidinous prongs,
Seas of bright juice suffuse heaven.

The earth by the sky staid with . . . . the daily close of their
    junction,

The heaved challenge from the east that moment over my
      head,
The mocking taunt, See then whether you shall be master!

Dazzling and tremendous how quick the sunrise would kill me,
If I could not now and always send sunrise out of me.

We also ascend dazzling and tremendous as the sun,
We found our own my soul in the calm and cool of the
      daybreak.

My voice goes after what my eyes cannot reach,
With the twirl of my tongue I encompass worlds and
      volumes of worlds.

Speech is the twin of my vision . . . . it is unequal to
      measure itself.

It provokes me forever,
It says sarcastically, Walt, you understand enough . . . . why
      don't you let it out then?

Come now I will not be tantalized . . . . you conceive too
      much of articulation.

Do you not know how the buds beneath are folded?
Waiting in gloom protected by frost,
The dirt receding before my prophetical screams,
I underlying causes to balance them at last,
My knowledge my live parts . . . . it keeping tally with the
      meaning of things,
Happiness . . . . which whoever hears me let him or her set
      out in search of this day.

My final merit I refuse you . . . . I refuse putting from me
      the best I am.

Encompass worlds but never try to encompass me,
I crowd your noisiest talk by looking toward you.

Writing and talk do not prove me,
I carry the plenum of proof and every thing else in my face,
With the hush of my lips I confound the topmost skeptic.

I think I will do nothing for a long time but listen,
And accrue what I hear into myself . . . . and let sounds
    contribute toward me.

I hear the bravuras of birds . . . . the bustle of growing
    wheat . . . . gossip of flames . . . . clack of sticks
    cooking my meals.

I hear the sound of the human voice . . . . a sound I love,
I hear all sounds as they are tuned to their uses . . . .
    sounds of the city and sounds out of the city . . . .
    sounds of the day and night;
Talkative young ones to those that like them . . . . the
    recitative of fish-pedlars and fruit-pedlars . . . . the
    loud laugh of workpeople at their meals,
The angry base of disjointed friendship . . . . the faint tones
    of the sick,
The judge with hands tight to the desk, his shaky lips
    pronouncing a death-sentence,
The heave'e'yo of stevedores unlading ships by the wharves
    . . . . the refrain of the anchor-lifters;
The ring of alarm-bells . . . . the cry of fire . . . . the whirr
    of swift-streaking engines and hose-carts with
    premonitory tinkles and colored lights,
The steam-whistle . . . . the solid roll of the train of
    approaching cars;
The slow-march played at night at the head of the association,
They go to guard some corpse . . . . the flag-tops are
    draped with black muslin.

I hear the violincello or man's heart's complaint,
And hear the keyed cornet or else the echo of sunset.

I hear the chorus . . . . it is a grand-opera . . . . this
    indeed is music!

A tenor large and fresh as the creation fills me,
The orbic flex of his mouth is pouring and filling me full.

I hear the trained soprano . . . . she convulses me like the
  climax of my love-grip;
The orchestra whirls me wider than Uranus flies,
It wrenches unnamable ardors from my breast,
It throbs me to gulps of the farthest down horror,
It sails me . . . . I dab with bare feet . . . . they are licked
  by the indolent waves,
I am exposed . . . . cut by bitter and poisoned hail,
Steeped amid honeyed morphine . . . . my windpipe
  squeezed in the fakes of death,
Let up again to feel the puzzle of puzzles,
And that we call Being.

To be in any form, what is that?
If nothing lay more developed the quahaug and its callous
  shell were enough.

Mine is no callous shell,
I have instant conductors all over me whether I pass or stop,
They seize every object and lead it harmlessly through me.

I merely stir, press, feel with my fingers, and am happy,
To touch my person to some one else's is about as much as I
  can stand.

Is this then a touch? . . . . quivering me to a new identity,
Flames and ether making a rush for my veins,
Treacherous tip of me reaching and crowding to help them,
My flesh and blood playing out lightning, to strike what is
  hardly different from myself,
On all sides prurient provokers stiffening my limbs,
Straining the udder of my heart for its withheld drip,
Behaving licentious toward me, taking no denial,
Depriving me of my best as for a purpose,
Unbuttoning my clothes and holding me by the bare waist,
Deluding my confusion with the calm of the sunlight and
  pasture fields,

Immodestly sliding the fellow-senses away,
They bribed to swap off with touch, and go and graze at the
    edges of me,
No consideration, no regard for my draining strength or my
    anger,
Fetching the rest of the herd around to enjoy them awhile,
Then all uniting to stand on a headland and worry me.

The sentries desert every other part of me,
They have left me helpless to a red marauder,
They all come to the headland to witness and assist against me.

I am given up by traitors;
I talk wildly . . . . I have lost my wits . . . . I and nobody
    else am the greatest traitor,
I went myself first to the headland . . . . my own hands
    carried me there.

You villain touch! what are you doing? . . . . my breath is
    tight in its throat;
Unclench your floodgates! you are too much for me.

Blind loving wrestling touch! Sheathed hooded sharptoothed
    touch!
Did it make you ache so leaving me?

Parting tracked by arriving . . . . perpetual payment of the
    perpetual loan,
Rich showering rain, and recompense richer afterward.

Sprouts take and accumulate . . . . stand by the curb
    prolific and vital,
Landscapes projected masculine full-sized and golden.

All truths wait in all things,
They neither hasten their own delivery nor resist it,
They do not need the obstetric forceps of the surgeon,
The insignificant is as big to me as any,
What is less or more than a touch?

Logic and sermons never convince,
The damp of the night drives deeper into my soul.

Only what proves itself to every man and woman is so,
Only what nobody denies is so.

A minute and a drop of me settle my brain;
I believe the soggy clods shall become lovers and lamps,
And a compend of compends is the meat of a man or
    woman,
And a summit and flower there is the feeling they have for
    each other,
And they are to branch boundlessly out of that lesson until
    it becomes omnific,
And until every one shall delight us, and we them.

I believe a leaf of grass is no less than the journeywork of
    the stars,
And the pismire is equally perfect, and a grain of sand, and
    the egg of the wren,
And the tree-toad is a chef-d'ouvre for the highest,
And the running blackberry would adorn the parlors of
    heaven,
And the narrowest hinge in my hand puts to scorn all
    machinery,
And the cow crunching with depressed head surpasses any
    statue,
And a mouse is miracle enough to stagger sextillions of
    infidels,
And I could come every afternoon of my life to look at the
    farmer's girl boiling her iron tea-kettle and baking
    shortcake.

I find I incorporate gneiss and coal and long-threaded moss
    and fruits and grains and esculent roots,
And am stucco'd with quadrupeds and birds all over,
And have distanced what is behind me for good reasons,
And call any thing close again when I desire it.

In vain the speeding or shyness,
In vain the plutonic rocks send their old heat against my
approach,
In vain the mastadon retreats beneath its own powdered
bones,
In vain objects stand leagues off and assume manifold shapes,
In vain the ocean settling in hollows and the great monsters
lying low,
In vain the buzzard houses herself with the sky,
In vain the snake slides through the creepers and logs,
In vain the elk takes to the inner passes of the woods,
In vain the razorbilled auk sails far north to Labrador,
I follow quickly . . . . I ascend to the nest in the fissure of
the cliff.

I think I could turn and live awhile with the animals . . . .
they are so placid and self-contained,
I stand and look at them sometimes half the day long.

They do not sweat and whine about their condition,
They do not lie awake in the dark and weep for their sins,
They do not make me sick discussing their duty to God,
Not one is dissatisfied . . . . not one is demented with the
mania of owning things,
Not one kneels to another nor to his kind that lived
thousands of years ago,
Not one is respectable or industrious over the whole earth.

So they show their relations to me and I accept them;
They bring me tokens of myself . . . . they evince them
plainly in their possession.

I do not know where they got those tokens,
I must have passed that way untold times ago and
negligently dropt them,
Myself moving forward then and now and forever,
Gathering and showing more always and with velocity,
Infinite and omnigenous and the like of these among them;
Not too exclusive toward the reachers of my remembrancers,

Picking out here one that shall be my amie,
Choosing to go with him on brotherly terms.

A gigantic beauty of a stallion, fresh and responsive to my
    caresses,
Head high in the forehead and wide between the ears,
Limbs glossy and supple, tail dusting the ground,
Eyes well apart and full of sparkling wickedness . . . . ears
    finely cut and flexibly moving.

His nostrils dilate . . . . my heels embrace him . . . . his
    well built limbs tremble with pleasure . . . . we speed
    around and return.

I but use you a moment and then I resign you stallion . . . .
    and do not need your paces, and outgallop them,
And myself as I stand or sit pass faster than you.

Swift wind! Space! My Soul! Now I know it is true what I
    guessed at;
What I guessed when I loafed on the grass,
What I guessed while I lay alone in my bed . . . . and again
    as I walked the beach under the paling stars of the
    morning.

My ties and ballasts leave me . . . . I travel . . . . I sail
    . . . . my elbows rest in the sea-gaps,
I skirt the sierras . . . . my palms cover continents,
I am afoot with my vision.

By the city's quadrangular houses . . . . in log-huts, or
    camping with lumbermen,
Along the ruts of the turnpike . . . . along the dry gulch
    and rivulet bed,
Hoeing my onion-patch, and rows of carrots and parsnips
    . . . . crossing savannas . . . trailing in forests,
Prospecting . . . . gold-digging . . . . girdling the trees of
    a new purchase,
Scorched ankle-deep by the hot sand . . . . hauling my boat
    down the shallow river;

Where the panther walks to and fro on a limb overhead
. . . . where the buck turns furiously at the hunter,
Where the rattlesnake suns his flabby length on a rock . . . .
where the otter is feeding on fish,
Where the alligator in his tough pimples sleeps by the
bayou,
Where the black bear is searching for roots or honey . . . .
where the beaver pats the mud with his paddle-tail;
Over the growing sugar . . . . over the cottonplant . . . .
over the rice in its low moist field;
Over the sharp-peaked farmhouse with its scalloped scum
and slender shoots from the gutters;
Over the western persimmon . . . . over the longleaved
corn and the delicate blueflowered flax;
Over the white and brown buckwheat, a hummer and a
buzzer there with the rest,
Over the dusky green of the rye as it ripples and shades in
the breeze;
Scaling mountains . . . . pulling myself cautiously up . . . .
holding on by low scragged limbs,
Walking the path worn in the grass and beat through the
leaves of the brush;
Where the quail is whistling betwixt the woods and the
wheatlot,
Where the bat flies in the July eve . . . . where the great
goldbug drops through the dark;
Where the flails keep time on the barn floor,
Where the brook puts out of the roots of the old tree and
flows to the meadow,
Where cattle stand and shake away flies with the tremulous
shuddering of their hides,
Where the cheese-cloth hangs in the kitchen, and andirons
straddle the hearth-slab, and cobwebs fall in festoons
from the rafters;
Where triphammers crash . . . . where the press is whirling
its cylinders;
Wherever the human heart beats with terrible throes out of
its ribs;
Where the pear-shaped balloon is floating aloft . . . .
floating in it myself and looking composedly down;

Where the life-car is drawn on the slipnoose . . . . where
    the heat hatches pale-green eggs in the dented sand,
Where the she-whale swims with her calves and never
    forsakes them,
Where the steamship trails hindways its long pennant
    of smoke,
Where the ground-shark's fin cuts like a black chip out of
    the water,
Where the half-burned brig is riding on unknown currents,
Where shells grow to her slimy deck, and the dead are
    corrupting below;
Where the striped and starred flag is borne at the head of
    the regiments;
Approaching Manhattan, up by the long-stretching island,
Under Niagara, the cataract falling like a veil over my
    countenance;
Upon a door-step . . . . upon the horse-block of hard wood
    outside,
Upon the race-course, or enjoying pic-nics or jigs or a good
    game of base-ball,
At he-festivals with blackguard jibes and ironical license and
    bull-dances and drinking and laughter,
At the cider-mill, tasting the sweet of the brown sqush . . . .
    sucking the juice through a straw,
At apple-pealings, wanting kisses for all the red fruit I
    find,
At musters and beach-parties and friendly bees and huskings
    and house-raisings;
Where the mockingbird sounds his delicious gurgles, and
    cackles and screams and weeps,
Where the hay-rick stands in the barnyard, and the dry-stalks
    are scattered, and the brood cow waits in the hovel,
Where the bull advances to do his masculine work, and the
    stud to the mare, and the cock is treading the hen,
Where the heifers browse, and the geese nip their food with
    short jerks;
Where the sundown shadows lengthen over the limitless and
    lonesome prairie,
Where the herds of buffalo make a crawling spread of the
    square miles far and near;

Where the hummingbird shimmers . . . . where the neck of
    the longlived swan is curving and winding;
Where the laughing-gull scoots by the slappy shore and
    laughs her near-human laugh;
Where beehives range on a gray bench in the garden half-hid
    by the high weeds;
Where the band-necked partridges roost in a ring on the
    ground with their heads out;
Where burial coaches enter the arched gates of a cemetery;
Where winter wolves bark amid wastes of snow and icicled
    trees;
Where the yellow-crowned heron comes to the edge of the
    marsh at night and feeds upon small crabs;
Where the splash of swimmers and divers cools the warm
    noon;
Where the katydid works her chromatic reed on the walnut-
    tree over the well;
Through patches of citrons and cucumbers with silver-wired
    leaves,
Through the salt-lick or orange glade . . . . or under conical
    firs;
Through the gymnasium . . . . through the curtained
    saloon . . . . through the office or public hall;
Pleased with the native and pleased with the foreign . . . .
    pleased with the new and old,
Pleased with women, the homely as well as the handsome,
Pleased with the quakeress as she puts off her bonnet and
    talks melodiously,
Pleased with the primitive tunes of the choir of the
    whitewashed church,
Pleased with the earnest words of the sweating Methodist
    preacher, or any preacher . . . . looking seriously at the
    camp-meeting;
Looking in at the shop-windows in Broadway the whole
    forenoon . . . . pressing the flesh of my nose to the
    thick plate-glass,
Wandering the same afternoon with my face turned up to
    the clouds;
My right and left arms round the sides of two friends and I
    in the middle;

Coming home with the bearded and dark-cheeked bush-boy
   . . . . riding behind him at the drape of the day;
Far from the settlements studying the print of animals' feet,
   or the moccasin print;
By the cot in the hospital reaching lemonade to a feverish
   patient,
By the coffined corpse when all is still, examining with a
   candle;
Voyaging to every port to dicker and adventure;
Hurrying with the modern crowd, as eager and fickle as any,
Hot toward one I hate, ready in my madness to knife him;
Solitary at midnight in my back yard, my thoughts gone
   from me a long while,
Walking the old hills of Judea with the beautiful gentle god
   by my side;
Speeding through space . . . . speeding through heaven and
   the stars,
Speeding amid the seven satellites and the broad ring and
   the diameter of eighty thousand miles,
Speeding with tailed meteors . . . . throwing fire-balls like
   the rest,
Carrying the crescent child that carries its own full mother in
   its belly;
Storming enjoying planning loving cautioning,
Backing and filling, appearing and disappearing,
I tread day and night such roads.

I visit the orchards of God and look at the spheric product,
And look at quintillions ripened, and look at quintillions
   green.

I fly the flight of the fluid and swallowing soul,
My course runs below the soundings of plummets.

I help myself to material and immaterial,
No guard can shut me off, no law can prevent me.

I anchor my ship for a little while only,
My messengers continually cruise away or bring their returns
   to me.

I go hunting polar furs and the seal . . . . leaping chasms
    with a pike-pointed staff . . . . clinging to topples of
    brittle and blue.

I ascend to the foretruck . . . . I take my place late at night
    in the crow's nest . . . . we sail through the arctic sea
    . . . . it is plenty light enough,
Through the clear atmosphere I stretch around on the
    wonderful beauty,
The enormous masses of ice pass me and I pass them . . . .
    the scenery is plain in all directions,
The white-topped mountains point up in the distance . . . .
    I fling out my fancies toward them;
We are about approaching some great battlefield in which we
    are soon to be engaged,
We pass the colossal outposts of the encampments . . . .
    we pass with still feet and caution;
Or we are entering by the suburbs some vast and ruined city
    . . . . the blocks and fallen architecture more than all
    the living cities of the globe.

I am a free companion . . . . I bivouac by invading
    watchfires.

I turn the bridegroom out of bed and stay with the bride
    myself,
And tighten her all night to my thighs and lips.

My voice is the wife's voice, the screech by the rail of the
    stairs,
They fetch my man's body up dripping and drowned.

I understand the large hearts of heroes,
The courage of present times and all times;
How the skipper saw the crowded and rudderless wreck of the
    steamship, and death chasing it up and down the storm,
How he knuckled tight and gave not back one inch, and was
    faithful of days and faithful of nights,
And chalked in large letters on a board, Be of good cheer,
    We will not desert you;

How he saved the drifting company at last,
How the lank loose-gowned women looked when boated
　　from the side of their prepared graves,
How the silent old-faced infants, and the lifted sick, and the
　　sharp-lipped unshaved men;
All this I swallow and it tastes good . . . . I like it well, and
　　it becomes mine,
I am the man . . . . I suffered . . . . I was there.

The disdain and calmness of martyrs,
The mother condemned for a witch and burnt with dry
　　wood, and her children gazing on;
The hounded slave that flags in the race and leans by the
　　fence, blowing and covered with sweat,
The twinges that sting like needles his legs and neck,
The murderous buckshot and the bullets,
All these I feel or am.

I am the hounded slave . . . . I wince at the bite of the dogs,
Hell and despair are upon me . . . . crack and again crack
　　the marksmen,
I clutch the rails of the fence . . . . my gore dribs thinned
　　with the ooze of my skin,
I fall on the weeds and stones,
The riders spur their unwilling horses and haul close,
They taunt my dizzy ears . . . . they beat me violently over
　　the head with their whip-stocks.

Agonies are one of my changes of garments;
I do not ask the wounded person how he feels I
　　myself become the wounded person,
My hurt turns livid upon me as I lean on a cane and observe.

I am the mashed fireman with breastbone broken . . . .
　　tumbling walls buried me in their debris,
Heat and smoke I inspired . . . . I heard the yelling shouts
　　of my comrades,
I heard the distant click of their picks and shovels;
They have cleared the beams away . . . . they tenderly lift
　　me forth.

I lie in the night air in my red shirt . . . . the pervading
    hush is for my sake,
Painless after all I lie, exhausted but not so unhappy,
White and beautiful are the faces around me . . . . the
    heads are bared of their fire-caps,
The kneeling crowd fades with the light of the torches.

Distant and dead resuscitate,
They show as the dial or move as the hands of me . . . .
    and I am the clock myself.

I am an old artillerist, and tell of some fort's bombardment
    . . . . and am there again.

Again the reveille of drummers . . . . again the attacking
    cannon and mortars and howitzers,
Again the attacked send their cannon responsive.

I take part . . . . I see and hear the whole,
The cries and curses and roar . . . . the plaudits for well
    aimed shots,
The ambulanza slowly passing and trailing its red drip,
Workmen searching after damages and to make indispensible
    repairs,
The fall of grenades through the rent roof . . . . the fan-
    shaped explosion,
The whizz of limbs heads stone wood and iron high in the air.

Again gurgles the mouth of my dying general . . . . he
    furiously waves with his hand,
He gasps through the clot . . . . Mind not me . . . . mind
    . . . . the entrenchments.

I tell not the fall of Alamo . . . . not one escaped to tell the
    fall of Alamo,
The hundred and fifty are dumb yet at Alamo.

Hear now the tale of a jetblack sunrise,
Hear of the murder in cold blood of four hundred and
    twelve young men.

Retreating they had formed in a hollow square with their
    baggage for breastworks,
Nine hundred lives out of the surrounding enemy's nine
    times their number was the price they took in advance,
Their colonel was wounded and their ammunition gone,
They treated for an honorable capitulation, received writing
    and seal, gave up their arms, and marched back
    prisoners of war.

They were the glory of the race of rangers,
Matchless with a horse, a rifle, a song, a supper or a
    courtship,
Large, turbulent, brave, handsome, generous, proud and
    affectionate,
Bearded, sunburnt, dressed in the free costume of hunters,
Not a single one over thirty years of age.

The second Sunday morning they were brought out in squads
    and massacred . . . . it was beautiful early summer,
The work commenced about five o'clock and was over by
    eight.

None obeyed the command to kneel,
Some made a mad and helpless rush . . . . some stood stark
    and straight,
A few fell at once, shot in the temple or heart . . . . the
    living and dead lay together,
The maimed and mangled dug in the dirt . . . . the new-
    comers saw them there;
Some half-killed attempted to crawl away,
These were dispatched with bayonets or battered with the
    blunts of muskets;
A youth not seventeen years old seized his assassin till two
    more came to release him,
The three were all torn, and covered with the boy's blood.

At eleven o'clock began the burning of the bodies;
And that is the tale of the murder of the four hundred and
    twelve young men,
And that was a jetblack sunrise.

Did you read in the seabooks of the oldfashioned frigate-
      fight?
Did you learn who won by the light of the moon and stars?

Our foe was no skulk in his ship, I tell you,
His was the English pluck, and there is no tougher or truer,
      and never was, and never will be;
Along the lowered eve he came, horribly raking us.

We closed with him . . . . the yards entangled . . . . the
      cannon touched,
My captain lashed fast with his own hands.

We had received some eighteen-pound shots under the water,
On our lower-gun-deck two large pieces had burst at the
      first fire, killing all around and blowing up overhead.

Ten o'clock at night, and the full moon shining and the leaks
      on the gain, and five feet of water reported,
The master-at-arms loosing the prisoners confined in the
      after-hold to give them a chance for themselves.

The transit to and from the magazine was now stopped by
      the sentinels,
They saw so many strange faces they did not know whom
      to trust.

Our frigate was afire . . . . the other asked if we demanded
      quarters? if our colors were struck and the fighting done?

I laughed content when I heard the voice of my little
      captain,
We have not struck, he composedly cried, We have just
      begun our part of the fighting.

Only three guns were in use,
One was directed by the captain himself against the enemy's
      mainmast,
Two well-served with grape and canister silenced his
      musketry and cleared his decks.

The tops alone seconded the fire of this little battery,
    especially the maintop,
They all held out bravely during the whole of the action.

Not a moment's cease,
The leaks gained fast on the pumps . . . . the fire eat
    toward the powder-magazine,
One of the pumps was shot away . . . . it was generally
    thought we were sinking.

Serene stood the little captain,
He was not hurried . . . . his voice was neither high nor low,
His eyes gave more light to us than our battle-lanterns.

Toward twelve at night, there in the beams of the moon they
    surrendered to us.

Stretched and still lay the midnight,
Two great hulls motionless on the breast of the darkness,
Our vessel riddled and slowly sinking . . . . preparations to
    pass to the one we had conquered,
The captain on the quarter deck coldly giving his orders
    through a countenance white as a sheet,
Near by the corpse of the child that served in the cabin,
The dead face of an old salt with long white hair and
    carefully curled whiskers,
The flames spite of all that could be done flickering aloft and
    below,
The husky voices of the two or three officers yet fit for duty,
Formless stacks of bodies and bodies by themselves . . . .
    dabs of flesh upon the masts and spars,
The cut of cordage and dangle of rigging . . . . the slight
    shock of the soothe of waves,
Black and impassive guns, and litter of powder-parcels, and
    the strong scent,
Delicate sniffs of the seabreeze . . . . smells of sedgy grass
    and fields by the shore . . . death-messages given in
    charge to survivors,
The hiss of the surgeon's knife and the gnawing teeth of his
    saw,

The wheeze, the cluck, the swash of falling blood . . . . the
    short wild scream, the long dull tapering groan,
These so . . . . these irretrievable.

O Christ! My fit is mastering me!
What the rebel said gaily adjusting his throat to the rope-
    noose,
What the savage at the stump, his eye-sockets empty, his
    mouth spirting whoops and defiance,
What stills the traveler come to the vault at Mount Vernon,
What sobers the Brooklyn boy as he looks down the shores
    of the Wallabout and remembers the prison ships,
What burnt the gums of the redcoat at Saratoga when he
    surrendered his brigades,
These become mine and me every one, and they are but little,
I become as much more as I like.

I become any presence or truth of humanity here,
And see myself in prison shaped like another man,
And feel the dull unintermitted pain.

For me the keepers of convicts shoulder their carbines and
    keep watch,
It is I let out in the morning and barred at night.

Not a mutineer walks handcuffed to the jail, but I am
    handcuffed to him and walk by his side,
I am less the jolly one there, and more the silent one with
    sweat on my twitching lips.

Not a youngster is taken for larceny, but I go up too and
    am tried and sentenced.

Not a cholera patient lies at the last gasp, but I also lie at
    the last gasp,
My face is ash-colored, my sinews gnarl . . . . away from
    me people retreat.

Askers embody themselves in me, and I am embodied in them,
I project my hat and sit shamefaced and beg.

I rise extatic through all, and sweep with the true gravitation,
The whirling and whirling is elemental within me.

Somehow I have been stunned. Stand back!
Give me a little time beyond my cuffed head and slumbers
 and dreams and gaping,
I discover myself on a verge of the usual mistake.

That I could forget the mockers and insults!
That I could forget the trickling tears and the blows of the
 bludgeons and hammers!
That I could look with a separate look on my own
 crucifixion and bloody crowning!

I remember . . . . I resume the overstaid fraction,
The grave of rock multiplies what has been confided to it
 . . . . or to any graves,
The corpses rise . . . . the gashes heal . . . . the fastenings
 roll away.

I troop forth replenished with supreme power, one of an
 average unending procession,
We walk the roads of Ohio and Massachusetts and Virginia
 and Wisconsin and New York and New Orleans and
 Texas and Montreal and San Francisco and Charleston
 and Savannah and Mexico,
Inland and by the seacoast and boundary lines . . . . and we
 pass the boundary lines.

Our swift ordinances are on their way over the whole
 earth,
The blossoms we wear in our hats are the growth of two
 thousand years.

Eleves I salute you,
I see the approach of your numberless gangs . . . . I see
 you understand yourselves and me,
And know that they who have eyes are divine, and the blind
 and lame are equally divine,
And that my steps drag behind yours yet go before them,

And are aware how I am with you no more than I am with
    everybody.

The friendly and flowing savage . . . . Who is he?
Is he waiting for civilization or past it and mastering it?

Is he some southwesterner raised outdoors? Is he
    Canadian?
Is he from the Mississippi country? or from Iowa, Oregon
    or California? or from the mountains? or prairie life or
    bush-life? or from the sea?

Wherever he goes men and women accept and desire him,
They desire he should like them and touch them and speak
    to them and stay with them.

Behaviour lawless as snow-flakes . . . . words simple as
    grass . . . . uncombed head and laughter and naivete;
Slowstepping feet and the common features, and the
    common modes and emanations,
They descend in new forms from the tips of his fingers,
They are wafted with the odor of his body or breath . . . .
    they fly out of the glance of his eyes.

Flaunt of the sunshine I need not your bask . . . . lie
    over,
You light surfaces only . . . . I force the surfaces and the
    depths also.

Earth! you seem to look for something at my hands,
Say old topknot! what do you want?

Man or woman! I might tell how I like you, but cannot,
And might tell what it is in me and what it is in you, but
    cannot,
And might tell the pinings I have . . . . the pulse of my
    nights and days.

Behold I do not give lectures or a little charity,
What I give I give out of myself.

You there, impotent, loose in the knees, open your scarfed
    chops till I blow grit within you,
Spread your palms and lift the flaps of your pockets,
I am not to be denied . . . . I compel . . . . I have stores
    plenty and to spare,
And any thing I have I bestow.

I do not ask who you are . . . . that is not important to me,
You can do nothing and be nothing but what I will infold you.

To a drudge of the cottonfields or emptier of privies I lean
    . . . . on his right cheek I put the family kiss,
And in my soul I swear I never will deny him.

On women fit for conception I start bigger and nimbler babes,
This day I am jetting the stuff of far more arrogant republics.

To any one dying . . . . thither I speed and twist the knob
    of the door,
Turn the bedclothes toward the foot of the bed,
Let the physician and the priest go home.

I seize the descending man . . . . I raise him with resistless
    will.

O despairer, here is my neck,
By God! you shall not go down! Hang your whole weight
    upon me.

I dilate you with tremendous breath . . . . I buoy you up;
Every room of the house do I fill with an armed force . . . .
    lovers of me, bafflers of graves:
Sleep! I and they keep guard all night;
Not doubt, not decease shall dare to lay finger upon you,
I have embraced you, and henceforth possess you to myself,
And when you rise in the morning you will find what I tell
    you is so.

I am he bringing help for the sick as they pant on their backs,
And for strong upright men I bring yet more needed help.

I heard what was said of the universe,
Heard it and heard of several thousand years;
It is middling well as far as it goes . . . . but is that all?

Magnifying and applying come I,
Outbidding at the start the old cautious hucksters,
The most they offer for mankind and eternity less than a spirt
    of my own seminal wet,
Taking myself the exact dimensions of Jehovah and laying
    them away,
Lithographing Kronos and Zeus his son, and Hercules his
    grandson,
Buying drafts of Osiris and Isis and Belus and Brahma and
    Adonai,
In my portfolio placing Manito loose, and Allah on a leaf,
    and the crucifix engraved,
With Odin, and the hideous-faced Mexitli, and all idols and
    images,
Honestly taking them all for what they are worth, and not a
    cent more,
Admitting they were alive and did the work of their day,
Admitting they bore mites as for unfledged birds who have
    now to rise and fly and sing for themselves,
Accepting the rough deific sketches to fill out better in myself
    . . . . bestowing them freely on each man and woman I
    see,
Discovering as much or more in a framer framing a house,
Putting higher claims for him there with his rolled-up
    sleeves, driving the mallet and chisel;
Not objecting to special revelations . . . . considering a curl
    of smoke or a hair on the back of my hand as curious as
    any revelation;
Those ahold of fire-engines and hook-and-ladder ropes more
    to me than the gods of the antique wars,
Minding their voices peal through the crash of destruction,
Their brawny limbs passing safe over charred laths . . . .
    their white foreheads whole and unhurt out of the
    flames;
By the mechanic's wife with her babe at her nipple interceding
    for every person born;

Three scythes at harvest whizzing in a row from three lusty
    angels with shirts bagged out at their waists;
The snag-toothed hostler with red hair redeeming sins past
    and to come,
Selling all he possesses and traveling on foot to fee lawyers
    for his brother and sit by him while he is tried for
    forgery:
What was strewn in the amplest strewing the square rod
    about me, and not filling the square rod then;
The bull and the bug never worshipped half enough,
Dung and dirt more admirable than was dreamed,
The supernatural of no account . . . . myself waiting my
    time to be one of the supremes,
The day getting ready for me when I shall do as much good
    as the best, and be as prodigious,
Guessing when I am it will not tickle me much to receive
    puffs out of pulpit or print;
By my life-lumps! becoming already a creator!
Putting myself here and now to the ambushed womb of the
    shadows!

. . . . A call in the midst of the crowd,
My own voice, orotund sweeping and final.

Come my children,
Come my boys and girls, and my women and household and
    intimates,
Now the performer launches his nerve . . . . he has passed
    his prelude on the reeds within.

Easily written loosefingered chords! I feel the thrum of their
    climax and close.

My head evolves on my neck,
Music rolls, but not from the organ . . . . folks are around
    me, but they are no household of mine.

Ever the hard and unsunk ground,
Ever the eaters and drinkers . . . . ever the upward and
    downward sun . . . . ever the air and the ceaseless tides,

Ever myself and my neighbors, refreshing and wicked
    and real,
Ever the old inexplicable query . . . . ever that thorned
    thumb—that breath of itches and thirsts,
Ever the vexer's hoot! hoot! till we find where the sly one
    hides and bring him forth;
Ever love . . . . ever the sobbing liquid of life,
Ever the bandage under the chin . . . . ever the tressels
    of death.

Here and there with dimes on the eyes walking,
To feed the greed of the belly the brains liberally spooning,
Tickets buying or taking or selling, but in to the feast never
    once going;
Many sweating and ploughing and thrashing, and then the
    chaff for payment receiving,
A few idly owning, and they the wheat continually claiming.

This is the city . . . . and I am one of the citizens;
Whatever interests the rest interests me . . . . politics,
    churches, newspapers, schools,
Benevolent societies, improvements, banks, tariffs, steamships,
    factories, markets,
Stocks and stores and real estate and personal estate.

They who piddle and patter here in collars and tailed coats
    . . . . I am aware who they are . . . . and that they are
    not worms or fleas,
I acknowledge the duplicates of myself under all the scrape-
    lipped and pipe-legged concealments.

The weakest and shallowest is deathless with me,
What I do and say the same waits for them,
Every thought that flounders in me the same flounders in
    them.

I know perfectly well my own egotism,
And know my omniverous words, and cannot say any
    less,
And would fetch you whoever you are flush with myself.

My words are words of a questioning, and to indicate reality;
This printed and bound book . . . . but the printer and the
    printing-office boy?
The marriage estate and settlement . . . . but the body and
    mind of the bridegroom? also those of the bride?
The panorama of the sea . . . . but the sea itself?
The well-taken photographs . . . . but your wife or friend
    close and solid in your arms?
The fleet of ships of the line and all the modern
    improvements . . . . but the craft and pluck of the
    admiral?
The dishes and fare and furniture . . . . but the host and
    hostess, and the look out of their eyes?
The sky up there . . . . yet here or next door or across the
    way?
The saints and sages in history . . . . but you yourself?
Sermons and creeds and theology . . . . but the human
    brain, and what is called reason, and what is called love,
    and what is called life?

I do not despise you priests;
My faith is the greatest of faiths and the least of faiths,
Enclosing all worship ancient and modern, and all between
    ancient and modern,
Believing I shall come again upon the earth after five
    thousand years,
Waiting responses from oracles . . . . honoring the gods
    . . . . saluting the sun,
Making a fetish of the first rock or stump . . . . powowing
    with sticks in the circle of obis,
Helping the lama or brahmin as he trims the lamps of
    the idols,
Dancing yet through the streets in a phallic procession . . . .
    rapt and austere in the woods, a gymnosophist,
Drinking mead from the skull-cup . . . . to shasta and vedas
    admirant . . . . minding the koran,
Walking the teokallis, spotted with gore from the stone and
    knife—beating the serpent-skin drum;
Accepting the gospels, accepting him that was crucified,
    knowing assuredly that he is divine,

To the mass kneeling—to the puritan's prayer rising—sitting
    patiently in a pew,
Ranting and frothing in my insane crisis—waiting dead-like
    till my spirit arouses me;
Looking forth on pavement and land, and outside of
    pavement and land,
Belonging to the winders of the circuit of circuits.

One of that centripetal and centrifugal gang,
I turn and talk like a man leaving charges before a journey.

Down-hearted doubters, dull and excluded,
Frivolous sullen moping angry affected disheartened
    atheistical,
I know every one of you, and know the unspoken
    interrogatories,
By experience I know them.

How the flukes splash!
How they contort rapid as lightning, with spasms and spouts
    of blood!

Be at peace bloody flukes of doubters and sullen mopers,
I take my place among you as much as among any;
The past is the push of you and me and all precisely the same,
And the night is for you and me and all,
And what is yet untried and afterward is for you and me
    and all.

I do not know what is untried and afterward,
But I know it is sure and alive, and sufficient.

Each who passes is considered, and each who stops is
    considered, and not a single one can it fail.

It cannot fail the young man who died and was buried,
Nor the young woman who died and was put by his side,
Nor the little child that peeped in at the door and then drew
    back and was never seen again,
Nor the old man who has lived without purpose, and feels it
    with bitterness worse than gall,

Nor him in the poorhouse tubercled by rum and the bad
    disorder,
Nor the numberless slaughtered and wrecked . . . . nor the
    brutish koboo, called the ordure of humanity,
Nor the sacs merely floating with open mouths for food to
    slip in,
Nor any thing in the earth, or down in the oldest graves of
    the earth,
Nor any thing in the myriads of spheres, nor one of the
    myriads of myriads that inhabit them,
Nor the present, nor the least wisp that is known.

It is time to explain myself . . . . let us stand up.

What is known I strip away . . . . I launch all men and
    women forward with me into the unknown.

The clock indicates the moment . . . . but what does
    eternity indicate?

Eternity lies in bottomless reservoirs . . . . its buckets are
    rising forever and ever,
They pour and they pour and they exhale away.

We have thus far exhausted trillions of winters and summers;
There are trillions ahead, and trillions ahead of them.

Births have brought us richness and variety,
And other births will bring us richness and variety.

I do not call one greater and one smaller,
That which fills its period and place is equal to any.

Were mankind murderous or jealous upon you my brother
    or my sister?
I am sorry for you . . . . they are not murderous or jealous
    upon me;
All has been gentle with me . . . . . . I keep no account
    with lamentation;
What have I to do with lamentation?

I am an acme of things accomplished, and I an encloser of
    things to be.

My feet strike an apex of the apices of the stairs,
On every step bunches of ages, and larger bunches between
    the steps,
All below duly traveled—and still I mount and mount.

Rise after rise bow the phantoms behind me,
Afar down I see the huge first Nothing, the vapor from the
    nostrils of death,
I know I was even there . . . . I waited unseen and
    always,
And slept while God carried me through the lethargic
    mist,
And took my time . . . . and took no hurt from the fœtid
    carbon.

Long I was hugged close . . . . long and long.

Immense have been the preparations for me,
Faithful and friendly the arms that have helped me.

Cycles ferried my cradle, rowing and rowing like cheerful
    boatmen;
For room to me stars kept aside in their own rings,
They sent influences to look after what was to hold me.

Before I was born out of my mother generations guided me,
My embryo has never been torpid . . . . nothing could
    overlay it;
For it the nebula cohered to an orb . . . . the long slow
    strata piled to rest it on . . . . vast vegetables gave it
    sustenance,
Monstrous sauroids transported it in their mouths and
    deposited it with care.

All forces have been steadily employed to complete and
    delight me,
Now I stand on this spot with my soul.

Span of youth! Ever-pushed elasticity! Manhood balanced
    and florid and full!

My lovers suffocate me!
Crowding my lips, and thick in the pores of my skin,
Jostling me through streets and public halls . . . . coming
    naked to me at night,
Crying by day Ahoy from the rocks of the river . . . .
    swinging and chirping over my head,
Calling my name from flowerbeds or vines or tangled
    underbrush,
Or while I swim in the bath . . . . or drink from the
    pump at the corner . . . . or the curtain is down at the
    opera . . . . or I glimpse at a woman's face in the
    railroad car;
Lighting on every moment of my life,
Bussing my body with soft and balsamic busses,
Noiselessly passing handfuls out of their hearts and giving
    them to be mine.

Old age superbly rising! Ineffable grace of dying days!

Every condition promulges not only itself . . . . it promulges
    what grows after and out of itself,
And the dark hush promulges as much as any.

I open my scuttle at night and see the far-sprinkled
    systems,
And all I see, multiplied as high as I can cipher, edge but
    the rim of the farther systems.

Wider and wider they spread, expanding and always
    expanding,
Outward and outward and forever outward.

My sun has his sun, and round him obediently wheels,
He joins with his partners a group of superior circuit,
And greater sets follow, making specks of the greatest inside
    them.

There is no stoppage, and never can be stoppage;
If I and you and the worlds and all beneath or upon their
    surfaces, and all the palpable life, were this moment
    reduced back to a pallid float, it would not avail in the
    long run,
We should surely bring up again where we now stand,
And as surely go as much farther, and then farther and farther.

A few quadrillions of eras, a few octillions of cubic leagues,
    do not hazard the span, or make it impatient,
They are but parts . . . . any thing is but a part.

See ever so far . . . . there is limitless space outside of that,
Count ever so much . . . . there is limitless time around that.

Our rendezvous is fitly appointed . . . . God will be there
    and wait till we come.

I know I have the best of time and space—and that I was
    never measured, and never will be measured.

I tramp a perpetual journey,
My signs are a rain-proof coat and good shoes and a staff
    cut from the woods;
No friend of mine takes his ease in my chair,
I have no chair, nor church nor philosophy;
I lead no man to a dinner-table or library or exchange,
But each man and each woman of you I lead upon a knoll,
My left hand hooks you round the waist,
My right hand points to landscapes of continents, and a
    plain public road.

Not I, not any one else can travel that road for you,
You must travel it for yourself.

It is not far . . . . it is within reach,
Perhaps you have been on it since you were born, and did
    not know,
Perhaps it is every where on water and on land.

Shoulder your duds, and I will mine, and let us hasten forth;
Wonderful cities and free nations we shall fetch as we go.

If you tire, give me both burdens, and rest the chuff of your
    hand on my hip,
And in due time you shall repay the same service to me;
For after we start we never lie by again.

This day before dawn I ascended a hill and looked at the
    crowded heaven,
And I said to my spirit, When we become the enfolders of
    those orbs and the pleasure and knowledge of every
    thing in them, shall we be filled and satisfied then?
And my spirit said No, we level that lift to pass and
    continue beyond.

You are also asking me questions, and I hear you;
I answer that I cannot answer . . . . you must find out for
    yourself.

Sit awhile wayfarer,
Here are biscuits to eat and here is milk to drink,
But as soon as you sleep and renew yourself in sweet clothes
    I will certainly kiss you with my goodbye kiss and open
    the gate for your egress hence.

Long enough have you dreamed contemptible dreams,
Now I wash the gum from your eyes,
You must habit yourself to the dazzle of the light and of
    every moment of your life

Long have you timidly waded, holding a plank by the shore,
Now I will you to be a bold swimmer,
To jump off in the midst of the sea, and rise again and nod
    to me and shout, and laughingly dash with your hair.

I am the teacher of athletes,
He that by me spreads a wider breast than my own proves
    the width of my own,
He most honors my style who learns under it to destroy the
    teacher.

The boy I love, the same becomes a man not through derived
    power but in his own right,
Wicked, rather than virtuous out of conformity or fear,
Fond of his sweetheart, relishing well his steak,
Unrequited love or a slight cutting him worse than a wound
    cuts,
First rate to ride, to fight, to hit the bull's eye, to sail a skiff,
    to sing a song or play on the banjo,
Preferring scars and faces pitted with smallpox over all
    latherers and those that keep out of the sun.

I teach straying from me, yet who can stray from me?
I follow you whoever you are from the present hour;
My words itch at your ears till you understand them.

I do not say these things for a dollar, or to fill up the time
    while I wait for a boat;
It is you talking just as much as myself . . . . I act as the
    tongue of you,
It was tied in your mouth . . . . in mine it begins to be
    loosened.

I swear I will never mention love or death inside a house,
And I swear I never will translate myself at all, only to him
    or her who privately stays with me in the open air.

If you would understand me go to the heights or water-shore,
The nearest gnat is an explanation and a drop or the motion
    of waves a key,
The maul the oar and the handsaw second my words.

No shuttered room or school can commune with me,
But roughs and little children better than they.

The young mechanic is closest to me . . . . he knows me
    pretty well,
The woodman that takes his axe and jug with him shall take
    me with him all day,
The farmboy ploughing in the field feels good at the sound
    of my voice,

In vessels that sail my words must sail . . . . I go with
    fishermen and seamen, and love them,
My face rubs to the hunter's face when he lies down alone in
    his blanket,
The driver thinking of me does not mind the jolt of his
    wagon,
The young mother and old mother shall comprehend me,
The girl and the wife rest the needle a moment and forget
    where they are,
They and all would resume what I have told them.

I have said that the soul is not more than the body,
And I have said that the body is not more than the soul,
And nothing, not God, is greater to one than one's-self is,
And whoever walks a furlong without sympathy walks to his
    own funeral, dressed in his shroud,
And I or you pocketless of a dime may purchase the pick of
    the earth,
And to glance with an eye or show a bean in its pod
    confounds the learning of all times,
And there is no trade or employment but the young man
    following it may become a hero,
And there is no object so soft but it makes a hub for the
    wheeled universe,
And any man or woman shall stand cool and supercilious
    before a million universes.

And I call to mankind, Be not curious about God,
For I who am curious about each am not curious about God,
No array of terms can say how much I am at peace about
    God and about death.

I hear and behold God in every object, yet I understand
    God not in the least,
Nor do I understand who there can be more wonderful than
    myself.

Why should I wish to see God better than this day?
I see something of God each hour of the twenty-four, and
    each moment then,

In the faces of men and women I see God, and in my own
    face in the glass;
I find letters from God dropped in the street, and every one
    is signed by God's name,
And I leave them where they are, for I know that others will
    punctually come forever and ever.

And as to you death, and you bitter hug of mortality . . . .
    it is idle to try to alarm me.

To his work without flinching the accoucheur comes,
I see the elderhand pressing receiving supporting,
I recline by the sills of the exquisite flexible doors . . . . and
    mark the outlet, and mark the relief and escape.

And as to you corpse I think you are good manure, but that
    does not offend me,
I smell the white roses sweetscented and growing,
I reach to the leafy lips . . . . I reach to the polished breasts
    of melons.

And as to you life, I reckon you are the leavings of many
    deaths,
No doubt I have died myself ten thousand times before.

I hear you whispering there O stars of heaven,
O suns . . . . O grass of graves . . . . O perpetual transfers
    and promotions . . . . if you do not say anything how
    can I say anything?

Of the turbid pool that lies in the autumn forest,
Of the moon that descends the steeps of the soughing
    twilight,
Toss, sparkles of day and dusk . . . . toss on the black stems
    that decay in the muck,
Toss to the moaning gibberish of the dry limbs.

I ascend from the moon . . . . I ascend from the night,
And perceive of the ghastly glitter the sunbeams
    reflected,

And debouch to the steady and central from the offspring
　　great or small.

There is that in me . . . . I do not know what it is . . . .
　　but I know it is in me.

Wrenched and sweaty . . . . calm and cool then my body
　　becomes;
I sleep . . . . I sleep long.

I do not know it . . . . it is without name . . . . it is a word
　　unsaid,
It is not in any dictionary or utterance or symbol.

Something it swings on more than the earth I swing on,
To it the creation is the friend whose embracing awakes me.

Perhaps I might tell more . . . . Outlines! I plead for my
　　brothers and sisters.

Do you see O my brothers and sisters?
It is not chaos or death . . . . it is form and union and plan
　　. . . . it is eternal life . . . . it is happiness.

The past and present wilt . . . . I have filled them and
　　emptied them,
And proceed to fill my next fold of the future.

Listener up there! Here you . . . . what have you to confide
　　to me?
Look in my face while I snuff the sidle of evening,
Talk honestly, for no one else hears you, and I stay only a
　　minute longer.

Do I contradict myself?
Very well then . . . . I contradict myself;
I am large . . . . I contain multitudes.

I concentrate toward them that are nigh . . . . I wait on
　　the door-slab.

Who has done his day's work and will soonest be through
    with his supper?
Who wishes to walk with me?

Will you speak before I am gone? Will you prove already too
    late?

The spotted hawk swoops by and accuses me . . . . he
    complains of my gab and my loitering.

I too am not a bit tamed . . . . I too am untranslatable,
I sound my barbaric yawp over the roofs of the world.

The last scud of day holds back for me,
It flings my likeness after the rest and true as any on the
    shadowed wilds,
It coaxes me to the vapor and the dusk.

I depart as air . . . . I shake my white locks at the runaway
    sun,
I effuse my flesh in eddies and drift it in lacy jags.

I bequeath myself to the dirt to grow from the grass I
    love,
If you want me again look for me under your bootsoles.

You will hardly know who I am or what I mean,
But I shall be good health to you nevertheless,
And filter and fibre your blood.

Failing to fetch me at first keep encouraged,
Missing me one place search another,
I stop some where waiting for you

———————

Come closer to me,
Push close my lovers and take the best I possess,
Yield closer and closer and give me the best you
    possess.

This is unfinished business with me . . . . how is it with you?
I was chilled with the cold types and cylinder and wet paper
    between us.

I pass so poorly with paper and types . . . . I must pass
    with the contact of bodies and souls.

I do not thank you for liking me as I am, and liking the touch
    of me . . . . I know that it is good for you to do so.

Were all educations practical and ornamental well displayed
    out of me, what would it amount to?
Were I as the head teacher or charitable proprietor or wise
    statesman, what would it amount to?
Were I to you as the boss employing and paying you, would
    that satisfy you?

The learned and virtuous and benevolent, and the usual terms;
A man like me, and never the usual terms.

Neither a servant nor a master am I,
I take no sooner a large price than a small price . . . . I will
    have my own whoever enjoys me,
I will be even with you, and you shall be even with me.

If you are a workman or workwoman I stand as nigh as the
    nighest that works in the same shop,
If you bestow gifts on your brother or dearest friend, I
    demand as good as your brother or dearest friend,
If your lover or husband or wife is welcome by day or night,
    I must be personally as welcome;
If you have become degraded or ill, then I will become so
    for your sake;
If you remember your foolish and outlawed deeds, do you
    think I cannot remember my foolish and outlawed deeds?
If you carouse at the table I say I will carouse at the
    opposite side of the table;
If you meet some stranger in the street and love him or her,
    do I not often meet strangers in the street and love
    them?

If you see a good deal remarkable in me I see just as much
remarkable in you.

Why what have you thought of yourself?
Is it you then that thought yourself less?
Is it you that thought the President greater than you? or
the rich better off than you? or the educated wiser than
you?

Because you are greasy or pimpled—or that you was once
drunk, or a thief, or diseased, or rheumatic, or a
prostitute—or are so now—or from frivolity or
impotence—or that you are no scholar, and never saw
your name in print . . . . do you give in that you are
any less immortal?

Souls of men and women! it is not you I call unseen,
unheard, untouchable and untouching;
It is not you I go argue pro and con about, and to settle
whether you are alive or no;
I own publicly who you are, if nobody else owns . . . . and
see and hear you, and what you give and take;
What is there you cannot give and take?

I see not merely that you are polite or whitefaced . . . .
married or single . . . . citizens of old states or citizens
of new states . . . . eminent in some profession . . . .
a lady or gentleman in a parlor . . . . or dressed in the
jail uniform . . . . or pulpit uniform,
Not only the free Utahan, Kansian, or Arkansian . . . . not
only the free Cuban . . . not merely the slave . . . .
not Mexican native, or Flatfoot, or negro from Africa,
Iroquois eating the warflesh—fishtearer in his lair of rocks
and sand . . . . Esquimaux in the dark cold snowhouse
. . . . Chinese with his transverse eyes . . . .
Bedowee—or wandering nomad—or tabounschik at the
head of his droves,
Grown, half-grown, and babe—of this country and every
country, indoors and outdoors I see . . . . and all else
is behind or through them.

The wife—and she is not one jot less than the husband,
The daughter—and she is just as good as the son,
The mother—and she is every bit as much as the father.

Offspring of those not rich—boys apprenticed to trades,
Young fellows working on farms and old fellows working on
    farms;
The naive . . . . the simple and hardy . . . . he going to
    the polls to vote . . . . he who has a good time, and he
    who has a bad time;
Mechanics, southerners, new arrivals, sailors, mano'warsmen,
    merchantmen, coasters,
All these I see . . . . but nigher and farther the same I see;
None shall escape me, and none shall wish to escape me.

I bring what you much need, yet always have,
I bring not money or amours or dress or eating . . . . but I
    bring as good;
And send no agent or medium . . . . and offer no
    representative of value—but offer the value itself.

There is something that comes home to one now and
    perpetually,
It is not what is printed or preached or discussed . . . .
    it eludes discussion and print,
It is not to be put in a book . . . . it is not in this book,
It is for you whoever you are . . . . it is no farther from
    you than your hearing and sight are from you,
It is hinted by nearest and commonest and readiest . . . .
    it is not them, though it is endlessly provoked by
    them . . . . What is there ready and near you now?

You may read in many languages and read nothing about it;
You may read the President's message and read nothing
    about it there,
Nothing in the reports from the state department or treasury
    department . . . . or in the daily papers, or the weekly
    papers,
Or in the census returns or assessors' returns or prices current
    or any accounts of stock.

The sun and stars that float in the open air . . . . the
    appleshaped earth and we upon it . . . . surely the drift
    of them is something grand;
I do not know what it is except that it is grand, and that it
    is happiness,
And that the enclosing purport of us here is not a speculation,
    or bon-mot or reconnoissance,
And that it is not something which by luck may turn out
    well for us, and without luck must be a failure for us,
And not something which may yet be retracted in a certain
    contingency.

The light and shade—the curious sense of body and
    identity—the greed that with perfect complaisance
    devours all things—the endless pride and outstretching
    of man—unspeakable joys and sorrows,
The wonder every one sees in every one else he sees . . . .
    and the wonders that fill each minute of time forever
    and each acre of surface and space forever,
Have you reckoned them as mainly for a trade or farmwork?
    or for the profits of a store? or to achieve yourself a
    position? or to fill a gentleman's leisure or a lady's
    leisure?

Have you reckoned the landscape took substance and form
    that it might be painted in a picture?
Or men and women that they might be written of, and
    songs sung?
Or the attraction of gravity and the great laws and harmonious
    combinations and the fluids of the air as subjects for the
    savans?
Or the brown land and the blue sea for maps and charts?
Or the stars to be put in constellations and named fancy
    names?
Or that the growth of seeds is for agricultural tables or
    agriculture itself?

Old institutions . . . . these arts libraries legends collections—
    and the practice handed along in manufactures . . . .
    will we rate them so high?

Will we rate our prudence and business so high? I
have no objection,
I rate them as high as the highest . . . . but a child born of
a woman and man I rate beyond all rate.

We thought our Union grand and our Constitution grand;
I do not say they are not grand and good—for they are,
I am this day just as much in love with them as you,
But I am eternally in love with you and with all my fellows
upon the earth.

We consider the bibles and religions divine . . . . I do not
say they are not divine,
I say they have all grown out of you and may grow out of
you still,
It is not they who give the life . . . . it is you who give the
life;
Leaves are not more shed from the trees or trees from the
earth than they are shed out of you.

The sum of all known value and respect I add up in you
whoever you are;
The President is up there in the White House for you . . . .
it is not you who are here for him,
The Secretaries act in their bureaus for you . . . . not you
here for them,
The Congress convenes every December for you,
Laws, courts, the forming of states, the charters of cities,
the going and coming of commerce and mails are all
for you.

All doctrines, all politics and civilization exurge from you,
All sculpture and monuments and anything inscribed
anywhere are tallied in you,
The gist of histories and statistics as far back as the records
reach is in you this hour—and myths and tales the same;
If you were not breathing and walking here where would
they all be?
The most renowned poems would be ashes . . . . orations
and plays would be vacuums.

All architecture is what you do to it when you look upon it;
Did you think it was in the white or gray stone? or the lines
of the arches and cornices?

All music is what awakens from you when you are reminded
by the instruments,
It is not the violins and the cornets . . . . it is not the oboe
nor the beating drums—nor the notes of the baritone
singer singing his sweet romanza . . . . nor those of
the men's chorus, nor those of the women's chorus,
It is nearer and farther than they.

Will the whole come back then?
Can each see the signs of the best by a look in the
lookingglass? Is there nothing greater or more?
Does all sit there with you and here with me?

The old forever new things . . . . you foolish child! . . . .
the closest simplest things—this moment with you,
Your person and every particle that relates to your person,
The pulses of your brain waiting their chance and
encouragement at every deed or sight;
Anything you do in public by day, and anything you do in
secret betweendays,
What is called right and what is called wrong . . . . what
you behold or touch . . . . what causes your anger or
wonder,
The anklechain of the slave, the bed of the bedhouse, the
cards of the gambler, the plates of the forger;
What is seen or learned in the street, or intuitively learned,
What is learned in the public school—spelling, reading,
writing and ciphering . . . . the blackboard and the
teacher's diagrams:
The panes of the windows and all that appears through them
. . . . the going forth in the morning and the aimless
spending of the day;
(What is it that you made money? what is it that you got
what you wanted?)
The usual routine . . . . the workshop, factory, yard, office,
store, or desk;

The jaunt of hunting or fishing, or the life of hunting or
　　fishing,
Pasturelife, foddering, milking and herding, and all the
　　personnel and usages;
The plum-orchard and apple-orchard . . . . gardening . .
　　seedlings, cuttings, flowers and vines,
Grains and manures . . marl, clay, loam . . the subsoil
　　plough . . the shovel and pick and rake and hoe . .
　　irrigation and draining;
The currycomb . . the horse-cloth . . the halter and bridle
　　and bits . . the very wisps of straw,
The barn and barn-yard . . the bins and mangers . . the
　　mows and racks:
Manufactures . . commerce . . engineering . . the building
　　of cities, and every trade carried on there . . and the
　　implements of every trade,
The anvil and tongs and hammer . . the axe and wedge . .
　　the square and mitre and jointer and smoothingplane;
The plumbob and trowel and level . . the wall-scaffold, and
　　the work of walls and ceilings . . or any mason-work:
The ship's compass . . the sailor's tarpaulin . . the stays and
　　lanyards, and the ground-tackle for anchoring or
　　mooring,
The sloop's tiller . . the pilot's wheel and bell . . the yacht
　　or fish-smack . . the great gay-pennanted three-hundred-
　　foot steamboat under full headway, with her proud fat
　　breasts and her delicate swift-flashing paddles;
The trail and line and hooks and sinkers . . the seine, and
　　hauling the seine;
Smallarms and rifles . . . . the powder and shot and caps
　　and wadding . . . . the ordnance for war . . . . the
　　carriages:
Everyday objects . . . . the housechairs, the carpet, the bed
　　and the counterpane of the bed, and him or her
　　sleeping at night, and the wind blowing, and the
　　indefinite noises:
The snowstorm or rainstorm . . . . the tow-trowsers . . . .
　　the lodge-hut in the woods, and the still-hunt:
City and country . . fireplace and candle . . gaslight and
　　heater and aqueduct;

The message of the governor, mayor, or chief of police . . . .
  the dishes of breakfast or dinner or supper;
The bunkroom, the fire-engine, the string-team, and the car
  or truck behind;
The paper I write on or you write on . . and every word we
  write . . and every cross and twirl of the pen . . and the
  curious way we write what we think . . . . yet very
  faintly;
The directory, the detector, the ledger . . . . the books in
  ranks or the bookshelves . . . . the clock attached to
  the wall,
The ring on your finger . . the lady's wristlet . . the hammers
  of stonebreakers or coppersmiths . . the druggist's
  vials and jars;
The etui of surgical instruments, and the etui of oculist's or
  aurist's instruments, or dentist's instruments;
Glassblowing, grinding of wheat and corn . . casting, and
  what is cast . . tinroofing, shingledressing,
Shipcarpentering, flagging of sidewalks by flaggers . .
  dockbuilding, fishcuring, ferrying;
The pump, the piledriver, the great derrick . . the coalkiln
  and brickkiln,
Ironworks or whiteleadworks . . the sugarhouse . . steam-
  saws, and the great mills and factories;
The cottonbale . . the stevedore's hook . . the saw and buck
  of the sawyer . . the screen of the coalscreener . . the
  mould of the moulder . . the workingknife of the
  butcher;
The cylinder press . . the handpress . . the frisket and
  tympan . . the compositor's stick and rule,
The implements for daguerreotyping . . . . the tools of the
  rigger or grappler or sailmaker or blockmaker,
Goods of guttapercha or papiermache . . . . colors and
  brushes . . . . glaziers' implements,
The veneer and gluepot . . the confectioner's ornaments
  . . the decanter and glasses . . the shears and
  flatiron;
The awl and kneestrap . . the pint measure and quart
  measure . . the counter and stool . . the writingpen of
  quill or metal;

Billiards and tenpins . . . . the ladders and hanging ropes of
    the gymnasium, and the manly exercises;
The designs for wallpapers or oilcloths or carpets . . . . the
    fancies for goods for women . . . . the bookbinder's
    stamps;
Leatherdressing, coachmaking, boilermaking, ropetwisting,
    distilling, signpainting, limeburning, coopering,
    cottonpicking,
The walkingbeam of the steam-engine . . the throttle and
    governors, and the up and down rods,
Stavemachines and plainingmachines . . . . the cart of the
    carman . . the omnibus . . the ponderous dray;
The snowplough and two engines pushing it . . . . the ride
    in the express train of only one car . . . . the swift go
    through a howling storm:
The bearhunt or coonhunt . . . . the bonfire of shavings in
    the open lot in the city . . the crowd of children
    watching;
The blows of the fighting-man . . the upper cut and one-
    two-three;
The shopwindows . . . . the coffins in the sexton's
    wareroom . . . . the fruit on the fruitstand . . . . the
    beef on the butcher's stall,
The bread and cakes in the bakery . . . . the white and red
    pork in the pork-store;
The milliner's ribbons . . the dressmaker's patterns . . . .
    the tea-table . . the homemade sweetmeats:
The column of wants in the one-cent paper . . the news by
    telegraph . . . . the amusements and operas and shows:
The cotton and woolen and linen you wear . . . . the money
    you make and spend;
Your room and bedroom . . . . your piano-forte . . . . the
    stove and cookpans,
The house you live in . . . . the rent . . . . the other
    tenants . . . . the deposite in the savings-bank . . . .
    the trade at the grocery,
The pay on Saturday night . . . . the going home, and the
    purchases;
In them the heft of the heaviest . . . . in them far more
    than you estimated, and far less also,

In them, not yourself . . . . you and your soul enclose all
    things, regardless of estimation,
In them your themes and hints and provokers . . if not, the
    whole earth has no themes or hints or provokers, and
    never had.

I do not affirm what you see beyond is futile . . . . I do not
    advise you to stop,
I do not say leadings you thought great are not great,
But I say that none lead to greater or sadder or happier than
    those lead to.

Will you seek afar off? You surely come back at last,
In things best known to you finding the best or as good as
    the best,
In folks nearest to you finding also the sweetest and strongest
    and lovingest,
Happiness not in another place, but this place . . not for
    another hour, but this hour,
Man in the first you see or touch . . . . always in your
    friend or brother or nighest neighbor . . . . Woman in
    your mother or lover or wife,
And all else thus far known giving place to men and women.

When the psalm sings instead of the singer,
When the script preaches instead of the preacher,
When the pulpit descends and goes instead of the carver that
    carved the supporting desk,
When the sacred vessels or the bits of the eucharist, or the
    lath and plast, procreate as effectually as the young
    silversmiths or bakers, or the masons in their overalls,
When a university course convinces like a slumbering woman
    and child convince,
When the minted gold in the vault smiles like the
    nightwatchman's daughter,
When warrantee deeds loafe in chairs opposite and are r
    friendly companions,
I intend to reach them my hand and make as much /
    as I do of men and women.

To think of time . . . . to think through the retrospection,
To think of today . . and the ages continued henceforward.

Have you guessed you yourself would not continue? Have
     you dreaded those earth-beetles?
Have you feared the future would be nothing to you?

Is today nothing? Is the beginningless past nothing?
If the future is nothing they are just as surely nothing.

To think that the sun rose in the east . . . . that men and
     women were flexible and real and alive . . . . that every
     thing was real and alive;
To think that you and I did not see feel think nor bear our
     part,
To think that we are now here and bear our part.

Not a day passes . . not a minute or second without an
     accouchement;
Not a day passes . . not a minute or second without a
     corpse.

When the dull nights are over, and the dull days also,
When the soreness of lying so much in bed is over,
When the physician, after long putting off, gives the silent
     and terrible look for an answer,
When the children come hurried and weeping, and the
     brothers and sisters have been sent for,
When medicines stand unused on the shelf, and the camphor-
     smell has pervaded the rooms,
When the faithful hand of the living does not desert the hand
     of the dying,
When the twitching lips press lightly on the forehead of the
     dying,
When the breath ceases and the pulse of the heart ceases,
Then the corpse-limbs stretch on the bed, and the living look
     upon them,
They are palpable as the living are palpable.

The living look upon the corpse with their eyesight,
But without eyesight lingers a different living and looks
    curiously on the corpse.

To think that the rivers will come to flow, and the snow fall,
    and fruits ripen . . and act upon others as upon us now
    . . . . yet not act upon us;
To think of all these wonders of city and country . . and
    others taking great interest in them . . and we taking
    small interest in them.

To think how eager we are in building our houses,
To think others shall be just as eager . . and we quite
    indifferent.

I see one building the house that serves him a few years
    . . . . or seventy or eighty years at most;
I see one building the house that serves him longer than
    that.

Slowmoving and black lines creep over the whole earth . . . .
    they never cease . . . . they are the burial lines,
He that was President was buried, and he that is now
    President shall surely be buried.

Cold dash of waves at the ferrywharf,
Posh and ice in the river . . . . half-frozen mud in the streets,
A gray discouraged sky overhead . . . . the short last
    daylight of December,
A hearse and stages . . . . other vehicles give place,
The funeral of an old stagedriver . . . . the cortege mostly
    drivers.

Rapid the trot to the cemetery,
Duly rattles the deathbell . . . . the gate is passed . . . . the
    grave is halted at . . . . the living alight . . . . the
    hearse uncloses,
The coffin is lowered and settled . . . . the whip is laid on
    the coffin,

The earth is swiftly shovelled in . . . . a minute . . no one
    moves or speaks . . . . it is done,
He is decently put away . . . . is there anything more?

He was a goodfellow,
Freemouthed, quicktempered, not badlooking, able to take
    his own part,
Witty, sensitive to a slight, ready with life or death for a
    friend,
Fond of women, . . played some . . eat hearty and drank
    hearty,
Had known what it was to be flush . . grew lowspirited
    toward the last . . sickened . . was helped by a
    contribution,
Died aged forty-one years . . and that was his funeral.

Thumb extended or finger uplifted,
Apron, cape, gloves, strap . . . . wetweather clothes . . . .
    whip carefully chosen . . . . boss, spotter, starter, and
    hostler,
Somebody loafing on you, or you loafing on somebody . . . .
    headway . . . . man before and man behind,
Good day's work or bad day's work . . . . pet stock or
    mean stock . . . . first out or last out . . . . turning in
    at night,
To think that these are so much and so nigh to other drivers
    . . and he there takes no interest in them.

The markets, the government, the workingman's wages . . . .
    to think what account they are through our nights
    and days;
To think that other workingmen will make just as great
    account of them . . yet we make little or no account.

The vulgar and the refined . . . . what you call sin and
    what you call goodness . . to think how wide a
    difference;
To think the difference will still continue to others, yet we
    lie beyond the difference.

To think how much pleasure there is!
Have you pleasure from looking at the sky? Have you
    pleasure from poems?
Do you enjoy yourself in the city? or engaged in business?
    or planning a nomination and election? or with your
    wife and family?
Or with your mother and sisters? or in womanly housework?
    or the beautiful maternal cares?

These also flow onward to others . . . . you and I flow
    onward;
But in due time you and I shall take less interest in them.

Your farm and profits and crops . . . . to think how
    engrossed you are;
To think there will still be farms and profits and crops . . yet
    for you of what avail?

What will be will be well—for what is is well,
To take interest is well, and not to take interest shall be well.

The sky continues beautiful . . . . the pleasure of men with
    women shall never be sated . . nor the pleasure of
    women with men . . nor the pleasure from poems;
The domestic joys, the daily housework or business, the
    building of houses—they are not phantasms . . they
    have weight and form and location;
The farms and profits and crops . . the markets and wages
    and government . . they also are not phantasms;
The difference between sin and goodness is no apparition;
The earth is not an echo . . . . man and his life and all the
    things of his life are well-considered.

You are not thrown to the winds . . you gather certainly and
    safely around yourself,
Yourself! Yourself! Yourself forever and ever!

It is not to diffuse you that you were born of your mother
    and father—it is to identify you,

It is not that you should be undecided, but that you should
    be decided;
Something long preparing and formless is arrived and
    formed in you,
You are thenceforth secure, whatever comes or goes.

The threads that were spun are gathered . . . . the weft
    crosses the warp . . . . the pattern is systematic.

The preparations have every one been justified;
The orchestra have tuned their instruments sufficiently . . . .
    the baton has given the signal.

The guest that was coming . . . . he waited long for reasons
    . . . . he is now housed,
He is one of those who are beautiful and happy . . . .
    he is one of those that to look upon and be with is
    enough.

The law of the past cannot be eluded.
The law of the present and future cannot be eluded,
The law of the living cannot be eluded . . . . it is eternal,
The law of promotion and transformation cannot be eluded,
The law of heroes and good-doers cannot be eluded,
The law of drunkards and informers and mean persons
    cannot be eluded.

Slowmoving and black lines go ceaselessly over the earth,
Northerner goes carried and southerner goes carried . . . .
    and they on the Atlantic side and they on the Pacific,
    and they between, and all through the Mississippi
    country . . . . and all over the earth.

The great masters and kosmos are well as they go . . . . the
    heroes and good-doers are well,
The known leaders and inventors and the rich owners and
    pious and distinguished may be well,
But there is more account than that . . . . there is strict
    account of all.

The interminable hordes of the ignorant and wicked are not
      nothing,
The barbarians of Africa and Asia are not nothing,
The common people of Europe are not nothing . . . . the
      American aborigines are not nothing,
A zambo or a foreheadless Crowfoot or a Camanche is not
      nothing,
The infected in the immigrant hospital are not nothing . . . .
      the murderer or mean person is not nothing,
The perpetual succession of shallow people are not nothing
      as they go,
The prostitute is not nothing . . . . the mocker of religion
      is not nothing as he goes.

I shall go with the rest . . . . we have satisfaction:
I have dreamed that we are not to be changed so much . . . .
      nor the law of us changed;
I have dreamed that heroes and good-doers shall be under
      the present and past law,
And that murderers and drunkards and liars shall be under
      the present and past law;
For I have dreamed that the law they are under now is enough.

And I have dreamed that the satisfaction is not so much
      changed . . . . and that there is no life without
      satisfaction;
What is the earth? what are body and soul without satisfaction?

I shall go with the rest,
We cannot be stopped at a given point . . . . that is no
      satisfaction;
To show us a good thing or a few good things for a space of
      time—that is no satisfaction;
We must have the indestructible breed of the best, regardless
      of time.

If otherwise, all these things came but to ashes of dung;
If maggots and rats ended us, then suspicion and treachery
      and death.

Do you suspect death? If I were to suspect death I should
    die now,
Do you think I could walk pleasantly and well-suited toward
    annihilation?

Pleasantly and well-suited I walk,
Whither I walk I cannot define, but I know it is good,
The whole universe indicates that it is good,
The past and the present indicate that it is good.

How beautiful and perfect are the animals! How perfect is
    my soul!
How perfect the earth, and the minutest thing upon it!
What is called good is perfect, and what is called sin is just
    as perfect;
The vegetables and minerals are all perfect . . and the
    imponderable fluids are perfect;
Slowly and surely they have passed on to this, and slowly
    and surely they will yet pass on.

O my soul! if I realize you I have satisfaction,
Animals and vegetables! if I realize you I have satisfaction,
Laws of the earth and air! if I realize you I have satisfaction.

I cannot define my satisfaction . . yet it is so,
I cannot define my life . . yet it is so.

I swear I see now that every thing has an eternal soul!
The trees have, rooted in the ground . . . . the weeds of the
    sea have . . . . the animals.

I swear I think there is nothing but immortality!
That the exquisite scheme is for it, and the nebulous float is
    for it, and the cohering is for it,
And all preparation is for it . . and identity is for it . . and
    life and death are for it.

I wander all night in my vision,
Stepping with light feet . . . . swiftly and noiselessly
    stepping and stopping,
Bending with open eyes over the shut eyes of sleepers;
Wandering and confused . . . . lost to myself . . . . ill-
    assorted . . . . contradictory,
Pausing and gazing and bending and stopping.

How solemn they look there, stretched and still;
How quiet they breathe, the little children in their cradles.

The wretched features of ennuyees, the white features of
    corpses, the livid faces of drunkards, the sick-gray faces
    of onanists,
The gashed bodies on battlefields, the insane in their strong-
    doored rooms, the sacred idiots,
The newborn emerging from gates and the dying emerging
    from gates,
The night pervades them and enfolds them.

The married couple sleep calmly in their bed, he with his
    palm on the hip of the wife, and she with her palm on
    the hip of the husband,
The sisters sleep lovingly side by side in their bed,
The men sleep lovingly side by side in theirs,
And the mother sleeps with her little child carefully wrapped.

The blind sleep, and the deaf and dumb sleep,
The prisoner sleeps well in the prison . . . . the runaway son
    sleeps,
The murderer that is to be hung next day . . . . how does he
    sleep?
And the murdered person . . . . how does he sleep?

The female that loves unrequited sleeps,
And the male that loves unrequited sleeps;
The head of the moneymaker that plotted all day sleeps,
And the enraged and treacherous dispositions sleep.

I stand with drooping eyes by the worstsuffering and
    restless,
I pass my hands soothingly to and fro a few inches from them;
The restless sink in their beds . . . . they fitfully sleep.

The earth recedes from me into the night,
I saw that it was beautiful . . . . and I see that what is not
    the earth is beautiful.

I go from bedside to bedside . . . . I sleep close with the
    other sleepers, each in turn;
I dream in my dream all the dreams of the other dreamers,
And I become the other dreamers.

I am a dance . . . . Play up there! the fit is whirling me fast.

I am the everlaughing . . . . it is new moon and twilight,
I see the hiding of douceurs . . . . I see nimble ghosts
    whichever way I look,
Cache and cache again deep in the ground and sea, and
    where it is neither ground or sea.

Well do they do their jobs, those journeymen divine,
Only from me can they hide nothing and would not if they
    could;
I reckon I am their boss, and they make me a pet besides,
And surround me, and lead me and run ahead when I walk,
And lift their cunning covers and signify me with stretched
    arms, and resume the way;
Onward we move, a gay gang of blackguards with
    mirthshouting music and wildflapping pennants of joy.

I am the actor and the actress . . . . the voter . . the
    politician,
The emigrant and the exile . . the criminal that stood in the
    box,
He who has been famous, and he who shall be famous after
    today,
The stammerer . . . . the wellformed person . . the wasted
    or feeble person.

I am she who adorned herself and folded her hair
    expectantly,
My truant lover has come and it is dark.

Double yourself and receive me darkness,
Receive me and my lover too . . . . he will not let me go
    without him.

I roll myself upon you as upon a bed . . . . I resign myself
    to the dusk.

He whom I call answers me and takes the place of my lover,
He rises with me silently from the bed.

Darkness you are gentler than my lover . . . . his flesh was
    sweaty and panting,
I feel the hot moisture yet that he left me.

My hands are spread forth . . I pass them in all directions,
I would sound up the shadowy shore to which you are
    journeying.

Be careful, darkness . . . . already, what was it touched me?
I thought my lover had gone . . . . else darkness and he
    are one,
I hear the heart-beat . . . . I follow . . I fade away.

O hotcheeked and blushing! O foolish hectic!
O for pity's sake, no one must see me now! . . . . my
    clothes were stolen while I was abed,
Now I am thrust forth, where shall I run?

Pier that I saw dimly last night when I looked from the
    windows,
Pier out from the main, let me catch myself with you and
    stay . . . . I will not chafe you;
I feel ashamed to go naked about the world,
And am curious to know where my feet stand . . . . and
    what is this flooding me, childhood or manhood . . . .
    and the hunger that crosses the bridge between.

The cloth laps a first sweet eating and drinking,
Laps life-swelling yolks . . . . laps ear of rose-corn, milky
    and just ripened:
The white teeth stay, and the boss-tooth advances in
    darkness,
And liquor is spilled on lips and bosoms by touching glasses,
    and the best liquor afterward.

I descend my western course . . . . my sinews are flaccid,
Perfume and youth course through me, and I am their wake.

It is my face yellow and wrinkled instead of the old
    woman's,
I sit low in a strawbottom chair and carefully darn my
    grandson's stockings.

It is I too . . . . the sleepless widow looking out on the
    winter midnight,
I see the sparkles of starshine on the icy and pallid earth.

A shroud I see—and I am the shroud . . . . I wrap a body
    and lie in the coffin;
It is dark here underground . . . . it is not evil or pain here
    . . . . it is blank here, for reasons.

It seems to me that everything in the light and air ought to
    be happy;
Whoever is not in his coffin and the dark grave, let him
    know he has enough.

I see a beautiful gigantic swimmer swimming naked through
    the eddies of the sea,
His brown hair lies close and even to his head . . . . he
    strikes out with courageous arms . . . . he urges
    himself with his legs.

I see his white body . . . . I see his undaunted eyes;
I hate the swift-running eddies that would dash him
    headforemost on the rocks.

What are you doing you ruffianly red-trickled waves?
Will you kill the courageous giant? Will you kill him in the
     prime of his middle age?

Steady and long he struggles;
He is baffled and banged and bruised . . . . he holds out
     while his strength holds out,
The slapping eddies are spotted with his blood . . . . they
     bear him away . . . . they roll him and swing him and
     turn him:
His beautiful body is borne in the circling eddies . . . . it is
     continually bruised on rocks,
Swiftly and out of sight is borne the brave corpse.

I turn but do not extricate myself;
Confused . . . . a pastreading . . . . another, but with
     darkness yet.

The beach is cut by the razory ice-wind . . . . the wreck-
     guns sound,
The tempest lulls and the moon comes floundering through
     the drifts.

I look where the ship helplessly heads end on . . . . I hear
     the burst as she strikes . . I hear the howls of dismay
     . . . . they grow fainter and fainter.

I cannot aid with my wringing fingers;
I can but rush to the surf and let it drench me and freeze
     upon me.

I search with the crowd . . . . not one of the company is
     washed to us alive;
In the morning I help pick up the dead and lay them in
     rows in a barn.

Now of the old war-days . . the defeat at Brooklyn;
Washington stands inside the lines . . he stands on the
     entrenched hills amid a crowd of officers,

His face is cold and damp . . . . he cannot repress the
    weeping drops . . . . he lifts the glass perpetually
    to his eyes . . . . the color is blanched from his
    cheeks,
He sees the slaughter of the southern braves confided to him
    by their parents.

The same at last and at last when peace is declared,
He stands in the room of the old tavern . . . . the
    wellbeloved soldiers all pass through,
The officers speechless and slow draw near in their turns,
The chief encircles their necks with his arm and kisses them
    on the cheek,
He kisses lightly the wet cheeks one after another . . . . he
    shakes hands and bids goodbye to the army.

Now I tell what my mother told me today as we sat at
    dinner together,
Of when she was a nearly grown girl living home with her
    parents on the old homestead.

A red squaw came one breakfasttime to the old homestead,
On her back she carried a bundle of rushes for
    rushbottoming chairs;
Her hair straight shiny coarse black and profuse
    halfenveloped her face,
Her step was free and elastic . . . . her voice sounded
    exquisitely as she spoke.

My mother looked in delight and amazement at the
    stranger,
She looked at the beauty of her tallborne face and full and
    pliant limbs,
The more she looked upon her she loved her,
Never before had she seen such wonderful beauty and
    purity;
She made her sit on a bench by the jamb of the fireplace . . . .
    she cooked food for her,
She had no work to give her but she gave her remembrance
    and fondness.

The red squaw staid all the forenoon, and toward the middle
    of the afternoon she went away;
O my mother was loth to have her go away,
All the week she thought of her . . . . she watched for her
    many a month,
She remembered her many a winter and many a summer,
But the red squaw never came nor was heard of there again.

Now Lucifer was not dead . . . . or if he was I am his
    sorrowful terrible heir;
I have been wronged . . . . I am oppressed . . . . I hate
    him that oppresses me,
I will either destroy him, or he shall release me.

Damn him! how he does defile me,
How he informs against my brother and sister and takes pay
    for their blood,
How he laughs when I look down the bend after the
    steamboat that carries away my woman.

Now the vast dusk bulk that is the whale's bulk . . . . it
    seems mine,
Warily, sportsman! though I lie so sleepy and sluggish, my
    tap is death.

A show of the summer softness . . . . a contact of something
    unseen . . . . an amour of the light and air;
I am jealous and overwhelmed with friendliness,
And will go gallivant with the light and the air myself,
And have an unseen something to be in contact with them
    also.

O love and summer! you are in the dreams and in me,
Autumn and winter are in the dreams . . . . the farmer goes
    with his thrift,
The droves and crops increase . . . . the barns are wellfilled.

Elements merge in the night . . . . ships make tacks in the
    dreams . . . . the sailor sails . . . . the exile returns
    home,

The fugitive returns unharmed . . . . the immigrant is back
  beyond months and years;
The poor Irishman lives in the simple house of his
  childhood, with the wellknown neighbors and faces,
They warmly welcome him . . . . he is barefoot again . . . .
  he forgets he is welloff;
The Dutchman voyages home, and the Scotchman and
  Welchman voyage home . . and the native of the
  Mediterranean voyages home;
To every port of England and France and Spain enter
  wellfilled ships;
The Swiss foots it toward his hills . . . . the Prussian goes
  his way, and the Hungarian his way, and the Pole goes
  his way,
The Swede returns, and the Dane and Norwegian return.

The homeward bound and the outward bound,
The beautiful lost swimmer, the ennuyee, the onanist, the
  female that loves unrequited, the moneymaker,
The actor and actress . . those through with their parts and
  those waiting to commence,
The affectionate boy, the husband and wife, the voter, the
  nominee that is chosen and the nominee that has
  failed,
The great already known, and the great anytime after to
  day,
The stammerer, the sick, the perfectformed, the homely,
The criminal that stood in the box, the judge that sat and
  sentenced him, the fluent lawyers, the jury, the
  audience,
The laugher and weeper, the dancer, the midnight widow,
  the red squaw,
The consumptive, the erysipalite, the idiot, he that is
  wronged,
The antipodes, and every one between this and them in the
  dark,
I swear they are averaged now . . . . one is no better than
  the other,
The night and sleep have likened them and restored them.

I swear they are all beautiful,
Every one that sleeps is beautiful . . . . every thing in the
    dim night is beautiful,
The wildest and bloodiest is over and all is peace.

Peace is always beautiful,
The myth of heaven indicates peace and night.

The myth of heaven indicates the soul;
The soul is always beautiful . . . . it appears more or it
    appears less . . . . it comes or lags behind,
It comes from its embowered garden and looks pleasantly on
    itself and encloses the world;
Perfect and clean the genitals previously jetting, and perfect
    and clean the womb cohering,
The head wellgrown and proportioned and plumb, and the
    bowels and joints proportioned and plumb.

The soul is always beautiful,
The universe is duly in order . . . . every thing is in its place,
What is arrived is in its place, and what waits is in its place;
The twisted skull waits . . . . the watery or rotten blood
    waits,
The child of the glutton or venerealee waits long, and the
    child of the drunkard waits long, and the drunkard
    himself waits long,
The sleepers that lived and died wait . . . . the far advanced
    are to go on in their turns, and the far behind are to go
    on in their turns,
The diverse shall be no less diverse, but they shall flow and
    unite . . . . they unite now.

The sleepers are very beautiful as they lie unclothed,
They flow hand in hand over the whole earth from east to
    west as they lie unclothed;
The Asiatic and African are hand in hand . . . . the European
    and American are hand in hand,
Learned and unlearned are hand in hand . . and male and
    female are hand in hand;

The bare arm of the girl crosses the bare breast of her lover
    . . . . they press close without lust . . . . his lips press
    her neck,
The father holds his grown or ungrown son in his arms with
    measureless love . . . . and the son holds the father in
    his arms with measureless love,
The white hair of the mother shines on the white wrist of
    the daughter,
The breath of the boy goes with the breath of the man . . . .
    friend is inarmed by friend,
The scholar kisses the teacher and the teacher kisses the
    scholar . . . . the wronged is made right,
The call of the slave is one with the master's call . . and the
    master salutes the slave,
The felon steps forth from the prison . . . . the insane
    becomes sane . . . . the suffering of sick persons is
    relieved,
The sweatings and fevers stop . . the throat that was
    unsound is sound . . the lungs of the consumptive are
    resumed . . the poor distressed head is free,
The joints of the rheumatic move as smoothly as ever, and
    smoother than ever,
Stiflings and passages open . . . . the paralysed become
    supple,
The swelled and convulsed and congested awake to themselves
    in condition,
They pass the invigoration of the night and the chemistry of
    the night and awake.

I too pass from the night;
I stay awhile away O night, but I return to you again and
    love you;
Why should I be afraid to trust myself to you?
I am not afraid . . . . I have been well brought forward
    by you;
I love the rich running day, but I do not desert her in whom
    I lay so long;
I know not how I came of you, and I know not where I go
    with you . . . . but I know I came well and shall go well.

I will stop only a time with the night . . . . and rise betimes.

I will duly pass the day O my mother and duly return to you;
Not you will yield forth the dawn again more surely than you
    will yield forth me again,
Not the womb yields the babe in its time more surely than I
    shall be yielded from you in my time.

The bodies of men and women engirth me, and I engirth
    them,
They will not let me off nor I them till I go with them and
    respond to them and love them.

Was it dreamed whether those who corrupted their own live
    bodies could conceal themselves?
And whether those who defiled the living were as bad as they
    who defiled the dead?

The expression of the body of man or woman balks account,
The male is perfect and that of the female is perfect.

The expression of a wellmade man appears not only in his face,
It is in his limbs and joints also . . . . it is curiously in the
    joints of his hips and wrists,
It is in his walk . . the carriage of his neck . . the flex of his
    waist and knees . . . . dress does not hide him,
The strong sweet supple quality he has strikes through the
    cotton and flannel;
To see him pass conveys as much as the best poem . .
    perhaps more,
You linger to see his back and the back of his neck and
    shoulderside.

The sprawl and fulness of babes . . . . the bosoms and heads
    of women . . . . the folds of their dress . . . . their
    style as we pass in the street . . . . the contour of their
    shape downwards;
The swimmer naked in the swimmingbath . . seen as he
    swims through the salt transparent greenshine, or lies
    on his back and rolls silently with the heave of the water;

Framers bare-armed framing a house . . hoisting the
    beams in their places . . or using the mallet and
    mortising-chisel,
The bending forward and backward of rowers in rowboats
    . . . . the horseman in his saddle;
Girls and mothers and housekeepers in all their exquisite
    offices,
The group of laborers seated at noontime with their open
    dinnerkettles, and their wives waiting,
The female soothing a child . . . . the farmer's daughter in
    the garden or cowyard,
The woodman rapidly swinging his axe in the woods . . . .
    the young fellow hoeing corn . . . . the sleighdriver
    guiding his six horses through the crowd,
The wrestle of wrestlers . . two apprentice-boys, quite
    grown, lusty, goodnatured, nativeborn, out on the
    vacant lot at sundown after work,
The coats vests and caps thrown down . . the embrace of
    love and resistance,
The upperhold and underhold—the hair rumpled over and
    blinding the eyes;
The march of firemen in their own costumes—the play of
    the masculine muscle through cleansetting trowsers and
    waistbands,
The slow return from the fire . . . . the pause when the
    bell strikes suddenly again—the listening on the alert,
The natural perfect and varied attitudes . . . . the bent head,
    the curved neck, the counting:
Suchlike I love . . . . I loosen myself and pass freely . . . .
    and am at the mother's breast with the little child,
And swim with the swimmer, and wrestle with wrestlers,
    and march in line with the firemen, and pause and listen
    and count.

I knew a man . . . . he was a common farmer . . . . he was
    the father of five sons . . . and in them were the fathers
    of sons . . . and in them were the fathers of sons.

This man was of wonderful vigor and calmness and beauty
    of person;

The shape of his head, the richness and breadth of his
    manners, the pale yellow and white of his hair and
    beard, the immeasurable meaning of his black eyes,
These I used to go and visit him to see . . . . He was wise
    also,
He was six feet tall . . . . he was over eighty years old . . . .
    his sons were massive clean bearded tanfaced and
    handsome,
They and his daughters loved him . . . all who saw him
    loved him . . . they did not love him by allowance . . .
    they loved him with personal love;
He drank water only . . . . the blood showed like scarlet
    through the clear brown skin of his face;
He was a frequent gunner and fisher . . . he sailed his boat
    himself . . . he had a fine one presented to him by a
    shipjoiner . . . . he had fowling-pieces, presented to
    him by men that loved him;
When he went with his five sons and many grandsons to
    hunt or fish you would pick him out as the most
    beautiful and vigorous of the gang,
You would wish long and long to be with him . . . . you
    would wish to sit by him in the boat that you and he
    might touch each other.

I have perceived that to be with those I like is enough,
To stop in company with the rest at evening is enough,
To be surrounded by beautiful curious breathing laughing
    flesh is enough,
To pass among them . . to touch any one . . . . to rest my
    arm ever so lightly round his or her neck for a moment
    . . . . what is this then?
I do not ask any more delight . . . . I swim in it as in a sea.

There is something in staying close to men and women and
    looking on them and in the contact and odor of them
    that pleases the soul well,
All things please the soul, but these please the soul well.

This is the female form,
A divine nimbus exhales from it from head to foot,

It attracts with fierce undeniable attraction,

I am drawn by its breath as if I were no more than a helpless
    vapor . . . . all falls aside but myself and it,

Books, art, religion, time . . the visible and solid earth . .
    the atmosphere and the fringed clouds . . what was
    expected of heaven or feared of hell are now consumed,

Mad filaments, ungovernable shoots play out of it . . the
    response likewise ungovernable,

Hair, bosom, hips, bend of legs, negligent falling hands — all
    diffused . . . . mine too diffused,

Ebb stung by the flow, and flow stung by the ebb . . . .
    loveflesh swelling and deliciously aching,

Limitless limpid jets of love hot and enormous . . . .
    quivering jelly of love . . . white-blow and delirious
    juice,

Bridegroom-night of love working surely and softly into the
    prostrate dawn,

Undulating into the willing and yielding day,

Lost in the cleave of the clasping and sweetfleshed day.

This is the nucleus . . . after the child is born of woman the
    man is born of woman,

This is the bath of birth . . . this is the merge of small and
    large and the outlet again.

Be not ashamed women . . your privilege encloses the rest . .
    it is the exit of the rest,

You are the gates of the body and you are the gates of the
    soul.

The female contains all qualities and tempers them . . . .
    she is in her place . . . . she moves with perfect balance,

She is all things duly veiled . . . . she is both passive and
    active . . . . she is to conceive daughters as well as sons
    and sons as well as daughters.

As I see my soul reflected in nature . . . . as I see through a
    mist one with inexpressible completeness and beauty
    . . . . see the bent head and arms folded over the breast
    . . . . the female I see,

I see the bearer of the great fruit which is immortality . . . .
    the good thereof is not tasted by roues, and never can be.

The male is not less the soul, nor more . . . . he too is in
    his place,
He too is all qualities . . . . he is action and power . . . .
    the flush of the known universe is in him,
Scorn becomes him well and appetite and defiance become
    him well,
The fiercest largest passions . . bliss that is utmost and
    sorrow that is utmost become him well . . . . pride is
    for him,
The fullspread pride of man is calming and excellent to the
    soul;
Knowledge becomes him . . . . he likes it always . . . . he
    brings everything to the test of himself,
Whatever the survey . . whatever the sea and the sail, he
    strikes soundings at last only here,
Where else does he strike soundings except here?

The man's body is sacred and the woman's body is sacred
    . . . . it is no matter who,
Is it a slave? Is it one of the dullfaced immigrants just landed
    on the wharf?

Each belongs here or anywhere just as much as the welloff
    . . . . just as much as you,
Each has his or her place in the procession.

All is a procession,
The universe is a procession with measured and beautiful
    motion.

Do you know so much that you call the slave or the dullface
    ignorant?
Do you suppose you have a right to a good sight . . . and
    he or she has no right to a sight?
Do you think matter has cohered together from its diffused
    float, and the soil is on the surface and water runs and
    vegetation sprouts for you . . and not for him and her?

A slave at auction!
I help the auctioneer . . . . the sloven does not half know
    his business.

Gentlemen look on this curious creature,
Whatever the bids of the bidders they cannot be high enough
    for him,
For him the globe lay preparing quintillions of years without
    one animal or plant,
For him the revolving cycles truly and steadily rolled.

In that head the allbaffling brain,
In it and below it the making of the attributes of heroes.

Examine these limbs, red black or white . . . . they are very
    cunning in tendon and nerve;
They shall be stript that you may see them.

Exquisite senses, lifelit eyes, pluck, volition,
Flakes of breastmuscle, pliant backbone and neck, flesh not
    flabby, goodsized arms and legs,
And wonders within there yet.

Within there runs his blood . . . . the same old blood . .
    the same red running blood;
There swells and jets his heart . . . . There all passions and
    desires . . all reachings and aspirations:
Do you think they are not there because they are not
    expressed in parlors and lecture-rooms?

This is not only one man . . . . he is the father of those
    who shall be fathers in their turns,
In him the start of populous states and rich republics,
Of him countless immortal lives with countless embodiments
    and enjoyments.

How do you know who shall come from the offspring of his
    offspring through the centuries?
Who might you find you have come from yourself if you
    could trace back through the centuries?

A woman at auction,
She too is not only herself . . . . she is the teeming mother
    of mothers,
She is the bearer of them that shall grow and be mates to the
    mothers.

Her daughters or their daughters' daughters . . who knows
    who shall mate with them?
Who knows through the centuries what heroes may come
    from them?

In them and of them natal love . . . . in them the divine
    mystery . . . . the same old beautiful mystery.

Have you ever loved a woman?
Your mother . . . . is she living? . . . . Have you been much
    with her? and has she been much with you?
Do you not see that these are exactly the same to all in all
    nations and times all over the earth?

If life and the soul are sacred the human body is sacred;
And the glory and sweet of a man is the token of manhood
    untainted,
And in man or woman a clean strong firmfibred body is
    beautiful as the most beautiful face.

Have you seen the fool that corrupted his own live body? or
    the fool that corrupted her own live body?
For they do not conceal themselves, and cannot conceal
    themselves.

Who degrades or defiles the living human body is cursed,
Who degrades or defiles the body of the dead is not more
    cursed.

Sauntering the pavement or riding the country byroad here
    then are faces,
Faces of friendship, precision, caution, suavity, ideality,

The spiritual prescient face, the always welcome common
    benevolent face,
The face of the singing of music, the grand faces of natural
    lawyers and judges broad at the backtop,
The faces of hunters and fishers, bulged at the brows . . . .
    the shaved blanched faces of orthodox citizens,
The pure extravagant yearning questioning artist's face,
The welcome ugly face of some beautiful soul . . . . the
    handsome detested or despised face,
The sacred faces of infants . . . . the illuminated face of the
    mother of many children,
The face of an amour . . . . the face of veneration,
The face as of a dream . . . . the face of an immobile rock,
The face withdrawn of its good and bad . . a castrated face,
A wild hawk . . his wings clipped by the clipper,
A stallion that yielded at last to the thongs and knife of the
    gelder.

Sauntering the pavement or crossing the ceaseless ferry, here
    then are faces;
I see them and complain not and am content with all.

Do you suppose I could be content with all if I thought
    them their own finale?

This now is too lamentable a face for a man;
Some abject louse asking leave to be . . cringing for it,
Some milknosed maggot blessing what lets it wrig to its
    hole.

This face is a dog's snout sniffing for garbage;
Snakes nest in that mouth . . I hear the sibilant threat.

This face is a haze more chill than the arctic sea,
Its sleepy and wobbling icebergs crunch as they go.

This is a face of bitter herbs . . . . this an emetic . . . . they
    need no label,
And more of the drugshelf . . laudanum, caoutchouc, or
    hog's lard.

This face is an epilepsy advertising and doing business . . . .
    its wordless tongue gives out the unearthly cry,
Its veins down the neck distend . . . . its eyes roll till they
    show nothing but their whites,
Its teeth grit . . the palms of the hands are cut by the
    turned-in nails,
The man falls struggling and foaming to the ground while
    he speculates well.

This face is bitten by vermin and worms,
And this is some murderer's knife with a halfpulled
    scabbard.

This face owes to the sexton his dismalest fee,
An unceasing deathbell tolls there.

Those are really men! . . . . the bosses and tufts of the great
    round globe.

Features of my equals, would you trick me with your creased
    and cadaverous march?
Well then you cannot trick me.

I see your rounded never-erased flow,
I see neath the rims of your haggard and mean disguises.

Splay and twist as you like . . . . poke with the tangling
    fores of fishes or rats,
You'll be unmuzzled . . . . you certainly will.

I saw the face of the most smeared and slobbering idiot they
    had at the asylum,
And I knew for my consolation what they knew not;
I knew of the agents that emptied and broke my brother,
The same wait to clear the rubbish from the fallen
    tenement;
And I shall look again in a score or two of ages,
And I shall meet the real landlord perfect and unharmed,
    every inch as good as myself.

The Lord advances and yet advances:
Always the shadow in front . . . . always the reached hand
    bringing up the laggards.

Out of this face emerge banners and horses . . . . O superb!
    . . . . I see what is coming,
I see the high pioneercaps . . . . I see the staves of runners
    clearing the way,
I hear victorious drums.

This face is a lifeboat;
This is the face commanding and bearded . . . . it asks no
    odds of the rest;
This face is flavored fruit ready for eating;
This face of a healthy honest boy is the programme of
    all good.

These faces bear testimony slumbering or awake,
They show their descent from the Master himself.

Off the word I have spoken I except not one . . . . red
    white or black, all are deific,
In each house is the ovum . . . . it comes forth after a
    thousand years.

Spots or cracks at the windows do not disturb me,
Tall and sufficient stand behind and make signs to me;
I read the promise and patiently wait.

This is a fullgrown lily's face,
She speaks to the limber-hip'd man near the garden pickets,
Come here, she blushingly cries . . . . Come nigh to me
    limber-hip'd man and give me your finger and thumb,
Stand at my side till I lean as high as I can upon you,
Fill me with albescent honey . . . . bend down to me,
Rub to me with your chafing beard . . rub to my breast and
    shoulders.

The old face of the mother of many children:
Whist! I am fully content.

Lulled and late is the smoke of the Sabbath morning,
It hangs low over the rows of trees by the fences,
It hangs thin by the sassafras, the wildcherry and the catbrier
    under them.

I saw the rich ladies in full dress at the soiree,
I heard what the run of poets were saying so long,
Heard who sprang in crimson youth from the white froth
    and the water-blue.

Behold a woman!
She looks out from her quaker cap . . . . her face is clearer
    and more beautiful than the sky.

She sits in an armchair under the shaded porch of the
    farmhouse,
The sun just shines on her old white head.

Her ample gown is of creamhued linen,
Her grandsons raised the flax, and her granddaughters spun
    it with the distaff and the wheel.

The melodious character of the earth!
The finish beyond which philosophy cannot go and does not
    wish to go!
The justified mother of men!

A young man came to me with a message from his brother,
How should the young man know the whether and when of
    his brother?
Tell him to send me the signs.

And I stood before the young man face to face, and took his
    right hand in my left hand and his left hand in my right
    hand,
And I answered for his brother and for men . . . . and I
    answered for the poet, and sent these signs.

Him all wait for . . . . him all yield up to . . . . his word is
    decisive and final,
Him they accept . . . . in him lave . . . . in him perceive
    themselves as amid light,
Him they immerse, and he immerses them.

Beautiful women, the haughtiest nations, laws, the landscape,
    people and animals,
The profound earth and its attributes, and the unquiet ocean,
All enjoyments and properties, and money, and whatever
    money will buy,
The best farms . . . . others toiling and planting, and he
    unavoidably reaps,
The noblest and costliest cities . . . . others grading and
    building, and he domiciles there;
Nothing for any one but what is for him . . . . near and far
    are for him,
The ships in the offing . . . . the perpetual shows and
    marches on land are for him if they are for any body.

He puts things in their attitudes,
He puts today out of himself with plasticity and love,
He places his own city, times, reminiscences, parents,
    brothers and sisters, associations employment and
    politics, so that the rest never shame them afterward,
    nor assume to command them.

He is the answerer,
What can be answered he answers, and what cannot be
    answered he shows how it cannot be answered.

A man is a summons and challenge,
It is vain to skulk . . . . Do you hear that mocking and
    laughter? Do you hear the ironical echoes?

Books friendships philosophers priests action pleasure pride
    beat up and down seeking to give satisfaction;
He indicates the satisfaction, and indicates them that beat up
    and down also.

Whichever the sex . . . whatever the season or place he may
go freshly and gently and safely by day or by night,
He has the passkey of hearts . . . . to him the response of
the prying of hands on the knobs.

His welcome is universal . . . . the flow of beauty is not
more welcome or universal than he is,
The person he favors by day or sleeps with at night is
blessed.

Every existence has its idiom . . . . every thing has an idiom
and tongue;
He resolves all tongues into his own, and bestows it upon
men . . and any man translates . . and any man
translates himself also:
One part does not counteract another part . . . . He is the
joiner . . he sees how they join.

He says indifferently and alike, How are you friend? to the
President at his levee,
And he says Good day my brother, to Cudge that hoes in
the sugarfield;
And both understand him and know that his speech is right.

He walks with perfect ease in the capitol,
He walks among the Congress . . . . and one representative
says to another, Here is our equal appearing and new.

Then the mechanics take him for a mechanic,
And the soldiers suppose him to be a captain . . . . and the
sailors that he has followed the sea,
And the authors take him for an author . . . . and the artists
for an artist,
And the laborers perceive he could labor with them and love
them;
No matter what the work is, that he is one to follow it or
has followed it,
No matter what the nation, that he might find his brothers
and sisters there.

The English believe he comes of their English stock,
A Jew to the Jew he seems . . . . a Russ to the Russ . . . .
    usual and near . . removed from none.

Whoever he looks at in the traveler's coffeehouse claims him,
The Italian or Frenchman is sure, and the German is sure, and
    the Spaniard is sure . . . . and the island Cuban is sure.

The engineer, the deckhand on the great lakes or on the
    Mississippi or St Lawrence or Sacramento or Hudson or
    Delaware claims him.

The gentleman of perfect blood acknowledges his perfect
    blood,
The insulter, the prostitute, the angry person, the beggar, see
    themselves in the ways of him . . . . he strangely
    transmutes them,
They are not vile any more . . . . they hardly know
    themselves, they are so grown.

You think it would be good to be the writer of melodious
    verses,
Well it would be good to be the writer of melodious verses;
But what are verses beyond the flowing character you
    could have? . . . . or beyond beautiful manners and
    behaviour?
Or beyond one manly or affectionate deed of an
    apprenticeboy? . . or old woman? . . or man that has
    been in prison or is likely to be in prison?

Suddenly out of its stale and drowsy lair, the lair of slaves,
Like lightning Europe le'pt forth . . . . half startled at itself,
Its feet upon the ashes and the rags . . . . Its hands tight to
    the throats of kings.

O hope and faith! O aching close of lives! O many a sickened
    heart!
Turn back unto this day, and make yourselves afresh.

And you, paid to defile the People . . . . you liars mark:
Not for numberless agonies, murders, lusts,
For court thieving in its manifold mean forms,
Worming from his simplicity the poor man's wages;
For many a promise sworn by royal lips, And broken, and
    laughed at in the breaking,
Then in their power not for all these did the blows strike of
    personal revenge . . or the heads of the nobles fall;
The People scorned the ferocity of kings.

But the sweetness of mercy brewed bitter destruction, and
    the frightened rulers come back:
Each comes in state with his train . . . . hangman, priest
    and tax-gatherer . . . . soldier, lawyer, jailer and
    sycophant.

Yet behind all, lo, a Shape,
Vague as the night, draped interminably, head front and
    form in scarlet folds,
Whose face and eyes none may see,
Out of its robes only this . . . . the red robes, lifted by
    the arm,
One finger pointed high over the top, like the head of a
    snake appears.

Meanwhile corpses lie in new-made graves . . . . bloody
    corpses of young men:
The rope of the gibbet hangs heavily . . . . the bullets of
    princes are flying . . . . the creatures of power laugh
    aloud,
And all these things bear fruits . . . . and they are good.

Those corpses of young men,
Those martyrs that hang from the gibbets . . . those hearts
    pierced by the gray lead,
Cold and motionless as they seem . . live elsewhere with
    unslaughter'd vitality.

They live in other young men, O kings,
They live in brothers, again ready to defy you:

They were purified by death . . . . They were taught and
   exalted.

Not a grave of the murdered for freedom but grows seed for
   freedom . . . . in its turn to bear seed,
Which the winds carry afar and re-sow, and the rains and the
   snows nourish.

Not a disembodied spirit can the weapons of tyrants let loose,
But it stalks invisibly over the earth . . whispering counseling
   cautioning.

Liberty let others despair of you . . . . I never despair of you.

Is the house shut? Is the master away?
Nevertheless be ready . . . . be not weary of watching,
He will soon return . . . . his messengers come anon.

Clear the way there Jonathan!
Way for the President's marshal! Way for the government
   cannon!
Way for the federal foot and dragoons . . . . and the
   phantoms afterward.

I rose this morning early to get betimes in Boston town;
Here's a good place at the corner . . . . I must stand and see
   the show.

I love to look on the stars and stripes . . . . I hope the fifes
   will play Yankee Doodle.

How bright shine the foremost with cutlasses,
Every man holds his revolver . . . . marching stiff through
   Boston town.

A fog follows . . . . antiques of the same come limping,
Some appear wooden-legged and some appear bandaged and
   bloodless.

Why this is a show! It has called the dead out of the earth,
The old graveyards of the hills have hurried to see;
Uncountable phantoms gather by flank and rear of it,
Cocked hats of mothy mould and crutches made of mist,
Arms in slings and old men leaning on young men's
    shoulders.

What troubles you, Yankee phantoms? What is all this
    chattering of bare gums?
Does the ague convulse your limbs? Do you mistake your
    crutches for firelocks, and level them?

If you blind your eyes with tears you will not see the
    President's marshal,
If you groan such groans you might balk the government
    cannon.

For shame old maniacs! . . . . Bring down those tossed
    arms, and let your white hair be;
Here gape your smart grandsons . . . . their wives gaze at
    them from the windows,
See how well-dressed . . . . see how orderly they conduct
    themselves.

Worse and worse . . . . Can't you stand it? Are you
    retreating?
Is this hour with the living too dead for you?

Retreat then! Pell-mell! . . . . Back to the hills, old limpers!
I do not think you belong here anyhow.

But there is one thing that belongs here . . . . Shall I tell
    you what it is, gentlemen of Boston?

I will whisper it to the Mayor . . . . he shall send a
    committee to England,
They shall get a grant from the Parliament, and go with a
    cart to the royal vault,
Dig out King George's coffin . . . . unwrap him quick from
    the graveclothes . . . . box up his bones for a journey:

Find a swift Yankee clipper . . . . here is freight for you
    blackbellied clipper,
Up with your anchor! shake out your sails! . . . . steer
    straight toward Boston bay.

Now call the President's marshal again, and bring out the
    government cannon,
And fetch home the roarers from Congress, and make
    another procession and guard it with foot and dragoons.

Here is a centrepiece for them:
Look! all orderly citizens . . . . look from the windows
    women.

The committee open the box and set up the regal ribs and
    glue those that will not stay,
And clap the skull on top of the ribs, and clap a crown on
    top of the skull.

You have got your revenge old buster! . . . . The crown is
    come to its own and more than its own.

Stick your hands in your pockets Jonathan . . . . you are a
    made man from this day,
You are mighty cute . . . . and here is one of your bargains.

———————

There was a child went forth every day,
And the first object he looked upon and received with
    wonder or pity or love or dread, that object he became,
And that object became part of him for the day or a certain
    part of the day . . . . or for many years or stretching
    cycles of years.

The early lilacs became part of this child,
And grass, and white and red morningglories, and white and
    red clover, and the song of the phœbe-bird,
And the March-born lambs, and the sow's pink-faint litter,
    and the mare's foal, and the cow's calf, and the noisy

brood of the barnyard or by the mire of the pond-side
. . and the fish suspending themselves so curiously
below there . . and the beautiful curious liquid . . and
the water-plants with their graceful flat heads . . all
became part of him.

And the field-sprouts of April and May became part of him
. . . . wintergrain sprouts, and those of the light-
yellow corn, and of the esculent roots of the garden,
And the appletrees covered with blossoms, and the fruit
afterward . . . . and woodberries . . and the
commonest weeds by the road;
And the old drunkard staggering home from the outhouse
of the tavern whence he had lately risen,
And the schoolmistress that passed on her way to the school
. . and the friendly boys that passed . . and the
quarrelsome boys . . and the tidy and freshcheeked
girls . . and the barefoot negro boy and girl,
And all the changes of city and country wherever he went.

His own parents . . he that had propelled the fatherstuff at
night, and fathered him . . and she that conceived him
in her womb and birthed him . . . . they gave this
child more of themselves than that,
They gave him afterward every day . . . . they and of them
became part of him.

The mother at home quietly placing the dishes on the
suppertable,
The mother with mild words . . . . clean her cap and gown
. . . . a wholesome odor falling off her person and
clothes as she walks by:
The father, strong, selfsufficient, manly, mean, angered, unjust,
The blow, the quick loud word, the tight bargain, the crafty
lure,
The family usages, the language, the company, the furniture
. . . . the yearning and swelling heart,
Affection that will not be gainsayed . . . . The sense of
what is real . . . . the thought if after all it should
prove unreal,

The doubts of daytime and the doubts of nighttime . . .
    the curious whether and how,
Whether that which appears so is so . . . . Or is it all flashes
    and specks?
Men and women crowding fast in the streets . . if they are
    not flashes and specks what are they?
The streets themselves, and the facades of houses . . . .
    the goods in the windows,
Vehicles . . teams . . the tiered wharves, and the huge
    crossing at the ferries;
The village on the highland seen from afar at sunset . . . .
    the river between,
Shadows . . aureola and mist . . light falling on roofs and
    gables of white or brown, three miles off,
The schooner near by sleepily dropping down the tide . . the
    little boat slacktowed astern,
The hurrying tumbling waves and quickbroken crests and
    slapping;
The strata of colored clouds . . . . the long bar of
    maroontint away solitary by itself . . . . the spread of
    purity it lies motionless in,
The horizon's edge, the flying seacrow, the fragrance of
    saltmarsh and shoremud;
These became part of that child who went forth every day,
    and who now goes and will always go forth every day,
And these become of him or her that peruses them now.

Who learns my lesson complete?
Boss and journeyman and apprentice? . . . . churchman and
    atheist?
The stupid and the wise thinker . . . . parents and offspring
    . . . . merchant and clerk and porter and customer
    . . . . editor, author, artist and schoolboy?

Draw nigh and commence,
It is no lesson . . . . it lets down the bars to a good lesson,
And that to another . . . . and every one to another still.

The great laws take and effuse without argument,
I am of the same style, for I am their friend,
I love them quits and quits . . . . I do not halt and make
     salaams.

I lie abstracted and hear beautiful tales of things and the
     reasons of things,
They are so beautiful I nudge myself to listen.

I cannot say to any person what I hear . . . . I cannot say it
     to myself . . . . it is very wonderful.

It is no little matter, this round and delicious globe, moving
     so exactly in its orbit forever and ever, without one jolt
     or the untruth of a single second;
I do not think it was made in six days, nor in ten thousand
     years, nor ten decillions of years,
Nor planned and built one thing after another, as an
     architect plans and builds a house.

I do not think seventy years is the time of a man or woman,
Nor that seventy millions of years is the time of a man or
     woman,
Nor that years will ever stop the existence of me or any
     one else.

Is it wonderful that I should be immortal? as every one is
     immortal,
I know it is wonderful . . . . but my eyesight is equally
     wonderful . . . . and how I was conceived in my
     mother's womb is equally wonderful,
And how I was not palpable once but am now . . . . and
     was born on the last day of May 1819 . . . . and passed
     from a babe in the creeping trance of three summers
     and three winters to articulate and walk . . . . are all
     equally wonderful.

And that I grew six feet high . . . . and that I have become
     a man thirty-six years old in 1855 . . . . and that I am
     here anyhow—are all equally wonderful;

And that my soul embraces you this hour, and we affect each
    other without ever seeing each other, and never perhaps
    to see each other, is every bit as wonderful:
And that I can think such thoughts as these is just as
    wonderful,
And that I can remind you, and you think them and know
    them to be true is just as wonderful,
And that the moon spins round the earth and on with the
    earth is equally wonderful,
And that they balance themselves with the sun and stars is
    equally wonderful.

Come I should like to hear you tell me what there is in
    yourself that is not just as wonderful,
And I should like to hear the name of anything between
    Sunday morning and Saturday night that is not just as
    wonderful.

Great are the myths . . . . I too delight in them,
Great are Adam and Eve . . . . I too look back and accept
    them;
Great the risen and fallen nations, and their poets, women,
    sages, inventors, rulers, warriors and priests.

Great is liberty! Great is equality! I am their follower,
Helmsmen of nations, choose your craft . . . . where you
    sail I sail,
Yours is the muscle of life or death . . . . yours is the perfect
    science . . . . in you I have absolute faith.

Great is today, and beautiful,
It is good to live in this age . . . . there never was any
    better.

Great are the plunges and throes and triumphs and falls of
    democracy,
Great the reformers with their lapses and screams,
Great the daring and venture of sailors on new explorations.

Great are yourself and myself,
We are just as good and bad as the oldest and youngest or
    any,
What the best and worst did we could do,
What they felt . . do not we feel it in ourselves?
What they wished . . do we not wish the same?

Great is youth, and equally great is old age . . . . great are
    the day and night;
Great is wealth and great is poverty . . . . great is expression
    and great is silence.

Youth large lusty and loving . . . . youth full of grace and
    force and fascination,
Do you know that old age may come after you with equal
    grace and force and fascination?

Day fullblown and splendid . . . . day of the immense sun,
    and action and ambition and laughter,
The night follows close, with millions of suns, and sleep and
    restoring darkness.

Wealth with the flush hand and fine clothes and hospitality:
But then the soul's wealth—which is candor and knowledge
    and pride and enfolding love:
Who goes for men and women showing poverty richer than
    wealth?

Expression of speech . . in what is written or said forget not
    that silence is also expressive,
That anguish as hot as the hottest and contempt as cold as
    the coldest may be without words,
That the true adoration is likewise without words and
    without kneeling.

Great is the greatest nation . . the nation of clusters of equal
    nations.

Great is the earth, and the way it became what it is,
Do you imagine it is stopped at this? . . . . and the increase
    abandoned?
Understand then that it goes as far onward from this as
    this is from the times when it lay in covering waters and
    gases.

Great is the quality of truth in man,
The quality of truth in man supports itself through all
    changes,
It is inevitably in the man . . . . He and it are in love, and
    never leave each other.

The truth in man is no dictum . . . . it is vital as eyesight,
If there be any soul there is truth . . . . if there be man or
    woman there is truth . . . . If there be physical or moral
    there is truth,
If there be equilibrium or volition there is truth . . . .
    if there be things at all upon the earth there is
    truth.

O truth of the earth! O truth of things! I am determined to
    press the whole way toward you,
Sound your voice! I scale mountains or dive in the sea after
    you.

Great is language . . . . it is the mightiest of the sciences,
It is the fulness and color and form and diversity of the earth
    . . . . and of men and women . . . . and of all qualities
    and processes;
It is greater than wealth . . . . it is greater than buildings or
    ships or religions or paintings or music.

Great is the English speech . . . . What speech is so great as
    the English?
Great is the English brood . . . . What brood has so vast a
    destiny as the English?
It is the mother of the brood that must rule the earth with
    the new rule,

The new rule shall rule as the soul rules, and as the love and
    justice and equality that are in the soul rule.

Great is the law . . . . Great are the old few landmarks of
    the law . . . . they are the same in all times and shall
    not be disturbed.

Great are marriage, commerce, newspapers, books, freetrade,
    railroads, steamers, international mails and telegraphs
    and exchanges.

Great is Justice;
Justice is not settled by legislators and laws . . . . it is in the
    soul,
It cannot be varied by statutes any more than love or pride or
    the attraction of gravity can,
It is immutable . . it does not depend on majorities . . . .
    majorities or what not come at last before the same
    passionless and exact tribunal.

For justice are the grand natural lawyers and perfect judges
    . . . . it is in their souls,
It is well assorted . . . . they have not studied for nothing
    . . . . the great includes the less,
They rule on the highest grounds . . . . they oversee all eras
    and states and administrations.

The perfect judge fears nothing . . . . he could go front to
    front before God,
Before the perfect judge all shall stand back . . . . life and
    death shall stand back . . . . heaven and hell shall
    stand back.

Great is goodness;
I do not know what it is any more than I know what health
    is . . . . but I know it is great.

Great is wickedness . . . . I find I often admire it just as
    much as I admire goodness:
Do you call that a paradox? It certainly is a paradox.

The eternal equilibrium of things is great, and the eternal
    overthrow of things is great,
And there is another paradox.

Great is life . . and real and mystical . . wherever and
    whoever,
Great is death . . . . Sure as life holds all parts together,
    death holds all parts together;
Sure as the stars return again after they merge in the light,
    death is great as life.

from *Leaves of Grass* (1860)

Chants Democratic and Native American: 5

Respondez! Respondez!
Let every one answer! Let those who sleep be waked! Let
    none evade—not you, any more than others!
(If it really be as is pretended, how much longer must we go
    on with our affectations and sneaking?
Let me bring this to a close—I pronounce openly for a new
    distribution of roles,)
Let that which stood in front go behind! and let that which
    was behind advance to the front and speak!
Let murderers, thieves, bigots, fools, unclean persons, offer
    new propositions!
Let the old propositions be postponed!
Let faces and theories be turned inside out! Let meanings be
    freely criminal, as well as results!
Let there be no suggestion above the suggestion of
    drudgery!
Let none be pointed toward his destination! (Say! do you
    know your destination?)
Let trillions of men and women be mocked with bodies and
    mocked with Souls!
Let the love that waits in them, wait! Let it die, or pass still-
    born to other spheres!
Let the sympathy that waits in every man, wait! or let it also
    pass, a dwarf, to other spheres!

Let contradictions prevail! Let one thing contradict another!
 and let one line of my poems contradict another!
Let the people sprawl with yearning aimless hands! Let
 their tongues be broken! Let their eyes be discouraged!
 Let none descend into their hearts with the fresh
 lusciousness of love!
Let the theory of America be management, caste,
 comparison! (Say! what other theory would you?)
Let them that distrust birth and death lead the rest! (Say!
 why shall they not lead you?)
Let the crust of hell be neared and trod on! Let the days be
 darker than the nights! Let slumber bring less slumber
 than waking-time brings!
Let the world never appear to him or her for whom it was all
 made!
Let the heart of the young man exile itself from the heart of
 the old man! and let the heart of the old man be exiled
 from that of the young man!
Let the sun and moon go! Let scenery take the applause of
 the audience! Let there be apathy under the stars!
Let freedom prove no man's inalienable right! Every one
 who can tyrannize, let him tyrannize to his
 satisfaction!
Let none but infidels be countenanced!
Let the eminence of meanness, treachery, sarcasm, hate,
 greed, indecency, impotence, lust, be taken for
 granted above all! Let writers, judges, governments,
 households, religions, philosophies, take such for
 granted above all!
Let the worst men beget children out of the worst women!
Let priests still play at immortality!
Let Death be inaugurated!
Let nothing remain upon the earth except the ashes of
 teachers, artists, moralists, lawyers, and learned and
 polite persons!
Let him who is without my poems be assassinated!
Let the cow, the horse, the camel, the garden-bee — Let the
 mud-fish, the lobster, the mussel, eel, the sting-ray, and
 the grunting pig-fish — Let these, and the like of these,
 be put on a perfect equality with man and woman!

Let churches accommodate serpents, vermin, and the corpses
    of those who have died of the most filthy of diseases!
Let marriage slip down among fools, and be for none but
    fools!
Let men among themselves talk and think obscenely of
    women! and let women among themselves talk and
    think obscenely of men!
Let every man doubt every woman! and let every woman
    trick every man!
Let us all, without missing one, be exposed in public, naked,
    monthly, at the peril of our lives! Let our bodies be
    freely handled and examined by whoever chooses!
Let nothing but copies, pictures, statues, reminiscences,
    elegant works, be permitted to exist upon the earth!
Let the earth desert God, nor let there ever henceforth be
    mentioned the name of God!
Let there be no God!
Let there be money, business, imports, exports, custom,
    authority, precedents, pallor, dyspepsia, smut,
    ignorance, unbelief!
Let judges and criminals be transposed! Let the prison-
    keepers be put in prison! Let those that were prisoners
    take the keys! (Say! why might they not just as well be
    transposed?)
Let the slaves be masters! Let the masters become slaves!
Let the reformers descend from the stands where they are
    forever bawling! Let an idiot or insane person appear
    on each of the stands!
Let the Asiatic, the African, the European, the American
    and the Australian, go armed against the murderous
    stealthiness of each other! Let them sleep armed! Let
    none believe in good-will!
Let there be no unfashionable wisdom! Let such be scorned
    and derided off from the earth!
Let a floating cloud in the sky—Let a wave of the sea—Let
    one glimpse of your eye-sight upon the landscape or
    grass—Let growing mint, spinach, onions, tomatoes—
    Let these be exhibited as shows at a great price for
    admission!

Let all the men of These States stand aside for a few
    smouchers! Let the few seize on what they choose!
    Let the rest gawk, giggle, starve, obey!
Let shadows be furnished with genitals! Let substances be
    deprived of their genitals!
Let there be wealthy and immense cities—but through
    any of them, not a single poet, saviour, knower,
    lover!
Let the infidels of These States laugh all faith away! If one
    man be found who has faith, let the rest set upon him!
    Let them affright faith! Let them destroy the power of
    breeding faith!
Let the she-harlots and the he-harlots be prudent! Let them
    dance on, while seeming lasts! (O seeming! seeming!
    seeming!)
Let the preachers recite creeds! Let them teach only what
    they have been taught!
Let the preachers of creeds never dare to go meditate
    candidly upon the hills, alone, by day or by night!
    (If one ever once dare, he is lost!)
Let insanity have charge of sanity!
Let books take the place of trees, animals, rivers,
    clouds!
Let the daubed portraits of heroes supersede heroes!
Let the manhood of man never take steps after itself! Let it
    take steps after eunuchs, and after consumptive and
    genteel persons!
Let the white person tread the black person under his heel!
    (Say! which is trodden under heel, after all?)
Let the reflections of the things of the world be studied
    in mirrors! Let the things themselves continue
    unstudied!
Let a man seek pleasure everywhere except in himself! Let a
    woman seek happiness everywhere except in herself!
    (Say! what real happiness have you had one single time
    through your whole life?)
Let the limited years of life do nothing for the limitless
    years of death! (Say! what do you suppose death will
    do, then?)

from *Leaves of Grass* (*1891 – 92*)

from *Inscriptions*

EIDÓLONS

I met a seer,
Passing the hues and objects of the world,
The fields of art and learning, pleasure, sense,
        To glean eidólons.

        Put in thy chants said he,
No more the puzzling hour nor day, nor segments, parts, put
    in,
Put first before the rest as light for all and entrance-song of all,
        That of eidólons.

        Ever the dim beginning,
Ever the growth, the rounding of the circle,
Ever the summit and the merge at last, (to surely start again,)
        Eidólons! eidólons!

        Ever the mutable,
Ever materials, changing, crumbling, re-cohering,
Ever the ateliers, the factories divine,
        Issuing eidólons.

        Lo, I or you,
Or woman, man, or state, known or unknown,
We seeming solid wealth, strength, beauty build,
        But really build eidólons.

        The ostent evanescent,
The substance of an artist's mood or savan's studies long,
Or warrior's, martyr's, hero's toils,
        To fashion his eidólon.

        Of every human life,
(The units gather'd, posted, not a thought, emotion, deed,
    left out,)
The whole or large or small summ'd, added up,
        In its eidólon.

The old, old urge,
Based on the ancient pinnacles, lo, newer, higher pinnacles,
From science and the modern still impell'd,
    The old, old urge, eidólons.

The present now and here,
America's busy, teeming, intricate whirl,
Of aggregate and segregate for only thence releasing,
    To-day's eidólons.

These with the past,
Of vanish'd lands, of all the reigns of kings across the sea,
Old conquerors, old campaigns, old sailors' voyages,
    Joining eidólons.

Densities, growth, façades,
Strata of mountains, soils, rocks, giant trees,
Far-born, far-dying, living long, to leave,
    Eidólons everlasting.

Exaltè, rapt, ecstatic,
The visible but their womb of birth,
Of orbic tendencies to shape and shape and shape,
    The mighty earth-eidólon.

All space, all time,
(The stars, the terrible perturbations of the suns,
Swelling, collapsing, ending, serving their longer, shorter use,)
    Fill'd with eidólons only.

The noiseless myriads,
The infinite oceans where the rivers empty,
The separate countless free identities, like eyesight,
    The true realities, eidólons.

Not this the world,
Nor these the universes, they the universes,
Purport and end, ever the permanent life of life,
    Eidólons, eidólons.

Beyond thy lectures learn'd professor,
Beyond thy telescope or spectroscope observer keen, beyond
    all mathematics,
Beyond the doctor's surgery, anatomy, beyond the chemist
    with his chemistry,
        The entities of entities, eidólons.

Unfix'd yet fix'd,
Ever shall be, ever have been and are,
Sweeping the present to the infinite future,
        Eidólons, eidólons, eidólons.

The prophet and the bard,
Shall yet maintain themselves, in higher stages yet,
Shall mediate to the Modern, to Democracy, interpret yet
    to them,
        God and eidólons.

And thee my soul,
Joys, ceaseless exercises, exaltations,
Thy yearning amply fed at last, prepared to meet,
        Thy mates, eidólons.

Thy body permanent,
The body lurking there within thy body,
The only purport of the form thou art, the real I myself,
        An image, an eidólon.

Thy very songs not in thy songs,
No special strains to sing, none for itself,
But from the whole resulting, rising at last and floating,
        A round full-orb'd eidólon.

from *Children of Adam*

FROM PENT-UP ACHING RIVERS

From pent-up aching rivers,
From that of myself without which I were nothing,
From what I am determin'd to make illustrious, even if I
    stand sole among men,
From my own voice resonant, singing the phallus,
Singing the song of procreation,
Singing the need of superb children and therein superb
    grown people,
Singing the muscular urge and the blending,
Singing the bedfellow's song, (O resistless yearning!
O for any and each the body correlative attracting!
O for you whoever you are your correlative body! O it, more
    than all else, you delighting!)
From the hungry gnaw that eats me night and day,
From native moments, from bashful pains, singing them,
Seeking something yet unfound though I have diligently
    sought it many a long year,
Singing the true song of the soul fitful at random,
Renascent with grossest Nature or among animals,
Of that, of them and what goes with them my poems
    informing,
Of the smell of apples and lemons, of the pairing of birds,
Of the wet of woods, of the lapping of waves,
Of the mad pushes of waves upon the land, I them
    chanting,
The overture lightly sounding, the strain anticipating,
The welcome nearness, the sight of the perfect body,
The swimmer swimming naked in the bath, or motionless on
    his back lying and floating,
The female form approaching, I pensive, love-flesh tremulous
    aching,
The divine list for myself or you or for any one making,
The face, the limbs, the index from head to foot, and what it
    arouses,

The mystic deliria, the madness amorous, the utter
abandonment,
(Hark close and still what I now whisper to you,
I love you, O you entirely possess me,
O that you and I escape from the rest and go utterly off, free
and lawless,
Two hawks in the air, two fishes swimming in the sea not
more lawless than we;)
The furious storm through me careering, I passionately
trembling.
The oath of the inseparableness of two together, of the
woman that loves me and whom I love more than my
life, that oath swearing,
(O I willingly stake all for you,
O let me be lost if it must be so!
O you and I! what is it to us what the rest do or think?
What is all else to us? only that we enjoy each other and
exhaust each other if it must be so;)
From the master, the pilot I yield the vessel to,
The general commanding me, commanding all, from him
permission taking,
From time the programme hastening, (I have loiter'd too
long as it is,)
From sex, from the warp and from the woof,
From privacy, from frequent repinings alone,
From plenty of persons near and yet the right person not
near,
From the soft sliding of hands over me and thrusting of
fingers through my hair and beard,
From the long sustain'd kiss upon the mouth or bosom,
From the close pressure that makes me or any man drunk,
fainting with excess,
From what the divine husband knows, from the work of
fatherhood,
From exultation, victory and relief, from the bedfellow's
embrace in the night,
From the act-poems of eyes, hands, hips and bosoms,
From the cling of the trembling arm,
From the bending curve and the clinch,
From side by side the pliant coverlet off-throwing,

From the one so unwilling to have me leave, and me just as
    unwilling to leave,
(Yet a moment O tender waiter, and I return,)
From the hour of shining stars and dropping dews,
From the night a moment I emerging flitting out,
Celebrate you act divine and you children prepared for,
And you stalwart loins.

I HEARD YOU SOLEMN-SWEET PIPES
OF THE ORGAN

I heard you solemn-sweet pipes of the organ as last Sunday
    morn I pass'd the church,
Winds of autumn, as I walk'd the woods at dusk I heard your
    long-stretch'd sighs up above so mournful,
I heard the perfect Italian tenor singing at the opera, I heard
    the soprano in the midst of the quartet singing;
Heart of my love! you too I heard murmuring low through
    one of the wrists around my head,
Heard the pulse of you when all was still ringing little bells
    last night under my ear.

AS ADAM EARLY IN THE MORNING

As Adam early in the morning,
Walking forth from the bower refresh'd with sleep,
Behold me where I pass, hear my voice, approach,
Touch me, touch the palm of your hand to my body as I pass,
Be not afraid of my body.

Calamus

IN PATHS UNTRODDEN

In paths untrodden,
In the growth by margins of pond-waters,
Escaped from the life that exhibits itself,

From all the standards hitherto publish'd, from the pleasures,
    profits, conformities,
Which too long I was offering to feed my soul,
Clear to me now standards not yet publish'd, clear to me that
    my soul,
That the soul of the man I speak for rejoices in comrades,
Here by myself away from the clank of the world,
Tallying and talk'd to here by tongues aromatic,
No longer abash'd, (for in this secluded spot I can respond as
    I would not dare elsewhere,)
Strong upon me the life that does not exhibit itself, yet
    contains all the rest,
Resolv'd to sing no songs to-day but those of manly
    attachment,
Projecting them along that substantial life,
Bequeathing hence types of athletic love,
Afternoon this delicious Ninth-month in my forty-first year,
I proceed for all who are or have been young men,
To tell the secret of my nights and days,
To celebrate the need of comrades.

SCENTED HERBAGE OF MY BREAST

Scented herbage of my breast,
Leaves from you I glean, I write, to be perused best
    afterwards,
Tomb-leaves, body-leaves growing up above me above death,
Perennial roots, tall leaves, O the winter shall not freeze you
    delicate leaves,
Every year shall you bloom again, out from where you
    retired you shall emerge again;
O I do not know whether many passing by will discover you
    or inhale your faint odor, but I believe a few will;
O slender leaves! O blossoms of my blood! I permit you to
    tell in your own way of the heart that is under you,
O I do not know what you mean there underneath
    yourselves, you are not happiness,
You are often more bitter than I can bear, you burn and sting
    me,

Yet you are beautiful to me you faint tinged roots, you make
 me think of death,
Death is beautiful from you, (what indeed is finally beautiful
 except death and love?)
O I think it is not for life I am chanting here my chant of
 lovers, I think it must be for death,
For how calm, how solemn it grows to ascend to the
 atmosphere of lovers,
Death or life I am then indifferent, my soul declines to prefer,
(I am not sure but the high soul of lovers welcomes death
 most,)
Indeed O death, I think now these leaves mean precisely the
 same as you mean,
Grow up taller sweet leaves that I may see! grow up out of
 my breast!
Spring away from the conceal'd heart there!
Do not fold yourself so in your pink-tinged roots timid leaves!
Do not remain down there so ashamed, herbage of my breast!
Come I am determin'd to unbare this broad breast of mine, I
 have long enough stifled and choked;
Emblematic and capricious blades I leave you, now you serve
 me not,
I will say what I have to say by itself,
I will sound myself and comrades only, I will never again
 utter a call only their call,
I will raise with it immortal reverberations through the States,
I will give an example to lovers to take permanent shape and
 will through the States,
Through me shall the words be said to make death exhilarating,
Give me your tone therefore O death, that I may accord with
 it,
Give me yourself, for I see that you belong to me now above
 all, and are folded inseparably together, you love and
 death are,
Nor will I allow you to balk me any more with what I was
 calling life,
For now it is convey'd to me that you are the purports
 essential,
That you hide in these shifting forms of life, for reasons, and
 that they are mainly for you,

That you beyond them come forth to remain, the real reality,
That behind the mask of materials you patiently wait, no
    matter how long,
That you will one day perhaps take control of all,
That you will perhaps dissipate this entire show of appearance,
That may-be you are what it is all for, but it does not last so
    very long,
But you will last very long.

WHOEVER YOU ARE HOLDING
ME NOW IN HAND

Whoever you are holding me now in hand,
Without one thing all will be useless,
I give you fair warning before you attempt me further,
I am not what you supposed, but far different.

Who is he that would become my follower?
Who would sign himself a candidate for my affections?

The way is suspicious, the result uncertain, perhaps destructive,
You would have to give up all else, I alone would expect to
    be your sole and exclusive standard,
Your novitiate would even then be long and exhausting,
The whole past theory of your life and all conformity to the
    lives around you would have to be abandon'd,
Therefore release me now before troubling yourself any
    further, let go your hand from my shoulders,
Put me down and depart on your way.

Or else by stealth in some wood for trial,
Or back of a rock in the open air,
(For in any roof'd room of a house I emerge not, nor in
    company,
And in libraries I lie as one dumb, a gawk, or unborn, or
    dead,)
But just possibly with you on a high hill, first watching lest
    any person for miles around approach unawares,

Or possibly with you sailing at sea, or on the beach of the sea
    or some quiet island,
Here to put your lips upon mine I permit you,
With the comrade's long-dwelling kiss or the new
    husband's kiss,
For I am the new husband and I am the comrade.

Or if you will, thrusting me beneath your clothing,
Where I may feel the throbs of your heart or rest upon
    your hip,
Carry me when you go forth over land or sea;
For thus merely touching you is enough, is best,
And thus touching you would I silently sleep and be carried
    eternally.

But these leaves conning you con at peril,
For these leaves and me you will not understand,
They will elude you at first and still more afterward, I will
    certainly elude you,
Even while you should think you had unquestionably caught
    me, behold!
Already you see I have escaped from you.

For it is not for what I have put into it that I have written
    this book,
Nor is it by reading it you will acquire it,
Nor do those know me best who admire me and vauntingly
    praise me,
Nor will the candidates for my love (unless at most a very
    few) prove victorious,
Nor will my poems do good only, they will do just as much
    evil, perhaps more,
For all is useless without that which you may guess at many
    times and not hit, that which I hinted at;
Therefore release me and depart on your way.

FOR YOU O DEMOCRACY

Come, I will make the continent indissoluble,
I will make the most splendid race the sun ever shone upon,
I will make divine magnetic lands,
        With the love of comrades,
            With the life-long love of comrades.

I will plant companionship thick as trees along all the rivers
        of America, and along the shores of the great lakes, and
        all over the prairies,
I will make inseparable cities with their arms about each
        other's necks,
        By the love of comrades,
            By the manly love of comrades.

For you these from me, O Democracy, to serve you ma
        femme!
For you, for you I am trilling these songs.

THESE I SINGING IN SPRING

These I singing in spring collect for lovers,
(For who but I should understand lovers and all their sorrow
        and joy?
And who but I should be the poet of comrades?)
Collecting I traverse the garden the world, but soon I pass
        the gates,
Now along the pond-side, now wading in a little, fearing not
        the wet,
Now by the post-and-rail fences where the old stones thrown
        there, pick'd from the fields, have accumulated,
(Wild-flowers and vines and weeds come up through the
        stones and partly cover them, beyond these I pass,)
Far, far in the forest, or sauntering later in summer, before I
        think where I go,
Solitary, smelling the earthy smell, stopping now and then in
        the silence,
Alone I had thought, yet soon a troop gathers around me,

Some walk by my side and some behind, and some embrace
    my arms or neck,
They the spirits of dear friends dead or alive, thicker they
    come, a great crowd, and I in the middle,
Collecting, dispensing, singing, there I wander with them,
Plucking something for tokens, tossing toward whoever is
    near me,
Here, lilac, with a branch of pine,
Here, out of my pocket, some moss which I pull'd off a live-
    oak in Florida as it hung trailing down,
Here, some pinks and laurel leaves, and a handful of sage,
And here what I now draw from the water, wading in the
    pond-side,
(O here I last saw him that tenderly loves me, and returns
    again never to separate from me,
And this, O this shall henceforth be the token of comrades,
    this calamus-root shall,
Interchange it youths with each other! let none render it
    back!)
And twigs of maple and a bunch of wild orange and
    chestnut,
And stems of currants and plum-blows, and the aromatic
    cedar,
These I compass'd around by a thick cloud of spirits,
Wandering, point to or touch as I pass, or throw them
    loosely from me,
Indicating to each one what he shall have, giving something
    to each;
But what I drew from the water by the pond-side, that I
    reserve,
I will give of it, but only to them that love as I myself am
    capable of loving.

NOT HEAVING FROM MY RIBB'D BREAST ONLY

Not heaving from my ribb'd breast only,
Not in sighs at night in rage dissatisfied with myself,
Not in those long-drawn, ill-supprest sighs,
Not in many an oath and promise broken,

Not in my wilful and savage soul's volition,
Not in the subtle nourishment of the air,
Not in this beating and pounding at my temples and wrists,
Not in the curious systole and diastole within which will one
    day cease,
Not in many a hungry wish told to the skies only,
Not in cries, laughter, defiances, thrown from me when alone
    far in the wilds,
Not in husky pantings through clinch'd teeth,
Not in sounded and resounded words, chattering words,
    echoes, dead words,
Not in the murmurs of my dreams while I sleep,
Nor the other murmurs of these incredible dreams of every
    day,
Nor in the limbs and senses of my body that take you and
    dismiss you continually—not there,
Not in any or all of them O adhesiveness! O pulse of my life!
Need I that you exist and show yourself any more than in
    these songs.

OF THE TERRIBLE DOUBT OF APPEARANCES

Of the terrible doubt of appearances,
Of the uncertainty after all, that we may be deluded,
That may-be reliance and hope are but speculations after all,
That may-be identity beyond the grave is a beautiful fable
    only,
May-be the things I perceive, the animals, plants, men, hills,
    shining and flowing waters,
The skies of day and night, colors, densities, forms, may-be
    these are (as doubtless they are) only apparitions, and
    the real something has yet to be known,
(How often they dart out of themselves as if to confound me
    and mock me!
How often I think neither I know, nor any man knows,
    aught of them,)
May-be seeming to me what they are (as doubtless they

indeed but seem) as from my present point of view, and
    might prove (as of course they would) nought of what
    they appear, or nought anyhow, from entirely changed
    points of view;
To me these and the like of these are curiously answer'd by
    my lovers, my dear friends,
When he whom I love travels with me or sits a long while
    holding me by the hand,
When the subtle air, the impalpable, the sense that words and
    reason hold not, surround us and pervade us,
Then I am charged with untold and untellable wisdom, I am
    silent, I require nothing further,
I cannot answer the question of appearances or that of
    identity beyond the grave,
But I walk or sit indifferent, I am satisfied,
He ahold of my hand has completely satisfied me.

THE BASE OF ALL METAPHYSICS

And now gentlemen,
A word I give to remain in your memories and minds,
As base and finalè too for all metaphysics.

(So to the students the old professor,
At the close of his crowded course.)

Having studied the new and antique, the Greek and
    Germanic systems,
Kant having studied and stated, Fichte and Schelling and
    Hegel,
Stated the lore of Plato, and Socrates greater than Plato,
And greater than Socrates sought and stated, Christ divine
    having studied long,
I see reminiscent to-day those Greek and Germanic systems,
See the philosophies all, Christian churches and tenets see,
Yet underneath Socrates clearly see, and underneath Christ
    the divine I see,

The dear love of man for his comrade, the attraction of friend
    to friend,
Of the well-married husband and wife, of children and
    parents,
Of city for city and land for land.

RECORDERS AGES HENCE

Recorders ages hence,
Come, I will take you down underneath this impassive
    exterior, I will tell you what to say of me,
Publish my name and hang up my picture as that of the
    tenderest lover,
The friend the lover's portrait, of whom his friend his lover
    was fondest,
Who was not proud of his songs, but of the measureless
    ocean of love within him, and freely pour'd it forth,
Who often walk'd lonesome walks thinking of his dear
    friends, his lovers,
Who pensive away from one he lov'd often lay sleepless and
    dissatisfied at night,
Who knew too well the sick, sick dread lest the one he lov'd
    might secretly be indifferent to him,
Whose happiest days were far away through fields, in woods,
    on hills, he and another wandering hand in hand, they
    twain apart from other men,
Who oft as he saunter'd the streets curv'd with his arm the
    shoulder of his friend, while the arm of his friend rested
    upon him also.

WHEN I HEARD AT THE CLOSE OF THE DAY

When I heard at the close of the day how my name had been
    receiv'd with plaudits in the capitol, still it was not a
    happy night for me that follow'd,
And else when I carous'd, or when my plans were
    accomplish'd, still I was not happy,

But the day when I rose at dawn from the bed of perfect
    health, refresh'd, singing, inhaling the ripe breath of
    autumn,
When I saw the full moon in the west grow pale and
    disappear in the morning light,
When I wander'd alone over the beach, and undressing
    bathed, laughing with the cool waters, and saw the sun
    rise,
And when I thought how my dear friend my lover was on his
    way coming, O then I was happy,
O then each breath tasted sweeter, and all that day my food
    nourish'd me more, and the beautiful day pass'd well,
And the next came with equal joy, and with the next at
    evening came my friend,
And that night while all was still I heard the waters roll
    slowly continually up the shores,
I heard the hissing rustle of the liquid and sands as directed
    to me whispering to congratulate me,
For the one I love most lay sleeping by me under the same
    cover in the cool night,
In the stillness in the autumn moonbeams his face was
    inclined toward me,
And his arm lay lightly around my breast—and that night I
    was happy.

ARE YOU THE NEW PERSON DRAWN TOWARD ME?

Are you the new person drawn toward me?
To begin with take warning, I am surely far different from
    what you suppose;
Do you suppose you will find in me your ideal?
Do you think it so easy to have me become your lover?
Do you think the friendship of me would be unalloy'd
    satisfaction?
Do you think I am trusty and faithful?

Do you see no further than this façade, this smooth and
    tolerant manner of me?
Do you suppose yourself advancing on real ground toward a
    real heroic man?
Have you no thought O dreamer that it may be all maya,
    illusion?

ROOTS AND LEAVES THEMSELVES ALONE

Roots and leaves themselves alone are these,
Scents brought to men and women from the wild woods and
    pond-side,
Breast-sorrel and pinks of love, fingers that wind around
    tighter than vines,
Gushes from the throats of birds hid in the foliage of trees as
    the sun is risen,
Breezes of land and love set from living shores to you on the
    living sea, to you O sailors!
Frost-mellow'd berries and Third-month twigs offer'd fresh
    to young persons wandering out in the fields when the
    winter breaks up,
Love-buds put before you and within you whoever you are,
Buds to be unfolded on the old terms,
If you bring the warmth of the sun to them they will open
    and bring form, color, perfume, to you,
If you become the aliment and the wet they will become
    flowers, fruits, tall branches and trees.

NOT HEAT FLAMES UP AND CONSUMES

Not heat flames up and consumes,
Not sea-waves hurry in and out,
Not the air delicious and dry, the air of ripe summer,
    bears lightly along white down-balls of myriads of seeds,
Wafted, sailing gracefully, to drop where they may;
Not these, O none of these more than the flames of me,
    consuming, burning for his love whom I love,

O none more than I hurrying in and out;
Does the tide hurry, seeking something, and never give up?
   O I the same,
O nor down-balls nor perfumes, nor the high rain-emitting
   clouds, are borne through the open air,
Any more than my soul is borne through the open air,
Wafted in all directions O love, for friendship, for you.

TRICKLE DROPS

Trickle drops! my blue veins leaving!
O drops of me! trickle, slow drops,
Candid from me falling, drip, bleeding drops,
From wounds made to free you whence you were prison'd,
From my face, from my forehead and lips,
From my breast, from within where I was conceal'd, press
   forth red drops, confession drops,
Stain every page, stain every song I sing, every word I say,
   bloody drops,
Let them know your scarlet heat, let them glisten,
Saturate them with yourself all ashamed and wet,
Glow upon all I have written or shall write, bleeding drops,
Let it all be seen in your light, blushing drops.

CITY OF ORGIES

City of orgies, walks and joys,
City whom that I have lived and sung in your midst will one
   day make you illustrious,
Not the pageants of you, not your shifting tableaus, your
   spectacles, repay me,
Not the interminable rows of your houses, nor the ships at
   the wharves,
Nor the processions in the streets, nor the bright windows
   with goods in them,
Nor to converse with learn'd persons, or bear my share in the
   soiree or feast;

Not those, but as I pass O Manhattan, your frequent and
    swift flash of eyes offering me love,
Offering response to my own—these repay me,
Lovers, continual lovers, only repay me.

BEHOLD THIS SWARTHY FACE

Behold this swarthy face, these gray eyes,
This beard, the white wool unclipt upon my neck,
My brown hands and the silent manner of me without
    charm;
Yet comes one a Manhattanese and ever at parting kisses me
    lightly on the lips with robust love,
And I on the crossing of the street or on the ship's deck give
    a kiss in return,
We observe that salute of American comrades land and sea,
We are those two natural and nonchalant persons.

I SAW IN LOUISIANA A LIVE-OAK GROWING

I saw in Louisiana a live-oak growing,
All alone stood it and the moss hung down from the branches,
Without any companion it grew there uttering joyous leaves
    of dark green,
And its look, rude, unbending, lusty, made me think of
    myself,
But I wonder'd how it could utter joyous leaves standing alone
    there without its friend near, for I knew I could not,
And I broke off a twig with a certain number of leaves upon
    it, and twined around it a little moss,
And brought it away, and I have placed it in sight in my
    room,
It is not needed to remind me as of my own dear friends,
(For I believe lately I think of little else than of them,)
Yet it remains to me a curious token, it makes me think of
    manly love;

For all that, and though the live-oak glistens there in
    Louisiana solitary in a wide flat space,
Uttering joyous leaves all its life without a friend a lover near,
I know very well I could not.

TO A STRANGER

Passing stranger! you do not know how longingly I look
    upon you,
You must be he I was seeking, or she I was seeking, (it comes
    to me as of a dream,)
I have somewhere surely lived a life of joy with you,
All is recall'd as we flit by each other, fluid, affectionate,
    chaste, matured,
You grew up with me, were a boy with me or a girl with me,
I ate with you and slept with you, your body has become not
    yours only nor left my body mine only,
You give me the pleasure of your eyes, face, flesh, as we pass,
    you take of my beard, breast, hands, in return,
I am not to speak to you, I am to think of you when I sit
    alone or wake at night alone,
I am to wait, I do not doubt I am to meet you again,
I am to see to it that I do not lose you.

THIS MOMENT YEARNING AND THOUGHTFUL

This moment yearning and thoughtful sitting alone,
It seems to me there are other men in other lands yearning
    and thoughtful,
It seems to me I can look over and behold them in Germany,
    Italy, France, Spain,
Or far, far away, in China, or in Russia or Japan, talking
    other dialects,
And it seems to me if I could know those men I should
    become attached to them as I do to men in my own
    lands,
O I know we should be brethren and lovers,
I know I should be happy with them.

I HEAR IT WAS CHARGED AGAINST ME

I hear it was charged against me that I sought to destroy
      institutions,
But really I am neither for nor against institutions,
(What indeed have I in common with them? or what with
      the destruction of them?)
Only I will establish in the Mannahatta and in every city of
      these States inland and seaboard,
And in the fields and woods, and above every keel little or
      large that dents the water,
Without edifices or rules or trustees or any argument,
The institution of the dear love of comrades.

THE PRAIRIE-GRASS DIVIDING

The prairie-grass dividing, its special odor breathing,
I demand of it the spiritual corresponding,
Demand the most copious and close companionship of men,
Demand the blades to rise of words, acts, beings,
Those of the open atmosphere, coarse, sunlit, fresh, nutritious,
Those that go their own gait, erect, stepping with freedom
      and command, leading not following,
Those with a never-quell'd audacity, those with sweet and
      lusty flesh clear of taint,
Those that look carelessly in the faces of Presidents and
      governors, as to say *Who are you?*
Those of earth-born passion, simple, never constrain'd, never
      obedient,
Those of inland America.

WHEN I PERUSE THE CONQUER'D FAME

When I peruse the conquer'd fame of heroes and the victories
      of mighty generals, I do not envy the generals,
Nor the President in his Presidency, nor the rich in his great
      house,

But when I hear of the brotherhood of lovers, how it was
    with them,
How together through life, through dangers, odium,
    unchanging, long and long,
Through youth and through middle and old age, how
    unfaltering, how affectionate and faithful they were,
Then I am pensive—I hastily walk away fill'd with the
    bitterest envy.

WE TWO BOYS TOGETHER CLINGING

We two boys together clinging,
One the other never leaving,
Up and down the roads going, North and South excursions
    making,
Power enjoying, elbows stretching, fingers clutching,
Arm'd and fearless, eating, drinking, sleeping, loving,
No law less than ourselves owning, sailing, soldiering,
    thieving, threatening,
Misers, menials, priests alarming, air breathing, water
    drinking, on the turf or the sea-beach dancing,
Cities wrenching, ease scorning, statutes mocking, feebleness
    chasing,
Fulfilling our foray.

A PROMISE TO CALIFORNIA

A promise to California,
Or inland to the great pastoral Plains, and on to Puget sound
    and Oregon;
Sojourning east a while longer, soon I travel toward you, to
    remain, to teach robust American love,
For I know very well that I and robust love belong among
    you, inland, and along the Western sea;
For these States tend inland and toward the Western sea, and
    I will also.

HERE THE FRAILEST LEAVES OF ME

Here the frailest leaves of me and yet my strongest lasting,
Here I shade and hide my thoughts, I myself do not expose
    them,
And yet they expose me more than all my other poems.

NO LABOR-SAVING MACHINE

No labor-saving machine,
Nor discovery have I made,
Nor will I be able to leave behind me any wealthy bequest to
    found a hospital or library,
Nor reminiscence of any deed of courage for America,
Nor literary success nor intellect, nor book for the book-shelf,
But a few carols vibrating through the air I leave,
For comrades and lovers.

A GLIMPSE

A glimpse through an interstice caught,
Of a crowd of workmen and drivers in a bar-room around
    the stove late of a winter night, and I unremark'd seated
    in a corner,
Of a youth who loves me and whom I love, silently
    approaching and seating himself near, that he may hold
    me by the hand,
A long while amid the noises of coming and going, of
    drinking and oath and smutty jest,
There we two, content, happy in being together, speaking
    little, perhaps not a word.

A LEAF FOR HAND IN HAND

A leaf for hand in hand;
You natural persons old and young!
You on the Mississippi and on all the branches and bayous of
    the Mississippi!

You friendly boatmen and mechanics! you roughs!
You twain! and all processions moving along the streets!
I wish to infuse myself among you till I see it common for
        you to walk hand in hand.

EARTH, MY LIKENESS

Earth, my likeness,
Though you look so impassive, ample and spheric there,
I now suspect that is not all;
I now suspect there is something fierce in you eligible to
        burst forth,
For an athlete is enamour'd of me, and I of him,
But toward him there is something fierce and terrible in me
        eligible to burst forth,
I dare not tell it in words, not even in these songs.

I DREAM'D IN A DREAM

I dream'd in a dream I saw a city invincible to the attacks of
        the whole of the rest of the earth,
I dream'd that was the new city of Friends,
Nothing was greater there than the quality of robust love, it
        led the rest,
It was seen every hour in the actions of the men of that city,
And in all their looks and words.

WHAT THINK YOU I TAKE MY PEN IN HAND?

What think you I take my pen in hand to record?
The battle-ship, perfect-model'd, majestic, that I saw pass the
        offing to-day under full sail?
The splendors of the past day? or the splendor of the night
        that envelops me?
Or the vaunted glory and growth of the great city spread
        around me? — no;

But merely of two simple men I saw to-day on the pier in the
      midst of the crowd, parting the parting of dear friends,
The one to remain hung on the other's neck and passionately
      kiss'd him,
While the one to depart tightly prest the one to remain in his
      arms.

TO THE EAST AND TO THE WEST

To the East and to the West,
To the man of the Seaside State and of Pennsylvania,
To the Kanadian of the north, to the Southerner I love,
These with perfect trust to depict you as myself, the germs
      are in all men,
I believe the main purport of these States is to found a
      superb friendship, exaltè, previously unknown,
Because I perceive it waits, and has been always waiting,
      latent in all men.

SOMETIMES WITH ONE I LOVE

Sometimes with one I love I fill myself with rage for fear I
      effuse unreturn'd love,
But now I think there is no unreturn'd love, the pay is certain
      one way or another,
(I loved a certain person ardently and my love was not
      return'd,
Yet out of that I have written these songs.)

TO A WESTERN BOY

Many things to absorb I teach to help you become eleve of
      mine;
Yet if blood like mine circle not in your veins,
If you be not silently selected by lovers and do not silently
      select lovers,
Of what use is it that you seek to become eleve of mine?

FAST ANCHOR'D ETERNAL O LOVE!

Fast-anchor'd eternal O love! O woman I love!
O bride! O wife! more resistless than I can tell, the thought
    of you!
Then separate, as disembodied or another born,
Ethereal, the last athletic reality, my consolation,
I ascend, I float in the regions of your love O man,
O sharer of my roving life.

AMONG THE MULTITUDE

Among the men and women the multitude,
I perceive one picking me out by secret and divine signs,
Acknowledging none else, not parent, wife, husband,
    brother, child, any nearer than I am,
Some are baffled, but that one is not—that one knows me.

Ah lover and perfect equal,
I meant that you should discover me so by faint indirections,
And I when I meet you mean to discover you by the like
    in you.

O YOU WHOM I OFTEN AND SILENTLY COME

O you whom I often and silently come where you are that I
    may be with you,
As I walk by your side or sit near, or remain in the same
    room with you,
Little you know the subtle electric fire that for your sake is
    playing within me.

THAT SHADOW MY LIKENESS

That shadow my likeness that goes to and fro seeking a
    livelihood, chattering, chaffering,
How often I find myself standing and looking at it where it
    flits,

How often I question and doubt whether that is really me;
But among my lovers and caroling these songs,
O I never doubt whether that is really me.

FULL OF LIFE NOW

Full of life now, compact, visible,
I, forty years old the eighty-third year of the States,
To one a century hence or any number of centuries hence,
To you yet unborn these, seeking you.

When you read these I that was visible am become invisible,
Now it is you, compact, visible, realizing my poems,
    seeking me,
Fancying how happy you were if I could be with you and
    become your comrade;
Be it as if I were with you. (Be not too certain but I am now
    with you.)

Crossing Brooklyn Ferry

I

Flood-tide below me! I see you face to face!
Clouds of the west—sun there half an hour high—I see you
    also face to face.

Crowds of men and women attired in the usual costumes,
    how curious you are to me!
On the ferry-boats the hundreds and hundreds that cross,
    returning home, are more curious to me than you
    suppose,
And you that shall cross from shore to shore years hence are
    more to me, and more in my meditations, than you
    might suppose.

2

The impalpable sustenance of me from all things at all hours
    of the day,
The simple, compact, well-join'd scheme, myself disintegrated,
    every one disintegrated yet part of the scheme,
The similitudes of the past and those of the future,
The glories strung like beads on my smallest sights and
    hearings, on the walk in the street and the passage over
    the river,
The current rushing so swiftly and swimming with me far
    away,
The others that are to follow me, the ties between me and
    them,
The certainty of others, the life, love, sight, hearing of others.

Others will enter the gates of the ferry and cross from shore
    to shore,
Others will watch the run of the flood-tide,
Others will see the shipping of Manhattan north and west,
    and the heights of Brooklyn to the south and east,
Others will see the islands large and small;
Fifty years hence, others will see them as they cross, the sun
    half an hour high,
A hundred years hence, or ever so many hundred years
    hence, others will see them,
Will enjoy the sunset, the pouring-in of the flood-tide, the
    falling-back to the sea of the ebb-tide.

3

It avails not, time nor place—distance avails not,
I am with you, you men and women of a generation, or ever
    so many generations hence,
Just as you feel when you look on the river and sky, so I felt,
Just as any of you is one of a living crowd, I was one of a
    crowd,
Just as you are refresh'd by the gladness of the river and the
    bright flow, I was refresh'd,

Just as you stand and lean on the rail, yet hurry with the swift
current, I stood yet was hurried,
Just as you look on the numberless masts of ships and the
thick-stemm'd pipes of steamboats, I look'd.

I too many and many a time cross'd the river of old,
Watched the Twelfth-month sea-gulls, saw them high in the
air floating with motionless wings, oscillating their
bodies,
Saw how the glistening yellow lit up parts of their bodies and
left the rest in strong shadow,
Saw the slow-wheeling circles and the gradual edging toward
the south,
Saw the reflection of the summer sky in the water,
Had my eyes dazzled by the shimmering track of beams,
Look'd at the fine centrifugal spokes of light round the shape
of my head in the sunlit water,
Look'd on the haze on the hills southward and south-
westward,
Look'd on the vapor as it flew in fleeces tinged with
violet,
Look'd toward the lower bay to notice the vessels arriving,
Saw their approach, saw aboard those that were near me,
Saw the white sails of schooners and sloops, saw the ships at
anchor,
The sailors at work in the rigging or out astride the spars,
The round masts, the swinging motion of the hulls, the
slender serpentine pennants,
The large and small steamers in motion, the pilots in their
pilot-houses,
The white wake left by the passage, the quick tremulous
whirl of the wheels,
The flags of all nations, the falling of them at sunset,
The scallop-edged waves in the twilight, the ladled cups, the
frolicsome crests and glistening,
The stretch afar growing dimmer and dimmer, the gray walls
of the granite storehouses by the docks,
On the river the shadowy group, the big steam-tug closely
flank'd on each side by the barges, the hay-boat, the
belated lighter,

On the neighboring shore the fires from the foundry
          chimneys burning high and glaringly into the night,
Casting their flicker of black contrasted with wild red and
          yellow light over the tops of houses, and down into the
          clefts of streets.

4

These and all else were to me the same as they are to you,
I loved well those cities, loved well the stately and rapid river,
The men and women I saw were all near to me,
Others the same—others who look back on me because I
          look'd forward to them,
(The time will come, though I stop here to-day and to-night.)

5

What is it then between us?
What is the count of the scores or hundreds of years between
          us?

Whatever it is, it avails not—distance avails not, and place
          avails not,
I too lived, Brooklyn of ample hills was mine,
I too walk'd the streets of Manhattan island, and bathed in
          the waters around it,
I too felt the curious abrupt questionings stir within me,
In the day among crowds of people sometimes they came
          upon me,
In my walks home late at night or as I lay in my bed they
          came upon me,
I too had been struck from the float forever held in solution,
I too had receiv'd identity by my body,
That I was I knew was of my body, and what I should be I
          knew I should be of my body.

6

It is not upon you alone the dark patches fall,
The dark threw its patches down upon me also,
The best I had done seem'd to me blank and suspicious,

My great thoughts as I supposed them, were they not in
    reality meagre?
Nor is it you alone who know what it is to be evil,
I am he who knew what it was to be evil,
I too knotted the old knot of contrariety,
Blabb'd, blush'd, resented, lied, stole, grudg'd,
Had guile, anger, lust, hot wishes I dared not speak,
Was wayward, vain, greedy, shallow, sly, cowardly, malignant,
The wolf, the snake, the hog, not wanting in me,
The cheating look, the frivolous word, the adulterous wish,
    not wanting,
Refusals, hates, postponements, meanness, laziness, none of
    these wanting,
Was one with the rest, the days and haps of the rest,
Was call'd by my nighest name by clear loud voices of young
    men as they saw me approaching or passing,
Felt their arms on my neck as I stood, or the negligent
    leaning of their flesh against me as I sat,
Saw many I loved in the street or ferry-boat or public
    assembly, yet never told them a word,
Lived the same life with the rest, the same old laughing,
    gnawing, sleeping,
Play'd the part that still looks back on the actor or actress,
The same old role, the role that is what we make it, as great
    as we like,
Or as small as we like, or both great and small.

7

Closer yet I approach you,
What thought you have of me now, I had as much of you—I
    laid in my stores in advance,
I consider'd long and seriously of you before you were born.

Who was to know what should come home to me?
Who knows but I am enjoying this?
Who knows, for all the distance, but I am as good as looking
    at you now, for all you cannot see me?

8

Ah, what can ever be more stately and admirable to me than
    mast-hemm'd Manhattan?
River and sunset and scallop-edg'd waves of flood-tide?
The sea-gulls oscillating their bodies, the hay-boat in the
    twilight, and the belated lighter?
What gods can exceed these that clasp me by the hand, and
    with voices I love call me promptly and loudly by my
    nighest name as I approach?
What is more subtle than this which ties me to the woman or
    man that looks in my face?
Which fuses me into you now, and pours my meaning into
    you?

We understand then do we not?
What I promis'd without mentioning it, have you not
    accepted?
What the study could not teach—what the preaching could
    not accomplish is accomplish'd, is it not?

9

Flow on, river! flow with the flood-tide, and ebb with the
    ebb-tide!
Frolic on, crested and scallop-edg'd waves!
Gorgeous clouds of the sunset! drench with your splendor
    me, or the men and women generations after me!
Cross from shore to shore, countless crowds of passengers!
Stand up, tall masts of Mannahatta! stand up, beautiful hills
    of Brooklyn!
Throb, baffled and curious brain! throw out questions and
    answers!
Suspend here and everywhere, eternal float of solution!
Gaze, loving and thirsting eyes, in the house or street or
    public assembly!
Sound out, voices of young men! loudly and musically call
    me by my nighest name!
Live, old life! play the part that looks back on the actor or
    actress!

Play the old role, the role that is great or small according as
    one makes it!
Consider, you who peruse me, whether I may not in
    unknown ways be looking upon you;
Be firm, rail over the river, to support those who lean idly,
    yet haste with the hasting current;
Fly on, sea-birds! fly sideways, or wheel in large circles high
    in the air;
Receive the summer sky, you water, and faithfully hold it till
    all downcast eyes have time to take it from you!
Diverge, fine spokes of light, from the shape of my head, or
    any one's head, in the sunlit water!
Come on, ships from the lower bay! pass up or down, white-
    sail'd schooners, sloops, lighters!
Flaunt away, flags of all nations! be duly lower'd at sunset!
Burn high your fires, foundry chimneys! cast black shadows
    at nightfall! cast red and yellow light over the tops of the
    houses!
Appearances, now or henceforth, indicate what you are,
You necessary film, continue to envelop the soul,
About my body for me, and your body for you, be hung out
    divinest aromas,
Thrive, cities—bring your freight, bring your shows, ample
    and sufficient rivers,
Expand, being than which none else is perhaps more spiritual,
Keep your places, objects than which none else is more lasting.

You have waited, you always wait, you dumb, beautiful
    ministers,
We receive you with free sense at last, and are insatiate
    henceforward,
Not you any more shall be able to foil us, or withhold
    yourselves from us,
We use you, and do not cast you aside—we plant you
    permanently within us,
We fathom you not—we love you—there is perfection in
    you also,
You furnish your parts toward eternity,
Great or small, you furnish your parts toward the soul.

Sea-Drift

OUT OF THE CRADLE ENDLESSLY ROCKING

Out of the cradle endlessly rocking,
Out of the mocking-bird's throat, the musical shuttle,
Out of the Ninth-month midnight,
Over the sterile sands and the fields beyond, where the child
    leaving his bed wander'd alone, bareheaded, barefoot,
Down from the shower'd halo,
Up from the mystic play of shadows twining and twisting as
    if they were alive,
Out from the patches of briers and blackberries,
From the memories of the bird that chanted to me,
From your memories sad brother, from the fitful risings and
    fallings I heard,
From under that yellow half-moon late-risen and swollen as if
    with tears,
From those beginning notes of yearning and love there in the
    mist,
From the thousand responses of my heart never to cease,
From the myriad thence-arous'd words,
From the word stronger and more delicious than any,
From such as now they start the scene revisiting,
As a flock, twittering, rising, or overhead passing,
Borne hither, ere all eludes me, hurriedly,
A man, yet by these tears a little boy again,
Throwing myself on the sand, confronting the waves,
I, chanter of pains and joys, uniter of here and hereafter,
Taking all hints to use them, but swiftly leaping beyond
    them,
A reminiscence sing.

Once Paumanok,
When the lilac-scent was in the air and Fifth-month grass was
    growing,
Up this seashore in some briers,
Two feather'd guests from Alabama, two together,

And their nest, and four light-green eggs spotted with
    brown,
And every day the he-bird to and fro near at hand,
And every day the she-bird crouch'd on her nest, silent, with
    bright eyes,
And every day I, a curious boy, never too close, never
    disturbing them,
Cautiously peering, absorbing, translating.

Shine! shine! shine!
Pour down your warmth, great sun!
While we bask, we two together.

Two together!
Winds blow south, or winds blow north,
Day come white, or night come black,
Home, or rivers and mountains from home,
Singing all time, minding no time,
While we two keep together.

Till of a sudden,
May-be kill'd, unknown to her mate,
One forenoon the she-bird crouch'd not on the nest,
Nor return'd that afternoon, nor the next,
Nor ever appear'd again.

And thenceforward all summer in the sound of the sea,
And at night under the full of the moon in calmer weather,
Over the hoarse surging of the sea,
Or flitting from brier to brier by day,
I saw, I heard at intervals the remaining one, the he-bird,
The solitary guest from Alabama.

Blow! blow! blow!
Blow up sea-winds along Paumanok's shore;
I wait and I wait till you blow my mate to me.

Yes, when the stars glisten'd,
All night long on the prong of a moss-scallop'd stake,
Down almost amid the slapping waves,
Sat the lone singer wonderful causing tears.

He call'd on his mate,
He pour'd forth the meanings which I of all men know.

Yes my brother I know,
The rest might not, but I have treasur'd every note,
For more than once dimly down to the beach gliding,
Silent, avoiding the moonbeams, blending myself with the
    shadows,
Recalling now the obscure shapes, the echoes, the sounds
    and sights after their sorts,
The white arms out in the breakers tirelessly tossing,
I, with bare feet, a child, the wind wafting my hair,
Listen'd long and long.

Listen'd to keep, to sing, now translating the notes,
Following you my brother.

Soothe! soothe! soothe!
Close on its wave soothes the wave behind,
And again another behind embracing and lapping, every one close,
But my love soothes not me, not me.

Low hangs the moon, it rose late,
It is lagging — O I think it is heavy with love, with love.

O madly the sea pushes upon the land,
With love, with love.

O night! do I not see my love fluttering out among the breakers?
What is that little black thing I see there in the white?

Loud! loud! loud!
Loud I call to you, my love!

High and clear I shoot my voice over the waves,
Surely you must know who is here, is here,
You must know who I am, my love.

Low-hanging moon!
What is that dusky spot in your brown yellow?
O it is the shape, the shape of my mate!
O moon do not keep her from me any longer.

Land! land! O land!
Whichever way I turn, O I think you could give me my mate back
    again if you only would,
For I am almost sure I see her dimly whichever way I look.

O rising stars!
Perhaps the one I want so much will rise, will rise with some of
    you.

O throat! O trembling throat!
Sound clearer through the atmosphere!
Pierce the woods, the earth,
Somewhere listening to catch you must be the one I want.

Shake out carols!
Solitary here, the night's carols!
Carols of lonesome love! death's carols!
Carols under that lagging, yellow, waning moon!
O under that moon where she droops almost down into the sea!
O reckless despairing carols.

But soft! sink low!
Soft! let me just murmur,
And do you wait a moment you husky-nois'd sea,
For somewhere I believe I heard my mate responding to me,
So faint, I must be still, be still to listen,
But not altogether still, for then she might not come immediately
    to me.

Hither my love!
Here I am! here!
With this just-sustain'd note I announce myself to you,
This gentle call is for you my love, for you.

Do not be decoy'd elsewhere,
That is the whistle of the wind, it is not my voice,
That is the fluttering, the fluttering of the spray,
Those are the shadows of leaves.

O darkness! O in vain!
O I am very sick and sorrowful.

O brown halo in the sky near the moon, drooping upon the sea!
O troubled reflection in the sea!
O throat! O throbbing heart!
And I singing uselessly, uselessly all the night.

O past! O happy life! O songs of joy!
In the air, in the woods, over fields,
Loved! loved! loved! loved! loved!
But my mate no more, no more with me!
We two together no more.

The aria sinking,
All else continuing, the stars shining,
The winds blowing, the notes of the bird continuous echoing,
With angry moans the fierce old mother incessantly moaning,
On the sands of Paumanok's shore gray and rustling,
The yellow half-moon enlarged, sagging down, drooping, the
    face of the sea almost touching,
The boy ecstatic, with his bare feet the waves, with his hair
    the atmosphere dallying,
The love in the heart long pent, now loose, now at last
    tumultuously bursting,
The aria's meaning, the ears, the soul, swiftly depositing,
The strange tears down the cheeks coursing,
The colloquy there, the trio, each uttering,
The undertone, the savage old mother incessantly crying,

To the boy's soul's questions sullenly timing, some drown'd
     secret hissing,
To the outsetting bard.

Demon or bird! (said the boy's soul,)
Is it indeed toward your mate you sing? or is it really to me?
For I, that was a child, my tongue's use sleeping, now I have
     heard you,
Now in a moment I know what I am for, I awake,
And already a thousand singers, a thousand songs, clearer,
     louder and more sorrowful than yours,
A thousand warbling echoes have started to life within me,
     never to die.

O you singer solitary, singing by yourself, projecting me,
O solitary me listening, never more shall I cease perpetuating
     you,
Never more shall I escape, never more the reverberations,
Never more the cries of unsatisfied love be absent from me,
Never again leave me to be the peaceful child I was before
     what there in the night,
By the sea under the yellow and sagging moon,
The messenger there arous'd, the fire, the sweet hell within,
The unknown want, the destiny of me.

O give me the clew! (it lurks in the night here somewhere,)
O if I am to have so much, let me have more!

A word then, (for I will conquer it,)
The word final, superior to all,
Subtle, sent up—what is it?—I listen;
Are you whispering it, and have been all the time, you sea-
     waves?
Is that it from your liquid rims and wet sands?

Whereto answering, the sea,
Delaying not, hurrying not,
Whisper'd me through the night, and very plainly before
     daybreak,

Lisp'd to me the low and delicious word death,
And again death, death, death, death,
Hissing melodious, neither like the bird nor like my arous'd
  child's heart,
But edging near as privately for me rustling at my feet,
Creeping thence steadily up to my ears and laving me softly
  all over,
Death, death, death, death, death.

Which I do not forget,
But fuse the song of my dusky demon and brother,
That he sang to me in the moonlight on Paumanok's gray
  beach,
With the thousand responsive songs at random,
My own songs awaked from that hour,
And with them the key, the word up from the waves,
The word of the sweetest song and all songs,
That strong and delicious word which, creeping to my feet,
(Or like some old crone rocking the cradle, swathed in sweet
  garments, bending aside,)
The sea whisper'd me.

AS I EBB'D WITH THE OCEAN OF LIFE

1

As I ebb'd with the ocean of life,
As I wended the shores I know,
As I walk'd where the ripples continually wash you
  Paumanok,
Where they rustle up hoarse and sibilant,
Where the fierce old mother endlessly cries for her castaways,
I musing late in the autumn day, gazing off southward,
Held by this electric self out of the pride of which I utter
  poems,
Was seiz'd by the spirit that trails in the lines underfoot,
The rim, the sediment that stands for all the water and all the
  land of the globe.

Fascinated, my eyes reverting from the south, dropt, to
     follow those slender windrows,
Chaff, straw, splinters of wood, weeds, and the sea-gluten,
Scum, scales from shining rocks, leaves of salt-lettuce, left by
     the tide,
Miles walking, the sound of breaking waves the other side
     of me,
Paumanok there and then as I thought the old thought of
     likenesses,
These you presented to me you fish-shaped island,
As I wended the shores I know,
As I walk'd with that electric self seeking types.

2

As I wend to the shores I know not,
As I list to the dirge, the voices of men and women
     wreck'd,
As I inhale the impalpable breezes that set in upon me,
As the ocean so mysterious rolls toward me closer and
     closer,
I too but signify at the utmost a little wash'd-up drift,
A few sands and dead leaves to gather,
Gather, and merge myself as part of the sands and drift.

O baffled, balk'd, bent to the very earth,
Oppress'd with myself that I have dared to open my
     mouth,
Aware now that amid all that blab whose echoes recoil
     upon me I have not once had the least idea who or
     what I am,
But that before all my arrogant poems the real Me stands yet
     untouch'd, untold, altogether unreach'd,
Withdrawn far, mocking me with mock-congratulatory signs
     and bows,
With peals of distant ironical laughter at every word I have
     written,
Pointing in silence to these songs, and then to the sand
     beneath.

I perceive I have not really understood any thing, not a single
    object, and that no man ever can,
Nature here in sight of the sea taking advantage of me to dart
    upon me and sting me,
Because I have dared to open my mouth to sing at all.

3

You oceans both, I close with you,
We murmur alike reproachfully rolling sands and drift,
    knowing not why,
These little shreds indeed standing for you and me and all.

You friable shore with trails of debris,
You fish-shaped island, I take what is underfoot,
What is yours is mine my father.

I too Paumanok,
I too have bubbled up, floated the measureless float, and
    been wash'd on your shores,
I too am but a trail of drift and debris,
I too leave little wrecks upon you, you fish-shaped island.

I throw myself upon your breast my father,
I cling to you so that you cannot unloose me,
I hold you so firm till you answer me something.

Kiss me my father,
Touch me with your lips as I touch those I love,
Breathe to me while I hold you close the secret of the
    murmuring I envy.

4

Ebb, ocean of life, (the flow will return,)
Cease not your moaning you fierce old mother,
Endlessly cry for your castaways, but fear not, deny not me,
Rustle not up so hoarse and angry against my feet as I touch
    you or gather from you.

I mean tenderly by you and all,
I gather for myself and for this phantom looking down
    where we lead, and following me and mine.

Me and mine, loose windrows, little corpses,
Froth, snowy white, and bubbles,
(See, from my dead lips the ooze exuding at last,
See, the prismatic colors glistening and rolling,)
Tufts of straw, sands, fragments,
Buoy'd hither from many moods, one contradicting another,
From the storm, the long calm, the darkness, the swell,
Musing, pondering, a breath, a briny tear, a dab of liquid or
    soil,
Up just as much out of fathomless workings fermented and
    thrown,
A limp blossom or two, torn, just as much over waves
    floating, drifted at random,
Just as much for us that sobbing dirge of Nature,
Just as much whence we come that blare of the cloud-
    trumpets,
We, capricious, brought hither we know not whence, spread
    out before you,
You up there walking or sitting,
Whoever you are, we too lie in drifts at your feet.

TEARS

Tears! tears! tears!
In the night, in solitude, tears,
On the white shore dripping, dripping, suck'd in by the sand,
Tears, not a star shining, all dark and desolate,
Moist tears from the eyes of a muffled head;
O who is that ghost? that form in the dark, with tears?
What shapeless lump is that, bent, crouch'd there on the sand?
Streaming tears, sobbing tears, throes, choked with wild cries;
O storm, embodied, rising, careering with swift steps along
    the beach!
O wild and dismal night storm, with wind—O belching and
    desperate!

O shade so sedate and decorous by day, with calm
    countenance and regulated pace,
But away at night as you fly, none looking—O then the
    unloosen'd ocean,
Of tears! tears! tears!

TO THE MAN-OF-WAR-BIRD

Thou who hast slept all night upon the storm,
Waking renew'd on thy prodigious pinions,
(Burst the wild storm? above it thou ascended'st,
And rested on the sky, thy slave that cradled thee,)
Now a blue point, far, far in heaven floating,
As to the light emerging here on deck I watch thee,
(Myself a speck, a point on the world's floating vast.)

Far, far at sea,
After the night's fierce drifts have strewn the shore with
    wrecks,
With re-appearing day as now so happy and serene,
The rosy and elastic dawn, the flashing sun,
The limpid spread of air cerulean,
Thou also re-appearest.

Thou born to match the gale, (thou art all wings,)
To cope with heaven and earth and sea and hurricane,
Thou ship of air that never furl'st thy sails,
Days, even weeks untired and onward, through spaces,
    realms gyrating,
At dusk that look'st on Senegal, at morn America,
That sport'st amid the lightning-flash and thunder-cloud,
In them, in thy experiences, had'st thou my soul,
What joys! what joys were thine!

ABOARD AT A SHIP'S HELM

Aboard at a ship's helm,
A young steersman steering with care.

Through fog on a sea-coast dolefully ringing,
An ocean-bell—O a warning bell, rock'd by the waves.

O you give good notice indeed, you bell by the sea-reefs
ringing,
Ringing, ringing, to warn the ship from its wreck-place.

For as on the alert O steersman, you mind the loud
admonition,
The bows turn, the freighted ship tacking speeds away under
her gray sails,
The beautiful and noble ship with all her precious wealth
speeds away gayly and safe.

But O the ship, the immortal ship! O ship aboard the ship!
Ship of the body, ship of the soul, voyaging, voyaging,
voyaging.

ON THE BEACH AT NIGHT

On the beach at night,
Stands a child with her father,
Watching the east, the autumn sky.

Up through the darkness,
While ravening clouds, the burial clouds, in black masses
spreading,
Lower sullen and fast athwart and down the sky,
Amid a transparent clear belt of ether yet left in the east,
Ascends large and calm the lord-star Jupiter,
And nigh at hand, only a very little above,
Swim the delicate sisters the Pleiades.

From the beach the child holding the hand of her father,
Those burial-clouds that lower victorious soon to devour all,
Watching, silently weeps.

Weep not, child,
Weep not, my darling,

With these kisses let me remove your tears,
The ravening clouds shall not long be victorious,
They shall not long possess the sky, they devour the stars
     only in apparition,
Jupiter shall emerge, be patient, watch again another night,
     the Pleiades shall emerge,
They are immortal, all those stars both silvery and golden
     shall shine out again,
The great stars and the little ones shall shine out again, they
     endure,
The vast immortal suns and the long-enduring pensive moons
     shall again shine.

Then dearest child mournest thou only for Jupiter?
Considerest thou alone the burial of the stars?

Something there is,
(With my lips soothing thee, adding I whisper,
I give thee the first suggestion, the problem and indirection,)
Something there is more immortal even than the stars,
(Many the burials, many the days and night, passing away,)
Something that shall endure longer even than lustrous
     Jupiter,
Longer than sun or any revolving satellite,
Or the radiant sisters the Pleiades.

THE WORLD BELOW THE BRINE

The world below the brine,
Forests at the bottom of the sea, the branches and leaves,
Sea-lettuce, vast lichens, strange flowers and seeds, the thick
     tangle, openings, and pink turf,
Different colors, pale gray and green, purple, white, and
     gold, the play of light through the water,
Dumb swimmers there among the rocks, coral, gluten, grass,
     rushes, and the aliment of the swimmers,
Sluggish existences grazing there suspended, or slowly
     crawling close to the bottom,

The sperm-whale at the surface blowing air and spray, or
    disporting with his flukes,
The leaden-eyed shark, the walrus, the turtle, the hairy sea-
    leopard, and the sting-ray,
Passions there, wars, pursuits, tribes, sight in those ocean-
    depths, breathing that thick-breathing air, as so many
    do,
The change thence to the sight here, and to the subtle air
    breathed by beings like us who walk this sphere,
The change onward from ours to that of beings who walk
    other spheres.

ON THE BEACH AT NIGHT ALONE

On the beach at night alone,
As the old mother sways her to and fro singing her husky
    song,
As I watch the bright stars shining, I think a thought of the
    clef of the universes and of the future.

A vast similitude interlocks all,
All spheres, grown, ungrown, small, large, suns, moons,
    planets,
All distances of place however wide,
All distances of time, all inanimate forms,
All souls, all living bodies though they be ever so different,
    or in different worlds,
All gaseous, watery, vegetable, mineral processes, the fishes,
    the brutes,
All nations, colors, barbarisms, civilizations, languages,
All identities that have existed or may exist on this globe, or
    any globe,
All lives and deaths, all of the past, present, future,
This vast similitude spans them, and always has spann'd,
And shall forever span them and compactly hold and enclose
    them.

SONG FOR ALL SEAS, ALL SHIPS

1

To-day a rude brief recitative,
Of ships sailing the seas, each with its special flag or ship-
        signal,
Of unnamed heroes in the ships—of waves spreading and
        spreading far as the eye can reach,
Of dashing spray, and the winds piping and blowing,
And out of these a chant for the sailors of all nations,
Fitful, like a surge.

Of sea-captains young or old, and the mates, and of all
        intrepid sailors,
Of the few, very choice, taciturn, whom fate can never
        surprise nor death dismay,
Pick'd sparingly without noise by thee old ocean, chosen by
        thee,
Thou sea that pickest and cullest the race in time, and unitest
        nations,
Suckled by thee, old husky nurse, embodying thee,
Indomitable, untamed as thee.

(Ever the heroes on water or on land, by ones or twos
        appearing,
Ever the stock preserv'd and never lost, though rare, enough
        for seed preserv'd.)

2

Flaunt out O sea your separate flags of nations!
Flaunt out visible as ever the various ship-signals!
But do you reserve especially for yourself and for the soul of
        man one flag above all the rest,
A spiritual woven signal for all nations, emblem of man elate
        above death,
Token of all brave captains and all intrepid sailors and mates,
And all that went down doing their duty,

Reminiscent of them, twined from all intrepid captains
    young or old,
A pennant universal, subtly waving all time, o'er all brave
    sailors,
All seas, all ships.

PATROLING BARNEGAT

Wild, wild the storm, and the sea high running,
Steady the roar of the gale, with incessant undertone
    muttering,
Shouts of demoniac laughter fitfully piercing and pealing,
Waves, air, midnight, their savagest trinity lashing,
Out in the shadows there milk-white combs careering,
On beachy slush and sand spirts of snow fierce slanting,
Where through the murk the easterly death-wind breasting,
Through cutting swirl and spray watchful and firm advancing,
(That in the distance! is that a wreck? is the red signal flaring?)
Slush and sand of the beach tireless till daylight wending,
Steadily, slowly, through hoarse roar never remitting,
Along the midnight edge by those milk-white combs careering,
A group of dim, weird forms, struggling, the night
    confronting,
That savage trinity warily watching.

AFTER THE SEA-SHIP

After the sea-ship, after the whistling winds,
After the white-gray sails taut to their spars and ropes,
Below, a myriad myriad waves hastening, lifting up their
    necks,
Tending in ceaseless flow toward the track of the ship,
Waves of the ocean bubbling and gurgling, blithely prying,
Waves, undulating waves, liquid, uneven, emulous waves,
Toward that whirling current, laughing and buoyant, with
    curves,
Where the great vessel sailing and tacking displaced the surface,

Larger and smaller waves in the spread of the ocean
    yearnfully flowing,
The wake of the sea-ship after she passes, flashing and
    frolicsome under the sun,
A motley procession with many a fleck of foam and many
    fragments,
Following the stately and rapid ship, in the wake following.

from *Drum-Taps*

COME UP FROM THE FIELDS FATHER

Come up from the fields father, here's a letter from our
    Pete,
And come to the front door mother, here's a letter from thy
    dear son.

Lo, 'tis autumn,
Lo, where the trees, deeper green, yellower and redder,
Cool and sweeten Ohio's villages with leaves fluttering in the
    moderate wind,
Where apples ripe in the orchards hang and grapes on the
    trellis'd vines,
(Smell you the smell of the grapes on the vines?
Smell you the buckwheat where the bees were lately
    buzzing?)

Above all, lo, the sky so calm, so transparent after the rain,
    and with wondrous clouds,
Below too, all calm, all vital and beautiful, and the farm
    prospers well.

Down in the fields all prospers well,
But now from the fields come father, come at the daughter's
    call,
And come to the entry mother, to the front door come right
    away.

Fast as she can she hurries, something ominous, her steps
    trembling,
She does not tarry to smooth her hair nor adjust her cap.

Open the envelope quickly,
O this is not our son's writing, yet his name is sign'd,
O a strange hand writes for our dear son, O stricken
    mother's soul!
All swims before her eyes, flashes with black, she catches the
    main words only,
Sentences broken, *gunshot wound in the breast, cavalry
    skirmish, taken to hospital,*
At present low, but will soon be better.

Ah now the single figure to me,
Amid all teeming and wealthy Ohio with all its cities and
    farms,
Sickly white in the face and dull in the head, very faint,
By the jamb of a door leans.

Grieve not so, dear mother, (the just-grown daughter speaks
    through her sobs,
The little sisters huddle around speechless and dismay'd,)
See, dearest mother, the letter says Pete will soon be better.

Alas poor boy, he will never be better, (nor may-be needs to
    be better, that brave and simple soul,)
While they stand at home at the door he is dead already,
The only son is dead.

But the mother needs to be better,
She with thin form presently drest in black,
By day her meals untouch'd, then at night fitfully sleeping,
    often waking,
In the midnight waking, weeping, longing with one deep
    longing,
O that she might withdraw unnoticed, silent from life escape
    and withdraw,
To follow, to seek, to be with her dear dead son.

VIGIL STRANGE I KEPT ON
THE FIELD ONE NIGHT

Vigil strange I kept on the field one night;

When you my son and my comrade dropt at my side that
day,

One look I but gave which your dear eyes return'd with a
look I shall never forget,

One touch of your hand to mine O boy, reach'd up as you
lay on the ground,

Then onward I sped in the battle, the even-contested battle,

Till late in the night reliev'd to the place at last again I made
my way,

Found you in death so cold dear comrade, found your body
son of responding kisses, (never again on earth
responding,)

Bared your face in the starlight, curious the scene, cool blew
the moderate night-wind,

Long there and then in vigil I stood, dimly around me the
battle-field spreading,

Vigil wondrous and vigil sweet there in the fragrant silent
night,

But not a tear fell, not even a long-drawn sigh, long, long I
gazed,

Then on the earth partially reclining sat by your side leaning
my chin in my hands,

Passing sweet hours, immortal and mystic hours with you
dearest comrade—not a tear, not a word,

Vigil of silence, love and death, vigil for you my son and my
soldier,

As onward silently stars aloft, eastward new ones upward
stole,

Vigil final for you brave boy, (I could not save you, swift was
your death,

I faithfully loved you and cared for you living, I think we
shall surely meet again,)

Till at latest lingering of the night, indeed just as the dawn
appear'd,

My comrade I wrapt in his blanket, envelop'd well his form,

Folded the blanket well, tucking it carefully over head and
    carefully under feet,
And there and then and bathed by the rising sun, my son in
    his grave, in his rude-dug grave I deposited,
Ending my vigil strange with that, vigil of night and battle-
    field dim,
Vigil for boy of responding kisses, (never again on earth
    responding,)
Vigil for comrade swiftly slain, vigil I never forget, how as
    day brighten'd,
I rose from the chill ground and folded my soldier well in his
    blanket,
And buried him where he fell.

AS TOILSOME I WANDER'D VIRGINIA'S WOODS

As toilsome I wander'd Virginia's woods,
To the music of rustling leaves kick'd by my feet, (for 'twas
    autumn,)
I mark'd at the foot of a tree the grave of a soldier;
Mortally wounded he and buried on the retreat, (easily all
    could I understand,)
The halt of a mid-day hour, when up! no time to lose—yet
    this sign left,
On a tablet scrawl'd and nail'd on the tree by the grave,
Bold, cautious, true, and my loving comrade.

Long, long I muse, then on my way go wandering,
Many a changeful season to follow, and many a scene of life,
Yet at times through changeful season and scene, abrupt,
    alone, or in the crowded street,
Comes before me the unknown soldier's grave, comes the
    inscription rude in Virginia's woods,
Bold, cautious, true, and my loving comrade.

THE WOUND-DRESSER

1

An old man bending I come among new faces,
Years looking backward resuming in answer to children,
Come tell us old man, as from young men and maidens that
    love me,
(Arous'd and angry, I'd thought to beat the alarum, and urge
    relentless war,
But soon my fingers fail'd me, my face droop'd and I resign'd
    myself,
To sit by the wounded and soothe them, or silently watch the
    dead;)
Years hence of these scenes, of these furious passions, these
    chances,
Of unsurpass'd heroes, (was one side so brave? the other was
    equally brave;)
Now be witness again, paint the mightiest armies of earth,
Of those armies so rapid so wondrous what saw you to tell
    us?
What stays with you latest and deepest? of curious panics,
Of hard-fought engagements or sieges tremendous what
    deepest remains?

2

O maidens and young men I love and that love me,
What you ask of my days those the strangest and sudden
    your talking recalls,
Soldier alert I arrive after a long march cover'd with sweat
    and dust,
In the nick of time I come, plunge in the fight, loudly shout
    in the rush of successful charge,
Enter the captur'd works—yet lo, like a swift-running river
    they fade,
Pass and are gone they fade—I dwell not on soldiers' perils
    or soldier's joys,
(Both I remember well—many the hardships, few the joys,
    yet I was content.)

But in silence, in dreams' projections,
While the world of gain and appearance and mirth goes on,
So soon what is over forgotten, and waves wash the
     imprints off the sand,
With hinged knees returning I enter the doors, (while for
     you up there,
Whoever you are, follow without noise and be of strong
     heart.)

Bearing the bandages, water and sponge,
Straight and swift to my wounded I go,
Where they lie on the ground after the battle brought in,
Where their priceless blood reddens the grass the ground,
Or to the rows of the hospital tent, or under the roof'd
     hospital,
To the long rows of cots up and down each side I return,
To each and all one after another I draw near, not one do
     I miss,
An attendant follows holding a tray, he carries a refuse pail,
Soon to be fill'd with clotted rags and blood, emptied, and
     fill'd again.

I onward go, I stop,
With hinged knees and steady hand to dress wounds,
I am firm with each, the pangs are sharp yet unavoidable,
One turns to me his appealing eyes—poor boy! I never knew
     you,
Yet I think I could not refuse this moment to die for you, if
     that would save you.

3

On, on I go, (open doors of time! open hospital doors!)
The crush'd head I dress, (poor crazed hand tear not the
     bandage away,)
The neck of the cavalry-man with the bullet through and
     through I examine,

Hard the breathing rattles, quite glazed already the eye, yet
    life struggles hard,
(Come sweet death! be persuaded O beautiful death!
In mercy come quickly.)

From the stump of the arm, the amputated hand,
I undo the clotted lint, remove the slough, wash off the
    matter and blood,
Back on his pillow the soldier bends with curv'd neck and
    side-falling head,
His eyes are closed, his face is pale, he dares not look on the
    bloody stump,
And has not yet look'd on it.

I dress a wound in the side, deep, deep,
But a day or two more, for see the frame all wasted and
    sinking,
And the yellow-blue countenance see.

I dress the perforated shoulder, the foot with the bullet-
    wound,
Cleanse the one with a gnawing and putrid gangrene, so
    sickening, so offensive,
While the attendant stands behind aside me holding the tray
    and pail.

I am faithful, I do not give out,
The fractur'd thigh, the knee, the wound in the abdomen,
These and more I dress with impassive hand, (yet deep in my
    breast a fire, a burning flame.)

4

Thus in silence in dreams' projections,
Returning, resuming, I thread my way through the hospitals,
The hurt and wounded I pacify with soothing hand,
I sit by the restless all the dark night, some are so young,

Some suffer so much, I recall the experience sweet and sad,
(Many a soldier's loving arms about this neck have cross'd
    and rested,
Many a soldier's kiss dwells on these bearded lips.)

DIRGE FOR TWO VETERANS

      The last sunbeam
Lightly falls from the finish'd Sabbath,
On the pavement here, and there beyond it is looking,
      Down a new-made double grave.

      Lo, the moon ascending,
Up from the east the silvery round moon,
Beautiful over the house-tops, ghastly, phantom moon,
      Immense and silent moon.

      I see a sad procession,
And I hear the sound of coming full-key'd bugles,
All the channels of the city streets they're flooding,
      As with voices and with tears.

      I hear the great drums pounding,
And the small drums steady whirring,
And every blow of the great convulsive drums,
      Strikes me through and through.

      For the son is brought with the father,
(In the foremost ranks of the fierce assault they fell,
Two veterans son and father dropt together,
      And the double grave awaits them.)

      Now nearer blow the bugles,
And the drums strike more convulsive,
And the daylight o'er the pavement quite has faded,
      And the strong dead-march enwraps me.

In the eastern sky up-buoying,
The sorrowful vast phantom moves illumin'd,
('Tis some mother's large transparent face,
    In heaven brighter growing.)

        O strong dead-march you please me!
O moon immense with your silvery face you soothe me!
O my soldiers twain! O my veterans passing to burial!
    What I have I also give you.

    The moon gives you light,
And the bugles and the drums give you music,
And my heart, O my soldiers, my veterans,
    My heart gives you love.

RECONCILIATION

Word over all, beautiful as the sky,
Beautiful that war and all its deeds of carnage must in time
    be utterly lost,
That the hands of the sisters Death and Night incessantly
    softly wash again, and ever again, this soil'd world;
For my enemy is dead, a man divine as myself is dead,
I look where he lies white-faced and still in the coffin—I
    draw near,
Bend down and touch lightly with my lips the white face in
    the coffin.

from *Memories of President Lincoln*

WHEN LILACS LAST IN
THE DOORYARD BLOOM'D

I

When lilacs last in the dooryard bloom'd,
And the great star early droop'd in the western sky in the
    night,
I mourn'd, and yet shall mourn with ever-returning spring.

Ever-returning spring, trinity sure to me you bring,
Lilac blooming perennial and drooping star in the west,
And thought of him I love.

2

O powerful western fallen star!
O shades of night—O moody, tearful night!
O great star disappear'd—O the black murk that hides the
 star!
O cruel hands that hold me powerless—O helpless soul of
 me!
O harsh surrounding cloud that will not free my soul.

3

In the dooryard fronting an old farm-house near the white-
 wash'd palings,
Stands the lilac-bush tall-growing with heart-shaped leaves of
 rich green,
With many a pointed blossom rising delicate, with the
 perfume strong I love,
With every leaf a miracle—and from this bush in the
 dooryard,
With delicate-color'd blossoms and heart-shaped leaves of
 rich green,
A sprig with its flower I break.

4

In the swamp in secluded recesses,
A shy and hidden bird is warbling a song.

Solitary the thrush,
The hermit withdrawn to himself, avoiding the settlements,
Sings by himself a song.

Song of the bleeding throat,
Death's outlet song of life, (for well dear brother I know,
If thou wast not granted to sing thou would'st surely die.)

5

Over the breast of the spring, the land, amid cities,
Amid lanes and through old woods, where lately the violets
    peep'd from the ground, spotting the gray debris,
Amid the grass in the fields each side of the lanes, passing the
    endless grass,
Passing the yellow-spear'd wheat, every grain from its shroud
    in the dark-brown fields uprisen,
Passing the apple-tree blows of white and pink in the
    orchards,
Carrying a corpse to where it shall rest in the grave,
Night and day journeys a coffin.

6

Coffin that passes through lanes and streets,
Through day and night with the great cloud darkening the
    land,
With the pomp of the inloop'd flags with the cities draped in
    black,
With the show of the States themselves as of crape-veil'd
    women standing,
With processions long and winding and the flambeaus of the
    night,
With the countless torches lit, with the silent sea of faces and
    the unbared heads,
With the waiting depot, the arriving coffin, and the sombre
    faces,
With dirges through the night, with the thousand voices
    rising strong and solemn,
With all the mournful voices of the dirges pour'd around the
    coffin,
The dim-lit churches and the shuddering organs—where
    amid these you journey,
With the tolling tolling bells' perpetual clang,
Here, coffin that slowly passes,
I give you my sprig of lilac.

7

(Nor for you, for one alone,
Blossoms and branches green to coffins all I bring,
For fresh as the morning, thus would I chant a song for you
    O sane and sacred death.

All over bouquets of roses,
O death, I cover you over with roses and early lilies,
But mostly and now the lilac that blooms the first,
Copious I break, I break the sprigs from the bushes,
With loaded arms I come, pouring for you,
For you and the coffins all of you O death.)

8

O western orb sailing the heaven,
Now I know what you must have meant as a month since I
    walk'd,
As I walk'd in silence the transparent shadowy night,
As I saw you had something to tell as you bent to me night
    after night,
As you droop'd from the sky low down as if to my side,
    (while the other stars all look'd on,)
As we wander'd together the solemn night, (for something I
    know not what kept me from sleep,)
As the night advanced, and I saw on the rim of the west how
    full you were of woe,
As I stood on the rising ground in the breeze in the cool
    transparent night,
As I watch'd where you pass'd and was lost in the
    netherward black of the night,
As my soul in its trouble dissatisfied sank, as where you
    sad orb,
Concluded, dropt in the night, and was gone.

9

Sing on there in the swamp,
O singer bashful and tender, I hear your notes, I hear your
    call,

I hear, I come presently, I understand you,
But a moment I linger, for the lustrous star has detain'd me,
The star my departing comrade holds and detains me.

10

O how shall I warble myself for the dead one there I loved?
And how shall I deck my song for the large sweet soul that
     has gone?
And what shall my perfume be for the grave of him I love?

Sea-winds blown from east and west,
Blown from the Eastern sea and blown from the Western sea,
     till there on the prairies meeting,
These and with these and the breath of my chant,
I'll perfume the grave of him I love.

11

O what shall I hang on the chamber walls?
And what shall the pictures be that I hang on the walls,
To adorn the burial-house of him I love?

Pictures of growing spring and farms and homes,
With the Fourth-month eve at sundown, and the gray smoke
     lucid and bright,
With floods of the yellow gold of the gorgeous, indolent,
     sinking sun, burning, expanding the air,
With the fresh sweet herbage under foot, and the pale green
     leaves of the trees prolific,
In the distance the flowing glaze, the breast of the river, with
     a wind-dapple here and there,
With ranging hills on the banks, with many a line against the
     sky, and shadows,
And the city at hand with dwellings so dense, and stacks of
     chimneys,
And all the scenes of life and the workshops, and the
     workmen homeward returning.

12

Lo, body and soul—this land,
My own Manhattan with spires, and the sparkling and
    hurrying tides, and the ships,
The varied and ample land, the South and the North in the
    light, Ohio's shores and flashing Missouri,
And ever the far-spreading prairies cover'd with grass and corn.

Lo, the most excellent sun so calm and haughty,
The violet and purple morn with just-felt breezes,
The gentle soft-born measureless light,
The miracle spreading bathing all, the fulfill'd noon,
The coming eve delicious, the welcome night and the stars,
Over my cities shining all, enveloping man and land.

13

Sing on, sing on you gray-brown bird,
Sing from the swamps, the recesses, pour your chant from
    the bushes,
Limitless out of the dusk, out of the cedars and pines.

Sing on dearest brother, warble your reedy song,
Loud human song, with voice of uttermost woe.

O liquid and free and tender!
O wild and loose to my soul—O wondrous singer!
You only I hear—yet the star holds me, (but will soon depart,)
Yet the lilac with mastering odor holds me.

14

Now while I sat in the day and look'd forth,
In the close of the day with its light and the fields of spring,
    and the farmers preparing their crops,
In the large unconscious scenery of my land with its lakes and
    forests,
In the heavenly aerial beauty, (after the perturb'd winds and
    the storms,)

Under the arching heavens of the afternoon swift passing,
   and the voices of children and women,
The many-moving sea-tides, and I saw the ships how they
   sail'd,
And the summer approaching with richness, and the fields all
   busy with labor,
And the infinite separate houses, how they all went on, each
   with its meals and minutia of daily usages,
And the streets how their throbbings throbb'd, and the cities
   pent—lo, then and there,
Falling upon them all and among them all, enveloping me
   with the rest,
Appear'd the cloud, appear'd the long black trail,
And I knew death, its thought, and the sacred knowledge of
   death.

Then with the knowledge of death as walking one side of me,
And the thought of death close-walking the other side of me,
And I in the middle as with companions, and as holding the
   hands of companions,
I fled forth to the hiding receiving night that talks not,
Down to the shores of the water, the path by the swamp in
   the dimness,
To the solemn shadowy cedars and ghostly pines so still.

And the singer so shy to the rest receiv'd me,
The gray-brown bird I know receiv'd us comrades three,
And he sang the carol of death, and a verse for him I love.

From deep secluded recesses,
From the fragrant cedars and the ghostly pines so still,
Came the carol of the bird.

And the charm of the carol rapt me,
As I held as if by their hands my comrades in the night,
And the voice of my spirit tallied the song of the bird.

Come lovely and soothing death,
Undulate round the world, serenely arriving, arriving,
In the day, in the night, to all, to each,
Sooner or later delicate death.

Prais'd be the fathomless universe,
For life and joy, and for objects and knowledge curious,
And for love, sweet love—but praise! praise! praise!
For the sure-enwinding arms of cool-enfolding death.

Dark mother always gliding near with soft feet,
Have none chanted for thee a chant of fullest welcome?
Then I chant it for thee, I glorify thee above all,
I bring thee a song that when thou must indeed come, come
    unfalteringly.

Approach strong deliveress,
When it is so, when thou hast taken them I joyously sing the dead,
Lost in the loving floating ocean of thee,
Laved in the flood of thy bliss O death.

From me to thee glad serenades,
Dances for thee I propose saluting thee, adornments and feastings
    for thee,
And the sights of the open landscape and the high-spread sky are
    fitting,
And life and the fields, and the huge and thoughtful night.

The night in silence under many a star,
The ocean shore and the husky whispering wave whose voice I know,
And the soul turning to thee O vast and well-veil'd death,
And the body gratefully nestling close to thee.

Over the tree-tops I float thee a song,
Over the rising and sinking waves, over the myriad fields and the
    prairies wide,
Over the dense-pack'd cities all and the teeming wharves and ways,
I float this carol with joy, with joy to thee O death.

15

To the tally of my soul,
Loud and strong kept up the gray-brown bird,
With pure deliberate notes spreading filling the night.

Loud in the pines and cedars dim,
Clear in the freshness moist and the swamp-perfume,
And I with my comrades there in the night.

While my sight that was bound in my eyes unclosed,
As to long panoramas of visions.

And I saw askant the armies,
I saw as in noiseless dreams hundreds of battle-flags,
Borne through the smoke of the battles and pierc'd with
    missiles I saw them,
And carried hither and yon through the smoke, and torn and
    bloody,
And at last but a few shreds left on the staffs, (and all in
    silence,)
And the staffs all splinter'd and broken.

I saw battle-corpses, myriads of them,
And the white skeletons of young men, I saw them,
I saw the debris and debris of all the slain soldiers of the war,
But I saw they were not as was thought,
They themselves were fully at rest, they suffer'd not,
The living remain'd and suffer'd, the mother suffer'd,
And the wife and the child and the musing comrade suffer'd,
And the armies that remain'd suffer'd.

16

Passing the visions, passing the night,
Passing, unloosing the hold of my comrades' hands,
Passing the song of the hermit bird and the tallying song of
    my soul,
Victorious song, death's outlet song, yet varying ever-
    altering song,

As low and wailing, yet clear the notes, rising and falling,
 flooding the night,
Sadly sinking and fainting, as warning and warning, and yet
 again bursting with joy,
Covering the earth and filling the spread of the heaven,
As that powerful psalm in the night I heard from recesses,
Passing, I leave thee lilac with heart-shaped leaves,
I leave thee there in the door-yard, blooming, returning with
 spring.

I cease from my song for thee,
From my gaze on thee in the west, fronting the west,
 communing with thee,
O comrade lustrous with silver face in the night.

Yet each to keep and all, retrievements out of the night,
The song, the wondrous chant of the gray-brown bird,
And the tallying chant, the echo arous'd in my soul,
With the lustrous and drooping star with the countenance
 full of woe,
With the holders holding my hand nearing the call of the
 bird,
Comrades mine and I in the midst, and their memory ever to
 keep, for the dead I loved so well,
For the sweetest, wisest soul of all my days and lands—and
 this for his dear sake,
Lilac and star and bird twined with the chant of my soul,
There in the fragrant pines and the cedars dusk and dim.

O CAPTAIN! MY CAPTAIN!

O Captain! my Captain! our fearful trip is done,
The ship has weather'd every rack, the prize we sought is won,
The port is near, the bells I hear, the people all exulting,
While follow eyes the steady keel, the vessel grim and daring;
       But O heart! heart! heart!
        O the bleeding drops of red,
          Where on the deck my Captain lies,
           Fallen cold and dead.

O Captain! my Captain! rise up and hear the bells;
Rise up—for you the flag is flung—for you the bugle trills,
For you bouquets and ribbon'd wreaths—for you the shores
     a-crowding,
For you they call, the swaying mass, their eager faces turning;
           Here Captain! dear father!
             This arm beneath your head!
               It is some dream that on the deck,
                You've fallen cold and dead.

My Captain does not answer, his lips are pale and still,
My father does not feel my arm, he has no pulse nor will,
The ship is anchor'd safe and sound, its voyage closed and
     done,
From fearful trip the victor ship comes in with object won;
           Exult O shores, and ring O bells!
            But I with mournful tread,
              Walk the deck my Captain lies,
               Fallen cold and dead.

By Blue Ontario's Shore

1

By blue Ontario's shore,
As I mused of these warlike days and of peace return'd, and
     the dead that return no more,
A Phantom gigantic superb, with stern visage accosted me,
Chant me the poem, it said, *that comes from the soul of America,*
     chant me the carol of victory,
And strike up the marches of Libertad, marches more powerful yet,
And sing me before you go the song of the throes of Democracy.

(Democracy, the destin'd conqueror, yet treacherous lip-
     smiles everywhere,
And death and infidelity at every step.)

2

A Nation announcing itself,
I myself make the only growth by which I can be appreciated,
I reject none, accept all, then reproduce all in my own forms.

A breed whose proof is in time and deeds,
What we are we are, nativity is answer enough to objections,
We wield ourselves as a weapon is wielded,
We are powerful and tremendous in ourselves,
We are executive in ourselves, we are sufficient in the variety
    of ourselves,
We are the most beautiful to ourselves and in ourselves,
We stand self-pois'd in the middle, branching thence over the
    world,
From Missouri, Nebraska, or Kansas, laughing attacks to
    scorn.

Nothing is sinful to us outside of ourselves,
Whatever appears, whatever does not appear, we are
    beautiful or sinful in ourselves only.

(O Mother—O Sisters dear!
If we are lost, no victor else has destroy'd us,
It is by ourselves we go down to eternal night.)

3

Have you thought there could be but a single supreme?
There can be any number of supremes—one does not
    countervail another any more than one eyesight
    countervails another, or one life countervails another.

All is eligible to all,
All is for individuals, all is for you,
No condition is prohibited, not God's or any.

All comes by the body, only health puts you rapport with the
    universe.

Produce great Persons, the rest follows.

4

Piety and conformity to them that like,
Peace, obesity, allegiance, to them that like,
I am he who tauntingly compels men, women, nations,
Crying, Leap from your seats and contend for your lives!

I am he who walks the States with a barb'd tongue,
        questioning every one I meet,
Who are you that wanted only to be told what you knew
        before?
Who are you that wanted only a book to join you in your
        nonsense?

(With pangs and cries as thine own O bearer of many children,
These clamors wild to a race of pride I give.)

O lands, would you be freer than all that has ever been
        before?
If you would be freer than all that has been before, come
        listen to me.

Fear grace, elegance, civilization, delicatesse,
Fear the mellow sweet, the sucking of honey-juice,
Beware the advancing mortal ripening of Nature,
Beware what precedes the decay of the ruggedness of states
        and men.

5

Ages, precedents, have long been accumulating undirected
        materials,
America brings builders, and brings its own styles.

The immortal poets of Asia and Europe have done their
        work and pass'd to other spheres,
A work remains, the work of surpassing all they have done.

America, curious toward foreign characters, stands by its own
        at all hazards,

Stands removed, spacious, composite, sound, initiates the
    true use of precedents,
Does not repel them or the past or what they have produced
    under their forms,
Takes the lesson with calmness, perceives the corpse slowly
    borne from the house,
Perceives that it waits a little while in the door, that it was
    fittest for its days,
That its life has descended to the stalwart and well-shaped
    heir who approaches,
And that he shall be fittest for his days.

Any period one nation must lead,
One land must be the promise and reliance of the future.

These States are the amplest poem,
Here is not merely a nation but a teeming Nation of nations,
Here the doings of men correspond with the broadcast
    doings of the day and night,
Here is what moves in magnificent masses careless of
    particulars,
Here are the roughs, beards, friendliness, combativeness, the
    soul loves,
Here the flowing trains, here the crowds, equality, diversity,
    the soul loves.

6

Land of lands and bards to corroborate!
Of them standing among them, one lifts to the light a west-
    bred face,
To him the hereditary countenance bequeath'd both mother's
    and father's,
His first parts substances, earth, water, animals, trees,
Built of the common stock, having room for far and near,
Used to dispense with other lands, incarnating this land,
Attracting it body and soul to himself, hanging on its neck
    with incomparable love,
Plunging his seminal muscle into its merits and demerits,

Making its cities, beginnings, events, diversities, wars, vocal
    in him,
Making its rivers, lakes, bays, embouchure in him,
Mississippi with yearly freshets and changing chutes,
    Columbia, Niagara, Hudson, spending themselves
    lovingly in him,
If the Atlantic coast stretch or the Pacific coast stretch, he
    stretching with them North or South,
Spanning between them East and West, and touching
    whatever is between them,
Growths growing from him to offset the growths of pine,
    cedar, hemlock, live-oak, locust, chestnut, hickory,
    cottonwood, orange, magnolia,
Tangles as tangled in him as any canebrake or swamp,
He likening sides and peaks of mountains, forests coated with
    northern transparent ice,
Off him pasturage sweet and natural as savanna, upland,
    prairie,
Through him flights, whirls, screams, answering those of the
    fish-hawk, mocking-bird, night-heron, and eagle,
His spirit surrounding his country's spirit, unclosed to good
    and evil,
Surrounding the essences of real things, old times and
    present times,
Surrounding just found shores, islands, tribes of red
    aborigines,
Weather-beaten vessels, landings, settlements, embryo stature
    and muscle,
The haughty defiance of the Year One, war, peace, the
    formation of the Constitution,
The separate States, the simple elastic scheme, the immigrants,
The Union always swarming with blatherers and always sure
    and impregnable,
The unsurvey'd interior, log-houses, clearings, wild animals,
    hunters, trappers,
Surrounding the multiform agriculture, mines, temperature,
    the gestation of new States,
Congress convening every Twelfth-month, the members duly
    coming up from the uttermost parts,

Surrounding the noble character of mechanics and farmers,
    especially the young men,
Responding their manners, speech, dress, friendships, the
    gait they have of persons who never knew how it felt to
    stand in the presence of superiors,
The freshness and candor of their physiognomy, the
    copiousness and decision of their phrenology,
The picturesque looseness of their carriage, their fierceness
    when wrong'd,
The fluency of their speech, their delight in music, their
    curiosity, good temper and open-handedness, the whole
    composite make,
The prevailing ardor and enterprise, the large amativeness,
The perfect equality of the female with the male, the fluid
    movement of the population,
The superior marine, free commerce, fisheries, whaling, gold-
    digging,
Wharf-hemm'd cities, railroad and steamboat lines
    intersecting all points,
Factories, mercantile life, labor-saving machinery, the
    Northeast, Northwest, Southwest,
Manhattan firemen, the Yankee swap, southern plantation life,
Slavery—the murderous, treacherous conspiracy to raise it
    upon the ruins of all the rest,
On and on to the grapple with it—Assassin! then your life or
    ours be the stake, and respite no more.

                            7

(Lo, high toward heaven, this day,
Libertad, from the conqueress' field return'd,
I mark the new aureola around your head,
No more of soft astral, but dazzling and fierce,
With war's flames and the lambent lightnings playing,
And your port immovable where you stand,
With still the inextinguishable glance and the clinch'd and
    lifted fist,
And your foot on the neck of the menacing one, the scorner
    utterly crush'd beneath you,

The menacing arrogant one that strode and advanced with
    his senseless scorn, bearing the murderous knife,
The wide-swelling one, the braggart that would yesterday do
    so much,
To-day a carrion dead and damn'd, the despised of all the
    earth,
An offal rank, to the dunghill maggots spurn'd.)

8

Others take finish, but the Republic is ever constructive and
    ever keeps vista,
Others adorn the past, but you O days of the present, I
    adorn you,
O days of the future I believe in you—I isolate myself for
    your sake,
O America because you build for mankind I build for you,
O well-beloved stone-cutters, I lead them who plan with
    decision and science,
Lead the present with friendly hand toward the future.

(Bravas to all impulses sending sane children to the next age!
But damn that which spends itself with no thought of the
    stain, pains, dismay, feebleness, it is bequeathing.)

9

I listened to the Phantom by Ontario's shore,
I heard the voice arising demanding bards,
By them all native and grand, by them alone can these States
    be fused into the compact organism of a Nation.

To hold men together by paper and seal or by compulsion is
    no account,
That only holds men together which aggregates all in a living
    principle, as the hold of the limbs of the body or the
    fibres of plants.

Of all races and eras these States with veins full of poetical
    stuff most need poets, and are to have the greatest, and
    use them the greatest,
Their Presidents shall not be their common referee so much
    as their poets shall.

(Soul of love and tongue of fire!
Eye to pierce the deepest deeps and sweep the world!
Ah Mother, prolific and full in all besides, yet how long
    barren, barren?)

10

Of these States the poet is the equable man,
Not in him but off from him things are grotesque, eccentric,
    fail of their full returns,
Nothing out of its place is good, nothing in its place is bad,
He bestows on every object or quality its fit proportion,
    neither more nor less,
He is the arbiter of the diverse, he is the key,
He is the equalizer of his age and land,
He supplies what wants supplying, he checks what wants
    checking,
In peace out of him speaks the spirit of peace, large, rich,
    thrifty, building populous towns, encouraging
    agriculture, arts, commerce, lighting the study of man,
    the soul, health, immortality, government,
In war he is the best backer of the war, he fetches artillery as
    good as the engineer's, he can make every word he
    speaks draw blood,
The years straying toward infidelity he withholds by his
    steady faith,
He is no arguer, he is judgment, (Nature accepts him
    absolutely,)
He judges not as the judge judges but as the sun falling
    round a helpless thing,
As he sees the farthest he has the most faith,
His thoughts are the hymns of the praise of things,
In the dispute on God and eternity he is silent,

He sees eternity less like a play with a prologue and
    denouement,
He sees eternity in men and women, he does not see men
    and women as dreams or dots.

For the great Idea, the idea of perfect and free individuals,
For that, the bard walks in advance, leader of leaders,
The attitude of him cheers up slaves and horrifies foreign
    despots.

Without extinction is Liberty, without retrograde is
    Equality,
They live in the feelings of young men and the best women,
(Not for nothing have the indomitable heads of the earth
    been always ready to fall for Liberty.)

II

For the great Idea,
That, O my brethren, that is the mission of poets.

Songs of stern defiance ever ready,
Songs of the rapid arming and the march,
The flag of peace quick-folded, and instead the flag we know,
Warlike flag of the great Idea.

(Angry cloth I saw there leaping!
I stand again in leaden rain your flapping folds saluting,
I sing you over all, flying beckoning through the fight—O
    the hard-contested fight!
The cannons ope their rosy-flashing muzzles—the hurtled
    balls scream,
The battle-front forms amid the smoke—the volleys pour
    incessant from the line,
Hark, the ringing word *Charge!*—now the tussle and the
    furious maddening yells,
Now the corpses tumble curl'd upon the ground,
Cold, cold in death, for precious life of you,
Angry cloth I saw there leaping.)

12

Are you he who would assume a place to teach or be a poet
    here in the States?
The place is august, the terms obdurate.

Who would assume to teach here may well prepare himself
    body and mind,
He may well survey, ponder, arm, fortify, harden, make lithe
    himself,
He shall surely be question'd beforehand by me with many
    and stern questions.

Who are you indeed who would talk or sing to America?
Have you studied out the land, its idioms and men?
Have you learn'd the physiology, phrenology, politics,
    geography, pride, freedom, friendship of the land? its
    substratums and objects?
Have you consider'd the organic compact of the first day of
    the first year of Independence, sign'd by the
    Commissioners, ratified by the States, and read by
    Washington at the head of the army?
Have you possess'd yourself of the Federal Constitution?
Do you see who have left all feudal processes and poems
    behind them, and assumed the poems and processes of
    Democracy?
Are you faithful to things? do you teach what the land and
    sea, the bodies of men, womanhood, amativeness, heroic
    angers, teach?
Have you sped through fleeting customs, popularities?
Can you hold your hand against all seductions, follies, whirls,
    fierce contentions? are you very strong? are you really of
    the whole People?
Are you not of some coterie? some school or mere religion?
Are you done with reviews and criticisms of life? animating
    now to life itself?
Have you vivified yourself from the maternity of these
    States?
Have you too the old ever-fresh forbearance and impartiality?

Do you hold the like love for those hardening to maturity?
    for the last-born? little and big? and for the errant?

What is this you bring my America?
Is it uniform with my country?
Is it not something that has been better told or done before?
Have you not imported this or the spirit of it in some ship?
Is it not a mere tale? a rhyme? a prettiness? — is the good old
    cause in it?
Has it not dangled long at the heels of the poets, politicians,
    literats, of enemies' lands?
Does it not assume that what is notoriously gone is still here?
Does it answer universal needs? will it improve manners?
Does it sound with trumpet-voice the proud victory of the
    Union in that secession war?
Can your performance face the open fields and the seaside?
Will it absorb into me as I absorb food, air, to appear again
    in my strength, gait, face?
Have real employments contributed to it? original makers,
    not mere amanuenses?
Does it meet modern discoveries, calibres, facts, face to face?
What does it mean to American persons, progresses, cities?
    Chicago, Kanada, Arkansas?
Does it see behind the apparent custodians the real
    custodians standing, menacing, silent, the mechanics,
    Manhattanese, Western men, Southerners, significant
    alike in their apathy, and in the promptness of their
    love?
Does it see what finally befalls, and has always finally befallen,
    each temporizer, patcher, outsider, partialist,
    alarmist, infidel, who has ever ask'd any thing of America?
What mocking and scornful negligence?
The track strew'd with the dust of skeletons,
By the roadside others disdainfully toss'd.

13

Rhymes and rhymers pass away, poems distill'd from poems
    pass away,

The swarms of reflectors and the polite pass, and leave ashes,
Admirers, importers, obedient persons, make but the soil of
    literature,
America justifies itself, give it time, no disguise can deceive it
    or conceal from it, it is impassive enough,
Only toward the likes of itself will it advance to meet them,
If its poets appear it will in due time advance to meet them,
    there is no fear of mistake,
(The proof of a poet shall be sternly deferr'd till his country
    absorbs him as affectionately as he has absorb'd it.)

He masters whose spirit masters, he tastes sweetest who
    results sweetest in the long run,
The blood of the brawn beloved of time is unconstraint;
In the need of songs, philosophy, an appropriate native
    grand-opera, shipcraft, any craft,
He or she is greatest who contributes the greatest original
    practical example.

Already a nonchalant breed, silently emerging, appears on the
    streets,
People's lips salute only doers, lovers, satisfiers, positive
    knowers,
There will shortly be no more priests, I say their work is done,
Death is without emergencies here, but life is perpetual
    emergencies here,
Are your body, days, manners, superb? after death you shall
    be superb,
Justice, health, self-esteem, clear the way with irresistible
    power;
How dare you place any thing before a man?

14

Fall behind me States!
A man before all—myself, typical, before all.

Give me the pay I have served for,
Give me to sing the songs of the great Idea, take all the rest,
I have loved the earth, sun, animals, I have despised riches,

I have given alms to every one that ask'd, stood up for the
    stupid and crazy, devoted my income and labor to
    others,
Hated tyrants, argued not concerning God, had patience and
    indulgence toward the people, taken off my hat to
    nothing known or unknown,
Gone freely with powerful uneducated persons and with the
    young, and with the mothers of families,
Read these leaves to myself in the open air, tried them by
    trees, stars, rivers,
Dismiss'd whatever insulted my own soul or defiled my body,
Claim'd nothing to myself which I have not carefully
    claim'dfor others on the same terms,
Sped to the camps, and comrades found and accepted from
    every State,
(Upon this breast has many a dying soldier lean'd to breathe
    his last,
This arm, this hand, this voice, have nourish'd, rais'd,
    restored,
To life recalling many a prostrate form;)
I am willing to wait to be understood by the growth of the
    taste of myself,
Rejecting none, permitting all.

(Say O Mother, have I not to your thought been faithful?
Have I not through life kept you and yours before me?)

15

I swear I begin to see the meaning of these things,
It is not the earth, it is not America who is so great,
It is I who am great or to be great, it is You up there, or any
    one,
It is to walk rapidly through civilizations, governments,
    theories,
Through poems, pageants, shows, to form individuals.

Underneath all, individuals,
I swear nothing is good to me now that ignores individuals,
The American compact is altogether with individuals,

The only government is that which makes minute of
   individuals,
The whole theory of the universe is directed unerringly to
   one single individual—namely to You.

(Mother! with subtle sense severe, with the naked sword in
   your hand,
I saw you at last refuse to treat but directly with
   individuals.)

16

Underneath all, Nativity,
I swear I will stand by my own nativity, pious or impious so
   be it;
I swear I am charm'd with nothing except nativity,
Men, women, cities, nations, are only beautiful from nativity.

Underneath all is the Expression of love for men and women,
(I swear I have seen enough of mean and impotent modes of
   expressing love for men and women,
After this day I take my own modes of expressing love for
   men and women.)

I swear I will have each quality of my race in myself,
(Talk as you like, he only suits these States whose manners
   favor the audacity and sublime turbulence of the States.)

Underneath the lessons of things, spirits, Nature,
   governments, ownerships, I swear I perceive other lessons,
Underneath all to me is myself, to you yourself, (the same
   monotonous old song.)

17

O I see flashing that this America is only you and me,
Its power, weapons, testimony, are you and me,
Its crimes, lies, thefts, defections, are you and me,
Its Congress is you and me, the officers, capitols, armies,
   ships, are you and me,
Its endless gestations of new States are you and me,

The war, (that war so bloody and grim, the war I will
     henceforth forget), was you and me,
Natural and artificial are you and me,
Freedom, language, poems, employments, are you and me,
Past, present, future, are you and me.

I dare not shirk any part of myself,
Not any part of America good or bad,
Not to build for that which builds for mankind,
Not to balance ranks, complexions, creeds, and the sexes,
Not to justify science nor the march of equality,
Nor to feed the arrogant blood of the brawn belov'd of time.

I am for those that have never been master'd,
For men and women whose tempers have never been master'd,
For those whom laws, theories, conventions, can never
     master.

I am for those who walk abreast with the whole earth,
Who inaugurate one to inaugurate all.

I will not be outfaced by irrational things,
I will penetrate what it is in them that is sarcastic upon me,
I will make cities and civilizations defer to me,
This is what I have learnt from America—it is the amount,
     and it I teach again.

(Democracy, while weapons were everywhere aim'd at your
     breast,
I saw you serenely give birth to immortal children, saw in
     dreams your dilating form,
Saw you with spreading mantle covering the world.)

18

I will confront these shows of the day and night,
I will know if I am to be less than they,
I will see if I am not as majestic as they,
I will see if I am not as subtle and real as they,
I will see if I am to be less generous than they,

I will see if I have no meaning, while the houses and ships
    have meaning,
I will see if the fishes and birds are to be enough for
    themselves, and I am not to be enough for myself.

I match my spirit against yours you orbs, growths,
    mountains, brutes,
Copious as you are I absorb you all in myself, and become
    the master myself,
America isolated yet embodying all, what is it finally except
    myself?
These States, what are they except myself?

I know now why the earth is gross, tantalizing, wicked, it is
    for my sake,
I take you specially to be mine, you terrible, rude forms.

(Mother, bend down, bend close to me your face,
I know not what these plots and wars and deferments are for,
I know not fruition's success, but I know that through war
    and crime your work goes on, and must yet go on.)

19

Thus by blue Ontario's shore,
While the winds fann'd me and the waves came trooping
    toward me,
I thrill'd with the power's pulsations, and the charm of my
    theme was upon me,
Till the tissues that held me parted their ties upon me.

And I saw the free souls of poets,
The loftiest bards of past ages strode before me,
Strange large men, long unwaked, undisclosed, were
    disclosed to me.

20

O my rapt verse, my call, mock me not!
Not for the bards of the past, not to invoke them have I
    launch'd you forth,

Not to call even those lofty bards here by Ontario's shores,
Have I sung so capricious and loud my savage song.

Bards for my own land only I invoke,
(For the war the war is over, the field is clear'd,)
Till they strike up marches henceforth triumphant and
    onward,
To cheer O Mother your boundless expectant soul.

Bards of the great Idea! bards of the peaceful inventions! (for
    the war, the war is over!)
Yet bards of latent armies, a million soldiers waiting ever-
    ready,
Bards with songs as from burning coals or the lightning's
    fork'd stripes!
Ample Ohio's, Kanada's bards—bards of California! inland
    bards—bards of the war!
You by my charm I invoke.

from *Autumn Rivulets*

ITALIAN MUSIC IN DAKOTA

[*"The Seventeenth—the finest Regimental Band I ever heard."*]

Through the soft evening air enwinding all,
Rocks, woods, fort, cannon, pacing sentries, endless wilds,
In dulcet streams, in flutes' and cornets' notes,
Electric, pensive, turbulent, artificial,
(Yet strangely fitting even here, meanings unknown before,
Subtler than ever, more harmony, as if born here, related here,
Not to the city's fresco'd rooms, not to the audience of the
    opera house,
Sounds, echoes, wandering strains, as really here at home,
Sonnambula's innocent love, trios with *Norma's* anguish,
And thy ecstatic chorus *Poliuto;*)
Ray'd in the limpid yellow slanting sundown,
Music, Italian music in Dakota.

While Nature, sovereign of this gnarl'd realm,
Lurking in hidden barbaric grim recesses,
Acknowledging rapport however far remov'd,
(As some old root or soil of earth its last-born flower or fruit,)
Listens well pleas'd.

Proud Music of the Storm

1

Proud music of the storm,
Blast that careers so free, whistling across the prairies,
Strong hum of forest tree-tops—wind of the mountains,
Personified dim shapes—you hidden orchestras,
You serenades of phantoms with instruments alert,
Blending with Nature's rhythmus all the tongues of nations;
You chords left as by vast composers—you choruses,
You formless, free, religious dances—you from the Orient,
You undertone of rivers, roar of pouring cataracts,
You sounds from distant guns with galloping cavalry,
Echoes of camps with all the different bugle-calls,
Trooping tumultuous, filling the midnight late, bending me
        powerless,
Entering my lonesome slumber-chamber, why have you
        seiz'd me?

2

Come forward O my soul, and let the rest retire,
Listen, lose not, it is toward thee they tend,
Parting the midnight, entering my slumber-chamber,
For thee they sing and dance O soul.

A festival song,
The duet of the bridegroom and the bride, a marriage-march,
With lips of love, and hearts of lovers fill'd to the brim with
        love,
The red-flush'd cheeks and perfumes, the cortege swarming
        full of friendly faces young and old,
To flutes' clear notes and sounding harps' cantabile.

Now loud approaching drums,
Victoria! see'st thou in powder-smoke the banners torn but
    flying? the rout of the baffled?
Hearest those shouts of a conquering army?

(Ah soul, the sobs of women, the wounded groaning in
    agony,
The hiss and crackle of flames, the blacken'd ruins, the
    embers of cities,
The dirge and desolation of mankind.)

Now airs antique and mediæval fill me,
I see and hear old harpers with their harps at Welsh festivals,
I hear the minnesingers singing their lays of love,
I hear the minstrels, gleemen, troubadours, of the middle ages.

Now the great organ sounds,
Tremulous, while underneath, (as the hid footholds of the
    earth,
On which arising rest, and leaping forth depend,
All shapes of beauty, grace and strength, all hues we know,
Green blades of grass and warbling birds, children that
    gambol and play, the clouds of heaven above,)
The strong base stands, and its pulsations intermits not,
Bathing, supporting, merging all the rest, maternity of all the
    rest,
And with it every instrument in multitudes,
The players playing, all the world's musicians,
The solemn hymns and masses rousing adoration,
All passionate heart-chants, sorrowful appeals,
The measureless sweet vocalists of ages,
And for their solvent setting earth's own diapason,
Of winds and woods and mighty ocean waves,
A new composite orchestra, binder of years and climes, ten-
    fold renewer,
As of the far-back days the poets tell, the Paradiso,
The straying thence, the separation long, but now the
    wandering done,
The journey done, the journeyman come home,
And man and art with Nature fused again.

Tutti! for earth and heaven;
(The Almighty leader now for once has signal'd with his
    wand.)

The manly strophe of the husbands of the world,
And all the wives responding.

The tongues of violins,
(I think O tongues ye tell this heart, that cannot tell itself,
This brooding yearning heart, that cannot tell itself.)

3

Ah from a little child,
Thou knowest soul how to me all sounds became music,
My mother's voice in lullaby or hymn,
(The voice, O tender voices, memory's loving voices,
Last miracle of all, O dearest mother's, sister's, voices;)
The rain, the growing corn, the breeze among the long-
    leav'd corn,
The measur'd sea-surf beating on the sand,
The twittering bird, the hawk's sharp scream,
The wild-fowl's notes at night as flying low migrating north
    or south,
The psalm in the country church or mid the clustering trees,
    the open air camp-meeting,
The fiddler in the tavern, the glee, the long-strung sailor-song,
The lowing cattle, bleating sheep, the crowing cock at dawn.

All songs of current lands come sounding round me,
The German airs of friendship, wine and love,
Irish ballads, merry jigs and dances, English warbles,
Chansons of France, Scotch tunes, and o'er the rest,
Italia's peerless compositions.

Across the stage with pallor on her face, yet lurid passion,
Stalks Norma brandishing the dagger in her hand.

I see poor crazed Lucia's eyes' unnatural gleam,
Her hair down her back falls loose and dishevel'd.

I see where Ernani walking the bridal garden,
Amid the scent of night-roses, radiant, holding his bride by
    the hand,
Hears the infernal call, the death-pledge of the horn.

To crossing swords and gray hairs bared to heaven,
The clear electric base and baritone of the world,
The trombone duo, Libertad forever!

From Spanish chestnut trees' dense shade,
By old and heavy convent walls a wailing song,
Song of lost love, the torch of youth and life quench'd in
    despair,
Song of the dying swan, Fernando's heart is breaking.

Awaking from her woes at last retriev'd Amina sings,
Copious as stars and glad as morning light the torrents of her
    joy.

(The teeming lady comes,
The lustrious orb, Venus contralto, the blooming mother,
Sister of loftiest gods, Alboni's self I hear.)

4

I hear those odes, symphonies, operas,
I hear in the *William Tell* the music of an arous'd and angry
    people,
I hear Meyerbeer's *Huguenots,* the *Prophet,* or *Robert,*
Gounod's *Faust,* or Mozart's *Don Juan.*

I hear the dance-music of all nations,
The waltz, some delicious measure, lapsing, bathing me
    in bliss,
The bolero to tinkling guitars and clattering castanets.

I see religious dances old and new,
I hear the sound of the Hebrew lyre,
I see the crusaders marching bearing the cross on high, to the
    martial clang of cymbals,

I hear dervishes monotonously chanting, interspers'd with
    frantic shouts, as they spin around turning always
    towards Mecca,
I see the rapt religious dances of the Persians and the Arabs,
Again, at Eleusis, home of Ceres, I see the modern Greeks
    dancing,
I hear them clapping their hands as they bend their bodies,
I hear the metrical shuffling of their feet.

I see again the wild old Corybantian dance, the performers
    wounding each other,
I see the Roman youth to the shrill sound of flageolets
    throwing and catching their weapons,
As they fall on their knees and rise again.

I hear from the Mussulman mosque the muezzin calling,
I see the worshippers within, nor form nor sermon,
    argument nor word,
But silent, strange, devout, rais'd, glowing heads, ecstatic
    faces.

I hear the Egyptian harp of many strings,
The primitive chants of the Nile boatmen,
The sacred imperial hymns of China,
To the delicate sounds of the king, (the stricken wood and
    stone,)
Or to Hindu flutes and the fretting twang of the vina,
A band of bayaderes.

5

Now Asia, Africa leave me, Europe seizing inflates me,
To organs huge and bands I hear as from vast concourses of
    voices,
Luther's strong hymn, *Eine feste Burg ist unser Gott,*
Rossini's *Stabat Mater dolorosa,*
Or floating in some high cathedral dim with gorgeous
    color'd windows,
The passionate *Agnus Dei* or *Gloria in Excelsis.*

Composers! mighty maestros!
And you, sweet singers of old lands, soprani, tenori, bassi!
To you a new bard caroling in the West,
Obeisant sends his love.

(Such led to thee O soul,
All senses, shows and objects, lead to thee,
But now it seems to me sound leads o'er all the rest.)

I hear the annual singing of the children in St. Paul's
        cathedral,
Or, under the high roof of some colossal hall, the
        symphonies, oratorios of Beethoven, Handel, or Haydn,
The *Creation* in billows of godhood laves me.

Give me to hold all sounds, (I madly struggling cry,)
Fill me with all the voices of the universe,
Endow me with their throbbings, Nature's also,
The tempests, waters, winds, operas and chants, marches and
        dances,
Utter, pour in, for I would take them all!

6

Then I woke softly,
And pausing, questioning awhile the music of my dream,
And questioning all those reminiscences, the tempest in its
        fury,
And all the songs of sopranos and tenors,
And those rapt oriental dances of religious fervor,
And the sweet varied instruments, and the diapason of
        organs,
And all the artless plaints of love and grief and death,
I said to my silent curious soul out of the bed of the slumber-
        chamber,
Come, for I have found the clew I sought so long,
Let us go forth refresh'd amid the day,
Cheerfully tallying life, walking the world, the real,
Nourish'd henceforth by our celestial dream.

And I said, moreover,
Haply what thou hast heard O soul was not the sound of
    winds,
Nor dream of raging storm, nor sea-hawk's flapping wings
    nor harsh scream,
Nor vocalism of sun-bright Italy,
Nor German organ majestic, nor vast concourse of voices,
    nor layers of harmonies,
Nor strophes of husbands and wives, nor sound of marching
    soldiers,
Nor flutes, nor harps, nor the bugle-calls of camps,
But to a new rhythmus fitted for thee,
Poems bridging the way from Life to Death, vaguely wafted
    in night air, uncaught, unwritten,
Which let us go forth in the bold day and write.

Passage to India

I

Singing my days,
Singing the great achievements of the present,
Singing the strong light works of engineers,
Our modern wonders, (the antique ponderous Seven outvied,)
In the Old World the east the Suez canal,
The New by its mighty railroad spann'd,
The seas inlaid with eloquent gentle wires;
Yet first to sound, and ever sound, the cry with thee O soul,
The Past! the Past! the Past!

The Past—the dark unfathom'd retrospect!
The teeming gulf—the sleepers and the shadows!
The past—the infinite greatness of the past!
For what is the present after all but a growth out of the past?
(As a projectile form'd, impell'd, passing a certain line, still
    keeps on,
So the present, utterly form'd, impell'd by the past.)

2

Passage O soul to India!
Eclaircise the myths Asiatic, the primitive fables.

Not you alone proud truths of the world,
Nor you alone ye facts of modern science,
But myths and fables of eld, Asia's, Africa's fables,
The far-darting beams of the spirit, the unloos'd dreams,
The deep diving bibles and legends,
The daring plots of the poets, the elder religions;
O you temples fairer than lilies pour'd over by the rising sun!
O you fables spurning the known, eluding the hold of the
    known, mounting to heaven!
You lofty and dazzling towers, pinnacled, red as roses,
    burnish'd with gold!
Towers of fables immortal fashion'd from mortal dreams!
You too I welcome and fully the same as the rest!
You too with joy I sing.

Passage to India!
Lo, soul, seest thou not God's purpose from the first?
The earth to be spann'd, connected by network,
The races, neighbors, to marry and be given in marriage,
The oceans to be cross'd, the distant brought near,
The lands to be welded together.

A worship new I sing,
You captains, voyagers, explorers, yours,
You engineers, you architects, machinists, yours,
You, not for trade or transportation only,
But in God's name, and for thy sake O soul.

3

Passage to India!
Lo soul for thee of tableaus twain,
I see in one the Suez canal initiated, open'd,
I see the procession of steamships, the Empress Eugenie's
    leading the van,

I mark from on deck the strange landscape, the pure sky, the
      level sand in the distance,
I pass swiftly the picturesque groups, the workmen gather'd,
The gigantic dredging machines.

In one again, different, (yet thine, all thine, O soul, the same,)
I see over my own continent the Pacific railroad surmounting
      every barrier,
I see continual trains of cars winding along the Platte
      carrying freight and passengers,
I hear the locomotives rushing and roaring, and the shrill
      steam-whistle,
I hear the echoes reverberate through the grandest scenery in
      the world,
I cross the Laramie plains, I note the rocks in grotesque
      shapes, the buttes,
I see the plentiful larkspur and wild onions, the barren,
      colorless, sage-deserts,
I see in glimpses afar or towering immediately above me the
      great mountains, I see the Wind river and the Wahsatch
      mountains,
I see the Monument mountain and the Eagle's Nest, I pass
      the Promontory, I ascend the Nevadas,
I scan the noble Elk mountain and wind around its base,
I see the Humboldt range, I thread the valley and cross the
      river,
I see the clear waters of lake Tahoe, I see forests of majestic
      pines,
Or crossing the great desert, the alkaline plains, I behold
      enchanting mirages of waters and meadows,
Marking through these and after all, in duplicate slender lines,
Bridging the three or four thousand miles of land travel,
Tying the Eastern to the Western sea,
The road between Europe and Asia.

(Ah Genoese thy dream! thy dream!
Centuries after thou art laid in thy grave,
The shore thou foundest verifies thy dream.)

4

Passage to India!
Struggles of many a captain, tales of many a sailor dead,
Over my mood stealing and spreading they come,
Like clouds and cloudlets in the unreach'd sky.

Along all history, down the slopes,
As a rivulet running, sinking now, and now again to the
    surface rising,
A ceaseless thought, a varied train—lo, soul, to thee, thy
    sight, they rise,
The plans, the voyages again, the expeditions;
Again Vasco de Gama sails forth,
Again the knowledge gain'd, the mariner's compass,
Lands found and nations born, thou born America,
For purpose vast, man's long probation fill'd,
Thou rondure of the world at last accomplish'd.

5

O vast Rondure, swimming in space,
Cover'd all over with visible power and beauty,
Alternate light and day and the teeming spiritual darkness,
Unspeakable high processions of sun and moon and countless
    stars above,
Below, the manifold grass and waters, animals, mountains,
    trees,
With inscrutable purpose, some hidden prophetic intention,
Now first it seems my thought begins to span thee.

Down from the gardens of Asia descending radiating,
Adam and Eve appear, then their myriad progeny after them,
Wandering, yearning, curious, with restless explorations,
With questionings, baffled, formless, feverish, with never-
    happy hearts,
With that sad incessant refrain, *Wherefore unsatisfied soul?* and
    Whither O mocking life?

Ah who shall soothe these feverish children?
Who justify these restless explorations?

Who speak the secret of impassive earth?
Who bind it to us? what is this separate Nature so unnatural?
What is this earth to our affections? (unloving earth, without
     a throb to answer ours,
Cold earth, the place of graves.)

Yet soul be sure the first intent remains, and shall be carried
     out,
Perhaps even now the time has arrived.

After the seas are all cross'd, (as they seem already cross'd,)
After the great captains and engineers have accomplish'd their
     work,
After the noble inventors, after the scientists, the chemist, the
     geologist, ethnologist,
Finally shall come the poet worthy that name,
The true son of God shall come singing his songs.

Then not your deeds only O voyagers, O scientists and
     inventors, shall be justified,
All these hearts as of fretted children shall be sooth'd,
All affection shall be fully responded to, the secret shall be
     told,
All these separations and gaps shall be taken up and hook'd
     and link'd together,
The whole earth, this cold, impassive, voiceless earth, shall be
     completely justified,
Trinitas divine shall be gloriously accomplish'd and
     compacted by the true son of God, the poet,
(He shall indeed pass the straits and conquer the mountains,
He shall double the cape of Good Hope to some purpose,)
Nature and Man shall be disjoin'd and diffused no more,
The true son of God shall absolutely fuse them.

6

Year at whose wide-flung door I sing!
Year of the purpose accomplish'd!
Year of the marriage of continents, climates and oceans!
(No mere doge of Venice now wedding the Adriatic,)

I see O year in you the vast terraqueous globe given and
    giving all,
Europe to Asia, Africa join'd, and they to the New World,
The lands, geographies, dancing before you, holding a
    festival garland,
As brides and bridegrooms hand in hand.

Passage to India!
Cooling airs from Caucasus far, soothing cradle of man,
The river Euphrates flowing, the past lit up again.

Lo soul, the retrospect brought forward,
The old, most populous, wealthiest of earth's lands,
The streams of the Indus and the Ganges and their many
    affluents,
(I my shores of America walking to-day behold, resuming
    all,)
The tale of Alexander on his warlike marches suddenly
    dying,
On one side China and on the other side Persia and Arabia,
To the south the great seas and the bay of Bengal,
The flowing literatures, tremendous epics, religions, castes,
Old occult Brahma interminably far back, the tender and
    junior Buddha,
Central and southern empires and all their belongings,
    possessors,
The wars of Tamerlane, the reign of Aurungzebe,
The traders, rulers, explorers, Moslems, Venetians,
    Byzantium, the Arabs, Portuguese,
The first travelers famous yet, Marco Polo, Batouta the Moor,
Doubts to be solv'd, the map incognita, blanks to be fill'd,
The foot of man unstay'd, the hands never at rest,
Thyself O soul that will not brook a challenge.

The mediæval navigators rise before me,
The world of 1492, with its awaken'd enterprise,
Something swelling in humanity now like the sap of the earth
    in spring,
The sunset splendor of chivalry declining.

And who art thou sad shade?
Gigantic, visionary, thyself a visionary,
With majestic limbs and pious beaming eyes,
Spreading around with every look of thine a golden world,
Enhuing it with gorgeous hues.

As the chief histrion,
Down to the footlights walks in some great scena,
Dominating the rest I see the Admiral himself,
(History's type of courage, action, faith,)
Behold him sail from Palos leading his little fleet,
His voyage behold, his return, his great fame,
His misfortunes, calumniators, behold him a prisoner,
    chain'd,
Behold his dejection, poverty, death.

(Curious in time I stand, noting the efforts of heroes,
Is the deferment long? bitter the slander, poverty, death?
Lies the seed unreck'd for centuries in the ground? lo, to
    God's due occasion,
Uprising in the night, it sprouts, blooms,
And fills the earth with use and beauty.)

                              7

Passage indeed O soul to primal thought,
Not lands and seas alone, thy own clear freshness,
The young maturity of brood and bloom,
To realms of budding bibles.

O soul, repressless, I with thee and thou with me,
Thy circumnavigation of the world begin,
Of man, the voyage of his mind's return,
To reason's early paradise,
Back, back to wisdom's birth, to innocent intuitions,
Again with fair creation.

                              8

O we can wait no longer,
We too take ship O soul,
Joyous we too launch out on trackless seas,

Fearless for unknown shores on waves of ecstasy to sail,
Amid the wafting winds, (thou pressing me to thee, I thee to
    me, O soul,)
Caroling free, singing our song of God,
Chanting our chant of pleasant exploration.

With laugh and many a kiss,
(Let others deprecate, let others weep for sin, remorse,
    humiliation,)
O soul thou pleasest me, I thee.

Ah more than any priest O soul we too believe in God,
But with the mystery of God we dare not dally.

O soul thou pleasest me, I thee,
Sailing these seas or on the hills, or waking in the night,
Thoughts, silent thoughts, of Time and Space and Death,
    like waters flowing,
Bear me indeed as through the regions infinite,
Whose air I breathe, whose ripples hear, lave me all over,
Bathe me O God in thee, mounting to thee,
I and my soul to range in range of thee.

O Thou transcendent,
Nameless, the fibre and the breath,
Light of the light, shedding forth universes, thou centre of
    them,
Thou mightier centre of the true, the good, the loving,
Thou moral, spiritual fountain—affection's source—thou
    reservoir,
(O pensive soul of me—O thirst unsatisfied—waitest not
    there?
Waitest not haply for us somewhere there the Comrade
    perfect?)
Thou pulse—thou motive of the stars, suns, systems,
That, circling, move in order, safe, harmonious,
Athwart the shapeless vastnesses of space,
How should I think, how breathe a single breath, how speak,
    if, out of myself,
I could not launch, to those, superior universes?

Swiftly I shrivel at the thought of God,
At Nature and its wonders, Time and Space and Death,
But that I, turning, call to thee O soul, thou actual Me,
And lo, thou gently masterest the orbs,
Thou matest Time, smilest content at Death,
And fillest, swellest full the vastnesses of Space.

Greater than stars or suns,
Bounding O soul thou journeyest forth;
What love than thine and ours could wider amplify?
What aspirations, wishes, outvie thine and ours O soul?
What dreams of the ideal? what plans of purity, perfection,
    strength?
What cheerful willingness for others' sake to give up all?
For others' sake to suffer all?

Reckoning ahead O soul, when thou, the time achiev'd,
The seas all cross'd, weather'd the capes, the voyage done,
Surrounded, copest, frontest God, yieldest, the aim attain'd,
As fill'd with friendship, love complete, the Elder Brother
    found,
The Younger melts in fondness in his arms.

9

Passage to more than India!
Are thy wings plumed indeed for such far flights?
O soul, voyagest thou indeed on voyages like those?
Disportest thou on waters such as those?
Soundest below the Sanscrit and the Vedas?
Then have thy bent unleash'd.

Passage to you, your shores, ye aged fierce enigmas!
Passage to you, to mastership of you, ye strangling problems!
You, strew'd with the wrecks of skeletons, that, living, never
    reach'd you.

Passage to more than India!
O secret of the earth and sky!
Of you O waters of the sea! O winding creeks and rivers!

Of you O woods and fields! of you strong mountains of my
    land!
Of you O prairies! of you gray rocks!
O morning red! O clouds! O rain and snows!
O day and night, passage to you!

O sun and moon and all you stars! Sirius and Jupiter!
Passage to you!

Passage, immediate passage! the blood burns in my veins!
Away O soul! hoist instantly the anchor!
Cut the hawsers—haul out—shake out every sail!
Have we not stood here like trees in the ground long enough?
Have we not grovel'd here long enough, eating and drinking
    like mere brutes?
Have we not darken'd and dazed ourselves with books long
    enough?

Sail forth—steer for the deep waters only,
Reckless O soul, exploring, I with thee, and thou with me,
For we are bound where mariner has not yet dared to go,
And we will risk the ship, ourselves and all.

O my brave soul!
O farther farther sail!
O daring joy, but safe! are they not all the seas of God?
O farther, farther, farther sail!

from *Whispers of Heavenly Death*

CHANTING THE SQUARE DEIFIC

I

Chanting the square deific, out of the One advancing, out of
    the sides,
Out of the old and new, out of the square entirely divine,
Solid, four-sided, (all the sides needed,) from this side
    Jehovah am I,

Old Brahm I, and I Saturnius am;
Not Time affects me—I am Time, old, modern as any,
Unpersuadable, relentless, executing righteous judgments,
As the Earth, the Father, the brown old Kronos, with laws,
Aged beyond computation, yet ever new, ever with those
mighty laws rolling,
Relentless I forgive no man—whoever sins dies—I will have
that man's life;
Therefore let none expect mercy—have the seasons,
gravitation, the appointed days, mercy? no more have I,
But as the seasons and gravitation, and as all the appointed
days that forgive not,
I dispense from this side judgments inexorable without the
least remorse.

2

Consolator most mild, the promis'd one advancing,
With gentle hand extended, the mightier God am I,
Foretold by prophets and poets in their most rapt
prophecies and poems,
From this side, lo! the Lord Christ gazes—lo! Hermes I—
lo! mine is Hercules' face,
All sorrow, labor, suffering, I, tallying it, absorb in myself,
Many times have I been rejected, taunted, put in prison, and
crucified, and many times shall be again,
All the world have I given up for my dear brothers' and
sisters' sake, for the soul's sake,
Wending my way through the homes of men, rich or poor,
with the kiss of affection,
For I am affection, I am the cheer-bringing God, with hope
and all-enclosing charity,
With indulgent words as to children, with fresh and sane
words, mine only,
Young and strong I pass knowing well I am destin'd myself
to an early death;
But my charity has no death—my wisdom dies not, neither
early nor late,
And my sweet love bequeath'd here and elsewhere never dies.

3

Aloof, dissatisfied, plotting revolt,
Comrade of criminals, brother of slaves,
Crafty, despised, a drudge, ignorant,
With sudra face and worn brow, black, but in the depths of
    my heart, proud as any,
Lifted now and always against whoever scorning assumes to
    rule me,
Morose, full of guile, full of reminiscences, brooding, with
    many wiles,
(Though it was thought I was baffled and dispel'd, and my
    wiles done, but that will never be,)
Defiant, I, Satan, still live, still utter words, in new lands duly
    appearing, (and old ones also,)
Permanent here from my side, warlike, equal with any, real as
    any,
Nor time nor change shall ever change me or my words.

4

Santa Spirita, breather, life,
Beyond the light, lighter than light,
Beyond the flames of hell, joyous, leaping easily above hell,
Beyond Paradise, perfumed solely with mine own perfume,
Including all life on earth, touching, including God,
    including Saviour and Satan,
Ethereal, pervading all, (for without me what were all? what
    were God?)
Essence of forms, life of the real identities, permanent,
    positive, (namely the unseen,)
Life of the great round world, the sun and stars, and of man,
    I, the general soul,
Here the square finishing, the solid, I the most solid,
Breathe my breath also through these songs.

A NOISELESS PATIENT SPIDER

A noiseless patient spider,
I mark'd where on a little promontory it stood isolated,
Mark'd how to explore the vacant vast surrounding,
It launch'd forth filament, filament, filament, out of itself,
Ever unreeling them, ever tirelessly speeding them.

And you O my soul where you stand,
Surrounded, detached, in measureless oceans of space,
Ceaselessly musing, venturing, throwing, seeking the spheres
     to connect them,
Till the bridge you will need be form'd, till the ductile
     anchor hold,
Till the gossamer thread you fling catch somewhere, O my
     soul.

CHRONOLOGY

BIOGRAPHICAL NOTES

NOTE ON THE TEXTS

NOTES

INDEXES

Chronology

1800   The Library of Congress established.

1801   Washington Allston begins art studies at the Royal Academy in London, under tutelage of Benjamin West. The New York *Evening Post* founded as Federalist newspaper by Alexander Hamilton, under editorship of William Coleman. *The Port Folio* (1801–27) founded by Joseph Dennie under pseudonym "Oliver Oldschool" (early contributors include Charles Brockden Brown and Royall Tyler).

1802   *The Boston Weekly Magazine* (later *The Emerald*) begins publication under the editorship of Samuel Gilbert and Thomas Dean of Boston, publishing some poetry along with fiction and theatrical reviews.

1803   Phineas Adams founds *The Monthly Anthology and Boston Review* (1803–11); after six months Adams succeeded as editor by the Rev. William Emerson, father of Ralph Waldo Emerson (contributors will include Washington Allston, William Cullen Bryant, Daniel Webster, and Joseph Story).

1804   Joel Barlow returns to America after 17 years in Europe. The Anthology Club (associated with the *The Monthly Anthology* and devoted to raising standards of American literature) founded in Boston.

1805   Joel Barlow publishes *Prospectus of a National Institution to be Established in the United States*, proposal for a national institute devoted to artistic and scientific research. The Boston Athenaeum (which eventually encompasses a library, a museum, and a laboratory) founded by members of the Anthology Club. At age 13, John Howard Payne publishes theatrical paper *The Thespian Mirror* (1805–06) in New York City. Samuel Woodworth publishes juvenile paper *The Fly* (1805–06), to which John Howard Payne contributes. In Rome, Washington Allston spends time with the visiting Washington Irving.

1806　　John Howard Payne's *Thespian Mirror* attracts notice of William Coleman, editor of New York *Evening Post*; through Coleman's efforts Payne gains reputation as prodigy and becomes acquainted with New York literary and theatrical circles; his play *Julia, or The Wanderer* produced in New York. In Rome, Washington Allston forms close friendship with Samuel Taylor Coleridge.

1807　　Joel Barlow publishes *The Columbiad*, an extensive reworking of his epic *The Vision of Columbus* (1787). James Kirke Paulding collaborates with Washington Irving and Irving's brother William on *Salmagundi*. John Howard Payne issues first number of literary magazine *The Pastime* (1807–08), most of which he writes himself.

　　　　　Joel Barlow: *The Columbiad*.

1808　　At his father's urging, William Cullen Bryant publishes *The Embargo*, an anti-Jeffersonian poetic satire written at age 13. Washington Allston returns to the U.S. to marry Ann Channing, sister of William Ellery Channing. Convention of the Universalists of New England publishes *Hymns Composed by Different Authors*, containing only American hymns (written by Hosea Ballou, Abner Kneeland, and Edward Turner).

　　　　　William Cullen Bryant: *The Embargo*.

1809　　John Howard Payne makes acting debut in New York City. The Scottish poet Thomas Campbell publishes *Gertrude of Wyoming*, narrative poem about a Pennsylvania Indian massacre.

　　　　　Philip Freneau: *Poems Written and Published During the American Revolutionary War*.
　　　　　Samuel Woodworth: *New-Haven*.

1810　　Washington Allston reads a long poem (possibly "The Sylphs of the Seasons") at the Phi Beta Kappa Society of Harvard.

1811　　Joel Barlow appointed by President Madison to negotiate trade agreement with France.

　　　　　Samuel Woodworth: *Beasts at Law*.

1812   Joel Barlow writes "Advice to a Raven in Russia" while in Vilna (now Vilnius, Lithuania) on diplomatic mission; caught up in Napoleon's retreat from Russia, contracts pneumonia and dies December 24 in a village near Cracow, Poland. American Antiquarian Society founded in Worcester, Massachusetts, by Isaiah Thomas.

John Pierpont: *The Portrait.*
Samuel Woodworth: *Quarter-Day.*

1813   Joseph Rodman Drake meets Fitz-Greene Halleck in New York. John Howard Payne settles in England. *The Analectic Magazine* (1813–21) begins publication in Philadelphia under editorship of Washington Irving; contributors include James Kirke Paulding and Gulian Verplanck.

Washington Allston: *The Sylphs of the Seasons.*

1814   After being detained by the British during bombardment of Baltimore on September 14, Francis Scott Key writes "The Star-Spangled Banner"; the poem, published a few days later in *The Baltimore American*, achieves nationwide popularity. John Neal and John Pierpont open dry goods franchises in Baltimore, Boston, and Charleston; business fails within two years.

Francis Scott Key: "The Star-Spangled Banner."

1815   *The North American Review* begins publication under editorship of William Tudor. Edward Coote Pinkney commissioned as midshipman in U.S. Navy (serves until 1822).

Philip Freneau: *A Collection of Poems on American Affairs.*
John Howard Payne: *Lispings of the Muse.*
Lydia Huntley Sigourney: *Moral Pieces in Prose and Verse.*
Samuel Worcester: *Christian Psalmody.*

1816   John Pierpont publishes long poem *Airs of Palestine.* Joseph Rodman Drake writes fairy fantasy "The Culprit Fay" (poem not published until 14 years after his death). The Delphian Club founded in Baltimore; members include John Neal, John Pierpont, Tobias Watkins, Francis Scott Key, and Samuel Woodworth; Neal serves as editor of the club's literary organ *The Portico* (1816–18).

John Pierpont: *Airs of Palestine.*

1817   William Cullen Bryant's "Thanatopsis" and "Lines" (later
                retitled "Inscription for the Entrance to a Wood") sent by
                the poet's father (without Bryant's knowledge) to *The
                North American Review*; on publication there, the poems
                attract wide attention. Jared Sparks replaces William
                Tudor as editor of *North American Review*.

                Manoah Bodman: *An Oration on Death*.
                William Cullen Bryant: "Thanatopsis."

1818   Edward Tyrrel Channing becomes editor of *The North
                American Review*, with Richard Henry Dana as assistant;
                Dana contributes reviews of Irving, Hazlitt, and Washing-
                ton Allston. Joseph Rodman Drake tours Europe with his
                wife. Washington Allston returns to United States, after
                five-year residence in England, settling in Boston.

                William Cullen Bryant: "To a Waterfowl."
                John Neal: *Battle of Niagara*.
                James Kirke Paulding: *The Backwoodsman*.
                Samuel Woodworth: "The Bucket."

1819   In the New York *Evening Post*, Joseph Rodman Drake and
                Fitz-Greene Halleck publish "The Croaker Papers," anon-
                ymous series of satirical poems of New York life. Edward
                Everett replaces Edward Tyrrel Channing as editor of *The
                North American Review*; Richard Henry Dana resigns from
                staff of the *Review*. John Pierpont becomes minister of the
                Hollis Street Church in Boston. Thomas Cole emigrates
                with family from Liverpool to America.

                Joseph Rodman Drake and Fitz-Greene Halleck: "The
                    Croaker Papers."
                Fitz-Greene Halleck: *Fanny*.
                John Neal: *Otho*.
                Richard Henry Wilde: "The Lament of the Captive."

1820   John Neal resigns from Delphian Club. John Howard
                Payne imprisoned for debt in London. Joseph Rodman
                Drake dies in September in New York City.

                Maria Gowen Brooks: *Judith, Esther, and Other Poems*.
                James Wallis Eastburn and Robert C. Sands: *Yamoyden*.

1821   William Cullen Bryant reads "The Ages" to Phi Beta
                Kappa Society at Harvard. Richard Henry Dana founds

The Idle Man (1821–22); contributors include Bryant and Washington Allston. *The Saturday Evening Post* begins weekly publication in Philadelphia (early contributors include Edgar Allan Poe, Nathaniel Parker Willis, and James Fenimore Cooper). James Gates Percival publishes first verse collection, containing long poem "Prometheus."

Richard Henry Dana: "The Dying Raven."
Fitz-Greene Halleck: "On the Death of Joseph Rodman Drake."
James Gates Percival: *Poems.*

1822   William Cullen Bryant publishes first collection of verse. Fitz-Greene Halleck tours Europe. In New York City, the Bread and Cheese Club becomes informal gathering place for writers and artists including Bryant, Halleck, Thomas Cole, James Fenimore Cooper, and Asher B. Durand. The anthology *Specimens of the American Poets* published in London. Clement Moore reads "A Visit from St. Nicholas" to his family. Henry Rowe Schoolcraft appointed government agent for Indian affairs in the Great Lakes region, based at Sault Ste. Marie.

William Cullen Bryant: *Poems.*
Philip Freneau: "On the Civilization of the Western Aboriginal Country."
Fitz-Greene Halleck: "Alnwick Castle."
James Gates Percival: *Clio I*; *Clio II*; *Prometheus Part II with Other Poems.*
Lydia Huntley Sigourney: *Traits of the Aborigines.*
Carlos Wilcox: *The Age of Benevolence.*

1823   Clement Moore's "A Visit from St. Nicholas" published (without Moore's knowledge) in *The Troy Sentinel*. John Howard Payne writes "Home, Sweet Home" for the operetta *Clari*; song becomes immediate success. Maria Gowen Brooks moves to Cuba; begins epic poem *Zophiël, or the Bride of Seven*. George Pope Morris founds *The New-York Mirror and Ladies' Literary Gazette* (1823–57); Samuel Woodworth serves as editor for a year before being replaced by Morris (later editors include Nathaniel Parker Willis, Charles Fenno Hoffman, and Epes Sargent). John Neal challenged to a duel by Edward Coote Pinkney because of a satiric passage about Pinkney's father in Neal's novel *Randolph*; Neal begins four-year stay in England.

Clement Moore: "A Visit from St. Nicholas."
John Howard Payne: "Home, Sweet Home."
James Gates Percival: *Poems*.

1824   John Neal, in London, publishes survey of 135 American authors in *Blackwood's Magazine*. Thomas Cole, studying at Philadelphia Academy of Fine Arts, publishes poems in *The Saturday Evening Post*. Theophilus Parsons founds *The United States Literary Gazette* (1824–26) in Boston (contributors include William Cullen Bryant, Henry Wadsworth Longfellow, James Gates Percival, and Richard Henry Dana).

1825   William Cullen Bryant becomes co-editor of short-lived *New York Review and Athenaeum Magazine*, publishing among other work Fitz-Greene Halleck's "Marco Bozzaris"; delivers series of lectures on poetry to the American Athenaeum Society. Maria Gowen Brooks publishes the first canto of her epic poem *Zophiël, or the Bride of Seven*; begins correspondence with Robert Southey. Thomas Cole established as landscape painter in New York City. Henry D. Gilpin edits *The Atlantic Souvenir* (1825–31), first series of "gift book" anthologies designed as Christmas or New Year's presents (contributors include James Gates Percival, Lydia Maria Child, and James Kirke Paulding). Henry Wadsworth Longfellow and Nathaniel Hawthorne graduate from Bowdoin College.

William Cullen Bryant: "Forest Hymn."
Fitz-Greene Halleck: "Marco Bozzaris."
Edward Coote Pinkney: *Poems*.

1826   William Lloyd Garrison publishes poetry by John Greenleaf Whittier in Newburyport *Free Press*; Garrison visits Whittier at his family's farm in East Haverhill, and the two become close friends. With Charles Folsom, William Cullen Bryant co-edits *United States Review and Literary Gazette* (1826–27), merger of *United States Literary Gazette* and *New York Review and Athenaeum Magazine*. *The Casket* (renamed *Graham's Magazine* in 1841) begins publication under editorship of Samuel C. Atkinson.

Samuel Woodworth: *Melodies, Duets, Songs, and Ballads*.

1827   William Cullen Bryant, Robert Sands, and Gulian Verplanck publish *The Talisman*, first of three annual gift books. Bryant delivers lectures on mythology at National Academy of the Arts of Design (series repeated in 1828, 1829, and 1831). John Neal returns from England to the U.S.; settles in Portland, Maine.

Richard Henry Dana: *The Buccaneer*.
Fitz-Greene Halleck: *Alnwick Castle, with Other Poems*.
James Gates Percival: *Clio No. III*.
Edgar Allan Poe: *Tamerlane and Other Poems*.
William Gilmore Simms: *Lyrical and Other Poems*; *Early Lays*.
Nathaniel Parker Willis: *Sketches*.

1828   Three poems by George Moses Horton, a North Carolina slave, published in *Lancaster Gazette* (Massachusetts). John Neal becomes editor of the Portland (Maine) *Yankee* (1828–29); publishes work by Edgar Allan Poe, John Greenleaf Whittier, and Henry Wadsworth Longfellow. William Gilmore Simms edits *Southern Literary Gazette* (1828–29). Edward Coote Pinkney dies in April in Baltimore, at age 26.

Fitz-Greene Halleck: "Red Jacket."
Carlos Wilcox: *Remains*.

1829   William Cullen Bryant becomes editor of the New York *Evening Post* upon the death of William Coleman. George Moses Horton's *The Hope of Liberty* published in unsuccessful attempt to subsidize purchase of the poet's freedom from slavery. After three years abroad, Henry Wadsworth Longfellow begins tenure teaching modern languages at Bowdoin College. Ralph Waldo Emerson becomes minister of Second Church of Boston. Thomas Cole leaves for three-year European visit; Bryant writes "To an American Painter, Departing for Europe." Samuel Kettell publishes *Specimens of American Poetry*, a comprehensive three-volume anthology of work from the 17th century onward. Nathaniel Parker Willis founds *The American Monthly Magazine* (1829–31), writing most of it himself. John Greenleaf Whittier edits *The American Manufacturer*, political paper in which he publishes many of his early poems.

George Moses Horton: *The Hope of Liberty*.
Samuel Kettell (editor): *Specimens of American Poetry*.

Edgar Allan Poe: *Al Aaraaf, Tamerlane, and Other Poems.*
William Gilmore Simms: *The Vision of Cortes, Cain,
and Other Poems.*
Nathaniel Parker Willis: *Fugitive Poetry.*

1830   In Hartford, Connecticut, John Greenleaf Whittier edits
The New England Weekly Review (1830–32), contributing
many poems, articles, and sketches; forms friendship with
Lydia Huntley Sigourney. Editor Edwin James appends
translations of Ojibwa ritual songs to *A Narrative of the
Captivity and Adventures of John Tanner.*

Samuel Henry Dickson: "I Sigh for the Land of the
Cypress and Pine."
Oliver Wendell Holmes: "Old Ironsides."
George Pope Morris: "The Oak" ("Woodman, Spare
That Tree!").

1831   Maria Gowen Brooks visits Robert Southey in England.
As foreign correspondent for *New-York Mirror*, Nathaniel
Parker Willis sets out on four years of travel in Europe and
Middle East.

Edgar Allan Poe: *Poems.*
John Greenleaf Whittier: *Legends of New-England
in Prose and Verse.*

1832   William Cullen Bryant publishes first major collection of
his work; meets with President Andrew Jackson and vari-
ous members of his cabinet in Washington; on tour of
Illinois prairie, sees ancient Indian mounds. Ralph Waldo
Emerson resigns ministry and sails to Europe. Fitz-Greene
Halleck goes to work as confidential clerk for John Jacob
Astor. Fanny Kemble tours America with her father's the-
atrical company. John Howard Payne returns penniless
from Europe. William Davis Ticknor and John Allen
found publishing house Allen and Ticknor in Boston
(Allen leaves company after two years). Philip Freneau
dies in December in blizzard near his home at Mount
Pleasant, New Jersey.

John Quincy Adams: *Dermot MacMorrogh; or,
the Conquest of Ireland.*
William Cullen Bryant: *Poems.*

Thomas Holley Chivers: *The Path of Sorrow, or the Lament of Youth*.
Thomas Hastings and Lowell Mason: *Spiritual Songs for Social Worship*.

1833   Maria Gowen Brooks' *Zophiël* published in England by Robert Southey. *The Knickerbocker* (1833–65) begins publication in New York under editorship of Charles Fenno Hoffman (contributors include Longfellow, Irving, Willis, Paulding, Halleck, Whittier, Holmes, and Bryant). William Gilmore Simms travels to New York; forms friendships with William Cullen Bryant and publisher Evert Duyckinck. Charles Fenno Hoffman travels in the West, 1833–34. Ralph Waldo Emerson travels in Italy, France, and England, meeting Walter Savage Landor, John Stuart Mill, Thomas Carlyle, Samuel Taylor Coleridge, and William Wordsworth. Henry Wadsworth Longfellow publishes translation of *Coplas por la muerte de su padre* by 15th-century Spanish poet Jorge Manrique.

        Maria Gowen Brooks: *Zophiël, or the Bride of Seven*.
        Richard Henry Dana: *Poems and Prose Writings*.

1834   Ralph Waldo Emerson settles in Concord. Bronson Alcott founds Masonic Temple School in Boston. John Greenleaf Whittier elected as Whig to Massachusetts legislature. Fanny Kemble marries Pierce Mease Butler in Philadelphia; retires from stage. *Southern Literary Messenger* (1834–64) begins publication in Richmond under editorship of James A. Heath, replaced the following year by Thomas W. White (contributors include Edgar Allan Poe, Richard Henry Wilde, Nathaniel Parker Willis, Lydia Huntley Sigourney, Philip Pendleton Cooke, and William Gilmore Simms). *The Ladies' Companion* (1834–44) begins publication in New York under editorship of William Snowden (contributors include Poe, Simms, Willis, Henry Wadsworth Longfellow, and James Kirke Paulding). Following newspaper controversy over authorship of Richard Henry Wilde's "The Lament of the Captive" (first published anonymously in 1819), Wilde acknowledges the poem as his.

        Thomas Hastings: *The Mother's Nursery Songs*.
        Lydia Huntley Sigourney: *Poems*.

1835   Henry Wadsworth Longfellow appointed Smith Professor of Modern Languages at Harvard; travels to Europe for year of further study; in Heidelberg, Germany, meets and spends much time with William Cullen Bryant. *The Western Messenger* (1835–41) begins publication in Cincinnati under editorship of Ephraim Peabody, subsequently replaced by James Freeman Clarke (1836–39) and William Henry Channing (1840–41); initially associated closely with Unitarianism, the *Messenger*'s contributors include Ralph Waldo Emerson, Margaret Fuller, Jones Very, Christopher Pearse Cranch, William Ellery Channing, Charles Timothy Brooks, Theodore Parker, Elizabeth Peabody, and Francis Parkman. Daniel K. Whitaker founds *The Southern Literary Journal* (1835–38) in Charleston, with William Gilmore Simms as chief contributor. Edgar Allan Poe works as editor on *Southern Literary Messenger*, contributing poems, stories, and reviews. Charles Fenno Hoffman assumes editorship of *American Monthly Magazine*, 1835–37. Joseph Rodman Drake's *The Culprit Fay* (edited by daughter Janet Halleck Drake) published 14 years after Drake's death. Christopher Pearse Cranch begins career as Unitarian minister. Traveling in Georgia, John Howard Payne meets John Ross, head of Cherokee Nation, and solicits information on Cherokee history for prospective literary magazine; arrested with Ross by Georgia militia, charged with abolitionism, and jailed for 13 days; writes newspaper account complaining of ill-treatment. John Pierpont travels to Holy Land. In England, Nathaniel Parker Willis attacked by Harriet Martineau and Frederick Marryat for journalistic indiscretion in publishing private conversations. James Gates Percival begins seven-year service as state geologist of Connecticut. Richard Henry Wilde settles in Florence; studies Dante and Italian lyric poets.

    Joseph Rodman Drake: *The Culprit Fay*.
    Nathaniel Parker Willis: *Melanie and Other Poems*.

1836   In *Southern Literary Messenger*, Edgar Allan Poe attacks inflated reputation of Joseph Rodman Drake and Fitz-Greene Halleck: "That we have among us poets of the loftiest order we believe—but we do *not* believe that these poets are Drake and Halleck." Bronson Alcott publishes first volume of *Conversations with Children on the Gospels*;

Margaret Fuller works briefly as Alcott's assistant at his Temple School (1836–37), replacing Elizabeth Peabody. Fuller meets Ralph Waldo Emerson; spends three weeks as guest in his household. Emerson and Henry David Thoreau develop close friendship. In *The American Nations*, Constantine Rafinesque publishes translation of what he claims to be Leni-Lenâpé (Delaware) tribal chronicle "Walam Olum" with "the songs annexed thereto in the original language." Thomas Cole completes series of paintings "The Course of Empire."

Oliver Wendell Holmes: *Poems*.
Richard Henry Wilde: "To the Mocking Bird."

1837 The first issue of *The Gentleman's Magazine*, later *Burton's Gentleman's Magazine* (1837–40), appears in Philadelphia under editorship of William E. Burton (contributors include Edgar Allan Poe and Thomas Dunn English). *United States Magazine and Democratic Review* (1837–55) begins publication under editorship of John L. O'Sullivan and Samuel D. Langtree (contributors in early years include Poe, James Russell Lowell, John Greenleaf Whittier, William Gilmore Simms, and Bayard Taylor). At Lac-qui-parle mission, Stephen Return Riggs and his wife, Mary Ann, begin study of Sioux language. Charles Fenno Hoffman edits *The New-York Book of Poetry*, containing first book publication of Clement Moore's "A Visit from St. Nicholas." James Kirke Paulding appointed Secretary of the Navy by Martin Van Buren.

Thomas Holley Chivers: *Nacoochee*.
Charles Fenno Hoffman (editor): *The New-York Book of Poetry*.

1838 Following intense religious experience, Jones Very's sanity is questioned; he is forced to resign from Harvard Divinity School, and is briefly committed to McLean Asylum in Somerville, Massachusetts. Ralph Waldo Emerson delivers controversial address at Harvard Divinity School. Walt Whitman founds *The Long Islander* (1838–39). John Greenleaf Whittier becomes editor of *The Pennsylvania Freeman* (1838–40); in May, Pennsylvania Hall in Philadelphia is burned by anti-abolitionist mob, destroying Whittier's editorial office in the process. Oliver Wendell

Holmes becomes professor of anatomy and physiology at Dartmouth. Richard Henry Dana delivers lectures on Shakespeare in Providence, Rhode Island. Fanny Kemble begins six-month stay at her husband's Georgia plantation.

Josiah D. Canning: *Poems*.
Henry Wadsworth Longfellow: "A Psalm of Life."
John Greenleaf Whittier: *Poems*.

1839   Henry Wadsworth Longfellow publishes first verse collection, *Voices of the Night*, and romance *Hyperion*. Twenty-seven sonnets by Jones Very published by James Freeman Clarke in *The Western Messenger*, followed by *Essays and Poems* (prepared with the assistance of Ralph Waldo Emerson). Margaret Fuller initiates series of "conversations" in Boston, educational experiment (continued until 1844) intended to provide "a point of union to well-educated and thinking women, in a city which, with great pretensions to mental refinement, boasts, at present, nothing of the kind"; she interviews Washington Allston in connection with exhibit of his paintings in Boston. Bronson Alcott forced to close Masonic Temple School after charges of heterodoxy lead to decreased enrollment and severe indebtedness. Richard Henry Dana lectures on Shakespeare in Boston. George Graham takes over editorship of *The Casket*, eventually renaming it (in 1841) *Graham's Magazine*; turns it into important literary magazine (contributors include Edgar Allan Poe, James Russell Lowell, Lydia Huntley Sigourney, William Cullen Bryant, Thomas Buchanan Read, George Pope Morris, Henry Wadsworth Longfellow, Charles Fenno Hoffman, Fanny Osgood, and James Fenimore Cooper). *Littell's Living Age* founded under editorship of Eliakim Littell; contributors include Poe, Emerson, Fitz-Greene Halleck, and Nathaniel Parker Willis. *The Liberty Bell* (published irregularly between 1839 and 1857), abolitionist gift book, begins publication under editorship of Maria Weston Chapman and her sisters Anne Warren and Caroline (contributors include Emerson, Fuller, Longfellow, Lydia Maria Child, Frederick Douglass, James Russell Lowell, and Maria White Lowell). Henry Rowe Schoolcraft's *Algic Researches* is published, first major study of American Indian folklore. Herman Melville sails to Liverpool as crew member of trading ship *St. Lawrence*. Henry David Thoreau and his brother John make 13-day trip on the Concord and Merrimack rivers.

Henry Wadsworth Longfellow: *Voices of the Night*.
Jones Very: *Essays and Poems*.

1840   Ralph Waldo Emerson and Margaret Fuller bring out first
        issue of *The Dial* (1840–44) with Fuller as editor (other
        contributors will include Henry David Thoreau, Christopher Pearse Cranch, Bronson Alcott, George Ripley, Theodore Parker, and Elizabeth Peabody). Cornelius Mathews
        and Evert Duyckinck found *Arcturus* (1840–42) in New
        York (contributors include Henry Wadsworth Longfellow,
        Nathaniel Hawthorne, and James Russell Lowell). *The
        Union Magazine* (1847–52) begins publication, edited by
        Caroline M. Kirkland and others (contributors include
        Lowell, Longfellow, Nathaniel Parker Willis, Lydia Huntley Sigourney, Charles Fenno Hoffman, and Fanny Osgood). Edgar Allan Poe writes to Thomas Holley Chivers,
        then in New York, in effort to solicit funding for Poe's
        prospective *Penn Magazine* (never published). John
        Howard Payne travels from Washington with John Ross to
        the latter's home in Indian Territory (later Oklahoma);
        meets Sequoya, creator of Cherokee alphabet. Christopher
        Pearse Cranch meets Ralph Waldo Emerson in Boston.
        Lydia Huntley Sigourney travels to Europe, where she
        meets William Wordsworth and Thomas Carlyle.

        William Cullen Bryant (editor): *Selections from the
            American Poets*.
        Philip Pendleton Cooke: "Florence Vane."

1841   Cooperative community Brook Farm, offshoot of Transcendental Club, established near West Roxbury, Massachusetts, by George Ripley and others; residents include
        Nathaniel Hawthorne, George William Curtis, and
        Charles Anderson Dana. Edgar Allan Poe becomes literary
        editor of *Graham's Magazine*. Ephraim George Squier
        founds *The Poet's Magazine* in Albany. William Cullen
        Bryant and Thomas Cole go on walking tour of the
        Catskills. Lydia Maria Child moves to New York to assume editorship of *The National Anti-Slavery Standard* (remains as editor until 1844). Dismissed from position as
        Indian agent in Sault Ste. Marie, Henry Rowe Schoolcraft

moves to New York City. Herman Melville sails for South Seas on whaling ship *Acushnet*.

Ralph Waldo Emerson: *Essays*.
Henry Wadsworth Longfellow: *Ballads and Other Poems*.
James Russell Lowell: *A Year's Life*.
Cornelius Mathews: *Wakondah: The Master of Life*.
Lydia Huntley Sigourney: *Pocahontas and Other Poems*;
 Poems, Religious and Elegiac.

1842   Charles Dickens visits the United States and meets William Cullen Bryant, Richard Henry Dana, Sr. and Jr., Fitz-Greene Halleck, Cornelius Mathews, Edgar Allan Poe, and other literary figures. John Greenleaf Whittier runs for Congress as Liberty Party candidate. Ralph Waldo Emerson succeeds Margaret Fuller as editor of *The Dial*. Poe resigns from *Graham's Magazine*, complaining of inadequate compensation. Daniel K. Whitaker founds *Southern Quarterly Review* (1842–57). *Arcturus* absorbed into *Boston Miscellany of Literature and Fashion* (1842–43) under editorship of Nathan Hale, Jr. (contributors include Poe, James Russell Lowell, Cornelius Mathews, and Evert Duyckinck). Nathaniel Hawthorne settles in Concord with his wife, Sophia Peabody. With financial assistance from Emerson, Bronson Alcott travels to England; meets Thomas Carlyle. William Ellery Channing marries Ellen Fuller, sister of Margaret Fuller; settles in Concord. William Cullen Bryant visits William Gilmore Simms in Florida. John Howard Payne appointed American consul at Tunis by President John Tyler. Herman Melville deserts whaling ship *Acushnet* in the Marquesas.

Charles Timothy Brooks (editor and translator): *Songs and Ballads*.
William Cullen Bryant: *The Fountain and Other Poems*.
Christopher Pearse Cranch (translator): *The Aeneid*.
Rufus Griswold (editor): *The Poets and Poetry of America*.
Henry Wadsworth Longfellow: *Poems on Slavery*.

1843   Bronson Alcott attempts to establish utopian community at Fruitlands, a farm near Harvard, Massachusetts (experiment abandoned in 1845). James Russell Lowell and Robert Carter found short-lived magazine *The Pioneer* (January–June); contributors include Jones Very, William

Wetmore Story, John Neal, John Greenleaf Whittier, and Edgar Allan Poe ("The Rationale of Verse"). Poe lectures on "Poets and Poetry of America." Ralph Waldo Emerson completes translation of Dante's *La Vita Nuova*. Henry David Thoreau's translation of Aeschylus' *Prometheus Bound* and *Seven Against Thebes* published in *The Dial*. Daniel Decatur Emmett's Virginia Minstrels make debut at Bowery Amphitheatre in New York City. James T. Fields admitted as junior partner of Ticknor and Company. Washington Allston dies in Cambridge, Massachusetts.

William Ellery Channing: *Poems*.
Thomas Dunn English: "Ben Bolt."
Henry Wadsworth Longfellow: *The Spanish Student*.
Cornelius Mathews: *Poems on Man in His Various Aspects under the American Republic*.
James Gates Percival: *The Dream of a Day, and Other Poems*.
John Pierpont: *Anti-Slavery Poems*.
John Greenleaf Whittier: *Lays of My Home and Other Poems*.
Nathaniel Parker Willis: *Poems of Passion*.

1844   Margaret Fuller moves to New York, upon invitation of Horace Greeley to become book reviewer for *New-York Daily Tribune*; during three-year residence, immerses herself in literary life, meeting writers and critics including Edgar Allan Poe, Lydia Maria Child, Anne Lynch, William Gilmore Simms, Evert Duyckinck, Cornelius Mathews, and Christopher Pearse Cranch. James Russell Lowell marries Maria White. At 19, Bayard Taylor publishes first collection of poetry and begins two years of travel in Europe as foreign correspondent for *The Saturday Evening Post* and other papers. Whittier asks Longfellow to run for Congress as candidate of the abolitionist Liberty Party; Longfellow turns down the offer, stating, "I am not a member of any society, and fight under no single banner . . . Partizan warfare becomes too violent—too vindictive for my taste." William Cullen Bryant builds new residence, Springbank, in Roslyn, New York. Translations of Pindar by Henry David Thoreau published in *The Dial*.

William Cullen Bryant: *The White Footed Deer and Other Poems*.

Christopher Pearse Cranch: *Poems*.
Samuel Henry Dickson: *Poems*.
Ralph Waldo Emerson: *Essays: Second Series*.
Fanny Kemble: *Poems*.
Clement Moore: *Poems*.
Bayard Taylor: *Ximena, or The Battle of the Sierra Morena*.
Dan Emmit's Original Banjo Melodies (including
    "The Blue-Tail Fly").

1845   Edgar Allan Poe's "The Raven" published in the *New-York Mirror*. Poe becomes editor of the *Broadway Journal* (1845–46); other contributors include Richard Henry Dana, Lydia Maria Child, Thomas Dunn English, Margaret Fuller, and William Gilmore Simms. In the *Journal's* pages, Poe resumes attacks on Longfellow (begun in *Burton's Gentleman's Magazine* and New York *Evening Mirror*), charging him with plagiarism. Longfellow, in response to the *Journal's* attacks, remarks in letter to James Russell Lowell: "I have had nothing to do with the discussion, and shall have nothing to do with it; as I consider, with you, life too precious to be wasted in street brawls." Poe meets Evert Duyckinck (who selects 12 stories for *Tales*, published in July) and is visited at *Broadway Journal* office by Walt Whitman. Thomas Holley Chivers arrives in New York to arrange for publication of *The Lost Pleiad*; meets Poe; Poe reviews Chivers' book favorably in the *Broadway Journal*. Critical discussion of Poe's work published in leading French literary journal *La Revue des Deux Mondes*. James Russell Lowell writes editorials for abolitionist paper *The Pennsylvania Freeman*. William Gilmore Simms edits *The Southern and Western Monthly Magazine and Review* (January–December), writing most of it himself; other contributors include Thomas Holley Chivers, James Mathewes Legaré, Albert Pike, Caroline Lee Hentz, and Evert Duyckinck. George Ripley edits Fourierist journal *The Harbinger* (1845–49); contributors include Christopher Pearse Cranch, James Russell Lowell, Thomas Wentworth Higginson, Horace Greeley, John Greenleaf Whittier, and William Wetmore Story. Thomas Dunn English edits short-lived magazine *The Aristidean*, to which Poe and Whitman contribute. After years of conflict with his congregation over his temperance and anti-slavery views, John Pierpont resigns ministry of Hollis Street Unitarian Church in Boston. William Cullen Bryant sails for

Europe; meets Thomas Moore and Leigh Hunt. William Wetmore Story commissioned to sculpt memorial to his late father, the Supreme Court justice Joseph Story. Fanny Kemble, separated from husband Pierce Butler, returns to London. Henry David Thoreau begins 26-month residence at Walden Pond. Maria Gowen Brooks dies in November in Cuba. Henry Rowe Schoolcraft publishes examples of Ojibwa poetry in *Oneóta; or, Characteristics of the Red Race of America.*

Thomas Holley Chivers: *The Lost Pleiad.*
George Moses Horton: *The Poetical Works of George M. Horton, the Colored Bard of North Carolina.*
James Russell Lowell: *Conversations on Some of the Old Poets.*
Edgar Allan Poe: *The Raven and Other Poems.*
Henry Rowe Schoolcraft: *Oneóta; or, Characteristics of the Red Race of America.*

1846   Margaret Fuller departs for Europe as foreign correspondent for the *New-York Tribune.* In *Godey's Lady's Book*, Poe publishes series of sketches of "The Literati of New York City"; Thomas Dunn English, incensed at description of him, attacks Poe's character in *Evening Mirror*; Poe successfully sues for damages. Poe moves with family to cottage in Fordham, New York. Walt Whitman works for Brooklyn *Daily Eagle. The National Press* begins publication under editorship of George Pope Morris and Nathaniel Parker Willis; name changes within the year to *The Home Journal* (1846–1901). Christopher Pearse Cranch travels to Italy; forms close friendship with Robert and Elizabeth Barrett Browning.

Ralph Waldo Emerson: *Poems.*
Frances Sargent Osgood: *Poems.*
William Gilmore Simms: *Areytos; or, Songs of the South.*
John Greenleaf Whittier: *Voices of Freedom.*

1847   Oliver Wendell Holmes becomes professor of anatomy and physiology at Harvard Medical School. John Greenleaf Whittier becomes an editor of *The National Era* (remains until 1860). *The Literary World* (1847–53) begins weekly publication in New York under editorship of Evert Duyckinck (temporarily replaced by Charles Fenno Hoffman, May 1847–September 1848); contributors include

Charles Timothy Brooks, James Kirke Paulding, and William Gilmore Simms. Herman Melville marries Elizabeth Shaw and moves to New York City. Edgar Allan Poe's young wife, Virginia, dies of tuberculosis. Ralph Waldo Emerson visits England; meets with Thomas Carlyle, Charles Dickens, William Wordsworth, and Alfred Tennyson. Richard Henry Wilde dies in September in New Orleans.

Henry Howard Brownell: *Poems.*
Philip Pendleton Cooke: *Froissart Ballads and Other Poems.*
William Ellery Channing: *Conversations in Rome between an Artist, a Catholic, and a Critic; Poems: Second Series.*
Fitz-Greene Halleck: *Works.*
Henry Wadsworth Longfellow: *Evangeline.*
Edgar Allan Poe: *Eureka: A Prose Poem.*
Epes Sargent: *Songs of the Sea with Other Poems.*
William Wetmore Story: *Poems.*
A Collection of Millenial Hymns, Shaker hymnal.

1848   In a single year, James Russell Lowell publishes four important books of poetry. Edgar Allan Poe delivers "The Poetic Principle" as lecture in Providence, Rhode Island. Poe meets Sarah Helen Whitman; proposes marriage to her; engagement is broken off after three months. George Boyer Vashon becomes first black lawyer in the state of New York. Walt Whitman founds *Brooklyn Freeman* (1848–49). Bayard Taylor becomes literary editor of *New-York Tribune* under Horace Greeley's editorship. Charles Godfrey Leland briefly caught up in revolutionary struggle in Paris. Ralph Waldo Emerson, also in Paris, meets Alexis de Tocqueville. Thomas Cole dies in February in Catskill, New York; eulogized by William Cullen Bryant at New York's Academy of Music.

John Quincy Adams: *Poems of Religion and Society.*
George Henry Boker: *A Lesson of Life.*
Stephen Foster: *Songs of the Sable Harmonists.*
Rufus Griswold (editor): *The Female Poets of America.*
James Mathewes Legaré: *Orta-Undis and Other Poems.*
James Russell Lowell: *The Biglow Papers; A Fable for Critics; The Vision of Sir Launfal; Poems: Second Series.*
William Gilmore Simms: *Lays of the Palmetto.*
Music of the Ethiopian Serenaders (including "Buffalo Gals").

1849 Edgar Allan Poe dies after being found delirious on Baltimore street. Longfellow writes to a correspondent: "What a melancholy death is that of Mr. Poe, a man so richly endowed with genius! . . . The harshness of his criticisms, I have never attributed to anything but the irritation of a sensitive nature chafed by some indefinite sense of wrong." Rufus Griswold writes damaging obituary of Poe for *New-York Tribune*. Asher B. Durand paints "Kindred Spirits," double portrait of William Cullen Bryant and Thomas Cole in the Catskills. Bryant travels to Cuba in the early part of the year, then sails for Europe in June. Bayard Taylor reports on California gold rush for *New-York Tribune*. Josiah Gilbert Holland becomes assistant editor of *The Springfield Republican* in Massachusetts. William Gilmore Simms takes over editorship of *Southern Quarterly Review*. Ticknor and Company changes imprint to Ticknor, Reed and Fields. Henry Rowe Schoolcraft receives U.S. government commission to compile survey of American Indians (published in six volumes as *History, Condition and Prospects of the Indian Tribes of the United States*, 1851–57). Margaret Fuller, involved in Italian revolution, flees from Rome to Italian mountain village with the Marchese Ossoli and their child after the fall of the Roman republic. Following recurrent attacks of mental illness, Charles Fenno Hoffman confined to Harrisburg (Pennsylvania) Insane Asylum (remains there until his death in 1884).

William Ellery Channing: *The Woodman and Other Poems*.
Stephen Foster: *Foster's Ethiopian Melodies*.
Henry Wadsworth Longfellow: *The Seaside and the Fireside*.
Edgar Allan Poe: "Annabel Lee"; "The Bells."
William Gilmore Simms: *The Cassique of Accabee*.
Bayard Taylor: *Rhymes of Travel, Ballads, and Poems*.
Henry David Thoreau: *A Week on the Concord and Merrimack Rivers*.
John Greenleaf Whittier: *Poems*.

1850 John Greenleaf Whittier writes "Ichabod" to protest Daniel Webster's support of Fugitive Slave Law. Returning from Europe, Margaret Fuller dies on July 19 with husband and son in shipwreck off Fire Island; at Ralph Waldo Emerson's request, Henry David Thoreau goes to site of wreck to search for her effects and manuscripts. Thomas Holley Chivers, charged by Jedediah Hunt with imitating Poe and others, responds: "Poe stole every thing that is worthy any thing from me . . . Poe stole all his *Raven* from me; but was the greatest Poetical Critic that ever existed." Rufus Griswold publishes edition of the works of Poe, altering some letters included in it, and further attacks Poe's character in attached "Memoir." Nathaniel Hawthorne settles in Lenox, Massachusetts, and forms friendship with Herman Melville, who had recently published highly favorable review of Hawthorne's short stories. Alice Cary travels from Ohio to New England and meets John Greenleaf Whittier; later in the year moves to New York City, joined by her sisters Phoebe and Elmina. Bayard Taylor reads Phi Beta Kappa poem at Harvard; wins prize offered by P. T. Barnum for poem to be sung by celebrated Swedish singer Jenny Lind on her appearance at New York's Castle Garden. In Washington, with John Howard Payne in the audience, Jenny Lind sings "Home, Sweet Home." *Harper's New Monthly Magazine* founded under editorship of Henry J. Raymond. Rufus Griswold edits *International Weekly Miscellany* (1850–52), assisted by Charles Godfrey Leland; contributors include Bayard Taylor, Alice Cary, Constance Fenimore Woolson, Nathaniel Hawthorne, and William Gilmore Simms. Philip Pendleton Cooke dies in January in Martinsburg, Virginia, at age 33.

Washington Allston: *Lectures on Art, and Poems* (edited by Richard Henry Dana).
Alice and Phoebe Cary: *Poems*.
Thomas Holley Chivers: *Eonchs of Ruby*.
William H. C. Hosmer: *Indian Traditions and Songs*; *Legends of the Senecas*.
William Gilmore Simms: *The City of the Silent*.
John Greenleaf Whittier: *Songs of Labor*; "Ichabod!"

1851   Bayard Taylor departs for two years of travel in Egypt, Abyssinia, the Middle East, India, China, and Japan.

Stephen Foster: "Old Folks at Home."
Henry Wadsworth Longfellow: *The Golden Legend*.
Herman Melville: *Moby-Dick*.
Bayard Taylor: *A Book of Romances, Lyrics, and Songs*.

1852   On visit to U.S., William Makepeace Thackeray meets Henry Wadsworth Longfellow, Christopher Pearse Cranch, Richard Henry Dana, Oliver Wendell Holmes, and James Russell Lowell. John James Piatt and William Dean Howells become friends while working on the staff of *The Ohio State Journal*. *The Golden Era* (1852–94) founded in San Francisco under editorship of J. Macdonough Foard and Rollin M. Daggett; contributors include John Rollin Ridge, Bret Harte, Mark Twain, and Adah Isaacs Menken. At the New-York Historical Society, with Daniel Webster presiding, William Cullen Bryant eulogizes James Fenimore Cooper, who had died at end of 1851. John Howard Payne dies in April in Tunis while serving as American consul. Poems of Margaret Fuller included in posthumous *The Memoirs of Margaret Fuller Ossoli*. Charles Baudelaire publishes the first of his critical studies of Edgar Allan Poe.

    Josiah D. Canning: *The Harp and Plow*.
    Alice Cary: *Lyra and Other Poems*.
    Edmund Hamilton Sears: "It Came Upon the Midnight Clear."
    A Sacred Repository of Anthems and Hymns (Shaker hymnal).

1853   Nathaniel Hawthorne sails to Liverpool to serve as U.S. consul; Henry Wadsworth Longfellow gives him a farewell dinner where guests include Ralph Waldo Emerson, James Russell Lowell, and Charles Eliot Norton. Bronson Alcott embarks on first of his lecture tours in the West. *Putnam's Monthly Magazine* begins publication under editorship of Charles F. Briggs, with early contributions from Longfellow, Lowell, Henry David Thoreau, Herman Melville, Fitz-James O'Brien, and Bayard Taylor. Maria White Lowell dies in October.

    Charles Timothy Brooks: *Songs of Field and Flood*; (translator) *German Lyrics*.
    Thomas Holley Chivers: *Memoralia*; *Virginalia*; *Atlanta*.
    Stephen Foster: "My Old Kentucky Home."
    William Gilmore Simms: *Poems: Descriptive, Legendary, and Contemplative*.
    James Monroe Whitfield: *America and Other Poems*.
    Sarah Helen Whitman: *Hours of Life and Other Poems*.
    John Greenleaf Whittier: *The Chapel of the Hermits*.

1854   Frances Ellen Watkins Harper works for Underground
            Railroad. James T. Fields enters into full partnership with
            William Davis Ticknor; authors published under their im-
            print, Ticknor & Fields, include Longfellow, Emerson,
            Holmes, Lowell, Hawthorne, Thoreau, Harriet Beecher
            Stowe, Bayard Taylor, and Julia Ward Howe. Bret Harte
            moves from New York to California.

            Benjamin Paul Blood: *The Bride of the Iconoclast.*
            Phoebe Cary: *Poems and Parodies.*
            Stephen Foster: "Jeanie with the Light Brown Hair."
            Frances Ellen Watkins Harper: *Poems on Miscellaneous
                Subjects.*
            Bayard Taylor: *Poems of the Orient.*
            Henry David Thoreau: *Walden.*
            George Boyer Vashon: "Vincent Ogé."

1855   Walt Whitman publishes *Leaves of Grass* at his own ex-
            pense; Ralph Waldo Emerson writes to him upon receiv-
            ing it, "I give you joy of your free & brave thought . . . I
            greet you at the beginning of a great career, which yet
            must have had a long foreground somewhere, for such a
            start." James Russell Lowell succeeds Longfellow as pro-
            fessor of Romance languages and literature at Harvard;
            arranges for posthumous publication of *The Poems of
            Maria Lowell*; delivers lectures on English poets at Lowell
            Institute of Boston. Henry Wadsworth Longfellow pub-
            lishes *The Song of Hiawatha*; sends copy to Henry Rowe
            Schoolcraft, writing: "Without your books I could not
            have written mine." During visit to England, Frederick
            Goddard Tuckerman is guest at Alfred Tennyson's home
            on Isle of Wight. Evert and George Duyckinck publish
            Cyclopaedia of American Literature, containing biographical
            sketches of many poets.

            George Henry Boker: *Francesca da Rimini.*
            Alice Cary: *Poems.*
            Thomas Dunn English: *Poems.*
            Paul Hamilton Hayne: *Poems.*
            Henry Wadsworth Longfellow: *The Song of Hiawatha.*
            Maria White Lowell: *Poems.*
            Bayard Taylor: *Poems of Home and Travel.*
            Walt Whitman: *Leaves of Grass.*

1856   Bronson Alcott and Henry David Thoreau visit Walt Whitman in Brooklyn (Thoreau afterward writes of Whitman: "He occasionally suggests something a little more than human. You can't confound him with the other inhabitants of Brooklyn or New York"). William Gilmore Simms begins series of pro-slavery lectures in New York; forced to cancel tour after hostile public reaction in Buffalo and Rochester. William Makepeace Thackeray, on visit to New York, forms friendship with Bayard Taylor; later in the year Taylor visits Alexander von Humboldt in Berlin. Giving up law for career as artist, William Wetmore Story settles in Rome. Herman Melville sets out on voyage to Europe and the Holy Land; in Liverpool in November meets briefly with Nathaniel Hawthorne. James Gates Percival dies in May at Hazel Green, Wisconsin.

George Henry Boker: *Plays and Poems*.
Charles Timothy Brooks (translator): *Faust*.
George Clark (editor): *The Harp of Freedom* (abolitionist songbook).
Walt Whitman: *Leaves of Grass* (second enlarged edition).
John Greenleaf Whittier: *The Panorama and Other Poems*.

1857   *Atlantic Monthly* begins publication under editorship of James Russell Lowell; early contributors include Ralph Waldo Emerson, Henry Wadsworth Longfellow, John Greenleaf Whittier, Harriet Beecher Stowe, Rose Terry Cooke, and Thomas Wentworth Higginson; Oliver Wendell Holmes' series "The Autocrat of the Breakfast-Table" is widely popular. Paul Hamilton Hayne edits *Russell's Magazine* (1857–60) in Charleston, an outgrowth of literary circle centered on John Russell's bookstore; contributors include William Gilmore Simms, Henry Timrod, and Samuel Henry Dickson. *Harper's Weekly* begins publication with Theodore Sedgwick as editor (subsequent editors include George William Curtis, Carl Schurz, and John Kendrick Bangs). Charles Godfrey Leland publishes first Hans Breitmann poems in *Graham's Magazine*. Henry David Thoreau meets John Brown. William Cullen Bryant sails for Europe. Herman Melville keeps journal of his travels in the Holy Land, material later to be used in *Clarel*.

Paul Hamilton Hayne: *Sonnets and Other Poems*.

1858   In Florence, William Cullen Bryant meets Nathaniel Haw-
            thorne while staying with Robert Browning; also spends
            time with Walter Savage Landor. Thomas Holley Chivers
            dies in December in Decatur, Georgia.

            Josiah Gilbert Holland: *Bitter-Sweet*.
            Oliver Wendell Holmes: *The Autocrat of the
                Breakfast-Table*.
            Henry Wadsworth Longfellow: *The Courtship of Miles
                Standish*.
            John A. Stone: *Put's Golden Songster* (including
                "Sweet Betsey from Pike").

1859   Henry David Thoreau speaks in Concord, Boston, and
            Worcester in defense of John Brown; aids fugitive member
            of Brown's party in his escape to Canada. *Vanity Fair*
            (1859–63) begins publication under editorship of William
            Allan Stephens, an outgrowth of bohemian circle fre-
            quenting Pfaff's beer cellar in New York; contributors in-
            clude Thomas Bailey Aldrich, Charles Godfrey Leland,
            Fitz-James O'Brien, Ada Clare, Edmund Clarence Sted-
            man, and Fitz Hugh Ludlow.

            Daniel Decatur Emmett: "Dixie's Land" ("Dixie").

1860   In February, William Cullen Bryant introduces Abraham
            Lincoln at Cooper Union, New York. Walt Whitman
            meets in Boston with Ralph Waldo Emerson, who urges
            him to tone down sexual elements of "Children of Adam"
            poems in new third edition of *Leaves of Grass*. Sarah Helen
            Whitman defends Poe's reputation in *Edgar Poe and His
            Critics*. William Dean Howells publishes campaign biogra-
            phy of Lincoln. On visit to Concord, Howells meets
            Emerson, Hawthorne, Lowell, and Holmes. Charles God-
            frey Leland takes over editorship of *Vanity Fair*, 1860–61.
            Moncure Daniel Conway publishes *The Dial* in Cincin-
            nati; contributors include Emerson, Howells, and Frank-
            lin Sanborn; it fails after a year. As editorialist for *The
            Northern Californian* (Arcata, California), Bret Harte pro-
            tests massacre of Wiyot Indians at Humboldt Bay.

            Elizabeth Akers Allen: "Rock Me to Sleep."
            Stephen Foster: "Old Black Joe."
            Paul Hamilton Hayne: *Avolio*.

William Dean Howells and John James Piatt: *Poems of Two Friends*.
Thomas Buchanan Read: *Complete Poetical Works*.
Edmund Clarence Stedman: *Poems Lyrical and Idyllic*.
Henry Timrod: *Poems*.
Frederick Goddard Tuckerman: *Poems*.
John Greenleaf Whittier: *Home Ballads, Poems and Lyrics*.

1861   John Hay travels to Washington as Abraham Lincoln's assistant private secretary. George Henry Boker founds Union League of Philadelphia. William Dean Howells appointed American consul in Venice. Edmund Clarence Stedman works as Civil War correspondent for New York *World*. John Banister Tabb travels to England to help arrange transport of supplies to Confederacy. Henry Adams, as London correspondent of *New York Times*, reports British reaction to Civil War. Ambrose Bierce joins 9th Indiana Infantry Regiment of Union Army. Edward Rowland Sill delivers acclaimed commencement poem at Yale. Charles Godfrey Leland edits *The Knickerbocker*, 1861–62; during his term writes most material himself, but also publishes work by William Dean Howells, Thomas Bailey Aldrich, Fitz Hugh Ludlow, and Fitz-James O'Brien. Henry David Thoreau travels to Minnesota; visits Lower Sioux Agency at Redwood. John James Piatt and Sarah Morgan Bryan married in Louisville, Kentucky. On July 9 Henry Wadsworth Longfellow's wife, Fanny, is fatally burned when burning sealing wax sets her dress on fire; Longfellow, attempting to save her, also burned severely. Adah Isaacs Menken gives her first performance in title role of *Mazeppa* in Albany, New York. Spiritual "Let My People Go " published in *The National Anti-Slavery Standard* under title "The Contrabands' Freedom Hymn." First printed version of "John Brown's Body."

Rose Terry Cooke: *Poems*.
Henry Wadsworth Longfellow: "Paul Revere's Ride."
James Ryder Randall: "Maryland, My Maryland."
Henry Timrod: "Ethnogenesis."
Henry Clay Work: "Kingdom Coming."

1862   Walt Whitman works in army hospitals in New York. William Cullen Bryant meets with Abraham Lincoln. Abram Joseph Ryan joins Confederate Army as unofficial chaplain. On leave from his regiment, Henry Timrod works as Civil War correspondent for *Charleston Mercury*; soon is forced to withdraw from service because of poor health. Henry Howard Brownell accepts position as acting ensign under Admiral David Farragut, who is impressed by Brownell's nautical poetry. Bayard Taylor travels to St. Petersburg as secretary of American legation. Emily Dickinson in the course of the year writes over 360 poems; in April, encloses four poems in a letter to Thomas Wentworth Higginson. Henry David Thoreau dies in Concord; Emerson delivers address at his funeral.

Oliver Wendell Holmes: *Songs in Many Keys*.
Julia Ward Howe: "The Battle Hymn of the Republic."
Thomas Buchanan Read: *The Wagoner of the Alleghanies*.
Bayard Taylor: *The Poet's Journal*.

1863 Offices of New York *Evening Post* attacked by draft rioters. Walt Whitman settles in Washington, D.C., where he serves as volunteer nurse in military hospitals, caring for both Union and Confederate wounded; supports himself by working in Army Paymaster's office. Revised edition of Frederick Goddard Tuckerman's *Poems* published in London. Performing in San Francisco, Adah Isaacs Menken meets Bret Harte and other local literary figures.

Henry Wadsworth Longfellow: *Tales of a Wayside Inn*.

1864 Sidney Lanier captured on Confederate blockade runner and imprisoned for four months in Maryland. John Banister Tabb taken prisoner by Union forces; meets Lanier in prison. James Russell Lowell begins tenure as co-editor (with Charles Eliot Norton) of *The North American Review*. Henry Timrod becomes associate editor of *The Daily South Carolinian*. New York's Century Club celebrates 70th birthday of William Cullen Bryant. Adah Isaacs Menken opens as Mazeppa in Virginia City (where she meets Mark Twain) and in London (where she meets Charles Dickens and Charles Reade). Stephen Foster dies in January in Bellevue Hospital, New York City. Nathaniel Hawthorne dies in May in Concord. Henry Rowe Schoolcraft dies in December in Washington, D.C.

George Henry Boker: *Poems of the War*.
Henry Howard Brownell: *Lyrics of a Day, or Newspaper Poems*.
Robert Lowry: "Beautiful River" ("Shall We Gather at the River").
Edmund Clarence Stedman: *Alice of Monmouth*.
John Greenleaf Whittier: *In War Time and Other Poems*.

1865   Henry Timrod reduced to poverty by burning of Columbia, South Carolina, by Sherman's army. George Moses Horton escapes from slavery and reaches Sherman's army in Raleigh, North Carolina; publishes final collection of poems, *Naked Genius*. At Harvard ceremony on July 21, James Russell Lowell reads ode commemorating Harvard students who fought in Civil War. Helen Hunt Jackson meets Thomas Wentworth Higginson; with his encouragement begins to publish poetry and prose. Walt Whitman works briefly as clerk in Department of Interior; dismissed, allegedly because of official disapproval of his poetry. Opening in Paris, Adah Isaacs Menken meets George Sand and Théophile Gautier. Lydia Huntley Sigourney dies in June in Hartford, Connecticut.

George Moses Horton: *Naked Genius*.
J. N. Plotts (editor): *Poetical Tributes to the Memory of Abraham Lincoln*.
Thomas Buchanan Read: *A Summer Story, Sheridan's Ride, and Other Poems*.
Walt Whitman: *Drum-Taps*; *Sequel to Drum Taps*.
Henry Clay Work: "Marching Through Georgia."

1866   Herman Melville begins 19-year tenure as District Inspector of Customs in New York. William Cullen Bryant travels in Spain and in Italy (where he meets with Garibaldi). Joaquin Miller elected county judge in Canyon City, Oregon. *The Galaxy* (1866–78) founded under editorship of William C. Church and Francis P. Church; contributors include Mark Twain, Henry James, Walt Whitman, Sidney Lanier, Emma Lazarus, Bayard Taylor, and Edmund Clarence Stedman. Bret Harte edits *Outcroppings*, anthology of California poets. Adah Isaacs Menken opens in Paris in *Les Pirates de la Savane*; meets Aléxandre Dumas.

Henry Howard Brownell: *War Lyrics and Other Poems*.
Alice Cary: *Ballads, Lyrics and Hymns*.

Herman Melville: *Battle-Pieces and Aspects of the War*.
John James Piatt: *Poems in Sunshine and Firelight*.
Thomas Buchanan Read: *Poetical Works*.
Abram Joseph Ryan: "Lines" ("Gather the sacred dust").
Bayard Taylor: *The Picture of St. John*.
John Greenleaf Whittier: *Snow-Bound*.

1867   William Francis Allen, Charles Pickard Ware, and Lucy
        McKim Garrison publish *Slave Songs of the United States*,
        first important collection of spirituals. "Negro Spirituals,"
        by Thomas Wentworth Higginson, appears in *Atlantic
        Monthly*. Richard Henry Wilde's *Hesperia* published 20
        years after his death. In London, Adah Isaacs Menken
        meets Dante Gabriel Rossetti and Algernon Swinburne.
        Nathaniel Parker Willis dies in January at home near
        Tarrytown, New York; at funeral, pallbearers include Rich-
        ard Henry Dana, Henry Wadsworth Longfellow, Oliver
        Wendell Holmes, and James Russell Lowell. Henry
        Timrod dies in October in Columbia, South Carolina.
        Fitz-Greene Halleck dies in November in Guilford, Con-
        necticut.

        John Burroughs: *Notes on Walt Whitman as Poet and Person*.
        Ralph Waldo Emerson: *May-Day and Other Pieces*.
        Francis Miles Finch: "The Blue and the Gray."
        Emma Lazarus: *Poems and Translations*.
        James Russell Lowell: *The Biglow Papers (Second Series)*.
        Henry Wadsworth Longfellow: *Flower-de-Luce*;
          (translator) *The Divine Comedy*.
        John James Piatt: *Western Windows and Other Poems*.
        William Gilmore Simms (editor): *War Poetry of the South*.
        John Greenleaf Whittier: *The Tent on the Beach*.
        Richard Henry Wilde: *Hesperia*.
        Forceythe Willson: *The Old Sergeant, and Other Poems*.

1868   Bret Harte becomes first editor of San Francisco journal
        The Overland Monthly; under his editorship (1868–70)
        contributors include Mark Twain, Ina Coolbrith, Clarence
        King, and Charles Warren Stoddard. Adah Isaacs Menken
        dies in August in Paris; collected poems, *Infelicia*, pub-
        lished days after her death. John Wesley Powell begins col-
        lecting data, including song texts and myths, for ethno-
        graphic study of Ute and Southern Paiute tribes (works
        on project for 12 years, but never publishes findings).

Julia Ward Howe helps found New England Woman Suffrage Association. John M. Brown publishes "Songs of the Slave" in *Lippincott's Magazine*.

Benjamin Paul Blood: *The Colonnades*.
Augusta Cooper Bristol: *Poems*.
Phillips Brooks: "O Little Town of Bethlehem."
Alice Cary: *The Lover's Diary*.
Fitz-Greene Halleck: *Poetical Writings* (including first authorized book publication of "The Croakers" by Drake and Halleck).
Henry Wadsworth Longfellow: *The New-England Tragedies*.
Adah Isaacs Menken: *Infelicia*.
Joaquin Miller: *Specimens*.
John Rollin Ridge: *Poems*.
Edward Rowland Sill: *The Hermitage and Other Poems*.
William Wetmore Story: *Graffiti d'Italia*.

1869   William Cullen Bryant delivers commemorative address on Fitz-Greene Halleck at New-York Historical Society. Richard Watson Gilder edits *Hours at Home* (1869–70). Stephen Return Riggs includes translations of Sioux poetry in *Tah'-koo Wah-kan'; or, The Gospel Among the Dakotas*.

George Henry Boker: *Königsmark, The Legend of the Hounds, and Other Poems*.
Phoebe Cary: *Poems of Faith, Hope and Love*.
Frances Ellen Watkins Harper: *Moses: A Story of the Nile*.
James Russell Lowell: *Under the Willows*.
Edmund Clarence Stedman: *The Blameless Prince*.
John Townsend Trowbridge: *The Vagabonds and Other Poems*.
John Greenleaf Whittier: *Among the Hills*.

1870   Bret Harte's "Plain Language from Truthful James" (also known as "The Heathen Chinee"), published in *The Overland Monthly*, becomes enormously popular and is reprinted in many other papers. Josiah Gilbert Holland becomes founding editor of *Scribner's Monthly*, assisted by Richard Watson Gilder; contributors include Gilder, Helen Hunt Jackson, George Washington Cable, Emma Lazarus, and Joaquin Miller. Joaquin Miller travels to

England. Bayard Taylor publishes first installment of translation of *Faust*. Henry Adams assumes editorship of *The North American Review*. William Gilmore Simms dies in June in Columbia, South Carolina.

William Cullen Bryant (translator): *The Iliad*.
Bret Harte: "Plain Language from Truthful James."
Helen Hunt Jackson: *Verses*.
James Russell Lowell: *The Cathedral*.
Bayard Taylor (translator): *Faust*.
Rose Hartwick Thorpe: "Curfew Must Not Ring
   To-Night."
George Boyer Vashon: "Ode on the Proclamation
   of the Fifteenth Amendment."

1871   William Dean Howells succeeds James T. Fields as editor of *Atlantic Monthly*. George Henry Boker appointed minister to Turkey. Alice and Phoebe Cary die within five months of each other. Julia Ward Howe becomes president of Woman's International Peace Association. Bret Harte visits William Dean Howells and Ralph Waldo Emerson in Concord.

William Cullen Bryant: (translator) *The Odyssey*; (editor)
   A Library of Poetry and Song.
William Ellery Channing: *The Wanderer: A Colloquial
   Poem*.
Bret Harte: *East and West Poems*.
Frances Ellen Watkins Harper: *Poems*.
John Hay: *Pike County Ballads*.
Emma Lazarus: *Admetus and Other Poems*.
Charles Godfrey Leland: *The Breitmann Ballads*.
Henry Wadsworth Longfellow: *The Divine Tragedy*.
Joaquin Miller: *Pacific Poems*; *Songs of the Sierras*.
Walt Whitman: *Passage to India*.

1872   William Cullen Bryant travels in the Bahamas, Cuba, and Mexico; received with honor by President Juárez of Mexico. George Henry Boker and Charles Godfrey Leland meet Ralph Waldo Emerson while traveling in Egypt. Stéphane Mallarmé publishes the first of his translations of Poe's poetry.

Francis Ellen Watkins Harper: *Sketches of Southern Life*.
Bret Harte: *Poetical Works*; *Echoes of the Foot-Hills*.

Paul Hamilton Hayne: *Legends and Lyrics.*
Josiah Gilbert Holland: *The Marble Prophecy.*
Charles Godfrey Leland: *The Music Lesson of Confucius; and Other Poems.*
Henry Wadsworth Longfellow: *Christus, a Mystery.*
Theodore Seward: *Jubilee Songs: As Sung by the Jubilee Singers of Fisk University.*
Bayard Taylor: *The Masque of the Gods.*
Celia Thaxter: *Poems.*
Ella Wheeler Wilcox: *Drops of Water.*

1873   Paul Hamilton Hayne edits posthumous edition of Henry Timrod's poetry. Sidney Lanier becomes first flutist of Peabody Orchestra, Baltimore. Walt Whitman suffers stroke. Frederick Goddard Tuckerman dies in May at his home in Greenfield, Massachusetts.

William Ellery Channing: *Thoreau, the Poet-Naturalist.*
Paul Hamilton Hayne: *The Mountain of the Lovers.*
William Dean Howells: *Poems.*
Joaquin Miller: *Songs of the Sun-Lands.*
Edmund Clarence Stedman: *The Poetical Works of Edmund Clarence Stedman.*
Bayard Taylor: *Lars: A Pastoral of Norway.*
Henry Timrod: *Poems.*
Ella Wheeler Wilcox: *Shells.*

1874   Ralph Waldo Emerson omits both Whitman and Poe from his poetry anthology *Parnassus.* Edward Rowland Sill assumes chair of English at Berkeley. Richard Watson Gilder marries Helena de Kay, granddaughter of Joseph Rodman Drake. Benjamin Paul Blood sends his treatise on nitrous oxide, *The Anaesthetic Revelation and the Gist of Philosophy,* to William James and Alfred Tennyson. "O Little Town of Bethlehem" (written in 1868) published in *The Church Porch.* Text of murder ballad "Poor Naomi" published in Greensboro (North Carolina) *Patriot.*

James A. Bland: "Carry Me Back to Old Virginny."
Paul Bliss: *Gospel Songs.*
Christopher Pearse Cranch: *Satan: A Libretto.*
Ralph Waldo Emerson (editor): *Parnassus.*
Thomas P. Fenner: *Cabin and Plantation Songs: as Sung by the Hampton Students.*

Henry Wadsworth Longfellow: *The Hanging of the Crane*.
Sarah Morgan Piatt: *A Voyage to the Fortunate Isles*.
G. D. Pike: *The Jubilee Singers of Fisk University*.
Bayard Taylor: *The Prophet*.

1875   George Henry Boker appointed minister to Russia. Helen
Hunt Jackson settles in Colorado Springs, Colorado. Walt
Whitman attends unveiling of monument to Edgar Allan
Poe in Baltimore.

Christopher Pearse Cranch: *The Bird and the Bell*.
Richard Watson Gilder: *The New Day*.
Oliver Wendell Holmes: *Songs of Many Seasons*.
Edward King: *Negro Songs and Singers*.
J.B.T. Marsh: *The Story of the Jubilee Singers: With
Their Songs*.
John Townsend Trowbridge: *The Emigrant's Story
and Other Poems*.
John Greenleaf Whittier: *Hazel-Blossoms*.
Ella Wheeler Wilcox: *Maurine*.

1876   Bayard Taylor commissioned to write "Centennial Hymn"
commemorating Declaration of Independence. Emma
Lazarus visits Ralph Waldo Emerson in Concord. On
visit to the United States, Emperor Dom Pedro of Brazil
meets with Longfellow, Whittier, Bryant, and other liter-
ary figures.

Ralph Waldo Emerson: *Selected Poems*.
Brewster Higley: "Home on the Range."
Charles Godfrey Leland: *Pidgin-English Sing-Song; or,
Songs and Stories in the China-English Dialect*.
Henry Wadsworth Longfellow (editor): *Poems of Places*
(31 volumes, 1876–79).
Herman Melville: *Clarel: A Poem and Pilgrimage in the
Holy Land*.
Bayard Taylor: *The Echo Club and Other Literary
Diversions*.
Walt Whitman: *Leaves of Grass* (Centennial Edition).

1877   In Baltimore, Sara Sigourney Rice publishes *Edgar Allan
Poe: A Memorial Volume*, including Stéphane Mallarmé's
sonnet "Le tombeau d'Edgar Poe" and tributes by John
Greenleaf Whittier, Alfred Tennyson, Algernon Swin-

burne, and others. William Cullen Bryant delivers address at unveiling of statue of Fitz-Greene Halleck in New York's Central Park. John Greenleaf Whittier's 70th birthday celebrated at dinner given by *Atlantic Monthly* in Boston, attended by Emerson, Longfellow, Holmes, Howells, Cranch, Trowbridge, Higginson, and others; humorous speech by Mark Twain regarded as in poor taste by many in attendance; Twain later apologizes. James Russell Lowell appointed minister to Spain (1877–80) by Rutherford B. Hayes. In *Kokomo Dispatch*, James Whitcomb Riley publishes parody "Leonainie" as newly discovered poem by Poe. Stephen Powers publishes translations of California Indian poetry in *Tribes of California*. John Wesley Powell hires Albert S. Gatschet as philologist for Geographical and Geological Survey of the Rocky Mountain Region.

Oliver Wendell Holmes: *Poetical Works*.
Sidney Lanier: *Poems*.
Sarah Morgan Piatt: *That New World*.
Edmund Clarence Stedman: *Hawthorne and Other Poems*.
Albery Allson Whitman: *Not a Man and Yet a Man*.
Constance Fenimore Woolson: *Two Women: 1862*.

1878   Ernest Fenollosa goes to Japan to teach at Imperial University in Tokyo. Bret Harte appointed U.S. consul at Krefeld, Germany. John Hay appointed assistant secretary of state by Rutherford B. Hayes. James A. Bland joins Georgia Minstrels, first all-black minstrel troupe. William Cullen Bryant dies in June in New York City, from a fall following ceremonies for unveiling of Mazzini statue in Central Park. George Boyer Vashon dies in October in Rodney, Mississippi. Bayard Taylor, arriving to assume post as U.S. minister, dies in December in Berlin; body brought back to lie in state in New York's City Hall.

Richard Watson Gilder: *The Poet and His Master*.
Henry Wadsworth Longfellow: *Kéramos and Other Poems*.
Sarah Morgan Piatt: *A Woman's Poems*.

1879   James Whitcomb Riley joins staff of *The Indianapolis Journal*. The Bureau of Ethnology (later the Bureau of American Ethnology) created by Congress; first director is John Wesley Powell. Bureau sends first anthropological expedition to Zuni Pueblo, led by James Stevenson, Matilda

Coxe Stevenson, and Frank Hamilton Cushing. The Jubilee Singers of Fisk University visit John Greenleaf Whittier at his home in Amesbury, New Hampshire. Sidney Lanier becomes lecturer in English at Johns Hopkins. Richard Henry Dana dies in February in Cambridge, Massachusetts.

James A. Bland: "Oh, Dem Golden Slippers."
John James Piatt: *Poems of House and Home.*
Abram Joseph Ryan: *Father Ryan's Poems.*
Celia Thaxter: *Drift-Weed.*

1880   James Russell Lowell appointed minister to Great Britain (1880–85). Augusta Cooper Bristol attends International Convention of Freethinkers in Brussels. Jones Very dies in May in Salem, Massachusetts.

Thomas Dunn English: *American Ballads.*
Sidney Lanier: *The Science of English Verse.*
Henry Wadsworth Longfellow: *Ultima Thule.*

1881   Richard Watson Gilder becomes editor of *Scribner's Monthly*, renamed *The Century*; contributors include William Dean Howells, Mark Twain, George Washington Cable, Paul Laurence Dunbar, and John Hay. Ambrose Bierce becomes editor of *The Wasp* (San Francisco). Walt Whitman visits Ralph Waldo Emerson in Concord. Alice Fletcher begins fieldwork on Omaha reservation. James A. Bland tours England with Minstrel Carnival of Genuine Colored Minstrels. Sidney Lanier dies in September at Lynn, North Carolina, at age 39.

A. Bronson Alcott: *An Autobiographical Poem.*
Oliver Wendell Holmes: *Poetical Works.*
Emma Lazarus: *Poems and Ballads of Heine.*
John James Piatt: *Idyls and Lyrics of the Ohio Valley.*
John Townsend Trowbridge: *A Home Idyl and Other Poems.*

1882   Oscar Wilde makes lecture tour of U.S.; visits Walt Whitman in Camden; meets Oliver Wendell Holmes, Julia Ward Howe, Henry Wadsworth Longfellow, Charles Eliot Norton, and Joaquin Miller. Helen Hunt Jackson appointed special federal commissioner to investigate condition of Mission Indians in California. Daniel Garrison

Brinton publishes first titles in his *Library of Aboriginal American Literature* (eight volumes appear before series is discontinued in 1890). James Whitcomb Riley gives first of many reading tours of the U.S. Richard Watson Gilder helps found the Authors' Club. John James Piatt appointed American consul at Cork, Ireland. Henry Wadsworth Longfellow dies in March in Cambridge, Massachusetts. Ralph Waldo Emerson dies in April in Concord.

A. Bronson Alcott: *Sonnets and Canzonets*.
George Henry Boker: *The Book of the Dead*.
Paul Hamilton Hayne: *Collected Poems*.
Emma Lazarus: *Songs of a Semite*.

1883   Eugene Field joins staff of *The Chicago Morning News*. William Reed Huntington begins tenure as rector of Grace Church, New York.

Daniel Garrison Brinton: *Aboriginal American Authors and Their Productions*.
Horatio Hale: *The Iroquois Book of Rites*.
Henry Wadsworth Longfellow: *Michael Angelo*.
William Wells Newell: *Games and Songs of American Children*.
James Whitcomb Riley: *The Old Swimmin'-Hole*.
Edward Rowland Sill: *The Venus of Milo and Other Poems*.
Ella Wheeler Wilcox: *Poems of Passion*.

1884   John Banister Tabb ordained as Roman Catholic priest. Longfellow commemorated by a bust in Westminster Abbey, the first American poet so honored.

Daniel Garrison Brinton: *The Lenâpé and Their Legends*.
Helen Hunt Jackson: *Easter Bells; Pansies and Orchids*.
Louise Imogen Guiney: *Songs at the Start*.
Charles Godfrey Leland: *The Algonquin Legends of New England*.
Percy Montrose: "Oh My Darling Clementine."
Clinton Scollard: *Pictures in Song*.
Albery Allson Whitman: *The Rape of Florida* (reprinted 1885 as *Twasinta's Seminoles*).

1885   Bret Harte settles permanently in London. James Mooney meets John Wesley Powell and is given post with Bureau of Ethnology. Katharine Lee Bates appointed professor of English at Wellesley. Edmund Clarence Stedman publishes critical study *Poets of America*. Helen Hunt Jackson dies in August in San Francisco.

Charles Timothy Brooks: *Poems, Original and Translated*.
Charles Edward Carryl: *Davy and the Goblin*.
James Russell Lowell: *Under the Old Elm*.

1886   "The New Colossus" by Emma Lazarus recited at dedication of Statue of Liberty. William Dean Howells and Stuart Merrill separately take up defense of anarchist demonstrators condemned to death in connection with Haymarket riot in Chicago. George Washington Cable publishes translations of Creole slave songs in *The Century*. Jules Laforgue's translations of three Walt Whitman poems appear in French periodical *La Vogue*. Henry Adams tours Japan with John La Farge. The German anthropologist Franz Boas does first fieldwork on Northwest Coast, spending time among the Kwakiutl, Bella Coola, and Tsimshian; afterward settles in U.S. Emily Dickinson dies in May in Amherst, Massachusetts.

George Henry Boker: *Sonnets*.
William Ellery Channing: *John Brown and the Heroes of Harper's Ferry*.
Emma Lazarus: "The New Colossus."
Sarah Morgan Piatt: *Selected Poems*.
Clinton Scollard: *With Reed and Lyre*.

1887   James Whitcomb Riley introduced by James Russell Lowell at triumphant poetry reading at Chickering Hall, New York City. Stuart Merrill publishes first book, *Les Gammes*, in French (as all but one of his subsequent volumes will be); meets Walt Whitman in New York City and presents him with copies of Jules Laforgue's Whitman translations. Richard Hovey meets Bliss Carman. *Scribner's Magazine* begins publication under editorship of Edward L. Burlingame; contributors include Edith Wharton, Sarah Orne Jewett, Eugene Field, and James Whitcomb Riley. Madison Cawein's first book favorably reviewed by William Dean Howells in *Harper's*. Joaquin Miller settles in Oakland, California. Emma Lazarus dies in November at age 38 in New York City.

Katharine Lee Bates: *The College Beautiful.*
Madison Cawein: *Blooms of the Berry.*
Richard Watson Gilder: *The Celestial Passion.*
Louise Imogen Guiney: *The White Sail and Other Poems.*
Washington Matthews: *The Mountain Chant:
    A Navajo Ceremony.*
Stuart Merrill: *Les Gammes.*
Lizette Woodworth Reese: *A Branch of May.*
James Whitcomb Riley: *Afterwhiles.*
Rose Hartwick Thorpe: *Ringing Ballads.*
Comic and Popular Songs, Sung by Robert Jones (including
    earliest printed version of "Jesse James").

1888   In Japan, Ernest Fenollosa appointed director of newly
        opened Tokyo Fine Arts Academy and Imperial Museum.
        In Paris, Stéphane Mallarmé collects his prose translations
        of Edgar Allan Poe's poetry. Bronson Alcott dies in March
        in Concord, Massachusetts.

        Madison Cawein: *The Triumph of Music.*
        Rose Terry Cooke: *Poems.*
        James Owen Dorsey: *Osage Traditions.*
        James Russell Lowell: *Heartsease and Rue.*
        Stéphane Mallarmé: *Les Poèmes d'Edgar Poe: Traductions
            en Prose.*
        Herman Melville: *John Marr and Other Sailors.*
        James Whitcomb Riley: *Pipes o' Pan at Zekesbury.*
        Clinton Scollard: *Old and New World Lyrics.*
        Ernest Lawrence Thayer: "Casey at the Bat."
        Ella Wheeler Wilcox: *Poems of Pleasure.*

1889   Edmund Clarence Stedman begins publication of ten-
        volume *Library of American Literature.* George Santayana
        joins philosophy faculty at Harvard.

        Eugene Field: *A Little Book of Western Verse.*
        Emma Lazarus: *The Poems of Emma Lazarus.*

1890   First collection of poetry by Emily Dickinson published,
        edited by Thomas Wentworth Higginson and Mabel
        Loomis Todd. Ernest Fenollosa returns to America to be-
        come curator of Oriental department of Boston Museum
        of Fine Arts. Stuart Merrill publishes only English-
        language volume, *Pastels in Prose* (translations of contem-

porary French writers), with preface by William Dean
Howells. In London, on his way back to France, Merrill
meets Oscar Wilde. Henry Adams and John La Farge
travel in the Pacific and Asia. James Mooney collects Ghost
Dance songs in South Dakota. George Henry Boker dies
in January in Philadelphia.

Madison Cawein: *Lyrics and Idyls*.
Emily Dickinson: *Poems*.
Albert S. Gatschet: *The Klamath Indians of
    Southwestern Oregon*.
John Hay: *Poems*.
Stuart Merrill: *Pastels in Prose*.
James Whitcomb Riley: *Rhymes of Childhood*.
John Greenleaf Whittier: *At Sundown*.

1891   Walt Whitman publishes last poems in *Goodbye, My Fancy*
            and final "deathbed" edition of *Leaves of Grass*. Stuart Mer-
            rill publishes *Les Fastes*; settles permanently in Paris, where
            he becomes manager of the Théâtre d'Art. Ernest Fenol-
            losa meets painter Arthur Dow and works with him to
            introduce Asian art to American students. Richard Hovey
            publishes *Launcelot and Guenevere*, first volume of pro-
            jected verse-drama cycle on Arthurian themes. James Rus-
            sell Lowell dies in August in Cambridge, Massachusetts.
            Herman Melville dies in September in New York City.

            Emily Dickinson: *Poems: Second Series*.
            W. J. Hoffman: *The Midewiwin or "Grand Medicine
                Society" of the Ojibwa*.
            Richard Hovey: *Launcelot and Guenevere*.
            Herman Melville: *Timoleon*.
            Stuart Merrill: *Les Fastes*.
            James Mooney: *Sacred Formulas of the Cherokees*.
            Lizette Woodworth Reese: *A Handful of Lavendar*.
            Walt Whitman: *Goodbye, My Fancy*; *Leaves of Grass*
                (final edition).

1892   Ernest Fenollosa reads "East and West" to Phi Beta Kappa
            Society at Harvard. Harriet Monroe commissioned to
            write "The Columbian Ode" for dedication of World's
            Columbian Exposition in Chicago. Paul Laurence Dunbar
            invited to join Western Association of Writers in Dayton,
            Ohio. Christopher Pearse Cranch dies in January in Cam-

bridge, Massachusetts. Walt Whitman dies in March in Camden, New Jersey. John Greenleaf Whittier dies in September in Hampton Falls, New Hampshire.

Eugene Field: *Second Book of Verse*.
Harriet Monroe: *Valeria and Other Poems*.
James Whitcomb Riley: *Green Fields and Running Brooks*.
Clinton Scollard: *Songs of Sunrise Lands*.

1893   World's Columbian Exposition ("The White City") opens in Chicago, including influential displays of modern architecture and technology, and first major American exhibit of Japanese art and architecture; visitors include Henry Adams (who writes "the mental excitement and disturbance have upset my usual balance so much that I am not yet quite willing to trust myself to talk or write on the subject"), Mark Twain, Ernest Fenollosa, Edwin Markham, Hamlin Garland, Theodore Dreiser, Katharine Lee Bates, and Richard Watson Gilder; Paul Laurence Dunbar employed by Frederick Douglass at Haiti Building; Albery Allson Whitman reads poem "The Freedman's Triumphant Song" to audience including Douglass and Dunbar; Franz Boas supervises exhibit on physical anthropology.

Ambrose Bierce: *Black Beetles in Amber*.
Madison Cawein: *Red Leaves and Roses*.
Paul Laurence Dunbar: *Oak and Ivy*.
Ernest Fenollosa: *East and West, The Discovery of America and Other Poems*.
Alice Fletcher and Francis La Flesche: *A Study of Omaha Indian Music*.
Hamlin Garland: *Prairie Songs*.
Louise Imogen Guiney: *A Roadside Harp*.
Richard Hovey: *Seaward*.
Harriet Monroe: *The Columbian Ode*.
John Banister Tabb: *An Octave to Mary*.

1894   Robert Frost's poem "My Butterfly" appears in *The Independent* (New York); Frost arranges private printing of *Twilight* in an edition of only two copies. In San Francisco, Gelett Burgess edits *Wave*. Constance Fenimore Woolson dies in January in a fall from her balcony in Venice. Oliver Wendell Holmes dies in October in Cambridge, Massachusetts.

Thomas Dunn English: *Select Poems of Dr. Thomas Dunn English*.
Richard Hovey and Bliss Carman: *Songs from Vagabondia*.
Sarah Morgan Piatt: *Collected Poems*.
George Santayana: *Sonnets and Other Verses*.
Matilda Coxe Stevenson: *The Sia*.
John Banister Tabb: *Poems*.

1895   William Dean Howells writes glowing review of Paul Laurence Dunbar's *Majors and Minors*; Dunbar becomes well-known. In San Francisco, Gelett Burgess assumes editorship of *The Lark* (1895–97), associated with literary group Les Jeunes. In Paris, George Cabot Lodge and Trumbull Stickney study at the Sorbonne; Richard Hovey meets Stéphane Mallarmé and other members of symbolist movement. Louise Imogen Guiney travels in England; forms friendshp with Lionel Johnson.

Henry Adams: "Buddha and Brahma."
Katharine Lee Bates: "America the Beautiful."
Augusta Cooper Bristol: *The Web of Life*.
James Edwin Campbell: *Echoes from the Cabin and Elsewhere*.
Stephen Crane: *The Black Riders and Other Lines*.
Paul Laurence Dunbar: *Majors and Minors*.
Louise Imogen Guiney: *Nine Sonnets Written at Oxford*.
Sadakichi Hartmann: *Conversations with Walt Whitman*.
Stuart Merrill: *Petits Poèmes d'Automne*.
James Whitcomb Riley: *The Days Gone By*.

1896   On a visit to Paris, Henry Adams taken by George Cabot Lodge to hear singer Yvette Guilbert; in London, Adams attends dinner hosted by John Hay, whose guests include Henry James, Bret Harte, and John Singer Sargent. Stephen Crane shipwrecked en route to Cuba to report on revolution.

Franz Boas: "Songs of the Kwakiutl Indians."
Madison Cawein: *The Garden of Dreams*.
Ina Coolbrith: *Songs of the Golden Gate*.
Frank Hamilton Cushing: *Outlines of Zuñi Creation Myths*.
Emily Dickinson: *Poems: Third Series*.
Paul Laurence Dunbar: *Lyrics of Lowly Life*.
Richard Hovey and Bliss Carman: *More Songs from Vagabondia*.

James Mooney: *The Ghost-Dance Religion and the Sioux Outbreak of 1890*.
Lizette Woodworth Reese: *A Quiet Road*.
Edwin Arlington Robinson: *The Torrent and the Night Before*.

1897   John Hay appointed ambassador to Great Britain by William McKinley. Paul Laurence Dunbar goes on reading tour of England. Following divorce scandal in Boston, Ernest Fenollosa returns to Japan with second wife, Mary McNeill. Louise Imogen Guiney publishes edition of Irish poet James Clarence Mangan. First printed version of the spiritual "Were You There When They Crucified My Lord?" appears in *The Journal of American Folklore*.

Franz Boas: *The Social Organization and the Secret Societies of the Kwakiutl Indians*.
Gelett Burgess: "The Purple Cow."
Washington Matthews: *Navaho Legends*.
Joaquin Miller: *Complete Poetical Works*.
John James Piatt: *Odes in Ohio*.
Edwin Arlington Robinson: *Children of the Night*.
John Banister Tabb: *Lyrics*.

1898   Carl Sandburg goes to Puerto Rico as soldier in Spanish-American War; George Cabot Lodge enlists in navy, participates in American capture of Ponce, Puerto Rico; Stephen Crane reports on fighting in Cuba for *New York World* and *New York Journal*. English translations of Yiddish poems by New York poet Morris Rosenfeld published in *Songs of the Ghetto*. John Hay appointed Secretary of State by William McKinley.

John Jay Chapman: "Bismarck"; *Emerson and Other Essays*.
Jeremiah Curtin: *Creation Myths of Primitive America*.
Louise Imogen Guiney: *England and Yesterday*.
Richard Hovey: *Along the Trail*; *The Birth of Galahad*.
George Cabot Lodge: *The Song of the Wave*.
Edgar Lee Masters: *A Book of Verses*.
Morris Rosenfeld: *Songs of the Ghetto*.

1899   Edwin Markham's "The Man with the Hoe," published in *The San Francisco Examiner* in January, makes him instant celebrity; his collection *The Man with the Hoe and Other*

Poems becomes bestseller. Edwin Arlington Robinson moves to New York City. Alfred L. Kroeber does fieldwork among the Arapaho, Ute, Northern Shoshone, and Bannock.

Stephen Crane: *War Is Kind.*
Paul Laurence Dunbar: *Lyrics of the Hearthside.*
John Comfort Fillmore: *The Harmonic Structure of Indian Music.*
Louise Imogen Guiney: *The Martyrs' Idyl and Shorter Poems.*
Richard Hovey: *Taliesin: A Masque.*
William Reed Huntington: *Sonnets and a Dream.*
Edwin Markham: *The Man with the Hoe and Other Poems.*
Edward William Nelson: *The Eskimo About Bering Strait.*
Lizette Woodworth Reese: "Tears."
George Santayana: *Lucifer: A Theological Tragedy.*

1900   Trumbull Stickney's verse drama "Prometheus Pyrphoros" appears in *Harvard Monthly*. John Jay Chapman suffers nervous breakdown. Robert Frost farms in New Hampshire. Richard Hovey dies in February in New York City. Stephen Crane dies in June in Germany.

Gelett Burgess: *Goops and How To Be Them.*
Alice Fletcher: *Indian Story and Song from North America.*
Edwin Markham: "Lincoln, the Man of the People."
Stuart Merrill: *Les Quatre Saisons.*
William Vaughn Moody: *The Masque of Judgment.*
Edmund Clarence Stedman (editor): *An American Anthology, 1787–1899.*
Ridgely Torrence: *The House of a Hundred Lights.*
George Santayana: *Interpretations of Poetry and Religion.*
Trumbull Stickney: "Prometheus Pyrphoros."

Biographical Notes

JOHN QUINCY ADAMS (July 11, 1767–February 21, 1848) b. Braintree, Massachusetts. Eldest son of Abigail Smith and John Adams. In 1778 accompanied his father on diplomatic mission to France and attended school in Paris until their return to America the following year. Served (1781–82) as private secretary to Francis Dana, minister to Russia; subsequently rejoined father in the Netherlands, traveling with him to England after signing of the Treaty of Paris in September 1783. Returned to America and graduated Harvard College 1787. Began law practice in 1790 in Newburyport. Contributed articles to Benjamin Russell's *Columbian Centinel*, including reply to Thomas Paine's *The Rights of Man*. Appointed by George Washington as minister to the Netherlands. In 1797 married Louisa Johnson; they had a daughter and three sons (including Charles Francis Adams, diplomat and father of Henry Adams). Appointed minister to Prussia following his father's election as president; travels resulted in *Letters on Silesia* (1804) and translation of Christoph Wieland's heroic poem *Oberon*. Elected to the Senate in 1803; resigned in 1808 after being repudiated by fellow Massachusetts Federalists for supporting Jefferson's Embargo Act of 1807. Named Professor of Rhetoric and Belles-Lettres at Harvard in 1806; *Lectures on Rhetoric and Oratory* published 1810. Resumed diplomatic career in 1809 when James Madison appointed him minister to Russia; declined appointment to Supreme Court. As leader of American peace commissioners, helped negotiate Treaty of Ghent (1814) ending the War of 1812. Appointed minister to England in 1815. Served as secretary of state under James Monroe, 1817–25; supported Andrew Jackson's invasion of Florida; negotiated Spain's cession of Florida, abandonment of Spanish claims in the Pacific Northwest, and Anglo-American agreement on the Canadian boundary; played major role in formulating the Monroe Doctrine. In 1824 presidential election, ran second to Andrew Jackson in the electoral vote; when none of the four candidates received an electoral majority, Adams was elected president by the House of Representatives with the support of Henry Clay (whom Adams then appointed secretary of state). Presidency (1825–29) was clouded by bitter party conflict among Jacksonians, Democratic Republicans, and Adams-Clay National Republicans, and he was defeated decisively by Jackson in presidential election of 1828. Elected to Congress in 1830 as independent candidate and served until his death. As congressman, actively opposed extension of slavery and annexation of Texas; led long, ultimately successful fight (1836–44) to overturn "gag rule" preventing congressional debate of anti-slavery petitions. In 1841 successfully defended African mutineers of the slave ship *Amistad* before the Supreme Court. Published narrative poem *Dermot MacMorrogh; or, the Conquest of Ireland* (1832), and verse collection *Poems of Religion and Society* (1848). Suffered a stroke during a session of Congress and died in the Capitol two days later; last words said to have been, "This is the end of earth—I am content." Diary (1794–1846) published posthumously in twelve volumes as *Memoirs* (1874–77).

A. BRONSON ALCOTT (November 29, 1799–March 4, 1888)   b. at Spindle Hill near Wolcott, Connecticut. Son of Anna Bronson (daughter of Connecticut sea captain) and Joseph Chatfield Alcox (farmer of Puritan ancestry); given name Amos Bronson Alcox. Raised on family farm; received little formal education. Employed in clock factory and worked as itinerant peddler (1818–23) in Virginia and the Carolinas after efforts to establish teaching career in Virginia failed. Became schoolteacher in Bristol, Wolcott, and Cheshire, Connecticut. In 1830, married Abigail May, sister of well-known Unitarian clergyman, and they moved to Germantown, Pennsylvania, where Alcott opened a school; they had four daughters, Anna, Louisa May, Elizabeth, and Abby. Studied writings of Swiss educator Johann Pestalozzi. Founded the Masonic Temple School in Boston in 1834; developed conversational method aimed at discovering innate ethical ideas. Views on education (centered on "self-realization" and "personalism") attracted attention in the United States and Europe. Introduced organized play, gymnastics, the honor system, and children's libraries; minimized corporal punishment and sought to create recreational atmosphere for learning. In 1835 his assistant Elizabeth Peabody detailed Alcott's educational methods in anonymously published journal, *Record of a School, Exemplifying the General Principles of Spiritual Culture*. Alcott published *The Doctrine and Discipline of Human Culture* in 1836; in *Conversations with Children on the Gospels* (1836–37) gave detailed examples of his teaching practices. Margaret Fuller taught at school, 1836–37. Alcott and the school came under attack for unorthodox religious ideas, discussion of human physiology with students, and for admitting a black student; the school lost a majority of its pupils and Alcott went deeply into debt; school closed in 1839. In 1840 moved to Concord, Massachusetts; made failed attempt to support family by farming; "Orphic Sayings" published in *The Dial*. Intimate friend of Ralph Waldo Emerson, Henry David Thoreau, and William Ellery Channing; regarded as a leader among the Transcendentalists. (Emerson later remarked, "As pure intellect I have never seen his equal"; Thoreau called him "the sanest man I ever knew.") Went to England (with funds supplied by Emerson) in 1842 to meet English admirers who had founded a school called "Alcott House"; met and eventually quarreled with Thomas Carlyle. Returned home with three English disciples and tried unsuccessfully (1843–45) to establish a utopian community incorporating vegetarian principles, the "Con-Sociate Family," at Fruitlands, a farm near Harvard, Massachusetts. After the experiment failed in 1845, the family relied on earnings of Abigail and Louisa for support. Eventually eked out a living on the lyceum circuit with lectures and discussions (called "conversations") which, after 1853, he delivered in Cincinnati, Cleveland, Chicago, St. Louis, and other Western cities. Daughter Elizabeth died of scarlet fever in 1858. In 1859 became superintendent of the Concord schools. The success of Louisa's novel *Little Women* in 1868–69 brought the family financial security. Wife Abigail died in 1877; daughter Abigail May died in Paris in 1879. Alcott's conversations and lectures at home were later formalized into Concord Summer School of Philosophy and Literature, which held first sessions in 1879 and continued until Alcott's death. In later years published *Tablets* (1868), *Concord Days* (1872), *Table Talk* (1877), *New Connecticut, An Autobiographical Poem* (1881), and *Sonnets and Canzonets* (1882). Maintained voluminous correspondence on topics including abolition, vegetarianism, women's rights, philosophy, and health with Mary Baker Eddy, Oliver Wendell Holmes, Julia Ward Howe, Henry James, Sr., James Russell Lowell, Elizabeth Cady Stanton, Walt Whitman, and others. In 1882 suffered a stroke from which he never fully recovered; subsequently cared for by surviving daughters; Louisa died two days after him.

WASHINGTON ALLSTON (November 5, 1779–July 9, 1843) b. on family plantation in Waccamaw Neck, South Carolina. Son of Rachel Moore (of Huguenot descent) and Captain William Allston (who served under Francis Marion in the Revolutionary War). Father died suddenly in 1781, upon returning home from battle of Cowpens (rumored to have been poisoned by a servant). After early schooling in Charleston and mother's remarriage (to Dr. Henry C. Flagg, chief of General Greene's medical staff), sent for further education in 1787 to Newport, Rhode Island; remained there for nine years, studying at private boarding school of Robert Rogers; formed friendship with fellow students William Ellery Channing (uncle of the poet of the same name) and Edmund Dana (brother of Richard Henry Dana). Developed interest in painting while at Newport, and was influenced by local portrait painter Samuel King and miniaturist Edward Greene Malbone. Attended Harvard, 1796–1800. Became engaged to Ann Channing, sister of William Ellery Channing. Upon graduation, sold his interest in the family property to finance art study abroad, and sailed for England with Malbone; studied from 1801 to November 1803 at Royal Academy in London under Benjamin West and Henry Fuseli. Traveled to Paris with artist John Vanderlyn; painted first major works, "The Rising of a Thunderstorm at Sea" and "The Deluge." From Paris went to Italy by way of Switzerland; remained in Rome 1804–08, establishing artistic reputation (known in local art circles as "the American Titian"); became acquainted with artists Antonio Canova and Gottlieb Schick and formed close friendships with Washington Irving and Samuel Taylor Coleridge. Returned to America in 1808 to marry Ann Channing; settled in Boston, where he wrote most of the poems later collected in *The Sylphs of the Seasons*. In 1810 read a long poem (possibly the title work of that collection) before Phi Beta Kappa Society of Harvard. Returned to England in 1813, accompanied by wife Ann and friend and pupil Samuel F. B. Morse (later joined by painter Charles R. Leslie). Became close friend of John Howard Payne. Painted series of religious pictures, including "Dead Man Revived by Touching the Bones of the Prophet Elisha" and "Saint Peter in Prison." In 1813 *The Sylphs of the Seasons* published, receiving high praise from Coleridge; that summer suffered severe and prolonged illness that permanently affected his health; taken to Bristol for treatment. In 1814 met painters John Martin and William Collins; exhibited paintings at Bristol during summer. Wife Ann died in February 1815. Confirmed as Anglican and devoted himself intensively to religion. Completed paintings "Uriel in the Sun" and "Jacob's Ladder." Returned to America in 1818 (unanimously elected to Royal Academy after departure from England); opened studio in Boston. Contributed essays to Richard Henry Dana's magazine *The Idle Man*. Exhibited paintings at Boston Athenaeum in 1827. Worked on large painting "Belshazzar's Feast," begun in England; admirers raised thousands of dollars to encourage its completion, but in 25 years of work Allston did not finish it. In later paintings moved away from large-scale narrative to concentrate on landscapes and portraits. Married late wife's cousin, Martha Dana, sister of Edmund and Richard Henry Dana, in 1830; settled in Cambridgeport, Massachusetts. At urging of friends, mounted successful exhibit of 45 paintings in Boston in 1839; interviewed in connection with exhibit by Margaret Fuller, who published an admiring essay on his work in *The Dial*. In 1841 published *Monaldi, a Tale*, Gothic romance set in Italy among painters, written two decades earlier. *Lectures on Art, and Poems*, edited by Dana, appeared posthumously in 1850.

JOEL BARLOW (March 24, 1754–December 24, 1812) b. Redding, Connecticut. Son of Esther Hull and Samuel Barlow. In 1776, while an undergraduate at Yale College, volunteered for temporary military service in the Revolutionary Army. At Yale, tutored by Timothy Dwight; friends included Noah Webster and Oliver Wolcott; graduated 1778 (first important poem "The Prospect of Peace" read at commencement). Taught school briefly in New Haven, then returned to Yale for graduate work. Employed as usher at Timothy Dwight's school in Northampton in 1779; during that time outlined epic poem about Columbus. Served in the Revolution as chaplain in the 3rd Massachusetts brigade, 1780–83. Married Ruth Baldwin in 1781; they settled in Hartford the following year. Formed business partnership (1784–85) with Elisha Babcock, selling and publishing books (including Barlow's revision of Isaac Watts' version of the Psalms) and co-editing *The American Mercury*. In 1786 admitted to the bar. Associated with so-called "Connecticut Wits," group of poets with Federalist and Calvinist leanings including Timothy Dwight, John Trumbull, David Humphreys, and Lemuel Hopkins; with them collaborated on mock-heroic verse series *The Anarchiad* (published 1786–87 in *The New Haven Gazette* and *The Connecticut Magazine*). Columbus epic published in 1787 as *The Vision of Columbus*; advance subscribers to the edition included George Washington, Benjamin Franklin, Thomas Paine, Alexander Hamilton, and the Marquis de Lafayette. In 1788 traveled to France as agent of the Ohio Company, selling Ohio River Valley real estate. In Paris, formed lifelong friendship with Thomas Jefferson, socialized with the Marquis de Lafayette, and witnessed scenes of French Revolution. By 1791, land venture had collapsed amid accusations of fraud and threats against Barlow. Resided in London, 1791–92; associates there included Thomas Paine, Mary Wollstonecraft, William Godwin, and Joseph Priestley. In 1792 published writings defending French Revolution including *Advice to the Privileged Orders*, *A Letter to the National Convention of France, on the Defects in the Constitution of 1791*, and verse satire *The Conspiracy of Kings*. Found enthusiastic reception for his ideas in France; in February 1793 made honorary French citizen; defeated in Savoy as Girondist candidate for deputy to the National Convention. In early 1793 wrote mock epic *The Hasty Pudding* (published 1796), which was widely reprinted. Many French friends and associates killed during Reign of Terror. Entrusted by Thomas Paine with manuscript of the first part of *The Age of Reason* following his arrest in Paris in December 1793 (Barlow arranged book's publication the following year). Enriched himself as middle man involved in shipping goods in and out of France. Visited Hamburg, 1794–95, where he studied German language and literature; met German poet Friedrich Gottlieb Klopstock. Returning to Paris, established friendship with James Monroe. In 1795 appointed U.S. consul at Algiers; over 21-month period negotiated release of American prisoners held by Dey of Algiers. Returned to Paris in 1797; in 1798, letter bluntly criticizing Adams administration's policy toward France published in American newspapers; Barlow widely attacked as seditious and atheistic by critics including old friend Noah Webster; Barlow clarified his position in *Letters from Paris* (1799). Became close friend of inventor Robert Fulton, who lived with the Barlows in their Paris home over a period of seven years; Barlow and Fulton collaborated on uncompleted scientific poem *The Canal*. Returned to America after 17-year European stay in 1804. Settled near Washington in mansion Kalorama, which became meeting place for leading political and intellectual figures. Proposed national research institution in *Prospectus of a National Institution* (1805). Lived in Philadelphia for over a year to supervise publication of extensively revised version of his epic, now titled *The Columbiad* and dedicated to Fulton; the book was published in an elaborate and expensive edition in 1807. In 1811 appointed by President Madison to negotiate trade agreement with Napoleon. After delays by French government, arranged meeting with French foreign minister Petry in Vilna (now Vilnius, Lithuania); over two-month period journeyed from Paris to Vilna, passing through region devastated by war; during two-week stay in Vilna wrote "Advice to a Raven in Russia." In the meantime Napoleon had suffered military catastrophe in Russia, and the French army was in full retreat. Barlow left Vilna for Warsaw and was caught up in the retreat during his journey. Contracted lung inflammation; died a few days after leaving Warsaw in Zarnowiec, a village near Cracow.

MANOAH BODMAN (January 28, 1765–January 1, 1850) b. Sunderland, Massachusetts. First of seven children born to Esther Field and Joseph Bodman; sometimes known as Noah Bodman. In 1779 the family moved to Williamsburg, Massachusetts (where Joseph Bodman's brothers William and Samuel had settled), and became prominent in local business and politics. In his youth, by his own account, Bodman "participated in divine grace" during Calvinist religious revival that swept Williamsburg. Following brother's death at age 19 in 1790, experienced troubling visions he attributed to Satan. In 1799 married Theodosia Green; she died during the first year of their marriage; they had no children, and Bodman never remarried. Practiced law. Following wife's death, experienced another and more intense series of diabolical apparitions and religious visions. Delivered confessional speeches in Williamsburg and other neighboring towns. Published *An Oration on Death* (1817), an account of his religious experiences interspersed with occasional poems; other publications included *Washington's Birth Day, An Oration* (1814) and *Oration on the Birth of Our Savior* (1826).

CHARLES TIMOTHY BROOKS (June 20, 1813–June 14, 1883) b. Salem, Massachusetts. Son of Mary King Mason and Timothy Brooks. Heard Emerson preach at South Church, Boston, in 1831. Graduated Harvard College (where he studied German literature with refugee scholar Charles Follen) in 1832; classmates included Charles Sumner and Oliver Wendell Holmes; graduated Harvard Divinity School (where classmates included Theodore Parker and Christopher Pearse Cranch) in 1835. Officiated in several New England churches, including brief terms at Nahant, Massachusetts, Bangor and Augusta, Maine, and Windsor, Vermont; ordained (by the elder William Ellery Channing) pastor of Unitarian Congregational Church in Newport, Rhode Island, 1837; served at the church until 1870, when failing eyesight forced his retirement. Married Harriet Lyman Hazard, daughter of Rhode Island legislator, in 1837; they had two sons and two daughters. Published translations from German, including Schiller's *William Tell* (1837) and *Homage of the Arts* (1847); anthologies *Songs and Ballads* (1842), to which Henry Wadsworth Longfellow and others also contributed, and *German Lyrics* (1853); and Goethe's *Faust* (1856) in the original meters. Established friendship with Ralph Waldo Emerson. Original writings included two volumes of poetry, *Aquidneck and Other Commemorative Pieces* (1848) and *Songs of Field and Flood* (1853); *The Old Stone Mill Controversy* (1851), an archaeological essay on the Newport site alleged to have been built by Norsemen; a volume of sermons, *The Simplicity of Christ's Teachings* (1859); and *William Ellery Channing, A Centennial Memory* (1880). Traveled on several occasions for his health, including trips to India (1853–54) and Europe (1865–66). *Poems, Original and Translated* published posthumously in 1885 with a memoir of Brooks by Charles W. Wendt.

MARIA GOWEN BROOKS (1794?–November 11, 1845) b. Medford, Massachusetts, of Welsh ancestry. Daughter of Eleanor Cutter and William Gowen (a goldsmith); given name Abigail Gowen but legally changed it to Mary at the time of her marriage; "Maria" was her own adopted usage. Influenced by reading, at age nine, of Robert Southey's poem *Madoc*. Her father died bankrupt when she was 14. John Brooks, her guardian (previously married to her sister Lucretia), arranged for completion of her education and in 1810 married her; they had two sons, Horace (later a brigadier general in the U.S. Army) and Edgar. Husband, a Boston merchant, suffered heavy financial losses during War of 1812; thereafter they lived in Portland, Maine, in reduced circumstances. In 1820 Brooks published poetry collection *Judith, Esther and Other Poems* "by a Lover of the Fine Arts." Husband died in 1823 and she moved with sons and stepsons to an uncle's coffee plantation in Matanzas,

Cuba, where she built a small house and began *Zophiël, or the Bride of Seven*, epic poem concerning the love of a fallen angel for a mortal, based on episode in apocryphal Book of Tobit. In 1825 published first canto of *Zophiël*; began correspondence with Robert Southey, who called her "the most impassioned and most imaginative of all poetesses," and compared her favorably to Sappho. In 1829 inherited her uncle's Cuban property, and with income now secure, traveled with son Horace to Hanover, New Hampshire, where he attended Dartmouth college while she pursued studies in the college library; son Edgar remained in Cuba with stepbrothers, overseeing plantation. In 1830, with brother Hammond Gowen, traveled to Paris, where she met Washington Irving and the Marquis de Lafayette (whose recommendation helped son Horace gain entrance to West Point); in spring of 1831 visited Southey's English estate, Keswick, remaining for a number of weeks. Returned to U.S. in late spring 1831 and moved to West Point, where Horace was now a cadet; continued to write and publish in periodicals. Southey edited and published *Zophiël* in 1833 under pseudonym "Maria del Occidente"; poem praised by Charles Lamb and John Quincy Adams; American edition of *Zophiël* appeared in 1834, but sold few copies. Devastated by deaths of son Edgar (1838) and a stepson (1839), returned to Cuba to erect a small monument; dedicated *Ode to the Departed* (1843) to their memory. Rufus Griswold, in *Poets and Poetry of America* (1842), called her the foremost American woman poet. Autobiographical prose romance *Idomen, or the Vale of Yamuri* (said to be based on unhappy love affair with a Canadian army officer) serialized in Boston *Saturday Evening Gazette* in 1838; published privately in book form in 1843, while Brooks was living with Horace, stationed at Governor's Island, New York City. Late in life, returned to Cuban estate, where she died of tropical fever.

WILLIAM CULLEN BRYANT (November 32, 1794 – June 12, 1878)   b. Cummington, Massachusetts. Son of Sarah Snell and Dr. Peter Bryant. Began writing poems at early age, and published poems in *New Hampshire Gazette* in 1807; anti-Jeffersonian satire, *The Embargo . . . By a Youth of Thirteen*, published in Boston with father's help in 1808. After private tutoring, entered Williams College in 1810, but withdrew after a year without degree. At age 20 wrote, but made no attempt to publish, "To a Waterfowl" and "Thanatopsis." Studied law and was admitted to bar in 1815; began law practice in Great Barrington, Massachusetts. Gained immediate recognition as poet after publication of "Thanatopsis" in *North American Review* in 1817; contributed articles to the *Review*, including survey of American poetic achievement and essay on prosody. In 1820 elected town clerk of Great Barrington and appointed justice of the peace of Berkshire County. In 1821, married Frances Fairchild, whom he had met five years earlier; they had two daughters, Fanny and Julia. Read "The Ages" at Harvard as Phi Beta Kappa poem; published first verse collection, *Poems* (1822); became close friend of Richard Henry Dana and contributed poems to his short-lived magazine *The Idle Man*. Gave up law in 1825 to pursue literary career in New York; became co-editor with Henry Anderson of *New York Review and Athenaeum Magazine*; as member (later

president) of Bread and Cheese Club, associated with James Fenimore Coo-
per, Fitz-Greene Halleck, Gulian Verplanck, Robert Sands, Samuel F. B.
Morse, Asher B. Durand, and Thomas Cole. Lent support to artists, encour-
aging formation of National Academy of Design (1826). With Sands and Ver-
planck, published *The Talisman*, first of annual series of gift books, in 1827.
Became editor-in-chief of the New York *Evening Post* in 1829, remaining in
that position until his death. Most of his best-known poems were already
written by the time the *Poems* of 1832 appeared (in the same year, a London
edition with the same title was published, edited by Washington Irving, who
took the liberty of altering some lines to avoid offending British political
sensitivities). In 1832 visited Washington, D.C., where he met President Jack-
son and various cabinet members; moved to Hoboken, New Jersey; traveled
to Illinois and toured the prairie, visiting ancient Indian mounds along Illi-
nois River. Toured Canada and northern New England in 1833, and the fol-
lowing year sailed to Europe in 1834 with wife and daughters for two-year
visit, traveling in France, Italy, Austria, and Germany; spent much time in
Heidelberg with Henry Wadsworth Longfellow in the winter of 1835–36. Ar-
ranged publication of Richard Henry Dana Jr.'s *Two Years Before the Mast*
(1840). During late 1830s and 1840s shared vacations, visits, and walking tours
with William Gilmore Simms, Thomas Cole, Samuel Tilden, and Richard
Henry Dana; entertained Charles Dickens in New York in 1842; crusaded for
international copyright protection and against the death penalty; was a pro-
ponent of homeopathic medicine; served three terms as president of Ameri-
can Art Union. Published *The Fountain and Other Poems* (1842) and *The White
Footed Deer and Other Poems* (1844). Built residence Springbank in Roslyn,
New York, where he resided from 1844. In 1845 traveled in England, Scotland,
Ireland, France, Belgium, Holland, Germany, Bohemia, Austria, Italy, and
Switzerland, and over the next two years traveled widely in the United States.
In 1848 delivered funeral oration for Thomas Cole; the following year Asher
B. Durand presented him with the painting "Kindred Spirits," a portrait of
Bryant and Cole in the Catskills. Left Democratic party in 1848 to support
Free Soil candidates. In 1849 visited Georgia, South Carolina, and Cuba; later
in the year traveled to England and the Continent, recounting the voyage in
Letters of a Traveller (1850). In 1851 presided at dinner in honor of Hungarian
revolutionary Louis Kossuth. In 1852 eulogized Cooper, who had died in
September of the previous year; served reluctantly as intermediary in discus-
sions preceding divorce trial of actor Edwin Forrest; visited Europe, Egypt,
and the Holy Land. Two-volume edition of the collected poems published in
1854. In 1856 supported Republican John Charles Frémont for president. In
1857–58, traveled in Spain, France, Italy (where he spent time with Nathaniel
Hawthorne, Walter Savage Landor, and Robert and Elizabeth Barrett
Browning), and England. Became a Unitarian. In February 1860, introduced
Abraham Lincoln at Cooper Union. In April, eulogized Washington Irving,
who had died the year before. In 1861 advised Lincoln on cabinet appoint-
ments; conferred with him a year later in Washington. Elected president of
New York Medical College (1862) and president of American Free-Trade

League (1863). In 1864, on 70th birthday, honored by "Bryant Festival" at New York's Century Club, with speakers including Bayard Taylor, Oliver Wendell Holmes, George Henry Boker, and Julia Ward Howe. In 1865 wrote poems on death of Lincoln and abolition of slavery. Wife Frances died in July 1866. Sailed in October for Europe, visiting Spain and Italy (where he spent time with Giuseppe Garibaldi, whom he had met years earlier in New York). In 1869 delivered addresses in commemoration of Fitz-Greene Halleck and upon founding of Metropolitan Museum of Art. Published translations of Homer's *Iliad* (1870) and *Odyssey* (1871–72). In 1872 traveled in the Bahamas, Cuba, and Mexico (where he received honors from President Juárez). Prepared final edition of poems in 1876. In final years maintained busy schedule of dinners and addresses; last public address was an oration at unveiling of Mazzini statue in Central Park; died from injuries received in a fall following the ceremony.

JOSIAH D. CANNING (1816–March 25, 1892) b. Gill, Massachusetts. Son of the Rev. Josiah W. Canning. Informal education in the classics at home. While still in his teens, built his own printing press and taught himself to print; published local newspaper, *The Village Post*. For the next five years, attempted to establish himself as printer, first in Detroit, where his brother Ebenezer was associate editor of the *Detroit Courier*; then in Wheeling, Virginia (now West Virginia), where his brother Edward lived, and finally in the newly established territory of Wisconsin. In 1838 returned to Gill; a farmer most of his life, he also worked over the years as postmaster, town clerk, and treasurer. Published poetry in *The Knickerbocker*, whose editor Louis Gaylord Clarke dubbed him "the Peasant Bard" (a phrase which Canning adopted as pseudonym for several of his books), and in local newspapers and magazines. Published works included *Poems* (1838); *Thanksgiving Eve* (1847); *The Harp and Plow* (1852); *The Shad Fishers*, a self-published pamphlet (1854); and *Connecticut River Reeds* (1892), poems issued posthumously as commemorative volume.

WILLIAM ELLERY CHANNING (November 29, 1818–December 23, 1901) b. Boston, Massachusetts. Son of Barbara Perkins and Dr. Walter Channing (distinguished surgeon and Harvard professor); nephew of the Unitarian clergyman of the same name. Following his mother's death in 1823, raised in household of great-aunt Mrs. Bennett Forbes (born Margaret Perkins) in Milton, Massachusetts. Early education at Round Hill School (Northampton), the Boston Latin School, and Hubbard's Academy in Brookline. Entered Harvard College in 1834, but left after only a few months to devote himself to poetry. Began publishing poems, essays, and sketches in 1835 in the Boston *Mercantile Journal* and *New England Magazine*. Continued studies on his own; family distressed that he had not secured a vocation. In 1839 purchased a farm in McHenry County, Illinois, and relocated there, returning home for occasional visits. Emerson reviewed his verses favorably in *The Dial* in 1840; the two men met in December while Channing was visiting from

Illinois. In 1841, sold Illinois farm and moved to Cincinnati where he worked as tutor and journalist, and read desultorily for law; met Ellen Fuller (sister of Margaret Fuller), whom he married in September 1841 against the wishes of his family; the couple had two daughters and three sons. Returned to Massachusetts in 1842, living for a short time in Cambridge before settling with Ellen in Concord. During 1844–45, worked in New York on editorial staff of Horace Greeley's *New-York Tribune*; traveled briefly to Italy from March to July of 1846; published book based on 16-day stay in Rome, *Conversations in Rome between an Artist, a Catholic, and a Critic* (1847). Marriage troubled by Channing's neglect of family responsibilities; Ellen left him in 1853, returned in 1855, and died in 1856. Children reared by relatives as Channing lived alone in Concord, virtually cut off from family. Edited *New Bedford Mercury*, 1856–58. Continued friendship with Emerson; other friends included Nathaniel Hawthorne, Margaret Fuller, Bronson Alcott, James Russell Lowell, and especially Henry David Thoreau, whom he accompanied on trips to Cape Cod, Maine, and Canada, and on frequent excursions around Concord. (Wrote first biography of Thoreau, *Thoreau, The Poet-Naturalist*, 1873; edited a number of Thoreau's works in collaboration with Thoreau's sister Sophia.) Last years spent in the home of his friend Franklin B. Sanborn. Published verse collections *Poems* (1843), *Poems, Second Series* (1847), and *The Woodman* (1849), and book-length poems *Near Home* (1858), *The Wanderer* (1871), *Eliot* (1885), and *John Brown and the Heroes of Harper's Ferry* (1886).

LYDIA MARIA CHILD (February 11, 1802–October 20, 1880) b. Medford, Massachusetts. Daughter of Susannah Rand and Convers Francis (a baker); sister of prominent Unitarian minister Convers Francis. After mother's death in 1814, sent to live with older sister in Norridgewock, Maine. Moved to Boston in 1821 to rejoin brother Convers; met Emerson, then a student at Harvard; developed interest in Swedenborgianism, joining Boston Society of the New Jerusalem in 1822. *Hobomok* (1824), novel about Indians in 17th-century New England, established reputation as writer; she became acquainted with literary figures including George Ticknor, William Ellery Channing, and Nathaniel P. Willis. A second novel, *The Rebels, or Boston Before the Revolution* (1825), was less well received. Edited first American children's magazine, *The Juvenile Miscellany* (1826–29); during same period ran private school in Watertown, Massachusetts; made acquaintance of Margaret Fuller. Married David Lee Child, lawyer and newspaper editor, in 1828; they had no children. Wrote financially successful household manual *The Frugal Housewife* (1829). Husband's financial difficulties resulted in his being briefly jailed for debt in 1830. Along with her husband, became increasingly involved in abolitionist movement, and published series of controversial anti-slavery works: *An Appeal in Favor of That Class of Americans Called Africans* (1833), *The Oasis* (1834), and *An Anti-Slavery Catechism* (1836). In the same period published two-volume *History of the Condition of Women in Various Ages and Nations* (1835) and *Philothea* (1836), philosophical novel set in ancient Athens. Moved to New York to edit *The National Anti-Slavery Standard* (1841–44), boarding with family of abolitionist Isaac T. Hopper; newspaper articles collected in successful *Letters from New York* (1843); resigned from *Standard* following disagreements with other abolitionists. Remaining in New York, enjoyed renewed friendship with Margaret Fuller. In 1850 reunited with husband (who had undergone continual financial problems, and whom she had seen only sporadically since coming to New York) and returned with him to Massachusetts. After many years of work, published three-volume history *The Progress of Religious Ideas Through Successive Ages* in 1855. In October 1859, following John Brown's raid on Harpers Ferry, offered to help nurse Brown in prison; resulting controversy summarized in *Correspondence Between Lydia Maria Child, Governor Wise, and Mrs. Mason* (1860). Edited and wrote introduction for fugitive slave Harriet Jacobs' *Incidents in the Life of a Slave Girl* (1860); also published *The Duty of Disobedience to the Fugitive Slave Act* (1860) and *The Right Way, the Safe Way* (1860), pamphlet urging freeing of slaves. In 1865 published *Looking Toward Sunset*, anthology of prose and poetry for the elderly, and *The Freedmen's Book*, collection of educational readings intended for emancipated slaves. Closely involved in politics of Reconstruction under Johnson and Grant administrations. *A Romance of the Republic* (1867) gave fictional account of mulatto life in New Orleans. Husband David died in 1874. Final book, religious anthology *Aspirations of the World*, published 1878.

THOMAS HOLLEY CHIVERS (October 18, 1809–December 18, 1858) b. on cotton plantation near Washington, Georgia; son of a Miss Digby and wealthy landholder and slave-owner Colonel Robert Chivers. Married cousin Frances Chivers in 1827; deserted by wife within first year of marriage while she was pregnant with daughter Frances, whom he never met; series of lawsuits followed on both sides, including unsuccessful suit by Chivers for divorce. Graduated from Transylvania University in Kentucky with medical degree in 1830; soon gave up medicine to pursue literary career. While recuperating from illness, reported having vision of fountain of water and angels playing harps. Unhappy marital experience provided basis for first book of poetry, *The Path of Sorrow, or the Lament of Youth* (1832), published, like all of Chivers' books, at his own expense. In 1831–34 traveled in Mississippi Valley, Cherokee Nation, Cincinnati, St. Louis, New York, and Philadelphia; published *Conrad and Eudora* (1834), drama based on so-called "Kentucky tragedy," the Sharpe-Beauchamp murder of 1826; volume also contained 29 poems. Returned to Georgia, 1835–36. Married Harriette Hunt, 18-year-old jeweler's daughter from Springfield, Massachusetts, in New York in 1837 (divorce from first wife, Frances, not final until 1842, but marriage legal under Georgia law); with second wife had five children. The couple lived in New York City and Middletown, Connecticut, until 1842. Next poetic collection, *Nacoochee; or The Beautiful Star* (1837), contained preface formulating his view of poetry: "Poetry is that crystal river of the soul which runs through all the avenues of life, and after purifying the affections of the heart, empties itself into the Sea of God." Began long-term correspondence with Edgar Allan Poe beginning in 1840; Poe published several of Chivers' poems in *Graham's*

Magazine. Returned to Georgia in 1842; daughter Allegra Florence died in October of that year, a tragedy commemorated in the elegies of *The Lost Pleiad* (1845). While visiting New York in 1845 to arrange for the book's publication, met Poe on several occasions. In 1848 three of his other children died in rapid succession. Became increasingly interested in mystical experience and Swedenborgianism; published prose treatise *Search After Truth; or, A New Revelation of the Psycho-Physiological Nature of Man* (1848); contributed poetry and visionary prose to *The Univercoelum* (1848–49), periodical devoted to ideas of mesmerist Andrew Jackson Davis (known as "the Poughkeepsie seer"). After Poe's death in 1849, worked on a never-completed biography of Poe (first published 1952). Literary correspondent to *The Georgia Citizen*, 1850–54. Later volumes (some of whose contents were written decades earlier) were poetic collections *Eonchs of Ruby, A Gift of Love* (1851); *Memoralia; or, Phials of Amber Full of the Tears of Love* (1853) and *Virginalia; or, Songs of My Summer Nights* (1853), the long poem *Atlanta: or The True Blessed Island of Poesy, A Paul Epic—In Three Lustra* (1853), the play *The Sons of Usna: a Tragi-Apotheosis* (1854, published 1858), and a patriotic poem, *Birth-Day Song of Liberty* (1856). In 1853 published articles in *The Waverley Magazine* charging Poe with having plagiarized his work; heated tone of articles led to protracted controversy and attacks on Chivers by other writers. Spent much time in New York and Connecticut in later years. Returned to Georgia three years before his death, and moved from Washington to Decatur, where he died.

THOMAS COLE   (February 1, 1801–February 11, 1848)   b. Bolton-le-Moor, Lancashire, England, seventh of eight children of Mary and James Cole, unsuccessful woolen manufacturer. Attended school in Chester. From around 1815 worked in Liverpool as engraver's assistant; became engraver of designs for calico. Immigrated with family to America in 1819. Worked as wood engraver in Philadelphia, where father opened dry goods shop. Traveled in St. Eustatius in West Indies, then rejoined family in Steubenville, Ohio, where he assisted father in manufacturing wallpaper. After unsuccessful attempts to support himself as itinerant portraitist, stayed with family briefly at new home in Pittsburgh; returned to Philadelphia in 1823 for two years of study at Philadelphia Academy of Fine Arts. Wrote poetry and fiction, some published in *Saturday Evening Post*. Rejoined family in New York City in 1825, painting in their house on Greenwich Street. Made sketching trips to Weehawken, the Palisades, the Highlands, and elsewhere in Hudson River Valley. Met and received encouragement from artists John Trumbull, William Dunlap, and Asher B. Durand; rapidly achieved celebrity for paintings of American landscapes. Spent winters painting and exhibiting in New York City, his summers traveling and sketching in the Hudson Valley and elsewhere. As member of Bread and Cheese Club, associated with William Cullen Bryant, Samuel F. B. Morse, Asher B. Durand, James Fenimore Cooper; contributed art to Bryant's periodical *The Talisman*. Traveled in Europe, 1829–32; in England, visited poet Samuel Rogers and painters Thomas Lawrence, J. M. W. Turner, John Constable, and John Martin; paintings exhibited at Royal Academy and British Institution. Toured France and Italy; in Rome used Claude Lorrain's old studio and associated with Samuel F. B. Morse and Horatio Greenough. Between 1833 and 1836 painted allegorical series "The Course of Empire," praised as his masterpiece by Cooper and others. Married Maria Bartow in November 1836; settled in Catskill, New York. In 1840 completed four-part allegory "The Voyage of Life" and "The Architect's Dream," fanciful combination of Egyptian, Greek, Roman, Moorish, and Gothic styles. In 1841 traveled again to Europe, returning to Catskill the following year. Accepted Frederick Edwin Church as student in 1844. Died in Catskill of lung inflammation while working on uncompleted allegorical series "The Cross and the World."

PHILIP PENDLETON COOKE (October 26, 1816–January 20, 1850) b. Martinsburg, Virginia (now West Virginia). Son of Maria Pendleton and John Rogers Cooke (a prominent lawyer); brother of novelist John Esten Cooke and cousin of novelist John Pendleton Kennedy. As undergraduate at Princeton, began writing poems that were published in *The Knickerbocker* in 1833. Graduated 1834 and returned to family estate Glengary; studied law with father; admitted to bar before age 21. Contributed poetry and critical essays on English poets to *Southern Literary Messenger*, 1835–36. In 1837 married Willianne Burwell; they had five children. Father lost fortune in financial panic of 1837; Glengary burned two years later. Practiced law in Martinsburg. Best-known poem "Florence Vane" published (under editorial auspices of Edgar Allan Poe) in *Burton's Gentleman's Magazine* in 1840. Work praised by Poe (in *The Broadway Journal*) as "exquisitely graceful and delicate"; included in new edition of Rufus Griswold's *Poets and Poetry of America*. Wife inherited 1,000-acre estate ("Vineyard") near Winchester in 1845. Only published volume of poetry, *Froissart Ballads and Other Poems*, appeared 1847. In last years devoted himself mostly to prose tales published in *Southern Literary Messenger*, including "John Carper, the Hunter of Lost River," "The Two Country Houses," "The Gregories of Hackwood," and "The Crime of Andrew Blair," and only novel *The Chevalier Merlin* (left unfinished at his death). Favorite pursuit apart from writing was hunting. Died of pneumonia contracted on a hunting trip.

CHRISTOPHER PEARSE CRANCH (March 8, 1813–January 20, 1892) b. Arlington, Virginia (then part of District of Columbia). Son of Anna Greenleaf and William Cranch (a federal judge and Supreme Court reporter); aunt, Rebecca Greenleaf, was married to Noah Webster; grandmother, Mary Smith, was sister of Abigail Adams. Received early training as draftsman. Graduated from Columbian College (now George Washington University) in 1831 and from Harvard Divinity School in 1835 (classmates included Charles Timothy Brooks and Theodore Parker). As an itinerant Unitarian minister preached in Andover, Bangor, and Portland, Maine, and in Boston, Richmond, St. Louis (home of cousin William Greenleaf Eliot, grandfather of T. S. Eliot), Cincinnati, Peoria, Louisville, and elsewhere. While preaching in

Louisville, 1837–38, assisted James Freeman Clarke in editing *The Western Messenger*, Unitarian journal associated with the Transcendentalists, to which he contributed poetry and articles. In Boston in 1840, met Emerson (who published some of his poems in *The Dial*) and became frequent visitor at utopian community Brook Farm. Married a cousin, Elizabeth de Windt (great-granddaughter of John Adams), in 1843; they had two daughters and a son. *Poems*, dedicated to Emerson, published in 1844. Moved to New York to begin career as landscape painter. Traveled with his wife and author George William Curtis to Italy in 1846; remained there for three years, studying art and spending time with Robert and Elizabeth Barrett Browning, Margaret Fuller, William Wetmore Story, and others. After four years in New York, family moved in 1853 to Paris, where Cranch painted and cultivated many acquaintances, including friendship with James Russell Lowell; exhibited paintings in Paris. Returned to the U.S. in 1863, following death of son George in Civil War. Elected to National Academy of Design in 1864, and contributed to its exhibitions for a number of years. After period of residence on Staten Island settled in 1873 in Cambridge, Massachusetts. In 1880, made last trip to Europe; met Frank Duveneck, who painted his portrait. Later verse collected in *Satan: A Libretto* (1874), *The Bird and the Bell* (1875), and *Ariel and Caliban* (1887); also published children's books *The Last of the Huggermuggers* (1856) and *Kobboltozo* (1857), and a blank verse translation of *The Aeneid* (1842).

RICHARD HENRY DANA (November 15, 1787–February 2, 1879) b. Cambridge, Massachusetts. Son of Elizabeth Ellery (daughter of William Ellery, signer of Declaration of Independence, and a descendant of Anne Bradstreet) and Francis Dana (diplomat and jurist); close relationship with maternal grandfather William Ellery. Educated in Newport, Rhode Island, before entering Harvard in 1804; expelled in 1807 for participation in dining hall riot (known as "Rotten Cabbage Rebellion"). Under pressure of family financial difficulties decided to enter legal profession; from 1809 studied law in offices of cousin Francis Dana Channing; admitted to bar 1812, and began practice in Sutton, Massachusetts (he abandoned his largely unsuccessful legal career in 1819). In 1813 moved to Cambridgeport and married schoolteacher Ruth Charlotte Smith; they had four children (including Richard Jr., author of *Two Years Before the Mast*). From 1818 served as assistant editor of *North America Review* under his cousin Edward Tyrrel Channing; contributed literary criticism, including reviews of Washington Allston, William Hazlitt, and Washington Irving. Left staff of *Review* when, following Channing's resignation, he was passed over for editorship in favor of Edward Everett in 1819. In 1821, founded short-lived literary magazine *The Idle Man* in New York, with contributors including Washington Allston (college friend of Dana's brother Edmund) and close friend William Cullen Bryant. His wife and infant daughter died in 1822, and he discontinued publication of *The Idle Man*; last issue contained story "Paul Felton," criticized for its morbid tone. Converted to Congregationalism in 1826 under influence of Lyman Beecher, and became involved in controversy between Congregationalists and Unitarians in Cambridge. Sister Martha married Washington Allston in 1830. Poems, essays, and fiction appeared in Bryant's *New York Review* and other periodicals; published *The Buccaneer and Other Poems* (1827) and *Poems and Prose Writings* (1833). From 1835 taught classes for women on English literature; lectured on Shakespeare in Providence in 1838. Confirmed as Episcopalian in 1843, and the following year was a founder and senior warden of the Church of the Advent (first American church to embrace the Anglo-Catholic movement). After lecture series in 1849 and 1850 and publication of second edition of *Poems and Prose Writings* (1850), spent later life in retirement in Boston, Cambridge, and Cape Ann.

SAMUEL HENRY DICKSON (September 20, 1798–March 31, 1872) b. Charleston, South Carolina. Son of Mary Neilson and Samuel Dickson (a schoolmaster), Presbyterians who had emigrated from Belfast, Ireland, before American Revolution. Graduated Yale College 1814. Studied medicine with Dr. Philip Gendron Prioleau; practiced during yellow fever epidemic of 1817; received medical degree from University of Pennsylvania in 1819. Practiced in Charleston, primarily among yellow fever patients. Lectured on physiology; participated in founding of medical college in Charleston, of which he was made professor of medicine. Resigned after disagreement with college; in 1833 founded Medical College of South Carolina. Achieved minor literary celebrity for poem "I Sigh for the Land of the Cypress and Pine," written in 1830. Close friend of William Gilmore Simms, who dedicated *The Yemassee* (1835) to him. First wife, Elizabeth Brownlee Robertson, died in 1832; two years later married her sister Jane Robertson Robertson, who died in 1842; in 1845 married Marie Seabrook DePre. *Poems* appeared in privately printed edition in 1844; reviewed in *Southern Literary Messenger*. Pamphlet *Essays on Slavery* (1845) defended institution and asserted racial inferiority of blacks. In 1847 became professor of practice of medicine at New York University; after three years returned to former professorship in Charleston. Was among group of writers associated with Russell's Bookstore in Charleston during 1850s. Returned in 1858 to Philadelphia, assuming professorship at Jefferson Medical College, and remained at post until shortly before his death. Wrote and lectured prolifically on medicine and other topics, including early contributions to anthropometry (comparison of body measurements). Medical works included *Manual of Pathology and Practice* (1839), *Essays on Pathology and Therapeutics* (1845), *Essays on Life, Sleep, Pain, Intellection, and Hygiene* (1852), *Elements of Medicine* (1855) and *Studies in Pathology and Therapeutics* (1867).

JOSEPH RODMAN DRAKE (August 7, 1795–September 21, 1820) b. New York City. Fourth child and only son of Hannah Lawrence (of Flushing, Long Island) and Jonathan Drake (a dry goods merchant). Shortly after Drake's birth, father suffered financial ruin after investing in fraudulent "Yazoo" land companies, leaving family impoverished; he died in 1797. In 1809, mother married widower Robert Muir Welman, a merchant, and moved with him (and two of her daughters) to New Orleans. Drake remained in New York with sister Caroline under guardianship of relatives in Hunts Point in the Bronx; took position as clerk in mercantile house of Norris L. Martin. In 1813 began studying medicine, supported by great-uncle Colonel Joseph Drake; established friendship with James Ellsworth De Kay, physician and naturalist, who introduced him to poet Fitz-Greene Halleck; Drake and Halleck became close friends and literary associates (the two were described after Drake's death as "the Damon and Pythias of American letters"). In 1816 awarded medical degree from Queens College in New Brunswick, New Jersey (later Rutgers College); began private practice in New York. Later the same year married Sarah Eckford, daughter of prosperous Scottish-born shipbuilder and naval architect Henry Eckford; father-in-law enjoyed literary company, and his house in Love Lane (present-day West 24th St.) served as gathering place for Drake, Halleck, De Kay, and others. In 1816 Drake's poem "The Culprit Fay" (fairy fantasy set along the Hudson near West Point) was, according to Halleck, "written, begun and finished, in three days." In 1818 traveled with wife to Europe, visiting Great Britain, France, and Holland. After return to New York in fall of 1818, initiated "The Croakers," series of pseudonymous satirical poems dealing with political, social, and theatrical life of New York City; Halleck joined him as collaborator; the poems appeared throughout spring and summer in New York *Evening Post*, and were collected in a volume late in 1819. During same year, opened drugstore in partnership with William Langstaff. Began to suffer symptoms of tuberculosis, and in an effort to regain health visited sisters in New Orleans, March–April 1820. Died on September 21 at his New York home. (On deathbed, said to have asked De Kay to burn unpublished poems. In 1821 Halleck published elegy "On the Death of Joseph Rodman Drake" in a New York literary magazine. *The Culprit Fay and Other Poems*, edited by daughter Janet Halleck Drake, was published in 1835.)

RALPH WALDO EMERSON   (May 25, 1803–April 27, 1882)   b. Boston, Massachusetts, fourth of eight children of Ruth Haskins and William Emerson (minister of First Church of Boston). Father died when he was eight; raised by mother and by father's sister, Mary Moody Emerson, whose strong religious views influenced him. Early education at Boston Public Latin School where, at age eight, he began writing verses. The youngest member of the class of 1821, Emerson worked his way through Harvard as an orderly, a waiter, and a tutor; won prizes for oratory and essays. Began keeping a journal in 1820. After graduating, became teacher at a school for young women in Boston operated by his brother. Studied briefly at Harvard Divinity School in 1825; forced to interrupt courses because of eye trouble. In 1826 began career as minister; suffering from lung ailment, traveled to South Carolina and Florida for health. Ordained pastor of Second Church of Boston in March, 1829; later that year, married Ellen Tucker, who was already ill with tuberculosis; she died in 1831, aged 19. A year later, when research persuaded him that the sacrament of communion was not in fact divinely authorized, gave up position as minister and sailed for Europe; traveled in Italy, France, England, and Scotland; met Walter Savage Landor, John Stuart Mill, Samuel Taylor Coleridge, William Wordsworth, and Thomas Carlyle. Returned to Boston and resumed itinerant preaching; began long correspondence with Carlyle. In 1834 settled in Concord, Massachusetts; a year later married Lydia Jackson. What would eventually be called the Transcendental Club began to form around Emerson; members included Margaret Fuller, Bronson Alcott, and Orestes Brownson. Published first significant work in 1836, the long essay *Nature*; it was followed by two influential orations, "The American Scholar" (delivered at Harvard in 1837 before the Phi Beta Kappa Society), and the July 1838 address to the Harvard Divinity School, which created a scandal due to the unorthodoxy of its religious views. Became closely associated with Henry David Thoreau, sharing his walks and employing him in his house; befriended the poets Jones Very and William Ellery Channing, both of whose work he helped to publish. Virtually gave up preaching in favor of lecturing by 1838; collaborated with Margaret Fuller on *The Dial* (1840–44), succeeding her as editor in July 1842; regularly contributed to the journal. Published *Essays* in 1841 (later retitled *Essays: First Series*), and *Essays: Second Series* in 1844. Continued to lecture extensively. *Poems* published 1846. Launched public attacks on Mexican War and slavery; became involved with abolitionist movement. Returning to Europe in 1847, made contact with wide range of writers and thinkers (including Charles Dickens, George Eliot, Alexis de Tocqueville, Alfred Tennyson, and Harriet Martineau), having become internationally known through essays. Published further collections of essays and public addresses—*Nature; Addresses, and Lectures* (1849), *Representative Men* (1850), *English Traits* (1856), *The Conduct of Life* (1860)—while lecturing throughout Northeast, as well as in the western states and Canada; continued agitation against slavery. Responded enthusiastically to first editon of Whitman's *Leaves of Grass* (1855), but attempted to persuade poet to tone down sexual imagery prominent in poems added to subsequent editions. Spoke at meetings held to benefit John Brown's family after the latter's execution for his part in the Harpers Ferry raid. After Civil War, continued to lecture energetically; published verse collection *May-Day and Other Pieces* (1867), and *Society and Solitude* (1870). In 1872 health began to fail; traveled to Europe once more before returning to Concord and settling into a quieter routine as his memory gradually weakened. *Selected Poems* published in 1876. Died of pneumonia in Concord.

DANIEL DECATUR EMMETT (October 29, 1815–June 28, 1904) b. Clinton, Ohio. Son of Sarah Zerick and Abraham Emmett (a blacksmith). Worked from early age in father's blacksmith shop; received little schooling. Taught himself music. Apprenticed to printer, and in his teens worked for *Huron Reflector* in Norwalk, Ohio, and *Western Aurora* in Mount Vernon, Ohio. Moved to Cincinnati around 1834 to work as printer; enlisted for three-year stint in army, falsifying his age; stationed at Newport Barracks in Kentucky; played drums and fife; later relocated to Jefferson Barracks near

St. Louis. Discharged from army in 1835 because of discovery that he had misrepresented his age. Traveled with various circus troupes in the late 1830s. From around 1841 associated with Frank Brower in minstrel shows; with Brower, organized the Virginia Minstrels, musical quartet that made debut at Bowery Ampitheatre in New York in February 1843. The Minstrels were immensely successful in New York and other American cities (although British tour proved disappointment); they introduced many songs of which words or music were attributed to Emmett, including "My Old Aunt Sally," "The Blue-Tail Fly," "Old Dan Tucker," "Walk Along, John," "De Boatman's Dance," and "Jordan Is a Hard Road to Travel." Emmett performed widely as actor and musician with various ensembles. Around 1852 married Catherine Rives. In 1858 joined the Bryant Minstrels, for whom in 1859 he composed "Dixie's Land" ("Dixie"); played in 1861 at inauguration of Jefferson Davis, song was adopted as unofficial anthem of Confederacy. Emmett songs performed with Bryant Minstrels included "The Road to Richmond" and "Here We Are, or Cross Ober Jordan"; toured with them sporadically until 1866. Settled in Chicago in 1867; managed a saloon there, 1872–74; continued to perform, primarily as fiddler, until the late 1870s. Wife Catherine died in 1875; married Mary Louise Bird in 1879. Money raised for him in public benefits in 1880 and 1882; toured with Leavitt's Gigantean Minstrels, 1881–82. In 1888 retired to Mount Vernon, Ohio, where he lived in relative poverty, assisted by stipend from Actors' Fund of America. Made final tour in the South, 1895–96.

THOMAS DUNN ENGLISH (June 29, 1819–April 1, 1902)   b. in Philadelphia, Pennsylvania. Son of Robert English. Family were Irish Quakers, their original name Angelos. Educated at Wilson's Academy in Philadelphia and the Friends' Academy in Burlington, New Jersey; in 1839 graduated with degree in medicine from University of Pennsylvania; thesis was defense of phrenology. Subsequently studied law; called to bar in 1842. Began literary career early, contributing frequently to *Burton's Gentleman's Magazine* (one of whose editors at the time was Edgar Allan Poe). Formed friendship with Poe, which later turned to bitter enmity. Best-known work, the poem "Ben Bolt," first appeared in the *New-York Mirror* in September 1843. Settled in New York in 1844; briefly edited political paper, *Aurora*, that supported John Tyler; awarded with position as customs weigher in New York; founded short-lived magazine *The Aristidean* (1845). In New York, quarrel with Edgar Allan Poe in 1845 led to fistfight; subsequently caricatured Poe as mad poet Marmaduke Hammerhead in anonymous novella *1844* (1846) serialized in the *New-York Mirror*; other attacks on Poe by English in the *Mirror* led to Poe's successful libel suit against the paper. Became editor of short-lived humor magazine *John Donkey* (1848), which failed because of libel suits resulting from English's frequent attacks on contemporaries. Married Annie Maxwell Meade in 1849; they had four children. Practiced law and medicine in Lawnsville, Virginia (1852–56); served as town's mayor. After a year's residence in New York, established medical practice in 1856 near Newark, New Jersey. Served in New

Jersey legislature, 1863–64, as a "Copperhead" Democrat. Another magazine, *The Old Guard* (1870), also failed. In 1878 worked on staff of Newark *Sunday Call*. Served as Democratic congressman, 1891–95. Published three novels under his own name—*Walter Woolfe* (1844), *Ambrose Fecit* (1867), and *Jacob Schuyler's Millions* (1870)—and others under pseudonyms. Wrote many plays including *The Mormons: or, Life at Salt Lake* (1858). Poetry collected in *Poems* (1855), *American Ballads* (1880), *Boy's Book of Battle Lyrics* (1885), and *Select Poems of Dr. Thomas Dunn English* (1894).

PHILIP FRENEAU (January 2, 1752–December 19, 1832) b. New York City. Son of Agnes Watson and Pierre Fresneau. Of French Huguenot descent; grandfather André Fresneau established as wine importer in New York around 1709. Educated at College of New Jersey (now Princeton); classmates included James Madison and Hugh Henry Brackenridge; wrote satirical anti-Tory verses. With Brackenridge collaborated on *Father Bombo's Pilgrimage* (1770), sometimes called earliest example of American prose fiction, and *A Poem on the Rising Glory of America* (1772). Following graduation in 1771, employed briefly as teacher on Long Island and in Maryland. Pastoral poem *The American Village* (1772) followed by patriotic and satirical verse including *American Liberty* (1775), *A Voyage to Boston* (1775), *General Gage's Soliloquy* (1775), and *General Gage's Confession* (1775). Secretary to planter in Santa Cruz (now St. Croix) in West Indies, 1776–78. During Revolutionary War served intermittently as member of the Monmouth (N.J.) Militia, and in 1779 sailed as commander of privateering brig *Rebecca*; as militiaman, assisted in capture of British brig *Brittania* off New Jersey coast in December 1779. As third mate on privateer *Aurora*, captured by the British in May 1780; brutal treatment during six weeks as prisoner of war on prison ship *Scorpion* and hospital ship *Hunter* in New York harbor recounted in poem *The British Prison-Ship* (1781). Following release and recuperation at Mount Pleasant (family plantation near Middletown Point, New Jersey), moved to Philadelphia to work on the staff of Francis Bailey's *Freeman's Journal*, to which he contributed poetry and polemical prose; employed as clerk in Philadelphia post office, 1782–84. Worked sporadically as master of trading ships along the Atlantic coast, 1784–89. First major verse collection, *The Poems of Philip Freneau*, published in 1786, followed by *Journey from Philadelphia to New York* (1787) and *Miscellaneous Works* (1788). In 1790 married Eleanor Forman, with whom he had four daughters. Settled in New York; edited *Daily Advertiser*, 1790–91; following removal of federal government to Philadelphia, hired by Jefferson as translating clerk in State Department, 1791–93; in 1791 began publishing the *National Gazette*, launching virulent attacks on Alexander Hamilton; fervently supported French Revolution and controversial French envoy Edmond Charles Genêt. Washington, annoyed by Freneau's radicalism, suggested to Jefferson that his appointment be revoked; Jefferson responded, "I will not do it. . . . His paper has saved our constitution which was galloping fast into monarchy." Upon Jefferson's retirement from the State Department, Freneau resigned his government clerical job. Worked as printer and bookseller in

New Jersey; edited *Jersey Chronicle* (1795–96), in which he published satirical essays featuring "Tomo Cheeki, the Creek Indian in Philadelphia." In New York, edited Antifederalist newspaper *The Time-Piece*, 1797–98. Poetry collected in *The Village Merchant* (1794), *Poems Written Between the Years 1768 and 1794* (1795), and two-volume *Poems Written and Published During the American Revolutionary War* (1809); satirical journalism published under pseudonym "Robert Slender" collected in *Letters on Various Interesting and Important Subjects* (1799). After 1798 retired from journalism; in later years lived mostly at Mount Pleasant; served as ship's captain, 1802–04 and 1809. During War of 1812 wrote topical patriotic poems, some published in *A Collection of Poems on American Affairs* (1815). Many of his manuscript poems were destroyed in a fire at Mount Pleasant in 1818. Increasingly impoverished in later years; much of property sold to creditors. Died when caught in a blizzard while walking home.

MARGARET FULLER   (May 23, 1810–July 19, 1850) b. Cambridge, Massachusetts. Daughter of Margaret Crane (former schoolteacher) and Timothy Fuller (lawyer, state senator, and congressman); given name Sarah Margaret Fuller. Rigorously educated at home by father, by tutors, with Dr. John Park in Boston, and at boarding school conducted by Susan Prescott in Groton, Massachusetts (1823–24); by age 15 she was proficient in Latin, Greek, French, and Italian. Made intensive study of German literature; close friend of James Freeman Clarke. Family settled in Groton when father took up farming in 1833. Following father's death in 1835, taught for several months at Bronson Alcott's Temple School in Boston; left due to Alcott's inability to pay her. Became teacher at Hiram Fuller's Greene-Street School in Providence, Rhode Island (1836–38); formed friendship with Sarah Helen Whitman. Moved to Boston area, where she taught privately; contributed essays to Clarke's *Western Messenger*; published translation of Eckermann's *Conversations with Goethe* (1839). Conducted successful women's education program of "conversations" focusing on philosophy, education, and women's rights, 1839–44. Close friend of Ralph Waldo Emerson; became editor of *The Dial*, 1840–42, frequently contributing essays and poems. Friends and intellectual associates in Boston and Cambridge included George Ripley, Theodore Parker, Caroline Sturgis, William Henry Channing, and many others. Greatly impressed by meeting with English writer Harriet Martineau in 1835; occasionally visited Brook Farm community beginning in 1841. Sister Ellen married poet William Ellery Channing in 1841. In the summer of 1843 traveled in Illinois and Wisconsin; her account of the journey, *A Summer on the Lakes* (1844), led to invitation from Horace Greeley to serve as literary critic for *New-York Tribune*. During vacation in Hudson Valley with close friend Caroline Sturgis, wrote *Woman in the Nineteenth Century* (published 1845). Moved to New York in 1844; lived for a time in Greeley household; literary associates in New York included Lydia Maria Child, Anne Lynch, Christopher Pearse Cranch, Cornelius Mathews, William Gilmore Simms, and Evert Duyckinck. Criticism collected in *Papers on Literature and Art* (1846). Sailed to Europe in the summer of 1846; wrote for *Tribune* as foreign correspondent (articles reprinted in *At Home and Abroad* in 1856). In England met Thomas Carlyle, William Wordsworth, Thomas De Quincey, and Italian revolutionary leader Giuseppe Mazzini; in France, George Sand, Pierre de Beranger, and Polish poet Adam Mickiewicz. In Italy, associated with Robert and Elizabeth Barrett Browning and artists William Wetmore Story, Hiram Powers, and Horatio Greenough; renewed friendship with Christopher Pearse Cranch. Met the Marchese Angelo Ossoli, impoverished Roman aristocrat and republican, whose son she bore in September 1848 (exact date of marriage to Ossoli, or if they married, is unknown). Became involved in Italian revolution of 1848–49, and celebrated it in articles for *Tribune*; cared for wounded during siege of Rome by French and Austrian forces; fled with Ossoli to mountain village of Rieti after defeat of Roman republic in June 1849; soon relocated to Florence. In 1850 sailed with Ossoli and young child to America, carrying manuscript of her history of the failed revolution. Ship wrecked off Fire Island; Fuller perished with family and many others aboard. Letters, journals, and poems collected posthumously in *The Memoirs of Margaret Fuller Ossoli* (1852); complete works published in 1869 under Greeley's direction.

FITZ-GREENE HALLECK (July 8, 1790–November 19, 1867) b. Guilford, Connecticut. Son of Mary Eliot (farmer's daughter descended from missionary John Eliot) and Israel Halleck (associated with Tory cause during Revolution). Educated locally. Went to New York in 1811 to work for banking house of Jacob Barker, where he was employed for the next 18 years. Gained early reputation as wit and scholar. Co-author (with close friend Joseph Rodman Drake) of "The Croakers," series of local satires that appeared in New York *Evening Post* in 1819. Anonymously published *Fanny* (1819), satirical poem about New York society. Traveled in Europe in 1822. From 1825 contributed poetry frequently to William Cullen Bryant's *New York Review* and other publications; "Marco Bozzaris" achieved wide popularity as poem for recitation. Wrote little verse after publication of *Alnwick Castle, with Other Poems* (1827), but remained active in New York literary circles of New York, maintaining friendships with William Cullen Bryant, James Kirke Paulding, James Fenimore Cooper, and others. Worked as confidential clerk in counting house of John Jacob Astor beginning in 1832. Edited *The Works of Byron in Prose and Verse* (1833) and *Selections from the British Poets* (1840); in 1837 elected vice-president of Authors Club of New York, of which Washington Irving was president. *The Works of Fitz-Greene Halleck* (1847) went through three editions during his lifetime. Bryant called Halleck "the favorite poet of the city of New York, where his name is cherished with a peculiar fondness and enthusiasm." John Jacob Astor died in 1848, leaving Halleck an annuity and naming him trustee of the Astor Library; retired to Guilford.

NATHANIEL HAWTHORNE (July 4, 1804–May 19, 1864) b. Salem, Massachusetts. Son of Elizabeth Clarke Manning and Nathaniel Hawthorne (a sea captain). Father died in Dutch Guiana 1808; mother became recluse. Graduated 1825 from Bowdoin College; classmate of Henry Wadsworth Longfellow and close friend of Franklin Pierce. Returned to Salem and devoted himself to writing. *Fanshawe* (1828), first novel, published anonymously. Published stories in *The Token* under editorship of S. G. Goodrich, collected in *Twice-Told Tales* (1837). Edited *American Magazine of Useful and Entertaining Knowledge*, compiled *Peter Parley's Universal History* (1837), and wrote a number of children's books. Worked 1839–40 at Boston custom house; lost patronage job after Whig victory. Associated for six or seven months in 1841 with utopian community Brook Farm in West Roxbury, Massachusetts. Married Sophia Peabody in 1842; they had two daughters and a son. Moved to Concord, where he became acquainted with Transcendentalist circle including Ralph Waldo Emerson, Henry David Thoreau, and Bronson Alcott. Second volume of *Twice-Told Tales* (1842) followed by *Mosses from an Old Manse* (1846). Returned to Salem in 1846 as Surveyor of Port of Salem and served for three years. In 1850 published *The Scarlet Letter*. Moved to Lenox, Massachusetts; formed friendship with Herman Melville, who had reviewed his work enthusiastically. Published *The House of the Seven Gables* (1851), *The Snow-Image and Other Twice-Told Tales* (1851), *The Blithedale Romance* (1852), inspired by experiences at Brook Farm, and two books of stories for children, *A Wonder Book* (1852) and *Tanglewood Tales* (1853). In 1852 wrote campaign biography for Franklin Pierce; following Pierce's election as president, appointed U.S. consul in Liverpool. After holding position for four years (1853–57), lived in Italy (1858–59) and England (1859–60) before returning to Concord. Final novel, *The Marble Faun*, published in 1860. Published essays on England, *Our Old Home* (1863). In later years kept voluminous notebooks that were published posthumously, along with fragments of several unfinished novels.

JOSIAH GILBERT HOLLAND (July 24, 1819–October 12, 1881) b. Belchertown, Massachusetts. Son of Anna Gilbert and Harrison Holland. Childhood impoverished; worked in factory as a boy. After early experience as schoolteacher, attended Berkshire Medical College, graduating 1844. Practiced medicine briefly; worked as daguerrotypist; published *Bay State Weekly Courier* (which failed after six months); worked as educator, becoming superintendent of schools in Vicksburg, Mississippi. Married Elizabeth Chapin in 1845; they had three children. In 1849 returned to Massachusetts to become assistant editor of *Springfield Republican*, under Samuel Bowles. Wrote wide variety of items for the paper, including a series of moralistic letters under the pseudonym Timothy Titcomb. Journalistic writing collected in *History of Western Massachusetts* (1855), *The Bay-Path* (1857), and the widely popular *Timothy Titcomb's Letters to Young People, Single and Married* (1858). After 1857 devoted himself primarily to writing books. Published volumes of poetry— *Bitter-Sweet* (1858), *Kathrina, Her Life and Mine in a Poem* (1867), *The Marble Prophecy* (1872), and *The Puritan's Guest* (1881)—and novels including *Miss Gilbert's Career* (1860), *Arthur Bonnicastle* (1873), *Sevenoaks* (1875), and *Nicholas Minturn* (1877), as well as collections of moral essays. Was a friend of Emily

Dickinson, one of a small circle to whom she occasionally showed work. In later years, in addition to literary and editorial work, served as president of New York City Board of Education and chairman of board of trustees of City College. From 1870 until his death he was editor of *Scribner's Monthly*.

OLIVER WENDELL HOLMES (August 29, 1809–October 7, 1894) b. Cambridge, Massachusetts. Son of Sarah Wendell (merchant's daughter) and Abiel Holmes (minister of First Church of Boston). Graduated Harvard 1829; entered Harvard Law School but transferred a year later to private medical school. Poem "Old Ironsides," protesting the impending destruction of the frigate *Constitution*, appeared in *Boston Daily Advertiser* in 1830 and became widely popular. Reputation as writer enhanced by essays under rubric "The Autocrat of the Breakfast-Table" in *New England Magazine*, the first of which appeared in November 1831. After two years of medical study in France (1833–35), and further work at Harvard Medical School, granted M.D. from Harvard in 1836; began practice in Boston. Published first collection of verse, *Poems* (1836). As researcher, awarded three Boyleston prizes by Harvard for essays on medical subjects; taught medicine at Tremont Medical School, of which he was a founder; professor of anatomy at Dartmouth, 1838–40. In 1840 married Amelia Lee Jackson, daughter of Massachusetts supreme court justice; they had three children (the eldest, Oliver Wendell, became a justice of United States Supreme Court, 1902–32). Continued important medical research, including landmark paper on pueperal fever in 1843. Appointed Parkman Professor of Anatomy and Physiology at Harvard Medical School in 1847, a position he held until 1882, when he was named professor emeritus; dean of Harvard Medical School, 1847–53. Was a member of celebrated "Saturday Club" and was considered one of the great conversationalists of his era; friends included James Russell Lowell, Nathaniel Hawthorne, Ralph Waldo Emerson, John Greenleaf Whittier, Henry Wadsworth Longfellow, John Lothrop Motley, and William Dean Howells. In 1853 delivered well-received lecture series on the English poets, and in 1857 resumed his "Breakfast-Table" series for *Atlantic Monthly*, collected in *The Autocrat of the Breakfast-Table* (1858), *The Professor at the Breakfast-Table* (1860), *The Poet at the Breakfast-Table* (1872), and *Over the Teacups* (1891). Published three novels, all originally serialized in the *Atlantic*—*Elsie Venner* (1861), *The Guardian Angel* (1867), and *A Mortal Antipathy* (1885)—and a variety of other prose including *John Lothrop Motley: A Memoir* (1879), *Medical Essays* (1883), and *Ralph Waldo Emerson* (1884). Poetry collected in *Songs in Many Keys* (1862), *Songs of Many Seasons* (1875), *The Iron Gate* (1880), and *Before the Curfew* (1887).

GEORGE MOSES HORTON (1798?–1883?) b. into slavery on plantation of William Horton in Northampton County, North Carolina; in childhood moved with his master to Chatham, near Chapel Hill. Belonged in turn to son and grandson of his original owner. Taught himself to read. Worked on campus of University of North Carolina; said to have been paid by students to compose love poems for them. *The Lancaster Gazette*, a Massachusetts newspaper, published three of his poems in 1828, and others appeared in *Freedom's Journal*, *The Liberator*, and *Southern Literary Messenger*. *The Hope of Liberty* (1829), designed to earn his freedom and passage to Liberia, failed to earn enough to do so (subsequently reprinted as *Poems by a Slave* in 1837 and 1838). In the 1830s, the author Caroline Lee Hentz tutored him in poetic composition and transcribed his verses while he learned to write; he read poetry in volumes given him by students. Second book, *The Poetical Works of George M. Horton, the Colored Bard of North Carolina*, published 1845. Wrote letters and otherwise constantly attempted to gain freedom, while working on campus as handyman, waiter, and servant. In 1865 escaped and reached Sherman's army in Raleigh. That same year published final collection, *Naked Genius*. Settled after the war in Philadelphia, where he is believed to have died in about 1883.

JULIA WARD HOWE (May 27, 1819–October 17, 1910) b. New York City. Daughter of Julia Rush Cutler Ward (an occasional writer of poems) and Samuel Ward (a wealthy banker); sister-in-law of sculptor Thomas Crawford and aunt of popular novelist F. Marion Crawford. In 1843 married reformer Samuel Gridley Howe (18 years her senior) and moved to Boston; they had six children, four of whom survived their mother (children included writers Laura Richards and Maud Howe Elliott). With her husband, published abolitionist newspaper *The Commonwealth* beginning in 1851; their Boston home was frequented by Theodore Parker, Charles Sumner, and other anti-slavery activists. First collection of poetry, *Passion Flowers*, appeared in 1854, followed by *Words for the Hour* (1857) and *A Trip to Cuba* (1860). *Atlantic Monthly* published "The Battle Hymn of the Republic" in April 1862; song became unofficial anthem of Union Army. After the war, Howe campaigned for woman suffrage; was a founder in 1868 of New England Woman Suffrage Association and served as its first president; active from 1869 on in American Woman Suffrage Association; president of Association for the Advancement of Women, 1878–88. Campaigned for world peace; in "Appeal to Womanhood Throughout the World" (1870) called for international women's peace conference; became president (1871) of Woman's International Peace Association. Active in support of prison reform and Greek independence. Was first woman elected to National Academy of Arts and Letters. Marriage strained by husband's objection to many of her public activities (she later wrote, "I have never known my husband to approve of any act of mine which I myself valued"); he died in 1876. Poetry collected in *Later Lyrics* (1866) and *From Sunset Ridge: Poems Old and New* (1899); other writings included *Sex and Education* (1874), *Modern Society* (1881), *Margaret Fuller* (1883), *Is Polite Society Polite?* (1895), and memoirs *Reminiscences* (1899) and *At Sunset* (1910). Died in Newport, Rhode Island.

FANNY KEMBLE (November 27, 1809–January 15, 1893) b. London, England, into distinguished theatrical family; given name Frances Anne Kemble. Daughter of Maria Thérese De Camp and Charles Kemble; niece of John

Philip Kemble and Sarah Siddons. Grew up mostly under care of aunt Adelaide De Camp; as adolescent spent three years at school in Paris. Made debut as Juliet at Covent Garden (of which her father was manager) in 1829; became overnight stage success. After father, burdened by debt, was forced to cut ties with Covent Garden, accompanied him to the U.S. in 1832 and toured for two years, playing in New York, Philadelphia, Boston, Baltimore, and Washington, and enjoying great popularity; presented to Andrew Jackson; formed close friendship with novelist Catharine Maria Sedgwick and Unitarian minister William Ellery Channing. In June 1834 abandoned stage career to marry Pierce Mease Butler of Philadelphia, heir to large sea-island plantation in Georgia; they had two daughters, one of whom became the mother of novelist Owen Wister. A two-volume record of Kemble's American experiences, *Journal of a Residence in America* (1835), stirred some resentment for occasional criticisms of American life; husband objected to its publication and at his urging she omitted anti-slavery passages. Made six-month visit with husband and daughters to Georgia plantation in December 1838; shocked by first-hand exposure to slavery. (Record of Georgia stay published in England in 1863 as *Journal of a Residence on a Georgian Plantation*, in effort to sway British public opinion in favor of the Union.) Marital strains continued after family returned to Philadelphia and during three-year stay in England beginning in December 1840. Despite her efforts to keep family united, she and husband had increasingly long separations; Kemble often summered in Lenox, Massachusetts, home of Catharine Maria Sedgwick and her circle. *Poems* published in 1844. After final breakup of marriage, returned to London in 1845; the following year relocated to Italy. Published memoir *A Year of Consolation* (1847); the following year Butler sued her for divorce on grounds of abandonment, and she returned to America. In the case, which became notorious, Kemble was represented by celebrated counsel Rufus Choate, although the case never came before a jury; divorce, including custody of children, awarded to Butler in 1849. Kemble established successful career as Shakespearean reader in America and abroad. Purchased cottage in Lenox, Massachusetts. Continued to travel regularly between England and America, and gave readings until 1869. Became close friend of Henry James, whom she met in Rome in 1872. In later years published autobiographies *Records of a Girlhood* (1878) and *Records of Later Life* (1882); *Notes Upon Some of Shakespeare's Plays* (1882); *Far Away and Long Ago* (1889), a novel set in the Berkshires; and *Further Records* (1891), a final volume of memoirs. Returned to England in 1877 and remained in London until her death.

FRANCIS SCOTT KEY (August 1, 1779 – January 11, 1843) b. on family estate in Frederick (now Carroll) County, Maryland. Son of Ann Phoebe Charlton and John Ross Key (an officer in American Revolutionary Army). Graduated St. John's College, Annapolis in 1796; studied law, opening practice at Fredericktown in 1801. Married Mary Taylor Lloyd in 1802; they had six sons and five daughters. The family moved to Georgetown in the District of Columbia, where Key practiced law for a time with his uncle, future congressman Philip Barton Key. In 1814, during British withdrawal from Washington, was asked to intervene in plight of an American physician held prisoner aboard a British ship; after arranging his release, witnessed British bombardment of Baltimore. In response to the sight, on the dawn of September 14, of the American flag still flying over Fort McHenry, wrote "The Star-Spangled Banner." Poem published (as "Defence of Fort McHenry") in *Baltimore American* on September 21, it achieved immediate nationwide popularity. As lawyer, practiced extensively in federal courts; served as U.S. attorney for District of Columbia (1833–41). Died of pleurisy in Baltimore. Poetry collected posthumously in *Poems of the Late Francis S. Key, Esq.* (1857).

ABRAHAM LINCOLN (February 12, 1809–April 15, 1865) b. near Hodgenville, Kentucky. Son of Nancy Hanks and Thomas Lincoln, a farmer and carpenter. Family moved to Indiana in 1816; mother died in 1818. Received little formal education. In 1830 family moved to Illinois. Worked on flatboat to New Orleans in 1828 and again in 1831. Settled in New Salem, Illinois; worked as storekeeper, surveyor, postmaster; captain of volunteers in Black Hawk War (1832). Served in state legislature, 1834–41, as Whig. Studied law; began law practice in 1836 and moved to Springfield in 1837. Married Mary Todd in 1842 after long, sometimes troubled courtship; they had four sons, two of whom died in childhood. Established law practice with William Herndon as junior partner in 1844. Served one term as Whig congressman (1847–49); opposed Mexican War. Renewed involvement with politics after Kansas-Nebraska Act of 1854 repealed anti-slavery restriction in Missouri Compromise; spoke frequently against it and gained wide recognition. Helped found the Republican Party of Illinois in 1856. Campaigned in 1858 for U.S. Senate seat held by Democrat Stephen Douglas, author of the Kansas-Nebraska Act, and debated Douglas seven times on the slavery issue (debates were published in 1860 in edition prepared by Lincoln). Although Illinois legislature reelected Douglas to the Senate, campaign brought Lincoln national prominence in the Republican party. In February 1860 (after introduction by William Cullen Bryant) delivered address on slavery at Cooper Union in New York City. Received Republican presidential nomination in May and won election in fall with 180 of 303 electoral votes and 40 percent of popular vote; victory led to secession of seven Southern states. In early April 1861 sent naval expedition to provision Fort Sumter in Charleston harbor in South Carolina; when Confederates bombarded the fort, Lincoln called up militia, proclaimed blockade of Southern ports, and suspended habeas corpus. Preliminary and final emancipation proclamations issued September 23, 1862, and January 1, 1863. Delivered address at Gettysburg on November 19, 1863. After long series of command changes, appointed Ulysses S. Grant commander of all Union forces in March 1864. Reelected president; delivered second inaugural address March 4, 1865. Worked for passage of Thirteenth Amendment. Visited Richmond after its capture by Union Army and learned of Appomattox surrender on his return to Washington. Assassinated on April 14 by John Wilkes Booth at Ford's Theatre.

HENRY WADSWORTH LONGFELLOW (February 27, 1807–March 24, 1882) b. Portland, Maine (then part of Massachusetts). Son of Zilpah Wadsworth and Stephen Longfellow, a prominent lawyer. Schooled privately until age 14. After a year at Portland Academy, entered Bowdoin College and graduated in 1825; classmate of Nathaniel Hawthorne; in graduate oration "Our Native Writers" called for a national literature. Appointed to newly instituted Chair of Modern Languages at Bowdoin with stipulation that he first engage in further study abroad; spent three years (1826–29) in France, Spain (where he met Washington Irving), Italy, and Germany. Married Mary Storer Potter in 1831. During his years at Bowdoin, published many textbooks and scholarly articles on Romance languages and literature; in 1833 published a translation of the *Coplas* of the Spanish poet Jorge Manrique; *Outre-Mer*, a prose account of his European journey, appeared in 1835. Appointed Smith Professor of Modern Languages at Harvard (the chair formerly held by George Ticknor) in 1835; went to Europe for year of additional study; visited England, Germany, Denmark, and Sweden; in Holland, Mary suffered a miscarriage and died in November 1835. Spent the winter in Heidelberg, where he met William Cullen Bryant; in Switzerland the following summer met Frances (Fanny) Appleton. He arrived in Cambridge, Massachusetts, in 1836, and the following summer settled into Craigie House, where he would live for the rest of his life. Lectures at Harvard ranged widely over European literature, treating among other subjects Dante, Lope de Vega, Calderón, Moliere, Goethe, Jean Paul Richter, and Anglo-Saxon and Scandinavian literature. Achieved celebrity as poet with publication of "A Psalm of Life" in *The Knickerbocker* in 1838; the following year published first collection of poems, *Voices of the Night*, and the romance *Hyperion*; *Ballads and Other Poems* (1841) included "The Skeleton in Armour," "The Wreck of the Hesperus," and "The Village Blacksmith." Suffering from neuralgia and eyestrain, spent six months in Germany, mostly at Marienberg spa on the Rhine; on return journey met Charles Dickens. Anti-slavery poems collected in *Poems of Slavery* (1842); published verse play *The Spanish Student* (1843), influenced by his study of Spanish drama. In 1843 married Fanny Appleton, who had previously repeatedly rejected his proposal of marriage; they had six children, born between 1844 and 1855. Suffered partial blindness in 1843. Urged by John Greenleaf Whittier in 1844 to run for Congress as abolitionist, but refused on the grounds that "partizan warfare becomes too violent—too vindictive for my taste." In 1845 published verse collections *Poems* and *The Belfry of Bruges and Other Poems* and monumental anthology *The Poets and Poetry of Europe*, containing work from ten modern languages (much of it in Longfellow's own translations). The narrative poem *Evangeline* (1847) went through six editions in its first three months of publication. Daughter Fanny died in 1848. A novel of New England life, *Kavanaugh* (1849), was followed by verse collection *The Seaside and the Fireside* (1849) and verse drama *The Golden Legend* (1851), first published installment of trilogy also including *The New-England Tragedies* (1868) and *The Divine Tragedy* (1871), and later collected as *Christus: A Mystery* (1872). Resigned from Harvard position in 1854 to devote himself entirely to writing. His reading of the Finnish epic *The Kalevala* led to the adoption of its meter for *The Song of Hiawatha* (1855), an enormously popular narrative poem based on American Indian legends he had encountered in the writings of Henry Rowe Schoolcraft. The title poem of *The Courtship of Miles Standish* (1858) incorporated the figures of his mother's 17th-century ancestors John Alden and Priscilla Mullens. Close friends and associates included Nathaniel Hawthorne, James Russell Lowell, Charles Sumner, Charles Eliot Norton, and Louis Agassiz. Wife Fanny died when her dress caught fire in 1861; he was badly burned trying to put the flames out. Devoted himself to translation of Dante's *Divine Comedy* (1865–67) and to series of narrative poems collected in *Tales of a Wayside Inn* (1863). Later poetry published in *Flower-de-Luce* (1867), *Three Books of Song* (1872), *Aftermath* (1873), *The Hanging of the Crane* (1874), *The Masque of Pandora and Other Poems* (1875), *Kéramos* (1878), and *Ultima Thule* (1880–82); juvenilia collected in *The Early Poems* (1878); also edited 31-volume poetry anthology *Poems of Places* (1876–79). Aside from a year in Europe (1868–69), remained in Cambridge. Suffered serious nervous attack in 1881; died the following year of peritonitis. *Michael Angelo* published posthumously in 1883.

JAMES RUSSELL LOWELL (February 22, 1819–August 12, 1891) b. Cambridge, Massachusetts. Son of Harriet Brackett Spence and Charles Lowell (distinguished Unitarian minister); mother suffered from mental illness in later life, and was confined to a hospital for two years. Graduated Harvard 1838 and Harvard Law School 1840; admitted to Massachusetts bar, but within a year abandoned law practice in favor of a literary career. Published poems in *Southern Literary Messenger* and elsewhere; first collection of poetry, *A Year's Life*, appeared 1841, followed by *Poems* (1844). With Robert Carter co-edited *The Pioneer*, short-lived literary magazine of which three numbers (including work by Poe, Hawthorne, and Whittier) were published in 1843. Literary essays serialized in *Boston Miscellany* formed basis of *Conversations on Some of the Old Poets* (1845). Married Maria White (also a poet) in 1844, after long engagement; they had four children, three of whom died in infancy. Under influence of wife's ardent abolitionism, wrote editorials for *Pennsylvania Freeman* and became contributing editor of *National Anti-Slavery Standard*. In his most productive period as a poet published in rapid succession *Poems: Second Series* (1848), *A Fable for Critics* (1848), *The Biglow Papers* (1848), and *The Vision of Sir Launfal* (1848). The Lowells spent the years 1851–52 in Europe; son Walter died in Rome in April 1852. Maria died in October 1853, and two years later Lowell privately published *The Poems of Maria Lowell* for distribution to friends. Lowell delivered lectures on the English poets at Lowell Institute in Boston in 1855; succeeded Longfellow as professor of French and Spanish language and literature at Harvard, remaining there in various capacities until retirement in 1886. Following his appointment spent a year in Europe, studying in Germany, Italy, and elsewhere in preparation for duties at Harvard. In 1857 married Frances Dunlap, governess in whose care he had left daughter Mabel during his absence. Became founding editor of

Atlantic Monthly (1857–61); contributors during his editorship included Emerson, Whittier, Holmes, Hawthorne, Stowe, Motley, and Longfellow. Second series of *The Biglow Papers*, attacking disunionists and pro-slavery interests, serialized in *Atlantic Monthly* in 1862. From 1864 to 1872 co-edited *The North American Review* with Charles Eliot Norton, contributing articles on the Civil War (in which three of his nephews died) and its consequences (later collected in *Political Essays*, 1888). Delivered widely acclaimed "Ode" at Harvard Commemoration of July 21, 1865, in honor of Harvard men killed in the Civil War. Published verse collections *Under the Willows* (1869) and *The Cathedral* (1870); essays collected in *Fireside Travels* (1864), *Among My Books* (1870–76), and *My Study Windows* (1871). Made long visit to Europe (1872–75), and was awarded honorary degrees by Oxford and Cambridge. Served as delegate to Republican National Convention and as a presidential elector for Rutherford B. Hayes in 1876. Appointed minister to Spain (1877–80) and Great Britain (1880–85). Frances, after years of failing health and mental illness, died in 1885. In later years published further poetry (*Under the Old Elm*, 1885, and *Heartsease and Rue,* 1888) and literary essays collected in *The English Poets, Lessing, Rousseau* (1888) and *Books and Libraries and Other Papers* (1889).

CORNELIUS MATHEWS (October 28, 1817–March 25, 1889) b. Port Chester, New York. Son of Catherine Van Cott and Abijah Mathews, a cabinet maker. Attended Columbia College for several years; graduated from newly opened New York University in 1834. Studied law; admitted to New York bar in 1837, but turned to literary career. Strong advocate of American literary nationalism; with Evert Duyckinck and William Gilmore Simms, became part of literary group known as Young America. Contributed to *American Monthly Magazine, New York Review,* and *Knickerbocker Magazine.* Published *The Motley Book* (1838) and *Behemoth: A Legend of the Mound Builders* (1839), a novel based on American Indian history and lore. Founded, with Evert Duyckinck, monthly magazine *Arcturus* (1840–42), which Mathews edited and for which he wrote articles and fiction; other contributors included Hawthorne, Longfellow, and Lowell. Wrote play about New York, *The Politicians* (1840); narrative poem on Indian themes, *Wakondah: The Master of Life* (1841); and satirical novel *The Career of Puffer Hopkins* (1842). Chief poetic work, *Poems on Man in His Various Aspects under the American Republic*, appeared 1843, along with a collected volume, *The Various Writings of Cornelius Mathews.* Wrote several more plays, of which *Witchcraft, or the Martyrs of Salem* (1846) was produced with some success, and additional fiction, including the novel *Moneypenny: or, The Heart of the World* (1849). Campaigned for international copyright, and spoke on the subject at dinner in honor of Charles Dickens in 1842. During 1840s and 1850s worked as editor on a number of literary magazines (including *Yankee Doodle*), most of them short-lived. After *The Indian Fairy Book* (1855), an anthology based on writings of Henry Rowe Schoolcraft, published no more books, but continued to contribute journalism to *New York Dramatic Mirror*, and to work as an editor on the *New*

York Reveille, *The New-Yorker* (1858–76), and *Comic World* (1876–78). Died in New York City.

CLEMENT MOORE (July 15, 1779–July 10, 1863) b. New York City. Son of Charity Clarke (heiress to large tract of land in what is now Chelsea section of Manhattan) and Benjamin Moore (Episcopal bishop of New York, rector of Trinity Church, president of Columbia College). In early youth educated at home; graduated Columbia 1798. Devoted himself to study of Hebrew, and in 1809 published two-volume *A Compendious Lexicon of the Hebrew Language*. In 1813 married Catharine Elizabeth Taylor; they had three daughters. Having come into his inheritance upon his father's death, in 1819 donated land on which General Theological Seminary was built; taught there from 1823 as professor of Biblical studies and later of Oriental and Greek literature. "A Visit from St. Nicholas," originally written in 1822 for his family, was published without Moore's knowledge in *Troy Sentinel* in 1823. It was reprinted frequently thereafter, but Moore was not identified publicly as the author until 1837, when the poem appeared in *The New York Book of Poetry* (edited by Charles Fenno Hoffman). Moore included the poem, along with other verse, in *Poems* (1844); also published a historical work, *George Castriot, Surnamed Scanderbeg, King of Albania* (1850).

GEORGE POPE MORRIS (October 10, 1802–July 6, 1864) b. Philadelphia, Pennsylvania. In his youth worked in printing office. Founded *New-York Mirror and Ladies' Literary Gazette* in 1823, and hired Samuel Woodworth to edit it; after a year took over editorial responsibilities. The weekly magazine included among its contributors William Cullen Bryant, Fitz-Greene Halleck, James Kirke Paulding, and Nathaniel P. Willis (who was contributing editor, 1831–36); Charles Fenno Hoffman and Epes Sargent later played editorial roles as well. Morris's play of the American Revolution, *Brier Cliff*, was successfully produced in 1826. Poem "The Oak" (later known as "Woodman, Spare That Tree!") achieved great popularity upon publication in 1830. First collection of poetry, *The Deserted Bride* (1838), followed by a book of humorous sketches, *The Little Frenchman and His Water Lots* (1839). The *Mirror* failed in 1842, and was revived a few months later as *New Mirror* (with Nathaniel P. Willis as co-editor), but lasted only a year and a half under that title before becoming a daily paper as *Evening Mirror*, with supplement entitled *Weekly Mirror*; contributors included Edgar Allan Poe. (By 1845 the *Mirror* had passed out of the control of Morris and Willis, continuing publication until 1857 under the editorship of Hiram Fuller.) Poetry collected in 1844 as *The Songs and Ballads of George P. Morris*. In 1846, again with Willis, founded the weekly *National Press*, whose name was changed within a few months to *The Home Journal*; paper was very popular, and Morris continued as editor until his death. With Willis, co-edited anthology *Prose and Poetry of Europe and America* (1857). Although he had no military experience aside from a stint in the New York milita, he was generally known as "General Morris." Lived for much of his life with his wife Mary Worthington Hopkins and their children on a country estate near Cold Spring, New York.

JOHN NEAL (August 25, 1793–June 20, 1876) b. Falmouth (now Portland), Maine. Son of Rachel Hall and John Neal, a Quaker schoolmaster. Father died shortly after Neal's birth, and he was raised by his mother. Worked as clerk in dry goods business and itinerant teacher of penmanship. In partnership with John Pierpont, ran dry goods businesses in Boston, Baltimore, and Charleston, 1814–16. Was a member, with Pierpont and Tobias Watkins, of the Delphian Club (founded 1816), literary association that published monthly magazine *The Portico* (1816–18). Studied law and began to write for a living; wrote 150-page critical essay on Byron for *The Portico*. Published series of novels: *Keep Cool* (1817), *Logan, a Family History* (1822), *Seventy-Six* (1823), *Randolph* (1823), *Errata, or the Works of Will Adams* (1823), and *Brother Jonathan* (1825). Other early writings included narrative poems (published under pseudonym "Jehu O'Cataract") collected in *Battle of Niagara, a Poem, without Notes; and Goldau, or, the Maniac Harper* (1818) and verse tragedy *Otho* (1819). Wrote much of Paul Allen's *A History of the American Revolution* (1819); briefly edited *Federal Republican and Baltimore Telegraph* (February–July 1819). Close friendship with John Pierpont broken off following incident in which Neal entered the bedroom of Pierpont's sister-in-law Abby Lord (Neal aggravated the situation by describing the incident in his novel *Randolph*); Neal and Pierpont were later reconciled but were never again as close. Challenged to a duel by Edward Coote Pinkney (whose father he had criticized in *Randolph*), but ignored the challenge; accused of cowardice on handbills distributed by Pinkney. Admitted to bar in 1820, but practiced only briefly; resigned from Delphian Club; affiliation with Quakers formally dissolved following Neal's participation in a street brawl. Went to England in 1823 and began to write articles (initially under pseudonym "Carter Holmes") on American topics for *Blackwood's Magazine*, among them a five-part survey of 135 American authors, the first such overview. Met the utilitarian philosopher Jeremy Bentham in 1825, whose ideas he undertook to promulgate; lodged in Bentham's house for over a year, although their relations were ultimately strained. Returned to the U.S. in 1827; settled in Portland. Practiced law with little success. Married his cousin, Eleanor Hall, in 1828; they had five children. Wrote novel based on witchcraft trials, *Rachel Dyer* (1828), followed by *Authorship* (1830) and *The Down-Easters* (1833). Contributed short fiction, articles, art criticism, and poems to a variety of periodicals, including *The Token* and *The Atlantic Souvenir*; edited *The Yankee* (1828–29), which gave early literary encouragement to Poe, Whittier, Hawthorne, and Longfellow (with whom he formed close friendship); later edited *The New-England Galaxy* (1835), *The New World* (1840), *Brother Jonathan* (1843), and *The Portland Transcript* (1848). Bowdoin College awarded him honorary M.A. in 1836. Campaigned for women's rights; involved in civic life of Portland. In 1850 publicly defended Poe's reputation after attack by Rufus Griswold, stating that Poe "saw farther, and looked more steadily, and more inquisitively into the elements of darkness . . . than did most of the shining brotherhood about him." Last full-length novel, *True Womanhood*, appeared in 1859. Wrote three adventure stories for dime novel publishers Beadle and Adams: *The White-Faced Pacer* (1863), *The Moose-Hunter* (1864), and *Little Moccasin* (1866). Papers destroyed in Portland fire of 1866. Later writings included religious treatise *One Word More* (1854), autobiography *Wandering Recollections of a Somewhat Busy Life* (1869), and *Portland Illustrated* (1874).

JAMES KIRKE PAULDING   (August 22, 1778–April 6, 1860)   b. Great Nine Partners, Putnam County, New York. Son of Catharine Ogden and William Paulding; father and many others in family actively involved in American Revolution. Raised in Tarrytown; moved around 1796 to New York City to live with his brother (who later served as congressman and New York mayor). Worked in a public office and became friendly with Washington Irving and Irving's brother William (who had married Paulding's sister Julia in 1793), collaborating with them on *Salmagundi* (1807–08). *The Diverting History of John Bull and Brother Jonathan* (1812), a humorous history in the vein of Irving's *History of New York*, was followed by *The Lay of the Scottish Fiddle* (1813), a parody of Scott's *Lay of the Last Minstrel*. Served as major in New York militia during War of 1812. After the war, published other works critical of English politics and culture—*The United States and England* (1815), *A Sketch of Old England by a New-England Man* (1822), and *John Bull in America* (1825)—as well as account of a journey through Virginia, *Letters from the South* (1817), long narrative poem in heroic couplets, *The Backwoodsman* (1818), and unsuccessful sequel to Irving collaboration written by Paulding alone, *Salmagundi, Second Series* (1819–20). Served as secretary of Board of Navy Commissioners under James Madison, 1815–23. In 1818 married Gertrude Kemble (sister of Irving associate Gouverneur Kemble); they had several children. First novel, *Koningsmarke: The Long Finne* (1823), initiated series of fictional accounts of American life, including *The Dutchman's Fireside* (1831), *Westward Ho!* (1832), *The Old Continental* (1846), and *The Puritan and His Daughter* (1849). Also published anti-utopian satire *The Merry Tales of the Three Wise Men of Gotham* (1826); more than 70 stories, some collected in *Tales of the Good Woman* (1829) and *Chronicles of the City of Gotham* (1830); several plays, including *The Lion of the West* (1833) and *The Bucktails* (1847); a biography, *A Life of Washington* (1835); and *Slavery in the United States* (1836), a defense of the Southern view. From 1823 to 1838 served as naval agent for New York City; appointed Secretary of the Navy by Martin Van Buren in 1837. Wife Gertrude died in 1841. Published two more historical novels, *The Old Continental* (1846) and *The Puritan and His Daughters* (1849). After the end of Van Buren's term as president, toured the west with him. Retired to Hyde Park, New York, in 1846.

JOHN HOWARD PAYNE   (June 9, 1791–April 9, 1852)   b. New York City, one of nine children of Sarah Isaacs and William Payne. Brought up mostly in East Hampton, Long Island, and in Boston, where his father taught school.

Showed early interest in the theater, which his father discouraged. Sent to New York to work as counting-house clerk; published theatrical magazine *The Thespian Mirror* (1805–06), which attracted attention of William Coleman, editor of New York *Evening Post*, who for a time was Payne's mentor. Publicized in newspapers and magazines as child prodigy; play *Julia, or The Wanderer* produced in New York in 1806. Formed friendships with Washington Irving, Charles Brockden Brown, James Kirke Paulding, and other literary figures. Contracted numerous debts. With financial support of New York merchant John Seaman attended Union College in Schenectady, New York; published literary magazine *The Pastime* (1807–08). Left school for stage debut in New York City, 1809, in the role of Young Norval in *Douglas* (a role with which he remained permanently identified). Mother died 1807, father 1812. Enjoyed initial acclaim as actor and was called "the American Roscius"; toured Boston, Baltimore, Philadelphia, Richmond, Charleston; first professional American actor to play Hamlet; in Boston, acted with Elizabeth Poe, mother of the poet. Mired in debt, and disappointed at dwindling of celebrity and conflicts with theatrical managers, settled (with financial help of friends and admirers) in England in 1813. Befriended Benjamin West, Washington Allston, Peter Irving (brother of the writer), Samuel Taylor Coleridge, Charles Lamb, and William Hazlitt; acted for a season in provinces; established prolific if largely unprofitable career as playwright in London theater. Drew on variety of sources (including older English work and successful French plays by Pixerecourt, Scribe, and La Beaumelle) to create as many as 60 theatrical pieces. Plays included *Lover's Vows* (1809); *Trial Without Jury* (1815); *Accusation* (1816); *Brutus; or, The Fall of Tarquin* (1818), a successful vehicle for Edmund Kean, stitched together from seven earlier works; *Thérèse; or, The Orphan of Geneva* (1821); *The Two Galley Slaves* (1822); *Mrs. Smith* (1823); *The Fall of Algiers* (1825); *The Lancers* (1827); *Procrastination* (1829); *Oswali at Athens* (1831); *Woman's Revenge* (1832); and *Virginia* (1834). Also published collection of verse, *Lispings of the Muse* (1815). Worked at variety of theatrical jobs, serving as secretary at Covent Garden (1818–19). Leased Sadler's Wells Theatre in 1820, an enterprise that drove him into bankruptcy; imprisoned for debt in Fleet Prison (1820–21); moved to Paris upon release and continued to dodge his many creditors. Wrote the lyrics of "Home, Sweet Home" (with music by Henry Bishop) for inclusion in his play *Clari; or, the Maid of Milan* (1823); the song achieved immediate widespread popularity, but Payne realized little monetary gain from it. Washington Irving spent much time with Payne in Paris, frequently lending him money, and collaborating on a number of plays, including *Charles the Second* (1824) and *Richelieu* (1826). Met Mary Shelley around 1823 and courted her unsuccessfully. Settled in London again in 1826, where he edited and published theatrical newspaper *Opera Glass* (1826–27). Nearly penniless despite prolific output, returned to America in 1832, traveling at expense of friends. A benefit performance of his work, featuring Edwin Forrest and Charles and Fanny Kemble, earned him $10,000. Made plans to publish a magazine of the arts which never appeared, although Payne traveled throughout South securing subscriptions and materials for articles. In 1835 met John Ross, head of the Cherokee Nation, and requested information on tribal history for proposed magazine. As a result of involvement with Ross (at that time resisting state and federal efforts to remove the Cherokee) arrested in Georgia by militia and accused of being an abolitionist; released after 13 days. Published articles describing ordeal and denouncing injustices done to the Indians, and upon his return to New York City, began history of the Cherokee Nation (completed manuscript of first volume is believed lost, although copious notes survive). Maintained connection with Ross in Washington, D.C., assisting him in the preparation of petitions to the federal government; in 1840, following Cherokee removal, traveled with Ross from Washington to his home in Park Hill, Indian Territory (now Oklahoma); met Sequoya, creator of Cherokee alphabet. In 1842, in recognition of his literary talent, and partly through the endeavors of Daniel Webster, President Tyler appointed him American consul at Tunis, where he served from 1843 until his recall by President Polk in 1845. After extensive travels in Europe, returned to America in 1847 seeking a new diplomatic post; eventually relocated to Washington. At gala concert at National Hall in December 1850, attended by President Fillmore and other dignitaries, Jenny Lind acknowledged Payne's presence with a rendition of "Home, Sweet Home," causing great sensation. Returned to Tunis in 1851 after reappointment by Fillmore; died there the following year.

JAMES GATES PERCIVAL (September 15, 1795–May 2, 1856) b. Kensington, Connecticut. Second son of Elizabeth Hart and Dr. James Percival; elder brother Edward was a painter. Sickly in youth; voice permanently damaged by attack of typhoid at age 12. Following father's death in 1807, attended private school where he read extensively but was by his own later account unhappy. At Yale, studied chemistry under Benjamin Silliman; became known as a poet. Graduated 1815; studied botany under Eli Ives in New Haven; subsequent studies at University of Pennsylvania; transferred to Yale Medical Institution, from which he graduated in 1820. Briefly practiced medicine in Charleston, South Carolina. First verse collection, *Poems* (containing long poem "Prometheus"), published in 1821, followed by *Clio I* and *Clio II* (1822) and *Prometheus Part II with Other Poems* (1822); a two-volume collection of his poetry appeared in 1823. Of his circumstances he wrote in 1823: "They are low and sad enough, and they have made my spirits low. I could tell a tale of embarrassments, joined to a bad constitution, injured health, and a neglected orphanage, which would do much to excuse the wrong that is in me." Worked fitfully as newspaper editor, chemistry instructor at West Point, and surgeon in Boston recruiting office. After publication of *Clio No. III* (1827), shifted his ambitions to science, scholarship, and linguistics. Assisted Noah Webster in revising and proofreading *An American Dictionary of the English Language* (1828); translated Malte Brun's *A System of Universal Geography* (1834). In 1835 appointed (along with Charles Shepard) to survey the geology of Connecticut; slow working methods led to difficulties with state government; published *Report on the Geology of the State of Connecticut* (1842).

Translated poems from Russian, Serbian, Danish, Hungarian, and other languages, as well as composing original poems in some of these languages; wrote songs in support of William Henry Harrison, published in *The New Haven Whig Song Book* (1840); *The Dream of a Day, and Other Poems*, final collection of poems and translations, appeared in 1843. Lived in seclusion for some years at state hospital in New Haven. From 1851 to 1854 surveyed lead mines in Illinois and Wisconsin for American Mining Company; shortly before his death, appointed state geologist of Wisconsin; traveled throughout Wisconsin, spending time with Winnebago and Ojibwa tribes. Died at Hazel Green, Wisconsin. Two-volume edition of his collected works published posthumously in 1859.

JOHN PIERPONT (April 6, 1785–August 27, 1866) b. Litchfield, Connecticut. Second of ten children of Elizabeth Collins and James Pierpont, a clothier. Graduated Yale College 1804, teaching for a short time in an academy at Bethlehem, Connecticut; spent four years as tutor in Colonel William Alston's household in South Carolina. Studied law on his return north. Married Mary Sheldon Lord in 1810; they had six children. Admitted to bar in 1812, and opened law office in Newburyport, Massachusetts, with little success. Published Federalist political poem *The Portrait* (1812), originally delivered before Washington Benevolent Society of Newburyport. Left the law in 1814 to open dry goods franchises in Boston, Baltimore, and Charleston, in partnership with writer John Neal; the business failed in 1816, and Pierpont was briefly jailed in Baltimore for debt. Decided to enter ministry. *Airs of Palestine* (1816) established reputation as poet; proceeds from book helped defray cost of attending Harvard Divinity School. Graduated 1818, and ordained minister of Hollis Street Unitarian Church in Boston a year later. Friendship with John Neal broken off after 1823 because of incident involving Pierpont's sister-in-law (they reconciled after a few years, but were never again as close). Visited Europe and Palestine, 1835–36. A new edition of his poetry, *Airs of Palestine and Other Poems*, appeared in 1840; in 1843 published *The Anti-Slavery Poems of John Pierpont*. Anti-slavery and temperance views led to long conflict (known locally as "the Seven Years' War") with unsympathetic congregation; in 1845 resigned his position. Went on to serve as pastor of other Unitarian churches in Troy, New York, and West Medford, Massachusetts. Two years after death of first wife, married Harriet Louise Fowler in 1857. Served briefly as army chaplain during the Civil War, but finding the duty arduous resigned to take post as clerk in Treasury Department in Washington, D.C., which he held until his death.

EDWARD COOTE PINKNEY (October 1, 1802–April 11, 1828) b. London, England. Seventh of ten children of Anna Maria Rodgers and William Pinkney of Maryland. Father served in London as U.S. commissioner negotiating claims adjustments under Jay Treaty. After two-year visit to Maryland, family returned to England in 1806 when father was named minister to Britain (served until 1811). In 1815 Pinkney was commissioned as navy midshipman, continuing in navy until father's death in 1822; stationed mostly in Mediterranean; fought pirates in West Indies and received citation for bravery, but frequently was at odds with superiors. In 1823 published the song "Look Out Upon the Stars, My Love" and *Rodolph, A Fragment*. Resigned his commission in 1824 (following a quarrel with his superior officer that nearly resulted in a duel). Practiced law in Baltimore; married Georgiana McCausland, with whom he had one child. Angered by reference to his father in John Neal's novel *Randolph* (1823), challenged Neal to a duel, but was rebuffed; another such challenge was issued to Stephen Simpson, editor of *Philadelphia Mercury*, in response to published statement that Pinkney interpreted as personal slur. Growing reputation as poet furthered by publication of *Poems* (1825). Traveled to Mexico in unsuccessful attempt to gain commission in Mexican Navy; forced to leave country after duel in which he killed his Mexican adversary; became ill. On his return became editor of *The Marylander*, newspaper supporting John Quincy Adams; after a few months, forced to resign due to failing health.

EDGAR ALLAN POE (January 19, 1809–October 7, 1849) b. Boston, Massachusetts. Second of three children of Elizabeth Arnold and David Poe; parents were traveling actors (Elizabeth won acclaim as an actress, while David was regarded as amateurish). Father abandoned family in 1809; mother moved frequently before her death in Richmond, Virginia, in December 1811. Poe and siblings became wards of different foster parents; Poe was taken into home of Frances and John Allan (a Richmond tobacco merchant) but was not legally adopted; name changed to Edgar Allan. Accompanied the Allans to Great Britain; attended schools in London, 1815–20. Family returned to Richmond in 1820; after periods of financial difficulty, Allan became wealthy due to a legacy in 1825. Poe attended private academies in Richmond. Early engagement to Elmira Royster disapproved by Allans and ultimately broken off by her family. Entered University of Virginia in 1826; lost money while gambling and Allan refused to honor debt; returned to Richmond but left household in 1827 after quarrel with Allan. Went to Boston; first book of poetry, *Tamerlane and Other Poems* (1827), published anonymously. Enlisted in U.S. Army under assumed name "Edgar A. Perry" and giving false age; stationed at Fort Independence in Boston harbor; transferred to Fort Moultrie, South Carolina. Partially reconciled with Allan at request of dying foster mother; with Allan's help secured appointment to U.S. Military Academy at West Point. Lived, while waiting for news of appointment, in Baltimore with brother William and aunt Maria Clemm; published second volume of poetry, *Al Aaraaf, Tamerlane and Minor Poems* (1829), favorably reviewed by John Neal. Entered West Point May 1830; dismissed (as he had sought to be) January 1831 for neglect of duty. In New York City, published *Poems by Edgar A. Poe: Second Edition* (1831). Returned to Baltimore and lived with Mrs. Clemm and her eight-year-old daughter, Virginia. Published short fiction in magazines; won recognition in 1833 when "Ms. Found in a Bottle" won competition sponsored by Baltimore *Saturday Visiter*. Through John Pendleton

Kennedy obtained editorial position with *Southern Literary Messenger* in 1835; contributed stories, book reviews, and poems. Married Mrs. Clemm's daughter Virginia, then 13 (license taken out in September 1835, probably followed by private ceremony; public marriage in May 1836, after Virginia turned 14). Disputes over salary, editorial independence, and Poe's drinking led to his resignation from the *Messenger*. Moved to New York with Virginia and Mrs. Clemm in February 1837; published *The Narrative of Arthur Gordon Pym* (1838). Moved to Philadelphia in spring or summer of 1838; became co-editor of *Burton's Gentleman's Magazine*, 1839–40; contributed stories including "The Fall of the House of Usher" and "William Wilson." First collection of stories, *Tales of the Grotesque and Arabesque*, published in two volumes in 1839. Left *Burton's*; attempted to start his own periodical, *The Penn Magazine*; corresponded with Thomas Holley Chivers, from whom he attempted to raise money for the magazine. Literary editor of *Graham's Magazine*, 1841–42; contributions included "The Murders in the Rue Morgue," "The Oval Portrait," and "The Masque of the Red Death." Virginia began to show early symptoms of tuberculosis. Met Dickens on 1842 visit to America. Three poems included in Rufus Griswold's *Poets and Poetry of America* (1842), but subsequent relations with Griswold were poor. Invited by James Russell Lowell to contribute to short-lived magazine *The Pioneer* (1843); contributed "The Tell-Tale Heart" and "Lenore." Won prize in 1843 for "The Gold-Bug"; toured with lecture on "Poets and Poetry of America," 1843–44. Continued to solicit funds for his own magazine, now called *The Stylus*. Moved to New York in 1844; worked on editorial staff of *New-York Evening Mirror* (1844–45), and formed friendship with its co-editor, Nathaniel Parker Willis; with "The Raven," published in the *Mirror* in 1845, achieved fame as poet; published *Tales* (a collection edited by Evert Duyckinck) and *The Raven and Other Poems*. Met Thomas Holley Chivers. Became editor and (on borrowed money) proprietor of *The Broadway Journal* (1845–46); in the *Mirror*, the *Journal*, and elsewhere, launched attack on plagiarisms allegedly committed by Longfellow; attacked in turn by defenders of Longfellow. Published series of sketches on "The Literati of New York" in *Godey's Lady's Magazine* in 1845; successfully sued Thomas Dunn English for libel in 1846 after English (with whom Poe had a fistfight the year before) responded harshly to criticism of him in one of the sketches. A discussion of Poe appeared in the *Revue des Deux Mondes* (1845), followed by translations of a number of his stories; Poe aware of growing French interest in his work. Suffered increasingly from illness and nervous depression. Virginia died of tuberculosis in winter of 1847. Had close relationships with many contemporary women writers, including Fanny Osgood, Elizabeth Ellet, and Sarah Helen Whitman (to whom he briefly became engaged in 1848). In 1848 lectured in New York on "The Universe" and published metaphysical treatise *Eureka*. Returned to Richmond; may have become engaged to childhood sweetheart Elmira Royster (now Elmira Shelton). Stopped in Baltimore on way to New York on literary business and later found in delirious condition there; died four days later. "The Bells" and "Annabel Lee" were published posthumously.

EPES SARGENT (September 27, 1813–December 30, 1880) b. Gloucester, Massachusetts. Son of Hannah Dane Coffin and Epes Sargent, shipmaster from old Gloucester family. When Sargent was five the family moved to Roxbury, where father worked as merchant before returning to maritime pursuits. Traveled for several months with his father in Russia. Extracts from his letters describing the journey appeared in the *Literary Journal* published by students of the Boston Latin School, from which Sargent graduated in 1829. Editor and writer on staff of *Boston Daily Advertiser* and *Boston Daily Atlas* (for whom he also served as Washington correspondent). Became involved in Whig politics and wrote *Life and Public Services of Henry Clay* (1842). Wrote a number of fairly successful plays—including *The Bride of Genoa* (1837) and *Velasco* (1839)—and was active as journalist in New York, working for *New-York Mirror* and *The New World*; edited his own short-lived *Sargent's New Monthly Magazine* (1843) and *Modern Standard Drama* (1846). First collection of poetry, *Songs of the Sea with Other Poems*, appeared in 1847. Returning to Boston, edited *Boston Transcript*, 1847–53. In 1848 married Elizabeth Weld of Roxbury. Published prolific quantity of poetry, fiction, plays, travel books, school texts, and miscellaneous anthologies, including *Harper's Cyclopedia of British and American Poetry* (issued posthumously in 1881). Later in life, spiritualism became chief interest, discussed in *Planchette, or the Despair of Science* (1869), *The Proof Palpable of Immortality* (1875), and *The Scientific Basis of Spiritualism* (1880).

EDMUND HAMILTON SEARS (April 6, 1810–January 16, 1876) b. Sandisfield, Massachusetts. Son of Lucy Smith and Joseph Sears, a farmer. Attended Westfield Academy briefly; in 1831 became student at Union College, Schenectady, New York, where he was an editor of college paper and won prize for poetry. Taught at Brattleboro, Vermont; studied theology. Graduated from Harvard Divinity School in 1837 and became missionary for American Unitarian Association, serving mostly in Toledo, Ohio. Subsequently ordained as Unitarian minister in Wayland, Massachusetts. Married Ellen Bacon in 1839, the year of his ordination; they had three sons and a daughter. In 1840 transferred to church in Lancaster, Massachusetts, but due to illness retired after seven years to a small farm in Wayland; health recovered and in 1848 he again became minister in Wayland. Best-known work, the hymn "It Came Upon the Midnight Clear," appeared in anthology *Five Christmas Hymns* in 1852. From 1859 to 1871 was an editor of *The Monthly Religous Magazine*. In 1866 became minister in Weston, Massachusetts. Published numerous theological and devotional writings, including *Regeneration* (1853), *Athanasia; or Foregleams of Immortality* (1858), *The Fourth Gospel, the Heart of Christ* (1872), and *Songs and Sermons of the Christian Life* (1875); also published two works of family history, *Pictures of the Olden Time as Shown in the Fortunes of a Family of Pilgrims* (1857) and *Genealogies and Biographical Sketches of the Ancestry and Descendants of Richard Sears* (1857). In 1874 received serious injuries in a fall from a tree, which led to his death two years later.

LYDIA HUNTLEY SIGOURNEY (September 1, 1791–June 10, 1865) b. Norwich, Connecticut. Daughter of Zerviah Wentworth and Ezekiel Huntley, a groundskeeper. Father employed by Mrs. Daniel Lathrop, in whose home Sigourney was born and to whom she dedicated many poems. Spent much time in Hartford with the family of Daniel Wadsworth, a wealthy art collector. Ran schools in Norwich (1811–12) and Hartford (1812–19). With Wadsworth's help, published *Moral Pieces in Prose and Verse* in 1815. Married Charles Sigourney, Hartford hardware merchant, in 1819 (they had a son and daughter, in addition to a son and two daughters from his previous marriage); despite his initial objections, turned to writing as career in order to supplement family income. Indian epic *Traits of the Aborigines* (1822) published anonymously, as were nearly all of her publications until 1833. Met Lafayette on his 1824 trip to Hartford. Major collection of poems published 1834, revised and reprinted numerous times afterward. Contributed prose and verse to many periodicals, including *The North American Review*, *Graham's Magazine*, and *Southern Literary Messenger*; published 67 books in her lifetime, including *How to Be Happy* (1833), *Letters to Young Ladies* (1833), *Olive Buds* (1836), *Pocahontas and Other Poems* (1841), *Poems, Religious and Elegiac* (1841), *The Voice of Flowers* (1846), *The Weeping Willow* (1847), *Water-drops* (1848), and *Whisper to a Bride* (1850); illustrated edition of collected poems published by Carey & Hart of Philadelphia in 1848. Widely popular and known as "the American Hemans" (in reference to the popular English poet Felicia Hemans); noted in particular for commemorative poems, which she frequently wrote on request. Traveled to Europe in 1840 where she was introduced to King Louis Philippe of France and made acquaintance of William Wordsworth, Thomas Carlyle, and Samuel Rogers; stirred controversy in England when, on her return, she published without permission a letter from Mrs. Robert Southey detailing the poet's final illness. Following son's early death, published his death-bed journal in *The Faded Hope* (1852). Active in many causes, including higher education for women and temperance. Died in Hartford. Her autobiography, *Letters of Life*, was published posthumously in 1866.

WILLIAM GILMORE SIMMS (April 17, 1806–June 11, 1870) b. Charleston, South Carolina. Son of Harriet Singleton and William Gilmore Simms, an Irish immigrant. Mother died in 1808; father, a merchant, moved to Tennessee and then to Mississippi Territory, serving as soldier in Indian wars under Andrew Jackson and establishing himself as planter. Simms remained in Charleston under the care of his maternal grandmother, despite repeated urgings by father for the boy to come live with him (father at one point attempted to have son abducted off the street and brought to him in Mississippi); Simms chose to remain with grandmother, although he later said that he regretted the decision. Served apprenticeship to pharmacist; after six years turned to study of law. From age 16 published verse in Charleston press. In 1824 made long visit to father's plantation in Mississippi and to Indian territory west of the Mississippi. Married Anna Malcolm Giles, city clerk's daughter, in 1826; they had a daughter. Admitted to South Carolina bar in 1827 (gave up law practice 1829). In the course of his life published over 30 volumes of fiction, 18 volumes of verse, and a variety of biographies, histories, geographies, political treatises, and literary essays. Early verse publications included *Monody on the Death of Gen. Charles Cotesworth Pinckney* (1825), *Lyrical and Other Poems* (1827), *Early Lays* (1827), *The Vision of Cortes, Cain, and Other Poems* (1829) and *The Tri-Color* (1830). Edited *Southern Literary Gazette* (1828–29) and *Charleston City Gazette* (1830–32); threatened with mob action for opposition to Nullification. Following death of wife Anna in 1832, visited New York, New Haven, and Boston; formed friendships with William Cullen Bryant and Evert Duyckinck. Achieved literary success with novels *Martin Faber* (1833), *Guy Rivers* (1834), and *The Yemassee* (1835). *The Partisan* (1835) was first of his best-known series, later known as "the Revolutionary Novels," concerned with South Carolina during Revolutionary War; subsequent volumes in series included *Mellichampe* (1836), *Katharine Walton* (1851), *Woodcraft* (1854), *The Forayers* (1855), and *Eutaw* (1856). Returned to Charleston and in 1836 married Chevillette Eliza Roach, daughter of prosperous plantation owner; they had 13 children. Settled at her family estate Woodlands; gradually took over management and eventually ownership. Continued to publish fiction at rapid rate, including *Richard Hurdis* (1838), *Border Beagles* (1840), *The Wigwam and the Cabin* (1845–46), and *The Cassique of Kiawah* (1859); wrote biographies of Francis Marion, Captain John Smith, Chevalier Bayard, and Nathanael Greene. Later volumes of poetry included *Atalantis* (1832), *Southern Passages and Pictures* (1839), *Donna Florida* (1843), *Areytos; or, Songs of the South* (1846), *Lays of the Palmetto* (1848), *The Cassique of Accabee* (1849), and *The City of the Silent* (1850); poems collected in *Poems: Descriptive, Legendary, and Contemplative* (1853). Edited *The Magnolia* (1842–43), *Simms's Magazine* (1845, subsequently absorbed into *Southern Literary Messenger*), and *The Southern Quarterly Review*, 1849–54. Became ardent defender of slavery; close friend and adviser of South Carolina senator James Henry Hammond; published *Slavery in America* (1838); contributed to *The Pro-Slavery Argument, as Maintained by the Most Distinguished Writers of the Southern States* (1852). Series of pro-slavery lectures in New York state in 1856 canceled after hostile public reaction in Buffalo and Rochester. Wife Chevillette died in 1863. Woodlands (already damaged by a fire in 1862) was destroyed by stragglers from Sherman's army in 1865; fled to Columbia, South Carolina, and witnessed its burning. After the war struggled to support family by fiction and journalistic pieces; edited newspapers *Columbia Phoenix* (1865), *Daily South Carolinian* (1865–66), and *Courier* (1870), and anthology *War Poetry of the South* (1867).

WILLIAM WETMORE STORY (February 12, 1819–October 7, 1895) b. Salem, Massachusetts. Sixth child of Sarah Waldo Wetmore and Joseph Story (Supreme Court justice and leading commentator on American law). When Story was ten, family moved to Cambridge, where Charles Sumner was close family friend; enjoyed early friendship with James Russell Lowell and Thomas

Wentworth Higginson. Graduated Harvard in 1838 and Harvard Law School in 1840; began practice as lawyer. Increasingly drawn to artistic career, devoting himself to poetry, music, painting, and sculpture. Contributed regularly to *Boston Miscellany* and formed part of discussion group meeting regularly at home of George Ripley. In 1843 married Emelyn Eldredge; they had four children. During 1840s published two standard works on law and served as a bankruptcy commissioner and court reporter for several federal courts. Delivered Phi Beta Kappa poem "Nature and Art" at Harvard in 1844. Upon father's death in 1845, commissioned by trustees of Mount Auburn Cemetery to execute memorial sculpture; traveled in 1847 to Italy with his family to prepare himself for the task. In Rome, Story and his wife became close friends of Margaret Fuller. While in Europe, prepared two-volume biography of his father, *The Life and Letters of Joseph Story* (1851). Published collections of poems in 1847 and 1856. Eldest son Joseph died in Rome in 1853. Returned briefly to America and to law practice, but in 1856 gave up legal career to devote himself to sculpture; returned to Rome, where he lived for the rest of his life. The Storys settled in an apartment in the Palazzo Barberini, where their neighbors and closest friends were Robert and Elizabeth Barrett Browning. Circle of acquaintances included Christopher Pearse Cranch, Fanny Trollope, William Makepeace Thackeray, Hans Christian Andersen, Charles Eliot Norton, Walter Savage Landor, Elizabeth Gaskell, Russell Sturgis, and John Lothrop Motley; later knew Henry James, who wrote biography *William Wetmore Story and His Friends* (1903). Supporter of Italian independence; acquainted with Mazzini and Cavour. Achieved celebrity as sculptor with exhibition of "Cleopatra" (described at length by Nathaniel Hawthorne in *The Marble Faun*) and "The Libyan Sibyl" at London International Exhibition of 1862; other subjects included Salome, Medea, Alcestis, and Saul; executed posthumous bust of Elizabeth Barrett Browning for her husband; in later years commissioned to create portrait sculptures of Josiah Quincy, Joseph Henry, Edward Everett, James Russell Lowell, Theodore Parker, and John Marshall. During Civil War, contributed letters to London *Daily News* in support of the Union, collected in *The American Question* (1862). Later poetry published in *Graffiti d'Italia* (1868). Wrote series of prose books about Italy, including *Roba di Roma* (1862), *Vallombrosa* (1881), and *Excursions in Arts and Letters* (1891); a novel, *Fiammetta* (1886); and a treatise on art, *The Proportions of the Human Figure* (1866). Made final trip to America in 1877; lectured on art. Served as U.S. Commissioner of Fine Arts to the World's Fair in Paris, 1879. Wife Emelyn died in 1894; he died the next year at his daughter's summer home in Vallombrosa. Sons Thomas Waldo Story and Julian Russell Story were also artists.

HENRY DAVID THOREAU (July 12, 1817–May 6, 1862) b. Concord, Massachusetts. Son of Cynthia Dunbar and John Thoreau; given name David Henry Thoreau. Father worked successively as farmer, grocer, teacher, and manufacturer of pencils; until 1850s, family frequently in difficult financial straits. After studying at Concord Academy, admitted to Harvard in 1833, barely passing entrance examinations. Met Orestes Brownson and studied

German with him; attended lectures on mineralogy, anatomy, and natural history; graduated 1837. Formed close relationship with Ralph Waldo Emerson, who had moved to Concord in 1834, and through him with others associated with Transcendentalist group, including Margaret Fuller, Bronson Alcott, Jones Very, and Theodore Parker. Worked in father's pencil business while beginning (in October 1837) to keep journal which eventually ran to over two million words in 47 manuscript volumes. Taught at Center School, Concord, in 1837, but resigned after being forced by superiors to flog students. With brother John, ran Concord Academy, 1838–41, teaching foreign languages and science. Regularly published poems and essays in *The Dial* (which he helped edit), beginning with first issue in July 1840. Met William Ellery Channing (poet and nephew of Unitarian minister of the same name), who became intimate friend and companion. Shocked by early death of brother John in 1842. Worked in Emerson's household as handyman, 1841–43; continued studies in classical literature; met Nathaniel Hawthorne. In 1845 built a cabin on property of Emerson's at Walden Pond, where he stayed for a little over two years. (During this time maintained active social life in Concord.) Spent a night in jail in 1846 for nonpayment of poll tax; explained his motives (protest against slavery and war with Mexico) in essay "Resistance to Civil Government" (1848, posthumously retitled "Civil Disobedience"). In October 1847 began ten-month residence at Emerson's house, looking after the family while Emerson traveled in Europe. First book, *A Week on the Concord and Merrimack Rivers* (1849), most of it written at Walden Pond, was based on boat trip made in 1839 with brother John; book sold only a few hundred copies. Traveled with Channing to Cape Cod in 1849. Relationship with Emerson became more distant. In 1850s supported himself as surveyor and continued to work in family business, now supplying ground lead for electrotyping. Increasingly involved in abolitionist movement; sheltered escaped slaves en route to Canada. *Walden*, on which he had worked since residence at pond, went through multiple revisions before publication in 1854; it proved unexpectedly successful, selling more than 1700 copies by year's end. Small circle of close friends included William Ellery Channing, F. B. Sanborn, and H.G.O. Blake. On 1856 visit to Brooklyn met Walt Whitman, who presented him with signed copy of *Leaves of Grass*. Met John Brown in 1857, and following Harpers Ferry raid delivered "A Plea for Captain John Brown" in Concord, Boston, and Worcester. Compiled information on relationship of climate to periodic biological phenomena. Worked for many years on projected study of American Indians, compiling thousands of pages of notes and extracts; in 1861 traveled to Minnesota, visiting Lower Sioux Agency at Redwood. Chronic tuberculosis that had flared several times previously became acute in winter of 1860–61. Died at home; his last intelligible words were "moose" and "Indian." *The Maine Woods* (1864) and *Cape Cod* (1865) were published posthumously.

JONES VERY (August 28, 1813–May 8, 1880) b. Salem, Massachusetts. Eldest of six children of Lydia Very and Jones Very (parents were cousins);

father was a privateer in War of 1812, and afterward master of Boston ship *Aurelia*. In 1823 accompanied father on board the *Aurelia* to Kronstadt, Russia. The following year, traveled with him to New Orleans; attended school there while father conducted business. After father's death in 1824, continued schooling for three more years. Began work as errand boy for Salem auctioneer; continued to receive tutoring from J. E. Worcester. In 1832 became assistant at Fisk Latin School under direction of Henry Kemble Oliver; while working there, gained academic credits and earned money for tuition, enabling him to enter Harvard as sophomore in 1834. At Harvard, was noted for studious habits, and won a number of academic prizes and honors. Appointed Greek tutor for freshman class (1836–38); began studies at Harvard Divinity School. Around this time, underwent powerful religious experience and began to write poems that he said were "communicated" to him. In December 1837 delivered essay on epic poetry (originally his Bowdoin Prize Essay at Harvard); Elizabeth Palmer Peabody heard it and recommended Very to Ralph Waldo Emerson as lecturer for Concord Lyceum. Very and Emerson met in April 1838 and formed close relationship. Very's colleagues at Harvard questioned his sanity and requested his withdrawal from academic duties; in September 1838 he entered McLean Asylum in Somerville, Massachusetts, remaining there for a month. Retained ties to Emerson, James Freeman Clarke, and other Transcendentalists, and won attestations of mental health from them; Emerson declared him "profoundly sane." Enjoyed close friendship with Harvard professor Edward Tyrrell Channing. In 1839 Clarke published 27 sonnets by Very in the *Western Messenger*, and Emerson oversaw preparation of *Essays and Poems*, which appeared in September 1839. Poetry won praise from a number of contemporaries, including William Cullen Bryant. Intensity of Very's religious fervor waned after 1840; relationship with Emerson cooled. Returned to Salem; after receiving license to preach from Cambridge Association, served in Eastport, Maine, and North Beverly, Massachusetts, and in Rhode Island. Several of Very's poems were adapted and reprinted in Samuel Longfellow and Samuel Johnson's widely used *A Book of Hymns for Public and Private Devotion* (1846). Continued to preach occasionally for most of his life, and wrote for newspapers; lived with his sisters (one of whom, Lydia Louise Ann Very, also published a volume of poetry).

SARAH HELEN WHITMAN (January 19, 1803–June 27, 1878) b. Providence, Rhode Island. Daughter of Anna Marsh and Nicholas Power, a seaman. Father left home when she was ten (he returned after an absence of 19 years and took up residence in a Providence hotel). Educated at private school in Providence; received further schooling at home of an aunt in Jamaica, Long Island. In 1828 married John Winslow Whitman, attorney and inventor; they lived in Boston until his death in 1833, when she returned to mother's home in Providence, where she lived for more than forty years; cared for younger sister Anna, who suffered from mental illness. Published first poem in Sarah Josepha Hale's *American Ladies' Magazine* in 1829; continued to contribute poetry and articles to magazines and newspapers. Formed friendship with Margaret Fuller during her residence in Providence as a schoolteacher (1836–38); other literary associates included George William Curtis, Henry Wadsworth Longfellow, and Rufus Griswold. In September 1848 met Edgar Allan Poe, who praised her poetry and to whom she had already dedicated a poem; after a few days' acquaintance he proposed marriage; following a stormy courtship, engagement broken off by Whitman in December 1848. (She later said that "had he kept his promise never again to taste wine, I should never have broken the engagement.") Rufus Griswold included a large selection of her poetry in *The Female Poets of America* (1849). Published articles on spiritualism in *New-York Tribune* in 1851; became a medium and held séances. Associated with causes of educational reform, Fourierism, women's rights, universal suffrage, and prevention of cruelty to animals. In 1853 published *Hours of Life and Other Poems*. Defended Poe's reputation in *Edgar Poe and His Critics* (1860); frequently supplied information on Poe to students and biographers. Collected verse appeared posthumously as *Poems* in 1879.

WALT WHITMAN   (May 31, 1819–March 26, 1892) b. West Hills, Huntington Township, New York. Son of Louisa Van Velsor and Walter Whitman, a farmer and carpenter; parents descended from early settlers on Long Island. Family moved to Brooklyn in 1823; attended Brooklyn public schools until about 1830. Learned printing trade on Brooklyn newspapers *Patriot* and *Star*; worked as printer until 1836. Taught school on Long Island, 1836–38. Founded and edited newspaper *The Long-Islander* (1838–39) at Huntington, New York; worked on Jamaica *Democrat*, publishing early poetry there; electioneered for Martin Van Buren. Moving to Manhattan in 1841, worked as compositor for *New World*; contributed fiction and journalistic sketches to a variety of newspapers and magazines, including *The Democratic Review*, and published temperance novel *Franklin Evans; or, The Inebriate* (1842). Returning to Brooklyn, worked for the *Star* (1845–46) and *Daily Eagle*, Democratic party newspaper (1846–48); discharged from latter for bias toward Free-Soil party. Went to New Orleans; edited *The Crescent* for three months; traveled in Missouri, Illinois, and upstate New York. On his return, founded and edited *Brooklyn Freeman* (1848–49); ran printing, bookselling, and house-building business. Published four topical poems in 1850, and the following year addressed Brooklyn Art Union. In 1855 published at his own expense *Leaves of Grass*, collection of twelve poems including what was eventually retitled "Song of Myself." Sent copy to Emerson, from whom he received letter of praise; received visit in Brooklyn from Bronson Alcott and Henry David Thoreau. Enlarged second edition of *Leaves of Grass* published the following year. Edited Brooklyn *Times* (1857–59). Frequented Pfaff's, New York beer cellar known as bohemian meeting place, where associates included Fitz-James O'Brien and Adah Isaacs Menken. Went to Boston in 1860 to oversee third, greatly enlarged edition of *Leaves of Grass* issued by Thayer and Eldridge; met Emerson, who urged him to delete sexually frank passages from

"Children of Adam" poems. Continued work as freelance journalist. After outbreak of Civil War visited sick, injured, and wounded at New-York Hospital; visited war front in Virginia in December 1862 upon learning that his brother George had been wounded. Settled in Washington, D.C., becoming volunteer nurse in military hospitals; supported himself by part-time clerical work in Army Paymaster's office. Returned to Brooklyn on sick leave in 1864. In Washington a year later, appointed to Department of Interior clerkship; fired by Interior Secretary, supposedly because of immorality of his poetry; worked subsequently as clerk in Attorney General's office, 1865–73. Poems of war and its aftermath published in *Drum-Taps* and *Sequel to Drum-Taps* (1865). Reputation defended by close friend William Douglas O'Connor in *The Good Gray Poet* (1866) and by naturalist John Burroughs in *Notes on Walt Whitman as Poet and Person* (1867); *Poems of Walt Whitman*, edited by William Michael Rossetti, published in London in 1868. New editions of *Leaves of Grass* published in 1867 and 1870; prose collected in *Democratic Vistas* (1871) and *Memoranda During the War* (1875); long poem *Passage to India*, inspired by opening of Suez Canal, published 1870. Suffered paralyzing stroke in 1873; left Washington for Camden, New Jersey, where he lived for the rest of his life. "Centennial" edition of *Leaves of Grass* published 1876 (identical to previous edition). Lectured in Philadelphia and New York; traveled to the west as far as Colorado in 1879 and to Canada in 1880. Visited in Camden by Oscar Wilde in 1882. *Leaves of Grass* (1881 edition) withdrawn by publisher James R. Osgood in April 1882 after threat of obscenity charge from Boston district attorney; reprinted in Philadelphia by Rees Welsh & Co. along with prose collection *Specimen Days and Collect*; notoriety led to increased sales. Suffered second stroke in 1888; in the same year published prose collection *November Boughs* and *Complete Poems and Prose*. Poems of his old age, *Good-Bye My Fancy* (1891), followed by final, so-called "deathbed" edition of *Leaves of Grass*. He had prepared an edition of his *Complete Prose Works* before his death in March 1892.

JOHN GREENLEAF WHITTIER (December 17, 1807–September 7, 1892) b. Haverhill, Massachusetts. Son of Abigail Hussey and John Whittier. Raised in devout Quaker household; little formal schooling. William Lloyd Garrison's *Newburyport Free Press* published poem "The Exile's Departure" in 1826; became friend of Garrison. Attended Haverhill Academy, 1827–28. Supported himself as shoemaker and schoolteacher. Edited *American Manufacturer* in Boston (1829) and *Essex Gazette* (1830) in Haverhill before becoming editor of the important *New England Weekly Review* (1830–32); formed friendship with Lydia Huntley Sigourney. Published *Legends of New England in Prose and Verse* (1831) and *Moll Pitcher* (1832). Active in support of National Republican candidates; delegate in 1831 to National Republican Convention in support of Henry Clay, and the following year ran unsuccessfully for Congress. Became deeply involved in anti-slavery movement; in *Justice and Expediency* (1833) urged immediate abolition. Elected as Whig for one term to Massachusetts legislature in 1834; mobbed and stoned in Concord, New

Hampshire, in 1835. Moved in 1836 to Amesbury, New Hampshire. Corresponding secretary for American Anti-Slavery Society from 1837. Edited *Pennsylvania Freeman* (1838–40); in May 1838, paper's offices burned and sacked during destruction of Pennsylvania Hall by mob. *Poems*, first authorized collection, published 1838. Split in 1839 with Garrison over the latter's more radical tactics; founded the Liberty party (1840); edited abolitionist gift book *The North Star*; worked on *The American and Foreign and Anti-Slavery Reporter* and *The Emancipator*. Ran for Congress as a Liberty candidate in 1842. Published *Lays of My Home* (1843). Edited *The Middlesex Standard* (1844–45) and *The Essex Transcript* (1845). Lobbied in Washington against the admission of Texas to the Union. Abolitionist verse collected in *Voices of Freedom* (1846); served as corresponding editor of *The National Era* (1847–60), contributing to it much poetry and prose. *The Supernaturalism of New England* published 1847. Collected edition of verse, *Poems by John G. Whittier*, published 1849, followed by *Leaves from Margaret Smith's Journal*, novel about 17th-century Massachusetts. Wrote "Ichabod" in 1850 in response to Daniel Webster's support of Fugitive Slave Law; supported senatorial candidacy of Charles Sumner. Published *Songs of Labor* (1850), *The Chapel of the Hermits* (1853), *The Panorama* (1856), *Home Ballads* (1860), and *In War Time* (1864), as well as prose collections *Old Portraits and Modern Sketches* (1850) and *Literary Recreations and Miscellanies* (1854). Worked for the formation of the Republican party; supported presidential candidacy of John C. Frémont in 1856. *Poetical Works* (1857) published; in same year helped found *Atlantic Monthly*. Close relationship with old friend Elizabeth Lloyd Howell led to consideration of marriage, but in 1859 Whittier decided against it. Was a member of the electoral college for Lincoln. Close friends included Bayard Taylor, Lucy Larcom, and Celia Thaxter. Most popular work, *Snow-Bound*, published 1866 and sold 20,000 copies; followed by *The Tent on the Beach* (1867), *Among the Hills* (1869), *Miriam and Other Poems* (1871), *Hazel-Blossoms* (1875), *The Vision of Echard* (1878), *St. Gregory's Guest* (1886), and *At Sundown* (1890). Campaigned against Massachusetts legislature's censure of Charles Sumner, 1873–74. From 1876 lived most of the time with cousins in Danvers, Massachusetts, while retaining legal residence in Amesbury. Formed close friendship with Sarah Orne Jewett and Annie Fields around 1881. Seventieth birthday dinner in 1877 attended by Ralph Waldo Emerson, Henry Wadsworth Longfellow, Mark Twain, Oliver Wendell Holmes, James Russell Lowell, William Dean Howells, and others. In 1879 received Jubilee Singers of Fisk University at his home, where they sang "Swing Low, Sweet Chariot" and other spirituals. Seven-volume Riverside Edition of his works, *The Writings of John Greenleaf Whittier*, published 1888–89. Corresponded with Helen Keller, 1889–90. Died at Hampton Falls, New Hampshire.

CARLOS WILCOX (October 23, 1794–May 29, 1827) b. Newport, New Hampshire. Father, a farmer, moved to Orwell, Vermont, when Wilcox was four. Health frail from early age; childhood knee injury made him unsuited for farming. Studied at Middlebury College (where he was valedictorian in

1813) and at Andover Theological Seminary, from which he graduated in 1817. Preached in several Connecticut towns, and was ordained pastor of North Church in Hartford in 1824. Only volume of poetry published in his lifetime was *The Age of Benevolence* (1822), self-published book containing first book of projected five-book poem, of which three additional books remained in manuscript at Wilcox's death. In 1824 read poem "The Religion of Taste" before Phi Beta Kappa Society of Yale. Left the pulpit in 1826 due to heart problems; resumed preaching in Danbury after several months of recuperation. The posthumous *Remains* (1828) contained sermons and extracts from later books of "The Age of Benevolence," "The Religion of Taste," and a biographical essay on Wilcox.

RICHARD HENRY WILDE (September 24, 1789–September 10, 1847) b. Dublin, Ireland. Son of Mary Newitt and Richard Wilde. Family arrived in Baltimore, Maryland, in 1797; shortly thereafter father's property, still in Dublin, was confiscated due to business partner's participation in Irish rebellion; family forced to depend upon father's income as ironmonger and hardware merchant. Following father's death in 1802, Wilde moved to Augusta, Georgia, in search of work, and after establishing himself with his older brother Michael, sent for his mother, who joined them in 1803; within two years, she opened a dry goods store with her sons' assistance. The family owned slaves and Wilde would later own several. Assisted by mother, Wilde educated himself; began to write poetry and essays; helped organized Thespian Society and Library Company of Augusta. Studied law privately; admitted to bar 1809; became acting attorney general of Georgia, 1811–13. Elected to House of Representatives, where he served 1815–17; close friend of Henry Clay. Married Caroline Buckle in 1819, with whom he had three sons (one of whom died in infancy); she died in 1827. Served briefly as mayor of Augusta, 1821–22. Wrote popular lyric "The Lament of the Captive" (frequently known by its first line, "My life is like the summer rose"), an excerpt from an unfinished epic based on adventures of brother James in Florida during Seminole War. The poem was first published without Wilde's permission in 1819; after it became a popular song (having been set to music without Wilde's involvement or authorization), authorship was claimed for Irish poet Patrick O'Kelly, who incorporated the lines in a lyric of his own. Wilde was accused of plagiarism, a charge complicated when friend Anthony Barclay, English consul at Savannah, as a practical joke in 1834 translated the poem into Greek and sent it to a friend, who attributed it to Alcaeus; following newspaper controversy, Wilde declared authorship. Elected to further terms in Congress, 1827–35; opposed Jacksonians and failed to win reelection in 1834; retired from politics. In poor health, traveled to Europe in 1835 and settled in Florence; while in Italy met Horatio Greenough, Hiram Powers, Charles Sumner, and Edward Everett; translated Italian poetry and worked on biography (never completed) of Dante and unpublished study "The Italian Lyric Poets." Engaged in research in libraries and private collections; through his researches, instrumental in 1840 recovery of Giotto's portrait of Dante in the

Bargello by removing layer of whitewash. Returned to Augusta in difficult financial straits in 1841; published two-volume study of Italian poet Tasso, *Conjectures and Researches Concerning the Love, Madness, and Imprisonment of Torquato Tasso* (1842), which included translations of Tasso's poems. Worked for years on *Hesperia*, long poem in four cantos, never completed; poem, unpublished during Wilde's lifetime, was eventually edited by his son William Cumming Wilde and published in 1867. Established law practice in New Orleans in 1843; became professor of constitutional law at newly established University of Louisiana (now Tulane University). Died during yellow fever epidemic in New Orleans.

NATHANIEL PARKER WILLIS (January 20, 1806–January 20, 1867) b. Portland, Maine. Son of Hannah Parker and Nathaniel Willis. Grandfather and father both newspaper publishers. Raised in Boston; attended Boston Latin School and Phillips Andover. Published first poems at age 17 in father's newspaper; entered Yale in 1823 and published first book, *Sketches*, volume of Biblical paraphrases in verse, in 1827, the year of his graduation. Embarked on journalistic career, working for Samuel G. Goodrich as an editor of *The Legendary* (1828) and gift book *The Token* (1829) before establishing *American Monthly Magazine* (1829–31) in Boston, writing most of it himself. Continued to build poetic reputation with *Fugitive Poetry* (1829) and *Poems Delivered before the Society of United Brothers* (1831). Moved to New York in 1831; contributing editor on George Pope Morris's *New-York Mirror*, 1831–36; in 1831 went to Europe as foreign correspondent for *Mirror*, detailing travels in Europe and Asia Minor in newspaper pieces eventually collected in *Pencillings by the Way* (1835). Toured western Europe and Middle East; settled in England, where friends and acquaintances included Walter Savage Landor, Charles and Mary Lamb, Joanna Baillie, Jane Porter, Thomas Moore, and Mary Russell Mitford. In 1835 married Mary Stace, daughter of General William Stace; they had a daughter, Imogen. While in England, came under attack for indiscreet revelations of private conversations in American press; attacked in print by Harriet Martineau and Frederick Marryat. Returned to America in 1836. Two plays were produced in New York, *Bianca Visconti* (1837) and *Tortesa, or the Usurer Matched* (1839), the latter enjoying some popularity. Journalistic pieces and travel sketches collected in *Inklings of Adventure* (1836), *A l'Abri; or, the Tent Pitch'd* (1839), *American Scenery* (1840), *Loiterings of Travel* (1840), and *The Scenery and Antiquities of Ireland* (1842). Collections of poetry included *Melanie* (1835), *Poems of Passion* (1843), *The Lady Jane, and Other Humorous Poetry* (1843), *Poems, Sacred, Passionate, and Humorous* (1844), and *Poems of Early and After Years* (1848). With Dr. T. O. Porter, founded weekly *The Corsair*, 1839–40; after its failure, again entered into partnership with Morris as co-owner and co-editor of *New Mirror* (1843–44), succeeded by *Evening Mirror* and its supplement *Weekly Mirror* (1844–45). Employed Poe on *Mirror*; the two became friends. A year after first wife Mary's death in childbirth in 1845, married Cornelia Grinnell, 20 years his junior; with Cornelia had two daughters and two sons. From 1846, again in partnership with Morris on

National Press (soon renamed *The Home Journal*). Achieved fame as chronicler of New York fashionable life and writer of light fiction, in the pages of the *Journal* and in such collections as *Lectures on Fashion* (1844), *Dashes at Life with a Free Pencil* (1845), *Rural Letters* (1849), *People I Have Met* (1850), *Life Here and There* (1850), *Hurry-Graphs* (1851), and *Fun Jottings* (1853); characterized in James Russell Lowell's *A Fable for Critics* as "the topmost bright bubble on the wave of the Town." In 1849 published article defending Poe's reputation from the attacks of Rufus Griswold. His work and character came under harsh criticism from sister Sarah Payson Willis, who under pseudonym Fanny Fern satirized him in her novel *Ruth Hall* (1854) for his refusal to give her financial assistance or literary encouragement. Became involved in divorce trial of actor Edwin Forrest, siding with Mrs. Forrest and suffering a physical attack by Forrest (who accused of Willis of illicit conduct with his wife) in Washington Square Park. As health declined, traveled in Bermuda and West Indies, writing up journey in *Health Trip to the Tropics* (1853). In 1853 retired with wife and children to country home Idlewild near Tarrytown, New York, not far from Washington Irving's Sunnyside; journalism collected in *Famous Persons and Famous Places* (1854), *Out-doors at Idlewild* (1855), *The Rag-Bag* (1855), and *The Convalescent* (1859). Novel of European-American relations, *Paul Fane* (1857), was unsuccessful. With Morris, edited *The Prose and Poetry of Europe and America* (1857). During Civil War, stayed in Washington as correspondent and enjoyed friendship with Mrs. Lincoln. Following death of Morris in 1864, took on full editorship of *Home Journal*; health failed rapidly. Pallbearers at funeral included Richard Henry Dana, Henry Wadsworth Longfellow, Oliver Wendell Holmes, and James Russell Lowell.

SAMUEL WOODWORTH (January 13, 1785–December 9, 1842) b. Scituate, Massachusetts. Son of Abigail Bryant and Benjamin Woodworth, a farmer who fought in American Revolution. At 16 went to Boston and apprenticed himself to printer Benjamin Russell (publisher of *The Columbian Centinel*), remaining with him until 1806. From an early age embarked on journalistic enterprises, the earliest of which was *The Fly* (1805–06), a juvenile paper in which John Howard Payne was involved. Went to New Haven, Connecticut; founded *The Belles-Lettres Repository*, which lasted two months; moved to Baltimore, Maryland, where his stay was also brief. In 1809 settled permanently in New York. Early in his career published three volumes of satirical poetry— *New-Haven* (1809), *Beasts at Law* (1811), *Quarter-Day* (1812)—and some popular verses on War of 1812. Married Lydia Reeder in 1810; they had a large family. Continued to work as printer but attempted to augment income through publishing and editing long series of publications, most of brief duration. These included *The War* (1812–14), a weekly devoted to events of War of 1812, *The Halcyon Luminary and Theological Repository* (1812–13), a journal devoted to Swedenborgianism (which Woodworth espoused), *The Ladies' Literary Cabinet* (1819–22), *Woodworth's Literary Casket* (1821), *The New-Jerusalem Missionary* (1823–24), another Swedenborgian publication, and *The Parthenon* (1827). After his friend George Pope Morris founded *New-York Mirror* in 1823,

Woodworth became editor, but withdrew after a year. Author of a large quantity of newspaper verse, often published under pseudonym Selim. His best-known poems were "The Bucket" (better known as "The Old Oaken Bucket") and "The Hunters of Kentucky" (both included in *Melodies, Duets, Songs, and Ballads*, 1826). A novel, *The Champions of Freedom* (1819), took the War of 1812 for its background. Wrote a number of plays, including *The Deed of Gift* (1822), *La Fayette* (1824), and *The Forest Rose* (1825), which achieved popularity for the comic Yankee character Jonathan Ploughboy. Literary and publishing endeavors did not lift him out of poverty; theatrical benefits were given in 1828 and 1829 to provide financial relief. Suffered stroke in February 1837 and was paralyzed for the remainder of his life.

Note on the Texts

The choice of text for each of the poems selected for inclusion in this volume has been made on the basis of a study of its textual history and a comparison of editions printed during the author's lifetime, along with relevant manuscripts, periodical appearances, contemporary anthologies, and posthumous editions. In general, each text is from the earliest book edition prepared with the author's participation; revised editions are sometimes followed, in light of the degree of authorial supervision and the stage of the writer's career at which the revisions were made, but the preference has been for the authorially approved book version closest to the date of composition. For some popular poems widely disseminated in periodicals, however, the early periodical versions have been preferred; for example, Francis Scott Key's late revisions to "The Star-Spangled Banner" in his collected poems have been rejected in favor of the earlier periodical version (printed here as "Defence of Fort McHenry"). Manuscript sources (such as those for Thoreau's "Guido's Aurora," "Music," and "Inspiration") have been used only when no printed text appears to be authoritative.

The following is a list of the sources of all the texts included in this volume, listed alphabetically by the authors of the poems.

John Quincy Adams. The Wants of Man; To the Sun-Dial; To Sally: *Poems of Religion and Society* (New York: William Graham, 1850).

A. Bronson Alcott. Sonnet XIV; Sonnet XVIII; Sonnet XIX: *Sonnets and Canzonets* (Boston: Roberts Brothers, 1882).

Washington Allston. *from* The Sylphs of the Seasons; On a Falling Group in the Last Judgement of Michael Angelo; On the Group of the Three Angels Before the Tent of Abraham, by Raffaelle, in the Vatican; On Seeing the Picture of Æolus by Peligrino Tibaldi, in the Institute at Bologna; On Rembrant; Occasioned by His Picture of Jacob's Dream; On the Luxembourg Gallery; To My Venerable Friend, the President of the Royal Academy: *The Sylphs of the Seasons* (London: W. Pople, 1813). America to Great Britain: Samuel Taylor Coleridge (ed.), *Sibylline Leaves* (London: Rest Fenner, 1817). Coleridge: Rufus Griswold (ed.), *Gems from the American Poets* (Philadelphia: H. Hooker, 1844). Art; On the Statue of an Angel, by Bienaimé; On Kean's Hamlet; A Word: Man; On Michael Angelo; Rubens: *Lectures on Art, and Poems* (New York: Baker & Scribner, 1850).

Joel Barlow. *from* The Columbiad: *The Columbiad* (Philadelphia: C. & A. Conrad & Co.; Baltimore: Conrad, Lucas and Company, 1809). Advice to a Raven in Russia: *Huntington Library Quarterly*, October 1938. Reprinted with the permission of the Henry E. Huntington Library.

Manoah Bodman. *from* An Oration on Death: *An Oration on Death* (Williamsburgh, Massachusetts: Ephraim Whitman, 1817).

Charles Timothy Brooks. Our Island Home; Lines: Composed at the Old Temples of Maralipoor: *Poems, Original and Translated* (Boston: Roberts Brothers, 1885).

Maria Gowen Brooks. *from* Zophiël, or the Bride of Seven: Canto the Third, Palace of the Gnomes; Composed at the Request of a Lady, and Descriptive of Her Feelings: *Zophiël; or, The Bride of Seven* (Boston: Hilliard, Gray & Co., 1834).

William Cullen Bryant. Thanatopsis; "I Cannot Forget With What Fervid Devotion"; To a Waterfowl; Inscription for the Entrance to a Wood; Green River; A Winter Piece; "Oh Fairest of the Rural Maids"; The Ages; The Rivulet; Summer Wind; An Indian at the Burying-Place of His Fathers; After a Tempest; Autumn Woods; November; Forest Hymn; The Conjunction of Jupiter and Venus; October; The Damsel of Peru; To an American Painter Departing for Europe; To the Fringed Gentian: *Poems* (New York: E. Bliss, 1832). The Prairies: *Poems* (New York: Harper & Brothers, 1836). The Fountain; The Painted Cup: *Poems: Third Edition* (Philadelphia: Carey & Hart, 1847). The Night Journey of a River; The Constellations; Dante: *Poems, Collected and Arranged by the Author* (New York: D. Appleton & Co., 1872).

Josiah D. Canning. The Indian Gone!: *Poems* (Greenfield, Massachusetts: Phelps & Ingersoll, 1838).

William Ellery Channing. The Harbor: *Poems* (Boston: Little & Brown, 1843). Hymn of the Earth; The Barren Moors; Walden: *Poems: Second Series* (Boston: James Munroe, 1847). Murillo's Magdalen: F. B. Sanborn (ed.), *Poems of Sixty-Five Years* (Philadelphia and Concord: James H. Bentley, 1902).

Lydia Maria Child. The New-England Boy's Song About Thanksgiving Day: *Flowers for Children* (New York: C. S. Francis, 1844).

Thomas Holley Chivers. To Isa Sleeping: *The Lost Pleiad* (New York: Edward O. Jenkins, 1845). Avalon: *Eonchs of Ruby: A Gift of Love* (New York: Spalding & Shepard, 1851). Apollo; Lily Adair; The Wind: *Virginalia; or, Songs of My Summer Nights* (Philadelphia: Lippincott, Grambo, 1853).

Thomas Cole. "I saw a Cave of sable depth profound"; A Painter; Lines Suggested by Hearing Music on the Boston Common at Night; The Voyage of Life, Part 2nd; The Dial; Lago Maggiore: Thomas Cole Papers, Manuscripts and Special Collections section, New York State Library. The Lament of the Forest: *The Knickerbocker*, June 1841.

Philip Pendleton Cooke. Florence Vane; Orthone: *Froissart Ballads and Other Poems* (Philadelphia: Carey & Hart, 1847).

Christopher Pearse Cranch. Correspondences; Gnosis: *Poems* (Philadelphia: Carey & Hart, 1844). The Bird and the Bell; The Cataract Isle; In the Palais Royal Garden; Cornucopia; The Spirit of the Age; The Evening Primrose; December; My Old Palette; Music; Bird Language: *The Bird and the Bell, with Other Poems* (Boston: James R. Osgood & Co., 1875). An Old Cat's Confession: *The Riverside Magazine for Young People*, Vol. IV, 1870. *from* Seven Wonders of the World: *Ariel and Caliban with Other Poems* (Boston and New York: Houghton, Mifflin & Co., 1887).

Richard Henry Dana. The Dying Raven; The Pleasure Boat; Daybreak; The Husband's and Wife's Grave: *Poems* (Boston: Bowles & Dearborn, 1827). The Chanting Cherubs: *Poems and Prose Writings* (Boston: Russell, Odiorne & Co., 1833).

Samuel Henry Dickson. Song—Written at the North: *Verses* (privately printed, 1843).

Joseph Rodman Drake. The Mocking-Bird: *The Portfolio*, May 1812. The National Painting: *The National Advocate*, March 15, 1819. *from* The Culprit Fay; The American Flag; Niagara; To a Friend; Bronx: *The Culprit Fay and Other Poems* (New York: George Dearborn, 1835).

Ralph Waldo Emerson. The Sphinx; Each and All; The Problem; To Rhea; The Visit; Uriel; The World-Soul; Mithridates; Hamatreya; The Rhodora; The Humble-Bee; The Snow-Storm; *from* Woodnotes II; *from* Monadnoc; Fable; Ode, Inscribed to W. H. Channing; Astræa; Compensation; Forerunners; Sursum Corda; Give All to Love; Eros; *from* Initial, Dæmonic, and Celestial Love; Merlin I; Merlin II; Bacchus; Merops; Saadi; Xenophanes; The Day's Ration; Blight; Musketaquid; Threnody; Hymn: Sung at the Completion of the Concord Monument: *Poems* (Boston: James Munroe & Company, 1847). Brahma; Freedom; Voluntaries; Days; Sea-Shore; Song of Nature; Two Rivers; Waldeinsamkeit; Terminus; Suum Cuique; Memory; Compensation ("The wings of Time are black and white"); Spiritual Laws; Art; Experience; Fate; Worship: *May-Day and Other Pieces* (Boston: Ticknor & Fields, 1867). The Harp; Wealth: *Selected Poems* (Boston: James R. Osgood & Co., 1876). Nature (1836): *Nature; Addresses, and Lectures* (Boston: James Munroe & Co., 1849). History; Self-Reliance; Circles: *Essays: First Series* (Boston: James Munroe & Co., 1847). Nature (1844); Nominalist and Realist: *Essays: Second Series* (Boston: James Munroe & Co., 1844). Illusions: *The Conduct of Life* (Boston: Ticknor & Fields, 1860). Grace; "Awed I behold once more"; "Dear brother, would you know the life"; "Who knows this or that"; Intellect; "The patient Pan"; Maia: Ralph H. Orth et al. (eds.), *The Poetry Notebooks of Ralph Waldo Emerson* (Columbia, Missouri: University of Missouri Press, 1986). Copyright © 1986 by The Ralph Waldo Emerson Memorial Association.

Daniel Decatur Emmett. Dixie's Land: Sheet music, ca. 1860 (New York: Firth & Pond). Boatman's Dance: *Songs of the Virginia Minstrels* (Boston: C. H. Keith, 1843).

Thomas Dunn English. Ben Bolt: *American Ballads* (New York: Harper & Brothers, 1879).

Philip Freneau. On the Civilization of the Western Aboriginal Country: *True American*, July 20, 1822. On the Great Western Canal of the State of New York: *Fredonian*, August 8, 1822. To Mr. Blanchard, the Celebrated Aeronaut in America: *New York Weekly Museum*, September 21, 1816. On the Conflagrations at Washington: *A Collection of Poems on American Affairs* (New York: David Longworth, 1815).

Margaret Fuller. Sistrum: Arthur Fuller (ed.), *Life Without and Life Within*

(Boston: Brown, Taggart, & Chase, 1860). Flaxman: *Julia Ward Howe, Margaret Fuller* (Boston: Roberts Brothers, 1883).

Fitz-Greene Halleck. On the Death of Joseph Rodman Drake; Alnwick Castle; Marco Bozzaris: *Alnwick Castle, with Other Poems* (New York: G. & C. Carvill, 1827). Red Jacket: *Alnwick Castle,* second edition (New York: George Dearborn, 1836). *from* Connecticut: *Poetical Works* (New York: Redfield, 1852).

Nathaniel Hawthorne. "I left my low and humble home": *The Spectator,* August 21, 1820; "Oh could I raise the darken'd veil": *The Spectator,* September 4, 1820; The Ocean: *Salem Gazette* XXXIX, August 26, 1825. Reprinted by permission of Nathaniel Hawthorne Papers, James Duncan Phillips Library, Peabody & Essex Museum, Salem, Massachusetts.

Josiah Gilbert Holland. *from* The Marble Prophecy: *The Marble Prophecy and Other Poems* (New York: Scribner, Armstrong & Co., 1872).

Oliver Wendell Holmes. Old Ironsides: *Poems* (Boston: Otis, Broaders, 1836). The Chambered Nautilus; The Living Temple; The Deacon's Masterpiece: Or The Wonderful "One-Hoss-Shay"; Contentment; The Voiceless: *The Autocrat of the Breakfast-Table* (Boston: Phillips, Sampson & Co., 1858). The Two Streams: *The Professor at the Breakfast-Table* (Boston: Ticknor & Fields, 1860). *from* Wind-Clouds and Star-Drifts: III. Sympathies: *The Poet at the Breakfast-Table* (Boston: J. R. Osgood & Co., 1872). Nearing the Snow-Line: *Songs of Many Seasons* (Boston: James R. Osgood & Co., 1875). The Flaneur; Prelude to a Volume Printed in Raised Letters for the Blind: *Before the Curfew* (Boston: Houghton & Mifflin, 1888).

George Moses Horton. On Liberty and Slavery; On Hearing of the Intention of a Gentleman to Purchase the Poet's Freedom: *The Hope of Liberty* (Raleigh: Gales & Son, 1829).

Julia Ward Howe. My Last Dance: *Passion-Flowers* (Boston: Ticknor, Reed & Fields, 1853). Battle-Hymn of the Republic: *Later Lyrics* (Boston: J.E. Tilton & Co., 1887).

Fanny Kemble. To the Wissahiccon; Impromptu: *Poems* (Philadelphia: John Penington, 1844).

Francis Scott Key. Defence of Fort McHenry: *Analectic Magazine,* 1814.

Abraham Lincoln. My Childhood-Home I See Again: Roy P. Basler (ed.), *The Collected Works of Abraham Lincoln* (New Brunswick, New Jersey: Rutgers University Press, 1953–55).

Henry Wadsworth Longfellow. The Spirit of Poetry; Hymn to the Night: *Voices of the Night* (Cambridge: John Owen, 1839). A Psalm of Life; Seaweed; Curfew: *Poems* (Philadelphia: Carey & Hart, 1845). The Wreck of the Hesperus: *Poems* (Boston: Ticknor & Fields, 1856). The Village Blacksmith; The Skeleton in Armour: *Ballads and Other Poems* (Cambridge: John Owen, 1842). The Warning: *Poems on Slavery* (Cambridge: John Owen, 1842). Mezzo Cammin: Samuel Longfellow, *Life of Henry Wadsworth Longfellow,* vol. 1 (Boston: Ticknor & Co., 1886). The Day Is Done; Afternoon in February; The Bridge; The Evening Star; Autumn: *The Belfry of Bruges and Other Poems* (Cambridge: John Owen, 1846). The Fire of Drift-

Wood: *The Seaside and the Fireside* (Boston: Ticknor, Reed & Fields, 1850). *from* Evangeline: *Evangeline* (Boston: W.D. Ticknor & Co., 1847). The Jewish Cemetery at Newport; My Lost Youth: *The Courtship of Miles Standish and Other Poems* (Boston: Ticknor & Fields, 1858). *from* The Song of Hiawatha: *The Song of Hiawatha* (Boston: Ticknor & Fields, 1855). The Children's Hour; Prelude: The Wayside Inn; Snow-Flakes: *Tales of a Wayside Inn* (Boston: Ticknor & Fields, 1863). The Landlord's Tale: Paul Revere's Ride: *Poetical Works* (Boston: Ticknor & Fields, 1866). The Spanish Jew's Tale: Azrael; Aftermath: *Aftermath* (Boston: James R. Osgood, 1873). Divina Commedia: *Complete Works*: Revised Edition, vol. 4 (Boston: James R. Osgood, 1873). Belisarius; Chaucer: *The Masque of Pandora and Other Poems* (Boston: James R. Osgood, 1875). Kéramos; Venice; The Harvest Moon: *Kéramos and Other Poems* (Boston: Houghton, Osgood & Co., 1878). The Cross of Snow: Samuel Longfellow, *Life of Henry Wadsworth Longfellow*, vol. 2 (Boston: Ticknor & Co., 1886). The Tide Rises, the Tide Falls: *Poetical Works*, Subscription Edition (Boston: Houghton, Osgood & Co., 1880). Night: *Ultima Thule* (Boston: Houghton, Mifflin & Co., 1880). Couplet: February 24, 1847; Fragment: December 18, 1847; The Poet's Calendar; *from* Elegiac Verse; The Bells of San Blas: *In the Harbor. Ultima Thule—Part II* (Boston: Houghton, Mifflin & Co., 1882).

James Russell Lowell. *from* The Present Crisis: *Poems, Second Series* (Boston: George Nichols, 1848). *from* A Fable for Critics: *A Fable for Critics* (New York: G. P. Putnam, 1848, second printing). *from* The Biglow Papers: Letter Six—The Pious Editor's Creed: *The Biglow Papers* (Boston: George Nichols, 1848). *from* The Vision of Sir Launfal: Prelude to Part the First: *The Vision of Sir Launfal* (Cambridge, Massachusetts: George Nichols, 1848). Remembered Music—A Fragment: *Poems, Second Series* (Boston: George Nichols, 1848). *from* Under the Willows; Ode Recited at the Harvard Comemoration, July 21, 1865: *Under the Willows and Other Poems* (Boston: Fields, Osgood & Co., 1869).

Cornelius Mathews. *from* Poems on Man in His Various Aspects Under the American Republic: *Poems on Man in His Various Aspects Under the American Republic* (New York: Wiley & Putnam, 1843).

Clement Moore. A Visit from St. Nicholas: *Poems* (New York: Bartlett & Welford, 1844).

George Pope Morris. The Oak: *The Deserted Bride and Other Poems* (New York: Adlard & Saunders, 1838).

John Neal. *from* The Battle of Niagara: *The Battle of Niagara . . . and Goldau* (Baltimore: N. G. Maxwell, 1818).

James Kirke Paulding. *from* The Backwoodsman: *The Backwoodsman* (Philadelphia: M. Thomas, 1818).

John Howard Payne. Home, Sweet Home!: *Clari; or, The Maid of Milan* (London: John Miller, 1823).

James Gates Percival. The Coral Grove: *Poems* (New York: Wiley, 1823).

John Pierpont. *from* Airs of Palestine: *Airs of Palestine* (Baltimore: B. Edes, 1816). *from* A Word from a Petitioner; The Fugitive Slave's Apostrophe to the North Star: *Airs of Palestine, and Other Poems* (Boston: James Munroe and Co., 1840).

Edward Coote Pinkney. Italy; The Voyager's Song; To . . . .; Serenade; A Health; On Parting; The Widow's Song: *Poems* (Baltimore: Joseph Robinson, 1825).

Edgar Allan Poe. "Stanzas": *Tamerlane and Other Poems* (Boston: Calvin F. S. Thomas, 1827). The Lake— To——; To Science; Al Aaraaf; Romance; Fairy-Land; To Helen; The Valley of Unrest; The City in the Sea; To F——; Silence: *The Raven and Other Poems* (New York: Wiley & Putnam, 1845). "Alone"; Israfel; The Haunted Palace; The Bells: Reprinted by permission of the publishers from *The Collected Works of Edgar Allan Poe*, Volume I, Thomas Ollive Mabbott, editor, Cambridge, Mass.: The Belknap Press of Harvard University Press, Copyright © 1969 by the President and Fellows of Harvard College. The Coliseum; For Annie: Rufus Wilmot Griswold (ed.), *The Works of the Late Edgar Allan Poe* (New York: J. S. Redfield, 1850–56). The Conqueror Worm; Dream-Land; Ulalume— A Ballad: Floyd Stovall (ed.), *The Poems of Edgar Allan Poe* (Charlottesville, Virginia: University Press of Virginia, 1965; reprinted by permission). Lenore: *Richmond Daily Whig*, September 18, 1849. The Raven: *Semi-Weekly Examiner* (Richmond), September 25, 1849. Eldorado: *Flag of Our Union* (Boston) April 12, 1849. Annabel Lee: *Southern Literary Messenger* (Richmond, Va.) November 1849.

Epes Sargent. The Planet Jupiter; The Sea-Breeze at Matanzas; Rockall: *Songs of the Sea, with Other Poems* (Boston: James Munroe & Co., 1847).

Edmund Hamilton Sears. "It came upon the midnight clear": *Songs and Sermons of the Christian Life* (Boston: Noyes, Holmes, 1875).

Lydia Huntley Sigourney. Indian Names: *Poems* (Philadelphia: Key & Biddle, 1834).

William Gilmore Simms. The Lost Pleiad: *The Vision of Cortes, Cain, and Other Poems* (Charleston: James S. Burges, 1829). By the Swanannoa: *Grouped Thoughts and Scattered Fancies* (Richmond: William Macfarlane, 1845). *from* The City of the Silent: *The City of the Silent* (Charleston: Walker & James, 1850). The New Moon: *Poems* (New York: Redfield, 1853).

William Wetmore Story. Cleopatra: *Graffiti d'Italia* (Edinburgh & London: William Blackwood & Sons, 1868). *from* A Contemporary Criticism: *Poems* (Edinburgh & London: William Blackwood & Sons, 1885).

Henry David Thoreau. "They who prepare my evening meal below"; "On fields oer which the reaper's hand has passd"; Fog: John C. Broderick (general ed.), *The Writings of Henry David Thoreau: Journal, Vol. 1: 1837–1844*. Copyright © 1981 by Princeton University Press. Reprinted by permission. "Dong, sounds the brass in the east"; Rumors from an Æolian Harp; "My life has been the poem I would have writ"; "I am a parcel of vain strivings tied": *A Week on the Concord and Merrimack Rivers* (Boston: Ticknor & Fields, 1868). "Light-winged Smoke, Icarian bird": *Walden* (Boston: Ticknor & Fields, 1854). Guido's Aurora; Music: The Pierpont Morgan Library, New York. MA 920. Inspiration: Photograph of a lost manuscript offered for sale in 1924 with the Stephen H. Workman collection.

Jones Very. The New Birth; "In Him we live, & move, & have our being"; The Morning Watch; The Garden; The Song; The Latter Rain; The Dead; Thy Brother's Blood; The Earth; The Cup; The New World; The New Man; The Created; Autumn Leaves; The Hand and the Foot; The Eye and Ear; Yourself; The Lost; The Prayer; The Cottage; The Strangers; The Wild Rose of Plymouth; The Lament of the Flowers; Autumn Flowers; The Origin of Man, I: Helen Deese (ed.), *Jones Very: The Complete Poems* (University of Georgia Press, 1993); copyright © 1993 Helen R. Deese.

Sarah Helen Whitman. To ——: *Poems* (Boston: Houghton, Osgood & Co., 1879).

Walt Whitman. *Leaves of Grass* (1855): *Leaves of Grass* (Brooklyn, 1855). from *Leaves of Grass* (1860): *Leaves of Grass* (Boston: Thayer & Eldridge, 1860). from *Leaves of Grass* (1891–92): *Leaves of Grass* (Philadelphia: David McKay, 1891–92).

John Greenleaf Whittier. Proem: *Poems* (Boston: B. B. Mussey & Co., 1849). Song of Slaves in the Desert; The Haschish; Maud Muller; The Barefoot Boy: *The Panorama* (Boston: Ticknor & Fields, 1856). *from* Songs of Labor: Dedication; Ichabod!: *Songs of Labor and Other Poems* (Boston: Ticknor, Reed & Fields, 1850). Astræa; First-Day Thoughts: *The Chapel of the Hermits and Other Poems* (Boston: Ticknor & Fields, 1852). Skipper Ireson's Ride; Telling the Bees; My Playmate: *Home Ballads and Poems* (Boston: Ticknor & Fields, 1860). Barbara Frietchie: *In War Time and Other Poems* (Boston: Ticknor & Fields, 1868). What the Birds Said: *The Tent on the Beach and Other Poems* (Boston: Ticknor & Fields, 1867). Snow-Bound: *Snow-Bound* (Boston: Ticknor & Fields, 1866). from *Among the Hills: Prelude*: *Among the Hills and Other Poems* (Boston: Fields, Osgood & Co., 1869). My Triumph: *Miriam and Other Poems* (Boston: Fields, Osgood & Co., 1871). Burning Drift-Wood: *At Sundown* (Cambridge: Riverside, 1890).

Carlos Wilcox. *from* The Age of Benevolence: *Remains* (Hartford: Hopkins, 1828).

Richard Henry Wilde. The Lament of the Captive: *New York Mirror*, February 28, 1835. To the Mocking-Bird; *from* Hesperia: *Hesperia. A Poem* (Boston: Ticknor & Fields, 1867).

Nathaniel Parker Willis. January 1, 1829; Psyche, Before the Tribunal of Venus: *Fugitive Poetry* (Boston: Pierce & Williams, 1829). *from* Melanie; The Confessional: *Melanie, and Other Poems* (London: Saunders & Oatley, 1835). Unseen Spirits; City Lyrics; The Lady in the White Dress, Whom I Helped Into the Omnibus: *Poems, Sacred, Passionate, and Humorous* (New York: Clarke & Austin, 1844). To Charles Roux, of Switzerland: *Sacred Poems* (New York: Clarke, Austin & Smith, 1859).

Samuel Woodworth. The Bucket: *Melodies, Duets, Songs, and Ballads* (New York: James M. Campbell, 1826).

The following is a list of pages where a stanza break coincides with the foot of the page (except where such breaks are apparent from the regular stanzaic structure of the poem): 66, 80, 82, 98, 249, 270, 282, 283, 288, 289, 333, 353, 355, 360, 415, 421, 436, 438, 463, 464, 483, 508, 516, 518, 523, 527, 533, 536, 537, 541, 548, 567, 571, 590, 613, 620, 621, 652, 668, 670, 678, 680, 685, 693, 714, 721, 723, 724, 725, 726, 729, 730, 736, 737, 738, 739, 740, 741, 746, 747, 748, 749, 750, 756, 759, 760, 761, 763, 765, 766, 769, 772, 773, 774, 775, 776, 780, 781, 783, 784, 786, 792, 794, 796, 797, 799, 800, 801, 802, 804, 806, 808, 813, 814, 816, 817, 818, 819, 820, 821, 822, 824, 830, 831, 833, 863, 872, 873, 874, 877, 878, 879, 881, 887, 891, 895, 901, 904, 911, 921, 922, 923, 924, 926, 927, 933, 935.

This volume presents the texts listed here without change except for the correction of typographical errors, but it does not attempt to reproduce features of their typographic design. For untitled poems, the first line is used as a title. The following is a list of typographical errors in the source texts that have been corrected, cited by page and line number: 1.15, year an,; 2.22, home,; 36.8, moontide; 55.13, uknnown; 64.3, mountain's; 65.31, scence; 106.5, whale's; 110.5, there'e; 110.11, lovely; 130.11, bum; 156.2, not not; 158.21, expatiated; 178.7, 'Twas; 182.12, Soul; 184.18, These; 185.6, XIV.; 219.25, ocean.; 355.3, *hol*; 378.17, grew,"; 494.11, knell; 498.30, you!'); 500.14, untrod.; 604.32, built, 647.16, ell; 666.28, wars; 716.33, Dids't; 783.18, aud. Error corrected second printing: 638.9, of of *(LOA)*.

Notes

In the notes below, the reference numbers denote page and line of this volume (the line count includes titles). No note is made for material included in standard desk-reference books, such as *Webster's Ninth New Collegiate Dictionary* or *Webster's Biographical Dictionary*. Quotations from Shakespeare are keyed to *The Riverside Shakespeare* (Boston: Houghton Mifflin, 1974), edited by G. Blakemore Evans. References to the Bible have been keyed to the King James Version.

2.19   *Helots*]   "All of servile conditions among the ancient Athenians were denominated *Helots*."—Freneau's note.

3.5   *Great Western Canal*]   The Erie Canal, extending from Albany to Buffalo and connecting the Hudson River to Lake Erie, opened in 1825.

3.7–8   *Meliusne . . . undas?*]   Horace, *Odes* III, 27, lines 42–44, rewritten and metrically rearranged by Freneau. The original passage, from Europa's complaint about having been borne by the bull over the ocean, reads: "*Meliusne fluctus / ire per longos fuit an recentis / carpere floras?*" (Was it better to travel over vast seas or pick fresh flowers?)

3.16   *Holland . . . Spain's*]   The struggle for Dutch independence from Hapsburg Spain lasted from 1566 to 1648.

6.1   *Mr. Blanchard*]   The French aeronaut Jean-Pierre François Blanchard (1753–1809) made the first balloon ascent over North America at Philadelphia in 1793.

6.3–4   *Nil . . . stuttistra.*]   Horace, *Odes* I, 3, 37–38, apparently garbled by the typesetter; the original reads, "*Nil mortalibus ardui est; / caelum ipsum petimus stultitia*" (No ascent is too steep for mortals; we seek heaven itself in our folly). Horace's allusion is to Daedalus, who "tried the empty air on wings not given to man."

6.17   Phæton's sad fate]   "See the second Book of Ovid's Metamorphosis, for the history of Phaeton."—Freneau's note. Ovid's account tells how Phaethon attempted (against the warning of his father, the sun god Phoebus) to drive Phoebus's fiery chariot; Juno killed him and destroyed the chariot with a thunderbolt when Phoebus lost control of the steeds, threatening the world with conflagration.

6.26   Herschell]   Name sometimes applied to the planet Uranus, discovered by the German-British astronomer William Herschel in 1781; Herschel also discovered two of Saturn's moons.

7.19   Polypheme]   Polyphemus, a Cyclops, son of Poseidon is represented in *The Odyssey* as a one-eyed giant.

8.10–12   *Jam . . . Ucalegon.*]   Virgil, *Aeneid* II, 310–12: "And now the big house of Deiphobus has collapsed, and already his neighbor Ucalegon's burns."

8.15   George the vandal]   George IV (1762–1830), who assumed the regency of England in 1811, after his father, George III, went mad.

8.21   *Beersheba* to *Dan*]   Biblical phrase denoting the full length of Palestine; Beersheba was the southernmost village in the kingdom and Dan the northernmost.

9.1   Cockburn]   Rear Admiral Sir George Cockburn (1772–1853), commander of British naval forces that participated in the capture of Washington, D.C., in August 1814.

9.14   *Rodgers*]   Captain John Rodgers (1773–1838), commander of the naval flotilla that patrolled the northern Atlantic coast of the United States from 1807 to 1814.

9.15   *a seventy-four*]   A ship of war equipped with seventy-four guns, and thus more powerful than a frigate.

9.17   *Ross*]   Major General Robert Ross (1766–1814), British expeditionary commander responsible for the burning of Washington in 1814.

12.5   Laurence]   The St. Lawrence River.

12.30   the Hero]   The poem's protagonist, Christopher Columbus.

13.29   Hesper]   The "radiant seraph" who reveals to the dying Columbus the vision with which *The Columbiad* is concerned.

14.9   Enceladus]   One of the Titans of Greek myth, son of Uranus and Ge, buried under Mt. Aetna on Sicily; legends hold that earthquakes are caused by his stirrings and volcanic eruptions by his breath.

14.27–28   nitric . . . muriatic]   In this passage the powers of frost are likened to the numbing and life-destroying qualities of various acids.

15.37   Palfrey]   William Palfrey (1741–80) served as paymaster-general in the Continental Army; he was lost at sea on the ship *Shelaly* that was taking him to France to serve as consul-general.

16.8   five great Caspians] The Great Lakes; "Caspian" is here used to denote an inland sea.

20.22   Now grateful . . . war] British forces led by General Cornwallis surrendered to George Washington at Yorktown on October 19, 1781.

21.11–13   Brunswick's . . . Crown] Hesse-Kassel, Hesse-Kanau, Brunswick, and Anspach-Bayreuth were among six German states that supplied mercenary troops to support the British forces in the Revolutionary War.

21.20   gerb] A sheaf of grain.

22.30   Kenhawa] The Great Kanawha, principal river in West Virginia.

24.2   *December, 1812*] Napoleon's retreat from Russia, begun in October 1812, had by December become a catastrophic rout.

24.15   Neustria] The western part of the Frankish empire in the Merovingian period, located between the Meuse and the Loire.

24.25   Lussian] Portuguese.

24.29   Domingo's . . . India's] Napoleon sent an army to Haiti in 1801 to reestablish French control. After fierce fighting with Haitian rebels and heavy losses to yellow fever, it surrendered to the British in 1803. French forces and their Indian allies were defeated by the British in a series of campaigns, 1799–1801.

25.2   the BAN?] The *ban* was, in the French military system, the portion of the population liable for conscription into the militia or national guard.

25.4   joles] Jaws.

28.1–8   Is dull . . . see.] In Bodman's *Oration on Death*, this stanza is separated from the preceding ones by a prose passage in which Bodman, having addressed the variety of the physical world, proceeds to contemplate the spiritual: "Now, is the pure intellectual world alone destitute of this delightful variety? . . . Has [God] poured out all the various glories of divine art and workmanship in the inanimate and brutal or animal world, and left the higher sort of creatures all of one genius, and turn, and mould, to replenish all the intellectual regions? Surely it is hard to believe it."

29.6   GOLDSMITH'S HERMIT] Oliver Goldsmith, "The Hermit, or Edwin and Angelina," lines 31–32; the poem appears in chapter 8 of *The Vicar of Wakefield* (1766), where it is titled "A Ballad." The "Hermit" is the character in the poem to whom these lines are given.

31.3   Guido's] Guido Reni (1575–1642), Italian painter.

31.4   Claudes] Claude Gellée, known as Claude Lorrain (1600–82), French landscape painter.

36.19–20   *"Integer . . . arcu."*] Horace, *Odes* I, 22, 1–2: "He who is upright in his life and pure of guilt, needs not Moorish arrows, nor bow." Adams's poem is a strict imitation of the *Ode* from which he takes his epigraph.

36.27   Zara's] The Sahara Desert.

36.31   Simoon's] Or simoom; a strong, hot desert wind.

37.6   Bohan Upas] Tropical Asian tree (*Antiaris toxicaria*) with a poisonous sap which was used for poisoning darts; mere proximity to the tree was popularly believed to be fatal.

39.19   PUTNAM's] Rufus Putnam (1738–1824), Revolutionary soldier, who helped fortify West Point.

39.26   Arnold] Benedict Arnold (1741–1801), Revolutionary general and traitor who conspired to betray the Continental forces at West Point.

39.27   André] Major John André (1751–80), British officer who acted as an intermediary between Benedict Arnold and the British commander Sir Henry Clinton. Captured by the Americans in civilian disguise, he was hanged as a spy.

39.29   The HONEST THREE] The three New York militiamen who on September 24, 1780, stopped and searched Major John André and found papers on him that led them to suspect treason.

44.26   *Donder* and *Blitzen*] German for Thunder and Lightning.

51.8   old Hecla's] Hecla, or Hekla, is a volcano in southwest Iceland; its first recorded eruption was in the 12th century.

54.24–26   *Group . . . Vatican*] Illustrating Genesis 18:1–10; one of a series of frescoes of biblical scenes, designed by Raphael and known as "Raphael's Bible," on the ceiling of Raphael's Loggia.

55.8–9   *Peligrino Tibaldi*] Pellegrino Tibaldi (1527–96), Italian painter.

55.11   Bonarroti] Michelangelo Buonarroti, also called Michelangelo.

55.25   *Jacob's Dream*] Genesis 28:11–16.

56.7   *Luxembourg Gallery*] The Grand, or East, Gallery of the Luxembourg Palace in Paris contained a series of 24 scenes from the life of Maria de Medicis that Rubens painted for the Gallery; they are now in the Louvre.

56.22   *the President*] Benjamin West (1738–1820), American painter, president of the Royal Academy (1792–1820).

59.7   the noble Tuscan] Michelangelo.

59.14   through Elisha's faith]   Cf. 2 Kings 2:11–12.

59.16   *Bienaimé*]   Angelo Bienaimé, a sculptor whose works were displayed at the Royal Academy a number of times between 1829 and 1850.

60.29   the unbending Roman]   "Coriolanus."—Allston's note.

60.31   Cooke . . . Jew]   George Frederick Cooke (1756–1811), English actor famed for his portrayals of Shylock, Iago, and Richard III.

60.31   the unrelenting Jew]   "Shylock."—Allston's note.

63.19   Cephissus]   A river of ancient Phocis, in central Greece.

63.21   Tempè]   Valley in northeastern Thessaly, Greece.

63.22   Peneus]   A river in Thessaly, Greece.

63.26   Citheron]   A mountain in east central Greece.

63.30   Hæmus . . . Hebrus]   Latin names for the Balkan Mountains and for the river Maritsa, which originates in Bulgaria to form part of the border between Greece and Turkey.

64.11   lamentable . . . vale]   Cf. Matthew 2:18.

64.23   tear . . . daughters]   Cf. Psalm 137.

64.31   Vallombrosa]   A village in Tuscany, situated in the Apennines.

64.34   Mont Alto]   Montalto is the highest peak in the Aspromonte ridge of the South Apennines.

68.30   "my hiding-place"]   Cf. Psalm 32:7.

69.10–16   the Eagle . . . Virgin's]   "The constellations, *Aquila*, *Leo*, and *Virgo*, are here meant by the astronomical fugitive."—Pierpont's note.

69.20   Queen . . . free!]   Slavery was abolished throughout the British Empire by the Abolition Act of 1833, which provided for the gradual emancipation of slaves in the West Indies. Emancipation was completed in 1838, a year after Queen Victoria ascended to the throne.

83.16   *The Chanting Cherubs*]   Title of a sculptural group (1828–30), now lost, by Horatio Greenough (1805–52).

86.20   Saint Anastasia's isle]   Anastasia Island, off the Florida coast south of St. Augustine.

86.25   The Constitution's column]   "The column of the Constitution, still standing [1826] in the public square of St. Augustine . . . 'Tis said, I know not how truly, to be the only one remaining in any of the present or former dominions of the Spanish monarchy."—from Wilde's note. The liberal Spanish constitution of 1812 was overthrown by Ferdinand VII after his restoration to the throne in 1814; East Florida was ceded to the United States by Spain in 1821.

88.27 Mount Auburn! . . . dead] The Mount Auburn Cemetery in Cambridge and Watertown, Massachusetts. The line alludes to the opening of Oliver Goldsmith's *The Deserted Village*: "Sweet Auburn, loveliest Village of the Plain!"

89.8 Warren's . . . rest] "The obelisk on Breed's, usually, though erroneously, called Bunker's Hill. Warren was the first officer of rank who fell in the Revolutionary war."—from Wilde's note. Joseph Warren (1741–75), physician, Revolutionary patriot, and a major general in the Massachusetts militia, was killed in action at Breed's Hill, June 17, 1775.

89.18 Beltrami] Giacomo Constantino Beltrami (1779–1855), Italian soldier, scholar, and explorer who journeyed to what he believed to be the source of the Mississippi in 1822–23; author of *La Découverte des Sources du Mississippi et de la Rivière Sanglante* (1824); published in English in 1828 as *A Pilgrimage in Europe and America leading to the Discovery of the Sources of the Mississippi and Bloody River*.

89.24 Bruce . . . Nile] Scottish traveler James Bruce (1730–94) reached the source of the Blue Nile in Abyssinia in 1770.

91.11 BOONE] Daniel Boone (1734–1820).

91.20–21 native orator . . . Colors,"] Little Turtle (c. 1752–1812), chief of the Miami Indian nation, in an oration quoted by the French scholar and traveler Constantin Volney (1757–1820), called the sun the father of colors because it turned the races into their respective colors.

91.22 Tully] Marcus Tullius Cicero (106–43 B.C.), Roman statesman, orator, and writer.

91.26 Volney] "It was Volney who preserved in his travels this among other specimens of Mi-shi-kin-a-kwa, or the Little Turtle's sagacity and eloquence (p. 407, Lond. ed. 1804)."—Wilde's note. The volume referred to is *View of the Climate and Soil of the United States of America* (1803, English translation 1804) by Constantin François Chasseboeuf, Comte de Volney (1757–1820).

91.28 Mirabeau's] Comte de Mirabeau (1749–91), a leading advocate of constitutional monarchy during the early years of the French Revolution.

93.11 Pharos] A lighthouse, one of the Seven Wonders of the World, on the island of Pharos off Alexandria, Egypt.

93.13 Sioux's tower of hunger] Starved Rock, a cliff along the south bank of the Illinois River where, according to legend, a group of Illinois

Indians held out and finally died, besieged by a hostile tribe variously identified as Ottawa or Pottawattomi.

93.14–16   Ugolino . . . Dante]   Conte Ugolino, imprisoned and starved to death in 1289 in the tower of Guaiandi alle Sette Vie at Pisa; he figures as a traitor in Cantos 32 and 33 of Dante's *Inferno*.

93.19–23   modern saint . . . temple]   Joseph Smith (1805–44), Mormon prophet and founder of the Church of Jesus Christ of the Latter-day Saints, in 1839 established the Mormon city of Nauvoo in western Illinois and began the building of a grand temple there, completed after his death.

93.27   "the march of mind,"]   Cf. Edmund Burke's remark in his speech on conciliation with America, March 22, 1775: "The march of the human mind is slow."

94.6   Oolaïtha's]   Daughter of a Sioux chief, who jumped from a high cliff on the shore of Lake Pepin out of disappointment in love, according to Beltrami's *Sources du Mississippi* and Henry Rowe Schoolcraft's *Narrative Journal of Travels through the Northwestern Regions of the United States*.

94.21   Or more Apollo-like]   "West is reported to have said, when he saw the Apollo, 'Good God! how like a young Indian!' "—from Wilde's note. The reference is to the painter Benjamin West's remark on seeing the Apollo Belvedere.

94.27   my   countryman]   "Hiram   Powers."—Wilde's   note.   Powers (1805–73) was an American sculptor.

94.28   artist . . . "Divine"]   Michelangelo.

95.5   Chastellux]   François Jean, Marquis de Chastellux (1734–88), French general who fought in the Revolutionary War and author of *Voyages dans l'Amérique Septentrionale* (1786) on travels in America.

95.7   Atala's]   Indian heroine of Chateaubriand's novel (1801) of the same name.

95.12   "Faithful . . . faithless"]   Cf. John Milton, *Paradise Lost*, Book 5, line 896–97: ". . . faithful found / Among the faithless, faithful only he."

95.13   the sinking mountain]   "A few miles below Wabashaw's village, an isolated mountain of singular appearance rises out of the centre of the river to a height of four or five hundred feet, when it terminates in crumbling peaks of naked rock, whose lines of stratification and massy walls, impress forcibly upon the mind the image of some gigantic battlement of former generations."—Henry Rowe Schoolcraft, cited by Wilde.

95.33   Fata Morgana]   Mirage, often visible in the Straits of Messina.

96.9   Ozolapaida]   Legendary Dakota Indian maiden, whose abduction precipitated a feud between warring families of the Assiniboins and the Sioux.

97.3   *Joseph Rodman Drake*]   See biographical note, p. 999.

98.1   *Alnwick Castle*]   Northumberland home of the Percy family since 1309.

98.19–20   gallant Hotspur . . . Katherine]   Harry Percy and his wife, Katherine, in Shakespeare, *1 Henry IV*.

98.28   the Cheviot day]   The Cheviots are a range of hills along the Scottish-English border. Stories of border warfare between the Percys and the Scottish Douglas family are recounted in "Chevy Chase, or The Hunting a' the Cheviat" and "The Battle of Otterbourne," two ballads collected in Percy's *Reliques of Ancient English Poetry* (1763).

99.13   "tongues in trees,"]   "And this our life, exempt from public haunt, / Finds tongues in trees, books in the running brooks, / Sermons in stones, and good in every thing."—Shakespeare, *As You Like It*, II, i, 15–17.

99.26   him . . . standard set]   "One of the ancestors of the Percy family was an Emperor of Constantinople."—Note from *Poetical Writings of Fitz-Greene Halleck* (1868).

99.29–30   him . . . King George]   Sir Hugh Percy, second Duke of Northumberland (1742–1817); commander of the relief column that met the British troops retreating from Concord at Lexington on April 19, 1775. He later served in the 1776 campaign around New York.

100.7   royal Berwick]   The county of Berwick is situated in southeast Scotland; the town of Berwick-upon-Tweed changed hands 13 times during the medieval border warfare between England and Scotland before becoming part of England in 1482. Due to its contested status, the town was often listed as a separate possession of the king in medieval documents.

100.15   Bailie Jarvie . . . Rob Roy]   Bailie Nicol Jarvie, Glasgow magistrate and merchant, and the heroic outlaw Rob Roy Macgregor, based on a historical figure (1671–1734), in Walter Scott's novel *Rob Roy* (1818).

100.16   Munro]   President James Monroe.

100.17   "the era . . . feeling"]   The phrase, referring to the decline of party conflict in American political life during the Monroe administrations (1817–25), has been traced to the Boston *Columbian Centinel* of July 12, 1817.

100.30–31   The age . . . Has come]   Cf. Edmund Burke, *Reflections on the Revolution in France* (1790): "The age of chivalry has gone. That of sophisters, economists, and calculators has succeeded, and the glory of Europe is extinguished forever."

101.18   *Marco Bozzaris*]   Markos Botsaris (c. 1788–1823) led a Souliot force during the siege of Missolonghi (1822–23). He was killed on August 21, 1823, leading a successful attack on an Albanian force advancing on Missolonghi.

101.31   Suliote]   Souliote; inhabitant of Suli, a mountainous district of northern Greece.

109.9   Monmouth's GEOFFRY]   Geoffrey of Monmouth (c. 1100–54), author of the *Historia Regum Britanniae* (*History of the Kings of Britain*), written around 1135.

109.27   'bids the desert blossom like the rose,']   Cf. Isaiah 35:1.

113.3   *Battle of Niagara*]   The battle of Lundy's Lane, fought in Ontario near Niagara Falls on July 25, 1814, during the War of 1812, was claimed as a victory by Americans.

122.3   *Thanatopsis*]   Greek for "contemplation, or view, of death."

123.18   the Barcan desert]   Barka, region in northeastern Libya, in Cyrenaica.

158.37–159.1   shameful . . . Missolonghi fallen]   In 1823 the insurgent Greek government raised a large loan in London, but was forced to spend much of the money in efforts to suppress internal strife; the resulting lack of funds contributed to the success of the renewed Ottoman offensive in 1825. Missolonghi (or Mesolongion) was captured by the Ottoman forces after a long siege in 1826.

160.27   now Peru is free]   Peru's independence was declared in 1821, and secured by Spanish military defeats in 1824.

160.31   Cole]   Thomas Cole; see biographical note, p. 996.

163.7   A race . . . away]   For much of the nineteenth century it was widely believed that the mounds such as those that Bryant visited in Illinois were the work of an unknown race unrelated to the American Indians.

163.10   Pentelicus]   Or Pentelikon; a mountain in Greece from which a superior marble was quarried.

175.3   from *Zophiël*]   *Zophiël*, a poem in six cantos based on an episode in the apocryphal Book of Tobit, concerns the unrequited love of the fallen angel Zophiël for the maiden Egla. As with each canto of her poem, Brooks begins the third canto with an Argument synopsizing its narrative: "Midnight.— Zophiël and Phraerion sit conversing together near a ruin on the banks of the Tigris.— Zophiël laments his former crimes; speaks of a change in his designs; dwells on the purity of his love for Egla; and expresses a wish to preserve her life and beauty beyond the period allotted to mortals.— Phraerion is induced to lead the way to the palace of Tahathyam.— Palace and banquet of Gnomes.—Zophiël, by force of entreaty and promise, obtains from Tahathyam a drop of the elixir of life."

180.9 seven long months] "From the blooming of the roses at Ecbatana, to the coming in of spices at Babylon."—Brooks's note.

181.5 that vague, wondrous lore] "It is said to have been believed by the Egyptians that many *wonderful secrets* were engraved by one of the Mercuries, on tablets of emerald, which still remain hidden in some part of their country."—from Brooks's note.

190.5 Tsavaven] "Tsavaven signifies tint-gem."—Brooks's note.

191.2−5 Ramaöur . . . Marmorak] "These names are formed from Hebraic words, expressive of the various qualities and employments of the beings who bear them. Aishalat signifies fire-control; Psaämayim, black-water; Ramaour, light-direct; Nahalcoul, guide-sound; Zotzaraven, shape-spar; Rouamasak, mingle-air; Talhazak, dew-congeal; Marmorak (partly Greek) marble-stain."—from Brooks's note.

196.1 That baffling . . . art] Alchemy.

197.14 hydromel] A kind of mead made of water and honey.

198.9 Ragasycheon] "This name is compounded of a Hebraic and a Greek word, and signifies to move or affect the soul."—Brooks's note.

201.21 Evanath] "From eva, life; and nathan, to give."—Brooks's note.

202.25 grenadilla] "The grenadilla is a melon produced from a blossom more rich and beautiful than it is easy to describe. Though much larger, it resembles the cerulean passion-flower so nearly as to seem of the same species; but the leaf of its vine is curled, and of a very different shape." —Brooks's note.

205.24 Maro] Virgil.

205.30−31 Campbell's war-blast . . . Elsinore] The reference is to Thomas Campbell's poem "The Battle of the Baltic," first collected in *Gertrude of Wyoming* (1809). The poem describes the naval battle of Copenhagen, April 2, 1801.

206.1 *The National Painting*] John Trumbull's "The Declaration of Independence."

206.6 T*******] John Trumbull (1756−1843), American painter and Revolutionary soldier.

206.9 Guido] Guido Reni; see note 31.3.

206.24   S*****d]   Jacob Sherred, a wealthy glazier and painter in New York City.

207.9   Cronest]   "The Crow's Nest, a mountain in the Hudson Highlands."—Note from *The Culprit Fay and Other Poems* (1835).

208.24   ising-stars]   Bits of mica.

208.37   Ouphe]   An elf or goblin.

211.6–9   Forever float . . . o'er us?]   On Drake's manuscript, the last four lines are written in the hand of Fitz-Greene Halleck, who with Drake's approval substituted them for four canceled lines by Drake.

213.1   *To a Friend*]   A final stanza exists in manuscript but was omitted from the poem as originally published:

> Come! shake these trammels off—let fools rehearse
> Their loves and raptures in unmeaning chime;
> Cram close their rude conceits in mawkish verse,
> And torture hackneyed thoughts in timeless rhyme.
> But thou shalt soar in glorious flight sublime,
> With heavenly voice of music, strength, and fire,
> Waft wide the wonders of your native clime,
> With patriot pride and patriot heart inspire,
> Till wondering Europe hear Columbia's matchless lyre.

213.2   *"You damn . . . praise."*]   Cf. Alexander Pope, *Epistle to Dr. Arbuthnot*, l. 201: "Damn with faint praise, assent with civil leer."

213.9   Strangford]   Percy Clinton Sidney Smythe, 6th Viscount Stranford, poet and diplomat, whose translations of the Portuguese poet Luis de Camoens (1524–80) were published in 1803; Drake refers to a satirical passage in Byron's "English Bards and Scotch Reviewers" (1809): "Mend, Strangford! mend thy morals to thy taste; / Be warm, but pure; be amorous, but be chaste; / Cease to deceive; thy pilfer'd harp restore, / Nor teach the Lusian bard to copy Moore."

214.23   the sweet Mc Rea]   Jane McCrea (1753–77), killed in upstate New York by two Indians scouting for the British Army under General Burgoyne.

214.32   Wyoming]   Wyoming Valley in Pennyslvania, site of an Indian massacre described in "Gertrude of Wyoming" (1809) by the Scottish poet Thomas Campbell.

215.9   "Pride . . . eye,"]   Cf. Goldsmith, "The Traveller," l. 327: "Pride in their port, defiance in their eye."

215.32   Pacolet]   A dwarf who rode a magic wooden horse in the medieval French romance of Valentine and Orson.

215.35   Manitou's]   In American Indian mythology, a spirit.

216.3   Areouski]   Areskoui, or Agreskoui, the Iroquois god of war.

216.10   Kanawa's]   An Indian tribe (also Conoy or Canawese) and, thence, a river in West Virginia; also spelled Kenhawa and Kanawha.

218.2   dog-trees]   Dogwood.

226.4–10   *"Ye blessed . . .* WORDSWORTH]   From William Wordsworth's "Ode: Intimations of Immortality from Recollections of Early Childhood," ll. 36–41.

226.26–30   *"Thus sing . . .* MORE]   From the preface "To the Reader" in *Philosophical Poems* (1642) by English theologian and poet Henry More (1614–87).

227.13–20   *"But else . . .* MILTON.]   From "Arcades" ll. 61–67.

227.21   Romancer]   Nathaniel Hawthorne.

235.27   Wolga's]   The river Volga.

236.1   *The Voyage . . . 2nd*]   In 1839–40 Cole produced a series of four paintings (commissioned by Lumen Reed) representing "The Voyage of Life": "Childhood," "Youth," "Manhood," and "Old Age." The present poem complements the second of these.

243.5   Know'st thou the land]   Cf. the lines about Italy at the opening of the song in Bk. III, chap. 1, of Goethe's *Wilhelm Meister's Apprenticeship*: "Kennst du das Land wo die Citronen blühn?" ("Know'st thou the land where the lemons bloom?")

243.10   vernant]   Flourishing; verdant.

244.23   ROBERTSON'S AMERICA]   *History of America* (1777) by William Robertson (1721–93).

254.15   Dædalian plan]   I.e., worthy of Daedalus, renowned in Greek myth for his ingenuity.

259.33   hand . . . Peter's dome]   Michaelangelo, chief architect of St. Peter's in Rome.

261.6   *Chrysostom*]   St. John Chrysostom (347–407), Archbishop of Constantinople, admired for his eloquence. His name means "golden mouth" (see following note).

261.8–9   younger . . . Taylor]   Jeremy Taylor (1613–67), English bishop and theologian renowned for his eloquence.

261.14   *Rhea*]   Greek goddess, daughter of Uranus (heaven) and Gaea (earth), both wife and mother of Kronos, and mother of Zeus and other Olympians.

264.10   *Uriel*]   One of the seven archangels of Christian legend, whose name means "fire of God."

264.18   SAID]   Or Sa'adi (Mosharref od-Din ibn Mosleh od-Din Sa'adi, c. 1213–92), Persian poet.

269.1   *Mithridates*]   Mithridates VI, king of Pontus in Asia Minor in the first century B.C., took daily doses of poisons to develop immunity to them.

269.8   cantharids]   Spanish blister beetles (called Spanish fly), pulverized to make a toxic powder used in aphrodisiac and medicinal potions.

269.16   blinding dog-wood]   Poison sumac, a member of the dogwood family, known commonly as "blind-your-eyes."

269.18   prussic juice]   Prussic acid, a form of cyanide, used as a poison.

269.19   upas]   Cf. note 37.6.

270.1   *Hamatreya*]   Emerson's variant of Maitreya, a figure from *The Vishnu Parana; a System of Hindu Mythology and Tradition*, translated by H. H. Wilson in 1840.

270.2   Minott . . . Flint]   Founders of Concord.

282.28   evil time's sole patriot]   William Henry Channing (1810–84), clergyman and abolitionist, who had been urging Emerson to engage himself more actively in the anti-slavery campaign.

283.15   Contoocook]   River in southern New Hampshire.

283.16   Agiochook]   Mountain in New Hampshire.

285.12   Cossack eats Poland]   Polish nationalists rose against Russian rule in 1830, and their defeat the following year precipitated intense political and cultural repression.

285.20   *Astræa*]   Goddess of Justice in Greek mythology; she left the world at the end of the Golden Age and became the constellation Virgo.

288.14   *Sursum Corda*]   "Let us lift up our hearts," Lamentations 3:41 (Vulgate); it occurs in the Roman Catholic Mass as "Lift up your hearts," the thanksgiving before the consecration of the bread and wine.

294.31   *Merlin*]   Here, a legendary Welsh poet of the sixth century.

300.16   *Merops*]   From Greek, "articulate speech"; Merops was a soothsayer in the *Iliad*.

300.29   *Saadi*]   Cf. note 264.18.

303.7   Dschami's]   Jami (Mowlana Nur od-Din 'Abd or-Rahman ebn Ah-mad, 1414—92), Persian poet and mystic.

305.22   *Xenophanes*]   Greek philosopher (c. 570—480 B.C.) who satirized the anthropomorphizing of divinity and argued for a single god, sometimes interpreted to mean the universe itself.

311.12   he, the wondrous child]   The poet's son Waldo, who died in January of 1842.

318.28   the shot . . . world]   The fighting at Concord between Massachusetts militia and British regular troops on April 19, 1775, was the first battle of the Revolutionary War.

319.10—11   If . . . slain]   Cf. *Katha Upanishad* 2:19—22: "If the slayer thinks he slays, / If the slain thinks he is slain, / Both these have no knowledge, / He slays not, is not slain," or *Bhagavad-Gita* 2:19—22: "Who thinks that he can be a slayer, / Who thinks that he is slain, / Both these have no right knowledge: / He slays not, is not slain." Translations of both works were in Emerson's library.

324.33   Giant's Stairs]   Giant's Causeway, a volcanic formation of basaltic columns on the coast of County Antrim, Ireland.

329.22   *Waldeinsamkeit*]   "Forest solitude," a word coined by Ludwig Tieck and a favorite term of German romanticism.

331.13   *Terminus*]   Roman god of boundaries.

332.6   Baresark]   Berserker.

332.19   *Suum Cuique*]   Latin: "to each his own."

346.4   Hants Franklin Berks]   Emerson refers to three counties in western Massachusetts: Hampshire (here called by its English nickname "Hants"), Franklin, and Berkshire.

347.26   *Maia*]   "Illusion" in Hindu thought.

354.15—17   Egeria's . . . mount]   Egeria, a Roman water goddess and nymph of the springs, was believed to have been worshipped at the Grotto of Egeria on the Via Appia Pigantelli in the environs of Rome. Nearby is Bosco Sacro, the hill where Numius Pompilius, legendary second king of Rome, received counsel from the goddess.

354.19   Caracalla's Baths]   Large hot baths in Rome, begun in A.D. 212 by emperor Aurelius Antoninus Bassianus (A.D. 188—217), called Caracalla.

354.23   Albano's hill]   The Colli Albani (Alban Hills), a volcanic mountain formation southeast of Rome, of which Albanus Mons is the highest peak.

355.2—7   "*When* . . . WORTLEY]   Lady Emmeline Charlotte Elizabeth

Stuart-Wortley (1806–55), playwright and poet; the lines are from "Stanzas," published in *The Keepsake*, 1832.

355.32   Contadina] Peasant woman.

355.33   Val d'Arno] The Arno River Valley.

356.12   Vallombrosa's] See note 64.31.

356.15   Milton . . . Paradise] Milton traveled in Italy, 1638–39.

357.9   Lais and Leontium] Lais was a Greek courtesan said to have been the mistress of the philosopher Aristippus of Cyrene (c. 435–356 B.C.); Leontium (or Leontion) was a courtesan and Epicurean philosopher of the early 3rd century B.C.

357.20   fount . . . Helen drank] "In the Scamander,—before contending for the prize of beauty on Mount Ida. Its head waters fill a beautiful tank near the walls of Troy."—Willis's note.

359.21   City Hotel] Hotel built in 1792 on Broadway near present-day Cedar Street.

359.28   the Astor] The Astor House hotel, a large luxury hotel overlooking City Hall Park in lower Manhattan.

365.1   *Swanannoa*] River in western North Carolina; also spelled Swannanoa.

366.20   Lucumones] Etruscan princes or chiefs.

367.38   "Esar"] "Esar, the Supreme Being of the ancient Etrurians."—Simms's note.

372.2   Ἀσπασίη, τρίλλιστος.] "Welcome, thrice (or often) prayed to": the phrase is evidently Longfellow's own.

374.28   Norman's Woe] Dangerous reef off Gloucester Harbor, Massachusetts.

377.7   *The Skeleton in Armour*] "The following Ballad was suggested to me while riding on the seashore at Newport. A year or two previous a skeleton had been dug up at Fall River, clad in broken and corroded armour; and the idea occurred to me of connecting it with the Round Tower at Newport, generally known hitherto as the Old Wind-Mill, though now claimed by the Danes as a work of their early ancestors."—from Longfellow's note.

382.15   *Mezzo Cammin*] Italian "mid-journey," from the first line of Dante's *Inferno*: "Nel mezzo del cammin di nostra vita" (in the middle of the journey of our life").

395.23   Têche] The Bayou Têche, a river in Louisiana.

396.1   Walleway] Wallowa, river in northeastern Oregon.

396.1   Owyhee]   River in southeastern Oregon, connecting with the Snake.

399.1–2   *The Song of Hiawatha*]   "This Indian Edda—if I may so call it—is founded on a tradition, prevalent among the North American Indians, of a personage of miraculous birth, who was sent among them to clear their rivers, forests, and fishing-grounds, and to teach them the arts of peace . . . Into this old tradition I have woven other curious Indian legends, drawn chiefly from the various and valuable writings of Mr. Schoolcraft, to whom the literary world is greatly indebted for his indefatigable zeal in rescuing from oblivion so much of the legendary lore of the Indians. The scene of the poem is among the Ojibways on the southern shore of Lake Superior, in the region between the Pictured Rocks and the Grand Sable."—from Longfellow's note. For the life and work of Henry Rowe Schoolcraft, see biographical note, *American Poetry: The Nineteenth Century, Melville to Stickney*, page 942.

399.9   Medas]   "Medicine-men."—Longfellow's note.

399.10   Wabenos]   "Magicians."—Longfellow's note.

400.11   Gitche Manito]   "The Great Spirit, the Master of Life."—Longfellow's note.

400.20   Kenabeek]   "A serpent."—Longfellow's note.

401.24   Jossakeeds]   "A Prophet."—Longfellow's note.

404.14   Nokomis]   Hiawatha's grandmother.

406.6   Ponemah]   "Hereafter."—Longfellow's note.

406.9   the beautiful town]   Portland, Maine, where Longfellow was born.

406.14   verse . . . Lapland song]   Adapted from Johannes Scheffer, *The History of Lapland* (English translation, 1674): "A Youth's desire is the desire of the wind, / All his essaies / Are long delaies, / No issue can they find."

407.20   Deering's Woods]   Woods near Portland, Maine, which Longfellow roamed as a child; now preserved as a park.

409.28–29   Bishop . . . Rhine!]   A medieval watch-tower on the Rhine, supposedly so named because of the tradition that Archbishop Hatto was devoured there by mice in the 10th century; the story is told in Robert Southey's poem "God's Judgment on a Wicked Bishop."

410.9   *Wayside Inn*]   In a letter to Frances Farrer dated December 28, 1863, Longfellow wrote of this poem: "The Wayside Inn has more foundation in fact than you may suppose. The town of Sudbury is about twenty miles from Cambridge. Some two hundred years ago, an English family, by the name of Howe, built there a country house, which has remained in the family down to the present time, the last of the race dying but two years ago. Losing their fortune, they became inn-keepers; and for a century the Red-Horse Inn has flourished, going down from father to son. The place is just as I have described it, though no longer an inn . . . All the characters are real. The musician is Ole Bull; the Spanish Jew, Israel Edrehi, whom I have seen as I have painted him, etc., etc." (Edrehi's first name was actually Isaac.)

411.31   Princess Mary's]   Daughter of James II and Anne Hyde; as Mary II (1662–94) assumed the English throne with her husband William of Orange in 1689.

412.5   Major Molineaux]   William Molineux (d. 1774) of Boston, said to have been at the Boston Tea Party; he figures in Hawthorne's 1832 short story, "My Kinsman, Major Molineux."

414.6–9   Flores . . . Gawain]   Characters in medieval romances.

414.15   Palermo's fatal siege]   The city fell to royalist troops in April 1849 during the suppression of the Sicilian revolution of 1848–49.

414.17   King Bomba's]   King Ferdinand II (1810–59) of the Two Sicilies (Sicily and Naples) was called "King Bomba" because he had the principal cities in Sicily bombarded during the suppression of the 1848–49 revolution.

414.30–31   Immortal Four of Italy]   Dante, Petrarch, Ariosto, and Tasso.

415.5   Meli]   Giovanni Meli (1740–1815), Sicilian poet noted for his poems in dialect.

415.27   Pierre Alphonse]   Pedro Alfonso (also known as Petrus Alfonsi), 11th-century author of *Disciplina Clericalis*; he prepared an edition of Aesop's fables.

415.29   Parables of Sandabar]   The *Misklo Sandabar,* a medieval Hebrew collection of stories.

415.30   Pilpay]   More commonly Bidpai, supposed author of a version of the Sanskrit collection of tales, the *Panchatantra.*

415.33   Targum]   Aramaic paraphrase of the Old Testament.

417.8   Strömkarl]   In Norse myth, a water sprite, usually having musical abilities and weeping when it hears the harp.

417.18   Elivagar's river]   In Norse mythology, poisonous waters gushing from the center of Niflheim, the land of mist.

425.24   Lethe and Eunoe]   Two sides of a stream in Dante's *Purgatorio* XXVIII, 127–32; the waters called Lethe ("forgetfulness") remove the memory of sin and those called Eunoe ("kindly thoughts, remembrance of good") restore the memory of good deeds.

427.1   *Belisarius*] According to legend, the Byzantine general Belisarius (505–65) became a blind beggar after losing favor with Emperor Justinian.

427.21   Ausonian realm] Italy; according to legend, the people of Italy were descendants of Auson, son of Ulysses and Calypso.

427.22   Parthenope] In ancient poetry, a name for Naples; from its legendary founder, the siren Parthenope, who was cast up on its shores.

427.29   Zabergan] Zaberganes, Persian ambassador to Byzantium.

428.3   the Vandal monarch] Gelimer, whom Belisarius defeated in A.D. 534.

428.15   the Monk of Ephesus] Theodosius, the adopted son of Belisarius, became the lover of Belisarius's wife, Antonina; according to the *Anecdota* (*Secret History*) of Procopius, he enrolled himself for a time as a monk at Ephesus in order to avoid danger.

429.1   *Kéramos*] Greek: "potter."

432.11   Palissy] Bernard Palissy (c. 1509–89), French potter and enameller, noted for his scientific and technical experiments; he devoted 16 years of labor to developing a process to produce enamels.

433.13   Gubbio] Town in Umbria, in central Italy, noted for production of majolica ware in the 16th century.

433.19   Faenza . . . Pesaro] Faenza is a north central Italian town known for production of majolica; Pesaro is a town in the Marches of north central Italy famed for its majolica ware in the 15th–18th centuries.

433.25   Francesco Xanto] Avelli Xanto, Italian painter and ceramicist of the 16th century, who worked in Urbino 1530–42.

433.29   Maestro Giorgio] Giorgio di Pietro Andreoli (c. 1500), Italian sculptor and ceramicist; also called "Maestro Giorgio." He developed a carmine tint for which the majolica of Gubbio became famous.

435.8   Ausonian] See note 427.21.

436.8   the Thebaid] The Roman province of Upper Egypt.

436.27   Emoth] Ammit or Ammut; in Egyptian religion, a monster stationed by the scales of judgment in Osiris's hall in the underworld.

437.13   King-te-tching] Jingdezhen, city in northeast Jiangxi (Kiangsi) province, China; formerly one of China's leading producers of porcelain.

438.8   Tower of Porcelain] Octagonal tower, about 260 feet high, whose outer walls were cased with porcelain bricks; begun in 1413 by

Emperor Yung Lo (1403–28), it was destroyed during the T'ai P'ing rebellion of the 1850s.

439.3   Fusiyama]   Mt. Fuji in Japan.

451.8   Marvel]   Andrew Marvell (1621–78), English poet.

451.11   *Song . . . Desert*]   The poem was suggested by the following passage in the African journal of the English abolitionist James Richardson (1806–51), as cited by Whittier in the 1888 Riverside Edition of his poems: "*Sebah, Oasis of Fezzan, 10th March, 1846.*—This evening the female slaves were unusually excited in singing, and I had the curiosity to ask my negro servant, Said, what they were singing about. As many of them were natives of his own country, he had no difficulty in translating the Mandara or Bornou language. I had often asked the Moors to translate their songs for me, but got no satisfactory account from them. Said at first said, 'Oh, they sing of *Rubee*' (God). 'What do you mean?' I replied, impatiently. 'Oh, don't you know?' he continued, 'they asked God to give them their *Atka?*' (certificate of freedom). I inquired, 'Is that all?' Said: 'No; they say, "Where are we going? The world is large. *O God! Where are we going? O God!*"' I inquired, 'What else?' Said: 'They remember their country, Bornou, and say, "*Bornou was a pleasant country, full of all good things; but this is a bad country, and we are miserable!*"' 'Do they say anything else?' Said: 'No; they repeat these words over and over again, and add, "O God! give us our *Atka, and let us return again to our dear home.*"'"

451.22   Bornou]   Region of West Africa, mostly lying in what is now northeast Nigeria.

451.24   Dourra]   Indian millet, common grain in parts of Africa.

454.6   *Ichabod!*]   Hebrew: "inglorious"; a child (I Samuel 4:21) so named by his mother who died giving him birth. Whittier here applies the epithet to Daniel Webster, for his support of the Compromise of 1850, including the passage of a new Fugitive Slave Law.

455.13   *Astræa*]   See note 285.20.

455.14–18   "*Jove . . .* 1615.]   Cf. Jonson's masque *The Golden Age Restored* (1615), 11–14: "And therefore means to settle / Astraea in her seat again, / And let down in his golden chain / The age of better metal."

456.17   *First-Day*]   Quaker term for Sunday.

457.13   Almeh]   An Egyptian dancing-girl.

457.14   Eblis]   In Islamic tradition, an equivalent of Satan: a fallen angelic prince, now the devil.

457.20   Mollah]   Variant of "mullah."

457.29   Shitan]   Form of Arabic *shaitan*, "satan-like."

458.12   raving Cuban filibuster] Pro-slavery expansionists advocated the annexation of Cuba in the years before the Civil War, and had supported two filibustering expeditions in 1850–51.

458.22   Gentoo]   Hindu.

465.25   Calendar's horse of brass]   Featured in "The Tale of the Third Kalandar" in *The Arabian Nights*.

465.27   Al-Borak]   White winged animal, somewhere between a donkey and a mule in height, on which Muhammad is said to have made a journey to the seven heavens.

465.30   Floyd Ireson]   In a headnote to this poem added in the Riverside Edition of his collected works (1888), Whittier says: "In the valuable and carefully prepared *History of Marblehead*, published in 1879 by Samuel Roads, Jr., it is stated that the crew of Captain Ireson, rather than himself, were responsible for the abandonment of the disabled vessel. To screen themselves they charged their captain with the crime."

466.20   Chaleur Bay]   Inlet of the Gulf of St. Lawrence between the Gaspé Peninsula of Quebec and New Brunswick.

468.12   *Telling the Bees*]   "A remarkable custom, brought from the Old Country, formerly prevailed in the rural districts of New England. On the death of a member of the family, the bees were at once informed of the event, and their hives dressed in mourning. This ceremonial was supposed to be necessary to prevent the swarms from leaving their hives and seeking a new home."—Whittier's note.

470.6   Ramoth hill]   "A hill in South Hampton, N.H., only a few miles from Amesbury, used to be called Ramoth-Gilead."—Samuel T. Pickard, *Life and Letters of John Greenleaf Whittier* (1894).

471.8   Follymill]   ". . . To give the thing a local stand-point, I have introduced the neighboring woods of Follymill, famous hereaway for their may-flowers, or ground laurel."—Whittier to James Russell Lowell, February 18, 1860, in Pickard, *Life and Letters of John Greenleaf Whittier* (1894).

472.5   *Barbara Frietchie*]   "This poem was written in strict conformity to the account of the incident as I had it from respectable and trustworthy sources. It has since been the subject of a good deal of conflicting testimony, and the story was probably incorrect in some of its details. It is admitted by all that Barbara Frietchie was no myth, but a worthy and highly esteemed gentlewoman, intensely loyal and a hater of the Slavery Rebellion, holding her Union flag sacred and keeping it with her Bible; that when the Confederates halted before her house, and entered her dooryard, she denounced them in vigorous language, shook her cane in their faces, and drove them out; and when General Burnside's troops followed close upon Jackson's, she waved her flag and cheered them. It is stated that May Quantrell, a brave and

loyal lady in another part of the city, did wave her flag in sight of the Confederates. It is possible that there has been a blending of the two incidents."—Whittier's headnote in the Riverside Edition (1888).

478.16   Amun]   Ram-headed Egyptian deity.

481.26   "The Chief . . . shore."]   A line from "The African Chief" by Sarah Wentworth Morton; the poem was collected in Caleb Bingham's *The American Preceptor*, the "school-book" to which Whittier refers at 481.25.

481.30   Dame Mercy Warren]   Mercy Warren (1728–1814), playwright, poet, historian, and political activist in the American Revolution.

481.36   Memphremagog's]   A lake, largely in Quebec, but extending into Vermont.

482.1   St. François's]   Probably a reference to Lake Saint François (also known as Lake Saint Francis), in southern Quebec to southeast Ontario.

482.9   Salisbury's level marshes]   Marshland adjacent to the town of Salisbury, northeastern Massachusetts, near the coast at the mouth of the Merrimack River.

482.14–15   Boar's . . . Shoals]   Little Boar's Head on the New Hampshire coast and the Isles of Shoals, nine small islands off the Maine and New Hampshire coast.

482.31   Cochecho town]   Dover, on the Cocheco River in New Hampshire, was attacked by Indians on June 28, 1689.

483.2   wizard's conjuring-book]   "I have in my possession the wizard's 'conjuring book' . . . It is a copy of Cornelius Agrippa's *Magic*, printed in 1651 . . . The full title of the book is *Three Books of Occult Philosophy, by Henry Cornelius Agrippa, Knight, Doctor of both Laws, Counsellor to Caesar's Sacred Majesty and Judge of the Prerogative Court.*"—from Whittier's headnote to the Riverside Edition (1888).

483.6   Piscataqua]   A river in New Hampshire.

483.18   Sewell's ancient tome]   *The History, Rise, Increase and Progress of the Christian People Called Quakers* (London, 1722) by William Sewell (1654–1720).

483.21   Chalkley's Journal]   Thomas Chalkley (1675–1741), an itinerant Quaker preacher; his *Journal* (1766) was extremely popular among Quakers and often reprinted.

484.14   Apollonius of old]   Apollonius of Tyana (3 B.C.–A.D. 97), Greek philosopher, supposedly a seer and miracle worker.

484.26   White of Selborne's]   Gilbert White (1720–93), English naturalist, author of *The Natural History and Antiquities of Selborne* (1789).

488.15   Pindus]   Range of mountains in west central to northwest Greece;

in classical times, the mountains forming the boundary between Epirus and Thessaly.

488.15   Araxes]   Ancient name for the Aras, a river in Turkey. In later editions, Whittier changed "Araxes" to "Aracthus"; his biographer, Samuel T. Pickard, in *Life and Letters of John Greenleaf Whittier* (1894), notes, "Mr. Whittier found that the similarity of names had misled him. It was the Aracthus he had in mind when the poem was written."

489.10   Another guest]   Harriet Livermore (1788–1867). "The portrait of that strange pilgrim, Harriet Livermore, the erratic daughter of Judge Livermore of New Hampshire, who used to visit us, is as near the life as I can give it."—Whittier in a letter to James T. Fields, October 3, 1865. In a headnote added to the 1888 Riverside Edition, Whittier described her as "a young woman of fine natural ability, enthusiastic, eccentric, with slight control over her violent temper, which sometimes made her religious profession doubtful . . . She early embraced the doctrine of the Second Advent, and felt it her duty to proclaim the Lord's speedy coming. With this message she crossed the Atlantic and spent the greater part of a long life in travelling over Europe and Asia."

489.36   Petruchio's Kate]   In Shakespeare's *The Taming of the Shrew*.

489.37   Siena's saint]   Saint Catherine of Siena (1347–80), Dominican mystic and diplomat.

490.16   Queen of Lebanon]   Lady Hester Lucy Stanhope (1776–1839), eldest daughter of Charles, Viscount Mahon (afterwards 3rd Earl of Stanhope). In 1814, she established a fortified estate at Mt. Lebanon and, adopting Eastern dress, proclaimed a religion that combined Christian and Islamic beliefs. She engaged in intrigues against the British consuls in the district and exercised almost despotic power over the tribal people in the area, who considered her a prophet.

493.29–32   Ellwood's . . . Jews.]   Thomas Ellwood (1639–1713), Quaker poet and pamphleteer, author of *Davideis: The Life of King David in Israel, a Sacred Poem* (1712).

494.2   McGregor]   Sir Gregory McGregor, Scottish adventurer who arrived in Caracas in 1817 and fought under Bolivar for independence; after this, he made a number of raids around the Caribbean before settling on the Mosquito Coast of Central America and calling himself His Highness, the Cacique of Pogair.

494.4   Taygetos]   Mountains in southern Peloponnesus, Greece.

494.5   Ypsilanti's Mainote Greeks]   Demetrius Ypsilanti (1793–1832), Greek patriot and commander, successfully defended Argos in a key battle with the Turks.

498.29   knife-grinder . . . Canning]   George Canning (1770–1827), En-

glish statesman and poet, wrote "The Friend of Humanity and the Knife-Grinder."

508.16   *Al Aaraaf*]   "A star was discovered by Tycho Brahe which appeared suddenly in the heavens—attained, in a few days, a brilliancy surpassing that of Jupiter—then as suddenly disappeared, and has never been seen since."—Poe's note. (In the first appearance of "Al Aaraaf" in *Al Aaraaf, Tamerlane, and Other Poems*, it was accompanied by extensive footnotes on the page, which are reproduced here.)

509.1   Nesace]   Greek: "lady of the island."

509.29   Capo Deucato]   The formerly used Italian name for Leucadia, the island off the western coast of Greece. "On Santa Maura—olim Deucadia."—Poe's note.

509.32   her who lov'd a mortal]   "Sappho."—Poe's note.

509.35   gemmy flower]   "This flower is much noticed by Lewenhoeck and Tournefort. The bee, feeding upon its blossom, becomes intoxicated."—Poe's note.

509.35   Trebizond]   Ancient city and region on the Black Sea, celebrated for its gardens; now the city and province of Trabzon in northeastern Turkey.

510.18   Clytia]   "The Chrysanthemum Peruvianum, or, to employ a better-known term, the turnsol—which turns continually towards the sun, covers itself, like Peru, the country from which it comes, with dewy clouds which cool and refresh its flowers during the most violent heat of the day—*B. de St. Pierre*."—Poe's note.

510.20   that aspiring flower]   "There is cultivated in the king's garden at Paris, a species of serpentine aloes without prickles, whose large and beautiful flower exhales a strong odour of the vanilla, during the time of its expansion, which is very short. It does not blow till towards the month of July—you then perceive it gradually open its petals—expand them—fade and die.—*St. Pierre*."—Poe's note.

510.24   Valisnerian lotus]   "There is found, in the Rhone, a beautiful lily of the Valisnerian kind. Its stem will stretch to the length of three or four feet—thus preserving its head above water in the swellings of the river."—Poe's note.

510.26   lovely purple perfume]   "The Hyacinth."—Poe's note.

510.26–27   Zante! . . . Levante!]   Island in the Ionian Sea, also known as Zakinthos or Zacynthus, and popularly invoked as "flower of the Levant." *Isola d'oro* means "golden isle."

510.28   Nelumbo bud]   "It is a fiction of the Indians, that Cupid was first seen floating in one of these down the river Ganges—and that he still loves the cradle of his childhood."—Poe's note.

510.31   To bear . . . Heaven]   "And golden vials full of odors which are the prayers of the saints.—*Rev. St. John.*"—Poe's note.

511. 15—16   Have dream'd . . . own—]   "The Humanitarians held that God was to be understood as having really a human form.—*Vide Clarke's Sermons*, vol. I, page 26, fol. edit.

"The drift of Milton's argument, leads him to employ language which would appear, at first sight, to verge upon their doctrine; but it will be seen immediately, that he guards himself against the charge of having adopted one of the most ignorant errors of the dark ages of the church.—*Dr. Sumner's Notes on Milton's Christian Doctrine.*

"This opinion, in spite of many testimonies to the contrary, could never have been very general. Andeus, a Syrian of Mesopotamia, was condemned for the opinion, as heretical. He lived in the beginning of the fourth century. His disciples were called Anthropmorphites.—*Vide Du Pin.*

"Among Milton's minor poems are these lines:—

> Dicite sacrorum præsides nemorum Deæ, &c.
> Quis ille primus cujus ex imagine
> Natura solers finxit humanum genus?
> Eternus, incorruptus, æquævus polo,
> Unusque et universus exemplar Dei.—And afterwards,
> Non cui profundum Cæcitas lumen dedit
> Dircæus augur vidit hunc alto sinu, &c."—Poe's note.

511.25   By winged Fantasy]   "Seltsamen Tochter Jovis / Seinem Schosskinde / Der Phantasie.—*Göethe.*"—Poe's note.

512.5   sightless]   "Too small to be seen.—*Legge.*"—Poe's note.

512.17   like fire-flies . . . night]   "I have often noticed a peculiar movement of the fire-flies;—they will collect in a body and fly off, from a common centre, into innumerable radii."—Poe's note.

512.30   Therasæan reign]   "Therasæa, or Therasea, the island mentioned by Seneca, which, in a moment, arose from the sea to the eyes of astonished mariners."—Poe's note.

513.12   stars . . . such as fall]   "Some star which, from the ruin'd roof / Of shak'd Olympus, by mischance, did fall.—*Milton.*"—Poe's note.

513.32   Tadmor and Persepolis]   Tadmor is a biblical name for Palmyra, ancient city (destroyed A.D. 273) of central Syria, and Persepolis was an ancient city of Persia. "Voltaire, in speaking of Persepolis, says, 'Je connois bien l'admiration qu'inspirent ces ruines—mais un palais erigé au pied d'une chaine des rochers sterils—peut il être un chef d'œuvre des arts!' "—Poe's note.

513.34   O, the wave] "Ula Deguisi is the Turkish appellation; but, on its own shores, it is called Bahar Loth, or Almotanah. There were undoubtedly more than two cities engulphed in the 'dead sea.' In the valley of Siddim were five—Adrah, Zeboin, Zoar, Sodom and Gomorrah. Stephen of Byzantium mentions eight, and Strabo thirteen, (engulphed)—but the last is out of all reason."—Poe's note.

513.38   Eyraco] "Chaldea."—Poe's note.

514.4   Is not . . . loud?] "I have often thought I could distinctly hear the sound of darkness as it stole over the horizon."—Poe's note.

514.17   Young . . . whispering] "Fairies use flowers for their charactery.—Merry Wives of Windsor."—Poe's note.

514.27–28   That keeps . . . away] "In Scripture is this passage—'The sun shall not harm thee by day, nor the moon by night.' It is perhaps not generally known that the moon, in Egypt, has the effect of producing blindness to those who sleep with the face exposed to its rays, to which circumstance the passage evidently alludes."—Poe's note.

515.28–29   Albatross . . . night] "The Albatross is said to sleep on the wing."—Poe's note.

516.9–10   The murmur . . . grass] "I met with this idea in an old English tale, which I am now unable to obtain and quote from memory:—' The verie essence and, as it were, springe-heade and origine of all musiche is the verie pleasaunte sounde which the trees of the forest do make when they growe.' "—Poe's note.

516.26   Have slept . . . bee] "The wild bee will not sleep in the shade if there be moonlight.

"The rhyme in this verse, as in one about sixty lines before, has an appearance of affectation. It is, however, imitated from Sir W. Scott, or rather from Claud Halcro—in whose mouth I admired its effect:

> O! were there an island,
>   Tho' ever so wild
> Where woman might smile, and
>   No man be beguil'd, &c."—Poe's note.

517.10   Simoom] See note 36.31.

517.18   Apart . . . Hell!] "With the Arabians there is a medium between Heaven and Hell, where men suffer no punishment, but yet do not attain that tranquil and even happiness which they suppose to be characteristic of heavenly enjoyment.

> Un no rompido sueno—
> Un dia puro—allegre—libre
> Quiera—
> Libre de amor—de zelo—
> De odio—de esperanza—de rezelo.—Luis Ponce de Leon.

"Sorrow is not excluded from 'Al Aaraaf,' but it is that sorrow which the living love to cherish for the dead, and which, in some minds, resembles the delirium of opium. The passionate excitement of Love and the buoyancy of spirit attendant upon intoxication are its less holy pleasures—the price of which, to those souls who make choice of 'Al Aaraaf' as their residence after life, is final death and annihilation."—Poe's note.

517.26   "tears . . . moan."]   "There be tears of perfect moan / Wept for thee in Helicon.—*Milton*."—Poe's note.

518.22   Parthenon]   "It was entire in 1687—the most elevated spot in Athens."—Poe's note.

518.24   Than ev'n . . . withal]   "Shadowing more beauty in their airy brows / Than have the white breasts of the Queen of Love.—*Marlowe*."—Poe's note.

519.2   pennon'd]   "Pennon—for pinion.—*Milton*."—Poe's note.

519.14   Dædalion]   A fabulously crafted thing (as by a maker like Daedalus).

521.27   atomies]   Atoms.

529.23   Porphyrogene]   Greek: "born to the purple," i.e. imperial.

532.30   *Peccavimus*]   Latin: "we have sinned."

533.17   Eidolon]   An insubstantial image, or phantom.

538.34   *is* there . . . Gilead?]   Cf. Jeremiah 8:22.

539.6   Aidenn]   Eden, here used in the sense of paradise or heaven.

556.3   *Old Ironsides*]   The poem, written in response to the proposal by the Navy Department to scrap the frigate *Constitution*, was published in the Boston *Daily Advertiser* on September 16, 1830, and was widely reprinted; its popularity led to the preservation of the ship, which had captured three British frigates in separate engagements during the War of 1812. Holmes subsequently included it in his Phi Beta Kappa address of 1836, "Poetry, a Metrical Essay," prefacing it with these lines:

> There was an hour when patriots dared profane
> The mast that Britain strove to bow in vain;
> And one, who listened to the tale of shame,
> Whose heart still answered to that sacred name,
> Whose eye still followed o'er his country's tides
> Thy glorious flag, our brave Old Ironsides!
> From yon lone attic, on a summer's morn,
> Thus mocked the spoilers with his school-boy scorn.

557.28   Triton . . . wreathèd horn!]   Cf. Wordsworth, "The World Is Too Much With Us": "Have sight of Proteus rising from the sea; / Or hear old Triton blow his wreathèd horn."

560.13–14   *Georgius* . . . hive!]   George II (1683–1760) succeeded to the throne of Great Britain in 1727; he was of the German House of Hanover.

560.15–16   year . . . gulp her down]   On November 1, 1755, an earthquake destroyed most of the city of Lisbon.

560.17   Braddock's army]   Edward Braddock (1695–1755), British general, commanded British forces in the North American campaign against the French in 1755; on July 9 of that year, French and Indian forces ambushed Braddock's army near Fort Duquesne, Pennsylvania. He lost half of his men, and was himself mortally wounded.

560.23   felloe]   The rim of a wheel.

563.18   *"Man . . . below."*]   See note 29.6.

564.7   Plenipo]   Minister plenipotentiary.

564.8   near St. James]   Diplomatic envoys to Great Britain are officially accredited to the Court of St. James.

564.10   Gubernator]   Governor.

566.5   Leucadian]   See note 509.29.

569.25   *Humani nihil*]   Latin: "nothing human"; the allusion is to Terence, *"Homo sum; humani nihil a me alienum puto"* ("I'm a man—I count nothing human as alien to me"), from his play *Heauton Timoroumenos* ("The Self-Tormentor").

569.30   Vallombrosa]   See note 64.31.

570.13   Orleans . . . Bourbon throne]   Louis Philippe, eldest son of the duke of Orleans, became king of France after the revolution of 1830, following the deposition of the Bourbon ruler Charles X; he was forced to abdicate in 1848.

571.30   simar]   A woman's robe; a loose, light garment.

572.33   "singing as they shine"]   From the conclusion of Joseph Addison's "Ode" (1712), referring to the heavenly bodies: "For ever singing, as they shine, ' The Hand that made us is Divine.' "

573.2   The Tuscan's hand]   Galileo Galilei (1564–1642) built a refracting telescope in 1609.

574.5   ROGERS]   Samuel Rogers (1763–1855), English poet.

574.21   DAVID]   Psalm 49:4.

574.23   PSALMS]   Psalm 42:7.

574.25   MILTON]   From "An Epitaph on the Marchioness of Winchester,"
ll. 55–56.

576.21   Micro-Uranos]   "Little heaven."

578. 14–19   Florence . . . Eugene Percy]   Children of Chivers.

579.14   Four . . . Death]   Chivers' daughter Florence died in October
1842; three other children died within a three-month period in 1848.

581.19   Æonian]   Aonia, a district of Boeotia in ancient Greece containing
the mountains Helicon and Cathaeron, sacred to the Muses.

585.3   *Wissahiccon*]   Wissahickon Creek, in southeastern Pennsylvania.

585.7   White Island's]   Albion, oldest name of Great Britain and poetical
name for England.

585.18   the river]   The Schuylkill River, Philadelphia.

587.17   *Flaxman*]   John Flaxman (1755–1826), sculptor and neo-classic il-
lustrator of Homer and the Greek tragedians.

594.10   Santa Maria Novella's Church]   Dominican church in Florence,
erected 1278–1350; its façade was later embellished from designs by Leon Bat-
tista Alberti (1404–72).

610.17   *Palais Royal*]   The palace and gardens, surrounded by arcades, in
Paris, built originally for Cardinal Richelieu in the 17th century.

610.20   "Casta Diva"]   Italian: "chaste goddess"; the most celebrated aria
in Vincenzo Bellini's *Norma*.

620.12   "Music, Heavenly Maid,"]   "When Music, heavenly maid, was
young, / While yet in early Greece was sung"—William Collins, "The Pas-
sions. An Ode for Music" (1746), lines 1–2.

620.18   Chickerings]   A well-known make of piano.

621.24   Pandean flutes]   Panpipes.

621.31   Boehm-flutes]   Theobald Boehm (1794–1881), German flutist and
inventor, produced the prototype for the modern flute in 1847.

624.22   weird bulls . . . tame]   In Greek mythology, Medea gives Jason a
magic ointment that protects him from the fire-breathing bulls that Aeetes
(Medea's father) had commanded him to yoke.

627.2   *Old Temples of Maralipoor*]   "They stand on the very verge of the
sea, about thirty-six miles south of Madras, where Southey, in his ' Curse of

Kehama,' lays the scene of the chapter called 'The City of Baly.' " — Brooks's note.

629.18   *"In Him . . . being"*]   Acts 17:28.

644.1   *Rockall*]   "Rockall is a solid block of granite, growing, as it were, out of the sea, at a greater distance from the main land, probably, than any other island or rock of the same diminutive size in the world. It is only seventy feet high, and not more than a hundred yards in circumference. It lies at a distance of no fewer than one hundred and eighty-four miles nearly due west of St. Kilda, the remotest part of the Hebrides, and is two hundred and sixty miles from the north of Ireland." — Sargent's note.

646.3   *Dixie's Land*]   An alternate version of the first part of the first stanza appears in the text of the song published in 1859 in *Bryant's Power of Music* (New York: Robert M. De Witt), a booklet containing lyrics without music for songs made popular by the Bryant Minstrel Show: "I wish I was in de land of cotton, / 'Cimmon seed 'an sandy bottom— / CHOR.—Look away— look 'way— away—Dixie Land."

662.12   *"I am . . . tied"*]   "I have seen a bunch of violets in a glass vase, tied loosely with straw, which reminded me of myself." — Thoreau's commentary in *A Week on the Concord and Merrimack Rivers*.

664.1   *Guido's Aurora*]   Painting by the Bolognese artist Guido Reni (1575–1642), commissioned by Cardinal Scipione Borghese in 1613.

674.17   *Walden*]   Walden Pond, in Concord, Massachusetts, where Thoreau lived from 1845 to 1847.

674.26   one attracted]   Thoreau.

675.22   *Murillo's Magdalen*]   Painting by Bartolome Esteban Murillo (1617–82).

677.4   J.L.M.]   John Lothrop Motley (1814–1877), historian, author of *The Rise of the Dutch Republic* (1856).

677.5   Charmian]   Cleopatra's attendant in Shakespeare's *Antony and Cleopatra*.

686.20   transdiurnal]   Beyond the domain of the day.

686.27   Flaxman]   See note 587.17.

687.32   Fouqué . . . Tieck]   Friedrich Heinrich Karl, Baron de la Motte-Fouqué (1777–1843) and Ludwig Tieck (1773–1853), German Romantic writers.

688.3 Dwight] John Sullivan Dwight (1813–93), Boston music critic and writer of verses.

688.9 Barnaby Rudge] Title character of Dickens' 1841 novel; he had a raven named Grip.

688.15 Mathews] Cornelius Mathews; see biographical note, p. 1013 in this volume.

688.35 Melesigenes] Ancient Greek epithet for Homer, from the river Meles in Ionia, near which Homer was said to have been born.

689.14 *The Pious Editor's Creed*] Within the fiction of *The Biglow Papers*, "The Pious Editor's Creed" is by Hosea Bigelow, a Yankee farmer fiercely opposed to the Mexican War and to slavery.

692.4 bagnets] Bayonets.

693.1 benedicite] Latin: "God bless you."

711.4 Laocöon!] The Laocöon group, a famous Hellenistic sculpture from Rhodes, shows the Trojan priest Laocöon and his sons entwined in the coils of a serpent as punishment for warning the Trojans against the wooden horse of the Greeks. It was dug up on the Esquiline hill in Rome in 1506.

711.14 the beautiful Apollo] The Apollo Belvedere, another celebrated classical piece, stands like the Laocöon in a courtyard in the Vatican.

715.37 De Fredis] Felice de Fredis, from whose vineyard the Laocöon group was first excavated.

716.28 Humbled Angelo] Michelangelo went with the architect Sangallo to see the piece while it was still in the ground; he identified the group from Pliny's description of it in *Historia Naturalis*.

720.3 *Leaves of Grass* (*1855*)] These poems had no titles in this edition. Whitman eventually added the titles that appear in parentheses in the Contents and Index in the present edition..

722.2 entretied] Cross-braced.

724.10 kelson] Keelson: a line of timbers laid over the keel of a ship to steady it.

724.31 Kanuck] Canuck, French Canadian.

724.31 Tuckahoe] Tidewater Virginian.

724.31 Cuff] Negro.

728.34 limpsey] Limp.

732.13 king-pin] Extended spoke of a pilot-wheel.

732.26 jour printer] Journeyman printer.

738.28   fold with powders] Powdered medicine used to be dispensed in folded papers.

739.14   carlacue] Variant of curlicue.

744.28   tilth] The depth to which soil may be cultivated.

748.12   fakes] Coils of a rope.

751.34   omnigenous] Of all kinds.

754.1   life-car . . . slipnoose] Water-tight boat traveling along a rope, to remove passengers from a wrecked ship to the shore.

754.22   bull-dances] A dance in which only men participate; a stag dance.

754.27   musters] Assemblies; here, convivial.

757.2   topples] Overhangs, projections.

757.30   crowded . . . wreck] The *San Francisco* was caught in a gale and wrecked a few hundred miles from New York City in late December 1853; the disaster was reported in the New York *Weekly Tribune* of January 21, 1854.

759.31   tale . . . sunrise] Mexican troops captured about 400 men under the command of Colonel James Walker Fannin near the village of Goliad, Texas, on March 20, 1836, most of whom were volunteers from the southern United States. Having previously decreed that all foreigners caught under arms on Mexican soil would be treated as pirates, President Santa Anna ordered their execution, and about 300 of the prisoners were shot on March 27, 1836.

761.1−2   frigate-fight] Between *Bon Homme Richard*, commanded by John Paul Jones, and the British *Serapis*, September 23, 1779.

763.11   Wallabout] Wallabout Bay, inlet in the East River where American prisoners were held on British prison ships during the Revolutionary War. It later became the site of the Brooklyn Navy Yard.

763.12   Saratoga] Now Schuylerville, on the Hudson River, north of Albany; scene of the surrender of General Burgoyne's British army to the Americans under Major-General Horatio Gates, October 17, 1777.

764.29   Eleves] French: pupils, disciples.

765.25   old topknot] Frontier slang for an Indian.

767.10   Kronos] Or Cronus; a Titan, son of Uranus and Gaea; ruler of the universe until overthrown by Zeus.

767.12   Belus] A legendary ancient king of Egypt.

767.16   Mexitli] Aztec war-god.

768.10   the bull and the bug]   E.g., as worshipped by Greeks (bull) and Egyptians (the scarab as an image of the sun god, Khepera).

769.8   tressels]   Trestles, here as supporting coffins.

770.29   obis]   Obeah, or obi is a form of West African sorcery practiced in the West Indies and in the southern United States. The plural here probably means "obi-men," or sorcerers.

770.34   shasta]   Shastras are ancient Hindu sacred texts.

770.36   teokallis]   Aztec temples.

772.4   koboo]   Or Kubu; native of Palembang, Sumatra.

773.29   sauroids]   Huge prehistoric reptiles, mistakenly alleged to have carried their eggs in their mouths.

776.3   chuff]   Here, the heel of the hand.

783.32   Bedowee]   Or badawi; in Arabic, singular of bedouin.

783.32   tabounschik]   Russian: horse-drover.

786.28   exurge]   Exsurge, rise up into view.

789.16   aurist]   Otologist, ear specialist.

793.22   posh]   Slush, crushed ice.

797.6   zambo]   A person of mixed African and American Indian blood; often spelled "Sambo."

799.10   ennuyees]   French: wearied, bored people.

800.14   douceurs]   Gifts or bribes.

800.16   cache]   This may be used as the French verb, "hide," rather than "hiding-place."

803.30   defeat at Brooklyn]   The battle of Long Island, August 27, 1776, at which the British were victorious.

817.22   fores]   Snouts, fronts of faces.

818.29   albescent]   Growing or becoming white or whitish; light-colored honey is considered the most valuable.

821.18   Cudge]   Usually Cudjo; a common name for male black slaves in the South.

824.14   Jonathan]   Slang for a New England hick. This section is thought to have been written in response to the arrest of a fugitive slave, Anthony Burns, in Boston in 1854.

837.2   smouchers]   Cheats, pilferers.

838.3   EIDÓLONS]   Images (see note 533.17); here, signs of a higher, transcendent reality.

838.25   ostent]   A sign or token.

843.26   *Calamus*]   "It is the very large and aromatic grass, or rush, growing about water-ponds in the valleys—spears about three feet high—often called 'sweet flag'—grows all over the Northern and Middle States . . . The recherché or ethereal sense of the term, as used in my book, arises probably from the actual Calamus presenting the biggest and hardiest spears of grass—and their fresh, aquatic, pungent bouquet."—Whitman, in a letter of November 1, 1867. In antiquity, the calamus reed was used as a pipe or flute, and also as a pen.

844.17   Ninth-month]   Subsequent to the 1855 *Leaves of Grass*, Whitman adopted the Quaker system of naming days and months numerically; this date would thus be September 1859.

850.17   adhesiveness]   Here used in its phrenological sense of a propensity for friendship.

862.26   eleve]   See note 764.29.

871.31   Paumanok]   Long Island, in Algonquian (meaning "fish-shaped").

881.6   MAN-OF-WAR-BIRD]   The frigate-bird, or stormy petrel.

895.29   great star]   Venus, as evening star.

909.29   Year One]   The first year of American Independence, July 1776–July 1777.

921.29–30   *Somnambula's . . . Poliuto*]   The operas mentioned here are Vincenzo Bellini's *La Somnambula* (1831), in which the heroine sleepwalks into a stranger's room and is accused of unfaithfulness, *Norma* (1831), whose heroine is torn between love and vengeance, and Gaetano Donizetti's *Poliuto* (1840).

924.31   Norma]   See note 921.29–30.

924.32   Lucia's]   The heroine of Donizetti's *Lucia di Lammermoor* (1835), here envisioned in her celebrated "mad scene."

925.1   Ernani]   Hero of Giuseppe Verdi's opera (1844), a suicide for love.

925.7   trombone duo]   The famous trombone duet in Bellini's *I Puritani* (1835).

925.12   Fernando's]   Hero of Donizetti's *La Favorita* (1840).

925.13   Amina]   Heroine of Bellini's *La Somnambula*.

925.18   Alboni's]   Marietta Alboni (1826–94), celebrated operatic contralto.

925.21   *William Tell*] Gioachino Rossini's opera (1829).

925.23   *Robert*] *Robert le Diable* (1831).

926.22   king] Ancient Chinese percussion instrument.

926.24   vina] A Hindu stringed instrument; also veena.

926.25   bayaderes] Hindu dancing girls.

926.30   *Eine . . . Gott*] "A Mighty Fortress Is Our God."

926.31   *Stabat Mater dolorosa*] "A sorrowful mother was standing"; medieval devotional poem set to music by Rossini (1842).

926.34   *Agnus Dei . . . Excelsis*] "Lamb of God," "Glory (to God) in the highest": two sections of the Mass.

927.12   *Creation*] Haydn's 1798 oratorio.

928.21   antique ponderous Seven] The Seven Wonders of the ancient world.

928.22–24   Suez canal . . . wires] The Suez Canal was opened in 1869; the Union Pacific and Central Pacific railroads were also joined that year. The Atlantic cable was completed in 1866.

929.3   Eclaircise] Illuminate, clarify.

930.6–32   I see . . . Western sea] These lines follow the railroad route from Omaha to San Francisco.

930.34   Genoese] Christopher Columbus.

933.28   Batouta the Moor] Ibn Batutah (c. 1304–68), Moroccan geographer who traveled widely in Africa and Asia.

934.8   Admiral] Columbus, called "Admiral of the Ocean Sea."

934.10   Palos] The port in Spain from which Columbus sailed on his first voyage.

938.1   Brahm] Brahma.

938.1   Saturnius] Saturn.

938.4   Kronos] See note 767.10.

939.5   sudra] The lowest of the Hindu castes.

939.19   Santa Spirita] Holy Spirit. The phrase is Whitman's coinage; in all romance languages "spirit" is masculine rather than feminine (e.g., the Latin *spiritus sanctus*).

Index of Titles and First Lines

Index of Poets

Cataloging Information

American poetry : the nineteenth century.
   edited by John Hollander.

   (The Library of America : 66–67)
   Contents: v. 1. Freneau to Whitman — v. 2. Melville
to Stickney. American Indian poetry. Folk songs & spirituals.
   1. American poetry—19th century. I. Series.
ISBN 0–940450–60–7 (V. 1). — ISBN 0–940450–78–X (V. 2)
PS607.A56   1993   93-10702
811′308—dc20

THE LIBRARY OF AMERICA SERIES

This book is set in 10 point Linotron Galliard,
a face designed for photocomposition by Matthew Carter
and based on the sixteenth-century face Granjon. The paper
is acid-free Ecusta Nyalite and meets the requirements for perma-
nence of the American National Standards Institute. The binding
material is Brillianta, a 100% woven rayon cloth made by
Van Heek-Scholco Textielfabrieken, Holland. The com-
position is by Haddon Craftsmen, Inc., and The
Clarinda Company. Printing and binding
by R. R. Donnelley & Sons Company.
Designed by Bruce Campbell.